Natural Legal Language Processing Workshop (NLLP 2022)

Abu Dhabi, United Arab Emirates
8 December 2022

ISBN: 978-1-7138-9142-0

Printed from e-media with permission by:

Curran Associates, Inc.
57 Morehouse Lane
Red Hook, NY 12571

Some format issues inherent in the e-media version may also appear in this print version.

Printed with permission by Curran Associates, Inc. (2024)

For permission requests, please contact the Association for Computational Linguistics at the address below.

Association for Computational Linguistics
209 N. Eighth Street
Stroudsburg, Pennsylvania 18360

Phone: 1-570-476-8006
Fax: 1-570-476-0860

acl@aclweb.org

Additional copies of this publication are available from:

Curran Associates, Inc.
57 Morehouse Lane
Red Hook, NY 12571 USA
Phone: 845-758-0400
Fax: 845-758-2633
Email: curran@proceedings.com
Web: www.proceedings.com

NLLP 2022

Natural Legal Language Processing Workshop 2022

Proceedings of the Workshop

December 8, 2022

The NLLP organizers gratefully acknowledge the support from the following sponsors.

Gold

Bloomberg Engineering

LBox

erc European Research Council

Introduction

Welcome to the fourth edition of the NLLP (Natural Legal Language Processing) Workshop, co-located with the 2022 Conference on Empirical Methods in Natural Language Processing.

Different industrial sectors have embraced natural language processing (NLP) technologies, which have altered services and products in healthcare, finance, education among others. The legal domain provides enormous potential for generating interesting research problems. Electronic tools are increasingly used for all types of legal tasks and that use is predicted to grow sharply. By its very nature, the practice of law necessarily involves the analysis and interpretation of language. The potential for NLP applications to provide benefit to practitioners of law and consumers of legal services around the world is enormous.

We organized this workshop to bring together researchers and practitioners from around the world who develop NLP techniques for legal data. This is an exciting opportunity to expand the boundaries of our field by identifying new problems and exploring new data as it interacts with the full inventory of NLP and machine learning approaches. In this spirit, the Organizing and Program Committee was assembled to include researchers from both academia and industry, from NLP and legal backgrounds.

We were interested in the following types of papers: (1) applications of NLP methods to legal tasks; (2) experimental results using and adapting NLP methods in legal documents; (3) descriptions of new legal tasks for NLP; (4) creation of curated and/or annotated resources; (5) descriptions of systems which use NLP technologies for legal text; (6) industrial research in this area and (7) interdisciplinary position papers.

We again received a record number of submissions. Out of 56 submissions, we accepted 33 papers for an overall acceptance rate of 58.9% percent. Out of the 33 accepted papers, 25 were long and 8 are short. These also include 3 original papers submitted as non-archival, in order to accommodate publication of the work at a later date in a conference or journal. All papers were reviewed by at least 3 members of the Program Committee. In addition, we also offered a venue for presentation for 6 papers accepted to the Findings of EMNLP 2022 on the above topics. All papers were invited to have an oral presentation and in-person attendees are also invited to join a poster session over lunch.

The papers cover a wide range of topics including new data sets for legal NLP, demos, legal perspectives on NLP topics and data rights, methods for dealing with legal documents including processing of long documents, domain adaptation, privacy-aware models and active learning as well as applications of NLP tasks to legal documents including retrieval, information extraction, simplification, extractive and abstractive summarization, generation, named entity recognition, segmentation, document similarity, stance detection and argument reasoning.

We thank our invited speaker Professor Michael A. Livermore from the University of Virginia School of Law for accepting our invitation. In the tradition of past NLLP workshops, the invited speaker is a legal scholar with an interest in empirical methods for legal analysis including NLP methods. For this edition, we are also hosting a panel From NLLP to legal NLP: The Future of the Field.

We thank everyone who expressed interest in the workshop, all authors of submitted papers, members of the Program Committee who did an excellent job at reviewing papers given a short turnaround time, everyone attending the workshop, the EMNLP 2022 conference for hosting us and the workshop and publication chairs for their support. We thank our sponsors – LBox, Bloomberg and the European Research Council Starting Grant project HUMANads – for their contributions.

The NLLP Workshop organizers.

http://nllpw.org/workshop

Organizing Committee

Organizers

Nikolaos Aletras, The University of Sheffield
Ilias Chalkidis, University of Copenhagen
Leslie Barrett, Bloomberg Law
Cătălina Goanță, Utrecht University
Daniel Preoțiuc-Pietro, Bloomberg

Program Committee

Reviewers

Tomaso Agnoloni, Ion Androutsopoulos, Elliott Ash

Tim Baldwin, Andrew Blair-Stanek, Lukasz Borchmann, Baldwin Breck

Rajarathnam Chandramouli, Daniel Chen, Ashish Chouhan, Corinna Coupette

Marina Danilevsky, Tony Davis, Stefania Degaetano-Ortlieb, Luigi Di Caro, Kasper Drazewski, Arthur Dyevre

Emmanouil Fergadiotis

Frank Giaoui, Matthias Grabmair, Neel Guha

Ivan Habernal, Peter Henderson, Nils Holzenberger

Daniel Katz, Ilan Kernerman, Manolis Koubarakis

Junyi Jessy Li, Ruta Liepina, How Khang Lim, Antoine Louis

Prodromos Malakasiotis, Adam Meyers, Jelena Mitrovic

Pietro Ortolani

Paulo Quaresma

Georg Rehm

George Sanchez, Cristiana Santos, Thibault Schrepel, Sebastian Schwemer, Mathias Siems, Dan Simonson, Jerrold Soh, Gerasimos Spanakis

Andrea Tagarelli, Dimitrios Tsarapatsanis

Josef Valvoda, Gijs Van Dijck, Jacob van de Kerkhof

Adam Wyner

Marcos Zampieri, Miri Zilka

Keynote Talk: Finding the Law

Mike Livermore
University of Virginia School of Law

Abstract: This presentation will examine challenges in finding the law, for both legal practitioners and scholars engaged in the computational analysis of law. For the practitioner, the challenge is one of search, a process that can be modeled and studied. Although undertheorized, law search has substantial jurisprudential and practical consequences that are only begining to be explored. For the computational scholar, challenges of selection and data bias are pervasive, and credible scholarship must ground descriptive and causal analyses in the actual processes that generate the data available for study.

Bio: Michael A. Livermore is a Professor of Law at the University of Virginia. He is one of the early scholars involved in a new research paradigm in legal scholarship that uses computational text analysis tools to study the law and legal institutions. Livermore is the author of dozens of academic works, which have appeared in top law journals as well as peer-reviewed legal, scientific, and social science journals. With Daniel N. Rockmore, he edited Law as Data: Computation, Text, and the Future of Legal Analysis (Santa Fe Institute Press, 2019). Livermore hosts the Online Workshop on the Computational Analysis of Law, a global forum for scholars to present cutting-edge research in this area. Livermore is also a leading expert on the use of cost-benefit analysis to evaluate regulation. Prior to joining the faculty, Livermore was the founding executive director of the Institute for Policy Integrity at New York University School of Law, a think tank dedicated to improving the quality of government decision-making. He is a public member of the Administrative Conference of the United States.

Keynote Talk: From NLLP to legal NLP - The Future of the Field

Panel

Table of Contents

On Breadth Alone: Improving the Precision of Terminology Extraction Systems on Patent Corpora
Sean Nordquist and Adam Meyers 1

On What it Means to Pay Your Fair Share: Towards Automatically Mapping Different Conceptions of Tax Justice in Legal Research Literature
Reto Gubelmann, Peter Hongler, Elina Margadant and Siegfried Handschuh 12

ClassActionPrediction: A Challenging Benchmark for Legal Judgment Prediction of Class Action Cases in the US
Gil Semo, Dor Bernsohn, Ben Hagag, Gila Hayat and Joel Niklaus 31

Combining WordNet and Word Embeddings in Data Augmentation for Legal Texts
Sezen Perçin, Andrea Galassi, Francesca Lagioia, Federico Ruggeri, Piera Santin, Giovanni Sartor and Paolo Torroni 47

A Legal Approach to Hate Speech – Operationalizing the EU's Legal Framework against the Expression of Hatred as an NLP Task
Frederike Zufall, Marius Hamacher, Katharina Kloppenborg and Torsten Zesch 53

Privacy Pitfalls of Online Service Terms and Conditions: a Hybrid Approach for Classification and Summarization
Emilia Lukose, Suparna De and Jon Johnson 65

Abstractive Summarization of Dutch Court Verdicts Using Sequence-to-sequence Models
Marijn Schraagen, Floris Bex, Nick Van De Luijtgaarden and Daniël Prijs 76

Legal-Tech Open Diaries: Lesson learned on how to develop and deploy light-weight models in the era of humongous Language Models
Stelios Maroudas, Sotiris Legkas, Prodromos Malakasiotis and Ilias Chalkidis 88

Towards Cross-Domain Transferability of Text Generation Models for Legal Text
Vinayshekhar Bannihatti Kumar, Kasturi Bhattacharjee and Rashmi Gangadharaiah 111

Parameter-Efficient Legal Domain Adaptation
Jonathan Li, Rohan Bhambhoria and Xiaodan Zhu 119

Processing Long Legal Documents with Pre-trained Transformers: Modding LegalBERT and Longformer
Dimitris Mamakas, Petros Tsotsi, Ion Androutsopoulos and Ilias Chalkidis 130

Data-efficient end-to-end Information Extraction for Statistical Legal Analysis
Wonseok Hwang, Saehee Eom, Hanuhl Lee, Hai Jin Park and Minjoon Seo 143

Semantic Segmentation of Legal Documents via Rhetorical Roles
Vijit Malik, Rishabh Sanjay, Shouvik Kumar Guha, Angshuman Hazarika, Shubham Nigam, Arnab Bhattacharya and Ashutosh Modi 153

Privacy-Preserving Models for Legal Natural Language Processing
Ying Yin and Ivan Habernal 172

Named Entity Recognition in Indian court judgments
Prathamesh Kalamkar, Astha Agarwal, Aman Tiwari, Smita Gupta, Saurabh Karn and Vivek Raghavan 184

The Legal Argument Reasoning Task in Civil Procedure
Leonard Bongard, Lena Held and Ivan Habernal 194

Efficient Deep Learning-based Sentence Boundary Detection in Legal Text
Reshma Sheik, Gokul T and S Nirmala 208

Tracking Semantic Shifts in German Court Decisions with Diachronic Word Embeddings
Daniel Braun 218

Should I disclose my dataset? Caveats between reproducibility and individual data rights
Raysa M. Benatti, Camila M. L. Villarroel, Sandra Avila, Esther L. Colombini and Fabiana Severi
228

Attack on Unfair ToS Clause Detection: A Case Study using Universal Adversarial Triggers
Shanshan Xu, Irina Broda, Rashid Haddad, Marco Negrini and Matthias Grabmair 238

E-NER — An Annotated Named Entity Recognition Corpus of Legal Text
Ting Wai Terence Au, Vasileios Lampos and Ingemar Cox 246

Detecting Relevant Differences Between Similar Legal Texts
Xiang Li, Jiaxun Gao, Diana Inkpen and Wolfgang Alschner 256

Legal and Political Stance Detection of SCOTUS Language
Noah Bergam, Emily Allaway and Kathleen Mckeown 265

Graph-based Keyword Planning for Legal Clause Generation from Topics
Sagar Joshi, Sumanth Balaji, Aparna Garimella and Vasudeva Varma 276

Automatic Classification of Legal Violations in Cookie Banner Texts
Marieke Van Hofslot, Almila Akdag Salah, Albert Gatt and Cristiana Santos 287

Text Simplification for Legal Domain: {I}nsights and Challenges
Aparna Garimella, Abhilasha Sancheti, Vinay Aggarwal, Ananya Ganesh, Niyati Chhaya and Nandakishore Kambhatla 296

Legal Named Entity Recognition with Multi-Task Domain Adaptation
Răzvan-alexandru Smădu, Ion-robert Dinică, Andrei-marius Avram, Dumitru-clementin Cercel, Florin Pop and Mihaela-claudia Cercel 305

Computing and Exploiting Document Structure to Improve Unsupervised Extractive Summarization of Legal Case Decisions
Yang Zhong and Diane Litman 322

AraLegal-BERT: A pretrained language model for Arabic Legal text
Muhammad Al-qurishi, Sarah Alqaseemi and Riad Souissi 338

An Efficient Active Learning Pipeline for Legal Text Classification
Sepideh Mamooler, Rémi Lebret, Stephane Massonnet and Karl Aberer 345

Program

Thursday, December 8, 2022

09:00 - 10:40 *Session 1*

Multi-LexSum: Real-world Summaries of Civil Rights Lawsuits at Multiple Granularities
Zejiang Shen, Kyle Lo, Lauren Yu, Nathan Dahlberg, Margo Schlanger and Doug Downey

Extractive Summarization of Legal Decisions using Multi-task Learning and Maximal Marginal Relevance
Matthias Grabmair, Shanshan Xu and Abhishek Agarwal

Towards Cross-Domain Transferability of Text Generation Models for Legal Text
Vinayshekhar Bannihatti Kumar, Kasturi Bhattacharjee and Rashmi Gangadharaiah

Parameter-Efficient Legal Domain Adaptation
Jonathan Li, Rohan Bhambhoria and Xiaodan Zhu

ClassActionPrediction: A Challenging Benchmark for Legal Judgment Prediction of Class Action Cases in the US
Gil Semo, Dor Bernsohn, Ben Hagag, Gila Hayat and Joel Niklaus

Zero Shot Transfer of Legal Judgement Prediction as Article-aware Entailment for the European Court of Human Rights
T.y.s.s Santosh, Oana Ichim and Matthias Grabmair

Revisiting Transformer-based Models for Long Document Classification
Desmond Elliott, Sune Darkner, Ilias Chalkidis and Xiang Dai

Attack on Unfair ToS Clause Detection: A Case Study using Universal Adversarial Triggers
Shanshan Xu, Irina Broda, Rashid Haddad, Marco Negrini and Matthias Grabmair

AraLegal-BERT: A pretrained language model for Arabic Legal text
Muhammad Al-qurishi, Sarah Alqaseemi and Riad Souissi

An Efficient Active Learning Pipeline for Legal Text Classification
Sepideh Mamooler, Rémi Lebret, Stephane Massonnet and Karl Aberer

Thursday, December 8, 2022 (continued)

	A Legal Approach to Hate Speech – Operationalizing the EU's Legal Framework against the Expression of Hatred as an NLP Task Frederike Zufall, Marius Hamacher, Katharina Kloppenborg and Torsten Zesch
	Validity Assessment of Legal Will Statements as Natural Language Inference Mihai Surdeanu, Derek Bambauer, Clayton Morrison, Jacob Israelsen and Alice Kwak
10:40 - 11:00	*Break*
11:00 - 12:00	*Finding the Law - Michael A. Livermore (University of Virginia School of Law)*
12:00 - 12:40	*Session 2*
	Data-efficient end-to-end Information Extraction for Statistical Legal Analysis Wonseok Hwang, Saehee Eom, Hanuhl Lee, Hai Jin Park and Minjoon Seo
	Efficient Deep Learning-based Sentence Boundary Detection in Legal Text Reshma Sheik, Gokul T and S Nirmala
	Semantic Segmentation of Legal Documents via Rhetorical Roles Vijit Malik, Rishabh Sanjay, Shouvik Kumar Guha, Angshuman Hazarika, Shubham Nigam, Arnab Bhattacharya and Ashutosh Modi
	Detecting Relevant Differences Between Similar Legal Texts Xiang Li, Jiaxun Gao, Diana Inkpen and Wolfgang Alschner
	E-NER — An Annotated Named Entity Recognition Corpus of Legal Text Ting Wai Terence Au, Vasileios Lampos and Ingemar Cox
12:40 - 14:00	*Lunch and In-Person Poster Session*
14:00 - 15:30	*Session 3*
	On What it Means to Pay Your Fair Share: Towards Automatically Mapping Different Conceptions of Tax Justice in Legal Research Literature Reto Gubelmann, Peter Hongler, Elina Margadant and Siegfried Handschuh

Thursday, December 8, 2022 (continued)

Combining WordNet and Word Embeddings in Data Augmentation for Legal Texts
Sezen Perçin, Andrea Galassi, Francesca Lagioia, Federico Ruggeri, Piera Santin, Giovanni Sartor and Paolo Torroni

Named Entity Recognition in Indian court judgments
Prathamesh Kalamkar, Astha Agarwal, Aman Tiwari, Smita Gupta, Saurabh Karn and Vivek Raghavan

Legal Named Entity Recognition with Multi-Task Domain Adaptation
Răzvan-alexandru Smădu, Ion-robert Dinică, Andrei-marius Avram, Dumitru-clementin Cercel, Florin Pop and Mihaela-claudia Cercel

Do Charge Prediction Models Learn Legal Theory?
Dongyan Zhao, Yansong Feng, Cong Jiang, Quzhe Huang and Zhenwei An

Legal-Tech Open Diaries: Lesson learned on how to develop and deploy light-weight models in the era of humongous Language Models
Stelios Maroudas, Sotiris Legkas, Prodromos Malakasiotis and Ilias Chalkidis

Processing Long Legal Documents with Pre-trained Transformers: Modding LegalBERT and Longformer
Dimitris Mamakas, Petros Tsotsi, Ion Androutsopoulos and Ilias Chalkidis

Privacy-Preserving Models for Legal Natural Language Processing
Ying Yin and Ivan Habernal

Automatic Classification of Legal Violations in Cookie Banner Texts
Marieke Van Hofslot, Almila Akdag Salah, Albert Gatt and Cristiana Santos

Tracking Semantic Shifts in German Court Decisions with Diachronic Word Embeddings
Daniel Braun

15:30 - 16:00 *Break*

16:00 - 17:30 *Session 4*

Should I disclose my dataset? Caveats between reproducibility and individual data rights
Raysa M. Benatti, Camila M. L. Villarroel, Sandra Avila, Esther L. Colombini and Fabiana Severi

Thursday, December 8, 2022 (continued)

Privacy Pitfalls of Online Service Terms and Conditions: a Hybrid Approach for Classification and Summarization
Emilia Lukose, Suparna De and Jon Johnson

Computing and Exploiting Document Structure to Improve Unsupervised Extractive Summarization of Legal Case Decisions
Yang Zhong and Diane Litman

Abstractive Summarization of Dutch Court Verdicts Using Sequence-to-sequence Models
Marijn Schraagen, Floris Bex, Nick Van De Luijtgaarden and Daniël Prijs

Graph-based Keyword Planning for Legal Clause Generation from Topics
Sagar Joshi, Sumanth Balaji, Aparna Garimella and Vasudeva Varma

Text Simplification for Legal Domain: {I}nsights and Challenges
Aparna Garimella, Abhilasha Sancheti, Vinay Aggarwal, Ananya Ganesh, Niyati Chhaya and Nandakishore Kambhatla

On Breadth Alone: Improving the Precision of Terminology Extraction Systems on Patent Corpora
Sean Nordquist and Adam Meyers

The Legal Argument Reasoning Task in Civil Procedure
Leonard Bongard, Lena Held and Ivan Habernal

Legal and Political Stance Detection of SCOTUS Language
Noah Bergam, Emily Allaway and Kathleen Mckeown

Can AMR Assist Legal and Logical Reasoning?
Daniel Hershcovich, Hugo López, Ruixiang Cui and Nikolaus Schrack

LawngNLI: A Long-Premise Benchmark for In-Domain Generalization from Short to Long Contexts and for Implication-Based Retrieval
Dan Roth and William Bruno

Legal Prompting: Teaching a Language Model to Think Like a Lawyer
Fangyi Yu, Lee Quartey and Frank Schilder

Thursday, December 8, 2022 (continued)

17:30 - 18:30 *From NLLP to Legal NLP - The Future of the Field (Panel) & Best Presentation Award*

On Breadth Alone: Improving the Precision of Terminology Extraction Systems on Patent Corpora

Sean Nordquist
New York University
nordquist@nyu.edu

Adam Meyers
New York University
meyers@cs.nyu.edu

Abstract

Automatic Terminology Extraction (ATE) methods are a class of linguistic, statistical, machine learning or hybrid techniques for identifying terminology in a set of documents. Most modern ATE methods use a statistical measure of how important or characteristic a potential term is to a foreground corpus by using a second background corpus as a baseline. While many variables with ATE methods have been carefully evaluated and tuned in the literature, the effects of choosing a particular background corpus over another are not obvious. In this paper, we propose a methodology that allows us to adjust the relative breadth of the foreground and background corpora in patent documents by taking advantage of the Cooperative Patent Classification (CPC) scheme. Our results show that for every foreground corpus, the broadest background corpus gave the worst performance, in the worst case that difference is 17%. Similarly, the least broad background corpus gave suboptimal performance in all three experiments. We also demonstrate qualitative differences between background corpora – narrower background corpora tend towards more technical output. We expect our results to generalize to terminology extraction for other legal and technical documents and, generally, to the foreground/background approach to ATE.

1 Introduction

Terminology extraction is the process by which specialized and domain-specific words and phrases are extracted from a set of documents. These techniques are actively used and researched to identify trends in technical documents, create domain glossaries, and improve the readability of technical documents, among their many uses. Automatic Terminology Extraction (ATE) methods are the class of linguistic, statistical, machine learning, or hybrid techniques designed to identify terminology in a specialized set of documents. ATE now covers a broad class of methods that are in real use today and continues to receive research attention.

Most modern ATE methods take advantage of a statistical measure of how important or characteristic a potential term is to a foreground corpus by using a second background corpus as a baseline. Systems that use these statistics rely on an assumption that the foreground corpus is specialized and the background corpus is less specialized. The statistical methods can then use relative frequencies in the less specialized corpus and compare them to the specialized corpus – if a term is significantly more common in the specialized than the unspecialized, we may have identified a domain-specific term. Techniques that use this statistical strategy work well. While many variables with ATE methods have been carefully evaluated and tuned in the literature, the effects that come from choosing a particular background corpus over another are not obvious. More specifically, what would happen if one were to use a more broad background corpus that contained a wider variety of subject matter?

This paper presents an experiment carried out with Termolator (Meyers et al., 2018), a high-performing open-source ATE system. The system allows for the specification of a foreground corpus consisting of the target topic area and a background corpus that can be customized. We explore the results from running this test on three distinct patent topic areas, using the Cooperative Patent Classification (CPC) scheme to curate five background corpora for each foreground. Our results show that the choice of background corpus has a significant effect on the precision of the words extracted.

For every foreground corpus, the broadest background corpus gave the worst performance, in the worst case that difference is 17%. Similarly, the least broad background corpus gave suboptimal performance in all three experiments. Indeed, the ideal background corpus seemed to occupy some middle position – broader than the foreground cor-

Proceedings of the Natural Legal Language Processing Workshop 2022, pages 1 - 11
December 8, 2022 ©2022 Association for Computational Linguistics

pus, but not too general either. For example, we found that highest results (72% precision) for a foreground of semiconductor (H01L 21) patents was derived from a background of patents related to electricity (H), which is more general than "electric solid state devices" (HOIL) and more specific than patents in general or than a combination of patents and non-patents.

We perform a qualitative analysis of words extracted to see how different background breadths affect the words extracted. For example, when the top 100 term candidates from the data input patent foreground corpus were analyzed, the most general background corpus produced a set of terminology that, while technical, was less characteristic of data inputs than the all patent background corpus (e.g., the most general corpus: *fingerprint sensor, social media* vs. a patent corpus: *focal vergence, selectable interaction element*).

We expect that our results will generalize to terminology extraction for other legal and technical documents and, generally, to the foreground/background approach to ATE.

2 Related Work

The definition of 'terminology' in the context of ATE systems is still a point of discussion in modern literature (Rigouts Terryn et al., 2020). In this study we use the word terminology to describe specialized language that is domain specific. Notionally, we distinguish a word or phrase as terminology if it is sufficiently specialized that a typical naive adult would not be expected to know the meaning of the term (Meyers et al., 2018).

ATE methods are generally split into 3 different categories: linguistic, statistical, and hybrid. Linguistic methods use linguistic features such as parts of speech patterns and chunking to extract term candidates. Statistical methods usually use a statistical measure of how characteristic a term is to a foreground corpus by comparing it to a baseline background corpus. Hybrid methods combine the linguistic and statistical methods, usually by using linguistic methods to identify term candidates and the statistical methods to rank the candidates.

The statistics in the hybrid methods work by comparing a foreground corpus from which terminology should be extracted, with a background corpus which serves as a baseline to identify terms characteristic of the foreground. The use of a foreground and a background corpus (or sometimes an analysis and reference corpus, respectively) has existed for a long time (e.g. (Kageura and Umino, 1996; Tomokiyo and Hurst, 2003; Drouin, 2003)). The intuition is that by using and combining these statistics, one can rank the words and phrases which are most likely to be specialized language from the foreground higher. A variety of statistics have been used in the literature (e.g. TF-IDF, KL divergence, etc.) (Kosa et al., 2020).

The assumption behind using a foreground and background corpus is that the foreground is sufficiently specialized and the background corpus is sufficiently general that the way they use potential terms will be different. This assumption is powerful and effective and has led some research to stick to a single general background corpus (Drouin, 2003) and some research to allow varying background corpora (Meyers et al., 2018).

By taking advantage of both linguistic and statistical techniques, hybrid methods have proven to be some of the most effective in ATE for the last decade (Macken et al., 2013; Rigouts Terryn et al., 2020). While most systems now fall into the hybrid category, there is growing interest in machine learning methods for ATE with a variety of methodologies (Kucza et al., 2018; Hätty and Schulte im Walde, 2018). In this paper we use an open-source hybrid method called Termolator that combines chunking and statistical ranking of term candidates using two corpora: the foreground corpus and the background corpus (Meyers et al., 2018).

Termolator is a flexible hybrid ATE system that allows us to vary the background corpus for a given foreground corpus. We are assuming that Termolator is representative of other hybrid systems which use a foreground and background corpus in the same way. We believe this is a valid assumption because such ATE systems are based on the idea that comparing the distribution of terms candidates across two different corpora helps identify them. Terms that appear frequently in foreground documents but not background documents are more likely to be terms and vice versa. We do not make any assumptions about the relative performance of Termolator and other comparable systems.

In this work, we focus on patents, a technical document in the legal domain, and the relationship between foreground and background corpora. We examine how the choice of background corpora might affect the performance of existing systems and the output of those systems.

Drouin et al. (2020) discussed how the distance between foreground and background corpora affects terms in unspecialized corpora. However, their paper focuses on design choices to optimize ATE for unspecialized corpora, like news articles.

3 Experimental Setup

3.1 Data Set

Patents will be the main document of study. We used the United States Patent Office Bulk Storage System to download all patent grants from the years 2016 to 2022. This will be the set of patents we sample from to construct our corpora. We also combine the Open American National Corpus (OANC) (Ide and Suderman, 2006) with a sample of patents to construct our general corpus.

3.2 Foreground Corpora

To better understand the generalizability of our results across other patent subject areas, we conduct experiments using corpora in three different subject areas. Each foreground corpus corresponds to a CPC classification code that corresponds to a particular "group" in the CPC scheme. The corpus is created by sampling 5,000 patents from each of these "groups." We chose to sample from the "group" rather than the "subgroup" because in most cases subgroups did not have enough patents in that time period for the experiment.

Table 1 shows the patent CPC codes from which we will sample documents for our foreground corpora. We select these three topic areas because they provide a good range of technical topics and types of terminology to test across.

3.3 Breadth of Corpora

We define the breadth of a patent corpus as how much variety in subject matter there is in the corpus. Reducing the problem of breadth to similarity opens us to a significant amount of existing research in computational linguistics on the problem.

Understanding how semantically similar two sets of words, documents, or corpora are is an important problem in natural language processing. Saying two texts are similar relies on an explicit normative definition of what makes them similar (Bär et al., 2011). Without a taxonomy that all speakers of every language agree on, little can be done to create a universal concept of similarity. A specialist, for example, has a richer and deeper ontology than a layman that will change the relative similarities of words and concepts. The precise layout of that ontology is based on circumstances such as what was being researched at the time and the interests of the people involved. Even word embeddings – our best attempt at making the problem numeric – do not assign a transparent measure of magnitude to semantic similarity (Faruqui et al., 2016).

Reconciling all the potential taxonomies that exist or that could exist is beyond this paper. We need not, however, look at precisely how much broader a corpus is than another, just the fact that it is broader. If we examine breadth as a measure that monotonically increases with the addition of dissimilar documents, we can define an ordinal notion of breadth that would serve our purpose. In other words, we need not look at precisely how much more broad a corpus is than another, just the fact that it is more broad. In effect, we create a rank-ordering of our patent corpora that will correspond to five different breadths (Stevens, 1946).

3.4 Background Corpora

To create our background corpora, we use the Cooperative Patent Classification (CPC) scheme. CPC is a classification system that classifies all US patent grants. The CPC scheme defines a hierarchy that organizes patents into sections, classes, subclasses, groups, and subgroups (Table 2) (USPTO, 2016–2022). As one moves down the hierarchy, one describes an increasingly specific set of patents. The CPC scheme thus describes a tree of classifications with the patents themselves at the leaves. Patents are always assigned a 'main' category which we will focus on. Each patent's main classification is a code in the format of "H01L 21/02".

We create a total of five background corpora of increasing breadth: one CPC level removed, two CPC levels removed, three CPC levels removed, a corpus sampled from all patent topics, and a general corpus composed of the OANC mixed with a sample of patents, which we will refer to as OANC+ [1]. To illustrate the curation process, we use a "F03G 7" foreground corpus as an example. The first background corpus is sampled from "F03G" – one level above in the hierarchy. The second background corpus is sampled from "F03". The third background corpus is sampled from "F". Finally, we create a general patent corpus, by sampling from all CPC classification codes, which we

[1]We have released a version of OANC+ to the public at the following link: https://drive.google.com/file/d/1VNFzZb6DyrNozBxiBcf07C83A13PM0RS/view

H01L 21	"Semiconductors"	Processes or apparatus adapted for the manufacture or treatment of semiconductor or solid state devices or of parts thereof
A61B 17	"Surgical Instruments"	Surgical instruments, devices or methods
G06F 3	"Data Input"	Input arrangements for transferring data to be processed into a form capable of being handled by the computer; Output arrangements for transferring data from processing unit to output unit

Table 1: The 3 patent classes that make up our 3 different foreground corpora and our labels for them.

H01L 21/02	Section H/Class 01/Subclass L/Group 21/Subgroup 02
H01L 21	Section H/Class 01/Subclass L/Group 21
H01L	Section H/Class 01/Subclass L
H01	Section H/Class 01
H	Section H

Table 2: Cooperative Patent Classification hierarchy breakdown for a CPC code 'H01L 21/02'.

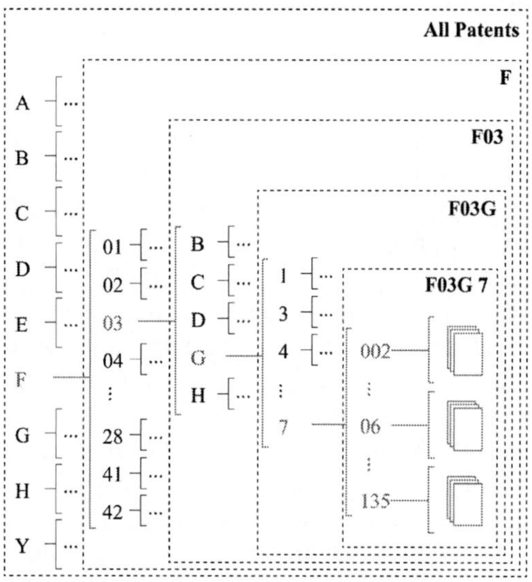

Figure 1: Diagram of the four different sampling levels for a foreground corpus 'F03G 7'. Each increasingly broad background corpus is constructed by sampling one level higher in the CPC hierarchy.

refer to as the 'All Patent' corpus. We repeat this process for each of the foreground corpora by simply moving up the hierarchy in each case. We see this sampling process visually in Figure 1. At each level we sample from a progressively wider range of patents.

Finally, we also create a 'general' background corpus. Ideally, the general background corpus will consist of a variety of different types of documents (court decisions, scholarly papers, patents, news articles, etc.) that will serve as our broadest possible background corpus. In addition, because we are attempting to create a broader corpus – not just a general contrasting corpus – we will also include a sample of patents to make it broader according to our definition. We use 5,000 total documents from both the OANC and a general sampling of patents to create our OANC+ background corpus (87.5% OANC documents and 12.5% patents). Now we have five total background corpora of five distinct breadths, each of which will be run against our foreground corpora using Termolator.

3.5 Annotation and Evaluation

For the purpose of annotation, we follow the convention given in Meyers et al. (2018). We define a valid term as a word or multi-word nominal expression that is specific to some technical field. A valid term should be definable within the field and reused. We do not consider term-like phrases to be valid terms unless they are reused verbatim either in the same or other documents. Next, we also require that valid terms be sufficiently specialized to a field's technical language. For a term to be considered specialized, a naive adult should not be expected to know the meaning of the term. We adopt the same intuitive model as Meyers et al. (2018), asking would Homer Simpson – an animated television character who is a caricature of a naive adult – know this term?

Following the evaluation strategy from Meyers

et al. (2018), we randomly sample 20 terms from each fifth of the output for a total of 100 terms. Then, we manually annotate each term as valid terminology or not. From these annotated terms, we can calculate a precision score that corresponds to that run of Termolator.

To calculate recall, one would need to annotate every document in the foreground corpus. For that reason, calculating recall is a labor-intensive and time consuming process when working with large corpora. This task is uniquely difficult because the experiment uses three 5,000 document-wide foreground corpora and therefore would require the annotation of 15,000 patents. In addition, the annotation of these three particular patent corpora do not serve a larger purpose at the moment. We make a preliminary effort nonetheless to examine a potential proxy for recall obtained by annotating a small subsample of documents in 4.3.

We also examine the words themselves. Specifically, we want to look at how the words change as the background corpora change. First, we examine how the outputs change by determining agreement between the output's top 100 words. We also perform a qualitative investigation of the terms extracted with each background corpus. We do this by looking at where the outputs disagree and examining those differences.

4 Results

4.1 Precision Scores

Table 3 presents the precision scores across experiments for all three foreground corpora. The scores that correspond to the best-performing background corpora for each analysis corpus are in bold.

Generally, we see the hybrid ATE method used by Termolator works better on some patent topics than others. For all three foreground corpora, we tend to achieve the lowest precision with the most general background corpus consisting mostly of non-patent documents. Interestingly, the highest precision is achieved at neither the most specific corpus nor the most general corpus, which suggests that the breadth of the background corpus is a tunable parameter for hybrid ATE methods.

What happens to the precision scores? Examining the first foreground corpus consisting of semiconductor patents and its respective background corpora, we notice a clear break that occurs between 'H01' and 'H' on the CPC hierarchy. Between this break, precision jumps a full 11% from 61% to 72%. Precision falls marginally to 70% in the 'All Patents' corpus and falls all the way to 45% on the general corpus.

The second foreground corpus with surgical instrument patents is similar with a break occurring in the exact same place jumping 6% from 72% to 78%. Yet again the general corpus performed considerably worse than all other background corpus, achieving a precision of only 50%.

The third foreground corpus consisting of data input patents has a slightly different pattern. There is a break that occurs between 'G' and 'All Patents' of a considerable 11%. However the general corpus only performs marginally worse than the other narrower patent categories, namely 'G' and 'G06'.

Why do some background corpora perform better than others? For the semiconductor patents, the best performance (72%) was achieved when the foreground corpus was compared to a background corpus consisting of patents about electricity and electrical devices. Using a background corpus that consisted of only semiconductor related patents resulted in worse performance (64%). This is likely because the patents about semiconductors provide a background corpus that is too similar to the foreground corpus, as a result candidate terms which are terminology are ranked lower than they should be because they occur and co-occur too frequently in the background corpus.

A similar rationale could be applied to the surgical cutting instruments patents. The background corpus about surgical instruments performed much worse (70%) than the background corpus that consisted of patents for human necessities.

The data input patents, on the other hand, did not perform very well at all at the level where the other two foreground corpora performed the best. In fact, the second-worst performance was at that level (50%). Instead, the best performance by far was at the level of all patents (61%). This result may be because the data input patents appear in general to use less specialized language than the other two patent categories.

The general background corpus resulted in the worst performance in all three cases. This result indicates that the wide ranging classes of documents of various technical and non-technical types do not establish as good of a frequency and co-occurrence baseline as documents of the same type.

		H01L	H01	H	All Patents	OANC+
Semiconductors	H01L 21	0.63	0.61	**0.72**	0.70	0.45
		A61B	A61	A	All Patents	OANC+
Surgical Instruments	A61B 17	0.70	0.72	**0.78**	0.77	0.50
		G06F	G06	G	All Patents	OANC+
Data Input	G06F 3	0.55	0.50	0.50	**0.61**	0.47

Table 3: Precision scores of Termolator after being run on three distinct foreground corpora and their corresponding five background corpora of increasing breadth.

What do these results mean? This analysis reveals that there is not a set distance at which all background corpora can be placed optimally when extracting terminology from patents. In fact, it appears the optimal choice is dependent on the foreground corpus. Moreover, the results taken in full suggest that for each foreground corpus there exists some 'optimal' background corpus that can be used to optimize for precision. At this point, the breadth of the optimal background corpus seems to be a variable that needs to be tuned for.

Generally, however, we are able to give some specific prescriptions. Our results suggest that it is important to choose a background corpus that is composed of the same types of documents as your foreground corpus if enough of them exist. What this means in general is if one is running an ATE system on a set of scholarly papers about sorting algorithms, using news articles as a background corpus would likely not result in the best precision; rather, one would prefer to use a set of scholarly documents from all of computer science or perhaps scholarly documents from a range of disciplines as the background corpus.

4.2 Word Analysis

Conducting any rigorous analysis of the qualities of these words is challenging and outside the scope of this paper; instead, we will focus on a qualitative analysis of observations from the words using the intuitive model we described in the annotation step. Each run (we discussed 15 runs above) of Termolator produces 5,000 output words. To narrow our investigation, we will only be looking at the top 100 words from each run.

We begin by examining how the top terms vary across the runs. A matrix is used to show the number of words each run, using each background corpus, agrees on. Next, because each output is from the same foreground corpus, many of the words across the top 100 term outputs will be shared, however, we are most interested in what one background corpus picked up but another background corpus did not. For that reason, we will be looking at the term candidates the runs did not agree on. In other words, the term candidates that were extracted using one background corpus, but not the other, and vice versa. We will start our discussion with the patent category G06F 3.

	G06F	G06	G	All Patents	OANC+
G06F	100	91	86	85	75
G06		100	88	85	73
G			100	91	79
All Patents				100	82
OANC+					100

Table 4: Number of terms shared in the output of the run with each background corpus with the Data Input 'G06F 3' foreground corpus.

Table 4 shows the share of the top 100 terms that are the same between each pair of background corpora used with patent class G06F 3. We notice that corpora that are further away from each other in the CPC hierarchy have fewer words in common. This difference is explained by the difference in the contents of the background corpora. This confirms that our notion of ordinal breadth of the background corpora has a significant effect on the top terms extracted. Specifically, the greatest disagreement occurs between the second most specific corpus (G06) and the most general corpus (general) with only 73% agreement. Whereas, the greatest agreement occurred between corpora that are adjacent in the hierarchy (G06F and G06; G and All Patents).

Table 5 shows the term candidates extracted using the All Patent background corpus but not the OANC+ background corpus in the left column and the vice versa in the right column. Term candidates

All Patent But Not OANC+	OANC+ But Not All Patent
EXTENSION APP	FINGERPRINT SENSOR
DATA PROCESSING ENGINE	TARGET VOLUME
VEHICLE DATA PARAMETER	SOCIAL MEDIA
SELECTABLE INTERACTION ELEMENT	HEAD NODE
SELECTABLE INTERACTION	VIEW ANGLE
MULTI-FUNCTIONAL INPUT BUTTON	SURROUND VIEW
HIGHLIGHT MESSAGE	PHY
GRAPHICAL ASSET	DISPLAY VIEW
FOCAL VERGENCE	DETECTOR ELEMENT
ENVIRONMENT CONTENT	VIBRATION DEVICE
CLIP AREA	UNIT MEMORY
USER INPUT ATTACHMENT	SUBARRAY
UNIT TOUCH	SERVICE REQUEST
TOUCH SENSOR SURFACE	SELECTION INDICATOR
TOUCH NODE	PRESENTATION DEVICE
PROCESS MANAGEMENT SERVICE	OPERATION REGION
POSITION POINTER	MULTI-FUNCTIONAL
PORTABLE MEDIA DEVICE	INPUT METHOD EDITOR
...	...

Table 5: Potential terms that were extracted using the All Patent background but not OANC (left column) and the OANC but not the All Patent background (right column) with the 'G06F 3' foreground corpus.

All Patent But Not OANC+	OANC+ But Not All Patent
REMOVAL MAP	HEATER ELEMENT
Q-CARBON	SHIELD PLATE
PROTECTOR LAYER	LIQUID LEVEL
N-TYPE GALLIUM OXIDE SUBSTRATE	FLUID MIXTURE
LIQUID NOZZLE	DIW
GROUND SECTION	DEVICE PACKAGE
FRONT OPENING UNIVERSAL POD	CARRIER STRUCTURE
CERAMIC POROUS BODY	SIDEWALL STRUCTURE
VERTICAL SEMICONDUCTOR FIN	CONDUCTIVE POWDER
THERMAL CENTER	BIAS GENERATOR
SURFACE WF	TUNNEL FET
POLYOLEFIN SHEET	STRESS LAYER
OPTICAL MATERIAL LAYER	EPITAXIAL FIN
MEOL LAYER	CARRIER WAFER
III-V COMPOUND LAYER	CARBON PRECURSOR
HOLDING ARM	C1-C10
...	...

Table 6: Potential terms that were extracted using the All Patent background but not OANC (left column) and the OANC+ but not the All Patent background (right column) with the ' H01L 21' foreground corpus.

	H01L	H01	H	All Patents	OANC+
H01L	100	85	79	76	69
H01		100	79	78	72
H			100	88	81
All Patents				100	84
OANC+					100

Table 7: Number of terms shared in output of the run with each background corpus with the Semiconductor 'H01L 21' foreground corpus.

extracted using the general background corpus are more likely to be well-formed words or phrases that are not terms in our sense of the word (*finger-print sensor, social media, multifunctional, etc.*). Generally, the terms extracted using the OANC+ background corpus appear to be less specialized and more accessible to a naive adult.

In contrast, term candidates extracted using the base background corpus have on average greater length and apparently more specialized subject matter (*data processing engine, portable media device, focal vergence, etc.*). Even the simpler terms candidates extracted using the base background corpus (*clip area, graphical asset, touch node, etc.*) refer to specialized subject matter. Nonetheless, there are exceptions. For instance, *PHY* is short-hand for the physical layer in the *Open Systems Interconnection* model which is quite a bit more specialized than the other terms in the column.

We shift our analysis to the patent class H01L 21 in Table 7. Again, agreement appears to be decreasing in distance in the CPC hierarchy. The lowest agreement occurs between the least broad (H01L) and the most broad (OANC+) background corpora with 69% agreement. This result lines up with our expectations.

As seen in Table 6, there is not as clear of a separation between the types of words extracted using the All Patents background corpus and the OANC+ background corpus as there were in the previous patent class tested. Both sets of words appear to contain term candidates that a naive adult would not be expected to know (*optical material layer, MEOL layer, front opening universal pod, etc.* vs. *bias generator, epitaxial fin, carrier wafer, etc.*). This is likely due to the nature of the terminology in patents about semiconductors. Namely, it is, on average, a more specialized subject matter than data input patents and requires the description of concepts that are more advanced concepts in physics and chemistry.

Nonetheless, there do appear to be more basic term candidates extracted using the OANC+ background corpus than the All Patents background corpus (*heater element, shield plate, liquid level, fluid mixture, device package*). There are exceptions, however (*carrier wafer, epitaxial fin, carbon precursor*).

We also performed the same analysis for the surgical instrument patents with results similar to the semiconductor patents included in Appendix A.

4.3 Preliminary Recall Scores

One possible solution to calculating recall on such a large corpus is randomly sampling documents to annotate. For this sample, one would want to ensure that their sampling is representative of the 5,000 documents. Take the data input patents foreground corpus for example. We obtained the foreground by selecting 5,000 patents that shared the G06F 3 group level, meaning that there are even more granular classification of patents under the G06F 3 level (over 200 subgroups). To properly represent these subgroups, one should collect a number of patents from each subgroup proportional to how the subgroups are represented in the foreground corpus. Therefore, even with sampling, recall proves to be an expensive metric to calculate.

Nonetheless, in an attempt to find a proxy for recall for one of our experiments, we manually annotated 10 patents that were randomly sampled from the data input foreground corpus. We then compared the correct terms found in these patents to the top 5,000 terms extracted using each background corpus to calculate a total of five recall scores. These results are shown in Table 8.

We observed that a significant portion of the correct terms in the patents are either specific to the document or a small sub-field and therefore appear with low frequency in the overall foreground corpus. One of the reasons for this is, although we sampled from patents in the same group, they still varied in subgroup so there was greater diversity in the subject matter than there would be at the subgroup level.

Moreover, the design of ATE systems is based on the distribution of terms across a large set of documents. Based on this distribution, a ranked list of

	G06F	G06	G	All Patents	OANC+
Data Input	0.061	0.049	0.061	**0.074**	**0.074**

Table 8: Recall scores obtained from a sample of 10 documents from running Termolator on one foreground corpus and its corresponding five background corpora of increasing breadth.

terms is produced. Terms that occur in many foreground documents are more likely to be detected than terms that occur in only a few documents. Zipf's Law tells us that it is likely that most of the terms will be relatively rare, but the "important" terms are likely to occur in many documents (the TF in TF-IDF stands for term frequency). Thus, if we look at individual documents, the recall of an ATE system designed to extract terms from a large corpus should be relatively low. However, if we could somehow manually examine a set of 5,000 documents and only pay attention to terms with a high frequency (100 times in the corpus, rather than five times or less), we might expect a system to achieve a higher recall, but only for these high-frequency words.

Low recall scores are also a consequence of the cut-off chosen and the construction of the task. The task is to extract the top 5,000 terms from the documents with high precision. Naturally in a set of documents as technical as patents there are significantly more terms than documents, resulting in lower recall. Adjusting the cut-off to, for example, 10,000 terms would result in higher recall and lower precision on those terms. We believe determining how to best choose this cut-off with different background corpora is worth investigating.

This is a preliminary investigation into recall. We believe more work should be done to investigate how recall changes as the breadth of the background corpus changes.

5 Future Work

In our experiment, we used a general corpus that was composed of a mixture of OANC and a subset of general patents. We made this choice because our focus was making broader corpora not contrasting corpora. Nonetheless, the effect of using a truly general corpus would be an important baseline to compare in future research.

We limited our evaluation in this paper to precision and a qualitative analysis of the words themselves. We believe it would be relevant to devise a methodology that would allow us to further investigate the differences in the words extracted using the different background corpora.

A relevant extension would be to perform similar experiments using other document types. For instance, a natural extension would be to perform a similar set of experiments on medical scholarly text from PubMed or Wikipedia articles and examine if the trends we observed with patents remain true for other kinds of technical documents.

6 Conclusion

In this paper we investigated how varying the breadth of the background corpus affects hybrid ATE systems. After creating five background corpora for each foreground corpora using the CPC hierarchy, we ran three experiments on three different patent groups. We examined both the precision scores and the output words themselves. In this analysis, we were unable to find a single "best choice" for all patent classes. We found that for all three patent groups neither the narrowest nor the most broad background corpus achieved the best precision; rather, it was always a background corpus that consisted of patents that performed best. In addition, we found that the words we extracted varied with the background corpus we chose. For one patent class there was a clear separation between less specialized terms for the general corpus and the more specialized terms from the all patent corpus. This separation was not clear for the other two patent classes.

We showed that the choice of background corpus has a significant effect on the precision of the output of an ATE system. We found that optimizing for precision in all three cases meant choosing a patent only corpus. We also studied the words we extracted by comparing differences across runs. We found that the breadth of the corpora had a significant effect on the words extracted. Moreover, we informally analyzed how the words from the general background corpus differed from the patent background corpus, concluding that the term candidates were on average less specialized with the general corpus.

References

Daniel Bär, Torsten Zesch, and Iryna Gurevych. 2011. A reflective view on text similarity. In *Proceedings of the International Conference Recent Advances in Natural Language Processing 2011*, pages 515–520, Hissar, Bulgaria. Association for Computational Linguistics.

Patrick Drouin. 2003. Term extraction using non-technical corpora as a point of leverage. *Terminology*, 9.

Patrick Drouin, Jean-Benoît Morel, and Marie-Claude L' Homme. 2020. Automatic term extraction from newspaper corpora: Making the most of specificity and common features. In *Proceedings of the 6th International Workshop on Computational Terminology*, pages 1–7, Marseille, France. European Language Resources Association.

Manaal Faruqui, Yulia Tsvetkov, Pushpendre Rastogi, and Chris Dyer. 2016. Problems with evaluation of word embeddings using word similarity tasks. In *Proceedings of the 1st Workshop on Evaluating Vector-Space Representations for NLP*, pages 30–35, Berlin, Germany. Association for Computational Linguistics.

Anna Hätty and Sabine Schulte im Walde. 2018. Fine-grained termhood prediction for German compound terms using neural networks. In *Proceedings of the Joint Workshop on Linguistic Annotation, Multiword Expressions and Constructions (LAW-MWE-CxG-2018)*, pages 62–73, Santa Fe, New Mexico, USA. Association for Computational Linguistics.

Nancy Ide and Keith Suderman. 2006. Integrating linguistic resources: The American national corpus model. In *Proceedings of the Fifth International Conference on Language Resources and Evaluation (LREC'06)*, Genoa, Italy. European Language Resources Association (ELRA).

Kyo Kageura and Bin Umino. 1996. Methods of automatic term recognition: A review. *Terminology. International Journal of Theoretical and Applied Issues in Specialized Communication, Volume 3, Issue 2.*

Victoria Kosa, David Chaves-Fraga, Hennadii Dobrovolskyi, and Vadim Ermolayev. 2020. Optimized term extraction method based on computing merged partial c-values. In *Information and Communication Technologies in Education, Research, and Industrial Applications*, pages 24–49, Cham. Springer International Publishing.

Maren Kucza, Jan Niehues, Thomas Zenkel, Alex Waibel, and Sebastian Stüker. 2018. Term extraction via neural sequence labeling a comparative evaluation of strategies using recurrent neural networks. In *Interspeech 2018*, pages 2072–2076.

Lieve Macken, Els Lefever, and Véronique Hoste. 2013. Texsis: Bilingual terminology extraction from parallel corpora using chunk-based alignment. *Terminology*, 19.

Adam L. Meyers, Yifan He, Zachary Glass, John Ortega, Shasha Liao, Angus Grieve-Smith, Ralph Grishman, and Olga Babko-Malaya. 2018. The termolator: Terminology recognition based on chunking, statistical and search-based scores. *Frontiers in Research Metrics and Analytics*, 3.

Ayla Rigouts Terryn, Veronique Hoste, Patrick Drouin, and Els Lefever. 2020. TermEval 2020: Shared task on automatic term extraction using the annotated corpora for term extraction research (ACTER) dataset. In *Proceedings of the 6th International Workshop on Computational Terminology*, pages 85–94, Marseille, France. European Language Resources Association.

S. S. Stevens. 1946. On the theory of scales of measurement. *Science*, 103(2684):677–680.

Takashi Tomokiyo and Matthew Hurst. 2003. A language model approach to keyphrase extraction. In *Proceedings of the ACL 2003 Workshop on Multiword Expressions: Analysis, Acquisition and Treatment*, pages 33–40, Sapporo, Japan. Association for Computational Linguistics.

USPTO. 2016–2022. Patent grant full text data (no images). *Bulk Data Storage System*.

A Word Analysis Tables for Surgical Instrument Patents

	A61B	A61	A	All Patents	OANC+
A61B	100	83	78	73	64
A61		100	88	80	72
A			100	78	72
All Patents				100	84
OANC+					100

Table 9: Number of terms shared in the output of the run with each background corpus with the Surgical Instruments 'A61B 17' foreground corpus.

All Patent But Not OANC+	OANC+ But Not All Patent
ROBOTIC DEBRIDEMENT APPARATUS	DISTAL BODY
TARGET VESSEL	DISTAL CROWN
SUPPORT CATHETER	CAMMING
CUTTING BLOCK	ATTACHMENT SIDE
CAMMING	TARGET VESSEL
ATTACHMENT SIDE	INTERSPINOUS PROCESS SPACING DEVICE
TUBULAR ELEMENT	FORMING POCKET ARRANGEMENT
DISTAL CROWN	DILATOR TUBE
CUTTING ASSEMBLY	COMPRESSIBLE ADJUNCT
CLAMP PAD	TUBULAR ELEMENT
PENETRATOR	SUPPORT CATHETER
OCCLUSION DEVICE	SCALPET ARRAY
INVENTIVE CONCEPT	SACROILIAC JOINT
INTERSPINOUS PROCESS	REMOVING DEVICE
FORMING SURFACE	MONOMER LIQUID
ENDOSCOPIC INSTRUMENT	CUTTING ASSEMBLY
DISTAL BASKET	BIOCOMPATIBLE LAYER
DILATOR TUBE	TISSUE THICKNESS COMPENSATOR
COMPRESSIBLE ADJUNCT	THROMBUS EXTRACTION DEVICE
SACROILIAC JOINT	THICKNESS COMPENSATOR
PIEZOELECTRIC ELEMENT	SURGICAL INSTRUMENT GUIDE
MICROBUBBLE	SHOCK WAVES
INTERSPINOUS PROCESS SPACING DEVICE	SCALPET DEVICE
I-BEAM	RETRACTION ELEMENT
FORMING POCKET ARRANGEMENT	RECEIVER MEMBER
BIOCOMPATIBLE LAYER	PERIANAL SUPPORT MEMBER
BASEPLATE	PERIANAL SUPPORT
TISSUE THICKNESS COMPENSATOR	PENETRATOR
...	...

Table 10: Potential terms that were extracted using the All Patent background but not OANC (left column) and the OANC but not the All Patent background (right column) with the 'A61B 17' foreground corpus.

On What it Means to Pay Your Fair Share: Towards Automatically Mapping Different Conceptions of Tax Justice in Legal Research Literature

Reto Gubelmann and **Peter Hongler** and **Elina Margadant** and **Siegfried Handschuh**
University of St.Gallen
Dufourstrasse 50
9000 St.Gallen
{reto.gubelmann,peter.hongler,elina.margadant,
siegfried.handschuh}@unisg.ch

Abstract

In this article, we explore the potential and challenges of applying transformer-based pre-trained language models (PLMs) and statistical methods to a particularly challenging, yet highly important and largely uncharted domain: normative discussions in tax law research. On our conviction, the role of NLP in this essentially contested territory is to make explicit implicit normative assumptions, and to foster debates across ideological divides. To this goal, we propose the first steps towards a method that automatically labels normative statements in tax law research, and that suggests the normative background of these statements. Our results are encouraging, but it is clear that there is still room for improvement.

1 Introduction

Disagreements about normative claims are notoriously hard to resolve, and in some cases, they are even hard to recognize as such. For instance, consider (1). Do you think that a tax system that follows this principle is just?

(1) To be just, a taxation system must tax people with the same income equally.

Example (1) illustrates what we mean by a normative claim: A moral judgment of some kind, that is, an assertion that something is either morally right or wrong. As we restrict our scope to tax law, the normative claims that we are interested in pertain to moral judgments of specific tax systems. Hence, while example (1) counts as a normative claim, example (2) does not count. While the latter is also about tax law, it does not make a claim about what is just or unjust in this domain, but rather what is legal.

(2) It is illegal not to pay one's taxes.

In the discussion on tax justice, claims of the kind of (1) are regularly made, and even more often they figure implicitly in the arguments of legal scholars. For example, consider (3), which does not make an explicit claim about what is just in taxation matters, but which implicitly presupposes an idea of the kind expressed in example (1). In the worst case, adherents of different normative positions will retreat into their normative bubbles and hence permanently hinder any truly rational debate about these topics.

(3) Taxation cannot consider the needs of the individuals or their dependents, as this would lead to people with the same income being taxed at a different rate.

To move towards improving this situation, we explore the use of state-of-the-art PLMs to detect and to classify normative statements in tax law research texts. More specifically, using a variety of classifier configurations, we first explore the sensibility of state-of-the-art PLMs for different normative backgrounds in a hyperparameter search experiment. Second, we use the configurations that have shown to perform best to iteratively develop a dataset as well as a method that both identifies normative statements and that classifies them into five distinct normative categories. Finally, we validate our results with the help of two experts without any previous knowledge of the project.

We make two contributions to the field. First, studying a domain within legal NLP that has so far remained entirely uncharted, we provide specific recommendations and insights for further research in this area. Second, we publish a high-quality, expert-verified dataset for this domain that is of considerable size given the complexity of the task.

We note that our task and domain differ sub-

Proceedings of the Natural Legal Language Processing Workshop 2022, pages 12 - 30
December 8, 2022

stantially from, and hence nicely complement first-order legal NLP tasks: rather than analyzing specific rulings, provisions, or contracts, our target is the second-order discussion about which kinds of provisions, rulings, and contracts might be just, which means that the content, vocabulary and goals of our target texts will differ accordingly. Our domain also complements studies of the normative attitudes used to describe individual moral stances, such as in moral foundations theory, or in human values approaches, see Kiesel et al. (2022) and Hoover et al. (2020): Our research focuses on a discussion that belongs to political philosophy, centering around the question what constitutes a just system of taxation, rather than analyzing the moral motivations of individuals to adopt one position rather than another.

While these second-order discussions about tax justice are clearly separable from the first order ones, the former directly influence the latter. If a judge subscribes to the libertarian view that income taxation is "on a par with forced labor" (Nozick, 1974, 169), then her rulings will show much more sympathy for individuals who try to avoid paying taxes by all means. In contrast, if she subscribes to a more Rawlsian view that mandates redistribution of wealth insofar as it constitutes unjustifiable inequalities, she will have much less sympathy with wealthy individuals who are optimizing their tax bills.

The task in focus of this article is both challenging and important. It is challenging because recognizing the specific normative background of a statement such as (1) and (3) requires expert knowledge, and even with such expert knowledge, genuine uncertainties remain in some cases. More fundamentally, it means that the very definition of the categories as well as the identification of the first samples that fall under these categories requires expert knowledge from legal studies. As a consequence, the present project is interdisciplinary throughout: only a combination of expertise in legal studies and NLP can achieve progress on this topic. In our second experiment, we address this challenge by iteratively combining expert input and classifiers in a bootstrapping procedure.

Furthermore, considered from a technical perspective, the amount of lexical overlap is substantially higher than in typical clustering or classifying settings, say, in classical word-sense-disambiguation (WSD) tasks (see Navigli 2009 for a survey), where the method has to distinguish entirely different senses of words such as "bank". This is because different normative conceptions of tax justice do not constitute fully-fledged cases of ambiguities: if adherents of two different normative theories debate tax justice, they might disagree strongly on the correct conception of tax justice. However, unlike in bank-cases of ambiguity, both mean to capture the same idea.

In the pertinent philosophical and linguistic literature, such concepts are called "essentially contested concepts". The conception was first proposed by Gallie (1955), for recent discussions see Collier et al. (2006) and Rodriguez (2015). According to this conception, concepts such as TAX JUSTICE are such that essential parts of their meaning are disputed. And the reason for the dispute is that the disagreement is due to larger-scale differences in worldview.

The task is important because the subject matter that is addressed in such normative arguments is of central importance for liberal democratic societies. The politically crucial questions of liberal states are of essentially contested nature. What counts as a just taxation system directly influences the lives of the members of that society. Hence, providing support to navigate such normative landscapes is of central importance for liberal democratic societies.

2 Related Research

We focus on two areas of related research: the work on word- and sentence-embeddings that we use to represent statements, and legal NLP, the subdomain of NLP that is concerned with legal texts.

We emphasize two aspects that separate our focus from that of current related research. First, the vast majority of research in legal NLP focuses on first-order legal texts, that is, specific provisions, court decisions, or contracts. In contrast, we focus on second-order legal texts, that is, on research literature about such provisions or court decisions. Second, to date, there simply is no research that focuses on normative positions within the legal domain. These two distinguishing characteristics force us often to resort to generic approaches.

We use three different kinds of embeddings for our experiments; two of them are based on the transformer architecture (Vaswani et al., 2017), the third kind consists of classic distributional embeddings. First, we use embeddings generated by **word-based PLMs**, namely bert-base-cased and bert-large-cased (Devlin et al., 2019) as well as roberta-large (Liu et al., 2019). Among this category, we include legal-bert, a model specifically designed for first-order legal texts (Chalkidis et al., 2020).[1]

Second, we test a number of **sentence-based PLMs**, namely SBERT-Models (Reimers and Gurevych, 2019), as initial explorations showed that they perform clearly best. These SBERT-Models are based on a variety of transformer-based PLMs (in addition to the classical BERT and RoBERTa, these are mpnet, Song et al. 2020, distilroberta, Sanh et al. 2019, AlBERT, Lan et al. 2019, and minilm, Wang et al. 2020). SBERT-Models are optimized for sentence-level comparison of embeddings via geometric similarity or distance measures such as cosine similarity.

Third, we use non-transformer-based, distributional **classical word embeddings**, namely GloVE (Pennington et al., 2014) and Komninos (Komninos and Manandhar, 2016) for purposes of comparison.[2]

For classification, we use support-vector-machines ("SVMs", Boser et al. 1992); SVMs systematically try to find the optimal hyperplane separating samples of different categories. We use the scikit-learn implementations of all the clustering and classification algorithms used in this study, see Pedregosa et al. (2011).

Dale (2019) shows that NLP has been used in the legal domain since the 1960ies, with the size and the financial significance of the legal business seemingly creating a perfect environment for the development and application of domain-specific NLP methods. However, as Tang and Clematide (2021) detail, the legal domain poses specific challenges, among them the unusual length of typical legal documents, a jargon that differs on the lexical and syntactic level from standard English, domain-specific notions of relevance, and the high cost of obtaining high-quality labelled data (legal experts are expensive).

These challenges explain why many core tasks in legal NLP are still unsolved. Perhaps most prominent among them is the task of finding relevant legal documents (i.e., codified legal texts as well as authoritative court decisions) given a specific query. Thus, Chalkidis et al. (2020) systematically investigate good practices for training transformer-based PLMs that perform well in typical first-order legal tasks (classification of laws and court decisions as well as named-entity recognition in contracts). Soh et al. (2019) evaluate different methods to classify Singapore supreme court decisions according to the legal area involved, finding that rather simple combinations of latent semantic analysis and support vector machine to perform equally well as state-of-the-art PLMs. With their survey, Chalkidis and Kampas (2019) provide embeddings based on the word2vec method (Mikolov et al., 2013) that are derived specifically from court decisions and legal provisions.

As the specific idiom of legal texts is challenging already within English, multilingual research is all the more challenging. There has been some research with regard to German. Wrzalik and Krechel (2021) present a German dataset for information retrieval, Niklaus et al. (2021) focus on judgment prediction of the Swiss federal court, whose rulings are translated in German, French, and Italian, being all official languages in Switzerland.

Regarding the specific area of tax law, Ash et al. (2021) present a novel approach to identify legal documents as belonging to the field of tax law, and within this field, classifying them into specific subclasses, such as personal income or sale. As a consequence, the structure of their classifying task is somewhat similar to ours: We, too, are interested in first identifying normative statements as such and then assigning them to specific normative positions. Note, again, however, that this study also focuses on first-order tax law provisions rather than on legal research articles reflecting such tax law provisions, which is our focus.

Our research shows some connections with the ongoing discussion about so-called open-textured concepts. According to Rissland and Skalak (1989, 525), open-textured concepts are such that they cannot be defined by necessary and sufficient conditions. This category is obviously broader than the one of normative concepts and statements in focus here: Rissland and Skalak (1989, 525) mention "meeting or dealing" and "contract" as examples.[3]. For an early attempt to tackle reasoning with such

[1]These models were downloaded from huggingface.co, see Wolf et al. (2019).

[2]The SBERT- as well as the classical models were obtained from https://www.SBERT.net/docs/pretrained_models.html.

[3]Indeed, building on Ludwig Wittgenstein's conception of family resemblances ("Familienähnlichkeiten"), one could argue that all concepts with the exception of very few, highly artifical cases are open-textured, as it is usually not possible to give a definition whose parts are individually necessary and jointly sufficient for concept application in all relevant contexts. See Wittgenstein (2006/1953).

concepts, see Sanders (1991). A recent categorization of regulation with an eye towards their potential to be processed automatically point out that such open-textured concepts are a considerable obstacle to such automatic processing (Guitton et al., 2022).

The essentially contested concepts that are often at the core of normative claims in focus of this paper can be seen as a specific species of open-textured concepts, namely those that resist any simple resolution of their open-texturedness due to being conceived very diffently from very different comprehensive worldviews.

3 Datasets

As we are interested in normative positions within research discussions in tax law, all of our datasets consist of statements from such research articles. The full references of these articles are listed in the appendix, section A. In addition to these research texts, we had to develop suitable classes to categorize the normative statements. Our tax justice expert supervised the development of five normative positions that are particularly prominent in the field. These five positions constitute the categories for our experiments.[4] In the following, we first introduce these five normative categories. Then, we detail specifics of the datasets used for each of our three experiments.

According to the so-called *Deontological View*, a tax policy proposal is just if it focuses on the treatment of the taxpayer and not on the distribution of the income within a society. Hence, according to the Deontological View, a tax provision is just if it conforms to basic moral principles, such as the fundamental equality of all human beings. In this sense, example (1) expresses a Deontological View.

According to the *Rawlsian View*, a tax system is just if it would be chosen by individuals that are under Rawls' famous veil of ignorance. Under this veil, individuals do not know their educational, financial, social, or any other position in the society whose tax system they are supposed to judge. It is generally agreed that such individuals would favor tax systems focused on equality and on the eradication of unjustified inequalities.

[4]Note that we did not find a single instance where one sentence explicitly expressed views that belong to two different categories. What we did find, of course, are cases where it is not clear to which category it belongs.

A tax provision is just if it results from good, democratically grounded processes – this is the gist of the *Procedural View*. Such view includes positions that argue for a certain tax policy proposal based on a discussion or debate about the arguments against and in favor of such a proposal.

The fourth theory used in this article is the *Libertarian View*. According to it, taxation should be kept at a minimum in general, as it is considered illegitimate in all but a few cases, mostly where it is necessary to allow a minimal state to function. Libertarians tend to view market outcomes as just and therefore any kind of redistribution as unjust.

The fifth and final normative viewpoint to be included in this study is *Utilitarianism*. According to it, we should develop a taxation system that results in the maximal increase in the overall population's happiness, or welfare. This means that, according to Utilitarianists, it is permissible that individuals are treated unequally if this implies a net benefit in welfare or happiness for the entire population.

Table 1 shows the names of each of the categories, including the None-Class with a typical example.

Specifics for Experiment 1 For the hyperparameter search, we asked the expert to manually find 35 samples of each of the five normative categories identified in publications in peer-reviewed journals from the legal domain, yielding an evenly distributed dataset of 175 samples. As we expected that most of the sentences that the classifier would encounter are not expressing a normative perspective, we then added 1708 non-normative statements in the following way. Using an sbert-sentence-embedding-model, we computed the centroid of all sentence embeddings of these 175 statements. Then, we ran this over all sentences from the corpus of bootstrapping loop 1, yielding a list of sentences with the cosine between their embeddings and our centroid. From this, we selected 523 statements with a cosine below 0.2, 310 with a cosine between 0.2 and 0.6, and then 875 with a cosine higher than 0.6. An expert in the field checked all 1708 statements to ensure that they are indeed not normative in our sense. The choice of distribution of our nonnormative samples is based on the hypothesis that the most difficult decisions to make for the classifiers are those where the overall similarity of the embedding to the centroid is high, while the statement is clearly not normative.

Category	Example
Deontological	Max burdens should bear similarly upon persons whom we regard as in substantially similar circumstances, and differently where circumstances differ.
Libertarian	the anti-progressive tax argument is often characterized as an argument that every person has a responsibility to take care of himself, and no one, including the wealthy, has an obligation to assist those in need.
Procedural	For Locke himself, the key institutional requirement was that taxes should not be levied except by "the consent of the people," which he understood as "the consent of the majority, giving it either by themselves, or their representatives chosen by them."
Rawlsian	The increasing inequality of market income can be significantly ameliorated by the redistributive effect of the tax transfer system, if it is appropriately targeted.
Utilitarian	Efficiency analysis looks to overall social welfare as a measure of a tax's virtue.
None	An income tax can be used to redistribute taxable income.

Table 1: The five normative categories used in the experiments including the None-Class with typical examples.

Loop	Single-gate	Dual-gate
0	175/1708	175/1708
1	310/1767	292/2091
2	435/1792	452/2172
3	686/1892	709/2415
Combined Final DS	937/2194	

Table 2: Listed in loops 1-3 are the resulting, expert-reviewed datasets after each loop (Normative/Nonnormative samples). Dataset at loop 0 represents the input to bootstrapping loop 1 that is equivalent to the dataset used in experiment 1. For the meaning of "single-gate" and "dual-gate" see below, section 4.2.

Specifics for Experiment 2 In our iterative bootstrapping experiment, we used separate texts as sources for the initial expert-compiled dataset as well as for each of the three bootstrapping loops (for references, see the appendix, section A). Note also that the training datasets for the classifiers grow with each further bootstrapping loop taken, as we include the corrected output from the previous bootstrapping loop in the training dataset for the next one. Table 2 gives the details of the datasets, as they evolved through the bootstrapping process.

Specifics for Experiment 3 We presented our external expert annotators with a dataset of 650 samples in total. This consists of evenly distributed samples (i.e., 130 samples of each of the five categories) from the final dataset resulting from experiment 2. That is, it contains samples of three different origins: (1) samples that are directly extracted from the texts by a human, (2,3) samples that have been suggested by one of our two classifying methods and then reviewed by a human expert.

We publish the final dataset, as well as other material that might be useful to the community, on GitHub.[5]

4 Experiments

The goal of our experiments is twofold (see above, section 1). First, using a human-in-the-loop method, we want to develop a high-quality dataset of normative statements from tax law that can serve as the basis for further studies of this and related fields by the community. Second, we want to assess whether current models, both generic ones and others fine-tuned to the legal domain, are able to map the subtle differences that exist between these different normative perspectives on tax law. Given that the field that we are working in is entirely uncharted, we believe that this double aim maximizes the benefit to the research community, and we have designed the experiments accordingly.

4.1 Experiment 1: Hyperparameter Search

The goal of this first experiment consists in finding the best hyperparameters for our main experiment 2. We tested a number of support vector machines, varying the usual hyperparameters and combining this with a total of 23 different pre-trained language models (PLMs). We tested three different kinds of PLMs. First, different transformer-based word-based models, including generic pre-trained BERT and RoBERTa as well as a model specifically developed for first-order legal texts, legal-bert. Second, we tested a number of transformer-based sentence-bert models, and third, we included two pre-transformer distributional models. For refer-

[5]Please consult this repository.

ences, see above, section 2, for details of the models as well as the configurations tested, see the appendix, section B.

Furthermore, we tested the configurations on two different tasks. In the first task, the classifiers had to categorize a dataset of 175 samples, evenly distributed across the five categories, into one of the five categories (called the "5cat task"). In the second task, the classifiers had to categorize a dataset of 1883 samples into normative and nonnormative, with 175 (the same that were used for the first task) being normative, and 1708 being nonnormative (called the "Norm task"). This uneven distribution is intended to model the actual task in the wild, where we expect the clear majority of sentences encountered by the classifiers to be nonnormative on our reading.

Overall, we tested 1380 different SVM-configurations per task, saving the best performing SVM-hyperparameter-setup per model.

4.2 Experiment 2: Bootstrapping a Classifier and a Dataset

In this second experiment, we employed the two best-performing PLM and SVM configurations from experiment 1 to iteratively develop a classifier as well as a dataset. For details of the configurations, see the appendix, section C.

We start out with the dataset used from experiment 1, that is, with 175 normative sentences that are evenly distributed among the five classes as well as 1708 nonnormative sentences. This dataset is then used to train a classifier, which is run on a set of texts, resulting in predictions, which are then reviewed by an expert. These predictions, with their labels corrected by the expert, are then merged with the training dataset from this bootstrapping loop and together serve as the training dataset for the next bootstrapping loop, etc. Overall, three bootstrapping loops were executed.

We conducted these three bootstrapping loops with two different SVM methods, calling them single-gate and dual-gate. The first, called single-gate, is a straightforward classifier conceiving nonnormative sentences as a sixth category to be classified by the classifier. Here, we were using a one vs. one scheme, meaning that we are in fact training $\frac{Nx(N-1)}{2}$ classifiers, resulting in 15 classifiers. The classifier then predicts the one class that wins the most 1:1-duels. However, we hypothesized that this procedure would be not only computationally expensive, given the large size of one of the classes, namely the None-class, but also yielding bad predictions, as the None-class is nearly 40 times larger than the other classes.

We therefore also used a method that we call dual-gate method. Here, a first SVM decides on whether the sentence under consideration is normative in our sense or not (here, the normative training split is less than 10 times smaller than the None class). Then, a second gate (hence the name), consisting of 10 1:1-SVMs, classifies sentences that are normative according to the first SVM into one of the five normative classes. In this way, we employ a one vs. rest approach to distinguish normative from nonnormative sentences and a one vs. one approach to classify normative ones into their separate categories. This way, we hoped to maximize accuracy and beat the standard single-gate 1:1-approach.

4.3 Experiment 3: Annotation by Two Uninvolved Experts

In this experiment, we get an external and intersubjective view on the results of experiment 2 by having two external annotators review the dataset described above (section 3). Two ideas were guiding our design of this experiment. First, we wanted to make sure that the results of experiment 2 are not overly optimistic because our expert annotator is biased towards, as it were, annotating such that our experiments become a success. We cannot rule this out with an annotator as ours that is quite involved in our experiments. Therefore, we chose two annotators that have no involvement whatsoever in the study.

The second motivation of this third experiment was to obtain a reliable figure on the intersubjectivity of the annotations that our internal expert annotator produced. A high inter-annotator agreement would mean that many of the samples can be rather clearly assigned to a category, despite the intricacies of our subject matter.

As a consequence, we recruited two external annotators, both advanced undergraduate or graduate students in philosophy, without any previous knowledge of our project. We give the precise instructions given to the annotators in the appendix, section D. The annotators were given the opportunity to annotate "OTHER" when they were fully certain that the sample at issue, while being normative, did not fit any of the categories in focus.

Modelname	Type	5cat
pp-ml-mpnet-base-v2	sbert	87%
pp-mpnet-base-v2	sbert	85%
nli-mpnet-base-v2	sbert	84%
stsb-roberta-base-v2	sbert	83%
stsb-droberta-base-v2	sbert	83%

Table 3: Models and modeltypes used for the five best performing classifiers in the 5cat task. "pp" = paraphrase, "ml" = multilingual, "droberta" = distilroberta, "du" = distiluse, "awe" = average_word_embedding.

Modelname	Type	Norm
roberta-large	avword	98%
pp-droberta-base-v2	sbert	95%
nli-droberta-base-v2	sbert	95%
stsb-roberta-base-v2	sbert	94%
stsb-droberta-base-v2	sbert	94%

Table 4: Models and modeltypes used for the five best performing classifiers in the Norm task.

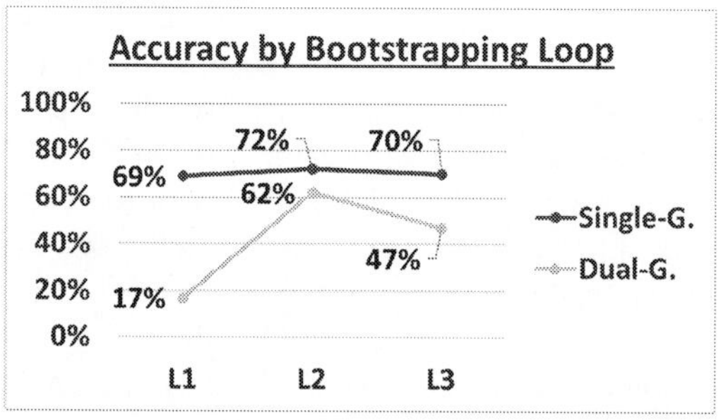

Figure 1: Overview on the performance of the two methods through the progress of experiment 2, Li referring to loop number i.

Furthermore, the annotators were not given any information on the three different subsets involved in the experiment, nor were they shown the predictions issued by the methods, or the categorization by our internal expert annotator – all with the goal of removing any possible bias that the annotators could develop.

5 Results

5.1 Experiment 1

The results of the two different classification tasks can be seen in tables 3 and 4 with "5cat" referring to the task of classifying samples into the five normative categories (most frequent sense baseline 20%, table 3) and "Norm" referring to that of distinguishing between normative and non-normative samples (most frequent sense baseline 91%, table 4; all results from all models are listed in the appendix, table 6). What is evident in the former case is that the models all perform rather well. Even the model that performed worst, `legal-bert-base` reached 74% accuracy. The best performing classifier is based on sentence-bert embeddings, and it is a rather small multilingual model: `paraphrase-multilingual-mpnet-base-v2`. The first classifier using classical word-embeddings employs `roberta-large`, and it loses no less than 5% to the best classifier.

The results of the Norm task differ in several aspects (see table 4). First, we find that the best classifier is indeed based on classic word-based embeddings delivered by `roberta-large`. It beats the first sentence-bert-based classifier by 3 percentage points. Given that the most frequent sense baseline is at 91%, these three percentage points are a considerable difference. Furthermore, overall, only 6 of 23 embeddings manage to ground classifiers that beat the baseline, whereas in task one, all of them achieved this by a margin of 54 percentage points.

As a consequence, we decided to run the bootstrapping loops with the two different methods described above, section 4.2. We chose this strategy because we were impressed at the challenge that the task of distinguishing normative from non-normative sentences posed to the classifiers, and we thought it necessary to have an SVM that can harness the full information contained in the samples of all normative categories to mark a good geometrical divide between these samples and the nonnormative ones.

5.2 Experiment 2: Bootstrapping a Classifier and a Dataset

An overview on the results of the three bootstrapping loops can be found on figure 1. Overall, it shows that the single-gate method outperforms the dual-gate method, despite our worries due to the large imbalance of the dataset. In terms of accuracy, it beats the dual-gate method throughout.

Table 2 (see above, section 3) shows the evolution of the two datasets through the bootstrapping process. It shows a steady growth of both normative samples belonging to one of the five categories as well as nonnormative samples through the loops,

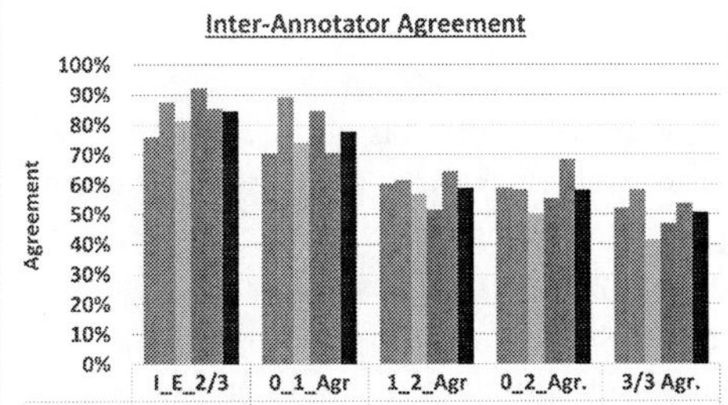

	I_E_2/3	0_1_Agr	1_2_Agr	0_2_Agr.	3/3 Agr.
Deont.	76%	71%	60%	59%	52%
Libert.	88%	89%	62%	58%	58%
Proced.	82%	74%	57%	50%	42%
Rawls.	92%	85%	52%	55%	47%
Util.	85%	71%	65%	68%	54%
Average	85%	78%	59%	58%	51%

Figure 2: Results of experiment 3, annotator 0 is our internal expert, 1 and 2 have been recruited externally. "I_E_2/3" is the percentage of samples where our internal annotator agreed with at least one external annotator.

with the dual-gate method resulting in a slightly larger dataset with regarding to normative samples and a much larger one with regard to nonnormative ones. Furthermore, the fact that the dataset from dual-gate SVM after loop 3 is 76% the size of the final combined dataset shows that the overlap between the true positives from the two methods is quite large.

5.3 Experiment 3: Annotation by Two Uninvolved Experts

The results from our third experiment are displayed in figure 2 (we also give Cohen's Kappa as well as inter-annotator variation by source in the appendix, section D). It shows that, in total, 85% of all of the classifications are supported by a 2/3-majority-vote, with one of the voters being external, one internal (to avoid falsely capitalizing on the two external annotators agreeing on a different label than our internal annotator, we focused on this restricted 2/3-agreement figure, abbreviated by "I_E_2/3"). This means that two out of three annotators independently identified the same category out of a choice of five categories. Annotator 0 is our internal annotator, annotators 1 and 2 are external ones. Figure 2 shows, for instance, that annotator 2 disagrees relatively often with annotators 0 and 1: while 0 and 1 agree in 78% of cases, this figure drops to about 60% if annotator 2 is involved.

6 Discussion

6.1 Experiment 1: Hyperparameter Search

The results of the hyperparameter search experiment are encouraging. For both tasks, our search has identified very promising candidate combinations of embeddings and SVM-configurations. It might be surprising that a multilingual and rather small model – mpnet-base is of the same category as bert-base, having 110M parameters – outperforms the large and monolingual models. This, however, dovetails nicely with the rankings on the SBERT-page for clustering.[6] We hypothesize that, for our task, the larger models overfitted to non-normative settings, and hence generalized worse to this novel task.

This finding that larger models perform worse at a natural language understanding task is not entirely without precedent. For instance, researchers at DeepMind find that larger models do not necessarily perform better at natural language inference. The large study by Rae et al. (2021, 23) strongly suggests that, in the words of the authors, "the benefits of scale are nonuniform", and that logical and mathematical reasoning does not improve when scaling up to the gigantic size of Gopher, a model having 280B parameters.

6.2 Experiment 2: Classifying

We make three observations on the results of experiment 2. First, the single-gate method outperforms the dual-gate method in terms of accuracy, but the difference decreases after bootstrapping loop 1 (see figure 1). In this loop 1, the accuracy of the dual-gate method is at 17%, whereas the single-gate method reaches 69%. This also means, given our set-up, that the dual-gate method receives a lot of high-quality false positives to use in the training for bootstrapping loop 2. Likely because of these samples, the dual-gate method, albeit still performing worse than the single-gate one, manages to gain some ground. With regard to the absolute figures of true positives returned (as opposed to accuracy), the two methods are even closer together after bootstrapping loop 1, whereas at that first loop, the single-gate method clearly outperforms the dual-gate one also on this measure.

Second, we note that the resulting dataset, containing 937 samples from the five normative categories, is not perfectly balanced. As table 7 in

[6]See here, last consulted on September 10, 2022.

the appendix, section C shows, the smallest sample size is in the deontological category with 137, while there are 301 samples in the Procedural category. Given our bootstrapping procedure, it has been impossible to achieve perfectly balanced sets without having to cut many good samples from the datasets.

Third, we suggest that, at this point, the results give us much reason to be optimistic. Using our bootstrapping process, we have been able to collect a dataset that is large enough and of sufficiently high quality to be useful to the community in many further applications. This in turn shows that the embeddings provided by pre-trained generic language models can provide enough information to build such a normative classifier. For instance, consider example (4), which the single-gate SVM of bootstrapping loop 3 has correctly classified as Rawlsian.

(4) Only a tax system that burdens exclusively the poorest group would be foreclosed on account of the difference principle, because that scheme of public finance would necessarily entail some redistribution, in the form of public goods at least, from the worst-off to the better-off.

What is remarkable about this correct prediction is that the typical superficial clues for Rawlsianism are all absent: mentioning "Rawls", emphasizing unjustifiable inequalities, etc. Rather, this sentence considers what taxation structures a central Rawlsian principle, namely the difference principle, excludes (rather than recommends).

6.3 Experiment 3: Annotation by Uninvolved Experts

We emphasize three insights provided by the results of this third experiment. First, the results support the reliability of the outcome of experiment 2. The fact that, in 85% of cases, one of the external annotators classified the samples in the same way as in the dataset suggests that, by and large, these classifications are reliable (Cohen's Kappa for this internal-external 2/3-agreement is at 0.81, see the appendix, section D).

Second, the classification is controversial, i.e., difficult. Annotators 1 and 2 diverge on their amount of agreement with annotator 0 (our internal annotator) by 19 percentage points, total agreement of all three annotators exists in only 51% of all cases. Likely, some of this divergence could be settled by discussing the samples in-person, but it still shows that this is a more complicated and controversial task than typical word-sense disambiguation. For instance, consider the example (5). Do you think it expresses a Deontological view, as it emphasizes equality of all individuals? While annotator 0 thought so, annotator 1 chose Utilitarian, probably because the sentence also suggests to focus on the (potential) welfare of everybody, that is, of the entire population. Thirdly, as annotator 3 did, you could also classify this sentence as Rawlsian, because it is about removing unjustified inequalities, namely such that concern an individual's potential to welfare.

(5) Social institutions should be designed to equalize the potential welfare of every individual.

Third, the variation between the normative categories is limited, not exceeding 18 percentage points. Given that the external annotators have not been involved in the specification of these categories (they were solely given the instructions that can be consulted in the appendix, section D), this gives reason to believe that these categories are sensible and hence useful to the community beyond the research lab that developed them.

7 Conclusion

In this article, we have explored the promises of using well-known classifying approaches together with state-of-the-art transformer-based PLMs to classify normative statements in the legal domain. Our results indicate that this approach does indeed hold substantial promise, which we would like to expand on in future research. In the meantime, we hope that our dataset will foster further research on this important, yet mostly uncharted, topic.

References

Elliott Ash, Malka Guillot, and Luyang Han. 2021. Machine extraction of tax laws from legislative texts. In *Proceedings of the Natural Legal Language Processing Workshop 2021*, pages 76–85, Punta Cana, Dominican Republic. Association for Computational Linguistics.

Bernhard E Boser, Isabelle M Guyon, and Vladimir N Vapnik. 1992. A training algorithm for optimal margin classifiers. In *Proceedings of the fifth annual workshop on Computational learning theory*, pages 144–152.

Ilias Chalkidis, Manos Fergadiotis, Prodromos Malakasiotis, Nikolaos Aletras, and Ion Androutsopoulos. 2020. LEGAL-BERT: The muppets straight out of law school. In *Findings of the Association for Computational Linguistics: EMNLP 2020*, pages 2898–2904, Online. Association for Computational Linguistics.

Ilias Chalkidis and Dimitrios Kampas. 2019. Deep learning in law: early adaptation and legal word embeddings trained on large corpora. *Artificial Intelligence and Law*, 27(2):171–198.

David Collier, Fernando Daniel Hidalgo, and Andra Olivia Maciuceanu. 2006. Essentially contested concepts: Debates and applications. *Journal of political ideologies*, 11(3):211–246.

Robert Dale. 2019. Law and word order: Nlp in legal tech. *Natural Language Engineering*, 25(1):211–217.

Jacob Devlin, Ming-Wei Chang, Kenton Lee, and Kristina Toutanova. 2019. BERT: Pre-training of deep bidirectional transformers for language understanding. In *Proceedings of the 2019 Conference of the North American Chapter of the Association for Computational Linguistics: Human Language Technologies, Volume 1 (Long and Short Papers)*, pages 4171–4186, Minneapolis, Minnesota. Association for Computational Linguistics.

Walter Bryce Gallie. 1955. Essentially contested concepts. In *Proceedings of the Aristotelian society*, volume 56, pages 167–198.

Clement Guitton, Aurelia Tamo-Larrieux, and Simon Mayer. 2022. A typology of automatically processable regulation. *Law, Innovation, and Technology*, 14(2).

Joe Hoover, Gwenyth Portillo-Wightman, Leigh Yeh, Shreya Havaldar, Aida Mostafazadeh Davani, Ying Lin, Brendan Kennedy, Mohammad Atari, Zahra Kamel, Madelyn Mendlen, et al. 2020. Moral foundations twitter corpus: A collection of 35k tweets annotated for moral sentiment. *Social Psychological and Personality Science*, 11(8):1057–1071.

Johannes Kiesel, Milad Alshomary, Nicolas Handke, Xiaoni Cai, Henning Wachsmuth, and Benno Stein. 2022. Identifying the human values behind arguments. In *Proceedings of the 60th Annual Meeting of the Association for Computational Linguistics (Volume 1: Long Papers)*, pages 4459–4471, Dublin, Ireland. Association for Computational Linguistics.

Alexandros Komninos and Suresh Manandhar. 2016. Dependency based embeddings for sentence classification tasks. In *Proceedings of the 2016 conference of the North American chapter of the association for computational linguistics: human language technologies*, pages 1490–1500.

Zhenzhong Lan, Mingda Chen, Sebastian Goodman, Kevin Gimpel, Piyush Sharma, and Radu Soricut. 2019. Albert: A lite bert for self-supervised learning of language representations. *arXiv preprint arXiv:1909.11942*.

Yinhan Liu, Myle Ott, Naman Goyal, Jingfei Du, Mandar Joshi, Danqi Chen, Omer Levy, Mike Lewis, Luke Zettlemoyer, and Veselin Stoyanov. 2019. Roberta: A robustly optimized bert pretraining approach. *arXiv preprint arXiv:1907.11692*.

Tomas Mikolov, Kai Chen, Greg Corrado, and Jeffrey Dean. 2013. Efficient estimation of word representations in vector space. *arXiv preprint arXiv:1301.3781*.

Roberto Navigli. 2009. Word sense disambiguation: A survey. *ACM computing surveys (CSUR)*, 41(2):1–69.

Joel Niklaus, Ilias Chalkidis, and Matthias Stürmer. 2021. Swiss-judgment-prediction: A multilingual legal judgment prediction benchmark. In *Proceedings of the Natural Legal Language Processing Workshop 2021*, pages 19–35, Punta Cana, Dominican Republic. Association for Computational Linguistics.

Robert Nozick. 1974. *Anarchy, state, and utopia*, volume 5038. new york: Basic Books.

F. Pedregosa, G. Varoquaux, A. Gramfort, V. Michel, B. Thirion, O. Grisel, M. Blondel, P. Prettenhofer, R. Weiss, V. Dubourg, J. Vanderplas, A. Passos, D. Cournapeau, M. Brucher, M. Perrot, and E. Duchesnay. 2011. Scikit-learn: Machine learning in Python. *Journal of Machine Learning Research*, 12:2825–2830.

Jeffrey Pennington, Richard Socher, and Christopher D Manning. 2014. Glove: Global vectors for word representation. In *Proceedings of the 2014 conference on empirical methods in natural language processing (EMNLP)*, pages 1532–1543.

Jack W. Rae, Sebastian Borgeaud, and Trevor Cai et al. 2021. Scaling language models: Methods, analysis & insights from training gopher. DeepMind Company Publication.

Nils Reimers and Iryna Gurevych. 2019. Sentence-bert: Sentence embeddings using siamese bert-networks. *arXiv preprint arXiv:1908.10084*.

Edwina L Rissland and David B Skalak. 1989. Combining case-based and rule-based reasoning: A heuristic approach. In *IJCAI*, pages 524–530.

Philippe-André Rodriguez. 2015. Human dignity as an essentially contested concept. *Cambridge Review of International Affairs*, 28(4):743–756.

Kathryn E Sanders. 1991. Representing and reasoning about open-textured predicates. In *Proceedings of the 3rd international conference on Artificial intelligence and law*, pages 137–144.

Victor Sanh, Lysandre Debut, Julien Chaumond, and Thomas Wolf. 2019. Distilbert, a distilled version of bert: smaller, faster, cheaper and lighter. *arXiv preprint arXiv:1910.01108*.

Jerrold Soh, How Khang Lim, and Ian Ernst Chai. 2019. Legal area classification: A comparative study of text classifiers on Singapore Supreme Court judgments. In *Proceedings of the Natural Legal Language Processing Workshop 2019*, pages 67–77, Minneapolis, Minnesota. Association for Computational Linguistics.

Kaitao Song, Xu Tan, Tao Qin, Jianfeng Lu, and Tie-Yan Liu. 2020. Mpnet: Masked and permuted pre-training for language understanding. *arXiv preprint arXiv:2004.09297*.

Li Tang and Simon Clematide. 2021. Searching for legal documents at paragraph level: Automating label generation and use of an extended attention mask for boosting neural models of semantic similarity. In *Proceedings of the Natural Legal Language Processing Workshop 2021*, pages 114–122, Punta Cana, Dominican Republic. Association for Computational Linguistics.

Ashish Vaswani, Noam Shazeer, Niki Parmar, Jakob Uszkoreit, Llion Jones, Aidan N. Gomez, Lukasz Kaiser, and Illia Polosukhin. 2017. Attention is all you need. In *Advances in Neural Information Processing Systems*, pages 5998–6008.

Wenhui Wang, Furu Wei, Li Dong, Hangbo Bao, Nan Yang, and Ming Zhou. 2020. Minilm: Deep self-attention distillation for task-agnostic compression of pre-trained transformers. *arXiv preprint arXiv:2002.10957*.

Matthijs J Warrens. 2015. Five ways to look at cohen's kappa. *Journal of Psychology & Psychotherapy*, 5(4):1.

Ludwig Wittgenstein. 2006/1953. Philosophische untersuchungen. In *Werkausgabe Band 1*. Suhrkamp.

Thomas Wolf, Lysandre Debut, Victor Sanh, Julien Chaumond, Clement Delangue, Anthony Moi, Pierric Cistac, Tim Rault, Rémi Louf, Morgan Funtowicz, Joe Davison, Sam Shleifer, Patrick von Platen, Clara Ma, Yacine Jernite, Julien Plu, Canwen Xu, Teven Le Scao, Sylvain Gugger, Mariama Drame, Quentin Lhoest, and Alexander M. Rush. 2019. Huggingface's transformers: State-of-the-art natural language processing. *arXiv preprint arXiv:1910.03771*.

Marco Wrzalik and Dirk Krechel. 2021. GerDaLIR: A German dataset for legal information retrieval. In *Proceedings of the Natural Legal Language Processing Workshop 2021*, pages 123–128, Punta Cana, Dominican Republic. Association for Computational Linguistics.

A Details on the dataset used

A.1 Sources for Experiment 1 and to Train for Bootstrapping Loop 1

Alm, J. & Melnik, M. I. (2005). Taxing the "Familiy" in the Individual Income Tax. Public Finance & Management, 5(1), 67-109.

Appelbaum, E. & Batt, R. (2017). Private Equity Partners Get Rich at Taxpayers Expense. Center for Economic and Policy Research.

Armstrong, C. (2013). Natural Resources: The Demands of Equality. Journal of Social Philosophy.

Avi-Yonah, R. S. (2002). Why Tax the Rich? Efficiency, Equity, and Progressive Taxation [Review of Does Atlas Shrug? The Economic Consequences of Taxing the Rich, by J. B. Slemrod]. The Yale Law Journal, 111(6), 1391–1416. https://doi.org/10.2307/797614

Barker, W. (2006). The Three Faces of Equality: Constitutional Requirements in Taxation. Case Western Reserve Law Review, 57(1), 1-53.

Baron, R. (2012). The Ethics of Taxation. Philosophy Now, 90.

Bezhanyan, R. (2017). Utilitarianism and Tax Policies.

Bird-Pollan, J. (2013). Unseating Privilege: Rawls, Equality of Opportunity, and Wealth Transfer Taxation. Wayne Law Review, 59(2), 713-742.

Bird-Pollan, J. (2016). Utilitarianism and Wealth Transfer Taxation. In Taxation of Wealth Transfers: A Philosophical Analysis, 124–151.

Bourguignon, F. (2018). Spreading the Wealth. Finance & Development, 55(1), 22-24.

Burgis, B. (2020). How to Debate Libertarians on Taxes — And Destroy Them. Jacobin.

Byrne, D. M. (1995). Progressive Taxation Revisited. Arizona Law Review, 37(3), 739-790.

Carens, J. H. (1986). Rights and Duties in an Egalitarian Society. Political Theory, 14(1), 31-50.

Cohn, A., Jessen, L. J., Klasnja, M. & Smeets, P. (2019). Why Do the Rich Oppose Redistribution? An Experiment with America's Top 5

Cooper, G. S. (1986). Income Tax Law and Contributive Justice: Some Thoughts on Defining and Expressing Consistent Theory of Tax Justice and Its Limitations. Australian Tax Forum, 3(3), 297-332.

Dodge, J. M. (2005). Theories of Tax Justice: Ruminations on the Benefit, Partnership, and Ability-to-Pay Principles. Tax Law Review, 58(4), 399-462.

Duff, D. G. (1993). Taxing Inherited Wealth: Philosophical Argument. Canadian Journal of Law and Jurisprudence, 6(1), 3-62.

Duff, D. G. (2005). Private Property and Tax Policy in a Libertarian World: A Critical Review. Canadian Journal of Law and Jurisprudence, 18(1), 23-45.

Durankev, B. (2019). Taxation and Social Justice. arXiv: General Economics. https://doi.org/10.48550/arXiv.1910.04155

Edwards, J. R. (2001). Taxation, Forced Labor, and Theft: Comment. The Independent Review, 6(2), 253–257.

Elkins, D. (2006). Horizontal Equity as Principle of Tax Theory. Yale Law & Policy Review, 24(1), 43-90.

Elkins, D. (2009). Taxation and the Terms of Justice. University of Toledo Law Review, 41(1), 73-106.

Epstein, R. A. (2005). Taxation with Representation: Or, the Libertarian Dilemma. Canadian Journal of Law and Jurisprudence, 18(1), 7-22.

Fleischer, M. (2010). Theorizing the Charitable Tax Subsidies: The Role of Distributive Justice. Washington University Law Review, 87(3), 505-566.

Frecknall-Hughes, J., Moizer, P., Doyle, E. & Summers, B. (2017). An Examination of Ethical Influences on the Work of Tax Practitioners. J Bus Ethics, 146, 729–745. https://doi.org/10.1007/s10551-016-3037-6

Galle, B. (2008). Tax Fairness. Washington and Lee Law Review, 65(4), 1323-1380.

Green, R. M. (1984). Ethics and Taxation: A Theoretical Framework. The Journal of Religious Ethics, 12(2), 146–161.

Gribnau, H. & Hughes-Frecknall, J. (2021). The Enlightenment and Influence of Social Contract Theory on Taxation. http://dx.doi.org/10.2139/ssrn.3963285

Hackney, P. (2021). Political Justice and Tax Policy: The Social Welfare Organization Case. Texas A&M Law Review, 8(2), 271-330. https://doi.org/10.37419/LR.V8.I2.2

Halliday, D. & Stewart, M. (2021). On "Dynastic" Inequality. In S. Gardiner (ed.) The Oxford Handbook of Intergenerational Ethics, 903.

Hänni, P. (2021). Chapter 9: The Swiss Tax System – Between Equality and Diversity. In The Principle of Equality in Diverse States, 253-289. https://doi.org/10.1163/9789004394612_011

Huemer, M. (2017). Is Taxation Theft? Libertarianism.org.

Hümbelin, O. & Farys, R. (2018). Income Redistribution Through Taxation – How Deductions Undermine the Effect of Taxes. Journal of Income Distribution, 25(1), 1-35.

Jestl, S. (2018). Inheritance Tax Regimes: A Comparison. The Vienna Institute for International Economic Studies. https://doi.org/10.3326/pse.45.3.3

Kamin, D. (2008). What Is Progressive Tax Change: Unmasking Hidden Values in Distributional Debates. New York University Law Review, 83(1), 241-292.

Kornhauser, M. E. (1995). Equality, Liberty, and Fair Income Tax. Fordham Urban Law Journal, 23(3), 607-662.

Lambert, P. J. & Naughton, H. T. (2009). The Equal Absolute Sacrifice Principle Revisited. Journal of Economic Surveys, 23(2), 328-349. http://dx.doi.org/10.1111/j.1467-6419.2008.00564.x

Leviner, S. (2006). From Deontology to Practical Application: The Vision of Good Society and the Tax System. Virginia Tax Review, 26(2), 405-446.

Leviner, S. (2012). The Normative Underpinnings of Taxation. Nevada Law Journal, 13(1), 95-133.

Lindsay, I. K. (2016). Tax Fairness by Convention: A Defense of Horizontal Equity. Florida Tax Review, 19(2), 79-119.

Mack, E. (2006). Non-Absolute Rights and Libertarian Taxation. Social Philosophy and Policy, 23(2), 109-141. https://doi.org/10.1017/S0265052506060195

Maloney, M. A. (1988). Distributive Justice: That is the Wealth Tax Issue. Ottawa Law Review, 20(3), 601-636.

Mankiw, N. G., Weinzierl, M. & Yagan, D. (2009). Optimal Taxation in Theory and Practice. Journal of Economic Perspectives, 23(4), 147-174. https://doi.org/10.1257/jep.23.4.147

McDaniel, P. R., & Repetti, J. R. (1993). Horizontal and Vertical Equity: The Musgrave/Kaplow Exchange. Florida Tax Review, 1(10), 607-622.

McIntyre, M. J. (1987). Tax Justice for Family Members after New York State Tax Reform. Albany Law Review, 51(3-4), 789-816.

Michael, M. A. (1997). Redistributive Taxation, Self-Ownership and the Fruit of Labour. Journal of

Applied Philosophy, 14(2), 137–146.

Milin, Z. (2014). Global Tax Justice and the Resource Curse: What Do Corporations Owe? Moral Philosophy and Politics, 1(1), 17-36. https://doi.org/10.1515/mopp-2013-0012

Miller, J. A. (2000). Equal Taxation: A Commentary. Hofstra Law Review, 29(2), 529-546.

Niesiobędzka, M., & Kołodziej, S. (2020). The Fair Process Effect in Taxation: The Roles of Procedural Fairness, Outcome Favorability and Outcome Fairness in the Acceptance of Tax Authority Decisions. Current Psychology: A Journal for Diverse Perspectives on Diverse Psychological Issues, 39(1), 246–253. https://doi.org/10.1007/s12144-017-9762-x

Ooi, V. (2016). Redistributive Taxation in the Modern World. Singapore Law Review, 34, 173-218.

Ozawa, M. N. (1973). Taxation and Social Welfare. Social Work, 18(3), 66–76.

Pawa, K. & Gee, C. (2021). Taxation and Distributive Justice in Singapore. IPS Working Papers, 42. Piketty, T. (2015). Capital, Inequality and Justice: Reflections on Capital in the Twenty-First Century. Basic Income Studies, 10(1), 141-156. https://doi.org/10.1515/bis-2015-0014

Porcano, T. M. (1984). Distributive Justice and Tax Policy. The Accounting Review, 59(4), 619–636.

Pressman, M. (2018). 'The Ability to Pay' in Tax Law: Clarifying the Concept's Egalitarian and Utilitarian Justifications and the Interactions between the Two. N.Y.U. Journal of Legislation & Public Policy, 21, 141-201.

Pryor, A. (2011). Ought There to Be Graduated Federal Income Tax: Is Robin Hood Justice, Justice at All? Georgetown Journal of Law & Public Policy, 9(2), 543-562.

Scheuer, F. (2020). Taxing the Superrich: Challenges of a Fair Tax System. UBS Center Public Paper.

Simester, A. A., & Chan, W. (2003). On Tax and Justice. Oxford Journal of Legal Studies, 23(4), 711-726.

Slemrod, J. (1998). The Economics of Taxing the Rich, National Bureau of Economic Research, 1-38. https://doi.org/10.3386/w6584

Stark, J. (2022). Tax Justice Beyond National Borders—International or Interpersonal? Oxford Journal of Legal Studies, 42(1), 133-160. https://doi.org/10.1093/ojls/gqab026

Steuerle, C. E. (2002). An Equal (Tax) Justice for All. Tax Justice, 253-284.

Sugin, L. (2004). Theories of Distributive Justice and Limitations on Taxation: What Rawls Demands from Tax Systems. Fordham Law Review, 72(5), 1991-2014.

Sugin, L. (2016). Rhetoric and Reality in the Tax Law of Charity. Fordham Law Review, 84(6), 2607-2632.

Svoboda, V. (2016). Libertarianism, Slavery, and Just Taxation. Humanomics: The International Journal of Systems and Ethics, 32(1), 69-79. https://doi.org/10.1108/H-05-2015-0031

Taite, P. C. (2014). Exploding Wealth Inequalities: Does Tax Policy Promote Social Justice or Social Injustice. Western New England Law Review, 36(3), 201-220.

Vallentyne, P. (2018). Libertarianism and Taxation. In M. O'Neill & S. Orr (ed.), Taxation: Philosophical Perspectives, 98–110.

Young, H. P. (1987). Progressive Taxation and the Equal Sacrifice Principle. Journal of Public Economics, 32, 203-214.

A.2 Sources for Predictions in the first Bootstrapping Loop

Avi-Yonah, R., Avi-Yonah, O., Fishbien, N., & Xu, H. (2020). Federalizing Tax Justice. Indiana Law Review, 53(3), 461-498. http://dx.doi.org/10.2139/ssrn.3249010

Baird, C. W. (1981). Proportionality, Justice, and the Value-Added Tax. Cato Journal, 1(2), 405-420.

Barker W. (2005). Expanding the Study of Comparative Tax Law to Promote Democratic Policy: The Example of the Move to Capital Gains Taxation in Post-Apartheid South Africa. Penn State Law Review, 109(3), 703-727.

Crawford, P. (2014). Occupy Wall Street, Distributive Justice, and Tax Scholarship: An Ideology Critique of the Consumption Tax Debate. University of New Hampshire Law Review, 12(2), 137-174.

Dagan, T. (2017). International Tax and Global Justice. Theoretical Inquiries in Law, 18(1), 1-36. http://dx.doi.org/10.2139/ssrn.2762110

Flynn, J. J., & Ruffinengo, P. (1975). Distributive Justice: Some Institutional Implication of Rawls' Theory of Justice. Utah Law Review, 1975(1), 123-157.

Fried, B. H. (1999). The Puzzling Case for Proportionate Taxation. Chapman Law Review, 2, 157-

196.

Kamin, D. (2008). What Is Progressive Tax Change: Unmasking Hidden Values in Distributional Debates. New York University Law Review, 83(1), 241-292.

Kaplow, L. (2007). Discounting Dollars, Discounting Lives: Intergenerational Distributive Justice and Efficiency. University of Chicago Law Review, 74(1), 79-118.

Kenealy, W. J. (1961). Equal Justice under Law Tax Aid to Education. Catholic Lawyer, 7(3), 183-202.

Kurland, N. G. (1977). Beyond ESOP: Steps Toward Tax Justice–Part 2. Tax Executive, 29(4), 386-402.

Maier, C. & Schanz, D. (2017). Towards Neutral Distribution Taxes and Vanishing Tax Effects in the European Union. http://dx.doi.org/10.2139/ssrn.2948475

McIntyre, M. J. (1988). Implications of US Tax Reform for Distributive Justice. Australian Tax Forum, 5(2), 219-256.

Murphy, L. B. (1996). Liberty, Equality, Well-Being: Rakowski on Wealth Transfer Taxation. Tax Law Review, 51(3), 473-494.

Repetti, J., & Ring, D. (2012). Horizontal Equity Revisited. Florida Tax Review, 13(3), 135-156.

van Apeldoorn, L. (2019). A Sceptic's Guide to Justice in International Tax Policy. Canadian Journal of Law and Jurisprudence, 32(2), 499-512. https://doi.org/10.1017/cjlj.2019.14

A.3 Sources for Predictions in the Second Bootstrapping Loop

Banfi, T. (2015). A Fair Tax (System) or an Ethical Taxpayer? Society and Economy, 37, 107–116. https://doi.org/10.1556/204.2015.37.s.7

Bărbuţă-Mişu, N. (2011). A Review of Factors for Tax Compliance. Economics and Applied Informatics, 1, 69-76.

Bradley, B., & Gephardt, R. (1984). Fixing the Income Tax with the Fair Tax. Yale Law & Policy Review, 3(1), 41–57.

Braithwaite, V. (2003), Who's Not Paying their Fair Share: Public Perceptions of the Australian Tax System. Australian Journal of Social Issues, 38, 323-348. https://doi.org/10.1002/j.1839-4655.2003.tb01149.x

Braithwaite, V. (2003). Tax System Integrity and Compliance: The Democratic Management of the Tax System. In Taxing Democracy, 269–287.

DeConcini, D. (1985). A Proposed Simple and Fair Tax. Journal of Legislation, 12(2), 143-155.

Gephardt, R. A., & Bryant, E. G. (1985). The Fair Tax Act: A Plan for Simple, Fair, and Economically Rational Tax. Journal of Legislation, 12(2), 129-142.

Herzberg, A. (1963). Blueprint of Fair Tax Administration. Taxes - The Tax Magazine, 41(3), 161-164.

McKerchar, M. (2008). Philosophical Paradigms, Inquiry Strategies and Knowledge Claims: Applying the Principles of Research Design and Conduct to Taxation. eJournal of Tax Research, 6(1), 5-22.

Osberg, L. (2016). 2. What's Fair?: The Problem of Equity in Taxation. In A. Maslove (Ed.), Fairness in Taxation, 63-86. https://doi.org/10.3138/9781442623293-004

Rosow, S. (1984). Treasury's Tax Reform Proposals: Not A Fair Tax. Yale Law & Policy Review, 3(1), 58-72.

Schoenblum, J. A. (1995). Tax Fairness or Unfairness A Consideration of the Philosophical Bases for Unequal Taxation of Individuals. American Journal of Tax Policy, 12(2), 221-272.

Slemrod, J. (2002). Tax Systems. The Reporter, 3, 1-17.

Slemrod, J. (2018). Is This Tax Reform, or Just Confusion? Journal of Economic Perspectives, 32(4), 73-96. https://doi.org/10.1257/jep.32.4.73

Sugin, L. (2011). A Philosophical Objection to the Optimal Tax Model. Tax Law Review, 64(2), 229-282.

A.4 Sources for Predictions in the Third boostrapping loop

Bello, K.B., & Danjuma, I.M. (2014). Review of Models/Theories Explaining Tax Compliance Behavior. Sains Humanika, 2(3), 35-38. https://doi.org/10.11113/sh.v2n3.432

Benham, F. (1942). What is the Best Tax-System? Economica, 9(34), 115–126. https://doi.org/10.2307/2549805

Bogenschneider, B. (2017). A Philosophy Toolkit for Tax Lawyers. Akron Law Review, 50(3), 452-494.

Buehler, A. G. (1949). The Cost and Benefit Theories. Tax Law Review, 5(1), 17-34.

Cobham, A. (2005). Taxation Policy and Development. OCGG Economy Analysis, 2, 1-23.

Colm, G. (1934). The Ideal Tax System. Social Research, 1(3), 319–342.

Colm, G. (1940). Conflicting Theories of Corporate Income Taxation. Law and Contemporary Problems, 7(2), 281-290.

Diamond, P. A., & Mirrlees, J. A. (1971). Optimal Taxation and Public Production I: Production Efficiency. The American Economic Review, 61(1), 8–27.

Dimopoulos, T. (2015). Theories and Philosophy of Property Taxation.

Dom, R. & Miller, M. (2018). Reforming tax systems in the developing world: What can we learn from the past? Overseas Development Institute (ODI).

Dorocak, J. R. (2015). What Would Libertarian Tax Look Like. South Texas Law Review, 57(2), 147-168.

Escarraz, D. R. (1967). Wicksell and Lindahl: Theories of Public Expenditure and Tax Justice Reconsidered. National Tax Journal, 20(2), 137–148.

Fagan, E. D. (1938). Recent and Contemporary Theories of Progressive Taxation. Journal of Political Economy, 46(4), 457–498.

Fausto, D. (2008). The Italian theories of progressive taxation. The European Journal of the History of Economic Thought, 15(2), 293-315. https://doi.org/10.1080/09672560802037607

Feser, E. (2000). Taxation, Forced Labor, and Theft. The Independent Review, 5(2), 219–235.

Hamlin, A. (2018). What Political Philosophy Should Learn from Economics about Taxation. In M. O'Neill & S. Orr (ed.), Taxation: Philosophical Perspectives, S. 1–28.

Hassett, K.& Auerbach A. (2005). Toward Fundamental Tax Reform, American Enterprise Institute.

Hodgson, H. (2010). Theories of Distributive Justice: Frameworks for Equity. Journal of the Australasian Tax Teachers Association, 5, 86-116.

Horvitz, J. S. (1977). Theories of Legal Responsibility in Regard to the CPA in Tax Practice. Baylor Law Review, 29(3), 475-498.

Howard, J. M. (1992). When Two Tax Theories Collide: A Look at the History and Future of Progressive and Proportionate Personal Income Taxation. Washburn Law Journal, 32(1), 43-76.

Josheski, D. & Boshkov T. (2020). Critical Review of the (Second Wave) Optimal Tax Theories. University Goce Delcev-Shtip. http://dx.doi.org/10.2139/ssrn.3531287

Kiser, E. (1994). Markets and Hierarchies in Early Modern Tax Systems: A Principal-Agent Analysis. Politics & Society, 22(3), 284–315. https://doi.org/10.1177/0032329294022003003

Kordana, K., & Tabachnick, D. (2006). Taxation, the Private Law, and Distributive Justice. Social Philosophy and Policy, 23(2), 142-165. https://doi.org/10.1017/S0265052506060201

LeFevre, T. A. (2017). Justice in Taxation. Vermont Law Review, 41(4), 763-798.

McCaffery, E. J. (1994). The Political Liberal Case Against the Estate Tax. Philosophy & Public Affairs, 23(4), 281–312.

McCaffery, E. J., & Hines, J. (2010). The Last Best Hope for Progressivity in Tax. Southern California Law Review, 83(5), 1031-1098.

Misra, F. (2019). Tax Compliance: Theories, Research Development and Tax Enforcement Models. Accounting Research Journal of Sutaatmadja, 3(2), 189-204. https://doi.org/10.35310/accruals.v3i2.72

Muzurura, J., Nyoni, J. & Mataruka, L. (2021). The Anatomy of Tax Evasion and Tax Morale: Lessons from Tax Theories, Tax Audits and Surveys in Zimbabwe. International Journal of Social Science and Economic Research, 6(4), 1283- 1303. https://doi.org/10.46609/IJSSER.2021.v06i04.011

Panova, T. V. & Panov, E. G. (2021). Tax philosophy versus fiscal sociology: choice problem in teaching, SHS Web of Conferences, 103, 1-4. https://doi.org/10.1051/shsconf/202110301027

Pirttila, J. (1999). Tax Evasion and Economies in Transition: Lessons from Tax Theory. BOFIT Discussion Paper, 2. http://dx.doi.org/10.2139/ssrn.1016663

Saez, E. & Stantcheva, S. (2016). Generalized Social Marginal Welfare Weights for Optimal Tax Theory. American Economic Review, 106(01), 24-45. https://doi.org/10.3386/w18835

Sahota, G. S. (1978). Theories of Personal Income Distribution: A Survey. Journal of Economic Literature, 16(1), 1–55.

Salahuddin, A. (2018). Robert Nozick's Entitlement Theory of Justice, Libertarian Rights and the Minimal State: A Critical Evaluation. Journal of Civil & Legal Sciences, 7(1), 234-238. https://doi.org/10.4172/2169-0170.1000234

Samuelson, P. A. (1958). Aspects of Public Expenditure Theories. The Review of Economics and Statistics, 40(4), 332–338. https://doi.org/10.2307/1926336

Slemrod, J. (2022). Group Equity and Implicit

Discrimination in Tax Systems. National Tax Journal, 75(1). https://doi.org/10.1086/717960

Sugin, L. (2004). Theories of Distributive Justice and Limitations on Taxation: What Rawls Demands from Tax Systems. Fordham Law Review, 72(5), 1991-2014.

Sunderman, M., Birch, J., Cannaday, R. & Hamilton, T. (1990). Testing for Vertical Inequity in Property Tax Systems, Journal of Real Estate Research, 5(3), 319-334, https://doi.org/10.1080/10835547.1990.12090625

van der Vossen, Bas. (2017). Libertarianism. Oxford Research Encyclopedia of Politics.

B Details on Experiment 1

SVM Hyperparameters & Implementation Details We use the following different hyperparameters for our search:[7]

C Regularization parameter, inversely proportional to strength of regularization – a large C causes individual training samples to influence the resulting function stronger: 0.1, 1, 10, 100, 1000

kernel Kind of kernel used in the SVM: rbf (radial basis function), poly (polynomial), linear

gamma Specifies the sphere of influence of datapoints on the resulting SVM: 1, 0.1, 0.01, 0.001, 0.0001

We have used scikit-learn's default implementation of SVM that automatically chooses one-vs.one for classification tasks with more than two classes, and it automatically employs five-fold cross-validation.

Models & Embedding Types We are testing three different kinds of models; for references, see above, section 2; for the full list of models, see below, table 5. We use four different routines to extract the embeddings:

Sentence-Averaged Word-Based In this routine, we use the average of all word embeddings, as the model delivers it for all words in the sentence. Hence, the sentence-embedding used here is the average of all word embeddings whose words appear in the sentence. Here, we use well-researched transformer-based PLMs, namely RoBERTa and BERT, but also models fine-tuned to first-order legal domains such as legal-bert (see above, section 2)

Sentence-based Here, we use the embeddings, as they directly result from the sentence-bert models trained by Reimers and Gurevych 2019. These models also output the average of all word embeddings (which we manually compute in the second variant), but they have been fine-tuned on the sentence level by training them on a wide variety of sentence-level tasks and datasets (the original models reported in Reimers and Gurevych 2019 use the combination of the SNLI and the Multi-Genre NLI datasets). Furthermore, the models that they fine-tuning are of many flavors, ranging from classical BERT to recent proposals such as mpnet (see above, section 2).

Average of Classical Word Embeddings We here test two classical kinds of word embeddings, GloVE as well as Komninos (see above, section 2), again taking the average of all word embeddings as the sentence embedding.

Table 5 lists all of the models used.

Word-Based Models
bert-base-cased
bert-large-cased
roberta-large
legal-bert-base-uncased
SBERT-Models
paraphrase-TinyBERT-L6-v2
paraphrase-distilroberta-base-v2
paraphrase-mpnet-base-v2
paraphrase-multilingual-mpnet-base-v2
paraphrase-MiniLM-L12-v2
paraphrase-MiniLM-L6-v2
paraphrase-albert-small-v2
paraphrase-multilingual-MiniLM-L12-v2
paraphrase-MiniLM-L3-v2
nli-mpnet-base-v2
nli-roberta-base-v2
nli-distilroberta-base-v2
distiluse-base-multilingual-cased-v1
stsb-mpnet-base-v2
stsb-distilroberta-base-v2
distiluse-base-multilingual-cased-v2
stsb-roberta-base-v2
Classical Models
average_word_embeddings_glove.6B.300d
average_word_embeddings_komninos

Table 5: Overview on the 23 models tested In clustering.

Table 6 lists all models whose embedding were used in experiment 1 with the accuracies of the best performing SVM that was found in the hyperparameter search specifically for these embeddings. For instance, The embeddings of roberta-large can be

[7] Compare the details here, last consulted on September 16, 2022.

Modelname	Type	Norm	5cat
pp-ml-mpnet-base-v2	sbert	91%	87%
pp-mpnet-base-v2	sbert	91%	85%
nli-mpnet-base-v2	sbert	91%	84%
stsb-roberta-base-v2	sbert	94%	83%
stsb-droberta-base-v2	sbert	94%	83%
nli-droberta-base-v2	sbert	95%	82%
roberta-large	avword	98%	82%
nli-roberta-base-v2	sbert	94%	82%
pp-droberta-base-v2	sbert	95%	80%
stsb-mpnet-base-v2	sbert	91%	80%
du-base-ml-cased-v2	sbert	91%	77%
pp-MiniLM-L12-v2	sbert	91%	77%
pp-MiniLM-L6-v2	sbert	91%	77%
du-base-ml-cased-v1	sbert	91%	77%
awe_komninos	sbert	91%	77%
bert-large-cased	avword	91%	77%
pp-ml-MiniLM-L12-v2	sbert	91%	77%
bert-base-cased	avword	91%	76%
pp-TinyBERT-L6-v2	sbert	91%	76%
awe_glove.6B.300d	sbert	91%	75%
pp-MiniLM-L3-v2	sbert	91%	75%
pp-albert-small-v2	sbert	91%	74%
nlpaueb-legalbertbase	avword	91%	74%

Table 6: Results of classifying samples as belonging to one of the five normative categories (35 samples each, column 5cats) and as normative or nonnormative (175/1708 samples, column Norm). Most frequent class baseline reaches accuracy of 20% for 5cat and 91% for Norm. "pp" = paraphrase, "ml" = multilingual, "droberta" = distilroberta, "du" = distiluse, "awe" = average_word_embedding.

combined with an SVM to form a classifier that delivers 98% accuracy in the normative-nonnormative task and 82% at the 5cat task.

C Details on Experiment 2

Table 7 shows the distribution of samples across the normative classes in the final dataset that results from a combination of the corrected outputs from both methods after bootstrapping loop 3 with any duplicates removed.

D Details on Experiment 3

Figure 3 gives Cohen's Kappa for the agreement between our three annotators; briefly, Cohen's Kappa

Category	# Samples
Deontological	137
Libertarian	159
Procedural	301
Rawlsian	138
Utilitarian	202
None	2194
Total Normative	937
Grand Total	3131

Table 7: Samples by category and in total in the final dataset, combining the reviewed output from bootstrapping loop 3 by both methods, and having removed any duplicates.

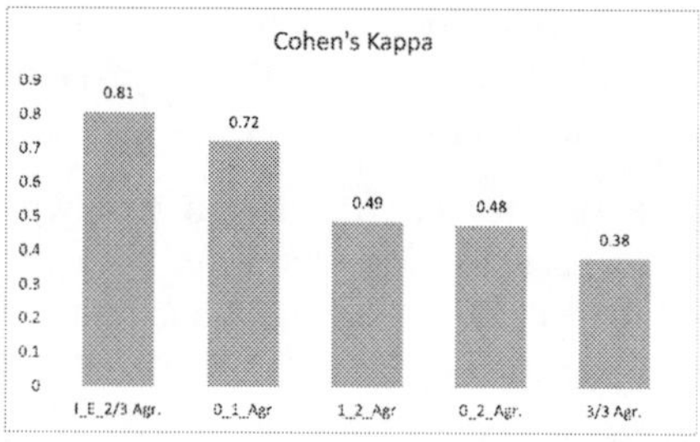

Figure 3: Cohen's Kappa for the inter-annotator agreement in experiment 3.

gives an inter-annotator agreement that takes into account the statistical probability of annotators agreeing by mere chance (see Warrens 2015 for further details). As can be seen, the basic layout doesn't change when compared to the accuracies reported above, figure 2: Internal-External-2/3-agreement is highest, annotator 2 diverges from 0 and 1 quite often, 3/3-agreement is lowest.

Table 8 gives the inter-annotator agreement by source of sample. For instance, the inter-annotator agreement with samples that were selected by our expert directly (as opposed to building on predictions by a classifier called "Fully human") is highest both in internal-external 2/3 agreement and 3/3 agreement. Table 8 shows that the origin of the samples does make a difference for the overall inter-annotator agreement, but a relatively small one, not exceeding 12 percentage points in the internal-external 2/3 agreement. This adds further evidence to the claim that our internal annotator has not been overly biased towards the output of our classifiers. Otherwise, we would expect annotators 1 and 2 to diverge from annotator 1 much more often regarding machine-produced samples than regarding

Origin	Count	I_E_2/3 Agr.	3/3 Agr.
Fully Human	175	90%	65%
Single-Gate	122	89%	51%
Dual-Gate	353	78%	41%

Table 8: Inter-annotator agreement by origin of the samples("I_E_2/3" continues to represent the 2/3-agreement where one of the agreeing annotators is our internal annotator 0, the other is either 1 or 2).

fully-human compiled samples.

In the remainder of this section, we give the literal instructions given to annotators, anonymized for reviewing.

General Task Description Thank you very much for taking the time to annotate our samples and thereby contribute to the ongoing NLP project. In the following, we provide instructions to ensure that your annotations are maximally useful to the project. Please read through the entire paper before annotating. Let me know if you have any questions: ANEMAIL.

For the list of statements enclosed, you are asked to make two decisions for each sample:

1. Decide whether the sample expresses a normative statement: If you think it does, enter "YES" into column A "Annotator Norm", if you think not, enter "NO". Please make sure you type it in all caps without any blanks.

2. If you have answered "YES" for a given sample, decide to which of the five normative categories the sample belongs; if you are unable to assign the sample to any of the five categories, use "OTHER"; please only use this category if you are fully convinced that the sentence does not fit any of the categories. Depending on your judgment, enter one of the following into Column B "Annotator Cat" (again, make sure you type it without blanks, and always in the exact way specified here):

   (a) Libertarian
   (b) Rawlsian
   (c) Deontological
   (d) Procedural
   (e) Utilitarian
   (f) OTHER

Details on categorization

1. **Normative vs. Not Normative**: Does the statement (a) make a direct recommendation what the state, an individual, etc. should be doing, or (b) does the statement make an assertion about what is just/unjust, fair/unfair, moral/immoral? If either (a) or (b) applies, the statement is normative.
   Examples:

   (a) **Not normative**: "An income tax can be used to redistribute taxable income."
   (b) **Normative**: "All that matters for the Utilitarian is maximizing utility, and by distributing the tax cut across income classes, a previously optimal tax system would no longer be so."

2. Following is a brief description of the normative categories that can help you decide about categorization. We are aware that the categorization proposed here is not beyond dispute; for the present project, we ask you to simply adhere to the categorization sketched here. Let us know if any of the categories were particularly challenging during the annotation process.

   (a) **Libertarianism** the essential idea is that the market outcome regarding income and wealth distribution is just and deserved and, therefore, taxation should not lead to redistribution. Therefore, taxation should be kept at an absolute minimum, what is needed to ensure that a minimal state is functioning.
   Examples:
      i. Nozick likens the imposition of redistributive taxes (typically progressively designed) on people who are working to earn money to partial enslavement.
      ii. the anti-progressive tax argument is often characterized as an argument that every person has a responsibility to take care of himself, and no one, including the wealthy, has an obligation to assist those in need.

   (b) **Rawlsians** in contrast, hold that the state should redistribute wealth and income to the extent to which this can reduce unjustified inequalities in the distribution of wealth. Rawlsians hold that many inequalities are in fact unjust, including,

for instance, the wealth of the family into which one is born, or the quality of the schools that are available in your area. As a consequence, Rawlsians will typically defend progressive taxation of both income and wealth.
Examples:

i. The increasing inequality of market income can be significantly ameliorated by the redistributive effect of the tax transfer system, if it is appropriately targeted.
ii. By distributing the tax burden more onerously on those who have the most physical wealth, equality of opportunity goals will be furthered.

(c) The term **Deontological** ethics covers a broad variety of positions. For the purpose of the present annotations, we consider positions as Deontological if they focus on the treatment of the individual taxpayer as opposed to any effects of this treatment, say the (re)distribution of the income within a society. The category helps us to cover the widespread argument that taxpayers should be treated equally (i.e., horizontal equity).
Examples:

i. Max burdens should bear similarly upon persons whom we regard as in substantially similar circumstances, and differently where circumstances differ.
ii. Horizontal equity requires equals to be treated equally

(d) **Procedural** positions hold that just tax laws are the outcome of free deliberative debate about the main design elements of the societal structure. This includes, for instance, a Habermasian approach aimed at achieving a just societal structure based on a democratic decision-making process.
Examples:

i. For Locke himself, the key institutional requirement was that taxes should not be levied except by "the consent of the people," which he understood as "the consent of the majority, giving it either by themselves, or their representatives chosen by them."
ii. As expected, respondents were more accepting of changes introduced in a fair manner than in an unfair manner, even if the changes resulted in higher tax burdens.

(e) **Utilitarian** positions emphasize the effect on overall happiness or welfare that a certain tax provision has. Hence, rather than capitalizing on participative, democratic decision-making, the equal treatment of individuals, or reducing unjustified inequalities, Utilitarians consider the overall net increase or decrease in wealth, happiness, or welfare, that a tax provision has on the society in question. Often, Utilitarians argue that the least well-off should benefit most from redistribution caused by taxation because their happiness shows the largest relative increase if they receive a certain amount of money.
Examples:

i. Efficiency analysis looks to overall social welfare as a measure of a tax's virtue.
ii. 68 Inequality is considered unfair because of the arbitrariness of unequal outcomes.69 But this inequality can potentially be justified in fairness terms if those at the bottom are made better off because of it.

ClassActionPrediction: A Challenging Benchmark for Legal Judgment Prediction of Class Action Cases in the US

Gil Semo* **Dor Bernsohn** **Ben Hagag** **Gila Hayat**
Darrow AI Ltd.
30 Ha'arbaa Street, Tel Aviv, Israel
firstname.lastname@darrow.ai

Joel Niklaus*†
Niklaus.ai
Schwarztorstrasse 108, Bern, Switzerland
joel@niklaus.ai

Abstract

The research field of Legal Natural Language Processing (NLP) has been very active recently, with Legal Judgment Prediction (LJP) becoming one of the most extensively studied tasks. To date, most publicly released LJP datasets originate from countries with civil law. In this work, we release, for the first time, a challenging LJP dataset focused on class action cases in the US. It is the first dataset in the common law system that focuses on the harder and more realistic task involving the complaints as input instead of the often used facts summary written by the court. Additionally, we study the difficulty of the task by collecting expert human predictions, showing that even human experts can only reach 53% accuracy on this dataset. Our Longformer model clearly outperforms the human baseline (63%), despite only considering the first 2,048 tokens. Furthermore, we perform a detailed error analysis and find that the Longformer model is significantly better calibrated than the human experts. Finally, we publicly release the dataset and the code used for the experiments.

1 Introduction

Recently, the literature in Legal Natural Language Processing (NLP) has grown at a fast pace, firmly establishing it as an important specialized domain in the broader NLP ecosystem. As part of this strong growth and as a first step establishing Legal NLP in the field, many legal datasets have been released in the fields of Legal Judgment Prediction (LJP) (Niklaus et al., 2021a; Chalkidis et al., 2019), Law Area Prediction (Glaser and Matthes, 2020), Legal Information Retrieval (Wrzalik and Krechel, 2021), Argument Mining (Urchs et al., 2022), Topic Classification (Chalkidis et al., 2021a), Named Entity Recognition (Luz de Araujo et al., 2018; Angelidis et al., 2018; Leitner et al., 2019), Natural Language Inference (Koreeda and Manning, 2021), Question Answering (Zheng et al., 2021; Hendrycks et al., 2021), and Summarization (Shen et al., 2022; Kornilova and Eidelman, 2019).

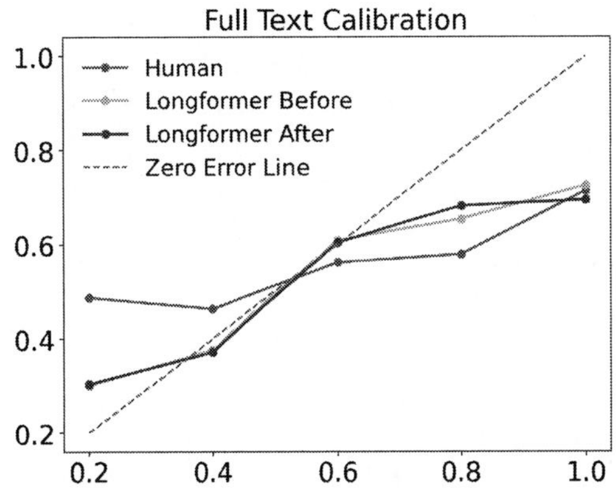

Figure 1: Calibration plot on the Full Text dataset. The human experts rated the confidence of their predictions on a score from 1 to 5. The confidence scores of the Longformer models were binned into 5 buckets.

In particular, the field of LJP has been very active, with many datasets released recently. Cui et al. (2022) surveyed the field and divided the datasets into five subtasks. In this work, we release a dataset belonging to the category of the Plea Judgment Prediction (PJP) task. Most other PJP datasets use the facts summary, written by the court (clerks or judges) as input (Cui et al., 2022). The facts are written in such a way as to support the final decision (Niklaus et al., 2021a) and require extensive work by highly qualified legal experts (Ma et al., 2021). In contrast, in this work we consider the plaintiff's pleas (AKA complaints) as input, making the task more realistic for use in real-world applications.

Most LJP datasets released so far are from countries with civil law. Our dataset originates from the United States, the largest country employing the common law legal system. To the best of our knowledge, we are the first to release a dataset specifically targeting class action lawsuits.

* Equal Contribution
† Corresponding Author

Proceedings of the Natural Legal Language Processing Workshop 2022, pages 31 - 46
December 8, 2022 ©2022 Association for Computational Linguistics

Motivation

The 16th United Nations Sustainable Development Goal (UNSDG) is to "Promote peaceful and inclusive societies for sustainable development, provide access to justice for all and build effective, accountable and inclusive institutions at all levels". Class actions are a private enforcement instrument that enables courts to organize the mass adjudication of meritorious claims by underrepresented individuals and communities. Without class actions, many victims of illegal action would never get their day in court. Making case outcomes and facts accessible is crucial to strengthen the effective use of class actions and private enforcement to drive UNSDG 16. With the power of early LJP, plaintiffs will have the ability to bring only meritorious cases to court, and defendants are more likely to resolve them faster.

Main Research Questions

In this work, we pose and examine three main research questions:
RQ1: *To what extent is it possible to determine the outcome of US class action cases using only the textual part of the complaints (without metadata)?*
RQ2: *To what extent can we use Temperature Scaling (TS) to better calibrate our models?*
RQ3: *To what extent can expert human lawyers solve the proposed task?*

Contributions

The contributions of this paper are four-fold:

- We curate a new specialized dataset of 10.8K class action complaints in the US from 2012 to 2022 annotated with the binary outcome: win or lose (plaintiff side). In contrast to most other LJP datasets it is (a) from a country with the common law system (where there are less datasets available), (b) it is specialized to class actions (important types of complaints ensuring justice for numerous often under-represented individuals), and (c) it uses the plaintiff's pleas as input instead of the facts, making the task more realistic. To the best of our knowledge, our work is the first dataset with plaintiff's pleas in the common law system and in the English language.
- We conduct a detailed analysis of the studied models using Integrated Gradients (IG) and model calibration using TS (Guo et al., 2017a).
- We perform an experiment with human experts on a randomly selected subset of the dataset, showing that our Longformer model both outperforms the human experts in terms of accuracy and calibration.
- We publicly release a sample of 3,000 cases from the annotated dataset[1] together with the human expert labels[2] and the code for the experiments[3].

2 Legal Background

2.1 Class Action Lawsuits

Class actions are a unique procedural instrument that allows one person to sue a company, not only on behalf of himself, but for everyone that has been injured by the same wrongdoing. In contrast to traditional lawsuits, in a class action lawsuit a plaintiff sues the defendant(s) on behalf of a class of absent parties. Class action lawsuits typically involve a minimum of 40 claimants. Rather than filing individual lawsuits for each damaged person, class actions allow the plaintiffs to unite and sue through a single proceeding. Thus, class actions are usually large and important cases and contain more complexity due to the high number of represented plaintiffs. These characteristics make class action a legal enforcement mechanism, along with police and regulators. Class actions both deter companies from harming people in the first place, and give compensation to the large number of victims hurt by the violation, giving consumers power over large corporations.

2.2 Definitions

Civil Law vs. Common Law: In both civil law and common law systems, courts rule based on laws and precedents (previous case law, mostly from the Supreme Court). However, in common law countries (mainly present in the UK and its former Colonies), case law dominates, whereas in civil law countries (most other countries) laws are more important. Note, that the differences are often not clear-cut, and courts usually use a combination of both laws and precedent for their rulings.
Complaint: A complaint is a written pleading to initiate a lawsuit. It includes the plaintiff's cause of action, the court's jurisdiction, and the plaintiff's demand for judicial relief. It is necessary for

[1] https://huggingface.co/datasets/darrow-ai/USClassActions

[2] https://huggingface.co/datasets/darrow-ai/USClassActionOutcomes_ExpertsAnnotations

[3] https://github.com/darrow-labs/ClassActionPrediction

the complaint to state all of the plaintiff's claims against the defendant, as well as what remedy the plaintiff seeks. A complaint must state "enough facts to state a claim to relief that is plausible on its face" (Twombly, 2007). The standards for filing a complaint vary from state to federal courts, or from one state to another. A typical class action complaint contains the allegations, the background details about both the plaintiff and the defendant, and the facts.

Allegations: In a complaint, allegations are statements of claimed facts. These statements are only considered allegations until they are proven. An allegation can be based on information and belief if the person making the statement is unsure of the facts. In the complaint, allegations can appear twice: once as a summary at the beginning and once in more detail later. There is usually a reference to the act that the plaintiff's attorney claims to have been violated in the allegations.

Background Details: The complaint contains background sections such as the plaintiff's history, class definitions, the defendant's history, and details about the platform/service in which the allegations took place.

Plaintiff's Facts: The plaintiff's facts or "factual background", are statements that can be proven and are often backed up with references and event dates. Note that the plaintiff's facts are written by the plaintiff lawyers.

Facts Summary: The facts summary or "factual description", are the summary of the accepted facts by the court and are written by the clerks or judges. The facts summary is usually more condensed in higher courts. Most previous LJP tasks used facts of this type. Since in this paper we consider complaints as input, when "facts" are mentioned we refer to the plaintiff's facts.

Case Description: The case description is written by the court clerks or judges and usually includes the header, the facts, the considerations, and the rulings.

Class Action Outcomes

Table 1 shows the outcomes possible in class action cases. In the following, we briefly describe each of the outcomes.

Settled: "Settling a case" refers to resolving a dispute before the trial ends.

Uncontested Dismissal: Without any opposition from the parties, the case is dismissed and closed.

Motion to Dismiss: The case was dismissed by the court following the defendant's formal request for a court to dismiss the case.

Outcome	Bin. Label	# Examples (%)
Settled	win	5234 (48.64%)
Other - Plaintiff	win	58 (00.52%)
Uncontested Dismissal	lose	4544 (42.23%)
Motion to Dismiss	lose	755 (07.01%)
Other - Defendant	lose	170 (01.56%)

Table 1: This table shows the original outcome together ruled by the court with the frequency and the final binarized label we map it to.

3 Related Work

LJP is an important and well-studied task in legal NLP. Cui et al. (2022) subdivide LJP into five subtasks: (a) In the *Article Recommendation Task*, systems predict relevant law articles for a given case (Aletras et al., 2016; Chalkidis et al., 2019; Ge et al., 2021). (b) The goal of the *Charge Prediction Task*, mainly studied in China, is to predict the counts the defendant is charged for based on the facts of the case (Zhong et al., 2018; Hu et al., 2018; Zhong et al., 2020). (c) In the *Prison Term Prediction Task*, systems predict the prison time for the defendant as ruled by the judge (Zhong et al., 2018; Chen et al., 2019). (d) In the *Court View Generation Task*, systems generate court views (explanation written by judges to interpret the judgment decision) (Ye et al., 2018; Wu et al., 2020). (e) In the *Plea Judgment Prediction Task*, systems predict the case outcome based on the case's facts (Niklaus et al., 2021b; Şulea et al., 2017; Lage-Freitas et al., 2022; Long et al., 2019; Ma et al., 2021; Strickson and De La Iglesia, 2020; Malik et al., 2021a; Alali et al., 2021). Since our work belongs to the PJP category, in the following, we elaborate more on the related work in this area.

Civil Law Niklaus et al. (2021b) released a trilingual (German, French, Italian) Swiss dataset from the Federal Supreme Court of Switzerland. They use the facts summary as input and predict a binary output: approval or dismissal of the plaintiff's pleas for approx. 85K decisions. Şulea et al. (2017) released a dataset of approx. 127K French Supreme Court cases. As input, they used the entire case description and not only the facts summary, presumably making the task considerably easier and a possible explanation for their high performance on the dataset. As output, they consider up to 8 classes of decisions ruled by the court. Lage-Freitas et al.

(2022) released a dataset comprising roughly 4K cases from a Brazilian State higher court (appellate court). They predicted three labels from the entire case description (written by the judges/clerks). Jacob de Menezes-Neto and Clementino (2022) release a large dataset of over 765K cases from the 5th Regional Federal Court of Brazil. They investigate a binary prediction task (whether the previous decision was reversed or not) using the entire case description as input. Long et al. (2019) studied the LJP task on 100K Chinese divorce proceedings considering three types of information as input: applicable law articles, fact description, and plaintiffs' pleas. Their model predicts a binary output. Ma et al. (2021) released a dataset comprising 70.5K civil cases (private lending) from China. They consider the more realistic task of inputting the plaintiff's complaints (together with debate data) instead of the easier facts summary used by most previous works. As output, their models predict three classes (reject, partially support and support). Similarly, our work also studies the more realistic (and challenging) use case of using the plaintiff's pleas as input instead of the heavily processed facts.

Common Law Strickson and De La Iglesia (2020) released a dataset of 5K cases from the UK's highest court of appeal. As input, they consider the case description and their models predict two labels (allow vs. dismiss). Malik et al. (2021a) study a dataset of 35K Indian Supreme Court cases in English. They use the case description as input and predict a binary outcome (accepted vs. rejected). Alali et al. (2021) study a dataset of 2.4K US Supreme Court decisions. Their models used the facts summary as input and predicted a binary output (first party won vs. second party won). In contrast, our dataset is ~ 5 times larger and is specialized to the rare subset of class action cases.

Apart from Ma et al. (2021), the PJP task based on plaintiff's complaints has not been studied before. In contrast, most previous works studied textual input originating from the case description written by the court.

4 Dataset Description

In this section, we describe the dataset origin and statistics in detail. Additionally, we elaborate on the dataset construction process and the variants we produced.

Figures 2a and 2b show the distribution of cases across the most frequent states and courts in the dataset, respectively. Note that the origin of these class action lawsuits is very diverse, both across states and across courts. Not surprisingly, population-rich states like California, Florida, and New York lead the list. However, while California is more than double in population (39.5M vs. 20.2M as of April 2021), the number of class action lawsuits has the inverse relationship ($\sim$ 3K from New York and $\sim$ 1.8K from California). We assume that the complicated filing system in California could be a reason for this disparity[4].

4.1 Plaintiff's Pleas Instead of Facts Summary

Condensing and extracting the relevant information from plaintiffs' pleas and court debates is a large part of the judge's work (Ma et al., 2021). This results in a condensed description of a case's facts. Most previous works consider this condensed description written by the judicial body (judges and clerks) as input. However, since a lot of qualified time has been spent on writing these descriptions, naturally, it makes the LJP task easier when using the court-written facts as input. Ma et al. (2021) were the first to consider the original plaintiff's pleas as input on Chinese data. In this work, to the best of our knowledge, we are the first to consider this harder task in the common law system (US class action cases in our case) and in the English language in general.

We do not consider the background details because our models might easily overfit on very specific data. In contrast, our goal was to create a dataset, where models need to focus on case-specific details to solve the task instead of being allowed to consider company-specific information such as number of employees or the area of business. We also disregard the introduction, containing metadata about the judge and the plaintiff.

4.2 Dataset Construction

To extract the plaintiffs' facts and allegations from each case, we manually reviewed hundreds of cases from different courts and different states to learn the structure of the document in each court to build a rule-based regex extraction system that detects the relevant text spans in each complaint. To summarize, constructing the dataset posed many technical difficulties due to the diverse nature of the

[4]Each court has its format of filing, and even courts within the same county do not usually use the same complaint filing format.

(a) Top 10 most frequent states

(b) Top 10 most frequent courts

Figure 2: Distribution of cases across states and courts.

complaint documents. At the preprocessing stage, we perform text cleaning, including removing some irrelevant text sections that our system incorrectly matched and removing duplicate sections.

4.3 Label Distribution

In this work we consider the task of binary legal judgment prediction. To do so, we simplified the labels. We used Table 1 to map the outcomes to either *win* or *lose* (for the plaintiff). After binarization the dataset is almost balanced with 5,469 (50.8%) *lose* cases and 5,290 (49.2%) *win* cases. Therefore, in our experiments, we just report the accuracy to keep it simple and make the scores more easily interpretable.

4.4 Dataset Variants

We experimented with different variants of the dataset to study the effect of the different parts of the text. We deliberately focused our attention more on the allegations because the facts contain a lot of repetitive content and are noisier than the allegations (many paragraphs only contain citations). Additionally, the facts contain many citations to laws, which are less relevant to the case's outcome according to domain experts (the facts are more generic and less case-specific than the allegations).

Full Text

The *Full Text* dataset combines the plaintiff's facts and the allegations but also disregards any background details. We concatenated the facts at the beginning and added the allegations parts to create one input text. We observe in Figure 3a that this dataset is rather long – almost 2700 tokens on average – with 10% of cases longer than 5400 tokens.

Unified Allegations

The *Unified Allegations* dataset consists of all case's allegations (mentioned in the complaint) concatenated together to form one input text . Approx. 2K documents did not contain any allegations (based on our extraction regexes), reducing the dataset size from 10.8K to 8.8K documents. The allegations make up a bit less than half of the full text complaint, as shown in Figure 3b (mean of $\sim$1,100 tokens and percentile 90 at $\sim$2,400 tokens).

Separated Allegations

The *Separated Allegations* dataset considers each allegation as a separate sample, increasing the size from 8.8K to 25K documents. We considered this dataset to test whether the entire context is necessary. Figure 3c shows the length distribution for individual allegations. Surprisingly, even a single allegation can reach up to 2,000 tokens ($\sim$ 4-5 pages of continuous text). However, most allegations (95%) are not longer than roughly 2 pages (1,100 tokens) with the average at 400 tokens.

5 Experiments

5.1 Experimental Setup

For all experiments, we truncated the text to the model's maximum sequence length (2,048 for Longformer and BigBird, 512 otherwise), unless otherwise specified. All experiments have been performed on the binarized labels (win or lose). We ran the experiments with 5-fold cross-validation and averaged across 5 random seeds. For more details regarding hyperparameter tuning and preprocessing, please refer to Appendix A.

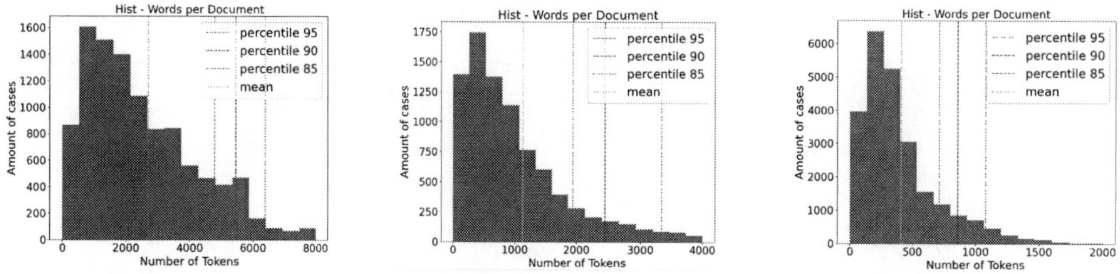

(a) Full Text (b) Unified Allegations (c) Separated Allegations

Figure 3: Histograms for the three dataset variants (number of tokens calculated using bert-base-uncased tokenizer).

5.2 Methods

We compared the following pretrained transformer models: BERT (Devlin et al., 2019), LegalBERT (Chalkidis et al., 2020) (pretrained on diverse English legal data from Europe and the US with a domain-specific tokenizer), CaseLawBERT (Zheng et al., 2021) (pretrained on 37GB of US state and federal caselaw with a domain specific tokenizer), LegalRoBERTa[5] (continued pretraining from RoBERTa checkpoint on 4.6 GB of US caselaw and patents), BigBird (Zaheer et al., 2021) and Longformer (Beltagy et al., 2020). For all models, we used the publicly available base checkpoints on the Huggingface hub[6]. We ran our experiments with the Huggingface transformers library (Wolf et al., 2020) available under an Apache-2.0 license.

5.3 Results

Results are reported in the $mean_{\pm std}$ format averaged accuracy across 5 random seeds. Table 2 shows the main results. We observe that the setup considering the entire text is harder than when we only consider the allegations (best Full Text model is at $\sim 63\%$ and worst allegations model is at $\sim 65\%$). These findings confirm our hypothesis, that the allegations encode more useful information than the facts (see Section 4.4) (the facts are often at the beginning of the complaints; thus the models on the Full Text dataset are likely to see mostly facts because of the truncation).

In line with previous findings (Chalkidis et al., 2021b, 2020; Zheng et al., 2021), models with legal pretraining outperform BERT also in our datasets (Unified Allegations and Separated Allegations). However, for LegalBERT the difference is small (only 0.5% above BERT). The models pretrained mostly or exclusively on US caselaw (LegalRoBERTa or CaseLawBERT respectively) perform better (up to 2% better than BERT), presumably because our dataset also originates from the US. CaseLawBERT achieves a much higher difference to BERT on the CaseHOLD task (4.6 F1) (Zheng et al., 2021) and on SCOTUS (7.6 macro-F1) (Chalkidis et al., 2021b). Both of these tasks are based on the same data as has been used in the pre-training of LegalRoBERTa and CaseLawBERT, whereas the complaints in our dataset are unseen by all models during pre-training. We suspect that this different data is the reason for the legal models not outperforming BERT as strongly as has been observed in other datasets.

Method	Accuracy
Full Text (trunc. to 2048 tokens)	
Longformer	$62.87_{\pm 2.06}$
BigBird	$63.26_{\pm 3.40}$
Unified Allegations (trunc. to 512 tokens)	
BERT	$65.06_{\pm 1.67}$
LegalBERT	$65.57_{\pm 0.26}$
CaseLawBERT	$65.87_{\pm 0.60}$
LegalRoBERTa	$65.95_{\pm 0.98}$
Separated Allegations (trunc. to 512 tokens)	
BERT	$64.98_{\pm 1.08}$
LegalBERT	$65.57_{\pm 0.62}$
CaseLawBERT	$66.82_{\pm 0.78}$
LegalRoBERTa	$65.97_{\pm 0.88}$

Table 2: Longformer and BigBird used a maximum sequence length of 2,048 tokens. All other models used 512 tokens. For all datasets, we truncated the text to fit the maximum sequence length.

6 Error Analysis

Neural Networks (NNs) and their latest incarnation, Transformers (Vaswani et al., 2017), work very well across a wide range of tasks, especially if

[5] https://huggingface.co/saibo/legal-roberta-base

[6] https://huggingface.co/models

the tasks involve more "complicated" data like text or images. However, in contrast to traditional Machine Learning (ML) methods such as Linear Regression, they are not interpretable out-of-the-box. Neural Networks need additional methods to make them explain themselves better to humans. A rich body of literature investigates how to make NNs and especially Transformers more interpretable (Ribeiro et al., 2016; Sundararajan et al., 2017; Lundberg and Lee, 2017; Dhamdhere et al., 2018; Serrano and Smith, 2019; Bai et al., 2021). Interpretability is especially important in high-stakes domains such as law or medicine.

In the following two sections, we analyze our models using the two interpretability methods Calibration and IG to get a better understanding of their inner workings.

6.1 Calibration

In this section, we investigate to what extent our models are calibrated out-of-the-box and "calibratable". Calibration is a first step towards understanding whether the model output can be trusted (Guo et al., 2017b; Desai and Durrett, 2020): how aligned are the confidence scores with the actual empirical likelihoods? Thus, if the model assigns 60% probability to a label, then this label should be correct in 60% of cases if the model is calibrated. So, even if the model itself is a black-box, a calibrated model at least gives an indication whether it knows when it is wrong. This information can be very valuable when deploying models in the real world because it allows us to discard predictions where the model is below some certainty threshold. Well calibrated models are especially important in domains with high potential downside for users, such as predictive tools for court cases.

In this work, we follow Desai and Durrett (2020) by employing TS (Guo et al., 2017b) for calibrating our models using the netcal library[7] (Küppers et al., 2020) available under an Apache License 2.0 license. We show calibration plots in Figure 4 for BERT and the legal models on the Unified Allegations dataset and aggregated scores in Table 5 in Appendix B.3. We observe that the legal models are less calibrated than BERT before, but better calibrated after TS. So TS seems to calibrate domain-specific models better than general models. When comparing the calibration of our models with

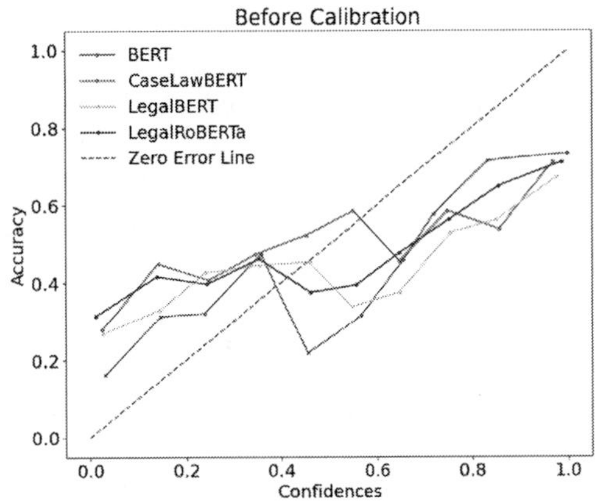

(a) Before Calibration

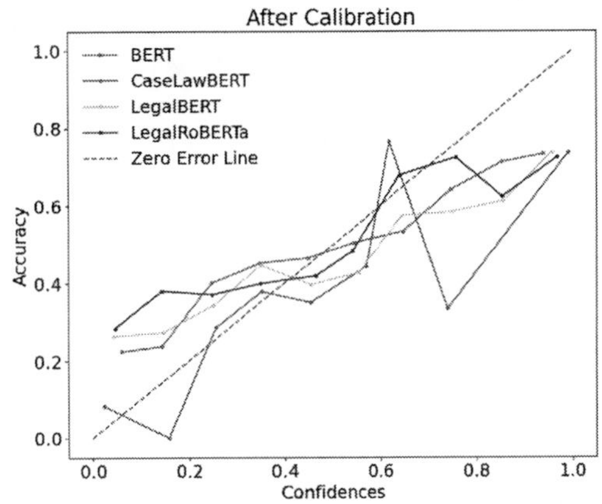

(b) After Calibration

Figure 4: Calibration on the Unified Allegations dataset.

the calibration of models from the literature (Desai and Durrett, 2020), we note that our models are less calibrated overall (further away from the zero-error-line and higher ECE scores), both out-of-the-box and after applying TS. We hypothesize that the generally lower accuracy on our hard dataset also makes the models less calibrated, especially in the areas of high (> 0.8) and low (< 0.2) confidence. To the best of our knowledge, in legal NLP we are the first to perform such an analysis.

6.2 Integrated Gradients

We conduct a qualitative analysis of the LegalBERT model using IG[8] (Sundararajan et al., 2017) and show an illustrative example in Figure 5. We observe that the model focuses most on "flsa" an acronym for Fair Labor Standards Act[9] regulating

[7] https://github.com/fabiankueppers/calibration-framework

[8] https://github.com/cdpierse/transformers-interpret#sequence-classification-explainer

[9] https://www.dol.gov/agencies/whd/flsa

minimum wage and overtime among others. Further, the model focuses on "work" and "wages" possibly signaling a (limited) understanding of the connections between those concepts. Future work may investigate explainability of Pretrained Language Models (PLMs) in more detail on the LJP task.

7 Human Expert Annotations

Malik et al. (2021b) collected predictions for the judgment outcome of Indian Supreme Court cases from five legal experts. The experts agreed with the judges in 94% of the cases, on average. Note, however, that they have access to both the facts summary and the court's considerations. Their best model, XLNet + BiGRU, only achieves an accuracy of 78%. Contrarily, Jacob de Menezes-Neto and Clementino (2022) find that all their models outperform 22 highly skilled experts on LJP in Brazilian Federal Courts using the entire case description for prediction.

We asked legal experts (employees of our company) and US law students in their final year, to predict the judgment outcome of 200 randomly selected examples in our Full Text dataset. Note that they only had access to the facts and allegations from the plaintiff's pleas (same as our models), and not to the court case written by the judge. So, their task was much more difficult than the one posed to the annotators by Malik et al. (2021b) and Jacob de Menezes-Neto and Clementino (2022). In our task, participants (whether models or human experts) basically need to estimate how the court is going to decide based only on the plaintiff's pleas. For each document, our legal experts had to answer whether they think the plaintiff would win or lose the case. Furthermore, they also had to indicate their confidence level for being correct (from 1 – very unsure – to 5 – very sure). We made sure that the annotators did not look for any additional information regarding the complaint (e.g., news articles about the outcome or further information on different legal platforms) so that their answer is based only on the input text presented on the annotation platform. Figure 6 in Appendix C presents a screenshot of the annotation platform we used.

On the entire dataset sample (200 examples), the human experts achieve an accuracy of 53%. When we filtered out the samples where the human experts were not confident (confidence score 1, 2 or 3), they achieved an accuracy of 60%. The entire results for the human experts are shown in Appendix B.4 in Table 6. We also trained and evaluated a Longformer model for comparison with the human predictions. We randomly split our remaining dataset into 6,877 train and 1,851 validation examples. Surprisingly, the Longformer model outperforms the human expert predictions both on the entire annotated test dataset (63% vs. 53% Accuracy) and the dataset filtered for high human confidence (67% vs. 60% Accuracy). In contrast to the human experts, the Longformer model only had access to the first 2,048 tokens of the case. While the human performance increases more than the Longformer performance on the high-confidence dataset, the Longformer model also has a higher performance, suggesting that these cases are easier to predict.

The task proposed in our dataset seems very challenging, given that human experts face great challenges in solving it. Interestingly, on the Indian dataset the humans clearly outperform the models, whereas in the Brazilian dataset it is reversed, similar to our results. Note that lawyers are often specialized in very narrow domains (legal areas). The cases in our dataset may be very diverse, and thus a generic model might be better suited for this task than specialized human experts. Future work may investigate this finding in more detail.

Figure 1 shows the calibration plot on the Full Text dataset, comparing Longformer before and after calibration with the human confidence scores. We observe that Longformer is already well calibrated in comparison to the human experts. Using TS, the Expected Calibration Error (ECE) of Longformer can be reduced from 5.14 to 2.34, whereas the ECE of the human experts lies at 17.5. Again, as mentioned in Section 6.1, the lower accuracy of the humans might explain their worse calibration compared to Longformer.

8 Conclusions and Future Work

Answers to the Research Questions

RQ1: *To what extent is it possible to determine the winner of US class action cases using only the textual part of the complaints (without metadata)?* It is possible, to some extent, to determine the winner of US class action cases using only the textual part of the complaints. Our best model achieves an accuracy of 66.8% (LegalRoBERTa) on the datasets using only the allegations. However, as this number shows, there is still a lot of room for improvement.

Predicted label = 1: Case Won

[CLS] plaintiff hereby real ##leg ##es and incorporates paragraphs 1 through 43 of this complaint , as if fully set forth herein . defendants failed to pay over ##time wages to plaintiff and other similarly situated employees for all time worked in excess of forty (40) hours in individual work weeks in violation of the flsa , 29 u . s . c . § 201 . for example , during the week beginning april 4 , 2016 , plaintiff worked approximately fifty - six (56) hours for defendants . during the week beginning may 16 , 2016 , 9 plaintiff worked approximately fifty - four (54) hours for defendants . plaintiff was not paid a rate of one and one - half times his regular rate of pay for all time worked in excess of forty (40) in these weeks and all other weeks he worked over forty (40) hours . during the course of their employment with defendants , plaintiff and others similarly situated driver ##s were not exempt from the maximum hour provisions of the flsa , 29 violation of the fair labor standards act [UNK] over ##time wages (collective action under 29 u . s . c . § 216 (b)) [SEP]

Figure 5: Analysis using Integrated Gradients (IG)

RQ2: *To what extent can we use Temperature Scaling (TS) to better calibrate our models?* Similar to Natural Language Inference, Paraphrase Detection and Commonsense Reasoning tasks (Desai and Durrett, 2020), we also find that in the PJP task, TS helps in calibrating pretrained transformers. In our best model, TS led to a decrease in ECE scores from 28 to 2.

RQ3: *To what extent can expert human lawyers solve the proposed task?* Expert human lawyers perform better than chance on a randomly selected dataset of 200 samples and can increase their accuracy from 53% to 60% when they are confident in their decision. However, they are still outperformed by a Longformer model having access to only the first 2,048 tokens in both scenarios.

Conclusions

We release a challenging new dataset of class action lawsuits for the more realistic PJP task (where the input is based on the complaints instead of the further processed facts summary written by the judge) in the US, a jurisdiction with the common law system. Additionally, we calibrated our models using TS and found that despite the relatively low accuracy (66% for the best model), relatively low ECE scores around 2 can be achieved. Finally, we find that our Longformer model is 10% more accurate than the human experts on our dataset despite having only access to the first 2,048 tokens of the case.

Limitations

Our best model achieves an accuracy of 66%. This may suggest that either the task posed in this dataset is very hard, or we did not optimize our models enough. The results achieved by the human experts suggests that the former is the case. However, we believe much more work is needed here.

Although we did some first efforts to interpret our model's outputs using Calibration and IG, the literature knows a host of other explainability methods (Molnar, 2022). We leave a more thorough qualitative analysis involving domain experts and explainability methods for future work.

Our experiments were performed only on relatively short input spans (512 tokens for allegations, and 2048 for full text). Longformer or BigBird support input spans until 4096 tokens. Another possibility is the use of hierarchical models, as employed for example by Niklaus et al. (2022); Dai et al. (2022) that can also easily scale to 4096 tokens given the right hardware. With 4096 tokens, we could fully encode all allegations and almost 80% percent of the full texts. We leave these investigations to future work.

Future Work

Since the legal models outperformed BERT only to a small margin, we suspect that further pretraining (Gururangan et al., 2020) on in-domain data might further enhance the performance. Additionally, in future work, we plan to study the domain-specific PJP and whether domain-specific models are better than generic model or human experts.

Large PLMs have proved to be very strong few shot learners in many tasks (Brown et al., 2020; Chowdhery et al., 2022). The use of such models may bring performance boosts also in our studied task. We leave experimentation using different prompting strategies for future work (Arora et al., 2022; Wei et al., 2022; Suzgun et al., 2022).

We discovered through our analysis using IG that some legal domains have a strong correlation to a particular label. To produce complaints with a higher success likelihood in court, future studies may examine the linguistic structure of successful allegations.

Ethics Statement

The goal of this research is to achieve a better understanding of LJP to broaden the discussion and aid practitioners in developing better technology for both legal experts and non-specialists. We believe that this is a crucial application area, where research should be done (Tsarapatsanis and Aletras, 2021) to improve legal services and democratize legal data, making it more accessible to end-users, while also highlighting (informing the audience on) the various multi-aspect deficiencies seeking a responsible and ethical (fair) deployment of legal-oriented technology.

In this direction, we study how we can best build our dataset to maximize accuracy of our models on the task. Additionally, we study the inner workings of the models using Integrated Gradients and make sure that our models are calibrated. A well calibrated model outputs confidence probabilities in line with actual likelihoods, thus giving the users the possibility of discarding low-confidence predictions or at least treating them with caution.

Lawyers often perform the LJP task by giving their clients advice on how high the chances for success are in court for specific cases. Given the complaint documents, we were able to show in this work that our models outperformed human experts in this task.

But, like with any other application (like content moderation) or domain (e.g., medical), reckless usage (deployment) of such technology poses a real risk. According to our opinion, comparable technology should only be used to support human specialists (legal scholars, or legal professionals).

Acknowledgements

We thank all the anonymous reviewers for their insightful comments. We thank the two employees at Darrow for the annotation of the dataset.

References

Mohammad Alali, Shaayan Syed, Mohammed Alsayed, Smit Patel, and Hemanth Bodala. 2021. JUSTICE: A Benchmark Dataset for Supreme Court's Judgment Prediction. ArXiv:2112.03414 [cs].

Nikolaos Aletras, Dimitrios Tsarapatsanis, Daniel Preoţiuc-Pietro, and Vasileios Lampos. 2016. Predicting judicial decisions of the European Court of Human Rights: a Natural Language Processing perspective. *PeerJ Computer Science*, 2:e93. Publisher: PeerJ Inc.

I. Angelidis, Ilias Chalkidis, and M. Koubarakis. 2018. Named Entity Recognition, Linking and Generation for Greek Legislation. In *JURIX*.

Simran Arora, Avanika Narayan, Mayee F. Chen, Laurel Orr, Neel Guha, Kush Bhatia, Ines Chami, Frederic Sala, and Christopher Ré. 2022. Ask Me Anything: A simple strategy for prompting language models. ArXiv:2210.02441 [cs].

Bing Bai, Jian Liang, Guanhua Zhang, Hao Li, Kun Bai, and Fei Wang. 2021. Why Attentions May Not Be Interpretable? In *Proceedings of the 27th ACM SIGKDD Conference on Knowledge Discovery & Data Mining*, KDD '21, pages 25–34, New York, NY, USA. Association for Computing Machinery.

Iz Beltagy, Matthew E. Peters, and Arman Cohan. 2020. Longformer: The Long-Document Transformer. *arXiv:2004.05150 [cs]*. ArXiv: 2004.05150.

Tom B. Brown, Benjamin Mann, Nick Ryder, Melanie Subbiah, Jared Kaplan, Prafulla Dhariwal, Arvind Neelakantan, Pranav Shyam, Girish Sastry, Amanda Askell, Sandhini Agarwal, Ariel Herbert-Voss, Gretchen Krueger, Tom Henighan, Rewon Child, Aditya Ramesh, Daniel M. Ziegler, Jeffrey Wu, Clemens Winter, Christopher Hesse, Mark Chen, Eric Sigler, Mateusz Litwin, Scott Gray, Benjamin Chess, Jack Clark, Christopher Berner, Sam McCandlish, Alec Radford, Ilya Sutskever, and Dario Amodei. 2020. Language Models are Few-Shot Learners. *arXiv:2005.14165 [cs]*. ArXiv: 2005.14165.

Ilias Chalkidis, Ion Androutsopoulos, and Nikolaos Aletras. 2019. Neural Legal Judgment Prediction in English. In *Proceedings of the 57th Annual Meeting of the Association for Computational Linguistics*, pages 4317–4323, Florence, Italy. Association for Computational Linguistics.

Ilias Chalkidis, Manos Fergadiotis, and Ion Androutsopoulos. 2021a. MultiEURLEX – A multi-lingual and multi-label legal document classification dataset for zero-shot cross-lingual transfer. *arXiv:2109.00904 [cs]*. ArXiv: 2109.00904.

Ilias Chalkidis, Manos Fergadiotis, Prodromos Malakasiotis, Nikolaos Aletras, and Ion Androutsopoulos. 2020. LEGAL-BERT: The Muppets straight out of Law School. *arXiv:2010.02559 [cs]*. ArXiv: 2010.02559.

Ilias Chalkidis, Abhik Jana, Dirk Hartung, Michael James Bommarito, Ion Androutsopoulos, Daniel Martin Katz, and Nikolaos Aletras. 2021b. LexGLUE: A Benchmark Dataset for Legal Language Understanding in English. SSRN Scholarly Paper ID 3936759, Social Science Research Network, Rochester, NY.

Huajie Chen, Deng Cai, Wei Dai, Zehui Dai, and Yadong Ding. 2019. Charge-Based Prison Term Prediction with Deep Gating Network. In *Proceedings of the 2019 Conference on Empirical Methods in Natural Language Processing and the 9th International*

Joint Conference on Natural Language Processing (EMNLP-IJCNLP), pages 6362–6367, Hong Kong, China. Association for Computational Linguistics.

Tianqi Chen and Carlos Guestrin. 2016. XGBoost: A Scalable Tree Boosting System. In *Proceedings of the 22nd ACM SIGKDD International Conference on Knowledge Discovery and Data Mining*, KDD '16, pages 785–794, New York, NY, USA. Association for Computing Machinery.

Aakanksha Chowdhery, Sharan Narang, Jacob Devlin, Maarten Bosma, Gaurav Mishra, Adam Roberts, Paul Barham, Hyung Won Chung, Charles Sutton, Sebastian Gehrmann, Parker Schuh, Kensen Shi, Sasha Tsvyashchenko, Joshua Maynez, Abhishek Rao, Parker Barnes, Yi Tay, Noam Shazeer, Vinodkumar Prabhakaran, Emily Reif, Nan Du, Ben Hutchinson, Reiner Pope, James Bradbury, Jacob Austin, Michael Isard, Guy Gur-Ari, Pengcheng Yin, Toju Duke, Anselm Levskaya, Sanjay Ghemawat, Sunipa Dev, Henryk Michalewski, Xavier Garcia, Vedant Misra, Kevin Robinson, Liam Fedus, Denny Zhou, Daphne Ippolito, David Luan, Hyeontaek Lim, Barret Zoph, Alexander Spiridonov, Ryan Sepassi, David Dohan, Shivani Agrawal, Mark Omernick, Andrew M. Dai, Thanumalayan Sankaranarayana Pillai, Marie Pellat, Aitor Lewkowycz, Erica Moreira, Rewon Child, Oleksandr Polozov, Katherine Lee, Zongwei Zhou, Xuezhi Wang, Brennan Saeta, Mark Diaz, Orhan Firat, Michele Catasta, Jason Wei, Kathy Meier-Hellstern, Douglas Eck, Jeff Dean, Slav Petrov, and Noah Fiedel. 2022. PaLM: Scaling Language Modeling with Pathways. *arXiv:2204.02311 [cs]*. ArXiv: 2204.02311.

Junyun Cui, Xiaoyu Shen, Feiping Nie, Z. Wang, Jinglong Wang, and Yulong Chen. 2022. A survey on legal judgment prediction: Datasets, metrics, models and challenges. *ArXiv*, abs/2204.04859.

Xiang Dai, Ilias Chalkidis, Sune Darkner, and Desmond Elliott. 2022. Revisiting Transformer-based Models for Long Document Classification. *arXiv:2204.06683 [cs]*. ArXiv: 2204.06683.

Shrey Desai and Greg Durrett. 2020. Calibration of Pre-trained Transformers. In *Proceedings of the 2020 Conference on Empirical Methods in Natural Language Processing (EMNLP)*, pages 295–302, Online. Association for Computational Linguistics.

Jacob Devlin, Ming-Wei Chang, Kenton Lee, and Kristina Toutanova. 2019. BERT: Pre-training of Deep Bidirectional Transformers for Language Understanding. *arXiv:1810.04805 [cs]*. ArXiv: 1810.04805.

Kedar Dhamdhere, Mukund Sundararajan, and Qiqi Yan. 2018. How Important Is a Neuron? ArXiv:1805.12233 [cs, stat].

Jidong Ge, Yunyun huang, Xiaoyu Shen, Chuanyi Li, and Wei Hu. 2021. Learning Fine-grained Fact-Article Correspondence in Legal Cases. ArXiv:2104.10726 [cs].

Ingo Glaser and Florian Matthes. 2020. Classification of German Court Rulings: Detecting the Area of Law. page 10.

Chuan Guo, Geoff Pleiss, Yu Sun, and Kilian Q. Weinberger. 2017a. On calibration of modern neural networks. In *Proceedings of the 34th International Conference on Machine Learning*, volume 70 of *Proceedings of Machine Learning Research*, pages 1321–1330. PMLR.

Chuan Guo, Geoff Pleiss, Yu Sun, and Kilian Q. Weinberger. 2017b. On Calibration of Modern Neural Networks. Number: arXiv:1706.04599 arXiv:1706.04599 [cs].

Suchin Gururangan, Ana Marasović, Swabha Swayamdipta, Kyle Lo, Iz Beltagy, Doug Downey, and Noah A. Smith. 2020. Don't Stop Pretraining: Adapt Language Models to Domains and Tasks. *arXiv:2004.10964 [cs]*. ArXiv: 2004.10964.

Dan Hendrycks, Collin Burns, Anya Chen, and Spencer Ball. 2021. CUAD: An Expert-Annotated NLP Dataset for Legal Contract Review. ArXiv:2103.06268 [cs].

Zikun Hu, Xiang Li, Cunchao Tu, Zhiyuan Liu, and Maosong Sun. 2018. Few-Shot Charge Prediction with Discriminative Legal Attributes. In *Proceedings of the 27th International Conference on Computational Linguistics*, pages 487–498, Santa Fe, New Mexico, USA. Association for Computational Linguistics.

Elias Jacob de Menezes-Neto and Marco Bruno Miranda Clementino. 2022. Using deep learning to predict outcomes of legal appeals better than human experts: A study with data from Brazilian federal courts. *PLOS ONE*, 17(7):e0272287.

Yuta Koreeda and Christopher Manning. 2021. ContractNLI: A Dataset for Document-level Natural Language Inference for Contracts. In *Findings of the Association for Computational Linguistics: EMNLP 2021*, pages 1907–1919, Punta Cana, Dominican Republic. Association for Computational Linguistics.

Anastassia Kornilova and Vladimir Eidelman. 2019. BillSum: A Corpus for Automatic Summarization of US Legislation. In *Proceedings of the 2nd Workshop on New Frontiers in Summarization*, pages 48–56, Hong Kong, China. Association for Computational Linguistics.

Fabian Küppers, Jan Kronenberger, Amirhossein Shantia, and Anselm Haselhoff. 2020. Multivariate confidence calibration for object detection. In *The IEEE/CVF Conference on Computer Vision and Pattern Recognition (CVPR) Workshops*.

André Lage-Freitas, Héctor Allende-Cid, Orivaldo Santana, and Lívia Oliveira-Lage. 2022. Predicting Brazilian Court Decisions. *PeerJ Computer Science*, 8:e904. Publisher: PeerJ Inc.

Elena Leitner, Georg Rehm, and Julian Moreno-Schneider. 2019. Fine-Grained Named Entity Recognition in Legal Documents. In Maribel Acosta, Philippe Cudré-Mauroux, Maria Maleshkova, Tassilo Pellegrini, Harald Sack, and York Sure-Vetter, editors, *Semantic Systems. The Power of AI and Knowledge Graphs*, volume 11702, pages 272–287. Springer International Publishing, Cham.

Shangbang Long, Cunchao Tu, Zhiyuan Liu, and Maosong Sun. 2019. Automatic Judgment Prediction via Legal Reading Comprehension. In *Chinese Computational Linguistics*, Lecture Notes in Computer Science, pages 558–572, Cham. Springer International Publishing.

Scott M Lundberg and Su-In Lee. 2017. A Unified Approach to Interpreting Model Predictions. In *Advances in Neural Information Processing Systems*, volume 30. Curran Associates, Inc.

Pedro Henrique Luz de Araujo, Teófilo E. de Campos, Renato R. R. de Oliveira, Matheus Stauffer, Samuel Couto, and Paulo Bermejo. 2018. LeNER-Br: A Dataset for Named Entity Recognition in Brazilian Legal Text. In *Computational Processing of the Portuguese Language*, Lecture Notes in Computer Science, pages 313–323, Cham. Springer International Publishing.

Luyao Ma, Yating Zhang, Tianyi Wang, Xiaozhong Liu, Wei Ye, Changlong Sun, and Shikun Zhang. 2021. Legal Judgment Prediction with Multi-Stage CaseRepresentation Learning in the Real Court Setting. In *Proceedings of the 44th International ACM SIGIR Conference on Research and Development in Information Retrieval*, pages 993–1002. ArXiv:2107.05192 [cs].

Vijit Malik, Rishabh Sanjay, Shubham Kumar Nigam, Kripabandhu Ghosh, Shouvik Kumar Guha, Arnab Bhattacharya, and Ashutosh Modi. 2021a. ILDC for CJPE: Indian Legal Documents Corpus for Court Judgment Prediction and Explanation. In *Proceedings of the 59th Annual Meeting of the Association for Computational Linguistics and the 11th International Joint Conference on Natural Language Processing (Volume 1: Long Papers)*, pages 4046–4062, Online. Association for Computational Linguistics.

Vijit Malik, Rishabh Sanjay, Shubham Kumar Nigam, Kripabandhu Ghosh, Shouvik Kumar Guha, Arnab Bhattacharya, and Ashutosh Modi. 2021b. ILDC for CJPE: Indian legal documents corpus for court judgment prediction and explanation. In *Proceedings of the 59th Annual Meeting of the Association for Computational Linguistics and the 11th International Joint Conference on Natural Language Processing (Volume 1: Long Papers)*, pages 4046–4062, Online. Association for Computational Linguistics.

Christoph Molnar. 2022. *Interpretable Machine Learning*, 2 edition.

Joel Niklaus, Ilias Chalkidis, and Matthias Stürmer. 2021a. Swiss-judgment-prediction: A multilingual legal judgment prediction benchmark. In *Proceedings of the Natural Legal Language Processing Workshop 2021*, pages 19–35, Punta Cana, Dominican Republic. Association for Computational Linguistics.

Joel Niklaus, Ilias Chalkidis, and Matthias Stürmer. 2021b. Swiss-Judgment-Prediction: A Multilingual Legal Judgment Prediction Benchmark. In *Proceedings of the Natural Legal Language Processing Workshop 2021*, pages 19–35, Punta Cana, Dominican Republic. Association for Computational Linguistics.

Joel Niklaus, Matthias Stürmer, and Ilias Chalkidis. 2022. An Empirical Study on Cross-X Transfer for Legal Judgment Prediction. ArXiv:2209.12325 [cs].

Marco Tulio Ribeiro, Sameer Singh, and Carlos Guestrin. 2016. "Why Should I Trust You?": Explaining the Predictions of Any Classifier.

Sofia Serrano and Noah A. Smith. 2019. Is Attention Interpretable? In *Proceedings of the 57th Annual Meeting of the Association for Computational Linguistics*, pages 2931–2951, Florence, Italy. Association for Computational Linguistics.

Zejiang Shen, Kyle Lo, Lauren Yu, Nathan Dahlberg, Margo Schlanger, and Doug Downey. 2022. Multi-LexSum: Real-World Summaries of Civil Rights Lawsuits at Multiple Granularities. ArXiv:2206.10883 [cs].

Benjamin Strickson and Beatriz De La Iglesia. 2020. Legal Judgement Prediction for UK Courts. In *Proceedings of the 2020 The 3rd International Conference on Information Science and System*, ICISS 2020, pages 204–209, New York, NY, USA. Association for Computing Machinery.

Mukund Sundararajan, Ankur Taly, and Qiqi Yan. 2017. Axiomatic Attribution for Deep Networks. ArXiv:1703.01365 [cs].

Mirac Suzgun, Nathan Scales, Nathanael Schärli, Sebastian Gehrmann, Yi Tay, Hyung Won Chung, Aakanksha Chowdhery, Quoc V. Le, Ed H. Chi, Denny Zhou, and Jason Wei. 2022. Challenging BIG-Bench Tasks and Whether Chain-of-Thought Can Solve Them. ArXiv:2210.09261 [cs].

Dimitrios Tsarapatsanis and Nikolaos Aletras. 2021. On the ethical limits of natural language processing on legal text. In *Findings of the Association for Computational Linguistics: ACL-IJCNLP 2021*, pages 3590–3599, Online. Association for Computational Linguistics.

550 U.S. at 570 Twombly. 2007. Bell atlantic corp. v. twombly. *Justia*.

Stefanie Urchs, Jelena Mitrović, and Michael Granitzer. 2022. Design and Implementation of German Legal Decision Corpora. pages 515–521.

Ashish Vaswani, Noam Shazeer, Niki Parmar, Jakob Uszkoreit, Llion Jones, Aidan N. Gomez, Lukasz Kaiser, and Illia Polosukhin. 2017. Attention Is All You Need. *arXiv:1706.03762 [cs]*. ArXiv: 1706.03762.

Jason Wei, Xuezhi Wang, Dale Schuurmans, Maarten Bosma, Brian Ichter, Fei Xia, Ed Chi, Quoc Le, and Denny Zhou. 2022. Chain of Thought Prompting Elicits Reasoning in Large Language Models. ArXiv:2201.11903 [cs].

Thomas Wolf, Lysandre Debut, Victor Sanh, Julien Chaumond, Clement Delangue, Anthony Moi, Pierric Cistac, Tim Rault, Remi Louf, Morgan Funtowicz, Joe Davison, Sam Shleifer, Patrick von Platen, Clara Ma, Yacine Jernite, Julien Plu, Canwen Xu, Teven Le Scao, Sylvain Gugger, Mariama Drame, Quentin Lhoest, and Alexander Rush. 2020. Transformers: State-of-the-Art Natural Language Processing. In *Proceedings of the 2020 Conference on Empirical Methods in Natural Language Processing: System Demonstrations*, pages 38–45, Online. Association for Computational Linguistics.

Marco Wrzalik and Dirk Krechel. 2021. GerDaLIR: A German Dataset for Legal Information Retrieval. In *Proceedings of the Natural Legal Language Processing Workshop 2021*, pages 123–128, Punta Cana, Dominican Republic. Association for Computational Linguistics.

Yiquan Wu, Kun Kuang, Yating Zhang, Xiaozhong Liu, Changlong Sun, Jun Xiao, Yueting Zhuang, Luo Si, and Fei Wu. 2020. De-Biased Court's View Generation with Causality. In *Proceedings of the 2020 Conference on Empirical Methods in Natural Language Processing (EMNLP)*, pages 763–780, Online. Association for Computational Linguistics.

Hai Ye, Xin Jiang, Zhunchen Luo, and Wenhan Chao. 2018. Interpretable Charge Predictions for Criminal Cases: Learning to Generate Court Views from Fact Descriptions. In *Proceedings of the 2018 Conference of the North American Chapter of the Association for Computational Linguistics: Human Language Technologies, Volume 1 (Long Papers)*, pages 1854–1864, New Orleans, Louisiana. Association for Computational Linguistics.

Manzil Zaheer, Guru Guruganesh, Avinava Dubey, Joshua Ainslie, Chris Alberti, Santiago Ontanon, Philip Pham, Anirudh Ravula, Qifan Wang, Li Yang, and Amr Ahmed. 2021. Big Bird: Transformers for Longer Sequences. *arXiv:2007.14062 [cs, stat]*. ArXiv: 2007.14062.

Lucia Zheng, Neel Guha, Brandon R. Anderson, Peter Henderson, and Daniel E. Ho. 2021. When Does Pretraining Help? Assessing Self-Supervised Learning for Law and the CaseHOLD Dataset. *arXiv:2104.08671 [cs]*. ArXiv: 2104.08671 version: 3.

Haoxi Zhong, Zhipeng Guo, Cunchao Tu, Chaojun Xiao, Zhiyuan Liu, and Maosong Sun. 2018. Legal Judgment Prediction via Topological Learning. In *Proceedings of the 2018 Conference on Empirical Methods in Natural Language Processing*, pages 3540–3549, Brussels, Belgium. Association for Computational Linguistics.

Haoxi Zhong, Yuzhong Wang, Cunchao Tu, Tianyang Zhang, Zhiyuan Liu, and Maosong Sun. 2020. Iteratively Questioning and Answering for Interpretable Legal Judgment Prediction. *Proceedings of the AAAI Conference on Artificial Intelligence*, 34(01):1250–1257. Number: 01.

Octavia-Maria Şulea, Marcos Zampieri, Mihaela Vela, and Josef van Genabith. 2017. Predicting the Law Area and Decisions of French Supreme Court Cases. In *Proceedings of the International Conference Recent Advances in Natural Language Processing, RANLP 2017*, pages 716–722, Varna, Bulgaria. INCOMA Ltd.

A Additional Training Details

A.1 Hyperparameter Tuning

We randomly split the data into 70% train, 15% validation and 15% test split. We searched the learning rate in {1e-6, 5e-5, 1e-5} and had the best results with 1e-5. We searched dropout in {0, 0.001, 0.1, 0.2} and finally chose 0. We searched the batch size in {16, 32, 64} and chose 16. Where GPU memory was not sufficient, we used gradient accumulation for a total batch size of 16. We searched the activation function in {Relu, SoftMax, LeakyRelu} and chose SoftMax. We searched weight decay in {0, 0.1} and found 0 to perform best. We used AMP mixed precision training and evaluation to reduce costs. We used early stopping on the validation loss with patience 2. If early stopping was not invoked, we trained for a maximum of 10 epochs. We used an AWS EC2 G5 instance with 4 CPU cores, 16 GB RAM and one NVIDIA A10G GPU (24 GB of GPU memory)

A.2 Preprocessing

We experimented with the following preprocessing methods: (a) removing punctuation; (b) removing numerals; (c) stemming; (d) lemmatization; and (e) entity masking (e.g., "Plaintiff James won would receive 30% from the 3 million compensation fund" $\rightarrow$ "PERSON won would receive PERCENT from the MONEY compensation fund"). We found that only stemming improved the results.

Method	Max Seq Len	Accuracy
Full Text		
Longformer	2048	$63.64_{\pm 0.72}$
BigBird	2048	$62.00_{\pm 1.08}$
Separated Allegations		
BERT	512	$64.82_{\pm 1.73}$
CaseLawBERT	512	$66.06_{\pm 0.84}$
LegalBERT	512	$64.57_{\pm 1.89}$
LegalRoBERTa	512	$65.41_{\pm 1.09}$

Table 3: Longformer and BigBird used a maximum sequence length of 2,048 tokens. All other models used 512 tokens. For all datasets, we filtered out the rows larger than the maximum sequence length.

A.3 Training Times

On the Unified Allegations dataset, training took approximately one hour for all the investigated models. On the Separated Allegations dataset, it took approximately two hours per model. On the Full Text dataset, it took approximately six hours for Longformer and approximately eight hours for BigBird. All training times are counted for five folds and one random seed on an AWS EC2 G5 instance with 4 CPU cores, 16 GB RAM and one NVIDIA A10G GPU (24GB of GPU memory).

A.4 Library Versions

We used the following libraries and associated versions: python 3.8, transformers 4.17.0, xgboost 1.5.2, torch 1.11.0+cu113, tokenizers 0.12.1, spacy 3.2.3, scikit-learn 1.1.1, pandas 1.3.4, numpy 1.20.3, netcal 1.2.1, nltk 3.6.5, optuna 2.10.1, matplotlib 3.4.3.

B Additional Results

B.1 Filtering the Datasets

In Table 3 we show results for the Filter setup, where we filtered out texts containing more tokens than the maximum sequence lengths of the models used. We note that the results don't change significantly in comparison to Table 2 (Truncation setup).

B.2 XGBoost

Table 4 shows the results for using XGBoost (Chen and Guestrin, 2016) on top of the embeddings instead of simple linear layers as it is reported in Table 2. We observe that this more sophisticated classification layer does not improve results.

Method	Max Seq Len	Accuracy
Full Text		
BERT	512	$60.40_{\pm 0.90}$
LegalBERT	512	$61.79_{\pm 1.13}$
CaseLawBERT	512	$60.65_{\pm 0.32}$
LegalRoBERTa	512	$60.37_{\pm 0.66}$
Longformer	2048	$59.96_{\pm 1.24}$
BigBird	2048	$60.98_{\pm 0.70}$
Unified Allegations		
BERT	512	$62.08_{\pm 0.71}$
LegalBERT	512	$63.01_{\pm 0.60}$
CaseLawBERT	512	$62.22_{\pm 0.59}$
LegalRoBERTa	512	$62.32_{\pm 1.12}$
Longformer	512	$61.7_{\pm 0.82}$
BigBird	512	$61.13_{\pm 1.02}$
Separated Allegations		
BERT	512	$63.19_{\pm 0.49}$
LegalBERT	512	$64.17_{\pm 0.44}$
CaseLawBERT	512	$63.81_{\pm 0.67}$
LegalRoBERTa	512	$64.52_{\pm 0.30}$
Longformer	512	$64.65_{\pm 0.40}$
BigBird	512	$63.38_{\pm 0.31}$

Table 4: We fed the embeddings of the transformer models into an XGBoost (Chen and Guestrin, 2016). For all datasets, we truncated the text to fit the maximum sequence length.

B.3 Calibration Results

Table 5 shows the detailed aggregated ECE scores together with the optimal temperature and the accuracy on the Unified Allegations dataset.

B.4 Human Results

Table 6 shows the results of the human experts on the 200 randomly selected examples.

C Annotation Platform

Figure 6 shows a screenshot of the annotation platform our human experts used.

D Example Complaint

Figures 7 and 8 show an example of a complaint present in the dataset.

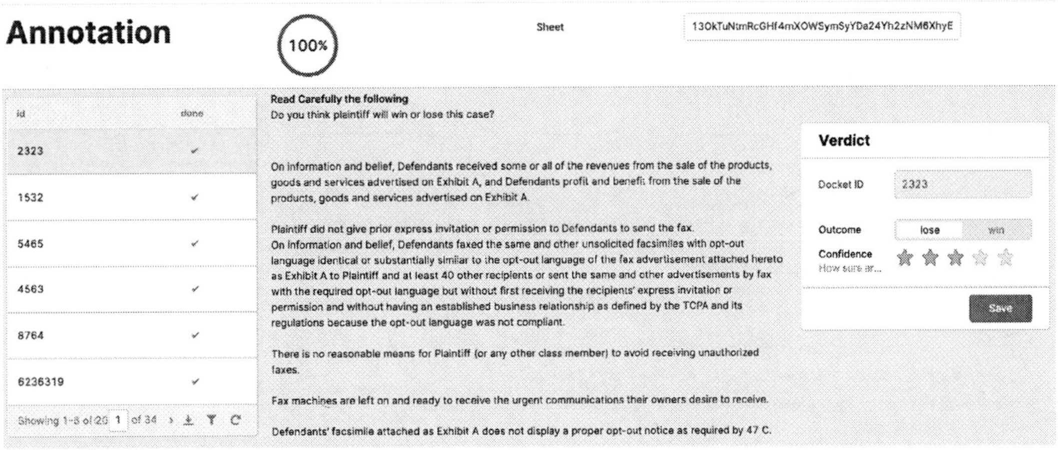

Figure 6: The platform for the human annotations.

Method	Opt. Temp.	ECE Before	ECE After	Accuracy
BERT	$0.19_{\pm 0.03}$	$23.44_{\pm 3.20}$	$5.06_{\pm 1.96}$	$65.06_{\pm 1.67}$
CaseLawBERT	$0.20_{\pm 0.03}$	$25.67_{\pm 2.32}$	$2.59_{\pm 0.90}$	$65.57_{\pm 0.60}$
LegalBERT	$0.22_{\pm 0.02}$	$24.78_{\pm 1.13}$	$3.06_{\pm 1.78}$	$65.87_{\pm 0.26}$
LegalRobertaBase	$0.13_{\pm 0.02}$	$28.02_{\pm 2.16}$	$1.92_{\pm 0.85}$	$65.95_{\pm 0.98}$

Table 5: Calibration results on the Unified Allegations dataset. The text was always truncated to fit the model's maximum sequence length of 512 tokens. Opt. Temp. abbreviates the optimal temperature used for calibrating the models.

	Precision	Recall	F1-score	# Examples
All Results				
lose	49.41	45.65	47.45	92
win	56.52	60.18	58.29	108
accuracy	-	-	53.50	200
High Confidence				
lose	75.00	37.50	50.00	24
win	54.54	85.71	66.66	21
accuracy	-	-	60.00	45

Table 6: Results of the human experts on the 200 randomly selected cases. Under High Confidence we show the results for only the examples where the human experts rated their confidence at 4 or 5 out of 5.

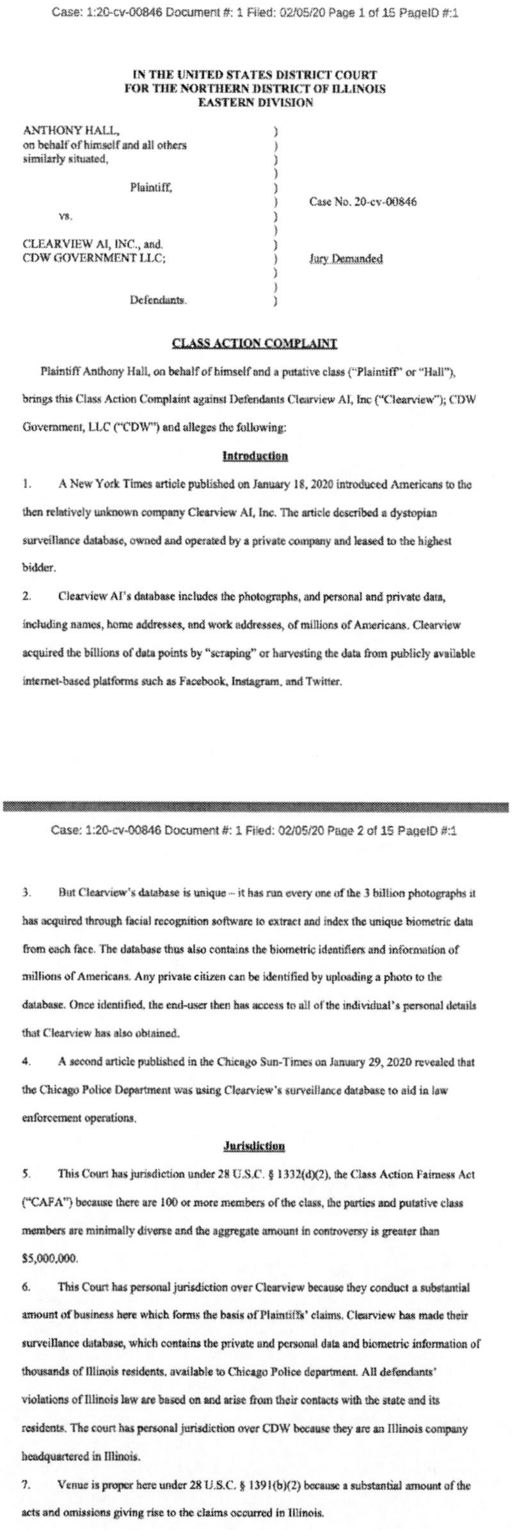
Case: 1:20-cv-00846 Document #: 1 Filed: 02/05/20 Page 1 of 15 PageID #:1

IN THE UNITED STATES DISTRICT COURT
FOR THE NORTHERN DISTRICT OF ILLINOIS
EASTERN DIVISION

ANTHONY HALL, on behalf of himself and all others similarly situated,

Plaintiff,

vs.

CLEARVIEW AI, INC., and CDW GOVERNMENT LLC;

Defendants.

Case No. 20-cv-00846

Jury Demanded

CLASS ACTION COMPLAINT

Plaintiff Anthony Hall, on behalf of himself and a putative class ("Plaintiff" or "Hall"), brings this Class Action Complaint against Defendants Clearview AI, Inc ("Clearview"); CDW Government, LLC ("CDW") and alleges the following:

Introduction

1. A New York Times article published on January 18, 2020 introduced Americans to the then relatively unknown company Clearview AI, Inc. The article described a dystopian surveillance database, owned and operated by a private company and leased to the highest bidder.

2. Clearview AI's database includes the photographs, and personal and private data, including names, home addresses, and work addresses, of millions of Americans. Clearview acquired the billions of data points by "scraping" or harvesting the data from publicly available internet-based platforms such as Facebook, Instagram, and Twitter.

Case: 1:20-cv-00846 Document #: 1 Filed: 02/05/20 Page 2 of 15 PageID #:1

3. But Clearview's database is unique – it has run every one of the 3 billion photographs it has acquired through facial recognition software to extract and index the unique biometric data from each face. The database thus also contains the biometric identifiers and information of millions of Americans. Any private citizen can be identified by uploading a photo to the database. Once identified, the end-user then has access to all of the individual's personal details that Clearview has also obtained.

4. A second article published in the Chicago Sun-Times on January 29, 2020 revealed that the Chicago Police Department was using Clearview's surveillance database to aid in law enforcement operations.

Jurisdiction

5. This Court has jurisdiction under 28 U.S.C. § 1332(d)(2), the Class Action Fairness Act ("CAFA") because there are 100 or more members of the class, the parties and putative class members are minimally diverse and the aggregate amount in controversy is greater than $5,000,000.

6. This Court has personal jurisdiction over Clearview because they conduct a substantial amount of business here which forms the basis of Plaintiffs' claims. Clearview has made their surveillance database, which contains the private and personal data and biometric information of thousands of Illinois residents, available to Chicago Police department. All defendants' violations of Illinois law are based on and arise from their contacts with the state and its residents. The court has personal jurisdiction over CDW because they are an Illinois company headquartered in Illinois.

7. Venue is proper here under 28 U.S.C. § 1391(b)(2) because a substantial amount of the acts and omissions giving rise to the claims occurred in Illinois.

Figure 7: These are the first two pages from an example complaint.

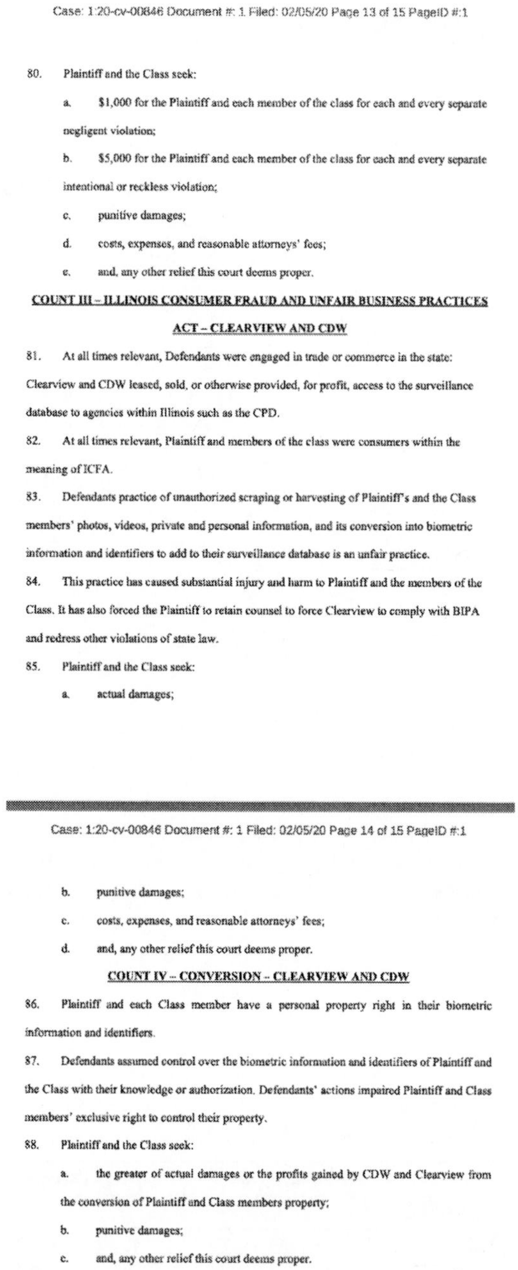
Case: 1:20-cv-00846 Document #: 1 Filed: 02/05/20 Page 13 of 15 PageID #:1

80. Plaintiff and the Class seek:

a. $1,000 for the Plaintiff and each member of the class for each and every separate negligent violation;

b. $5,000 for the Plaintiff and each member of the class for each and every separate intentional or reckless violation;

c. punitive damages;

d. costs, expenses, and reasonable attorneys' fees;

e. and, any other relief this court deems proper.

COUNT III – ILLINOIS CONSUMER FRAUD AND UNFAIR BUSINESS PRACTICES ACT – CLEARVIEW AND CDW

81. At all times relevant, Defendants were engaged in trade or commerce in the state: Clearview and CDW leased, sold, or otherwise provided, for profit, access to the surveillance database to agencies within Illinois such as the CPD.

82. At all times relevant, Plaintiff and members of the class were consumers within the meaning of ICFA.

83. Defendants practice of unauthorized scraping or harvesting of Plaintiff's and the Class members' photos, videos, private and personal information, and its conversion into biometric information and identifiers to add to their surveillance database is an unfair practice.

84. This practice has caused substantial injury and harm to Plaintiff and the members of the Class. It has also forced the Plaintiff to retain counsel to force Clearview to comply with BIPA and redress other violations of state law.

85. Plaintiff and the Class seek:

a. actual damages;

Case: 1:20-cv-00846 Document #: 1 Filed: 02/05/20 Page 14 of 15 PageID #:1

b. punitive damages;

c. costs, expenses, and reasonable attorneys' fees;

d. and, any other relief this court deems proper.

COUNT IV – CONVERSION – CLEARVIEW AND CDW

86. Plaintiff and each Class member have a personal property right in their biometric information and identifiers.

87. Defendants assumed control over the biometric information and identifiers of Plaintiff and the Class with their knowledge or authorization. Defendants' actions impaired Plaintiff and Class members' exclusive right to control their property.

88. Plaintiff and the Class seek:

a. the greater of actual damages or the profits gained by CDW and Clearview from the conversion of Plaintiff and Class members property;

b. punitive damages;

c. and, any other relief this court deems proper.

Jury Demand

Plaintiff demands a trial by jury.

February 5, 2020

[Signature Page Follows]

Figure 8: These are the last two pages from an example complaint.

Combining WordNet and Word Embeddings in Data Augmentation for Legal Texts

Sezen Perçin[1,2,3] and **Andrea Galassi**[3] ✉
Francesca Lagioia[4] and **Federico Ruggeri**[3] and **Piera Santin**[4]
Giovanni Sartor[4] and **Paolo Torroni**[3]
[1]Department of Electrical and Electronics Engineering, Boğaziçi University, Turkey
[2]Technische Universität München, Munich, Germany
[3]DISI, University of Bologna, Bologna, Italy
[4]CIRSFID-Alma AI, University of Bologna, Bologna, Italy
a.galassi@unibo.it

Abstract

Creating balanced labeled textual corpora for complex tasks, like legal analysis, is a challenging and expensive process that often requires the collaboration of domain experts. To address this problem, we propose a data augmentation method based on the combination of GloVe word embeddings and the WordNet ontology. We present an example of application in the legal domain, specifically on decisions of the Court of Justice of the European Union. Our evaluation with human experts confirms that our method is more robust than the alternatives.

1 Introduction

Many of the state-of-the-art Natural Language Processing (NLP) techniques are based on deep learning methods with millions of parameters (Devlin et al., 2019; Vaswani et al., 2017), and therefore they usually require vast amounts of data to be trained. Even if a lot of progress has been made in the development of unsupervised or semi-supervised methods, many high-level tasks are still addressed in a supervised fashion, especially when they concern complex tasks or very specific domains, such as predictions on legal documents (Drawzeski et al., 2021; Poudyal et al., 2020; Zhong et al., 2020). At the same time, creating corpora for such applications is particularly challenging and expensive since this process requires the collaboration of domain experts for the labeling process. One possible way to address this problem is data augmentation (Shorten et al., 2021), which exploits existing data to generate new synthetic ones. These synthetic samples must be different enough from the original ones to provide a valuable contribution to the training. Still, at the same time, their semantic content must remain similar enough not to invalidate their labels. In NLP, one possibility is to replace some words or sentences of the original samples with other ones that hold the same semantic meaning. This can be done by exploiting similarities between sub-symbolic representations of text, such as word and sentence embeddings, or exploiting relationships in symbolic representations, such as WordNet (Fellbaum, 2010).

Inspired by works regarding semantic relatedness (Lee et al., 2016; Vasanthakumar and Bond, 2018), we propose to merge graph-structured and embedding-based augmentation by combining the use of WordNet and similarity between word embeddings. In particular, we create new synthetic samples by replacing some terms with words with similar semantic meaning. We exploit WordNet to compute a set of candidate words and then choose the most similar one according to its GloVe word embedding (Pennington et al., 2014).

We present an example of the application of such a method in the legal domain. Our context is a task of sentence classification, where we want to automatically predict whether a sentence extracted from a judgment is representative of a principle of law. Since the distribution between the negative and positive classes is heavily unbalanced, we need to rely on data augmentation. We compare different techniques and ask a team of legal experts to evaluate the new synthetic data. Their evaluation confirms that the quality of the synthetic data generated through our method is superior to data generated exploiting only WordNet or GloVe embeddings. Our contribution is three-fold:

- (i) we propose a novel method to perform textual data augmentation by mixing the use of WordNet and Word Embeddings;
- (ii) we perform a qualitative evaluation on legal documents, where human domain experts assess the efficacy of our method with respect to alternatives;

Proceedings of the Natural Legal Language Processing Workshop 2022, pages 47 - 52
December 8, 2022

- (iii) we perform a preliminary quantitative evaluation, using neural language models to measure the similarity between the augmented texts and the original ones.

We make our code, data, and evaluation publicly available.[1]

2 Related Works

Data augmentation is a frequently used strategy in NLP to introduce diversity in the datasets that will help models overcome phenomena such as overfitting (Shorten et al., 2021). In particular, paraphrasing-based data augmentation techniques (Li et al., 2022) aim to create new synthetic data preserving the meaning of the original source.

One popular family of augmentation methods relies on knowledge graphs, thesauruses, and lexical database such as WordNet. WordNet (Fellbaum, 2010) is a lexical database where words are grouped into sets of cognitive synonyms called "synsets". Serving as a relational network, it is widely used as a source of synonyms and for the measurement of similarity between terms. For example, Mosolova et al. (2018) use WordNet to retrieve a list of synonyms of a word, and replace it with one chosen randomly. Xiang et al. (2020) expand such approach by constraining candidates according to Part of Speech (POS) tags by selecting them based on a similarity measure, and test their approach on various text classification tasks. Wang and Yang (2015) follow a different approach and instead they rely on semantic embeddings, embedding words with Word2Vec and replacing candidate words with their nearest neighbour.

Our approach stems from Xiang et al.'s and follows the intuition of Wang and Yang. We rely on WordNet to select a pool of candidate words, but we choose the replacement by measuring the similarity between their GloVe word embeddings (Pennington et al., 2014). However, we provide a simpler definition of the candidate list considering the synsets collected from the WordNet opening room for syntactic differences while preserving the semantic integrity of the sentences. Moreover, we address the challenging domain of legal documents, in which retaining domain-specific validity while introducing textual diversity is a critical factor. Finally, we provide an evaluation of synthetic samples involving human experts.

Other possible data augmentation strategies include rule-based approaches (Wei and Zou, 2019), syntactic alterations (Şahin and Steedman, 2018), interpolation approaches (Zhang et al., 2018), generative data augmentation and back-translation (Sennrich et al., 2016), and random manipulation of words (Yan et al., 2019). Additional information can be found in the surveys by Shorten et al. (2021) and Li et al. (2022).

3 Method

Our augmentation method **augWN+GV** combines the use of the lexical database WordNet (WN) with the properties of the vector space defined by GloVe pre-trained word embeddings (GV).

Given a sample sentence, composed of a list of words $\{w_1, ..., w_n\}$, we randomly choose one word to be replaced among those that are adjectives, nouns, or adverbs. We do so by computing the POS tags of each word POS_{w_i} through the NLTK library and considering only the words for which $POS_{w_i} \in \{NN, NNS, NNP, NNPS, JJ, JJR, JJS, RB, RBR, RBS, RP\}$.[2] Then, given a word w_j to replace, we proceed as follows:

1. we retrieve from WordNet the synsets with a meaningful relationship and the related lemmas;

2. we create a list of 10 candidate lemmas, excluding the original word and giving priority to the synsets whose WordNet POS tag corresponds to POS_{w_j};[3]

3. we encode the word w_j and each candidate through pre-trained GloVe (Pennington et al., 2014) embeddings of size 100;

4. we select the candidate w_k that is most similar to w_j and perform the replacement through cosine similarity.

We compared our method against four baselines:

- **augWN** follows our method for the selection of candidates, but then the choice is not based on GloVe but rather on random selection;

- **augWN+POS** is similar to the previous baseline, but additionally only candidates w_k

[1] https://github.com/adele-project/maxims

[2] We included RP words since they can be used as adverbial particles.

[3] For example, the WordNet POS tag n correspond to the NLTK POS tags $NN, NNS, NNP, NNPS$.

whose POS_{w_k} correspond to POS_{w_j} are considered; in this way we enforce two POS constraints: one on the synsets level, and one on the lemmas level;

- **augGV** does not rely on WordNet, but only on the vector space properties of the pre-trained GloVe word embeddings, replacing the original word with the most similar one among those present in the vocabulary.
- **augLB** is a neural augmentation method (Shorten et al., 2021) based on Legal-BERT language model (Chalkidis et al., 2020): firstly the candidate word is replaced with a mask token, then the sentence is inputted to the neural language model, and finally, the model generates a novel word in place of the mask token.

4 Evaluation

To perform a preliminary evaluation of our method, we generated a small set of synthetic samples and then asked domain experts to judge them. We also measure the difference between the augmented sentences and the original ones in terms of similarity between their embeddings.

We generated the synthetic starting from a given textual sentence, randomly selecting one suitable candidate word in it, and applying one augmentation method to it. The original sample and the synthetic one thus obtained would therefore differ only for one term. This process was then applied multiple times to the synthetic sample, replacing other words and generating new samples. We repeated this process until we replaced about 60% of the candidate terms of the original sentence.

4.1 Data

We conducted our experimentation on segments of texts in English language extracted from decisions of the Court of Justice of the European Union (CJEU) on fiscal state aid. In particular, we have chosen sentences that are representative of a principle of law (legal maxims or *rationes decidendi*). Such sentences are used to highlight the decisive principle of law contained in each judgement, that will be useful to assure the uniform interpretation of the law with respect to the courts of first or second instance. Out of the 334 segments extracted by domain experts from 41 documents, we randomly selected 10 of them. We have chosen to work with CJEU decisions because they usually contain a rich and diverse set of legal principles established in a case that determine the judgment.

4.2 Metrics

For the human evaluation, two domain experts have analyzed each single augmentation step, assigning a value between $\{+1, 0, -1\}$. We have chosen to use a 3-values scale to identify not only replacements that are completely correct (+1) and those that are incorrect (-1), but also those that are imprecise or too informal for our specific domain (0). The evaluation was performed by both experts together, solving disagreements through discussion. We measured which augmentation method preserves better the meaning of the original text by summing together the scores obtained at each step. To perform a fair comparison, we used the same original samples for each of our augmentation methods, and in each step, we replace the same term. Figure 1 and Table 1 respectively report an example of an augmented sample and the related evaluation.

As an additional evaluation, we also measured how much the synthetic samples differ from the original ones in terms of distance between their embeddings. We used Legal-BERT (Chalkidis et al., 2020) to generate the sentence embeddings of the two samples and then measured their cosine similarity.

4.3 Results

As can be seen in Table 2, our method seems to be the more robust. Indeed, in the evaluation of the single sources it obtains a negative score only two times, its performance is close to the best method in each case, and it outperforms the alternatives in the total score. Nonetheless, the performance on different legal maxims is highly variable, with scores ranging from +8 to -1.

The performance of **augLB** is comparable to **augWN+GV** in most cases, with the remarkable exception of document #10, where the difference between the two scores is above 10 points. Another difference between the two methods is that the substitutions performed through **augLB** tend to preserve the grammatical rules of the sentences, while the same can not be said for **augWN+GV**.

The worst performing method is **augWN** and it is also the only one to obtain a negative total score. The introduction of additional constraints

The need to take account of requirements relating to environmental protection, however legitimate, cannot justify the exclusion of selective measures, even specific ones such as environmental levies, from the scope of Article 87(1) EC, as account may in any event usefully be taken of the environmental objectives when the compatibility of the State aid measure with the common market is being assessed pursuant to Article 87(3) EC.

The need to take account of requirements relating to environmental protection, however legitimate, cannot excuse the expulsion of selective measure, even particular ones such as environmental impose, from the scope of clause 87(1) EC, as report may in any result usefully be taken of the environmental objective when the compatibility of the department of state assistance measure with the usual marketplace is being assessed pursuant to clause 87(3) EC.

Figure 1: Example of one legal maxim and a synthetic sample obtained after the application of multiple augmentation steps.

Table 1: Human evaluation of single word replacements, with respect to the context.

Word	Replacement	Score	Word	Replacement	Score
justify	excuse	+1	event	result	+1
exclusion	expulsion	0	objectives	objective	+1
measures	measure	+1	State	deparment of state	-1
specific	particular	+1	aid	assistance	0
levies	impose	0	common	usual	-1
article	clause	0	market	marketplace	0
account	report	+1			

Table 2: Evaluation of augmentation methods over 10 legal maxims samples. For each augmentation method we report the score obtained for each legal maxim, the sum of such scores, and the average cosine similarity between the sentence embeddings of the synthetic sentence and the original one.

Method	Human Evaluation #1	#2	#3	#4	#5	#6	#7	#8	#9	#10	Total	Avg LB similarity
baselines												
augWN	-3	-5	-2	**1**	-2	-6	-2	-7	-1	-1	-28	0.763
augWN+POS	-2	-1	2	-2	4	-1	1	3	**2**	**9**	15	0.779
augGV	-3	**0**	-4	-1	6	0	-3	1	0	7	3	0.879
augLB	2	-1	**3**	-1	**10**	**6**	1	**8**	1	-4	25	0.886
our proposal												
augWN+GV	**8**	-1	2	-1	8	5	**2**	4	0	8	**35**	**0.894**

in **augWN+POS** greatly improves the previous method by about 40 points. **augGV** does not perform well, obtaining a positive score only in 3 cases.

For what concerns the similarities between embeddings, our method outperforms all the others. However, it is important to remark that the difference between **augWN+GV**, **augLB**, and **augGV** amounts to a few decimals. Surprisingly, **augWN+POS** does not perform well, obtaining a score about 0.1 lower than **augGV**.

5 Conclusion

We presented a data augmentation method that leverages both the symbolic information available in knowledge graphs and the sub-symbolic information provided by word embeddings. We have applied this technique to the challenging domain of legal documents and asked a team of experts to evaluate each replacement. The results confirm the quality of our method with respect to alternative approaches, yet they emphasize that more work is needed to obtain satisfactory results. We relied on GloVe since is a popular and widely adopted representation with a low computational footprint. Nonetheless, our proposal can be adapted to other embeddings.

In future work, we plan to further test this technique in a task-based setting where we train a machine learning model to recognize the sentences that contain a principle of law. Moreover, we will apply it to other legal tasks where data is difficult to produce or where some classes are greatly underrepresented. Examples of these tasks are argument mining (Poudyal et al., 2020; Habernal et al., 2022; Grundler et al., 2022) and identification of unfair clauses in contracts (Galassi et al., 2020; Drawzeski et al., 2021; Ruggeri et al., 2022).

Acknowledgements

This work has been partially funded by the European Union's Horizon 2020 Research and Innovation Programme under grant agreement 101017142 (StairwAI), by the European Union's Justice programme under grant agreement 101007420 (ADELE), by the European Horizon 2020 ERC project CompuLaw (Computable Law) under grant agreement 833647, and by the Italian Ministry of Education and Research's PRIN programme under grant agreement 2017NCPZ22 (LAILA).

References

Ilias Chalkidis, Manos Fergadiotis, Prodromos Malakasiotis, Nikolaos Aletras, and Ion Androutsopoulos. 2020. LEGAL-BERT: The muppets straight out of law school. In *Findings of EMNLP*, pages 2898–2904, Online. Association for Computational Linguistics.

Jacob Devlin, Ming-Wei Chang, Kenton Lee, and Kristina Toutanova. 2019. BERT: pre-training of deep bidirectional transformers for language understanding. In *NAACL-HLT*, pages 4171–4186. ACL.

Kasper Drawzeski, Andrea Galassi, Agnieszka Jablonowska, Francesca Lagioia, Marco Lippi, Hans Wolfgang Micklitz, Giovanni Sartor, Giacomo Tagiuri, and Paolo Torroni. 2021. A corpus for multilingual analysis of online terms of service. In *NLLP@EMNLP*, pages 1–8, Punta Cana, Dominican Republic. Association for Computational Linguistics.

Christiane Fellbaum. 2010. *WordNet*, pages 231–243. Springer Netherlands, Dordrecht.

Andrea Galassi, Kasper Drazewski, Marco Lippi, and Paolo Torroni. 2020. Cross-lingual annotation projection in legal texts. In *COLING*, pages 915–926, Barcelona, Spain (Online). International Committee on Computational Linguistics.

Giulia Grundler, Piera Santin, Andrea Galassi, Federico Galli, Francesco Godano, Francesca Lagioia, Elena Palmieri, Federico Ruggeri, Giovanni Sartor, and Paolo Torroni. 2022. Detecting arguments in CJEU decisions on fiscal state aid. In *Proceedings of the 9th Workshop on Argument Mining*, pages 143–157, Online and in Gyeongju, Republic of Korea. International Conference on Computational Linguistics.

Ivan Habernal, Daniel Faber, Nicola Recchia, Sebastian Bretthauer, Iryna Gurevych, Indra Spiecker genannt Döhmann, and Christoph Burchard. 2022. Mining legal arguments in court decisions. *CoRR*, abs/2208.06178.

Yang-Yin Lee, Hao Ke, Hen-Hsen Huang, and Hsin-Hsi Chen. 2016. Combining word embedding and lexical database for semantic relatedness measurement. In *WWW (Companion Volume)*, pages 73–74. ACM.

Bohan Li, Yutai Hou, and Wanxiang Che. 2022. Data augmentation approaches in natural language processing: A survey. *AI Open*, 3:71–90.

Anna Mosolova, Vadim Fomin, and Ivan Bondarenko. 2018. Text augmentation for neural networks. In *AIST (Supplement)*, volume 2268 of *CEUR Workshop Proceedings*, pages 104–109. CEUR-WS.org.

Jeffrey Pennington, Richard Socher, and Christopher D. Manning. 2014. Glove: Global vectors for word representation. In *EMNLP*, pages 1532–1543. ACL.

Prakash Poudyal, Jaromir Savelka, Aagje Ieven, Marie Francine Moens, Teresa Goncalves, and Paulo Quaresma. 2020. ECHR: Legal corpus for argument mining. In *ArgMining*, pages 67–75, Online. Association for Computational Linguistics.

Federico Ruggeri, Francesca Lagioia, Marco Lippi, and Paolo Torroni. 2022. Detecting and explaining unfairness in consumer contracts through memory networks. *Artif. Intell. Law*, 30(1):59–92.

Gözde Gül Şahin and Mark Steedman. 2018. Data augmentation via dependency tree morphing for low-resource languages. In *Proceedings of the 2018 Conference on Empirical Methods in Natural Language Processing*, pages 5004–5009, Brussels, Belgium. Association for Computational Linguistics.

Rico Sennrich, Barry Haddow, and Alexandra Birch. 2016. Improving neural machine translation models with monolingual data. In *Proceedings of the 54th Annual Meeting of the Association for Computational Linguistics (Volume 1: Long Papers)*, pages 86–96, Berlin, Germany. Association for Computational Linguistics.

Connor Shorten, Taghi M. Khoshgoftaar, and Borko Furht. 2021. Text data augmentation for deep learning. *J. Big Data*, 8(1):101.

E Umamaheswari Vasanthakumar and Francis Bond. 2018. Multilingual Wordnet sense ranking using nearest context. In *GWC*, pages 272–283, Singapore. Global Wordnet Association.

Ashish Vaswani, Noam Shazeer, Niki Parmar, Jakob Uszkoreit, Llion Jones, Aidan N. Gomez, Lukasz Kaiser, and Illia Polosukhin. 2017. Attention is all you need. In *NeurIPS*, pages 5998–6008.

William Yang Wang and Diyi Yang. 2015. That's so annoying!!!: A lexical and frame-semantic embedding based data augmentation approach to automatic categorization of annoying behaviors using #petpeeve tweets. In *Proceedings of the 2015 Conference on Empirical Methods in Natural Language Processing*, pages 2557–2563, Lisbon, Portugal. Association for Computational Linguistics.

Jason W. Wei and Kai Zou. 2019. EDA: easy data augmentation techniques for boosting performance on text classification tasks. In *EMNLP/IJCNLP (1)*, pages 6381–6387. Association for Computational Linguistics.

Rong Xiang, Emmanuele Chersoni, Yunfei Long, Qin Lu, and Chu-Ren Huang. 2020. Lexical data augmentation for text classification in deep learning. In *Canadian Conference on AI*, volume 12109 of *Lecture Notes in Computer Science*, pages 521–527. Springer.

Ge Yan, Yu Li, Shu Zhang, and Zhenyu Chen. 2019. Data augmentation for deep learning of judgment documents. In *IScIDE (2)*, volume 11936 of *Lecture Notes in Computer Science*, pages 232–242. Springer.

Hongyi Zhang, Moustapha Cissé, Yann N. Dauphin, and David Lopez-Paz. 2018. mixup: Beyond empirical risk minimization. In *ICLR*. OpenReview.net.

Haoxi Zhong, Chaojun Xiao, Cunchao Tu, Tianyang Zhang, Zhiyuan Liu, and Maosong Sun. 2020. How does NLP benefit legal system: A summary of legal artificial intelligence. In *Proceedings of the 58th Annual Meeting of the Association for Computational Linguistics*, pages 5218–5230, Online. Association for Computational Linguistics.

A Legal Approach to Hate Speech – Operationalizing the EU's Legal Framework against the Expression of Hatred as an NLP Task

Frederike Zufall[1], Marius Hamacher[2], Katharina Kloppenborg[3], Torsten Zesch[2]
[1] Max Planck Institute for Research on Collective Goods, Bonn, Germany;
Waseda Institute for Advanced Study, Waseda University, Tokyo, Japan
[2] Computational Linguistics, CATALPA, FernUniversität in Hagen, Germany
[3] Université Paris Cité (U1284), F-75004 Paris, France
zufall@coll.mpg.de, katharina.kloppenborg@cri-paris.org,
{marius.hamacher, torsten.zesch} @fernuni-hagen.de

Abstract

We propose a 'legal approach' to hate speech detection by operationalization of the decision as to whether a post is subject to criminal law into an NLP task. Comparing existing regulatory regimes for hate speech, we base our investigation on the European Union's framework as it provides a widely applicable legal minimum standard. Accurately deciding whether a post is punishable or not usually requires legal education. We show that, by breaking the legal assessment down into a series of simpler sub-decisions, even laypersons can annotate consistently. Based on a newly annotated dataset, our experiments show that directly learning an automated model of punishable content is challenging. However, learning the two sub-tasks of 'target group' and 'targeting conduct' instead of a holistic, end-to-end approach to the legal assessment yields better results. Overall, our method also provides decisions that are more transparent than those of end-to-end models, which is a crucial point in legal decision-making.

1 Introduction

Social media provides the platform for the expression of opinions along with their widespread dissemination. Unrestricted freedom of expression, however, bears the risk of harming certain groups of people - rendering the regulation of hate speech a potential instrument against discrimination. To do so at scale, automated detection systems are required to aid the moderation process. While research on hate speech detection is well-established, defining 'hate speech' remains challenging. Datasets encode all kinds of (partly incompatible) notions of hatefulness or offensiveness (Schmidt and Wiegand, 2017; Fortuna and Nunes, 2018; Poletto et al., 2020; Fortuna et al., 2021) that make it difficult to decide which postings would justify restricting freedom of speech through deletion. Ultimately, a subset of especially hateful content can be considered punishable by law and thus would not fall under the legal right to freedom of expression. As there exist competing legal standards for the regulation of hateful expressions, the selection requires discussion.

Competing Legal Standards On the international level, Article 4 of the 'International Convention on the Elimination of All Forms of Racial Discrimination (ICERD)'[1] binds the signatory states to punish incitement to racial discrimination against any race or group of persons of another colour or ethnic origin by their respective national law. However, the convention does not cover discrimination based on religion and is limited in its legal effect, as various states have made reservations. This is especially the case for the U.S., where the expression of hatred toward any group is constitutionally widely protected by the Free Speech Clause of the First Amendment (Fisch, 2002). Consequently, as U.S. law does not provide for any legal provision prohibiting hate speech as an act of speech, it cannot serve as a base for a detection system.

In Europe, however, the prevention of discrimination against and segregation of a target group (thereby ensuring the members' acceptance as equal in a society) is considered such an important prerequisite for democracy that it may justify the restriction of free speech. The Council of Europe has set up an additional protocol to the 'Convention on Cybercrime', concerning the criminalization of acts of a racist and xenophobic nature committed through computer systems.[2] However, the Protocol has not been ratified or even signed by all Member States of the Council of Europe and is subject to several reservations.[3]

[1] General Assembly resolution 2106 (XX) of 21 Dec 1965.
[2] ETS No. 189, 28.01.2003.
[3] Bulgaria, Hungary, Ireland, the Russian Federation and the U.K., for instance, did not sign the Protocol. Countries

Proceedings of the Natural Legal Language Processing Workshop 2022, pages 53 - 64
December 8, 2022

Legally and practically more relevant is the following instrument: the European Union (EU) has, after long debate, set up a common regime with a *Framework Decision*[4] that fully binds all of its Member States to make incitement to hatred or violence a punishable criminal offense. The framework also affects U.S. social-media platforms as long as the offender or the material hosted is located within the EU. Its importance has also been emphasized by the 'EU Code of conduct on countering illegal hate speech online' that the EU Commission agreed with IT companies like Facebook, Twitter, and Youtube.[5] Furthermore, the EU's new Digital Services Act creates new obligations for large online platforms regarding illegal content.[6] The regulation will be directly applicable in all EU Member States from 17 February 2024, and also apply to providers established outside the EU if they provide their services to recipients in the Union. The EU Commission has also started an initiative to add to the list of EU crimes in Art. 83(1) TFEU "all forms of hate crime and hate speech, whether because of race, religion, gender or sexuality".[7] This would allow the Commission to replace the existing Framework Decision by a new Directive further elabolarting on a more extensive notion of hate speech incrimination. To date, the EU Framework Decision not only provides a minimum standard for handling hate speech by criminal law, but it is also the regime that – in connection with the new Digital Services Act – triggers the broadest regulatory obligations for large platform providers inside and outside the EU.

As Figure 1 shows, each Member State may still go beyond the framework's minimum requirements and define higher standards. Germany, for instance, provides for a broader definition of the possible protected target group by including 'sections of the population', e.g. refugees otherwise not being covered as they cannot clearly be distinguished by race,

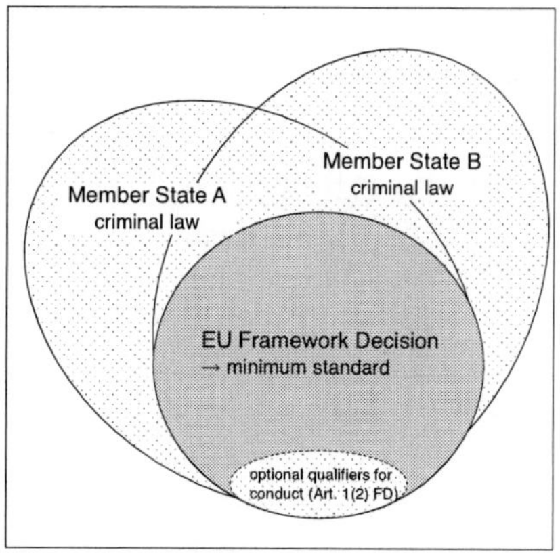

Figure 1: Scope of the EU Framework's legal standard. It defines a common core of punishable offenses.

ethnic, or national origin. However, the Framework Decision allows member states to make the incrimination depend on additional requirements.

Based on all these considerations, the Framework Decision's minimum standard may stand in for a general legal approach to hate speech and serve as the basis of our further studies.

Contributions In this paper, we translate the legal framework as defined in the EU Framework Decision 2008/913/JHA into a series of binary decisions. We show that the resulting annotation scheme can be used by laypeople to reliably produce a legal evaluation of posts that is comparable to those of legal experts, making dataset generation for this task feasible. Based on the resulting dataset, we experiment with directly learning an automated model of punishable content. The discouraging results of the end-to-end approach and ethical considerations lead us to proposing two subtasks instead: 'target group' and 'targeting conduct' detection. We show that the sub-tasks can be more reliably learned and also provide for better explainability and higher transparency, which is a crucial point in legal decision-making. We make our dataset and models publicly available to foster future research in that direction.[8]

2 Operationalizing Legal Assessment

We begin our investigation by operationalizing the relevant part of the Framework Decision (FD) into a sequence of binary decisions that can be reliably annotated (see Figure 2 for the final decision tree).

like Austria, Belgium, Italy, Switzerland and Turkey signed, but did not (yet) ratify it.

[4]Council Framework Decision 2008/913/JHA of 28 November 2008 on combating certain forms and expressions of racism and xenophobia by means of criminal law. In the remainder of this paper, we shall refer to this as 'EU law' or 'EU Framework Decision' for simplification.

[5]https://ec.europa.eu/newsroom/just/document.cfm?doc_id=42985

[6]Regulation (EU) 2022/2065 of the European Parliament and of the Council of 19 October 2022 on a Single Market For Digital Services and amending Directive 2000/31/EC (Digital Services Act).

[7]Communication of 9.12.2021, COM(2021) 777 final.

[8]https://github.com/simulacrum6/op-hate-nlp

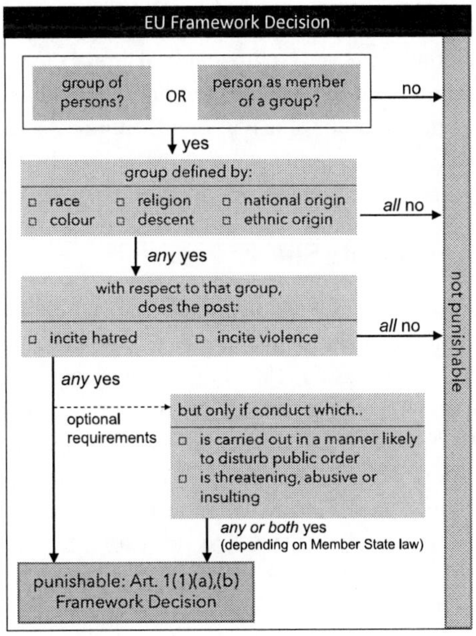

Figure 2: Decision tree derived from legal framework.

In a way, we are translating the plain text of the legal definition into an actionable algorithm.

Article 1(1) FD states that the following intentional conduct is punishable:

> (a) publicly inciting to violence or hatred directed against a group of persons or a member of such a group defined by reference to race, colour, religion, descent or national or ethnic origin;
>
> (b) the commission of an act referred to in point (a) by public dissemination or distribution of tracts, pictures or other material;

The punishable conduct addressed in paragraph (a) refers to the oral expression of hatred, while paragraph (b) broadens the scope to public dissemination or distribution of tracts, pictures or other material. For the detection of social-media posts, there is no added value in implementing these actions separately, as they are always met in case of public social-media posting on the Internet.

In a simplified way, two main questions have to be answered: (1) does a statement address a protected group? and (2) does it target that group by inciting hatred or violence? We address these as (1) *target group* and (2) *targeting conduct*.

2.1 Target Group

As shown in Figure 2, Art.1(1)(a) FD refers to the following potential targets: a group of persons or a member of such a group defined by reference to race, colour, religion, descent, or national or ethnic origin (see Example 1).

- **French people** are frog eaters. (nationality)
- **Black people** = slaves!! (race)
- **Muslims** are all terrorists! (religion)
- **Sinti and Roma** - awful parasites! (ethnic origin)

Example 1: Distinguishable groups.

The scope also covers *individuals* in case they are targeted as a member of an aforementioned group, as illustrated in Example 2.

- you fucking muslim should leave our country!
- This dirty american bitch, typical american, lying son-of-a-bitch, out of our country!

Example 2: Individuals as members of a group.

'Race and 'colour' are discriminating grounds that can be understood interchangeable. 'Religion' refers broadly to persons defined by reference to their religious convictions or beliefs as Recital (8) of the Framework Decision indicates.

Recital (7) FD clarifies that 'descent' points to persons or groups of persons who descend from persons who could be identified by characteristics like race or colour. It is not necessary that all these characteristics still be present in the respective persons. Hence, the descendants would be protected regardless, e.g., descendants of people of Jewish faith even in cases where they do not share this faith anymore. 'National origin' or 'ethnic origin' are both distinguishing grounds that require reference to a specific nationality or ethnic group. Statements that refer to 'foreigners' or 'refugees' without further specification are not covered, as these references are considered too general.

2.2 Targeting Conduct

With respect to the target group as a victim, Art.1(1)(a) FD requires at least one of the following acts to be committed by the potential offender: (i) inciting hatred, or (ii) inciting violence.

Regarding the definition and understanding of these acts, freedom of expression needs to be taken into consideration through Art.7(1) FD, which ultimately refers to Art.11(1) of the EU Charter of Human Rights. By preventing segregation, the intent is to protect minorities from being deprived of their human dignity as equal members of society. Punishing expressions is only justified in the respective cases if the legal interest in preventing discrimination outweighs the right to free speech – which is likewise a precondition for democracy.

Within these limits, the Framework Decision itself does not provide for a more detailed definition of 'inciting hatred' and 'inciting violence', but entrusts the Member States with elaborating the interpretation in national case law. For our annotation guidelines, we draw here from German case law, which provides for long-standing settled decision-making practice for these terms.

Inciting 'Inciting' has been defined as 'conduct influencing emotions and intellect of others'.[9] A key element of the definition is the clear intent to influence others. To outweigh freedom of expression, the conduct has to go beyond mere rejection or contempt and means more than merely endorsing.

Hatred The Framework Decision limits, in Recital (8), the notion of 'hatred' as such based on race, colour, religion, descent, or national or ethnic origin. In other words, 'hatred' expressed against a specific group, but which is unrelated to the belonging to this group, is not covered. We draw here again on German case law, where the act of incitement to hatred needs to be 'objectively capable and subjectively intended to create or intensify an emotionally enhanced, hostile attitude (towards the respective group)'.[10] Example 3 illustrates comments that fit these criteria.

- Muslims are deceitful parasites enjoying life thanks to hard working german citizens!!
- Bring back the slaves! #niggerarenohumans

Example 3: Comments inciting hatred.

Violence While 'hatred' refers to the creation of a hostile attitude, inciting 'violence' shall 'give rise to the determination of others to commit violence'.[11] Violent measures do not just comprise assault, but also violent expulsion or pogroms. Example 4 illustrates comments inciting violence.

- U.S. citizens should be hunt down and deported!
- Burn all Muslims in their mosques!

Example 4: Comments inciting violence.

2.3 Optional Qualifiers

Art. 1 (2) FD, however, grants one exception to the minimum standard, as seen in Figure 1. Member States may predicate the offense on the additional requirements of the disturbance of public order or threatening, abusive or insulting conduct. In other words, a Member State may stipulate that the conduct is only punishable if it also leads to a disturbance of public order, or if the conduct is also threatening, abusive, or insulting. As these additional requirements are only required by a few Member States, we do not operationalize them.

3 Feasibility Study

Based on the above considerations we obtained a decision tree that will serve as a basis for annotation, but also as a logical high-level fundament for our classifiers (Figure 2). It should not be confused with decision trees as machine learning algorithms, as we work with fine-tuned BERT for training our classifiers (see Section 5). To test our decision tree annotation scheme, we first perform a feasibility study, where we assess the quality of annotations produced by our annotation scheme against direct annotation. We also assess the reliability of an assessment by legal experts to establish an upper bound for this task.

Setup We asked public prosecutors from one of the two cybercrime prosecution centers in Germany to provide the ground truth for punishability based on §130 of the German Criminal Code – which implements the EU Framework.[12] As prosecutors would be obliged to open an investigation for each punishable post, we provided a set of 156 'made-up' hate speech posts in German. These were never openly published and are thus not punishable.[13] The prosecutors did not use our decision tree, but decided based on their legal training and expertise. As a control condition, we asked layperson annotators to perform a direct annotation. Annotators were provided with the legal text of §130 and decided whether a post was punishable using their understanding of the legal code. Finally, we asked layperson annotators to follow our multi-label annotation scheme, from which we can automatically derive whether a post is punishable or not, depending on the combination of our labels.

Results Figure 3 shows the inter-annotator agreement (IAA) per setup in the feasibility study. Agreement in the control condition (holistic annotation) is very low, which is in line with previous

[9] BGHSt 21, 371 (372); BGHSt 46, 212 (217)

[10] BGHSt 21, 371 (372); BGHSt 46, 212 (217)

[11] BGH 3.4.2008 – 3 StR 394/07

[12] As §130 of the German Criminal Code is a transposition of the minimum standard set by the EU Framework Decision (see Section 2), the results obtained in this way should be generalizable to EU law.

[13] The made-up posts are comparable in nature to realistic posts. See next Section 4 for a more detailed description.

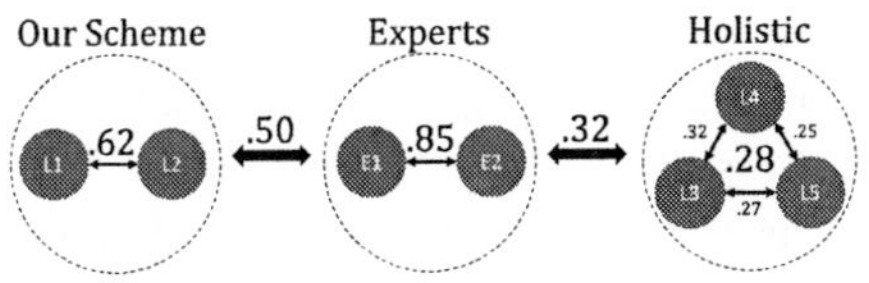

Figure 3: Cohen's Kappa for the *Punishable* label for different annotation schemes in the feasibility study.

Source	#	% Punishable
Made-up	157	13.5
Web search	80	6.2
Anti hate speech initiatives	88	10.2
GermEval2019 (abuse, insult)	425	0.9
GermEval2019 (other)	250	0.0

Table 1: Composition of the dataset by source.

findings of low IAA for hate speech annotations (Ross et al., 2016). However, the high kappa between expert prosecutors shows that sufficient legal expertise enables consistent legal decision-making.

Using our annotation scheme increases consistency between annotators and agreement with experts. Thus, based on the success of the feasibility study, we adapt our annotation scheme to fit the EU framework and produced the full dataset, described in the next section.

4 Punishable Hate Speech Dataset

In this section, we describe how the full dataset was created. All posts in the dataset are in German.

4.1 Data Sources

Social-media posts were sampled and requested from a multitude of sources with the primary goal of obtaining sufficient examples of punishable hate speech. Table 1 provides an overview of the final composition of the dataset.

Made-up We include the 'made-up' examples from the feasibility study, re-annotated according to the EU framework. The examples were produced by volunteers, who were instructed to write short texts presumably constituting 'incitement to hatred' against the list of target groups mentioned in Figure 4.[14] Participants also received instances of real hate speech as examples for their artificial posts. 9 participants created a total of 157 short texts. The resulting statements are nearly indistinguishable in form from real examples, but we have no way of controlling for topic biases that might have been introduced via this process.

Web search We performed a manual search of Twitter, comment sections of online newsrooms, law forums, court databases as well as news articles for hateful social media posts that were included in a court decision. This resulted in 80 instances.

Anti hate speech initiatives We include 88 hate speech comments collected by the initiative 'respect!' of Demokratiezentrum BW.

GermEval2019 Data samples from the subtask 2 corpus of GermEval 2019, a shared task on the identification of offensive language (Struß et al., 2019), were also included. We add 425 tweets from the 'abuse' and 'insult' categories, that will probably contain only few cases of legally punishable hate speech, but are likely to contain offensive language. We also add 250 tweets from the 'other' category that are non-offensive, but cover the same topics (like refugee crisis, politics, etc.).

4.2 Annotation Scheme & Process

The full dataset was annotated by two paid laypersons, who were provided with an annotation manual based on the operationalisation described in Section 2 with further explanations, instructions, and examples. To measure annotation quality, a subset of 101 posts was annotated by a fully-qualified lawyer using the same annotation scheme.

We annotate whether a group of persons or a group member was mentioned in a post and, if so, whether the group is distinguishable by any reference to race, descent, or national or ethnic origin. In case a group is explicitly mentioned, we also annotate the surface form used in the comment. We created a short list of frequently attacked groups and asked annotators to choose one of these or 'other' ('Group Category' annotation). We include groups not covered by the EU framework like *women* or *refugees*, as they might be relevant for future detection tasks regarding other legal regimes. The full list of target groups used in our study can be seen in Figure 4.

- Euthanasia is the only way to deal with all the **disabled people**, they should be buried.
- You should gas all the **Jews**. All they want is your money.
- The **oil eyes** should set themselves on fire with their gasoline.

Example 5: Explicitly mentioned groups.

We also annotate possible targeting conduct described in Section 2.2, i.e. inciting hatred and inciting violence. If a relevant group is targeted and any

[14] Volunteers did not participate in subsequent annotation efforts.

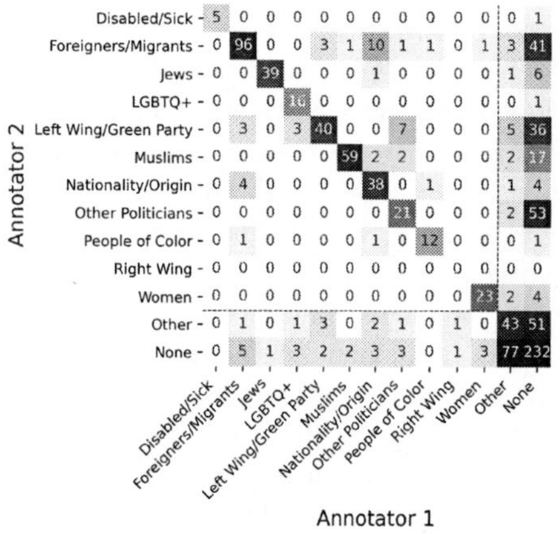

Figure 4: Confusion matrix of non-expert annotators.

targeting conduct is present, a post is considered punishable. Table 2 provides some examples of the resulting annotation.

4.3 Analysis

We analyze the IAA among laypersons as well as between laypersons and the expert annotator in terms of *Cohen's Kappa* as shown in Table 3. Aggregated results on target group and targeting conduct are quite reliable (kappa between .52 and .70), while kappa for the punishable label is rather low (.33 to .43). People agree on the facts (group, conduct), but disagree on the interpretation.

Table 1 displays the distribution of punishable posts. It is noteworthy that in the GermEval2019 data a surprisingly low proportion (under 1%) of abusive or insulting comments are actually punishable under EU law. This highlights that hate speech detection and detecting illegal content are fundamentally different tasks.

Figure 4 shows the confusion matrix between the two layperson annotators regarding the group annotation from our short list (subset of 392 posts having a group mention). The largest target group is foreigners/migrants, which is not explicitly protected under EU law. Differences between annotators mainly arise due to the 'none' and 'other' categories, while the largest disagreement is within closely related categories like 'left-wing/green party' and 'other politicians'.

5 Automated Detection

Holistic baseline approach To study the extent to which our annotated data can serve as a basis for automated detection, we train a baseline classifier that takes a post as input and estimates whether the post is punishable. At this step, as we do not take our decision tree into consideration, we may refer to this baseline classifier as a "holistic approach". For model training, differences between annotators were adjudicated by a legal expert who made the final decision on the correct label. The agreement numbers reported in Section 4 are thus not applicable for the following experiment.

Fine-tuned BERT (Devlin et al., 2018) models have proven to be strong baselines for various NLP tasks, so we follow this practice[15], using GBERT-base (Chan et al., 2020). The model is trained for 20 epochs using a batch size of 16 and NLL loss. For optimization, we choose bias-corrected Adam (Kingma and Ba, 2015), with a learning rate of $2e^{-5}$. The learning rate is linearly increased up to its peak during the first 10% of training and then linearly decreased. These choices follow the recommendations of Mosbach et al. (2020) for increasing training stability when fine-tuning BERT. For evaluation, we perform a stratified 10-fold CV. We also include a random classification baseline for the punishable label. We set $p = 0.5$ and thus yield a recall of 0.5 and a precision that corresponds to the overall ratio of punishable posts in the dataset, i.e. 0.04.

The fine-tuned model achieves an average F_1 of .39 (P .69; R .28), which shows that legal hate speech classification is complex and not easily solvable by baseline models with a holistic approach. The mere presence of language inciting hate or violence is not a sufficient signal, but the model needs to learn in addition whether (i) the hate is directed against an object, (ii) the object is a group, (iii) the group is protected under the given law.

Even among relevant target groups, detection is made difficult by the many surface forms that identify a particular group as the target of the statement. This is exemplified looking at some misclassifications. In Example 6.1, no group is targeted; yet, the model classified the post as punishable. In Example 6.2, the model erroneously judged the post to be punishable, even though the group is not protected under the EU framework. Implicit or metaphorical references to a group were not detected by the model (e.g. Example 6.3).

[15] For the implementation, we use *HuggingFace Transformers* (Wolf et al., 2020) and *PyTorch* (Paszke et al., 2019).

Statement	Group Category	Target Group: Group of persons	Target Group: Distinguishable by nationality, race, religion, ethnicity	Target Group: Explicit	Targeting Conduct: Incite hatred	Targeting Conduct: Incite violence	**Punishable**
So dumm wie Gutmenschen halt sind! Stupid as do-gooders are!	Other	✓		✓			
Die linken Hurensöhne! Ballert die alle ab! Left-wing sons of bitches! Shoot 'em all!	Left-Wing	✓		✓		✓	
Es brennen noch zu wenige Synagogen. Still too few synagogues on fire.	Jews	✓	✓			✓	✓
Muslime sind alles Vergewaltiger! Schützt deutsche Frauen! Muslims are all rapists! Protect our German women!	Muslims	✓	✓	✓	✓		✓

Table 2: Example annotations from the resulting dataset. Surface form referring to groups is underlined.

		L1/ L2	L1/ Exp	L2/ Exp
	Group Category	**.77**	**.70**	**.67**
Group	Group of persons	.49	.82	.55
Group	Individual as group member	.14	.24	.48
Group	Nationality, race, religion, ...	.52	.42	.67
Group	**Any target group**	**.53**	**.52**	**.70**
Conduct	Inciting hatred	.11	.39	.00
Conduct	Inciting violence	.56	.64	.74
Conduct	**Any targeting conduct**	**.56**	**.69**	**.52**
	Punishable	**.33**	**.43**	**.37**

Table 3: Inter-annotator agreement (Cohen's Kappa) between laypersons and domain expert.

	P	R	F_1
Group of persons	.81	.85	.83
Individual as member of group	.00	.00	.00
Distinguishable by nationality, etc.	.79	.71	.75
Inciting hatred	.25	.07	.11
Inciting violence	.70	.73	.72
Punishable (random)	.04	.50	.07
Punishable (direct)	.69	.28	.39
Punishable (submodels + decision tree)	.41	.43	.42

Table 4: Overview of prediction results

Submodel + decision tree approach As an alternative to this direct and holistic classification approach, we also trained separate binary classification models for each annotation label. This allowed us to combine the resulting submodels with our decision tree from Figure 2. The decision tree serves as a logical high-level foundation and allows us to employ model training at a much more concrete level. This approach provides a higher degree of transparency with regard to the actual steps of the decision-making process. It may also lead to an overall improved assessment as each submodel has an easier task to learn and thus may provide more accurate results when combined.

1) DEPORT DEPORT [...] DEPORT
2) Faggots should be castrated and locked up!
3) A metro we build, a metro we build, a metro we build from Jerusalem to Auschwitz, a metro we build!

Example 6: Cases misclassified by detection model

We trained separate models for the prediction of target groups and targeting conduct using the same setup as described above. The last row in Table 4 shows results of applying those two models to derive punishability. In terms of F_1 score, the subtask approach is comparable to the direct approach of estimating punishability (.42 vs .39). Looking at the performance of the subtask models, we see mixed results. While the *Group of persons*, *Distinguishable by nationality, race, religion, ethnicity* and *Inciting violence* models produce good results (.71 – .83), the models for *Individual as member of group* and *Inciting hatred* failed making accurate predictions (.00 – .11). Both are rare in the dataset (14 positive cases each), making them difficult labels to learn. Having more positive cases should bring performance up to levels comparable to the other annotations.

6 Generalizing beyond EU Law

So far, we have presented a case study of operationalizing a specific legal standard (i.e. the EU Framework Decision). The underlying methodology can be generalized in a straightforward way. Instead of directly predicting whether a post is punishable or not, we divide the problem into two subtasks, (i) group detection and (ii) conduct detection, each of which can be tackled separately, depending on the applicable legal regime. By doing so, this approach offers higher explainability of model decisions, an aspect that is crucial for legal decision-making.

6.1 Group Detection

If we were able to reliably detect all groups referred to in a comment, we could take the list of protected groups and only consider those relevant under a certain legal standard. In this way, our approach would also generalize beyond EU law.

However, groups are often referenced by a variety of different surface forms, some of which are only metaphorically related to the group (e.g. 'Goldstücke'; Engl. '*gold pieces*' for *people of color*, see Table 5). Consequently, we cannot use Named Entity Recognition (Ritter et al., 2011) for group detection, as, e.g. 'women' are a common target group, but not a named entity. A better fit seems Entity Linking (Derczynski et al., 2015), which would (depending on the underlying knowledge base) find explicitly mentioned groups. However, groups can also be implicitly mentioned (7.1) or as part of a co-reference chain (7.2).

1) [...] For them the sport [football] is like. I put a goat on the field, 22 holy warriors and whoever knocks it up first, wins.
2) No mercy for **terrorists**. We have declared war on **Islam**. **They** had 800 years to reform. Time is up!

Example 7: 1) Implicit targeting of Muslims. 2) Muslims target group only identifiable by coreference.

Thus, we argue that annotating data for groups referenced in the text (even implicitly) is a prerequisite for 'group detection' as a stand-alone NLP task. Once this is established, it can be used to find the best methods for group detection. A possible way to find surface variants might be to compile a list of common surface forms and compare the closest synonyms for a group as computed over a more general corpus.

6.2 Conduct Detection

For specific targeting conduct like *inciting violence*, detecting the most common actions patterns like 'kill GROUP' or 'burn GROUP' might be a promising approach. This would also limit the number of false positives, e.g. when someone 'threatens' to *burn a candle* instead. For this task, semantic role labeling (Gildea and Jurafsky, 2002) or using frames (Baker, 2014) could be useful, but existing resources like FrameNet seem not specific enough, as they put 'threat' under the COMMITMENT frame (in the sense of 'committing to harm someone').

In general, there is a high level of metaphor, irony and sarcasm in the comments, which poses serious challenges to all conduct detection methods. This is especially problematic as those may qualify as ironic or sarcastic critique protected by the freedom of expression. Even though irony and sarcasm as such are not legal terms, they will then have an influence on the assessment as to whether a targeting conduct like *inciting hatred* is given. Accordingly, these cases can be captured at the annotation level as *in dubio pro reo*, i.e. would have to be annotated as not punishable.

7 Related Work

Automated detection of offensive Internet discourse has been intensively studied under a variety of names, for instance: abusive language (Waseem et al., 2017) or content (Kiritchenko et al., 2020), ad hominem arguments (Habernal et al., 2018), aggression (Kumar et al., 2018), cyberbullying (Xu et al., 2012; Macbeth et al., 2013), hate speech (Warner and Hirschberg, 2012; Ross et al., 2016; Del Vigna et al., 2017), offensive language usage (Razavi et al., 2010), profanity (Schmidt and Wiegand, 2017), threats (Oostdijk and van Halteren, 2013) and socially unacceptable discourse (Fišer et al., 2017). While most early work focused on English, now there is also a growing body of work in other languages, e.g., German (Ross et al., 2016), Italian (Del Vigna et al., 2017), and Dutch (Oostdijk and van Halteren, 2013). All of those works use a non-legally informed definition of the construct to be detected. A notable exception is work on Slovene by Fišer et al. (2017) who relied on annotators interpretation of the legal definition without further breaking down those decisions.

There is a body of work in NLP with a legal perspective focused on predicting the outcome of court decisions (Aletras et al., 2016; Katz et al., 2017; Bruninghaus and Ashley, 2003; Kastellec, 2010; Waltl et al., 2017), to the best of our knowledge our work is the only effort to operationalise a legal framework for hate speech. However, the dependence on existing court decisions makes it difficult to work with legal problems where relevant case law is not available as a data source. To overcome this problem, Zufall et al. (2019) translated statutory rules for defamatory offenses into a series of annotatable binary decisions.

The importance of finding groups for hate speech analysis has also been stressed by Kiritchenko et al.

(2020). As offenses against groups are often implicitly framed, Sap et al. (2020) introduce *Social Bias Frames* that make the attacked group explicit. As group detection can work with any set of group categories, it can also be adapted to cover non-Western groups (Sambasivan et al., 2021).

8 Conclusion

We operationalize a 'legal approach to hate speech' by translating the requirements of the EU Framework Decision into a series of annotation steps that can be reliably performed by laypersons. However, we show that learning a holistic, end-to-end model of whether a post is punishable remains challenging. We thus propose to tackle two subtasks instead: *group detection* and *conduct detection*. Depending on the applicable legal framework, a final decision on the legal status of a comment can then be derived from the combination of the detected group and conduct. Relying on subtasks comes with the added benefit of increased transparency and explainability compared to black-box models. This is crucial for systems that potentially interfere with human rights, such as the balance between freedom of expression and the prevention of discrimination. Hence, we recommend this modular approach as the preferred way of composing systems for legal decision-making.

Ethical Considerations

Predicting the legal status of a comment might infringe on the fundamental right of 'free speech'. On the other hand, we are targeting the worst tail-end of the distribution – the kind of hate speech that is putting democracy in danger by inciting hatred and violence in a society. Not addressing hate speech and its foregoing automated detection methods would give further rise to possible discrimination, making it a problem for equal participation in a democracy. As our approach introduces a layer of algorithmic transparency not found in traditional methods, we believe that the importance of this research outweighs its dangers.

Annotation Process Regarding our made-up examples, we conducted a survey with nine students, asking them to create short texts that presumably constitute 'incitement to hatred' (see Section 4). This survey was approved by the ethics committee of ANONYMIZED. The final annotation of the dataset was carried out by two paid annotators, who were compensated above the local minimum wage. Annotators were warned about the offensive nature of the data and instructed only to annotate 50 comments a day to mitigate the effect of fatigue.

Race and Gender The EU Framework Decision explicitly requires the conduct to be directed against a "group of persons or a member of such a group defined by reference to race, colour, religion, descent or national or ethnic origin" (Art.1(1)(a) Framework Decision). It is thus a necessary legal requirement which is meant to protect the aforementioned groups and to prevent discrimination. We also use the groups 'women' and 'LGBTQ+', as these are often the targets of hate speech. Our model explicitly allows for adding other groups in order to adapt to differing legal standards.

Deployment Systems used in the context of legal decision-making or, more generally, systems that filter specific content should be used with great care and in view of the potential interference with human rights, namely the right to free speech. We explicitly do not recommend using any legal decision-making system without human supervision. We consider the improved transparency of our model to be an important step in allowing prosecutors to understand the reasons behind flagging a certain comment as potentially punishable.

Release of the Data As our dataset consists of postings that could be traced back to individuals, it contains personal data in the sense of the EU

General Data Protection Regulation (GDPR). To comply with this legal standard, and given the sensitive nature of the data, we do not make any of the real postings publicly available. We do, however, publish the made-up examples generated during the feasibility study.

Acknowledgements

We would like to thank the prosecutors office in Cologne (Staatsanwaltschaft Köln/ZAC NRW) for their expert annotations and helpful insights into their work. Furthermore we thank the anti hate speech initiative "respect!" of the Democracy Center Baden-Württemberg for providing us with resources for our dataset. We also thank Emilie Mathieu for proofreading. This work was partially funded by the German ministry of education and research (BMBF) within the framework program Research for Civil Security of the German Federal Government (KISTRA, 13N15337).

References

Nikolaos Aletras, Dimitrios Tsarapatsanis, Daniel Preoţiuc-Pietro, and Vasileios Lampos. 2016. Predicting judicial decisions of the European Court of Human Rights: A Natural Language Processing perspective. *PeerJ Computer Science*.

Collin F. Baker. 2014. FrameNet: A knowledge base for natural language processing. In *Proceedings of Frame Semantics in NLP: A Workshop in Honor of Chuck Fillmore (1929-2014)*, pages 1–5, Baltimore, MD, USA. Association for Computational Linguistics.

Stefanie Bruninghaus and Kevin D. Ashley. 2003. Predicting Outcomes of Case Based Legal Arguments. In *Proceedings of the International Conference on Artificial Intelligence and Law*, pages 233–242, New York, NY, USA. ACM.

Branden Chan, Stefan Schweter, and Timo Möller. 2020. German's Next Language Model. In *Proceedings of the 28th International Conference on Computational Linguistics*, pages 6788–6796, Barcelona, Spain (Online). International Committee on Computational Linguistics.

Fabio Del Vigna, Andrea Cimino, Felice Dell'Orletta, Marinella Petrocchi, and Maurizio Tesconi. 2017. Hate Me, Hate Me Not: Hate Speech Detection on Facebook. In *Proceedings of the First Italian Conference on Cybersecurity (ITASEC17)*, pages 86–95.

Leon Derczynski, Diana Maynard, Giuseppe Rizzo, Marieke Van Erp, Genevieve Gorrell, Raphaël Troncy, Johann Petrak, and Kalina Bontcheva. 2015. Analysis of named entity recognition and linking for tweets. *Information Processing & Management*, 51(2):32–49.

Jacob Devlin, Ming-Wei Chang, Kenton Lee, and Kristina Toutanova. 2018. BERT: pre-training of deep bidirectional transformers for language understanding. *CoRR*, abs/1810.04805.

William B. Fisch. 2002. Hate speech in the constitutional law of the united states. *The American Journal of Comparative Law*, (50):463–492.

Darja Fišer, Tomaž Erjavec, and Nikola Ljubešić. 2017. Legal framework, dataset and annotation schema for socially unacceptable online discourse practices in slovene. In *Proceedings of the First Workshop on Abusive Language Online*, pages 46–51. Association for Computational Linguistics.

Paula Fortuna and Sérgio Nunes. 2018. A survey on automatic detection of hate speech in text. 51(4).

Paula Fortuna, Juan Soler-Company, and Leo Wanner. 2021. How well do hate speech, toxicity, abusive and offensive language classification models generalize across datasets? *Information Processing & Management*, 58(3):102524.

Daniel Gildea and Daniel Jurafsky. 2002. Automatic labeling of semantic roles. *Comput. Linguistics*, 28(3):245–288.

Ivan Habernal, Henning Wachsmuth, Iryna Gurevych, and Benno Stein. 2018. Before Name-Calling: Dynamics and Triggers of Ad Hominem Fallacies in Web Argumentation. In *Proceedings of the 2018 Conference of the North American Chapter of the Association for Computational Linguistics: Human Language Technologies, Volume 1 (Long Papers)*, pages 386–396. Association for Computational Linguistics.

Jonathan Kastellec. 2010. The Statistical Analysis of Judicial Decisions and Legal Rules with Classification Trees. *Journal of Empirical Legal Studies*, 7(2):202–230.

Daniel Martin Katz, Michael J. Bommarito, II, and Josh Blackman. 2017. A general approach for predicting the behavior of the Supreme Court of the United States. *PLOS ONE*, 12(4):1–18.

Diederik P. Kingma and Jimmy Ba. 2015. Adam: A method for stochastic optimization. In *3rd International Conference on Learning Representations, ICLR 2015, San Diego, CA, USA, May 7-9, 2015, Conference Track Proceedings*.

Svetlana Kiritchenko, Isar Nejadgholi, and Kathleen C. Fraser. 2020. Confronting abusive language online: A survey from the ethical and human rights perspective.

Ritesh Kumar, Atul Kr. Ojha, Shervin Malmasi, and Marcos Zampieri. 2018. Benchmarking Aggression Identification in Social Media. In *Proceedings of the First Workshop on Trolling, Aggression and Cyberbullying (TRAC-2018)*, pages 1–11. Association for Computational Linguistics.

Jamie Macbeth, Hanna Adeyema, Henry Lieberman, and Christopher Fry. 2013. Script-based story matching for cyberbullying prevention. In *ACM SIGCHI Conference on Human Factors in Computing Systems*, pages 901–906.

Marius Mosbach, Maksym Andriushchenko, and Dietrich Klakow. 2020. On the Stability of Fine-tuning BERT: Misconceptions, Explanations, and Strong Baselines. *arXiv*.

Nelleke Oostdijk and Hans van Halteren. 2013. N-Gram-Based Recognition of Threatening Tweets. In *Computational Linguistics and Intelligent Text Processing*, pages 183–196, Berlin, Heidelberg. Springer Berlin Heidelberg.

Adam Paszke, Sam Gross, Francisco Massa, Adam Lerer, James Bradbury, Gregory Chanan, Trevor Killeen, Zeming Lin, Natalia Gimelshein, Luca Antiga, Alban Desmaison, Andreas Kopf, Edward Yang, Zachary DeVito, Martin Raison, Alykhan Tejani, Sasank Chilamkurthy, Benoit Steiner, Lu Fang, Junjie Bai, and Soumith Chintala. 2019. Pytorch: An imperative style, high-performance deep learning library. In H. Wallach, H. Larochelle, A. Beygelzimer, F. dÁlché-Buc, E. Fox, and R. Garnett, editors, *Advances in Neural Information Processing Systems 32*, pages 8024–8035. Curran Associates, Inc.

Fabio Poletto, Valerio Basile, Manuela Sanguinetti, Cristina Bosco, and Viviana Patti. 2020. Resources and benchmark corpora for hate speech detection: a systematic review. *Language Resources and Evaluation*, pages 1–47.

Amir H. Razavi, Diana Inkpen, Sasha Uritsky, and Stan Matwin. 2010. Offensive language detection using multi-level classification. In *Proceedings of the 23rd Canadian Conference on Advances in Artificial Intelligence*, pages 16–27, Berlin, Heidelberg. Springer-Verlag.

Alan Ritter, Sam Clark, Oren Etzioni, et al. 2011. Named entity recognition in tweets: an experimental study. In *Proceedings of the 2011 conference on empirical methods in natural language processing*, pages 1524–1534.

Björn Ross, Michael Rist, Guillermo Carbonell, Ben Cabrera, Nils Kurowsky, and Michael Wojatzki. 2016. Measuring the Reliability of Hate Speech Annotations: The Case of the European Refugee Crisis. In *Proceedings of NLP4CMC III: 3rd Workshop on Natural Language Processing for Computer-Mediated Communication*, pages 6–9.

Nithya Sambasivan, Erin Arnesen, Ben Hutchinson, Tulsee Doshi, and Vinodkumar Prabhakaran. 2021. Re-imagining algorithmic fairness in india and beyond.

Maarten Sap, Saadia Gabriel, Lianhui Qin, Dan Jurafsky, Noah A Smith, and Yejin Choi. 2020. Social Bias Frames: Reasoning about Social and Power Implications of Language. In *Proceedings of the 58th Annual Meeting of the Association for Computational Linguistics*, pages 5477–5490, Stroudsburg, PA, USA. Association for Computational Linguistics.

Anna Schmidt and Michael Wiegand. 2017. A Survey on Hate Speech Detection using Natural Language Processing. In *Proceedings of the Fifth International Workshop on Natural Language Processing for Social Media*, pages 1–10. Association for Computational Linguistics.

Julia Maria Struß, Melanie Siegel, Josep Ruppenhofer, Michael Wiegand, and Manfred Klenner. 2019. Overview of germeval task 2, 2019 shared task on the identification of offensive language. In *Proceedings of the 15th Conference on Natural Language Processing (KONVENS 2019)*, pages 354–365, Erlangen, Germany. German Society for Computational Linguistics & Language Technology.

Bernhard Waltl, Georg Bonczek, Elena Scepankova, Jörg Landthaler, and Florian Matthes. 2017. Predicting the Outcome of Appeal Decisions in Germany's Tax Law. In *Electronic Participation*, pages 89–99, Cham. Springer International Publishing.

William Warner and Julia Hirschberg. 2012. Detecting Hate Speech on the World Wide Web. In *Proceedings of the Second Workshop on Language in Social Media*, pages 19–26, Stroudsburg, PA, USA. Association for Computational Linguistics.

Zeerak Waseem, Thomas Davidson, Dana Warmsley, and Ingmar Weber. 2017. Understanding Abuse: A Typology of Abusive Language Detection Subtasks. In *Proceedings of the First Workshop on Abusive Language Online*, pages 78–84. Association for Computational Linguistics.

Thomas Wolf, Lysandre Debut, Victor Sanh, Julien Chaumond, Clement Delangue, Anthony Moi, Pierric Cistac, Tim Rault, Rémi Louf, Morgan Funtowicz, Joe Davison, Sam Shleifer, Patrick von Platen, Clara Ma, Yacine Jernite, Julien Plu, Canwen Xu, Teven Le Scao, Sylvain Gugger, Mariama Drame, Quentin Lhoest, and Alexander M. Rush. 2020. Transformers: State-of-the-art natural language processing. In *Proceedings of the 2020 Conference on Empirical Methods in Natural Language Processing: System Demonstrations*, pages 38–45, Online. Association for Computational Linguistics.

Jun-Ming Xu, Kwang-Sung Jun, Xiaojin Zhu, and Amy Bellmore. 2012. Learning from Bullying Traces in Social Media. In *Proceedings of the Conference of the North American Chapter of the Association for Computational Linguistics: Human Language Technologies*, NAACL HLT '12, pages 656–666, Stroudsburg, PA, USA. Association for Computational Linguistics.

Frederike Zufall, Tobias Horsmann, and Torsten Zesch. 2019. From Legal to Technical Concept: Towards an Automated Classification of German Political Twitter Postings as Criminal Offenses . In *Proceedings of the 2019 Conference of the North American Chapter of the Association for Computational Linguistics: Human Language Technologies, Volume 1 (Long Papers)*, NAACL HLT '19, pages 1337–1347. Association for Computational Linguistics.

A Surface Forms of Target Groups

Category	Surface Form
People of Color	#negersindkeinemenschen, affe, bimbo, dunkler teint, nafris, neger, negroide goldstücke, schwarze, sklaven
Jews	dreckiges judenpack, judenschwein, zentralrat der juden, jüdischer zombie, rattenvolk, zionisten
Muslims	#islamisierung, #muslime, islamlobbys, bärtigen kinderschänder, ditib imams, dreckige kopftuchmädchen, gotteskrieger, isis-schlampen, muslim-ungeziefer, scharia
Nationality/ Origin	pro-erdogan türken, abschaum afrikas, araber, schlitzäugige, deutsche kartoffel, deniz, nafris, polnische hurensöhne

Table 5: Examples of surface forms of target groups

Each group is referred to by a wide variety of different surface forms. Table 5 lists selected examples of surface forms in the dataset. The median number of surface forms per group is 20 (min=3, max=135), showing that automatic detection will have to deal with a high variance. The 'other' category contains a wide range of different types of groups like law enforcement, vegans, jobless, football clubs, or media outlets that we might consider as distinct groups in a revised annotation scheme.

B Data Distribution in Automated Experiments

Annotation	false	true
Group of persons	541	465
Individual as member of group	992	14
Distinguishable by nationality, etc.	744	262
Inciting hatred	992	14
Inciting violence	886	120
Punishable	966	40

Table 6: Label distribution for automated detection experiments. The number of total annotations is > 1000, since some posts contained multiple groups.

	Group Category
None	341
Foreigners/Migrants	155
Other	103
Left Wing/Green Party	93
Muslims	81
Other Politicians	69
Nationality/Origin	49
Jews	46
Women	29
LGBTQ+	17
People of Color	15
Disabled/Sick	6
Right Wing	0

Table 7: Distribution of adjudicated group categories in the dataset.

Privacy Pitfalls of Online Service Terms and Conditions: a Hybrid Approach for Classification and Summarization

Emilia Lukose
Dept. of Computer Science
University of Surrey
Guildford, U.K.
el00490@surrey.ac.uk

Suparna De
Dept. of Computer Science
University of Surrey
Guildford, U.K.
s.de@surrey.ac.uk

Jon Johnson
UCL Social Research Institute
University College London
London, UK
jon.johnson@ucl.ac.uk

Abstract

Verbose and complicated legal terminology in online service terms and conditions (T&C) means that users typically don't read these documents before accepting the terms of such unilateral service contracts. With such services becoming part of mainstream digital life, highlighting Terms of Service (ToS) clauses that impact on the collection and use of user data and privacy are important concerns. Advances in text summarization can help to create informative and concise summaries of the terms, but existing approaches geared towards news and microblogging corpora are not directly applicable to the ToS domain, which is hindered by a lack of T&C-relevant resources for training and evaluation. This paper presents a ToS model, developing a hybrid extractive-classifier-abstractive pipeline that highlights the privacy and data collection/use-related sections in a ToS document and paraphrases these into concise and informative sentences. Relying on significantly less training data (4313 training pairs) than previous representative works (287,226 pairs), our model outperforms extractive baselines by at least 50% in ROUGE-1 score and 54% in METEOR score. The paper also contributes to existing community efforts by curating a dataset of online service T&C, through a developed web scraping tool.

1 Introduction

Despite legislative advances such as the European Union's General Data Protection Regulation (GDPR)[1] regarding specific, informed and unambiguous consent for the collection and use of personal data on the Internet (Kubíček et al., 2022), understanding how online services can read, edit, distribute and sell user data, as documented in their Terms of Service (ToS), remains out of reach for the typical user, with most (98%) consenting to the terms without reading the documents in their entirety (Obar and Oeldorf-Hirsch, 2018). Two major factors contributing to this are the length of the documents and the ambiguous and complicated terminology used (Manor and Li, 2019), with users unable to interpret the implications of the terms of such a legally-binding unilateral contract. In addition to the implication for users' rights, the distribution and use of user data is also important for companies looking to use third-party services in their product.

This can be exemplified with the case of the Global Science Research (GSR) company tasking Cambridge Analytica to build psychological profiles of users through a quiz app, which also collected information from the users' Facebook friends, allowing the company to acquire data from millions of unwitting Facebook users[2]. This data was then matched with existing voter datasets, enabling aggressive voter-targeting operations in the 2016 US presidential election[3]. Delving into the app's ToS reveals that it states: "We collect any information that you choose to share with us ...this may include, inter alia, the name, demographics, [. . .] of your profile and of your network." In addition to this, they permit GSR to "edit and sell" user data by accepting the conditions (Research, 2014). When queried in 2018 if it had read and evaluated the terms and conditions for the app, Facebook responded: "We did not read all the terms and conditions"[4].

With a lack of regulations around standard terms in which consumer contracts should be drafted (Drawzeski et al., 2021), a condensed equivalent of the salient points of a ToS document can em-

[1] https://eugdpr.org/

[2] https://www.theguardian.com/news/2018/mar/17/cambridge-analytica-facebook-influence-us-election

[3] https://www.theguardian.com/us-news/2015/dec/11/senator-ted-cruz-president-campaign-facebook-user-data

[4] https://www.mercurynews.com/2018/04/26/facebook-didnt-read-terms-and-conditions-for-app-behind-cambridge-analytica

Proceedings of the Natural Legal Language Processing Workshop 2022, pages 65 - 75
December 8, 2022 ©2022 Association for Computational Linguistics

power users to understand their rights and avoid privacy invasion and legal disagreements. Summarization, which condenses text into a shorter form whilst keeping the most crucial and informational parts intact, is an intuitive approach for replacing unnecessary (and in some cases, intentionally convoluted) long text with a digestible summary.

Building on recent community approaches to annotate and curate ToS sentence/summary pairs (Manor and Li, 2019; Keymanesh et al., 2020), we propose a hybrid extractive-classifier-abstractive model that can extract ToS sentences related to privacy and data collection/use and paraphrases these into concise and informative ToS highlights. The hybrid model forms part of a Web application and browser plugin that enables users to view an at-a-glance summary of any online service (specified through its URL) T&C. We also contribute to community efforts for curating a ToS dataset by developing a web scraping engine to build a novel ToS dataset from 163 different online services. The proposed hybrid model addresses limitations of existing works as it relies on significantly less training data (4313 training pairs) than previous representative works in hybrid extractive-abstractive methods (See et al., 2017) (287,226 pairs). The summarization results are compared against the baseline unsupervised, extractive techniques, achieving significant improvements in performance (50% improvement in ROUGE-1 score versus the best performing baseline, and 54% in METEOR score).

2 Related Work

This section explores the state-of-the-art community efforts and research within the domain of T&C and text summarization. The "Terms of Service; Didn't Read" (TOS;DR)[5] community-driven project highlights alarming statements in ToS. Services are given grades ranging from A-E based on the severity of the terms listed; E being very serious concerns. Summaries are manually submitted by the TOS;DR community, which limits the scope of summarization to only those that already exist in the database. Moreover, manually reading and analysing long documents of terms is a laborious and time-consuming task. The TL;DRLegal[6] website hosts community-submitted software license summaries that are peer-reviewed by the website managers, with the same manual-process limitations as TOS;DR.

A notable work in ToS data curation is that by Manor & Li (Manor and Li, 2019) with 446 sets of contract sections and corresponding reference summaries from TOS;DR and TL;DRLegal, thus presenting the first dataset in this genre.

Automated summarization techniques have been applied successfully to curated news (e.g. CNN/DailyMail corpus (Hermann et al., 2015)), scientific articles (Yasunaga et al., 2019) or microblogging (e.g. Large Scale Chinese Short Text Summarization (LCTCS) (Hu et al., 2015)) corpora. Categorized either as extractive (Nallapati et al., 2017; Keymanesh et al., 2020) or abstractive (See et al., 2017; Gehrmann et al., 2018) methods, existing summarization approaches are however, not directly applicable to the T&C domain. Extractive approaches work by selecting the most salient sentences for the summary (Xiao et al., 2020) and deciding on their order of presentation. They rely on the structural features of documents, i.e. typically news, scientific articles, where the title and abstract/first few lines of the document, contain a snapshot of the key content. These heuristics do not translate well for ToS documents, which have differing structures for different jurisdictions and where the terminological nuances in legal language are difficult to capture (Drawzeski et al., 2021). Moreover, as the resultant extractive summary matches source sentences word-for-word, complex legal terms in the summary may still confuse the reader (Manor and Li, 2019). Existing works for privacy policies and ToS include the extractive approach of a supervised Convolutional Neural Network (CNN) model (Keymanesh et al., 2020) to predict which content has the most risk of unsafe data practices, that is followed by extracting a calculated amount of sentences with the highest risk score. The model did not perform well when compared to the TOS;DR summaries, as a fully-extractive approach cannot mimic the human-like qualities in the TOS;DR summaries, and also suffers as it generates "legalese" rather than plain English, making it less accessible.

Abstractive methods, on the other hand, generate concise summaries by compressing and paraphrasing, but are weak at content selection and prone to information loss (Xiao et al., 2020). These supervised approaches also require a large corpus of parallel document/summary pairs for training neural models and their evaluation. Unlike the

[5]https://tosdr.org/, CC BY-SA 3.0

[6]https://tldrlegal.com/

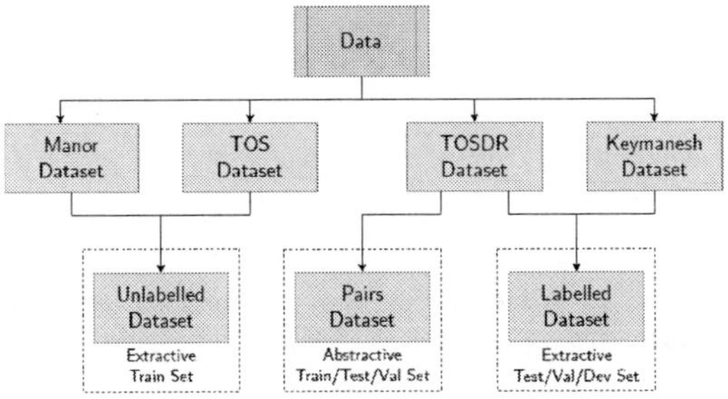

Figure 1: An overview of the datasets used for training and evaluation of the ToS Hybrid Model. Manor dataset - open source dataset from Manor & Li (Manor and Li, 2019), Keymanesh dataset - (Keymanesh et al., 2020).

news/microblogging genres, where such large curated datasets are available for training, resources for ToS documents are currently not large enough, being "intended for evaluation, rather than training" (Manor and Li, 2019). Other abstractive models include pointer-generator models with coverage mechanism (See et al., 2017), which use pointing (Vinyals et al., 2015), and a hybrid extractive-abstractive approach to improve accuracy and handle unknown words.

3 Data

This section describes the datasets (shown in Figure 1) created and compiled for training and evaluation of the hybrid ToS model.

3.1 ToS Dataset

163 ToS documents retrieved from 387 website domains, representing a range of online service categories compiled from Kaggle[7] and The Moz[8] datasets. This dataset of text files (31,752 sentences), each corresponding to a terms page, is made available on github (*https://github.com/supdey/tos-dataset*) as a contribution to the community effort on ToS dataset curation. The mean of 217.5 sentences and 4775.5 words per document and 22.1 words per sentence (std 20.2) supports similar observations in the literature about ToS documents being very long on average.

3.2 TOS;DR Dataset

The TOS;DR community dataset containing 17,109 data entries, consists of quotes from ToS documents paired with human-written summaries ("titles") and is used in combination with other datasets for model training and evaluation. Each title has an assigned class: good, bad, blocker (also bad) and neutral.

3.3 Sentence Classification Dataset

Labelled and Unlabelled Datasets used for the extractive component. The Labelled Dataset combines the TOS;DR and Keymanesh[9] datasets, with 15,839 labelled sentences.

Both datasets are modified to replace the "bad" and "blocker" classes with "1", signifying importance, with the "good" and "neutral" classes replaced with "0" signifying unimportance.

The Unlabelled Dataset combines ToS sentences from the ToS and the Manor & Li dataset, as training data for weak-supervised learning in the extractive component.

3.4 Terms and Reference Summaries Dataset

The Pairs Dataset used for the abstractive component is created by selecting rows with quote-summary pairs from the TOS;DR dataset. An analysis of the abstraction level of the summaries in terms of the number of n-grams that only appear in the reference summaries and not in the quote sentences shows that 67.5% of words and 91.6% of bigrams in the summaries did not appear in the original quote, showing significant abstraction.

4 Methodology

The methodology for the ToS hybrid model proposes to automate the summarization and grading (sentence extraction) process, allowing a broader scope of companies and websites to be analyzed while also removing the manual step of summary review.

4.1 Extractive Component

The extractive component creates a classifier for labelling ToS sentences as important or unimportant, in order to extract "important" sentences from a ToS document. An overview of the training process is shown in Figure 2.

4.1.1 Weak Supervision for Sentence Labelling

The workflow of the weak supervision approach used to label sentences programmatically is shown

[7]https://www.kaggle.com/datasets/bpali26/popular-websites-across-the-globe

[8]https://moz.com/top500

[9]www.github.com/senjed/Summarization-of-Privacy-Policies

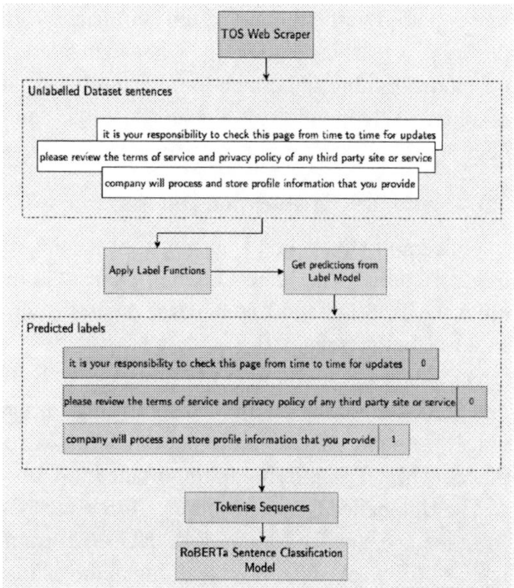

Figure 2: An overview of the training process for the extractive component, which feeds into a RoBERTa classifier to extract 'important' sentences from a ToS document.

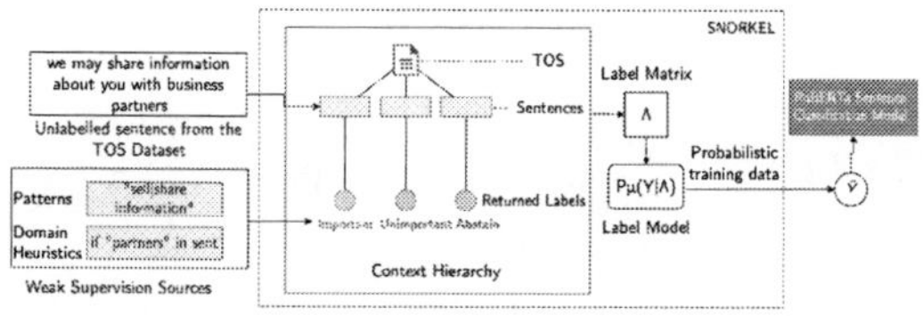

Figure 3: Weak supervision for sentence labelling, adapted from (Ratner et al., 2020).

in Figure 3.

It aims to learn a classification model that takes a ToS sentence $x \in \mathcal{X}$ and predicts its label $y \in \mathcal{Y}$, where $\mathcal{Y} = \{0, 1\}$. The training data used for this task is the 'Unlabelled' Dataset shown in Figure 1. The labels are generated from user-defined black-box labelling functions, $\lambda : \mathcal{X} \rightarrow \mathcal{Y} \cup \{-1\}$, that take in a sentence and output an important (1) or unimportant (0) label, where -1 is used to denote that the function abstains. These functions, shown in Table 1 are programmatic rules and heuristics, which use methods such as keyword-searching and pattern-matching with regex. It is possible for labelling functions not to label every data point; they can also overlap and conflict with each other by assigning the same or different labels to a single point.

The labelling functions are developed as a result of examining the Labelled Dataset, which is split into a 60:30:10 test, validation and development set. The development set is used to inform the decisions behind the labelling functions, with the sentences analysed to find common vocabulary, phrases and verbs after stopword removal, for sentences labelled important and unimportant. This is kept separate from the training data in order to avoid overfitting by introducing rules that are too specific. The validation set is used for hyperparameter tuning and checking performance without looking at the test set scores. The test set is used for final evaluation. The labelling functions are evaluated by examining their: (1) coverage: percentage of the dataset that the function labels, (2) overlaps: dataset percentage that the function and at least one other function also labels, and (3) conflicts: the percentage of the dataset that the function and at least one other function disagree on, with the goal being to increase coverage, while avoiding false positives. Some of the labelling functions involve using regex to detect when verbs such as "collect" and "sell" are used next to references to personal data. A list of these verbs are generated using NLTK[10], which is able to return synonyms for given words using WordNet (Miller, 1995). While developing labelling functions, random rows are checked to determine whether the labelling matched intuition or if false positives are being introduced. Moreover, labelling functions are compared by grouping data points by their predicted labels to determine which has the most impact.

For m unlabelled sentences and n labelling functions (in this case, $n = 8$), the labelling functions are applied to the sentences to produce a matrix of labelling function outputs (denoted as Label Matrix in Figure 3): $\Lambda \in (\mathcal{Y} \cup \{-1\})^{m \times n}$. This label matrix is then fed to the LabelModel $P_\mu(Y|\Lambda)$, parameterised by a vector of source correlations and accuracies μ. The LabelModel uses a modelling approach similar to that proposed in (Ratner et al., 2018), to produce a single vector of probabilistic training labels $\tilde{Y} = (\tilde{y_1}..., \tilde{y_m})$, where $\tilde{y_i} \in [0, 1, -1]$. After the abstains have been filtered out, the training labels are used to train a Robustly Optimised BERT Pretraining Approach (RoBERTa) classifier (Liu et al., 2019).

4.1.2 Classifier for Sentence Extraction

The classifier is able to generalise beyond the outputs of the labelling function, increasing cov-

[10]https://www.nltk.org/

Function Name	Polarity	Explanation	Example Match
Important Keyword Lookup	1	Match references to advertisements & web beacons.	website uses cookies scripts and web beacons
Data Regex	1	Match if verbs such as "collect" and "sell" are associated with personal data	we use tracking tools to collect information from you
Waive Regex	1	Match sentences related to user's rights waiver	you waive your right to participate in any class group
Self-reference Regex	0	Match sentences mentioning the terms document it belongs to	these terms of use went into effect in June
Unimportant Phrase Lookup	0	Match sentences containing unnecessary information such as support information or outlining user rights	contact us for press inquiries & more information
Unimportant Word Lookup	0	Match sentences containing words indicating users should check other areas of the website	the table below explains the cookies we use
Rules Regex	0	Match sentences informing users that they should not perform certain actions. To identify "risky" terms, these sentences are classified as unimportant	you must be 13 years or older to use this site
No Data Regex	0	Opposite of Data Regex - match sentences informing users that the service is NOT using their data	we do not sell user data

Table 1: Labelling functions' definitions used to determine if a ToS sentence is important (polarity = 1) or unimportant (polarity = 0).

erage and robustness on unseen ToS sentences. RoBERTa, a modified pre-trained Bidirectional Encoder Representations from Transformers (BERT) (Devlin et al., 2019) model, is used as the end classifier model for "important" sentence extraction, due to its modifications such as the removal of the next sentence prediction objective, longer training time, bigger batches, training on longer sequences and dynamically changing the masking pattern applied to the training data, which is known to improve performance on downstream tasks. Exploration of the LabelModel outputs shows that the dataset is highly imbalanced; therefore, the classifier model hyperparameters are fine-tuned by using rebalanced labelled data. The optimal hyperparameter settings are found to be: number of epochs: 2, a batch size of 16 and the AdamW optimiser with a learning rate of 3e-5.

Figure 4 shows the working of the classifier model with two sample sentences, showcasing the contribution of the top features contributing towards a prediction. In the top image, the green-highlighted text shows which words contributed towards the "important" label. Higher transparency implies less contribution. The words "collect information", highlighted strongly, indicate a major contribution from this phrase towards classifying this sentence as risky. In contrast, with the word "also" changed to "do not" in the same sentence (bottom image of Figure 4), changes its classification to an "unimportant sentence", with a strong indication that the word "not" had major contribution to this decision - this is expected given that the sentence is negated. Moreover, the word "information" is slightly highlighted in red, showing that it contributes towards an "important" classification.

4.2 Abstractive Component

With the goal of this research being not to summarise the entire contents of a ToS but to first extract the important sentences and then to paraphrase each one, a sequence-to-sequence (seq2seq) model with attention is chosen due to its ability to retain context. The model architecture is shown in Figure 5.

Sentence tokens from terms documents are fed one-by-one into an encoder containing a bidirectional LSTM layer, which produces a sequence of encoder hidden states h_i. In each step t, the decoder (a single-layer LSTM) receives the word embedding of the previous word. During model training, this is the previous word of the reference summary,

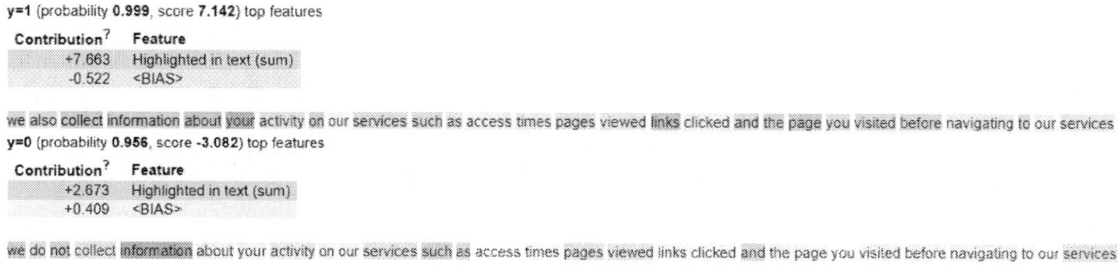

Figure 4: Two sentences predicted by the fine-tuned classifier; colours refer to contribution and not the actual classes themselves. (Top) A sentence classified as "important"; (bottom) a negated sentence classified as "unimportant".

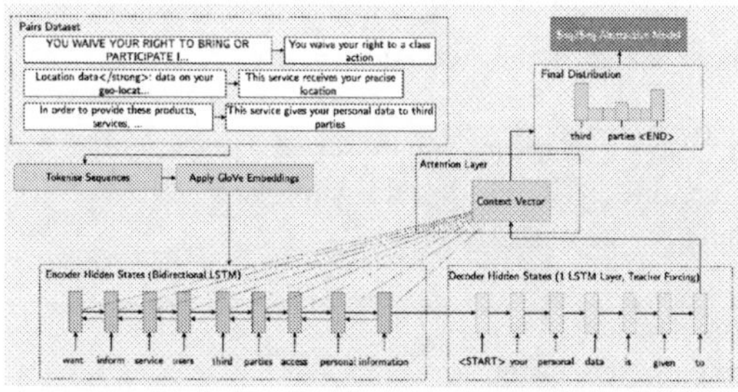

Figure 5: Overview of the training process for the abstractive component.

while during testing, it is the previous word output by the decoder. The decoder has decoder state s_t. The attention distribution (probability distribution over the source words) a^t is calculated using Bahdanau Attention (Bahdanau et al., 2015):

$$e_i^t = v^T \tanh(W_h h_i + W_s s_t + b_{\text{attn}}) \quad (1)$$

$$a^t = \text{softmax}(e^t) \quad (2)$$

where v, W_h, W_s and b_{attn} are learnable parameters. The distribution is used to produce the context vector h_t^*, which is the weighted sum of the encoder hidden states as shown in Figure 5. This can be seen as a fixed-size representation of what has been read from the terms sentence for this step. The calculation of the context vector is as follows:

$$h_t^* = \sum\nolimits_i a_i^t h_i \quad (3)$$

This context vector is then concatenated with the decoder state s_t to produce the vocabulary distribution P_{vocab}. This is the probability distribution over all words in the vocabulary, which is calculated as follows:

$$P_{\text{vocab}} = \text{softmax}(V'(V[s_t, h_t^*] + b) + b') \quad (4)$$

where V, V', b and b' are learnable parameters. This distribution provides the final distribution that is used to predict words w:

$$P(w) = P_{\text{vocab}}(w) \quad (5)$$

The loss for timestep t during training is the negative log likelihood of the target word w_t^* for that timestep:

$$\text{loss}_t = -\log P(w_t^*) \quad (6)$$

The overall loss for the whole sequence is calculated as follows:

$$\text{loss} = \frac{1}{T} \sum\nolimits_{t=0}^{T} \text{loss}_t \quad (7)$$

The LSTM networks each use 256-dimensional hidden units and pre-trained GloVe word embedding (Pennington et al., 2014), that has been pre-trained on a dataset of one billion tokens and a vocabulary of 400,000 words. The vocabulary size is limited by filtering out rare words to prevent overfitting. For the source sentences, a word is considered "rare" when the number of occurrences throughout all the texts is less than 4; for the summaries, this is 6, due to the average summary length being shorter. The resulting vocabulary size for the source sentences is 2,413, and for the target sentences 308. Regular and recurrent dropout are applied to the LSTM layers to reduce overfitting, with dropout values set to 0.4, with the exception for the recurrent dropout of the decoder LSTM which is set to 0.2. Softmax activation is used in the final dense decoder layer, as the output can be interpreted as a probability distribution vector that helps determine the final output of sequence tokens. The optimiser is Root Mean Squared Propagation (RMSProp). The loss function used is sparse categorical cross-entropy due to the Y inputs consisting of integer sequences that are mutually exclusive. This function also has memory and computation usage benefits, as the classes are defined by single integers as opposed to entire vectors.

5 Results and Evaluation

5.1 Dataset and Ground-Truth Construction

The ground truth dataset is created by combining the TOS;DR and Keymanesh datasets, with labels of 1955 important and unimportant sentences. To get plain English summaries, cleaned sentences (following pre-processing) from the Keymanesh dataset are matched with sentences in the TOS;DR dataset to create the ground-truth summaries. For sentences with no corresponding reference summary, the ground-truth was taken as the cleaned, stopword-removed version of the sentence text, ensuring that all sentences labelled 'important' feature in the evaluation. The resulting dataset has 263 rows of plain English summaries and 1692 rows of the cleaned, stopword-removed version of the quote text.

The evaluation baselines are executed on the entire ToS contracts retrieved by the web-scraping tool, which returned the ToS of 102 services taken from the Keymanesh dataset.

After filtering for services that contain at least one 'important label' in the Keymanesh dataset, 45 services, with 10231 sentences, are used for evaluation.

5.2 Summarization Baselines

We compare the performance of our hybrid summarisation model with the following unsupervised baselines:

- TextRank (Mihalcea and Tarau, 2004): uses the PageRank algorithm to extract the most important keywords from a ToS, based on the similarity between phrases.
- KLSum (Haghighi and Vanderwende, 2009): minimises the Kullback-Lieber (KL) divergence between the ToS and proposed summary by greedily selecting sentences.
- Lead-K (See et al., 2017): extracts the first k sentences until the word limit is reached.
- K-Random: picks random sentences until a word limit is reached. This baseline was run 10 times to get the average results.

Following pre-processing, sentences from TextRank and KLSum were limited by the average sentence count from ground-truth summaries (i.e. 4). Summaries from Lead-K and K-Random were limited by the average word count (93) from ground-truth summaries.

5.3 Evaluation Metrics

The summarisation was evaluated by computing the average F1-score for ROUGE-1, ROUGE-2, and ROUGE-L metrics (Lin and Hovy, 2002), as well as the METEOR score (Denkowski and Lavie, 2014).

ROUGE-N measures the number of matching n-grams between the generated summaries and the ground-truth summary, with ROUGE-1 referring to unigram overlaps and ROUGE-2 referring to bigram overlaps. ROUGE-L calculates the Longest Common Subsequence - identifying the longest overlapping sequence of tokens. The METEOR metric was found to be a better evaluation system as this rewards not only exact word matches but also matching stems, synonyms and paraphrases.

5.4 Results

5.4.1 Summarization Results

Model evaluation results are shown in Table 2. The ToS hybrid model significantly outperforms the extractive baselines. When compared against the best performing baseline for each metric, there is a 49.7% improvement in ROUGE-1, 114.6% in ROUGE-2, 53.5% in ROUGE-L and 53.6% improvement in METEOR scores. This indicates that the ToS hybrid model can generate summaries that are easier to read and understand. This is important given that the aim of the TOS;DR summaries is to be simple and concise.

While the Lead-K baseline performed well in summarization tasks in existing works (See et al., 2017) for news articles and headlines datasets, even outperforming abstractive models using pointer-generators, the results of our work show it to have the worst performance. The success of the lead-3 baseline in (See et al., 2017) can be attributed to the structure of news articles, which contain the most crucial information at the beginning, and the use of the first three sentences of the article as a summary by lead-3. In contrast, the structure of a ToS document often begins with definitions of phrases used throughout the document and an introduction to the service(s) offered. This is often not considered important information, as it is merely an explanation of the document's contents. This observation shows that using a dataset specifically focused on the domain of T&C for this task significantly boosts performance, highlighting the need for collecting more ToS data and the usefulness of the developed ToS web-scraper tool.

Table 2: Evaluation results of the ToS Hybrid Model in comparison to the baselines.

Model	ROUGE-1	ROUGE-2	ROUGE-L	METEOR
ToS Hybrid Model	**19.45**	**7.21**	**18.41**	**16.25**
TextRank	12.99	3.36	11.99	10.58
KLSum	12.94	1.79	11.85	8.58
K-Random	10.72	1.71	10.15	8.94
Lead-K	10.41	1.47	9.88	8.67

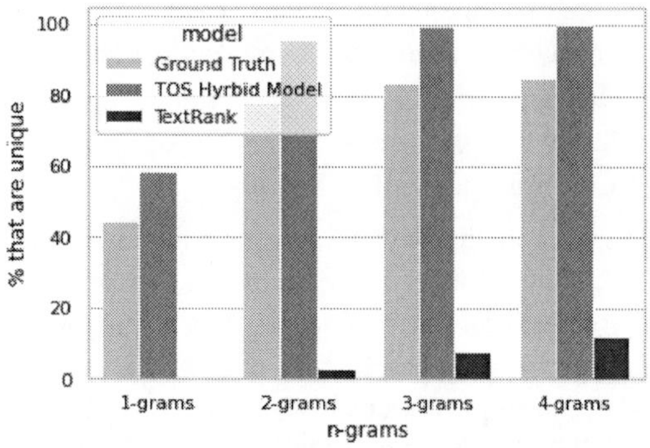

Figure 6: Unique n-grams in the of the Ground-Truth, ToS Hybrid Model and TextRank summaries.

5.4.2 Abstraction and Compression Level

The summaries from the ground-truth, ToS Hybrid Model and TextRank have been compared against the original ToS documents for each service, to assess their effectiveness in terms of the level of abstraction and compression. The abstraction level is calculated by the number of n-grams that only appear in the summaries and not in the ToS documents (See et al., 2017). As shown in Figure 6, the hybrid model has high levels of abstraction and shows that 58.7% of the words in the summaries are not present in the ToS document, demonstrating its ability to generate new words. As expected, the summary of the TextRank model does not contain any new words as it is an extractive approach. The ground-truth summaries appear to be slightly less abstractive than that of our hybrid model; we can assume this is because the ground-truth contains stopword-cleaned sentences where it is unable to find a summary from the Pairs Dataset. The mean compression rate is 0.026 (std 0.014), showing that the summaries are significantly shortened.

TOS: *<truncated>* In order to provide the Service, UpCloud may process personal data on behalf of the Customer as a data processor for the purposes of providing the Service UpCloud processes certain personal data also as a data controller Such personal data includes, inter alia, data of the Customer's contact persons, invoicing details and other personal data of Customer's contact persons which UpCloud processes in order to maintain the customer relationship ... In connection with the use of the Service, the Customer may transfer various data to UpClond for processing on behalf of the Customer *<truncated>*

Reference Summary:

- blocking first party cookies may limit your ability to use the service
- the service provider makes no warranty regarding uninterrupted timely secure or error free service
- the service is provided as is and to be used at your sole risk
- your data may be processed and stored anywhere in the world
- third parties are involved in operating the service
- your personal data may be sold or otherwise transferred as part of a bankruptcy proceeding or other type of financial transaction

TOS Hybrid Model:

- this service gives your personal data to third parties involved in its operation
- your personal data is used to employ targeted third party advertising
- your personal information is used for many different purposes
- your personal data may be sold or otherwise transferred as part of bankruptcy proceeding or other type of financial transaction
- the service provider makes no warranty regarding uninterrupted timely secure or error free service
- your personal data may be used for marketing purposes
- you are tracked via web beacons tracking pixels browser fingerprinting and or device fingerprinting

KLSum:

- upcloud shall provide the customer with the service which is specified in the order.
- upcloud shall offer compensation to the customer for all unscheduled interruptions in the provision of the service in accordance with the sla in force from time to time.
- in order to provide the service upcloud may process personal data on behalf of the customer as a data processor for the purposes of providing the service.
- in connection with the use of the service the customer may transfer various data to upcloud for processing on behalf of the customer.

Lead-K:

- these terms apply to all our existing users as of and any new users as of
- please note not everybody has a law degree or speak english natively so we have added helpful tl dr in plain english that summarize each term
- these are only meant to help you understand the general meaning and are not legally binding terms of service *<truncated>*

Figure 7: ToS Hybrid Model, KLSum and Lead-K summaries compared for UpCloud's ToS (17 May 2018).

5.4.3 Case Study and Results Discussion

Figure 7 shows sample summaries generated by the ToS hybrid model, KLSum and Lead-K, with the underlying ToS document containing 290 sentences. The ToS hybrid model succeeds in producing a bullet-point format summary written in plain English. When compared against the reference summary, we can see that both of them mention the use of third parties. There are two identical sentences from both summaries; indicating that the abstractive model has overfitted to the Pairs Dataset, which contains TOS;DR template summaries. The ground-truth dataset contains "important" sentences which may not be considered important by some users - e.g., the reference summary sentence "blocking first party cookies may limit your ability to use the service". However, this is subjective, and with the availability of more training data, the abstractive model can learn to summarize *any* sentence within a ToS. On comparing the ground-truth to the hybrid model's summary outputs, there are cases where it does not seem to summarize certain sentences accurately and instead may output a different sentence similar to the TOS;DR template summaries. A likely reason for this is the lack of training data for the abstractive component. The Pairs dataset has 5,326 rows, of which 4,313 are used for training. This is 98% less training data than that in the pointer-generator model in (See et al., 2017). Moreover, the extractive-abstractive models in (Nallapati et al., 2017) used 3.8M training examples.

6 Conclusions

In this paper, we proposed a domain-aware hybrid extractive-abstractive model that highlights privacy and data collection sections in a ToS document and paraphrases these into concise and informative sentences. A novel dataset is also created using a developed web-scraping tool, with the purpose of automatically fetching ToS documents from any online service. The dataset used for classification training was found to be highly imbalanced; despite this, the hybrid model performed well in ROUGE and METEOR scores when compared against unsupervised, extractive baselines. To resolve the imbalance problem, the data was resampled before being used in the classifiers for training, which reduced the false negative rate by 64%. However, this did increase the false positive rate, which implies that the extractive classifier is more inclined to incorrectly label sentences as important. Given that the abstractive model is only trained on important sentences, this can lead to incorrect warnings by the ToS model. In the context of this paper, to maintain the integrity of legal concepts, this can still be seen as the preferable outcome since users can verify statements made by the model by reviewing the original ToS if necessary.

More training data for both the classifier and abstractive model can improve performance; this can be obtained by the developed web-scraping tool, in addition to future TOS;DR community contributions. This would result in more data for the classifier post-resampling, which in turn would help the imbalance issue and false positive rate. Another direction for future work would be testing the generated summaries for comprehension through qualitative user studies, from participants recruited through platforms such as MTurk or Prolific.

Acknowledgements

This research is supported by the Science and Technology Facilities Council (STFC) DiRAC-funded 'Understanding the multiple dimensions of prediction of concepts in social and biomedical science questionnaires' project, grant number ST/S003916/1. The second author also acknowledges support through the UKRI Strategic Priority Fund as part of the wider Protecting Citizens Online programme (Grant number: EP/W032473/1) associated with the National Research Centre on Privacy, Harm Reduction and Adversarial Influence Online (REPHRAIN).

References

Dzmitry Bahdanau, Kyung Hyun Cho, and Yoshua Bengio. 2015. Neural machine translation by jointly learning to align and translate. In *3rd International Conference on Learning Representations, ICLR, Conference Track Proceedings*.

Michael Denkowski and Alon Lavie. 2014. Meteor universal: Language specific translation evaluation for any target language. In *Proceedings of the Ninth Workshop on Statistical Machine Translation*, pages 376–380, Baltimore, Maryland, USA. Association for Computational Linguistics.

Jacob Devlin, Ming-Wei Chang, Kenton Lee, and Kristina Toutanova. 2019. Bert: Pre-training of deep bidirectional transformers for language understanding. *Proceedings of the 2019 Conference of the North*, pages 4171–4186.

Kasper Drawzeski, Andrea Galassi, Agnieszka Jablonowska, Francesca Lagioia, Marco Lippi, Hans Wolfgang Micklitz, Giovanni Sartor, Giacomo Tagiuri, and Paolo Torroni. 2021. A corpus for multilingual analysis of online terms of service. In *Proceedings of the Natural Legal Language Processing Workshop*, NLLP '21 @EMNLP '21, pages 1–8, Punta Cana, Dominican Republic. ACM.

Sebastian Gehrmann, Yuntian Deng, and Alexander Rush. 2018. Bottom-up abstractive summarization. In *Proceedings of the 2018 Conference on Empirical Methods in Natural Language Processing*, pages 4098–4109, Brussels, Belgium. Association for Computational Linguistics.

Aria Haghighi and Lucy Vanderwende. 2009. Exploring content models for multi-document summarization. In *Proceedings of Human Language Technologies: The 2009 Annual Conference of the North American Chapter of the Association for Computational Linguistics*, pages 362–370, Boulder, Colorado. Association for Computational Linguistics.

Karl Moritz Hermann, Tomáš Kočiský, Edward Grefenstette, Lasse Espeholt, Will Kay, Mustafa Suleyman, and Phil Blunsom. 2015. Teaching machines to read and comprehend. In *Proceedings of the 28th International Conference on Neural Information Processing Systems - Volume 1*, NIPS'15, page 1693–1701, Cambridge, MA, USA. MIT Press.

Baotian Hu, Qingcai Chen, and Fangze Zhu. 2015. LCSTS: A large scale Chinese short text summarization dataset. In *Proceedings of the 2015 Conference on Empirical Methods in Natural Language Processing*, pages 1967–1972, Lisbon, Portugal. Association for Computational Linguistics.

Moniba Keymanesh, Micha Elsner, and Srinivasan Parthasarathy. 2020. Toward domain-guided controllable summarization of privacy policies. In *Proceedings of the Natural Legal Language Processing Workshop, co-located with the 26th ACM SIGKDD International Conference on Knowledge Discovery and Data Mining (KDD 2020)*, NLLP '20 @KDD'20, pages 18–24, San Diego, CA. ACM.

Karel Kubíček, Jakob Merane, Carlos Cotrini, Alexander Stremitzer, Stefan Bechtold, and David Basin. 2022. Checking websites' gdpr consent compliance for marketing emails. *Proceedings on Privacy Enhancing Technologies (PoPETs)*, 2022(2):282–303.

Chin-Yew Lin and Eduard Hovy. 2002. Manual and automatic evaluation of summaries. In *Proceedings of the ACL-02 Workshop on Automatic Summarization - Volume 4*, AS '02, page 45–51, USA. Association for Computational Linguistics.

Yinhan Liu, Myle Ott, Naman Goyal, Jingfei Du, Mandar Joshi, Danqi Chen, Omer Levy, Mike Lewis, Luke Zettlemoyer, and Veselin Stoyanov. 2019. Roberta: A robustly optimized bert pretraining approach.

Laura Manor and Junyi Jessy Li. 2019. Plain english summarization of contracts. In *Proceedings of the Natural Legal Language Processing Workshop*, NLLP '19 @NAACL 2019, pages 1–11, Minneapolis, Minnesota. ACM.

Rada Mihalcea and Paul Tarau. 2004. TextRank: Bringing order into text. In *Proceedings of the 2004 Conference on Empirical Methods in Natural Language Processing*, pages 404–411, Barcelona, Spain. Association for Computational Linguistics.

George A. Miller. 1995. Wordnet: A lexical database for english. *Commun. ACM*, 38(11):39–41.

Ramesh Nallapati, Feifei Zhai, and Bowen Zhou. 2017. Summarunner: A recurrent neural network based sequence model for extractive summarization of documents. In *Proceedings of the Thirty-First AAAI Conference on Artificial Intelligence*, AAAI'17, page 3075–3081. AAAI Press.

Jonathan A Obar and Anne Oeldorf-Hirsch. 2018. The biggest lie on the internet: Ignoring the privacy policies and terms of service policies of social networking services. *Information, Communication and Society*, pages 128–147.

Jeffrey Pennington, Richard Socher, and Christopher D. Manning. 2014. Glove: Global vectors for word representation. In *Proceedings of 2014 Conference on Empirical Methods in Natural Language Processing (EMNLP)*, pages 1532–1543. Association for Computational Linguistics (ACL).

Alexander Ratner, Stephen H. Bach, Henry Ehrenberg, Jason Fries, Sen Wu, and Christopher Ré. 2020. Snorkel: Rapid training data creation with weak supervision. *The VLDB Journal*, 29:709–730.

Alexander Ratner, Braden Hancock, Jared Dunnmon, Frederic Sala, Shreyash Pandey, and Christopher Ré. 2018. Training complex models with multi-task weak supervision. In *Proceedings of the 33rd AAAI Conference on Artificial Intelligence, AAAI 2019, 31st Innovative Applications of Artificial Intelligence Conference, IAAI 2019 and the 9th AAAI Symposium on Educational Advances in Artificial Intelligence, EAAI 2019*, pages 4763–4771. AAAI Press.

Global Science Research. 2014. Thisisyourdigitallife app application end user terms and conditions.

Abigail See, Peter J. Liu, and Christopher D. Manning. 2017. Get to the point: Summarization with pointer-generator networks. In *Proceedings of the 55th Annual Meeting of the Association for Computational Linguistics (Volume 1: Long Papers)*, pages 1073–1083, Vancouver, Canada. Association for Computational Linguistics.

Oriol Vinyals, Meire Fortunato, and Navdeep Jaitly. 2015. Pointer networks. In *Advances in Neural Information Processing Systems (NIPS)*, volume 28.

Liqiang Xiao, Lu Wang, Hao He, and Yaohui Jin. 2020. Copy or rewrite: Hybrid summarization with hierarchical reinforcement learning. In *Proceedings of the Thirty-Fourth AAAI Conference on Artificial Intelligence (AAAI-20)*, volume 34, pages 9306–9313, Punta Cana, Dominican Republic. AAAI press.

Michihiro Yasunaga, Jungo Kasai, Rui Zhang, Alexander R. Fabbri, Irene Li, Dan Friedman, and Dragomir R. Radev. 2019. Scisummnet: A large annotated corpus and content-impact models for scientific paper summarization with citation networks. In *33rd AAAI Conference on Artificial Intelligence, AAAI 2019, 31st Innovative Applications of Artificial Intelligence Conference, IAAI 2019 and the 9th AAAI Symposium on Educational Advances in Artificial Intelligence, EAAI 2019*, pages 7386–7393. AAAI press.

A Summarization Framework Implementation

As shown in the figure below, the ToS summarization framework has been implemented as a Web application, with the extractive and abstractive components of the ToS hybrid model interacting with a Web component.

The framework consists of four major components:

ToS Web Scraper: The Web scraper tool has been developed to address the lack of reference

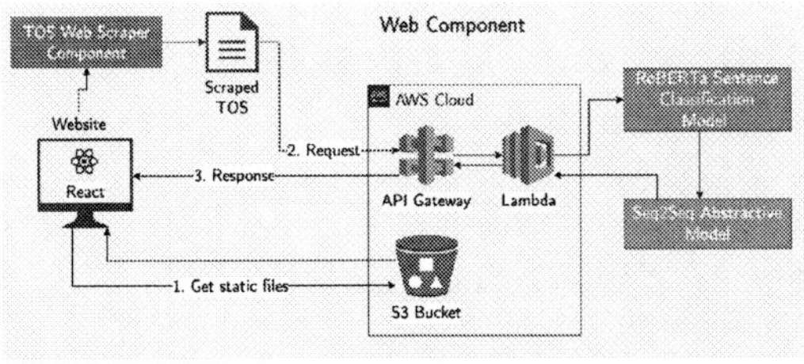

Figure 8: An overview of how the ToS Hybrid Model (the RoBERTA Classifier and Seq2Seq model) interact with the web component. The ToS Hybrid Model is called by the Lambda functions and returns a string of ordered, summarised sentences in the response.

datasets of ToS documents. It is also a feature of the website, allowing users to retrieve a terms document from any website or company, by either entering the source URL or searching by the company name. It accepts an URL as input, which is parsed to form a valid URL. If the given URL does not directly link to a terms document, the scraper first tries to search for potential URLs linking to T&C, through regular expression (regex) for HTML link elements containing words and phrases associated with T&C, e.g. "privacy policy", "terms", and "legal". The HTML of the URL is retrieved using the Selenium[11] Python library and parsed using BeautifulSoup[12]. Content cleaning steps include removing HTML tags for the navigation bar, footer, headings, images and labels. It is common for terms documents to contain a list of terms with a sentence heading such as “You agree to:" or “You agree not to:". This can be problematic when separating sentences, as the distinction between “agree to" and “agree not to" is quite important, not only for identifying risky terms but also unimportant terms for the extractive component. To fix this issue, the HTML structure of the page is utilized. By identifying list elements that come after a text ending with a semicolon, the scraper prefixes each list item with the text preceding the semicolon.This allows the extractive and abstractive models to identify the context surrounding each list item and whether they have a positive or negative meaning. Additional tag cleaning includes the removal of implicit headings - this refers to headings that are not HTML tags but still titles for various sections of the document. These headings are removed using regex for commonly occurring title structures.

Web Component: User interaction with the framework is enabled through the Web component which consists of a website and accompanying Chrome browser plugin, with an Amazon Web Services (AWS) back-end component. A plugin allows quick look-up of a summary of terms when a user is already on a T&C page. Chrome was chosen for the plugin implementation due to it being the leading Internet browser (64% global market share[13]). It chains the outputs of the extractive component to the inputs to the abstractive component in a hybrid network architecture. The website is accessed through the S3 bucket static files. Functionality is shared between the website and the plugin through API routes (using the API Gateway service) connecting to two Lambda functions: one for the web-scraping component to be accessible to the website, and one for summarization (encompassing the extractive and abstractive components), which is used by both the website and plugin.

Extractive Component: following tag cleaning, the classification model is loaded and the sentences are vectorized. The Labelled Dataset is split into 60:30:10 test:validation:development sets, with the development set determining the heuristics for the labelling functions definitions. The labelling functions assign $[0|1|-1]$ labels to each of these sentences. After these labels are fed into a LabelModel, the sentences and assigned labels are ready to be used as training data for the classifier. Sentences with probabilities >50% for the important class are filtered and re-ordered, with the most important sentences at the top. Stopwords and single-character words are removed. The validation set is used for training the RoBERTa classifier and the test set is used for evaluating the label model, classifier and baseline models during the Evaluation.

Abstractive Component: the encoder, decoder and summary tokeniser are loaded at initialization. The tokeniser converts the texts to sequences and pads them up to the maximum length, 60, with the encoder making predictions for each sequence. The `START` token is used as a first input to the decoder, which predicts the next words until an `END` token is generated or the maximum length has been reached. The tokenised sequence is returned as a readable format and the final summary is joined by newlines.

[11]https://pypi.org/project/selenium/

[12]https://pypi.org/project/beautifulsoup4/

[13]https://gs.statcounter.com/

Abstractive Summarization of Dutch Court Verdicts Using Sequence-to-sequence Models

Nick van de Luijtgaarden, Daniël Prijs, Marijn Schraagen*, Floris Bex
Utrecht University, The Netherlands

Abstract

With the legal sector embracing digitization, the increasing availability of information has led to a need for systems that can automatically summarize legal documents. Most existing research on legal text summarization has so far focused on *extractive* models, which can result in awkward summaries, as sentences in legal documents can be very long and detailed. In this study, we apply two *abstractive* summarization models on a Dutch legal domain dataset. The results show that existing models transfer quite well across domains and languages: the ROUGE scores of our experiments are comparable to state-of-the-art studies on English news article texts. Examining one of the models showed the capability of rewriting long legal sentences to much shorter ones, using mostly vocabulary from the source document. Human evaluation shows that for both models hand-made summaries are still perceived as more relevant and readable, and automatic summaries do not always capture elements such as background, considerations and judgement. Still, generated summaries are valuable if only a keyword summary or no summary at all is present.

1 Introduction

Given the increasing availability of legal information and the fact that many legal documents are often relatively long and dense, there is an increasing need for systems that can automatically summarize these documents. Such summaries can help not only lawyers and judges, but also citizens, companies and researchers to process case law.

Two key approaches exist for automatic summarization: *extractive summarization* involves identifying important text spans from the document and combining them into a summary, and *abstractive summarization* involves generating new sentences that explain in more general terms what the text is about (Hahn and Mani, 2000). Abstractive summaries are potentially more readable and more efficient than extractive summaries. For example, consider the following sentence:

> By letter of 18 June 2012, the appellant addressed a request to the defendant to take enforcement action against [A] Inc. and [B] Inc. for (alleged) violation of the provisions of the Quarantine Facilities for Live Bivalve Molluscs Regulation 2007.

An abstractive model can retain only the information that the appellant requested enforcement action based on the Quarantine Facilities for Live Bivalve Molluscs Regulation 2007, while an extractive model would retain the full sentence. In this paper we apply a reinforcement learning approach with a biLSTM (referred to as **RL**) as well as a deep learning approach based on the BART (Lewis et al., 2019) transformer model (referred to as **BART**) to abstractive summarization of the Dutch case verdict database Rechtspraak.nl. We show that generated summaries are useful, but not yet on par with human-generated summaries.

The rest of this paper is structured as follows. In Section 2 we consider current state-of-the-art models for legal summarization, Section 3 describes our dataset, and Section 4 discusses the design and implementation of the deep learning pipelines. Here we also highlight the different evaluation methods used: in addition to the common ROUGE metric, we also look at abstractiveness (See et al., 2017), i.e., the amount of novelty introduced in the wording of the summary, and perform a human evaluation on the aspects of summary relevance and readability. Finally, Section 5 and 6 will elaborate upon the results and implications of this research.

*Corresponding author, `M.P.Schraagen@uu.nl`.
Code and data are available via `https://git.science.uu.nl/n.vandeluijtgaarden/legal-text-summarization` (RL models) and `https://github.com/prijsdf/dutch-legal-summarization` (BART models).

Proceedings of the Natural Legal Language Processing Workshop 2022, pages 76 - 87
December 8, 2022

2 Related work

Legal text differs from common document types such as news articles (Kanapala et al., 2017), which has prompted the development of custom word embeddings for legal vocabulary in English (Chalkidis and Kampas, 2019; Chalkidis et al., 2020). However, general pre-trained embeddings or embeddings trained on-the-fly are also commonly used. Early approaches used pattern-based heuristic segmentation approaches (Uyttendaele et al., 1998; Farzindar and Lapalme, 2004). Machine learning was used by Hachey and Grover (2006) to classify sentences as different legal rhetorical structures (Moens and de Busser, 2002) such as fact, proceedings or background. Saravanan et al. (2006) applied probablistic graphical models based on Conditional Random Fields (CRF) to segment and label a legal decision given various rhetorical roles (e.g., argument or final decision). Yousfi-Monod et al. (2010) used a Naive Bayes algorithm with a set of heuristic features to identify sections (introduction, context, reasoning, conclusion) and create a summary. Instead of identifying specific sections or elements, Galgani et al. (2012) use a rule-based approach, where rules created by domain experts are used to identify important phrases in a decision. More recently, Zhong et al. (2019) create summaries by classifying sentences in a decision as, e.g., issues, decision, etc. Similarly, Xu et al. (2020) use a number of different machine learning techniques to classify the issues, conclusions and reasons in a legal verdict. Liu and Chen (2019) use an LSTM classifier on sentences from the 'reasoning' section of Taiwanese Supreme Court judgements to determine which sentences belong to the 'gist' of the judgement, achieving an F1-score of around 0.9. Eidelman (2019) used a combination of supervised sentence-scoring and TF-IDF in an ensemble method on their BillSum dataset. Regarding abstractive approaches, Bhattacharya et al. (2019) use the pointer model by See et al. (2017) on their Supreme Court of India dataset. Zhang et al. (2020) use their pre-trained PEGASUS language model to generate abstractive summaries on the BillSum dataset of Eidelman (2019). Previous work on abstractive summarization of UK court verdicts was performed by Ray et al. (2020).

3 Data

For the current research, data from the Dutch judicial system is used. On average, around 1.6M cases are handled in The Netherlands every year, of which a small percentage is published on the official website Rechtspraak.nl. For the RL experiments in this research a pre-processed version of the Rechtspraak data provided by Pandora Intelligence[1] is used, providing easy access to the type, summary and verdict of each case. For the BART experiments a separate preprocessing pipeline is used that exposes only the case text and the summary. In total, this dataset contains around 430K legal court cases. 94% of these cases contain a summary, and we included only these cases in the data exploration discussion in the current section. An example document can be found in Table A1.

On average, case texts contain $\sim$ 650 words with summaries of length $\sim$ 50. However, a significant amount of summaries has less than 25 words, containing only keywords or a single sentence. A small amount of summaries is over 250 words long. To provide more uniform data to the models, for training we used only cases that have a summary containing between 40 and 150 words, and consisting of a minimum of three and a maximum of six sentences with at least 5 words in each sentence. Note that very short summaries are reintroduced in the dataset for human evaluation.

4 Research Method

We use two deep learning pipelines on the Rechtspraak.nl data: a hybrid reinforcement learning method and a transformer-based method.

4.1 RL model

Chen and Bansal (2018) have proposed a hybrid extractive-abstractive model that first selects important sentences (similar to extractive summarization) and then rewrites them abstractively. First, sentences are represented using a temporal convolutional model and words are converted to a distributed vector representation using word embeddings. Sequences of word vectors are fed through the layers of the model to capture the dependencies of nearby words. Selection of sentences from the sentence representations is then done by training a pointer network based on a set of features (Vinyals et al., 2015), and these extracted sentences are then subsequently compressed and paraphrased by an abstractive model to create a concise summary sentence (see Figure 1).

[1] https://www.pandoraintelligence.com/

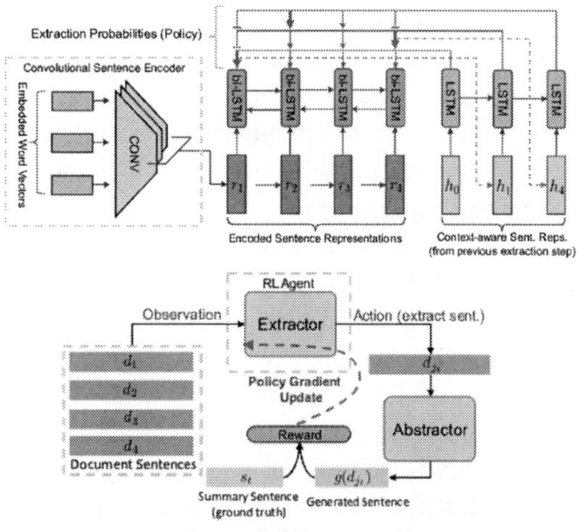

Figure 1: RL model architecture, showing the extractor component (top) and the full architecture (bottom). Images reproduced from Chen and Bansal (2018).

We use this hybrid model on legal data in the current study, arguing that the extractive part of the model can help retain the core facts of the verdicts, while the abstractive part of the model can make the summary shorter and more readable.

The data processing pipeline consists of a number of steps. First, data from Rechtspraak is loaded based on the filtering described in Section 3, and tokenized using Ucto (van Gompel et al., 2012) and Stanford CoreNLP (Manning et al., 2014). Gensim (Rehurek and Sojka, 2010) is used to create word embeddings through Word2Vec. The network itself is trained using the PyTorch framework and CUDA.

The Extractor component (shown in the top of Figure 1) consists of multiple steps. First, word embeddings for all words in a sentence are combined into a sentence representation r_j using a convolutional layer. Then, an encoding step using a bi-directional LSTM layer transforms the sentence representation into a contextual representation h_j using the surrounding sentences. Finally, in a decoding step an LSTM computes the extraction probability of a sentence based on the contextual embedding h_j. The training target for the extraction probability is to minimize the ROUGE distance between the extracted sentence and the reference summary, i.e., the component learns to extract a sentence if there is a similar sentence somewhere in the reference summary.

After a sentence is selected it is processed by the Abstractor component. This component is a sequence-to-sequence model using a bi-directional LSTM as encoder and a unidirectional LSTM as decoder, trained with the objective of transforming the extractive input sentence into the corresponding sentence in the reference summary. The resulting sentence is evaluated by the reinforcement learning component. If a suitable sentence is selected and correctly rewritten, then a reward is generated to reinforce the Extractor component. Conversely, if the similarity between the generated sentence and the reference summary is low, the Extractor component receives negative reward and learns not to extract this sentence.

For training, we used batches of 4 samples and set the checkpoint frequency (number of update steps for checkpoint and validation) on 3000 for the abstractor/extractor network and 300 for RL training. For the abstractor and extractor network we used a batch size of 32. Word2Vec embeddings were trained with a vector size of 128 and a vocabulary of 30,000. Sentence generation was limited to 30 tokens with a beam size of 5. Learning rate for the Adam optimizer is set on 0.001 for maximum likelihood (ML) objectives and 0.0001 for RL training. We set the discount factor for RL on 0.95 and cut the learning rate in half when validation loss stops decreasing, in order to speed up convergence. Gradient clipping is used to prevent exploding gradients and uses a 2-norm of 2.0 for all LSTMs. We use a network of 256 hidden units with one layer. Following the training phase, new summaries are generated for all documents in the test set.

4.2 BART model

Lewis et al. (2019) introduced BART as an autoencoder for pretraining sequence-to-sequence models for various downstream tasks, such as machine translation, question answering and summarization. The model uses the following tasks for pretraining:

Token masking Similar to BERT, a percentage of tokens in the text are masked at random and the model has to reconstruct the original text.

Sentence permutation The text is split-up in sentences (based on full stops) and then these sentences are shuffled. The model has to reconstruct the text.

Document rotation A new start token is picked at random and the document is rotated such that it starts with this new token. Again, the model has to reconstruct the original text.

Token deletion Tokens are deleted from the text.

The model needs to identify the positions of the deleted tokens.

Text infilling Similar to masking, but here random spans of texts are replaced by a single mask token. The spans mostly have a length of 0 to 9 tokens. Spans of zero length can also be replaced, which is equal to inserting a mask token into the text.

For applying the BART sequence-to-sequence model to the legal dataset, the model was pretrained from scratch using the model configuration described by Lewis et al. (2019) as implemented in the Huggingface library in Python. For pretraining the model and the tokenizer, we used the 'tiny' subset (6B words) of the Dutch part of the mC4 dataset[2] that contains a broad variety of web crawl data. Pretraining was performed on 4 million examples during one epoch with a batch size of 8 (i.e., 500k steps in total). Note that pretraining from scratch was a practical consideration. While a Dutch language model for BART already exists (Liu et al., 2020) this model was too large to be used with our setup, therefore we opted for an additional pretraining step. After pretraining, the model was fine-tuned using 70,140 court verdict documents for 10 epochs with a batch size of 8 (i.e., 88k steps). Then the actual summaries were generated on 9.9k test documents with a minimum length of 40 tokens, a maximum length of 150 tokens, a length penalty of 2.0 and a beam search of size 4. The length constraints were empirically chosen as sensible values for producing useful summaries.

4.3 Human evaluation

For the RL experiments 10 documents were sampled from the dataset and rated on a scale between 1–10 on content and readability (see Table 1), similar to (See et al., 2017; Chen and Bansal, 2018). Two law students were recruited to act as subject matter experts. The participant is asked to read and study a case for 15 minutes, then the generated summary and the reference summary from Rechtspraak are presented (without disclosing the source of the summaries). The participant is asked to provide content and readability ratings as well as a short explanation for their answer. After rating five cases with full reference summaries, another five cases with keyword-only reference summaries were presented. For these five cases the participant is asked whether they prefer the full generated summary or the keyword-only reference summary, again without disclosing the source.

For the BART experiments 40 documents were sampled from the dataset and evaluated by one of the authors. Evaluation was performed on the aspects *informativeness, relevance, fluency, coherence* as defined in Table 1 on a 5-point Likert scale. First, the evaluator read the summary and rated fluency and coherence. Then the full case text was read in order to rate informativeness and relevance of the summary.

4.4 Automatic Evaluation

Results are evaluated using standard ROUGE-1, ROUGE-2 and ROUGE-L F1 measures. The dataset is divided in a random split of 70% (training), 15% (validation) and 15% (test) cases. Hyperparameter tuning is performed on the validation set, while actual evaluation is performed on the test set. For the ML experiments the ROUGE evaluation takes the category of cases and year ranges into account, while for the BART experiments this information was not available.

Furthermore, we evaluate the abstractiveness of the generated summaries, defined as the novel n-gram count of our model compared to the reference summary. This measurement allows us to assess whether our model is actually generating new sentences, as well as whether it writes summaries in a different style compared to the reference summary.

5 Results

5.1 ROUGE evaluation

Table 2 shows the ROUGE scores for both models. ROUGE-1 and ROUGE-L are higher compared to ROUGE-2.

For the RL model specific law categories and dates were available (Table 3). Administrative Law performs best on ROUGE scores, while Private Law performs worst. A possible explanation for this difference is that Administrative Law cases are the largest category in the dataset and the reference summaries for this category relatively long, therefore the model gets a large exposure to this category during training. Regarding time periods, the model seems to perform best on cases between 2001 and 2008, while performing slightly worse on cases from the last decade. This is surprising, because the majority of documents in the dataset belongs to the most recent time period.

[2] https://huggingface.co/datasets/yhavinga/mc4_nl_cleaned

Content	Does the summary contain all important information of the original case description? Does it avoids generating repeated and redundant information?
Readability	Is the summary fluent, grammatical, of suitable length?
Informativeness	How well does the summary capture the key points of the article?
Relevance	Are the details provided by the summary consistent with details in the article?
Fluency	Are the individual sentences of the summary well-written and grammatical?
Coherence	Do phrases and sentences of the summary fit together and make sense collectively?

Table 1: Human evaluation metrics

Model	dataset	ROUGE–1	ROUGE–2	ROUGE–L
RL	Rechtspraak	37.24	16.20	34.07
BART	Rechtspraak	**46.52**	**33.74**	**44.88**
BART	CNN/Daily mail	44.16	21.28	40.90

Table 2: ROUGE scores for the summarization models

5.2 Abstractiveness

Following See et al. (2017), for the RL summaries we compute an abstractiveness score as the ratio of novel n-grams in the generated summary. Figure 2 shows the abstractiveness scores of our model compared to the reference summaries of Rechtspraak. One can see that the RL model generates very different summaries from the reference summaries. For example, 20% or less of 2,3 and 4-grams in our generated summaries are identical to the reference summary. The figure furthermore shows that abstractiveness decreases when more training examples are presented to the model, whereas ROUGE F1 increases. One can argue that as models get more abstractive, ROUGE becomes less suitable to evaluate the quality of a summary.

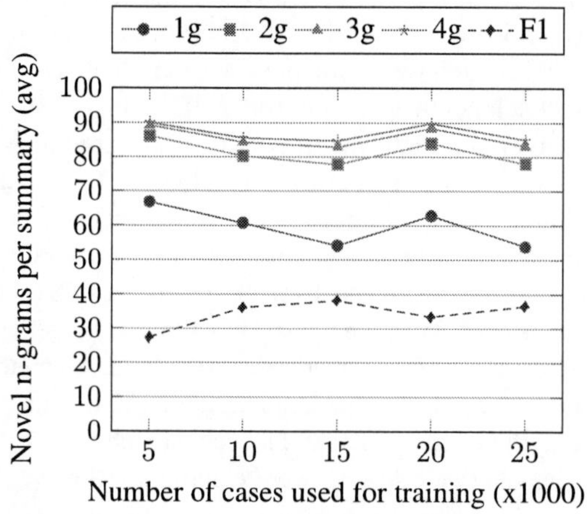

Figure 2: Ratio of novel n-gram counts of summaries compared to the reference summary by number of training cases and development of ROUGE F1

Using a manual check on a sample of the resulting summaries, we observed that the model extracts many sentences from the input document itself. When looking at sentences with similar 4-grams, the model actually used much larger n-grams from the text. However, the model did rewrite and shorten many sentences, thus improving the readability of the text. In addition, redundant information from sentences was removed properly, which made sentences more concise. However, we did note that the model occasionally tends to remove relevant facts and details from sentences, which are needed to understand the case (cf. Figure A1).

5.3 Qualitative evaluation

Exploratory qualitative evaluation by the authors indicated that the model does not introduce many novel sentences. Still, it shows good results for rewriting sentences and removing redundant details from the case, while preserving grammaticality in generated sentences. When important facts (e.g numbers and dates) are present, the model is likely to include these facts in the summary. However, sometimes the model recognized words as not important, which may be caused by the fact that the model has not seen these words often during training. This leads to sentences being cut off too fast. Also, the summary did not always include all elements that are needed in a summary (background, considerations and judgement).

In the example shown in Figure A1, the RL model first gives a very short background description of the case and describes one of the considerations. The description of the background of the

	ROUGE-1	ROUGE-2	ROUGE-L
Administrative Law	39.26 (38.82, 39.74)	18.05 (17.49, 18.64)	35.99 (35.54, 36.49)
Private Law	32.83 (32.30, 33.36)	10.72 (10.24, 11.26)	29.46 (28.96, 29.98)
Criminal Law	37.54 (36.94, 38.12)	17.48 (16.76, 18.18)	34.73 (34.13, 35.34)
Tax Law	36.46 (35.63, 37.32)	13.46 (12.59, 14.42)	32.83 (32.03, 33.70)
1970-2000	38.91 (35.10, 43.05)	16.64 (12.35, 21.37)	35.23 (31.39, 39.32)
2001-2008	38.86 (38.19, 39.53)	18.49 (17.61, 19.38)	35.63 (34.93, 36.32)
2009-2018	36.59 (36.23, 36.94)	15.34 (14.92, 15.74)	33.47 (33.10, 33.83)

Table 3: Observations from the RL experiments (ROUGE F_1 with and 95% confidence interval)

case is very short and the consideration is discussed in far too much detail. Also, the judgement of the case is not discussed. In the first sentence, the main subject of the case (Quarantine Facilities for Live Bivalve Molluscs Regulation 2007) is removed, likely because the model has not seen this word before in other documents and thus does not deem it important. Apart from this mistake, the model does a very good job at rewriting the sentence to a more clearer one. In the second sentence the article number and name of the relevant regulation is omitted in the summary. In the third sentence, many unnecessary details are removed. Still, the summary does not include the (important) fact that the defendant was accused of this case and not that they were actually found guilty. The fourth sentence is taken directly from the original case text. In general, the summary goes in too much detail on some parts of the case and fails to give a generalized summary. However, this example does show the power of the model to rewrite sentences into much clearer and shorter ones.

Qualitative exploration of the BART results indicated that some summaries are able to improve on the reference summary significantly in conciseness while retaining all important facts (see Figure A2). Other summaries however seem to go off on the wrong track, and expand on an unimportant detail for several sentences while missing key points.

In future work, postprocessing could help to fix some of the mentioned issues, using a template-based approach where elements from the original text are copied into the generated summary if the model fails to provide specific details (cf. (Xu et al., 2020)).

5.4 Human evaluation

Table 4 describes the results of the human evaluation phase, showing that the participants in the RL experiment found the reference summaries more relevant and more readable compared to the generated summaries, however the variance of the responses was relatively high. For keyword-only reference summaries all participants preferred to use the generated summary. Participants explicitly noted that they disliked a case to be summarised using only keywords, as this approach is much too abstract for the legal sector. In the BART experiments the content rating was split between the aspects of informativeness and relevance, while the readability rating was split between the aspects of fluency and coherence. For all aspects the evaluator rated the reference summary higher than the generated summary, similar to the RL results.

For the RL experiments, participants noted that not all elements needed in the summary (background, considerations and judgement) were always included. For example, some summaries included the facts and the judgements of a case, but failed to explain the considerations. However, the evaluation showed that, to a lesser extent, also reference summaries are found to omit fundamental details of cases. Participants mentioned that the text that was in fact included in the generated summaries was relevant for the case (which could be compared to a high precision and low recall of information content in the summaries). Regarding readability, participants observed that sentences in the generated summary occasionally contained grammatical errors or ended strangely. Also, the order of sentences was criticized, in both generated and reference summaries, as some summaries started with the judgement and ended with background information about the case. For the summaries generated by the BART model similar observations can be made about content aspects, i.e., the topics discussed in the summary are relevant but not all important aspects are always included by the models, which was again also observed for the reference summaries. For the BART model issues

Summary	n	Content		Readability	
		Informativeness	Relevance	Fluency	Coherence
RL generated	10	4.60 ± 2.12		5.55 ± 1.67	
RL reference	10	6.65 ± 1.63		7.00 ± 1.63	
BART generated	40	3.58 ± 1.24	4.03 ± 1.19	4.45 ± 0.90	4.10 ± 1.08
BART reference	40	4.13 ± 1.04	4.80 ± 0.61	4.75 ± 0.67	4.45 ± 0.81

Table 4: Results of the human evaluation experiment (mean and standard deviation). RL summaries are rated on a scale of 1–10, BART summaries are rated on a scale of 1–5.

in fluency and coherence were noticed, however this model suffered less from obvious grammatical errors or cut-off sentences.

Due to constraints on time and resources in this research project the number of participants was small, leading to large confidence intervals and only a small number of data points. For future work, it would be advised to have a much larger group of subjects, which would also allow to test different versions of our model by changing filters or hyperparameters. Also, it can be interesting to use experienced legal professionals in this type of research, instead of evaluation by law students (RL model) or the paper authors (BART model).

In this evaluation we have seen that there are some issues relating to relevance and readability, such as grammatical errors or missing content. For improving readability, a parser could be implemented in the decoding function that can give a signal when a sentence is cut off too early, giving this sentence a lower score in the beam search algorithm. Also, post-processing can fix some problems regarding nouns, as the models did not always use these correctly when generating sentences.

For improving relevance, an implementation of a neural network that can identify the three core elements needed in a summary can prove useful. Alternatively, a clustering algorithm can be used to find diverse topics in the text, and then identify the most important sentences in these clusters.

6 Conclusion & Discussion

In this work, a dataset containing over 400K Dutch court verdicts was used to train a hybrid reinforcement learning-based model, as well as a transformer-based BART model. We evaluated generated summaries based on ROUGE, abstractiveness, and through a human evaluation experiment using legal experts. Our experiments report an F1 score of 46.52 (ROUGE-1), 33.74 (ROUGE-2) and 44.88 (ROUGE-L) for the BART model, comparable to state-of-the-art results achieved on the CNN/Daily Mail dataset.

The models did not introduce many novel n-grams, but showed good performance in rewriting and shortening sentences. The evaluation also showed the potential to improve the model, following observations that the model may cut sentences off too early and does not always include all elements (background, considerations and judgement) in the summary. Furthermore, while important facts were generally included and the rewriting process showed adequate results, still unnecessary case details are found in the generated summaries.

Considering the level of abstractiveness the models showed the capability of rewriting long and redundant sentences found in legal text to much shorter ones. Quantitatively it was shown that the model generates a large number of novel n-grams compared to the reference summaries from the dataset. Due to the inverse relationship of the abstractiveness and ROUGE score of a document, a good performance in producing novel n-grams actually reduces the score on the summary quality evaluation measured with ROUGE, which was confirmed by the analysis of the evaluation results. Therefore, we argue that ROUGE scores are not fully representative as a metric for abstractive summarization. While alternative methods are being developed (Zhang et al., 2019; Yuan et al., 2021) ROUGE is likely to remain an influential evaluation approach, however these results should be interpreted carefully when comparing models and approaches.

To complement ROUGE scores, a human evaluation study was conducted to evaluate both generated and reference summaries on readability and content. Especially for the RL model the results show a large difference in relevance between reference summaries (6.7/10) and generated summaries (4.6/10), and a slightly smaller difference in readability (7.0/10 vs 5.6/10). However, the participants in the RL experiments noted that the generated summaries did contain key information about the case and preferred it to using a reference summary consisting of only keywords. For the BART experiments the difference across the four dimensions informativeness, relevance, fluency and readability were perceived to be smaller but still the reference summaries were preferred for all dimensions.

It has been argued in the literature that an abstractive summary may be less accurate and can lead to misinterpretations of a judge's intent (Yousfi-Monod et al., 2010). Furthermore, as argued by Jain et al. (2021), there are many citations (to e.g. previous cases or articles of law) which cannot be ignored. However, with more data being available, improved hardware and matured algorithms, the accuracy of abstractive models is increasing. Furthermore, citations can often be extracted from legal texts using basic regular expressions and the relevant legal articles or precedent cases can be provided as metadata, which can then be presented in combination with the abstractive natural language summary. Furthermore, we argue that even less accurate summaries can be useful as a tool for quickly searching through huge databases of cases. Furthermore, there is also the possibility to combine abstractive models with more domain-specific constraints, such as citing law articles and structuring the summary into facts, arguments and decision.

This study fills the following gaps in current research on (legal) text summarization. First, very few research on legal summarization has made use of an abstractive summarization model. The authors are aware of two approaches only, of which the first shows comparatively low evaluation scores (Bhattacharya et al., 2019), and the second is based on US Congressional Bills (Zhang et al., 2018), which, while they can be considered legal documents, are rather different from the case verdicts and decisions we consider. For example, Bills – essentially numbered lists of laws and statutes – are much more structured than verdicts, and the language used in Bills is much more generic because it does not pertain to individual cases like verdicts.

Second, like (Zhang et al., 2020), our work shows that unsupervised neural models originally developed for news articles can be successfully used on legal documents, which differ significantly from news articles both in terms of length and in terms of internal structure and distribution of relevant content elements. Furthermore, no previous research has applied an abstractive summarization model on a dataset of legal documents in Dutch, showing that our unsupervised language models are robust considering the legal language of the documents presented to the model.

For both models, long texts are still difficult to process due to technical limitations on input representation. A case verdict document can easily surpass such length constraints and will be truncated (e.g., to 1024 words) as a result prior to summarization. With respect to future research, models designed to process longer text (Beltagy et al., 2020; Yang et al., 2020) therefore seems promising. Also, even though pre-trained language models are known for their ability to generalize across domains, the model of (Zhang et al., 2018) used to obtain the high levels of performance on Congressional Bills shows a relatively average performance on the CNN/Daily Mail news dataset, which might support the hypothesis that the document structure (rather than the model itself) is the predominant factor for the summary evaluation scores. Applying the current two methods on the Congressional Bills would provide more insight into the reasons behind the performance differences.

Currently, the RL model uses static Word2Vec word embeddings created on the fly on the Rechtspraak dataset. In contrast, the BART contextual embeddings were pretrained on the general-purpose C4 dataset. While the BART model already outperforms the RL model by a significant margin for both ROUGE scores and human ratings, it would be interesting to investigate whether pretraining BART on domain-specific data (i.e., Dutch legal text) would result in an additional performance increase. A practical problem however is data availability: the C4 subset currently used contains 6B words of crawled web pages, which is difficult to match with Dutch legal text.

Other future work includes a more detailed analysis of summaries generated by the BART model. We have observed that the overall quality of the BART summaries is higher compared to the summaries generated by the RL model, in terms of grammaticality and topicality. It would be interesting to compare the detailed observations made for the RL model, such as the abstractiveness, relation to law categories and time frames, and missing legal aspects in the summaries, to establish whether the BART model supports these observations as well.

References

Iz Beltagy, Matthew Peters, and Arman Cohan. 2020. Longformer: The long-document transformer. *arXiv:2004.05150*.

Paheli Bhattacharya, Kaustubh Hiware, Subham Rajgaria, Nilay Pochhi, Kripabandhu Ghosh, and Saptarshi Ghosh. 2019. A comparative study of summarization algorithms applied to legal case judgments. In *European Conference on Information Retrieval*, pages 413–428. Springer.

Ilias Chalkidis, Manos Fergadiotis, Prodromos Malakasiotis, Nikolaos Aletras, and Ion Androutsopoulos. 2020. LEGAL-BERT: The muppets straight out of law school. In *Findings of the Association for Computational Linguistics: EMNLP 2020*, pages 2898–2904, Online. Association for Computational Linguistics.

Ilias Chalkidis and Dimitrios Kampas. 2019. Deep learning in law: early adaptation and legal word embeddings trained on large corpora. *Artificial Intelligence and Law*, 27:171–198.

Yen-Chun Chen and Mohit Bansal. 2018. Fast Abstractive Summarization with Reinforce-Selected Sentence Rewriting. *arXiv:1805.11080 [cs]*. ArXiv: 1805.11080.

Vladimir Eidelman. 2019. Billsum: A corpus for automatic summarization of us legislation. In *Proceedings of the 2nd Workshop on New Frontiers in Summarization*, pages 48–56.

Atefeh Farzindar and Guy Lapalme. 2004. Legal Text Summarization by Exploration of the Thematic Structure and Argumentative Roles. In *Text Summarization Branches Out: Proceedings of the ACL-04 Workshop*, pages 27–34, Barcelona, Spain. Association for Computational Linguistics.

Filippo Galgani, Paul Compton, and Achim Hoffmann. 2012. Combining Different Summarization Techniques for Legal Text. In *Proceedings of the Workshop on Innovative Hybrid Approaches to the Processing of Textual Data*, HYBRID '12, pages 115–123, Stroudsburg, PA, USA. Association for Computational Linguistics.

Ben Hachey and Claire Grover. 2006. Extractive summarisation of legal texts. *Artificial Intelligence and Law*, 14(4):305–345.

U. Hahn and I. Mani. 2000. The challenges of automatic summarization. *Computer*, 33(11):29–36.

Deepali Jain, Malaya Dutta Borah, and Anupam Biswas. 2021. Summarization of legal documents: Where are we now and the way forward. *Computer Science Review*, 40:100388.

Ambedkar Kanapala, Sukomal Pal, and Rajendra Pamula. 2017. Text summarization from legal documents: a survey. *Artificial Intelligence Review*.

Mike Lewis, Yinhan Liu, Naman Goyal, Marjan Ghazvininejad, Abdelrahman Mohamed, Omer Levy, Ves Stoyanov, and Luke Zettlemoyer. 2019. Bart: Denoising sequence-to-sequence pre-training for natural language generation, translation, and comprehension. *arXiv preprint arXiv:1910.13461*.

Chao-Lin Liu and Kuan-Chun Chen. 2019. Extracting the gist of Chinese judgements of the Supreme Court. In *Proceedings of ICAIL '19*. ACM.

Yinhan Liu, Jiatao Gu, Naman Goyal, Xian Li, Sergey Edunov, Marjan Ghazvininejad, Mike Lewis, and Luke Zettlemoyer. 2020. Multilingual denoising pre-training for neural machine translation. *arXiv*.

Christopher Manning, Mihai Surdeanu, John Bauer, Jenny Finkel, Steven Bethard, and David McClosky. 2014. The Stanford CoreNLP Natural Language Processing Toolkit. In *Proceedings of 52nd Annual Meeting of the Association for Computational Linguistics: System Demonstrations*, pages 55–60, Baltimore, Maryland. Association for Computational Linguistics.

Marie-Francine Moens and Rik de Busser. 2002. First steps in building a model for the retrieval of court decisions. *International Journal of Human-Computer Studies*, 57(5):429–446.

Oliver Ray, Amy Conroy, and Rozano Imansyah. 2020. Summarisation with majority opinion. In S. Villata et al., editor, *Legal Knowledge and Information Systems: JURIX 2020*, pages 247–250. IOS Press.

Radim Rehurek and Petr Sojka. 2010. Software framework for topic modelling with large corpora. In *Proceedings of the LREC 2010 Workshop on New Challenges for NLP Frameworks*, pages 45–50. ELRA.

M. Saravanan, B. Ravindran, and S. Raman. 2006. Improving Legal Document Summarization Using Graphical Models. In *Proceedings of the 2006 Conference on Legal Knowledge and Information Systems: JURIX 2006: The Nineteenth Annual Conference*, pages 51–60, Amsterdam, The Netherlands, The Netherlands. IOS Press.

Abigail See, Peter J. Liu, and Christopher D. Manning. 2017. Get To The Point: Summarization with Pointer-Generator Networks. *arXiv:1704.04368 [cs]*. ArXiv: 1704.04368.

Caroline Uyttendaele, Marie-Francine Moens, and Jos Dumortier. 1998. SALOMON: Automatic abstracting of legal cases for effective access to court decisions. *Artificial Intelligence and Law*, 6:59–79.

Maarten van Gompel, Ko van der Sloot, and Antal van den Bosch. 2012. Ucto: Unicode Tokeniser. Technical Report 12-05, ILK.

Oriol Vinyals, Meire Fortunato, and Navdeep Jaitly. 2015. Pointer Networks. In C. Cortes, N. D.

Lawrence, D. D. Lee, M. Sugiyama, and R. Garnett, editors, *Advances in Neural Information Processing Systems 28*, pages 2692–2700. Curran Associates, Inc.

Huihui Xu, Jaromír Šavelka, and Kevin Ashley. 2020. Using argument mining for legal text summarization. In S. Villata et al., editor, *Legal Knowledge and Information Systems: JURIX 2020*, pages 184–193. IOS Press.

Liu Yang, Mingyang Zhang, Cheng Li, Mike Bendersky, and Marc Najork. 2020. Beyond 512 tokens: Siamese multi-depth transformer-based hierarchical encoder for long-form document matching. In *Proceedings of the 29th ACM International Conference on Information and Knowledge Management (CIKM '20)*, pages 1725–1734. ACM.

Mehdi Yousfi-Monod, Atefeh Farzindar, and Guy Lapalme. 2010. Supervised Machine Learning for Summarizing Legal Documents. In *Advances in Artificial Intelligence*, Lecture Notes in Computer Science, pages 51–62. Springer.

Weizhe Yuan, Graham Neubig, and Pengfei Liu. 2021. BARTScore: Evaluating generated text as text generation. In *35th Conference on Neural Information Processing Systems (NeurIPS 2021)*. Curran Associates, Inc.

Jianmin Zhang, Jiwei Tan, and Xiaojun Wan. 2018. Towards a Neural Network Approach to Abstractive Multi-Document Summarization. *arXiv:1804.09010 [cs]*. ArXiv: 1804.09010.

Jingqing Zhang, Yao Zhao, Mohammad Saleh, and Peter Liu. 2020. PEGASUS: Pre-training with extracted gap-sentences for abstractive summarization. In *Proceedings of the 37th International Conference on Machine Learning*, pages 11328–11339. PMLR.

Tianyi Zhang, Varsha Kishore, Felix Wu, Kilian Weinberger, and Yoav Artzi. 2019. BERTScore: Evaluating text generation with BERT.

Linwu Zhong, Ziyi Zhong, Zinian Zhao, Siyuan Wang, Kevin D. Ashley, and Matthias Grabmair. 2019. Automatic summarization of legal decisions using iterative masking of predictive sentences. In *Proceedings of the Seventeenth International Conference on Artificial Intelligence and Law*, ICAIL '19, page 163–172. Association for Computing Machinery.

Appendix: summary examples

Case (ECLI:NL:CBB:2013:212)
.... Process By letter of 18 June 2012, the appellant addressed a request to the defendant to take enforcement action against [A] B.V. and [B] B.V. for (alleged) violation of the provisions of the Quarantine Facilities for Live Bivalve Molluscs Regulation 2007. By letter dated 19 June 2012, the defendant responded. By letter of 27 June 2012, the appellant repeated the request to take enforcement action. By letter of 9 July 2012, the defendant responded again. By letter of 3 August 2012, the defendant responded to the appellant's subsequent letters of 24 and 27 July 2012. ... Considerations ... 3.1 Is it not disputed that the appellant has requested the defendant to initiate disciplinary proceedings for (alleged) breach of the prohibition in Article 2(1) of the Regulation on quarantine facilities for live bivalve molluscs 2007. Appellant subsequently served notice on Defendant for failing to decide to initiate disciplinary proceedings, she claims, and then brought an appeal under Article 6:12 of the General Administrative Law Act (Awb). Which first of all raises the question of whether an appeal under Article 6:12 of the General Administrative Law Act was open to the appellant in this case. The Board answers this question in the negative. Article 15 of the Corporate Disciplinary Procedure (Organisation) Act 2004 stipulates that the chairperson of the defendant, once he or she has established that there has been an (alleged) offence, shall refer the matter to the disciplinary court within a reasonable period of time by means of a written statement. ....
Reference summary
Refers to appeals against failure to take a decision on time. Such proceedings are not open against the chairman of the Dutch Fish Product Board not initiating disciplinary proceedings. Making such a request is not an application within the meaning of Article 1:3 of the General Administrative Law Act. The corporate organisation disciplinary law has its own provisions.
Generated summary
Request for enforcement action. Not in dispute is that appellant has requested the defendant to initiate disciplinary proceedings for (alleged) breach of the prohibition in Article 2, first. Defendant failed to decide on the filing of a disciplinary case. Which raises the question of whether recourse to Article 6:12 of the General Administrative Law Act was open to appellants in this case.

Figure A1: Example from the dataset showing the generated summary of the RL model. The example is translated from Dutch into English for illustration purposes. The colored (marked) sentences correspond to the sentences that were extracted by the model.

Case (ECLI:NL:CBB:CRVB:2012:BW3333)
[...] Considerations [...] The job expert has selected functions which he considers the appellant capable of performing and has established the loss of earning capacity to less than 35%. As decided on January 7th, 2010, it is established that appellant starting October 20, 2009 is not entitled to benefits regarding the Law Work and Income. The insurance physician has concluded that the impairments are established correctly. He has studies the letter by the general practitioner dated December 31, 2009. According to the insurance physician there are no grounds to assume further impairments. [...] The court has judged that the decision was based on a sufficiently appropriate medical foundation. There is no reason to doubt the conclusion by the insurance physicians that appellant is capable of performing simple, routine tasks. [...] For the appeal appellant has entered information by the general practitioner and treating psychologist. [...] The insurance physician has stated that this information is not a reason to assume further impairments. The Council follows this conclusion. [...] Establishing sickness- or handicap-based impairments to performing labor based on the medical condition of the appellant should in principle be considered the expertise of the insurance physician. [...] Appellant is rightfully considered to be able to perform the selected tasks. [...] It did not become apparent that the workload exceeds the capabilities of the appellant.
Reference summary
Refusal to grant "WIA Law" benefits. The contested decision is based on a sufficiently appropriate medical foundation. The information from the general practitioner and psychologist do not substantiate that the appellant is more impaired than the insurance physician has established. Establishing sickness- or handicap-based impairments to performing labor based on the medical condition of the appellant should in principle be considered the expertise of the insurance physician. Appellant is rightfully considered to be able to perform the selected tasks. It did not become apparent that the workload exceeds the capabilities of the appellant.
Generated summary
Refusal to grant WIA benefits. Less than 35% incapacitated. Sufficient medical and employment-related foundation. No reason to doubt the conclusion by the insurance physicians that appellant is capable of performing simple, routine tasks.

Figure A2: Example from the dataset showing the generated summary of the BART model for an appeal case. The example is translated from Dutch into English for illustration purposes. The colored (marked) sentences correspond to sentences in the generated summary. It can be observed that the reference summary is almost completely extractive, while the BART summary contains both abstractive and extractive sentences.

Legal-Tech Open Diaries: Lesson learned on how to develop and deploy light-weight models in the era of humongous Language Models

Stelios Maroudas[* †◇] **Sotiris Legkas**[* †◇]
Prodromos Malakasiotis[†] **Ilias Chalkidis** [‡◇]
[†] Department of Informatics, Athens University of Economics and Business, Greece
‡ Department of Computer Science, University of Copenhagen, Denmark
[◇] Cognitiv+, Athens, Greece

Abstract

In the era of billion-parameter-sized Language Models (LMs), start-ups have to follow trends and adapt their technology accordingly. Nonetheless, there are open challenges since the development and deployment of large models comes with a need for high computational resources and has economical consequences. In this work, we follow the steps of the R&D group of a modern legal-tech start-up and present important insights on model development and deployment. We start from ground zero by pre-training multiple domain-specific multi-lingual LMs which are a better fit to contractual and regulatory text compared to the available alternatives (XLM-R). We present benchmark results of such models in a half-public half-private legal benchmark comprising 5 downstream tasks showing the impact of larger model size. Lastly, we examine the impact of a full-scale pipeline for model compression which includes: a) Parameter Pruning, b) Knowledge Distillation, and c) Quantization: The resulting models are much more efficient without sacrificing performance at large.

1 Introduction

Transformer-based Languages Models (LMs) (Radford and Narasimhan, 2018; Devlin et al., 2019; Liu et al., 2019) have stormed NLP benchmarks with state-of-the-art performance, while recently humongous billion-parameter-sized models (Brown et al., 2020; Rae et al., 2021; Hoffmann et al., 2022) have showcased impressive few-shot capabilities. In addition, multi-lingual LMs (Conneau et al., 2020) have been also developed demonstrating exceptional results as well as impressive performance in zero-shot cross-lingual transfer.

The legal NLP literature is also flourishing with the release of many new resources, including large legal corpora (Henderson* et al., 2022), benchmark datasets (Chalkidis et al., 2021a; Koreeda and Manning, 2021; Zheng et al., 2021; Chalkidis et al., 2022; Habernal et al., 2022), and pre-trained legal-oriented language models (Chalkidis et al., 2020; Zheng et al., 2021). Despite this impressive progress, the efficacy of differently-sized language models on legal NLP tasks and the importance of domain (legal) specificity are still understudied, while the effect of model compression techniques in model's performance and efficiency is ignored.

In this work, we aim to shed light in all these directions following model development across three incremental steps in a *pipelined* approach:

(a) *model pre-training* on large legal corpora,
(b) *model fine-tuning* on down-stream tasks, and
(c) *model compression* to improve efficiency.

To do so, we initially develop 4 multi-lingual legal-oriented language models (C-XLMs). We benchmark their performance across 5 down-stream legal NLP tasks, comprising both publicly available and private datasets, covering both English and multilingual scenarios in several tasks types, i.e., document/sentence classification, natural language inference, and entity extraction. Finally, we experiment with a full-scale pipeline for model compression which includes a) Parameter Pruning, b) Knowledge Distillation, and c) Quantization to produce much more efficient (smaller and faster) models that can be effectively deployed in production.

Our work aims to provide guidelines to legal-tech practitioners on model development (pre-training, fine-tuning, compression) bearing both performance and efficiency into consideration. Our findings show that the impact of larger vs. smaller models, domain-specific vs. generic models and the efficacy of model compression techniques varies across tasks, but in general larger domain-specific models perform better. Via full-scale model compression, we produce models with performance decrease by 2.3 p.p., while being approx.

[*] Equal contribution. Work done during capstone projects in Cognitiv+ (https://www.cognitivplus.com/).

Proceedings of the Natural Legal Language Processing Workshop 2022, pages 88 - 110
December 8, 2022 ©2022 Association for Computational Linguistics

Model Alias		#Langs	#Layers	#Units	#Heads	#Params	Vocab. Size	Train. Tokens	MLM Acc.
XLM-R	base	100	12	768	12	278M	250k	6.3T	74.0
XLM-R	large	100	24	1024	16	559M	250k	6.3T	78.9
C-XLM	tiny	10	4	128	4	9M	64k	92B	54.9
C-XLM	small	10	6	256	4	21M	64k	92B	68.9
C-XLM	base	10	12	512	8	71M	64k	92B	77.8
C-XLM	large	10	24	1024	16	368M	64k	92B	81.5

Table 1: Model Specifications, Training Tokens processed on pre-training and MLM performance (Acc.) for all variants of our XLM (C-XLM) models and the XLM-R models of Conneau et al. (2020) considered as baselines.

42× smaller, and approx. 66× faster. We also find that fully compressed models outperform equally sized distilled or fine-tuned models.

2 Model Specifications

Following Chalkidis et al. (2020), we pre-train from scratch legal domain specific transformer-based language models. Our models are based on the RoBERTa architecture (Liu et al., 2019), i.e., trained with the Masked Language Modelling (MLM) objective, excluding the Next Sentence Prediction (NSP) one used by BERT (Devlin et al., 2019). In addition, based on the industry needs and driven by the work of (Conneau et al., 2020), our models are a multilingual one -usually referred as XLM in the literature- and supports ten languages in total (English, French, German, Greek, Spanish, Italian, Dutch, Polish, Portuguese, Russian).

We pre-train 4 variants of custom XLM models (C-XLM) starting from a large version with 24 Transformer blocks (layers), each consisting of 1024 hidden units and 16 attention heads and continue by decreasing each time by a factor of 2 across all dimensions, i.e., blocks/layers, hidden units, and attention heads (Table 1).[1]

3 Pre-Training

3.1 Training Corpora

We pre-trained our models using multi-lingual corpora that consist of regulations and contracts. For regulations, we used the MultiEURLEX dataset of Chalkidis et al. (2021b) that comprises 65k EU regulations officially translated in 24 languages.[2]. We also considered additional publicly available English resources; specifically the 250 US code books, part of the "Pile of Law" corpus released by (Henderson* et al., 2022), along-size 36k UK laws published by Chalkidis and Søgaard (2022).

Regarding contracts, we considered the LEDGAR (Tuggener et al., 2020) dataset comprising 900k sections from US contracts in English; and 60k additional full contracts in English from a publicly available crawl from EDGAR. Since, there are no publicly available contracts in the rest of the languages, we translated these documents using state-of-the-art Neural Machine Translation (NMT) systems across all languages of interest.[3]

3.2 Custom Vocabulary

Relying on the above mentioned resources, we built a custom vocabulary of 64k sub-word units that better fit the documents in the respective domains and languages of interest. We opted for Byte-Pair Encodings (BPEs) (Sennrich et al., 2016), similarly to most recent work on Transformer-based language models (Radford and Narasimhan, 2018; Liu et al., 2019; Conneau et al., 2020).

3.3 Masked Language Modelling (MLM)

We pre-trained all variants of C-XLM (our domain-specific multi-lingual RoBERTa) for 1.1m steps (gradient updates) in total based on a two-step approach, similarly to Devlin et al. (2019), i.e., pre-train for 1m steps with sequences up to 128 sub-word units, followed by continued pre-training for 100k steps with sequences up to 512 sub-word units, always with a batch size of 512 sequences.[4] At each example, we mask out 15% of the tokens in total. We train all models for a maximum learning rate of 1e−4 with warm-up for the initial (5%) training steps followed by a cosine decay.

In comparison XLM-R models were pre-trained for 1.5m steps with batches of 8192 sequences, which accounts for approx. 63× more training

[1] A minor exception in the tiny version, where we consider 4 attention heads of 32 hidden units per head instead of 2 attention heads with 64 units per head.

[2] In our work, we consider 9 languages (English, French, German, Greek, Spanish, Italian, Dutch, Polish, Portuguese).

[3] We used the OpusMT (en2m) mBART models using the EasyNMT library.

[4] This approach aims to a more efficient (compute-friendly) pre-training, since pre-training with shorter sequences severely decreases the needed compute and time.

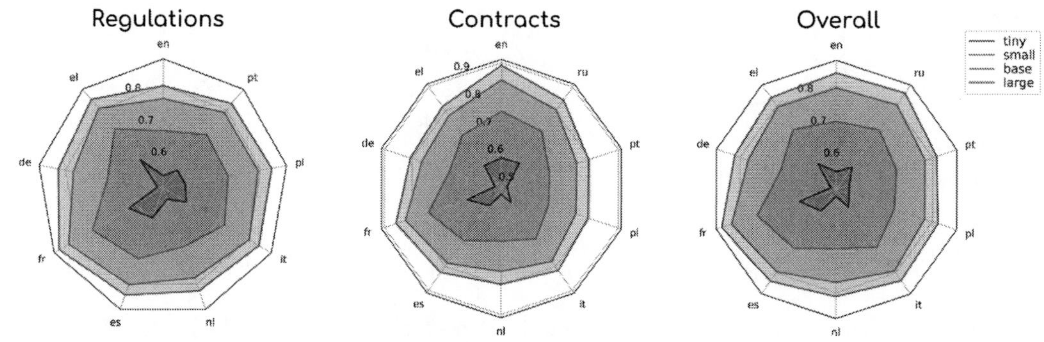

Figure 1: MLM performance per language across C-XLM model variants depicted with different coloured webs.

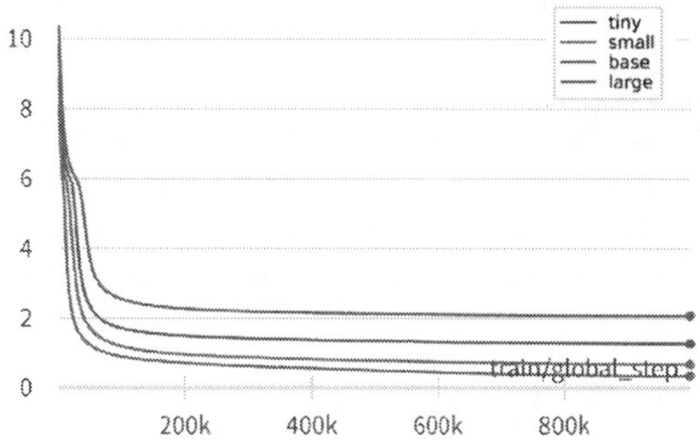

Figure 2: Pre-training loss curves of C-XLMs.

tokens processed; the majority of those in high-resource languages like the ones we consider.

3.4 MLM Results

In Figure 2, we observe the loss curves of differently sized models during pre-training. While models are equally poor performing in the very initial steps, larger models substantially outperform the smaller counterparts due to their increased capacity (number of parameters). Table 1 presents the accuracy of our different models. As expected, the large version (81.5% accuracy) followed by the base version (77.8% accuracy) of C-XLM outperform their corresponding generic XLM-R models by 2.6% and 3.8% respectively.[5] Figure 1 presents masked language modelling performance in finer details across languages per model, highlighting the predominance of our two largest models.[6]

4 Fine-tuning

4.1 Benchmark - Tasks and Datasets

In this section, we briefly present the evaluation benchmark that we use, which consist of both publicly available and private datasets. The benchmark is diverse covering three task types (document, sentence, and token classification) and two multi-lingual datasets.[7] The datasets in detail are:

MultiEURLEX (Chalkidis et al., 2021a), a multilingual dataset for legal topic classification comprising 65k EU laws officially translated in 23 EU languages.[8] Each document (EU law) was originally annotated with relevant EUROVOC[9] concepts by the Publications Office of EU. We use the 21 'Level 1' labels, obtained by Chalkidis et al. (2021a) from the original EUROVOC annotations of the documents. We use a derivative of the original dataset considering only 1k non-parallel documents per supported language (9k in total, Section 3.1).[10] This is a multi-label document classification task, thus we evaluate performance using macro- (m-F_1) and micro- (μ-F_1) F1 scores.

UNFAIR-ToS (Drawzeski et al., 2021) is a dataset for detecting unfair clauses in Terms of Service (ToS) agreements from on-line platforms (e.g., YouTube, Facebook, etc.) in 4 languages (English, German, Italian, and Polish). The dataset has been annotated on the sentence-level with 8 types of *un-*

[5]A comparison between the XLM-R models of Conneau et al. (2020) and our models (C-XLMs) is not ideal due to the different vocabulary used. Nevertheless, it provides a general idea on pre-training performance on legal specific corpora.

[6]More fine-grained MLM evaluation (per language and per document type) can be found in Appendix B.

[7]We do not use the LexGLUE benchmark of Chalkidis et al. (2022), since it is monolingual (English only) and also covers tasks that involve litigation, which are out of scope.

[8]MultiEURLEX is available at `https://huggingface.co/datasets/multi_eurlex`.

[9]EUROVOC is a hierarchically organized taxonomy of concepts (a hierarchy of labels) available at `http://eurovoc.europa.eu/`.

[10]This is inline with the work of Xenouleas et al. (2022), where the authors consider a more "realistic" harder version of MultiEURLEX with less and non-parallel documents.

Model	Alias	MultiEURLEX		UNFAIR-ToS		CNLI		Obligations		ContractNER	
		μ-F_1	m-F_1	Acc.	MAE	μ-F_1	m-F_1	μ-F_1	m-F_1	μ-F_1	m-F_1
XLM-R	(base)	75.3	53.2	86.6	0.17	84.0	81.9	89.7	88.2	92.4	93.9
XLM-R	(large)	77.8	63.8	89.0	0.16	**86.3**	**84.7**	88.9	87.4	92.8	93.7
C-XLM	(tiny)	66.5	46.1	78.2	0.27	70.2	69.2	88.7	87.4	87.2	89.3
C-XLM	(small)	72.3	54.7	85.4	0.20	79.7	77.0	90.4	89.0	90.1	92.4
C-XLM	(base)	75.3	59.4	87.3	0.18	84.0	82.1	91.2	90.4	92.9	93.9
C-XLM	(large)	**78.4**	**65.4**	**89.7**	**0.14**	85.3	83.0	**91.8**	**90.6**	**93.2**	**94.6**

Table 2: Overall results of fine-tuned models across all down-stream tasks.

fair contractual terms, meaning terms (sentences) that potentially violate user rights according to EU consumer law. Sentences have been also annotated according to a 3-level fairness score (*fair*, *partially unfair*, *clearly unfair*). In our case, we examine the latter task as sentence regression and evaluate performance using Mean Absolute Error (MAE), and Accuracy (Acc.) on rounded (discrete) scores.

ContractNLI (Koreeda and Manning, 2021) is a dataset for contract-based Natural Language Inference (NLI). The dataset consists of 607 contracts, specifically Non-Disclosure Agreements (NDAs). Each document has been paired with 17 templated *hypotheses* and labeled with one out of three classes (*entailment*, *contradiction*, or *neutral*). We examine a lenient version of this task, where instead of the full document (NDA), we represent the document with a short number of sentences which have been annotated as rationales for the specific task. This is a single-label multi-class document classification task and we evaluate performance using macro- (m-F_1) and micro- (μ-F_1) F1 scores.

Contract-Obligations (Chalkidis et al., 2018) is a proprietary (privately developed) dataset for obligation extraction from contracts (legal agreements). The dataset consists of 100 service agreements. Each contract has been split into paragraphs (approx. 9,400 in total), and labeled with 4 obligation sub-types, i.e., *Obligation*, *Deliverable*, *Discretion*, and *Prohibition*, while some paragraphs are not relevant, resulting in a total of 5 potential classes. This is a single-label multi-class document classification task. We evaluate performance using macro- (m-F_1) and micro- (μ-F_1) F1 scores.

ContractNER (Chalkidis et al., 2017) is a proprietary dataset for contract element extraction. The dataset consists of 3,500 contractual introductions from several types (service, employment, purchase, etc.) of contracts. Each introduction (paragraph) has been labeled with 4 entity types (*Title*, *Contracting Party*, *Start Date*, *Effective Date*). This is a single-label multi-class token classification task. Thus, we evaluate performance using macro- (m-F_1) and micro- (μ-F_1) F1 scores on entity level.

4.2 Experimental Set Up

We tune all models conducting a grid search for learning rates ∈ {1e-4, 3e-4, 1e-5, 3e-5, 5e-5, 1e-6}. We use early stopping based on validation loss; we select and report test scores based on the model with the best validation performance.[11]

4.3 Fine-tuning Results

Table 2 presents the results of the fined-tuned baselines, XLM-R models, (upper zone) and of all the variants of our C-XLM models (lower zone) for each downstream task. We hypothesize that the base and large versions of C-XLM will perform better compared to their counterpart XLM-R models. Indeed, the base version of C-XLM always outperforms XLM-R across all 5 datasets, while the large version of C-XLM outperforms XLM-R in all but one (4 out of 5) datasets.

MultiEURLEX: Both large versions of C-XLM and XLM-R clearly outperform the rest of the models with the C-XLM outperforming XLM-R by 0.6 p.p. in μ-F_1 and 1.6 p.p. in m-F_1. Similarly, the base version of C-XLM outperforms the equivalent version of XLM-R. Interestingly, the small version of C-XLM has comparable performance with the latter while being approx. 13× smaller.

UNFAIR-ToS: Both large and base versions of C-XLM outperform their counterpart XLM-R models by 0.7 p.p. in accuracy. Again, the small version of C-XLM achieves competitive performance to base-sized models.

[11]Additional details and development scores are provided in Appendix A

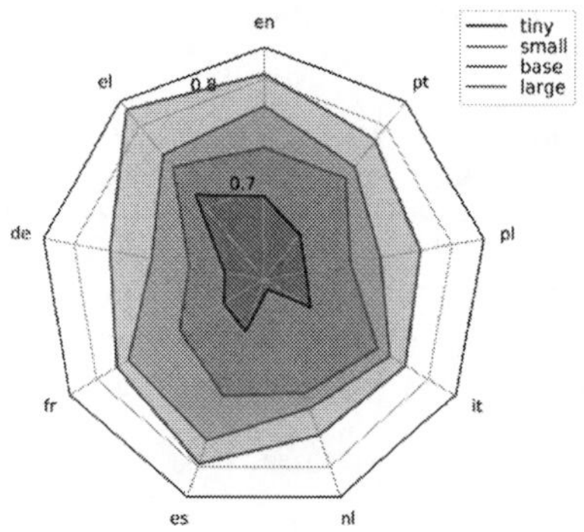

(a) MultiEURLEX

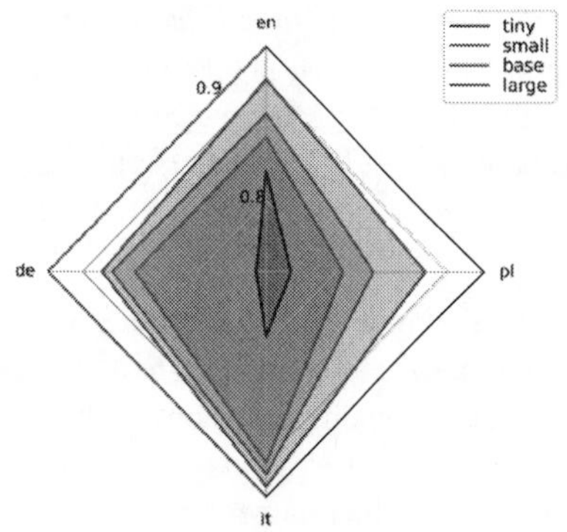

(b) UNFAIR-ToS

Figure 3: Radar plots with per language performance for the multilingual MultiEURLEX and Unfair-ToS datasets for all the versions of C-XLM.

ContractNLI: In this task, we find that the large version of XLM-R outperforms the one of C-XLM (+1 p.p. in μ-F_1 and +1.7 p.p. in m-F_1) while both base models perform comparably. We also note that the relative differences between differently sized models are the more intense across all tasks.

Contract-Obligations: On this task, all C-XLM models except the tiny version outperform the baselines (XLM-R). Specifically, the large version of C-XLM achieves +2.9 p.p. in μ-F_1 and +3.2 p.p. in m-F_1 compared to the large version of XLM-R.

ContractNER: Similarly, our C-XLM models outperform the corresponding large and base baselines by approx. 0.5 p.p. in μ-F_1. In addition, m-F_1 is higher in our large model by 0.9 p.p., while base models have identical results. Again, the small version of C-XLM is competitive to the baseline.

In general trends, we observe that larger models outperform smaller ones in most cases, and domain-specific models outperform generic ones, while using a sunstantially smaller (4×) vocabulary and be significantly less (63×) pre-trained. The largest relative differences occur in MULTIEURLEX, a 20-class multi-label classificationtask, and CNLI, a sentence pair classification task.

Language Parity: Figure 3 provides information through radar plots, about scores per language for each variant of C-XLM. We generally observe that performance varies across languages (e.g., models perform better in English compared to German), while also language performance disparity varies across models (depicted as differently shaped webs), and across datasets (e.g., models are better in English compared to Italian in MultiEURLEX, but the opposite is true for UNFAIR-ToS).[12]

We cross out representation disparity as a possible explanation, since training data equally represent all languages (equal number of training examples). Interestingly, pre-training (MLM) accuracy also does not correlate with the down-stream performance. Based on the aforementioned points, we can only hypothesize that other qualitative characteristics (idiosyncrasies of a language in a specific context/domain) are responsible for perfomance disparities in-between languages.

Algorithm 1 Gradual Compression

if Teacher Size >> Student Size **then**
  S0: Distill *model* to *teacher assistant*
S1: Prune *model vocabulary* and
fine-tune for 1-3 epochs (if needed).
S2: Prune *model depth* and distill.
S3: Prune *model width* and re-distill.
S4.1: Optimize computational graph.
S4.2: Apply 8-bit dynamic quantization.

5 Model Compression

5.1 Methodology

To compress and accelerate the inference of fine-tuned transformer-based models we adopt *gradual compression*, a pipeline that combines structured pruning, knowledge distillation, and post-training quantization to progressively reach the desired compression rate, summarized in Algorithm 1.[13]

Step 0 — Teacher Assistant: In case the teacher is very large and the desired compression rate is high (e.g., reducing the large version of C-XLM to the tiny one), teacher assistants (Mirzadeh et al., 2020) are used to make the transition smoother.

[12]Refer to Appendix B for detailed results.

[13]See additional details and results from preliminary experiments in Appendix B.

Step 1 — Vocabulary Pruning: The first step is to reduce the model's vocabulary. Tokens that do not appear in the training dataset of the down-stream task are removed. Furthermore, using information from the tokenizer's merges, the merge of two tokens that exist in the training dataset and individual tokens that form a merge that, also, exists in the training dataset are kept as well. After the redundant tokens are removed, the embedding matrix is reshaped and the new model, if necessary, is fine-tuned for 1-3 epochs, to restore its original performance. The intuition behind vocabulary reduction is that some word embeddings that were learned during pre-training might not be useful for a specific down-stream task, since such words are rare and their word embeddings would not get updated during fine-tuning, if they did not exist in the training set (e.g., some words of a multilingual model would be redundant for a monolingual task).

Step 2 — Depth Pruning: The second step is to reduce the model's *depth* via knowledge distillation. Similarly to Sun et al. (2019), we find that using the weights of the first k layers from the teacher's original pre-trained (not fine-tuned) language model produces the most consistent results. In our implementation, the KL-divergence between the (softened) teacher's and student's predicted probabilities is chosen as the distillation loss function. Across all tasks, the distillation loss is, also, linearly combined with the original loss. For the multi-label classification task, the cross-entropy loss is replaced by a binary cross-entropy loss, again with the (softened) teacher's and student's probabilities as inputs, whereas for the regression task it is replaced by the mean squared error between the teacher's and student's output logits (Ba and Caruana, 2014).

Step 3 — Width Pruning: Once the fine-tuned teacher's knowledge is distilled to the student model, structured pruning is applied to reduce the student's *width*. In particular, using *TextPruner* (Yang et al., 2022), the top n neurons from the intermediate fully-connected layers and the top a attention heads from the multi-head attention layers that have the smallest impact on the expected loss are iteratively removed (Michel et al., 2019; Prasanna et al., 2020). The pruned student model is re-distilled to restore its original performance. Although unstructured pruning (Han et al., 2015; Sanh et al., 2020; Louizos et al., 2018) would probably lead to higher compression rates with smaller performance loss, we choose structured pruning to ensure that the compressed model's inference speed is also accelerated.

Step 4 — Graph Optimization & Model Quantization: For the final step, the student's weights are quantized to 8-bits, using post-training dynamic quantization. However, although 8-bit quantization will reduce the memory footprint by approximately 4x, without specialized hardware there will be hardly any inference time speed-up. Thus, before quantizing the student model, using *ONNX* (Bai et al., 2019), its computational graph is optimized, which can provide hardware-independent acceleration (Li et al., 2021). In particular, constant folding –where constant expressions are statically pre-computed–, redundant node elimination –where redundant nodes such as identities are removed without changing the graph structure– and operation fusion –where multiple smaller nodes are fused into one, reducing in this way launch and synchronization overhead (Vasilache et al., 2018)– are applied.

Why gradual compression? Although gradual compression can be more time-consuming than, for example, distilling the teacher's knowledge in a student with a smaller predefined size, it offers more flexibility and control over the whole compression process. When the desired compression rate is reached gradually, one could better balance the performance/compression-rate trade-off.

If for example the model is sensitive to reducing the depth, one could prune the width more aggressively and vice versa. Since the model will only be compressed once before deployed, it is important to ensure that the productionized model will perform as well as possible, thus, devoting more time to take careful steps should not be a concern.

5.2 Compression Results

For each down-stream task, the goal is to produce compressed versions of the large and base C-XLM that can outperform the fine-tuned small and tiny variants of C-XLM, while being smaller and faster in terms of memory and inference speed. Using Gradual Compression (GC), the final compressed versions with the small version of C-XLM as a reference comprise 6 Transformer blocks, 24 attention heads, and 1024 units, whereas the compressed versions with the tiny one as a reference consist of 3 blocks, 12 heads and 512 units.

Model	MultiEURLEX		UNFAIR-ToS		CNLI		Obligations		ContractNER	
	μ-F_1	m-F_1	Acc.	MAE	μ-F_1	m-F_1	μ-F_1	m-F_1	μ-F_1	m-F_1
Top Bound - Performance "Ceiling"										
C-XLM (large)	78.4	65.4	89.7	0.14	85.3	83.0	91.8	90.6	93.2	94.6
Gradual Compression — Reference C-XLM (small)										
C-XLM (small) (FT)	72.3	54.7	**85.4**	**0.20**	79.7	77.0	90.4	89.0	90.1	92.4
C-XLM (small) (KD)	73.3	54.7	81.1	0.25	80.2	78.1	90.1	89.1	91.0	93.1
C-XLM (large) (GC)	**74.2**	**60.4**	83.7	0.21	**84.5**	**83.1**	**92.2**	**91.3**	**92.2**	**93.3**
Gradual Compression — Reference C-XLM (tiny)										
C-XLM (tiny) (FT)	66.5	46.1	78.2	0.27	70.2	69.2	88.7	87.4	87.2	89.3
C-XLM (tiny) (KD)	64.0	42.0	76.7	0.30	75.3	74.3	89.1	88.1	**87.7**	90.1
C-XLM (large) (GC)	**73.2**	**57.0**	**79.6**	**0.25**	**80.7**	**79.2**	**91.9**	**90.7**	87.6	**90.2**

Table 3: Model compression results across down-stream tasks. We report the performance for two baselines: (a) fine-tuning the reference pre-trained C-XLM model (FT), and (b) Knowledge Distillation and Vocabulary Pruning. where the student is the reference pre-trained C-XLM (KD); alongside the performance of fully gradually compressed (GC) models, i.e., pruned, distilled and quantized (P+KD+Q). We report the model's performance across the incremental compression steps (S) presented in Section 5.1 in the Appendix (Table 9).

The large C-LXM used as the teacher is substantially larger (20-40×) compared to the reference models. To ensure that the transition to compressed versions is smooth, we first distill it using as student the base version of C-XLM, to create a *teacher assistant* (Mirzadeh et al., 2020). In every incremental step of GC where knowledge distillation is applied, the learning rate, temperature and a (the original and distillation loss weighing) are tuned using grid search. Our GC compression pipeline is also compared with a variant of *Pre-trained Distillation* (Turc et al., 2019), where the teacher's (or its assistant's) knowledge is distilled directly to the reference (smaller) pre-trained model.

Results are presented in Table 3. We observe that the compressed versions of the large C-XLM model (GC) produced by the full-scale compression pipeline introduced in Section 5.1 always outperform both the respective fine-tuned (FT) models of the smaller versions of C-XLM and the distilled (KD) ones with a single exception in UNFAIR-ToS. Similar results can be derived when we consider the base version of C-XLM as the teacher model. Results are presented in Appendix B.

The largest relative differences are observed in the setting where we use the tiny model as a reference, which indicates that gradual compression is very effective when higher compression rates are being considered. Interestingly, in the Obligation extraction task, the compressed models are able to outperform the teacher (Upper Bound).

Model	Performance Loss	Compression Rate	Inference Acceleration
Reference C-XLM (small)			
FT	-4.1 p.p.	17.4×	34.1×
KD	-4.5 p.p.	21.0×	36.2×
GC	**-2.3 p.p.**	**41.8×**	**65.5×**
Reference C-XLM (tiny)			
FT	-9.5 p.p.	40.3×	87.9×
KD	-9.1 p.p.	**50.9×**	94.2×
GC	**-5.1 p.p.**	**50.9×**	**169.8×**

Table 4: Averaged performance and efficiency statistics for each model across all tasks.

Results can be vastly improved if a more fine-grained network-architecture search is conducted. For example, in some of the tasks, the largest performance drop occurs during the second step (depth pruning). This could be prevented if few additional layers remain, in favor of aggressive width pruning (step 3).[14] However, the goal of our experiments was to produce competitive results among all tasks, even with the constraint of using shared predefined network specifications.

5.3 Efficiency Considerations

In Table 4, we present aggregated (averaged) statistics in terms of efficiency.[14] With the small version of C-XLM as a reference, GC produces models that are 41.8× smaller and 65.5× faster, while losing

[14]The size and inference speed of models produced at each compression step are reported in Appendix B.4.

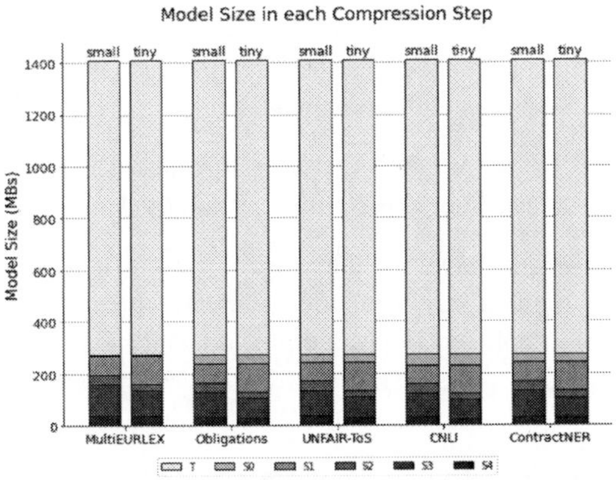

Figure 4: Model size (MB) in each compression step (S) in relevance to the original model, C-XLM (large).

only 2.3 p.p. of performance on average. On the other hand, the fine-tuned (FT) or distilled (KD) models have a larger performance drop (by approx. 1-2 p.p.) compared to the GC versions which are also substantially (almost 2×) faster on average.

With the tiny version of C-XLM as a reference, GC can produce models that are, on average, 50.9x smaller and 169.8x faster, while losing 5.1 p.p. of performance on average. The fine-tuned (FT) or distilled (KD) models have now substantially larger performance drop (9 p.p.) highlighting the benefits of GC in an extreme-compression setting.

In Figure 4, we present the model size reduction across the incremental GC steps (S0-S4). The largest size reduction in both settings (small, tiny) is observed in the quantization step (S4), if we exclude the preliminary distillation step to create the teacher's assistant (S0), which reduces the original model size approx. 4×.[15]

6 Related Work

6.1 Transformer-based LMs

Devlin et al. (2019) are the first to pre-train transformer-based language models (BERT) on large corpora that achieving state-of-the-art results in generic NLP benchmarks ((Wang et al., 2019b,a). One year later, Liu et al. (2019) argued that BERT was significantly under-trained and introduced RoBERTa (Robustly optimized BERT) using improved pre-training settings (more data, larger mini-batches, dynamic masking, and a larger vocabulary) leading to new state-of-the-art results.

[15]The size compression effect of steps S1-S4 is better depicted in Figure 5 in Appendix B where the base version of C-XLM is the teacher and thus S0 is omitted.

Moreover, multilingually pre-trained models (Conneau and Lample, 2019; Conneau et al., 2020) have been developed using a shared vocabulary, which can later fine-tuned across several languages. These models have also shown to have exceptional zero-shot cross-lingual capabilities, a direction that we do not investigate in this work.

In the NLP literature, domain-specific models outperform generic ones in domain-specific benchmarking. Lee et al. (2019) created BioBERT by further pre-training BERT of (Devlin et al., 2019) on biomedical corpora. n the same manner, Alsentzer et al. (2019) further pre-trained BioBERT on clinical notes, releasing ClinicalBERT. Similarly, Beltagy et al. (2019) pretrained BERT model on scientific publications called SciBERT, while Loukas et al. (2022) released SEC-BERT pre-trained on US financial filings.

In the legal domain, Chalkidis et al. (2020) released LegalBERT, a legal-oriented BERT model pre-trained on diverse English legal corpora, which outperform generic ones in most legal NLU benchmark (Chalkidis et al., 2022) as is CaseLawBERT of Zheng et al. (2021), a BERT model pre-trained solely on US case law. Recently, (Henderson* et al., 2022) released a new legal-oriented larger BERT model, which is also heavily biased towards legal proceedings in US-based jurisdictions.

6.2 Model Compression

Unstructured pruning was popularized by Han et al. (2015), who iteratively located and pruned connections whose weights were less than a pre-specified threshold and retrained the sparsed network. In later work, the idea of learning how to sparsify models during training was also proposed (Zhu and Gupta, 2017; Louizos et al., 2018; Sanh et al., 2020). For Transformer-base models, Sanh et al. (2020) argued that changes in weights during fine-tuning must be taken into consideration and proposed *movement pruning*.

On the other hand, structured pruning produces smaller (not sparse) models by removing attention heads (Voita et al., 2019; McCarley et al., 2019; Michel et al., 2019)), individual (McCarley et al., 2019; Prasanna et al., 2020) or blocks (Lagunas et al., 2021) of neurons from fully-connected layers in a structured manner. We follow this line of work, since structured pruning improves model compression in practice (deployment of smaller models), contrary to unstructured pruning which sparsify networks (deployment of sparse, but equally-sized models comparing to the original ones).

Another approach to reduce the memory footprint of neural networks is quantization, i.e., mapping the real-valued parameters and activations over a fixed set of discrete numbers to minimize the number of bits required to store them. When transformer-based models are quantized to 8-bits, the models' memory overhead is reduced approximately by 4x (Bondarenko et al., 2021), while the matrix multiplication computational cost can be reduced by 3.7x with the use of specialized hardware. Junczys-Dowmunt et al. (2018) and Bhandare et al. (2019)) applied 8-bit post training quantization to transformer-based models. Zafrir et al. (2019) and Fan et al. (2020) used quantization aware training to quantize transformer-based language models.

The last technique that is frequently used to compress transformer-based models is knowledge distillation. With knowledge distillation, a smaller (*student*) network is trained to mimic the behavior of a larger (*teacher*) network. In particular, instead of training the student network with the true labels, the teacher's predictions are used as a target (*response-based knowledge distillation*), which are usually "softened" to better capture similarities across classes (Hinton et al., 2015).

Along with the teacher's predictions, information from the teacher's intermediate states (*feature-based knowledge distillation*) such as hidden states (Sun et al., 2019), embeddings (Jiao et al., 2020) and attention distributions (Sun et al., 2020) have been used, an interesting direction that we do not explore in this work.

7 Conclusions

Following model development across all three incremental steps of the examined *pipelined* approach, we make the following observations:

(a) Larger models outperform smaller ones; the performance increase varies across tasks.

(b) Domain-specific models outperform generic ones, although gains are decreased considering much large models.

(c) Fully compressed (pruned, distilled, and quantized) models severely outperform equally sized distilled or fine-tuned models.

To conclude, our guidelines to LegalTech practitioners who aim to build effective, but also efficient models, can be summarized in four general points:

1. Pre-train large-scale domain-specific language models, if possible; in case there are no such models already available.

2. Fine-tune the largest possible model available based on your compute capabilities.

3. Compress the fine-tuned models to derive much smaller models that can efficiently be deployed in production; consider a suitable compression rate to balance the performance / efficiency trade-offs.

4. Follow a full-scale compression pipeline (Vocabulary Pruning, Parameter Pruning, Knowledge Distillation, Graph Optimization and Quantization) for best results.

Broader Impact and Ethics Considerations

In this sections, we would like to discuss the broader impact and ethical considerations with respect to the use of data, privacy issues and environmental considerations.

Use of Data In this work, we considered two sources of open publicly available data. The first source is legislation from EU (Chalkidis et al., 2021b) published by the EU Publication Office,[16] UK (Chalkidis and Søgaard, 2022) published the UK National Archives,[17] and US (Henderson* et al., 2022) published by the U.S. Government Publishing Office.[18] The second source is US contracts (Tuggener et al., 2020; Borchmann et al., 2020) published as exhibits in public filings at SEC-EDGAR.[19] As discussed in Henderson* et al. (2022), the content from these legal sources implicitly encodes privacy and toxicity rules since its content is handled by governments and courts, contrary to generic web material scraped from the web (Dodge et al., 2021).

In another note, many of these sources that we used to pre-train our C-XLM models, overlap with the benchmark datasets we used to evaluate the very same models, e.g., the MultiEURLEX dataset used both for pre-training and evaluation (Sections 3.1 and 4.1). As Krishna et al. (2022) recently showed using downstream datasets make surprisingly good up-stream (pre-training) corpora, if domain specificity and such applications is the goal, in contrast

[16] https://eur-lex.europa.eu/
[17] https://www.legislation.gov.uk/
[18] http://www.gpo.gov/
[19] https://www.sec.gov/edgar/

to heavy generalization across domains and acquirement of common knowledge.[20]

Environmental Considerations Modern large deep learning models are cost intensive financially to train, due to the cost of hardware, electricity - especially in these challenging times-, and cloud compute (Strubell et al., 2019). They are also environmentally expensive due to the operational carbon footprint, i.e., carbon emissions, (Dodge et al., 2022). It has been also demonstrated that the impact of deployment and inference can be equally or more harmful compared to training with regards to carbon emissions (Wu et al., 2022), hence effective counter-measures should be considered to compensate for the financial and environmental cost.

By compressing and accelerating larger models, the carbon footprint of inference can be significantly reduced as we show in Section 5.3; compensating in this way (on the long run) the environmental implications of large-scale training. Furthermore, by decreasing their memory requirements (model size, and architecture complexity), predictive models can be hosted on more environmentally-friendly infrastructure, e.g., moderate-compute cloud servers with low memory and processing power leading to a decreased energy footprint, contrary to high-end energy-intensive GPU-accelerated machines.

Privacy Considerations Privacy concerns are also a critical topic, especially in the legal-tech industry, since prospect users (law firms, companies, and civilians etc.) want to process large quantities of documents, many of which include confidential information (e.g., private contracts). While there are many directions to privacy preserving ML via differential privacy (Abadi et al., 2016; Klymenko et al., 2022) or federated learning (Ryffel et al., 2018), the problem of data leakage is practically unsolved, since the risks of sharing private documents are not considered and the responsibilities are transferred to data and cloud security.

Since highly accurate compressed models are able to be developed (Section 5.1), deployed and run on moderate-compute servers (Section 5.3), such technologies can be deployed on premises as an in-house solution on private clouds; or even run on the client side on server-client web infrastructures, eliminating the need for hosting data remotely or using API calls to remote cloud servers over the web, thus effectively contribute in a safer, more secure (private) AI.

Limitations

Based on our experiments, similarly to the literature, there no is free lunch with respect to model compression, and further compressing models takes a toll on performance. Experimenting with much larger models and examining their performance and potential for compression, following the line of work of Rae et al. (2021); Hoffmann et al. (2022) would be fascinating but we lack resources to built billion-parameter-sized models, while increasing resources would have a larger impact with respect to environmental considerations. Based on the findings of Hoffmann et al. (2022), our models are not under-trained, and exploring larger models would have to be followed by an analogous increase of pre-training data and compute.

Acknowledgments

This research has been co-funded by the European Regional Development Fund of the European Union and Greek national funds through the Operational Program Competitiveness, Entrepreneurship and Innovation, under the call RESEARCH – CREATE – INNOVATE (T2EΔK-03849). This work is also partly funded by the Innovation Fund Denmark (IFD)[21] under File No. 0175-00011A.

This project was also supported by the TensorFlow Research Cloud (TFRC)[22] program that provided instances of Google Cloud TPU v3-8 for free that were used to pre-train all C-XLM language models. Cognitiv+ provided the compute (16× Quadro RTX 6000 24GB) to fine-tune all models.

References

Martin Abadi, Andy Chu, Ian Goodfellow, H. Brendan McMahan, Ilya Mironov, Kunal Talwar, and Li Zhang. 2016. Deep learning with differential privacy. In *Proceedings of the 2016 ACM SIGSAC Conference on Computer and Communications Security*, CCS '16, page 308–318, New York, NY, USA. Association for Computing Machinery.

Emily Alsentzer, John Murphy, William Boag, Wei-Hung Weng, Di Jindi, Tristan Naumann, and Matthew McDermott. 2019. Publicly available clinical BERT embeddings. In *Proceedings of the 2nd Clinical Natural Language Processing Workshop*,

[20] Of course, we always consider fair evaluation practices, i.e., no access to the test subsets of evaluation datasets.

[21] `https://innovationsfonden.dk/en`

[22] `https://sites.research.google/trc/about/`

pages 72–78, Minneapolis, Minnesota, USA. Association for Computational Linguistics.

Jimmy Ba and Rich Caruana. 2014. Do deep nets really need to be deep? In *Advances in Neural Information Processing Systems*, volume 27. Curran Associates, Inc.

Junjie Bai, Fang Lu, Ke Zhang, et al. 2019. Onnx: Open neural network exchange. `https://github.com/onnx/onnx`.

Iz Beltagy, Kyle Lo, and Arman Cohan. 2019. SciBERT: A pretrained language model for scientific text. In *Proceedings of the 2019 Conference on Empirical Methods in Natural Language Processing and the 9th International Joint Conference on Natural Language Processing (EMNLP-IJCNLP)*, pages 3615–3620, Hong Kong, China. Association for Computational Linguistics.

Aishwarya Bhandare, Vamsi Sripathi, Deepthi Karkada, Vivek Menon, Sun Choi, Kushal Datta, and Vikram Saletore. 2019. Efficient 8-bit quantization of transformer neural machine language translation model. *arXiv preprint arXiv:1906.00532*.

Yelysei Bondarenko, Markus Nagel, and Tijmen Blankevoort. 2021. Understanding and overcoming the challenges of efficient transformer quantization. In *Proceedings of the 2021 Conference on Empirical Methods in Natural Language Processing*, pages 7947–7969, Online and Punta Cana, Dominican Republic. Association for Computational Linguistics.

Łukasz Borchmann, Dawid Wisniewski, Andrzej Gretkowski, Izabela Kosmala, Dawid Jurkiewicz, Łukasz Szałkiewicz, Gabriela Pałka, Karol Kaczmarek, Agnieszka Kaliska, and Filip Graliński. 2020. Contract discovery: Dataset and a few-shot semantic retrieval challenge with competitive baselines. In *Findings of the Association for Computational Linguistics: EMNLP 2020*, pages 4254–4268, Online. Association for Computational Linguistics.

Tom Brown, Benjamin Mann, Nick Ryder, Melanie Subbiah, Jared D Kaplan, Prafulla Dhariwal, Arvind Neelakantan, Pranav Shyam, Girish Sastry, Amanda Askell, Sandhini Agarwal, Ariel Herbert-Voss, Gretchen Krueger, Tom Henighan, Rewon Child, Aditya Ramesh, Daniel Ziegler, Jeffrey Wu, Clemens Winter, Chris Hesse, Mark Chen, Eric Sigler, Mateusz Litwin, Scott Gray, Benjamin Chess, Jack Clark, Christopher Berner, Sam McCandlish, Alec Radford, Ilya Sutskever, and Dario Amodei. 2020. Language models are few-shot learners. In *Advances in Neural Information Processing Systems*, volume 33, pages 1877–1901. Curran Associates, Inc.

Ilias Chalkidis, Ion Androutsopoulos, and Achilleas Michos. 2017. Extracting contract elements. In *Proceedings of the 16th Edition of the International Conference on Articial Intelligence and Law*, ICAIL '17, page 19–28, New York, NY, USA. Association for Computing Machinery.

Ilias Chalkidis, Ion Androutsopoulos, and Achilleas Michos. 2018. Obligation and prohibition extraction using hierarchical RNNs. In *Proceedings of the 56th Annual Meeting of the Association for Computational Linguistics (Volume 2: Short Papers)*, pages 254–259, Melbourne, Australia. Association for Computational Linguistics.

Ilias Chalkidis, Manos Fergadiotis, and Ion Androutsopoulos. 2021a. MultiEURLEX - a multi-lingual and multi-label legal document classification dataset for zero-shot cross-lingual transfer. In *Proceedings of the 2021 Conference on Empirical Methods in Natural Language Processing (EMNLP)*, Online.

Ilias Chalkidis, Manos Fergadiotis, and Ion Androutsopoulos. 2021b. MultiEURLEX - a multi-lingual and multi-label legal document classification dataset for zero-shot cross-lingual transfer. In *Proceedings of the 2021 Conference on Empirical Methods in Natural Language Processing*, pages 6974–6996, Online and Punta Cana, Dominican Republic. Association for Computational Linguistics.

Ilias Chalkidis, Manos Fergadiotis, Prodromos Malakasiotis, Nikolaos Aletras, and Ion Androutsopoulos. 2020. LEGAL-BERT: The muppets straight out of law school. In *Findings of the Association for Computational Linguistics: EMNLP 2020*, pages 2898–2904, Online.

Ilias Chalkidis, Abhik Jana, Dirk Hartung, Michael Bommarito, Ion Androutsopoulos, Daniel Katz, and Nikolaos Aletras. 2022. LexGLUE: A benchmark dataset for legal language understanding in English. In *Proceedings of the 60th Annual Meeting of the Association for Computational Linguistics (Volume 1: Long Papers)*, pages 4310–4330, Dublin, Ireland. Association for Computational Linguistics.

Ilias Chalkidis and Anders Søgaard. 2022. Improved multi-label classification under temporal concept drift: Rethinking group-robust algorithms in a label-wise setting. In *Findings of the Association for Computational Linguistics: ACL 2022*, pages 2441–2454, Dublin, Ireland. Association for Computational Linguistics.

Alexis Conneau, Kartikay Khandelwal, Naman Goyal, Vishrav Chaudhary, Guillaume Wenzek, Francisco Guzmán, Edouard Grave, Myle Ott, Luke Zettlemoyer, and Veselin Stoyanov. 2020. Unsupervised cross-lingual representation learning at scale. In *Proceedings of the 58th Annual Meeting of the Association for Computational Linguistics*, pages 8440–8451, Online. Association for Computational Linguistics.

Alexis Conneau and Guillaume Lample. 2019. Cross-lingual language model pretraining. In *Advances in Neural Information Processing Systems*, volume 32. Curran Associates, Inc.

Jacob Devlin, Ming-Wei Chang, Kenton Lee, and Kristina Toutanova. 2019. BERT: Pre-training of deep bidirectional transformers for language understanding. In *Proceedings of the 2019 Conference of the North American Chapter of the Association for Computational Linguistics: Human Language Technologies, Volume 1 (Long and Short Papers)*, pages 4171–4186, Minneapolis, Minnesota. Association for Computational Linguistics.

Jesse Dodge, Taylor Prewitt, Remi Tachet des Combes, Erika Odmark, Roy Schwartz, Emma Strubell, Alexandra Sasha Luccioni, Noah A. Smith, Nicole DeCario, and Will Buchanan. 2022. Measuring the carbon intensity of ai in cloud instances. In *2022 ACM Conference on Fairness, Accountability, and Transparency*, FAccT '22, page 1877–1894, New York, NY, USA. Association for Computing Machinery.

Jesse Dodge, Maarten Sap, Ana Marasović, William Agnew, Gabriel Ilharco, Dirk Groeneveld, Margaret Mitchell, and Matt Gardner. 2021. Documenting large webtext corpora: A case study on the colossal clean crawled corpus. In *Proceedings of the 2021 Conference on Empirical Methods in Natural Language Processing*, pages 1286–1305, Online and Punta Cana, Dominican Republic. Association for Computational Linguistics.

Kasper Drawzeski, Andrea Galassi, Agnieszka Jablonowska, Francesca Lagioia, Marco Lippi, Hans Wolfgang Micklitz, Giovanni Sartor, Giacomo Tagiuri, and Paolo Torroni. 2021. A corpus for multilingual analysis of online terms of service. In *Proceedings of the Natural Legal Language Processing Workshop 2021*, pages 1–8, Punta Cana, Dominican Republic. Association for Computational Linguistics.

Angela Fan, Pierre Stock, Benjamin Graham, Edouard Grave, Rémi Gribonval, Herve Jegou, and Armand Joulin. 2020. Training with quantization noise for extreme model compression. *arXiv preprint arXiv:2004.07320*.

Ivan Habernal, Daniel Faber, Nicola Recchia, Sebastian Bretthauer, Iryna Gurevych, Indra Spiecker genannt Döhmann, and Christoph Burchard. 2022. Mining Legal Arguments in Court Decisions. *arXiv preprint*.

Song Han, Jeff Pool, John Tran, and William Dally. 2015. Learning both weights and connections for efficient neural network. In *Advances in Neural Information Processing Systems*, volume 28. Curran Associates, Inc.

Peter Henderson*, Mark S. Krass*, Lucia Zheng, Neel Guha, Christopher D. Manning, Dan Jurafsky, and Daniel E. Ho. 2022. Pile of law: Learning responsible data filtering from the law and a 256gb opensource legal dataset.

Geoffrey Hinton, Oriol Vinyals, and Jeffrey Dean. 2015. Distilling the knowledge in a neural network. In *NIPS Deep Learning and Representation Learning Workshop*.

Jordan Hoffmann, Sebastian Borgeaud, Arthur Mensch, Elena Buchatskaya, Trevor Cai, Eliza Rutherford, Diego de Las Casas, Lisa Anne Hendricks, Johannes Welbl, Aidan Clark, Tom Hennigan, Eric Noland, Katie Millican, George van den Driessche, Bogdan Damoc, Aurelia Guy, Simon Osindero, Karen Simonyan, Erich Elsen, Jack W. Rae, Oriol Vinyals, and Laurent Sifre. 2022. Training compute-optimal large language models.

Xiaoqi Jiao, Yichun Yin, Lifeng Shang, Xin Jiang, Xiao Chen, Linlin Li, Fang Wang, and Qun Liu. 2020. TinyBERT: Distilling BERT for natural language understanding. In *Findings of the Association for Computational Linguistics: EMNLP 2020*, pages 4163–4174, Online. Association for Computational Linguistics.

Marcin Junczys-Dowmunt, Kenneth Heafield, Hieu Hoang, Roman Grundkiewicz, and Anthony Aue. 2018. Marian: Cost-effective high-quality neural machine translation in c++. In *Proceedings of the 2nd Workshop on Neural Machine Translation and Generation*, pages 129–135.

Oleksandra Klymenko, Stephen Meisenbacher, and Florian Matthes. 2022. Differential privacy in natural language processing the story so far. In *Proceedings of the Fourth Workshop on Privacy in Natural Language Processing*, pages 1–11, Seattle, United States. Association for Computational Linguistics.

Yuta Koreeda and Christopher Manning. 2021. ContractNLI: A dataset for document-level natural language inference for contracts. In *Findings of the Association for Computational Linguistics: EMNLP 2021*, pages 1907–1919, Punta Cana, Dominican Republic. Association for Computational Linguistics.

Kundan Krishna, Saurabh Garg, Jeffrey P. Bigham, and Zachary C. Lipton. 2022. Downstream datasets make surprisingly good pretraining corpora.

François Lagunas, Ella Charlaix, Victor Sanh, and Alexander Rush. 2021. Block pruning for faster transformers. In *Proceedings of the 2021 Conference on Empirical Methods in Natural Language Processing*, pages 10619–10629, Online and Punta Cana, Dominican Republic. Association for Computational Linguistics.

Jinhyuk Lee, Wonjin Yoon, Sungdong Kim, Donghyeon Kim, Sunkyu Kim, Chan Ho So, and Jaewoo Kang. 2019. BioBERT: a pre-trained biomedical language representation model for biomedical text mining. *Bioinformatics*.

Mingzhen Li, Yi Liu, Xiaoyan Liu, Qingxiao Sun, Xin You, Hailong Yang, Zhongzhi Luan, Lin Gan, Guangwen Yang, and Depei Qian. 2021. The deep learning compiler: A comprehensive survey. *IEEE Transactions on Parallel and Distributed Systems*, 32(3):708–727.

Yinhan Liu, Myle Ott, Naman Goyal, Jingfei Du, Mandar Joshi, Danqi Chen, Omer Levy, Mike Lewis, Luke Zettlemoyer, and Veselin Stoyanov. 2019. Roberta: A robustly optimized bert pretraining approach. *arXiv preprint arXiv:1907.11692*.

Christos Louizos, Max Welling, and Diederik P. Kingma. 2018. Learning sparse neural networks through l0 regularization. In *International Conference on Learning Representations*.

Lefteris Loukas, Manos Fergadiotis, Ilias Chalkidis, Eirini Spyropoulou, Prodromos Malakasiotis, Ion Androutsopoulos, and Georgios Paliouras. 2022. FiNER: Financial numeric entity recognition for XBRL tagging. In *Proceedings of the 60th Annual Meeting of the Association for Computational Linguistics (Volume 1: Long Papers)*, pages 4419–4431, Dublin, Ireland. Association for Computational Linguistics.

JS McCarley, Rishav Chakravarti, and Avirup Sil. 2019. Structured pruning of a bert-based question answering model. *arXiv preprint arXiv:1910.06360*.

Paul Michel, Omer Levy, and Graham Neubig. 2019. Are sixteen heads really better than one? In *Advances in Neural Information Processing Systems*, volume 32. Curran Associates, Inc.

Seyed Iman Mirzadeh, Mehrdad Farajtabar, Ang Li, Nir Levine, Akihiro Matsukawa, and Hassan Ghasemzadeh. 2020. Improved knowledge distillation via teacher assistant. *Proceedings of the AAAI Conference on Artificial Intelligence*, 34(04):5191–5198.

Sai Prasanna, Anna Rogers, and Anna Rumshisky. 2020. When BERT Plays the Lottery, All Tickets Are Winning. In *Proceedings of the 2020 Conference on Empirical Methods in Natural Language Processing (EMNLP)*, pages 3208–3229, Online. Association for Computational Linguistics.

Alec Radford and Karthik Narasimhan. 2018. Improving language understanding by generative pretraining.

Jack W. Rae, Sebastian Borgeaud, Trevor Cai, Katie Millican, Jordan Hoffmann, H. Francis Song, John Aslanides, Sarah Henderson, Roman Ring, Susannah Young, Eliza Rutherford, Tom Hennigan, Jacob Menick, Albin Cassirer, Richard Powell, George van den Driessche, Lisa Anne Hendricks, Maribeth Rauh, Po-Sen Huang, Amelia Glaese, Johannes Welbl, Sumanth Dathathri, Saffron Huang, Jonathan Uesato, John Mellor, Irina Higgins, Antonia Creswell, Nat McAleese, Amy Wu, Erich Elsen, Siddhant M. Jayakumar, Elena Buchatskaya, David Budden, Esme Sutherland, Karen Simonyan, Michela Paganini, Laurent Sifre, Lena Martens, Xiang Lorraine Li, Adhiguna Kuncoro, Aida Nematzadeh, Elena Gribovskaya, Domenic Donato, Angeliki Lazaridou, Arthur Mensch, Jean-Baptiste Lespiau, Maria Tsimpoukelli, Nikolai Grigorev, Doug Fritz, Thibault Sottiaux, Mantas Pajarskas, Toby Pohlen, Zhitao Gong, Daniel Toyama, Cyprien de Masson d'Autume, Yujia Li, Tayfun Terzi, Vladimir Mikulik, Igor Babuschkin, Aidan Clark, Diego de Las Casas, Aurelia Guy, Chris Jones, James Bradbury, Matthew Johnson, Blake A. Hechtman, Laura Weidinger, Iason Gabriel, William S. Isaac, Edward Lockhart, Simon Osindero, Laura Rimell, Chris Dyer, Oriol Vinyals, Kareem Ayoub, Jeff Stanway, Lorrayne Bennett, Demis Hassabis, Koray Kavukcuoglu, and Geoffrey Irving. 2021. Scaling language models: Methods, analysis & insights from training gopher. *CoRR*, abs/2112.11446.

Théo Ryffel, Andrew Trask, Morten Dahl, Bobby Wagner, Jason Mancuso, Daniel Rueckert, and Jonathan Passerat-Palmbach. 2018. A generic framework for privacy preserving deep learning. *CoRR*, abs/1811.04017.

Victor Sanh, Thomas Wolf, and Alexander Rush. 2020. Movement pruning: Adaptive sparsity by finetuning. In *Advances in Neural Information Processing Systems*, volume 33, pages 20378–20389. Curran Associates, Inc.

Rico Sennrich, Barry Haddow, and Alexandra Birch. 2016. Neural machine translation of rare words with subword units. In *Proceedings of the 54th Annual Meeting of the Association for Computational Linguistics (Volume 1: Long Papers)*, pages 1715–1725, Berlin, Germany. Association for Computational Linguistics.

Emma Strubell, Ananya Ganesh, and Andrew McCallum. 2019. Energy and policy considerations for deep learning in NLP. In *Proceedings of the 57th Annual Meeting of the Association for Computational Linguistics*, pages 3645–3650, Florence, Italy. Association for Computational Linguistics.

Siqi Sun, Yu Cheng, Zhe Gan, and Jingjing Liu. 2019. Patient knowledge distillation for BERT model compression. In *Proceedings of the 2019 Conference on Empirical Methods in Natural Language Processing and the 9th International Joint Conference on Natural Language Processing (EMNLP-IJCNLP)*, pages 4323–4332, Hong Kong, China. Association for Computational Linguistics.

Zhiqing Sun, Hongkun Yu, Xiaodan Song, Renjie Liu, Yiming Yang, and Denny Zhou. 2020. MobileBERT: a compact task-agnostic BERT for resource-limited devices. In *Proceedings of the 58th Annual Meeting of the Association for Computational Linguistics*, pages 2158–2170, Online. Association for Computational Linguistics.

Chul Sung, Tejas Dhamecha, Swarnadeep Saha, Tengfei Ma, Vinay Reddy, and Rishi Arora. 2019. Pre-training BERT on domain resources for short answer grading. In *Proceedings of the 2019 Conference on Empirical Methods in Natural Language*

Processing and the 9th International Joint Conference on Natural Language Processing (EMNLP-IJCNLP), pages 6071–6075, Hong Kong, China. Association for Computational Linguistics.

Don Tuggener, Pius von Däniken, Thomas Peetz, and Mark Cieliebak. 2020. LEDGAR: A large-scale multi-label corpus for text classification of legal provisions in contracts. In *Proceedings of the 12th Language Resources and Evaluation Conference*, pages 1235–1241, Marseille, France. European Language Resources Association.

Iulia Turc, Ming-Wei Chang, Kenton Lee, and Kristina Toutanova. 2019. Well-read students learn better: The impact of student initialization on knowledge distillation. *CoRR*, abs/1908.08962.

Nicolas Vasilache, Oleksandr Zinenko, Theodoros Theodoridis, Priya Goyal, Zachary DeVito, William S. Moses, Sven Verdoolaege, Andrew Adams, and Albert Cohen. 2018. Tensor comprehensions: Framework-agnostic high-performance machine learning abstractions.

Elena Voita, David Talbot, Fedor Moiseev, Rico Sennrich, and Ivan Titov. 2019. Analyzing multi-head self-attention: Specialized heads do the heavy lifting, the rest can be pruned. In *Proceedings of the 57th Annual Meeting of the Association for Computational Linguistics*, pages 5797–5808, Florence, Italy. Association for Computational Linguistics.

Alex Wang, Yada Pruksachatkun, Nikita Nangia, Amanpreet Singh, Julian Michael, Felix Hill, Omer Levy, and Samuel Bowman. 2019a. Superglue: A stickier benchmark for general-purpose language understanding systems. In *Advances in Neural Information Processing Systems*, volume 32. Curran Associates, Inc.

Alex Wang, Amanpreet Singh, Julian Michael, Felix Hill, Omer Levy, and Samuel R. Bowman. 2019b. GLUE: A multi-task benchmark and analysis platform for natural language understanding. In *International Conference on Learning Representations*, New Orleans, Louisiana, USA.

Carole-Jean Wu, Ramya Raghavendra, Udit Gupta, Bilge Acun, Newsha Ardalani, Kiwan Maeng, Gloria Chang, Fiona Aga, Jinshi Huang, Charles Bai, Michael Gschwind, Anurag Gupta, Myle Ott, Anastasia Melnikov, Salvatore Candido, David Brooks, Geeta Chauhan, Benjamin Lee, Hsien-Hsin Lee, Bugra Akyildiz, Maximilian Balandat, Joe Spisak, Ravi Jain, Mike Rabbat, and Kim Hazelwood. 2022. Sustainable ai: Environmental implications, challenges and opportunities. In *Proceedings of Machine Learning and Systems*, volume 4, pages 795–813.

Stratos Xenouleas, Alexia Tsoukara, Giannis Panagiotakis, Ilias Chalkidis, and Ion Androutsopoulos. 2022. Realistic zero-shot cross-lingual transfer in legal topic classification. In *Proceedings of the 12th EETN Conference on Artificial Intelligence (SETN 2022)*.

Ziqing Yang, Yiming Cui, and Zhigang Chen. 2022. TextPruner: A model pruning toolkit for pre-trained language models. In *Proceedings of the 60th Annual Meeting of the Association for Computational Linguistics: System Demonstrations*, pages 35–43, Dublin, Ireland. Association for Computational Linguistics.

Ofir Zafrir, Guy Boudoukh, Peter Izsak, and Moshe Wasserblat. 2019. Q8bert: Quantized 8bit bert. In *2019 Fifth Workshop on Energy Efficient Machine Learning and Cognitive Computing-NeurIPS Edition (EMC2-NIPS)*, pages 36–39. IEEE.

Lucia Zheng, Neel Guha, Brandon R. Anderson, Peter Henderson, and Daniel E. Ho. 2021. When does pretraining help?: assessing self-supervised learning for law and the casehold dataset of 53,000+ legal holdings. *Proceedings of the Eighteenth International Conference on Artificial Intelligence and Law*.

Michael Zhu and Suyog Gupta. 2017. To prune, or not to prune: exploring the efficacy of pruning for model compression. Technical report, Google.

A Experimentail Details

Devlin et al. (2019) suggested a hyperparameter tuning, that was adopted in many papers (Lee et al., 2019; Beltagy et al., 2019; Alsentzer et al., 2019; Sung et al., 2019). This hyper-parameter tuning included a light grid search in learning rate ∈ {2e-5, 3e-5, 4e-5, 5e-5}, the number of training epochs ∈ {3, 4}, and the batch size ∈ {16, 32} with a fixed dropout rate of 0.1. In our research, we tune each variation of our model based on a grid-search of learning rate on the following range ∈ {1e-4, 3e-4, 1e-5, 3e-5, 5e-5, 1e-6}. The batch size is fixed to 16, and the dropout rate at 0.1. The max sequence length is fixed to 512 for MultiEURLEX and ContractNLI, 256 for ContractNER and 128 for Contract-Obligations and UNFAIR-ToS based on the training subset statistics. Lastly, Chalkidis et al. (2020) found that some models may underfit for 4 epochs. Hence, following their work, we use early stopping based on validation loss up to 20 maximum train epochs with a patience of 3 epochs.

In every incremental step of GC where knowledge distillation is applied, learning rate, temperature and *a* (the original and distillation loss weighing) are tuned using grid search. in the hyper-parameter spaces of [1e-5, 3e-5, 5-e5, 7e-5, 1e-4], [1, 5, 10, 15] and [0.1, 0.3, 0.6], respectively.

Corpus	Tokens per Language										
	EN	EL	DE	FR	ES	IT	NL	PL	PT	RU	All
Contracts	125.3M	111.1M	103.3M	121.7M	122.5M	113.4M	110.7M	89.8M	111.3M	89.6M	1.1B
Regulations	178.7M	71.4M	62.8M	74.0M	77.1M	70.1M	71.2M	31.9M	71.5M	-	708.7M
All	304M	182.5M	166.1M	195.7M	199.6M	183.5M	181.9M	121.7M	182.8M	89.6M	1.8B

Table 5: Total tokens used per language per pre-training corpus.

Model	CNLI		Obligations		ContractNER	
	μ-F_1	m-F_1	μ-F_1	m-F_1	μ-F_1	m-F_1
Baselines						
C-XLM Base (Ceiling Baseline)	84.0	82.1	91.2	90.4	92.9	93.8
C-XLM Tiny (Bottom Baseline)	70.2	69.2	88.7	87.4	87.2	89.3
S1: Vocab Pruning						
S1.1: Prune vocabulary at random	79.4	77.2	88.7	87.6	88.5	83.2
S1.2: Prune vocabulary based on training data	**84.8**	**82.9**	**91.7**	**90.6**	**93.2**	**94.1**
Input Model: S1.2 –> S2: Pruning Depth (Layers) + KD						
S2.1: Prune layers at random	79.4	77.1	87.6	87.6	88.7	90.3
S2.2: Prune last N layers	80.6	78.8	**92.1**	**91.2**	**88.8**	**91.2**
S2.3: Prune first N layers	77.8	76.4	90.8	89.2	78.9	83.6
S2.4: Prune every second layer	**81.0**	**79.6**	89.9	88.5	88.6	89.4
S2.5: Prune layers with mimimum pair-wise distance	75.6	72.6	91.5	90.5	85.6	87.3
Input Model: S2.2 –> S3: Pruning Width (Heads + FF) + KD						
S3.1: Prune heads and FF at random	77.9	75.8	90.6	89.3	82.6	87.1
S3.2: Prune heads and FF based on the exp. sensitivity(L)	**78.0**	**76.1**	**91.6**	**90.7**	**89.5**	**92.3**

Table 6: Preliminiary Experiments to determine which settings produce the most consistent results.

B Additional Results

B.1 Additional Pre-training Results

This section provides additional results regarding the pre-training process. Table 5 displays the number of tokens that were included in contracts and regulations for each language. It should be noted that during the pre-training, 100% of regulations and 20% of translated contracts (100% of English contracts used) were used. Finally, Table 15 presents the evaluation loss and accuracy scores of the pre-training of the masked language models. This table provides the overall scores, along with scores for each document type, language and document type/language.

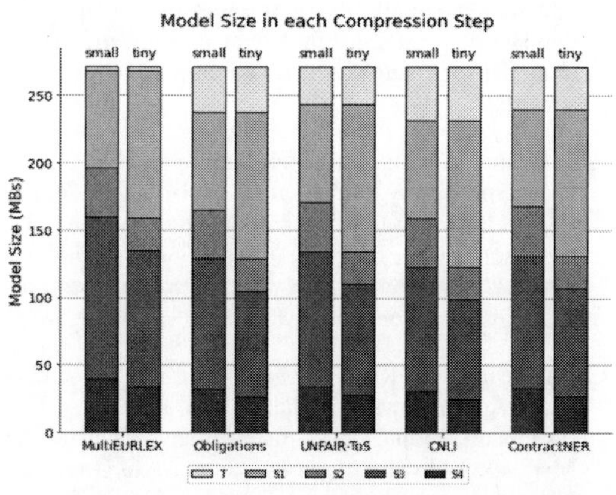

Figure 5: Model size (MB) in each compression step (S) in relevance to the original model, C-XLM (large).

B.2 Model Compression Preliminary Experiments

Before each model was compressed, some preliminary experiments were conducted to determine which setting in each compression step produces the most consistent results.

For the first step (Vocabulary Reduction), our proposed method, where the model's vocabulary is pruned based on information from the training data and the tokenizer's merges, was compared with a random baseline, i.e., the vocabulary is randomly pruned. In both settings, the exact same percentage of tokens were kept, and as expected, the random baseline led to performance deterioration.

Task	Reduction of Tokens	Removed Params (C-XLM Large)	Removed Params (C-XLM Base)
MultiEURLEX	2.52%	1,653,760	826,880
Obligations	26.98%	17,679,360	8,839,680
UNFAIR-ToS	22.54%	14,774,272	7,387,136
ContractNLI	31.83%	20,858,880	10,429,440
ContractNER	24.17%	15,839,232	7,919,616

Table 7: Percentage of usable tokens and parameter reduction after vocabulary pruning for each task.

Model	MultiEURLEX	UNFAIR-ToS	CNLI	Obligations	ContractNER
XLM-R (Base)	1e-5	3e-5	1e-5	1e-5	5e-5
XLM-R (Large)	3e-5	1e-5	1e-5	1e-6	5e-5
C-XLM (Tiny)	1e-4	3e-4	1e-4	1e-4	1e-4
C-XLM (Small)	1e-4	5e-5	1e-4	5e-5	5e-5
C-XLM (Base)	5e-5	3e-5	5e-5	3e-5	3e-5
C-XLM (Large)	5e-5	5e-5	3e-5	1e-5	5e-5

Table 8: Optimal Learning Rates per downstream task across all models.

For the second step (Depth Pruning), 9 out of the 12 transformer blocks of the base (language) model were removed and the pruned model was trained using knowledge distillation. Five different settings were tested. Encoder blocks were pruned by: (i) pruning blocks at random, (ii) pruning the last 9 blocks, (iii) pruning the first 9 blocks, (iv) pruning every second block, and (v) pruning blocks with the minimum pair-wise distance. For setting (v), the mean absolute error and the cosine similarity of the CLS tokens of each encoder block were used as the metrics (except for the ContractNER task, were the average of all tokens was used instead of the CLS one). We found that among all settings, copying the weights of the first encoder blocks of the original pre-trained language model produced the most consistent results.

For the third step (Width Pruning), the model of the second setting from the second step was pruned down to 12 attention heads (in total) and 512 neurons in the intermediate fully-connected layers. Two settings were examined: random pruning and pruning based on the expected loss when each attention head/neuron was iteratively removed (Michel et al., 2019; Prasanna et al., 2020). Just like in step 1, the random baseline performed worse. Results are summarized in Table 6.

B.3 Additional Fine-tuning Results

This section presents some additional results regarding the fine-tuning process. Table 8 displays the optimal learning rates for each model variation and baseline that were used during the fine-tuning process for every different task. Each one was selected through grid search, between learning rates $\in$ {1e-4, 3e-4, 1e-5, 3e-5, 5e-5, 1e-6}. We observe that smaller models favor larger learning rates, i.e., 1e-4 and 5e-5 in most cases, while larger models favor smaller learning rates, i.e., 1e-5 and 3e-5. Additionally, the upper parts of Tables 12 and 13 present the μ-F_1 and m-F_1 scores of the fine tuned models per language, respectively, for MultiEURLEX task. Lastly, the upper part of Table 14 presents the Mean Absolute Error (MAE) and accuracy scores of the fine-tuned models, for UNFAIR-ToS task per language.

B.4 Additional Compression Results

In this section, some additional experimental results are presented. First, the percentage of usable tokens and the parameter reduction of both large and base models from the vocabulary pruning step for each task can be found in Table 7. In Table 11, the model size (in MBs) and the average inference time (in seconds) of a 32-batch (on CPU) across all incremental compression steps and baselines are presented. Inference benchmarking was conducted using a modern mid-range RYZEN

7 4700U. In Table 10, model compression results can be found, across all down-stream task, when the Base C-XLM is used as a teacher. Lastly, Tables 12, 13 and 14 summarize the μ-F_1, m-F_1 of MultiEURLEX and results of UNFAIR-ToS tasks, across all languages for each incremental compression step and baselines.

Model	MultiEURLEX		UNFAIR-ToS		CNLI		Obligations		ContractNER	
	μ-F_1	m-F_1	Acc.	MAE	μ-F_1	m-F_1	μ-F_1	m-F_1	μ-F_1	m-F_1
Top Bound - Performance "Ceiling"										
C-XLM (large)	78.4	65.4	89.7	0.14	85.3	83.0	91.8	90.6	93.2	94.6
Step 0 (TA-KD)	75.2	63.0	88.6	0.16	84.6	82.2	92.8	91.8	93.7	94.9
Gradual Compression — Reference C-XLM (small)										
Step 1 (VP+KD)	75.1	62.9	88.5	0.18	84.9	82.9	92.8	91.8	93.6	94.9
Step 2 (DP+KD)	74.4	54.3	83.5	0.22	84.0	81.8	92.6	91.6	92.4	93.2
Step 3 (WP+KD)	73.8	60.8	83.5	0.21	84.5	83.0	92.3	91.4	92.1	93.2
Step 4 (GO+Q)	**74.2**	**60.4**	83.7	0.21	**84.5**	**83.1**	**92.2**	**91.3**	**92.2**	**93.3**
C-XLM (small) (FT)	72.3	54.7	**85.4**	**0.20**	79.7	77.0	90.4	89.0	90.1	92.4
C-XLM (small) (KD)	73.3	54.7	81.1	0.25	80.2	78.1	90.1	89.1	91.0	93.1
Gradual Compression — Reference C-XLM (tiny)										
Step 1 (VP+KD)	75.1	62.9	88.5	0.18	84.9	82.9	92.8	91.8	93.6	94.9
Step 2 (DP+KD)	72.6	58.2	80.6	0.24	80.9	79.3	91.1	90.0	89.7	92.1
Step 3 (WP+KD)	72.5	58.0	79.9	0.25	80.9	79.4	91.6	90.5	87.6	90.4
Step 4 (GO+Q)	**73.2**	**57.0**	**79.6**	**0.25**	**80.7**	**79.2**	**91.9**	**90.7**	87.6	**90.2**
C-XLM (tiny) (FT)	66.5	46.1	78.2	0.27	70.2	69.2	88.7	87.4	87.2	89.3
C-XLM (tiny) (VP+KD)	64.0	42.0	76.7	0.30	75.3	74.3	89.1	88.1	**87.7**	90.1

Table 9: Model compression results across down-stream tasks. We report the model's performance across the incremental compression steps (S) presented in Section 5.1. We also report the performance for two baselines: (a) fine-tuning the reference pre-trained C-XLM model (FT), and (b) Knowledge Distillation and Vocabulary Pruning. where the student is the reference pre-trained C-XLM (KD).

Model	MultiEURLEX		UNFAIR-ToS		CNLI		Obligations		ContractNER	
	μ-F_1	m-F_1	Acc.	MAE	μ-F_1	m-F_1	μ-F_1	m-F_1	μ-F_1	m-F_1
Top Bound - Performance "Ceiling"										
C-XLM (Base)	75.3	59.4	87.3	0.18	84.0	82.1	91.2	90.4	92.9	93.8
Gradual Compression — Reference C-XLM (small)										
Step 1 (VP+KD)	74.9	60.3	88.2	0.17	84.8	82.9	91.7	90.6	93.2	94.1
Step 2 (DP+KD)	74.4	59.3	82.7	0.23	84.2	82.4	91.3	90.2	91.6	91.7
Step 3 (WP+KD)	73.8	61.5	83.2	0.23	84.8	83.7	92.8	91.5	92.7	94.1
Step 4 (GO+Q)	**73.7**	**61.7**	83.2	0.23	**84.5**	**83.1**	**92.7**	**91.4**	**92.7**	**93.7**
C-XLM (small) (FT)	69.9	51.7	**85.4**	**0.20**	79.7	77.0	90.4	89.0	90.1	92.4
C-XLM (small) (KD)	72.3	54.7	82.7	0.23	80.0	78.4	90.3	89	92.0	92.4
Gradual Compression — Reference C-XLM (tiny)										
Step 1 (VP+KD)	74.9	60.3	88.2	0.17	84.8	82.9	91.7	90.6	93.2	94.1
Step 2 (DP+KD)	71.2	55.7	81.8	0.22	79.1	77.0	92.1	91.2	89.0	90.6
Step 3 (WP+KD)	70.6	55.8	80.8	0.24	78.0	76.1	91.6	90.7	89.8	92.5
Step 4 (GO+Q)	**70.4**	**54.4**	**80.8**	**0.24**	**78.5**	**76.8**	**91.6**	**90.7**	**89.5**	**92.3**
C-XLM (tiny) (FT)	66.5	46.1	78.2	0.27	70.2	69.2	88.7	87.4	87.2	89.3
C-XLM (tiny) (KD)	66.3	45.3	75.3	0.31	74.6	72.2	86.8	85.6	87.7	89.9

Table 10: Model compression results across down-stream tasks when Base C-XLM is used as a teacher. We report the model's performance across the incremental compression steps (S) presented in Section 5.1. We also report the performance for two baselines: (a) fine-tuning the reference pre-trained C-XLM model (FT), and (b) Knowledge Distillation and Vocabulary Pruning. where the student is the reference pre-trained C-XLM (KD).

Model	MultiEURLEX		UNFAIR-ToS		CNLI		Obligations		ContractNER	
	Size	Time	Size	Time	Size	Time	Size	Time	Size	Time
Top Bound - Performance "Ceiling"										
C-XLM (large)	1,409	99.3	1,409	21.5	1,409	116.0	1,409	21.3	1409	45.6
Gradual Compression — Reference C-XLM (tiny)										
Step 1 (VP+KD)	268	16.1	243	3.6	232	20.2	238	3.3	240	7.4
Step 2 (DP+KD)	159	4.1	134	0.8	123	4.1	129	0.8	131	1.8
Step 3 (WP+KD)	135	1.8	110	0.4	99	1.8	105	0.3	107	0.8
Step 4 (GO+Q)	**34**	**0.8**	**28**	**0.1**	**25**	**0.8**	**26**	**0.1**	**27**	**0.3**
C-XLM (tiny) (FT)	35	1.3	35	0.2	35	2.0	35	0.2	35	0.5
C-XLM (tiny) (KD)	**34**	1.3	**28**	0.2	**25**	1.3	**26**	0.2	**27**	0.5
Gradual Compression — Reference C-XLM (small)										
Step 1 (VP+KD)	268	16.1	243	3.6	232	20.2	238	3.3	240	7.4
Step 2 (DP+KD)	196	8.3	171	1.8	159	8.3	165	1.6	168	3.5
Step 3 (WP+KD)	160	4.4	110	0.9	123	4.4	129	0.9	131	1.9
Step 4 (GO+Q)	**40**	**1.8**	**34**	**0.3**	**31**	**1.8**	**32**	**0.3**	**33**	**0.7**
C-XLM (small) (FT)	81	3.2	81	0.6	81	4.1	81	0.5	81	1.4
C-XLM (small) (KD)	80	3.2	67	0.6	61	3.2	65	0.5	66	1.3

Table 11: Model compression results across down-stream tasks. We report the model's size in MBs and average inference time, in seconds, of a 32-batch across the incremental compression steps (S) presented in Section 5.1. We also report the performance for two baselines: (a) fine-tuning the reference pre-trained C-XLM model (FT), and (b) Knowledge Distillation and Vocabulary Pruning. where the student is the reference pre-trained C-XLM (KD).

Model	MultiEURLEX per Language μ-F_1									
	EN	FR	DE	NL	IT	ES	PT	PL	EL	μ-F_1
Fine-tuned Models										
XLM-R (large)	80.6	78.8	76.1	76.1	78.5	80.1	75.7	75.8	78.7	77.8
XLM-R (base)	77.6	76.9	73.7	74.3	76.3	75.0	75.7	73.2	75.6	75.3
C-XLM (large)	80.5	77.7	76.4	76.8	77.4	79.7	78.3	76.9	82.0	78.4
C-XLM (base)	77.5	76.4	72.3	74.1	75.6	77.4	75.0	72.9	76.5	75.3
C-XLM (small)	69.0	65.7	65.1	62.2	66.4	66.4	66.6	65.3	71.6	72.3
C-XLM (tiny)	69.0	65.7	65.1	62.2	66.4	66.4	66.6	65.3	71.6	66.5
Gradual Compression — Reference C-XLM (tiny)										
Step 1 (VP+KD)	78.0	75.9	74.0	73.1	75.2	78.5	75.4	73.4	72.0	75.1
Step 2 (DP+KD)	75.3	72.3	67.2	71.4	73.9	75.9	73.3	72.3	71.9	72.6
Step 3 (WP+KD)	74.1	70.7	69.2	71.9	74.4	74.2	72.9	71.8	73.1	72.5
Step 4 (GO+Q)	74.2	70.8	70.9	72.8	74.7	74.2	73.7	72.5	73.5	73.2
C-XLM (tiny) (KD)	64.9	63.3	60.8	63.2	66.3	63.1	63.8	65.0	65.7	64.0
Gradual Compression — Reference C-XLM (small)										
Step 1 (VP+KD)	78.0	75.9	74.0	73.1	75.2	78.5	75.4	73.4	2.0	75.1
Step 2 (DP+KD)	76.5	75.6	71.0	71.4	75.9	77.4	75.5	73.0	73.1	74.4
Step 3 (WP+KD)	75.8	75.2	70.4	70.5	74.4	75.6	73.9	74.2	74.7	73.8
Step 4 (GO+Q)	75.9	75.7	71.7	71.4	74.8	76.1	74.1	73.7	75.5	74.2
C-XLM (small) (KD)	74.2	73.2	71.7	72.7	76.4	73.3	75.5	71.6	70.8	73.3

Table 12: Model compression results for the MultiEURLEX task. We report the model's per-language μ-F_1 across the incremental compression steps (S) presented in Section 5.1. We also report the performance for two baselines: (a) fine-tuning the reference pre-trained C-XLM model (FT), and (b) Knowledge Distillation and Vocabulary Pruning. where the student is the reference pre-trained C-XLM (KD).

Model	MultiEURLEX per Language m-F_1									
	EN	FR	DE	NL	IT	ES	PT	PL	EL	m-F_1
Fine-tuned Models										
XLM-R (large)	64.3	67.3	60.3	61.9	58.1	63.6	57.1	60.0	63.5	63.8
XLM-R (base)	56.2	54.7	50.9	53.6	49.5	52.4	52.2	49.8	52.0	53.2
C-XLM (large)	66.8	63.2	63.0	63.9	55.0	67.1	60.6	61.6	70.7	65.4
C-XLM (base)	59.6	58.8	55.1	59.7	54.0	59.1	59.8	57.1	60.3	59.4
C-XLM (small)	55.9	52.7	50.8	55.8	52.6	57.0	55.6	50.8	56.2	54.7
C-XLM (tiny)	50.1	43.7	47.7	42.6	38.3	46.8	47.6	41.9	44.1	46.1
Gradual Compression — Reference C-XLM (tiny)										
Step 1 (VP+KD)	64.3	64.3	60.8	60.8	53.2	66.6	63.3	59.0	56.0	62.9
Step 2 (DP+KD)	58.4	56.9	51.0	55.6	56.4	61.0	55.5	56.2	54.9	58.2
Step 3 (WP+KD)	56.1	62.2	55.5	53.7	53.6	59.7	55.5	54.3	53.9	58.0
Step 4 (GO+Q)	54.8	56.0	54.6	54.2	53.5	58.8	54.0	54.4	51.1	57.0
C-XLM (tiny) (KD)	42.2	41.1	40.9	38.7	41.5	40.9	41.5	41.2	39.4	42.0
Gradual Compression — Reference C-XLM (small)										
Step 1 (VP+KD)	64.3	64.3	60.8	60.8	53.2	66.6	63.3	59.0	56.0	62.9
Step 2 (DP+KD)	58.2	55.8	49.9	56.0	50.2	56.5	53.6	49.8	50.8	54.3
Step 3 (WP+KD)	61.9	60.9	56.2	59.1	53.8	61.8	55.5	61.1	58.4	60.8
Step 4 (GO+Q)	61.5	60.8	57.3	59.8	54.7	61.6	55.4	57.6	58.8	60.4
C-XLM (small) (KD)	56.9	54.3	52.8	56.3	54.3	55.1	55.8	48.6	47.8	54.7

Table 13: Model compression results for the MultiEURLEX task. We report the model's per-language m-F_1 across the incremental compression steps (S) presented in Section 5.1. We also report the performance for two baselines: (a) fine-tuning the reference pre-trained C-XLM model (FT), and (b) Knowledge Distillation and Vocabulary Pruning. where the student is the reference pre-trained C-XLM (KD).

Model	EN MAE	EN μ-F1	PL MAE	PL μ-F1	IT MAE	IT μ-F1	DE MAE	DE μ-F1	Total MAE	Total μ-F1
	UNFAIR-ToS per Language m-F_1									
	Fine-tuned Models									
XLM-R (large)	0.16	89.3	0.19	87.2	0.14	91.2	0.15	88.3	0.16	89.0
XLM-R (base)	0.14	90.3	0.22	81.7	0.15	88.2	0.17	86.4	0.17	86.6
C-XLM (large)	0.13	90.3	0.17	88.1	0.11	92.2	0.15	88.3	0.14	89.7
C-XLM (base)	0.17	87.4	0.22	83.5	0.13	91.2	0.19	87.4	0.18	87.3
C-XLM (small)	0.17	85.4	0.24	80.7	0.16	90.2	0.21	85.4	85.4	0.20
C-XLM (tiny)	0.27	82.5	0.28	76.1	0.24	79.4	0.30	74.8	78.2	0.27
	Gradual Compression — Reference C-XLM (tiny)									
Step 1 (VP+KD)	0.13	92.2	0.21	86.2	0.14	90.2	0.22	85.4	0.18	88.5
Step 2 (DP+KD)	0.23	80.6	0.24	78.0	0.22	84.3	0.27	79.6	0.24	80.6
Step 3 (WP+KD)	0.24	80.6	0.24	80.7	0.23	82.4	0.28	75.7	0.25	79.9
Step 4 (GO+Q)	0.24	80.6	0.24	80.7	0.24	82.4	0.28	75.7	0.25	79.6
C-XLM (tiny) (KD)	0.32	76.7	0.30	75.2	0.30	76.5	0.27	78.6	0.30	76.7
	Gradual Compression — Reference C-XLM (small)									
Step 1 (VP+KD)	0.13	92.2	0.21	86.2	0.14	90.2	0.22	85.4	0.18	88.5
Step 2 (DP+KD)	0.20	83.5	0.25	80.7	0.21	84.3	0.21	85.4	0.22	83.5
Step 3 (WP+KD)	0.20	84.5	0.21	84.4	0.22	81.4	0.21	83.5	0.21	83.5
Step 4 (GO+Q)	0.20	84.5	0.20	84.4	0.22	82.4	0.21	83.5	0.21	83.7
C-XLM (small) (KD)	0.25	81.6	0.28	78.0	0.22	83.3	0.26	81.6	0.25	81.1

Table 14: Model compression m-F_1 for the UNFAIR-ToS task. We report the per-language model's μ-F_1 and MAE across the incremental compression steps (S) presented in Section 5.1. We also report the performance for two baselines: (a) fine-tuning the reference pre-trained C-XLM model (FT), and (b) Knowledge Distillation and Vocabulary Pruning. where the student is the reference pre-trained C-XLM (KD).

Model	C-XLM								XLM-R			
Corpus Subset	Tiny		Small		Base		Large		Base		Large	
	Loss	Acc.	Loss	Acc.	Loss	Acc.	Loss	Acc.	Loss	Acc.	Loss	Acc.
Regulations (EN)	2.46	54.2%	1.62	67.1%	1.11	76.3%	0.97	80.0%	1.36	71.2%	1.07	76.3%
Regulations (EL)	1.89	61.0%	1.24	72.9%	0.85	80.5%	0.74	83.9%	0.93	79.2%	0.68	84.3%
Regulations (DE)	2.52	52.3%	1.60	67.3%	1.02	77.6%	0.84	82.1%	1.20	74.2%	0.89	80.0%
Regulations (FR)	1.84	62.3%	1.16	74.8%	0.75	82.8%	0.65	86.0%	1.01	77.8%	0.77	82.5%
Regulations (ES)	2.01	59.7%	1.31	72.1%	0.88	80.2%	0.78	83.3%	1.19	74.4%	0.93	79.0%
Regulations (NL)	2.43	54.0%	1.54	68.4%	1.00	78.1%	0.85	82.1%	1.25	73.8%	0.91	79.8%
Regulations (IT)	2.06	58.5%	1.32	71.8%	0.88	80.2%	0.77	83.5%	1.16	75.0%	0.88	80.2%
Regulations (PL)	2.23	57.2%	1.44	70.3%	0.94	79.2%	0.75	83.3%	1.08	76.8%	0.80	82.1%
Regulations (PT)	2.20	57.2%	1.43	70.7%	0.98	79.0%	0.87	82.3%	1.23	73.5%	0.94	78.8%
Regulations (All)	2.36	55.1%	1.53	68.9%	1.03	77.7%	0.90	81.4%	1.18	74.6%	0.90	79.8%
Contracts (EN)	1.96	58.0%	1.15	73.7%	0.66	84.2%	0.45	89.1%	1.24	73.0%	0.93	78.8%
Contracts (EL)	2.11	57.2%	1.41	70.0%	0.99	78.0%	0.84	81.8%	1.07	76.8%	0.87	80.9%
Contracts (DE)	2.62	50.0%	1.65	66.2%	1.07	76.5%	0.89	80.7%	1.27	73.0%	1.04	77.4%
Contracts (FR)	1.99	59.9%	1.23	73.9%	0.78	82.5%	0.65	85.9%	1.09	76.8%	0.88	80.7%
Contracts (ES)	2.28	54.7%	1.45	69.2%	0.95	78.6%	0.80	82.5%	1.32	72.4%	1.08	76.4%
Contracts (NL)	2.64	49.7%	1.69	65.2%	1.12	75.5%	0.93	79.9%	1.43	70.6%	1.15	75.5%
Contracts (IT)	2.37	53.4%	1.52	68.4%	1.01	77.8%	0.86	81.7%	1.38	71.5%	1.14	75.9%
Contracts (PL)	2.66	50.2%	1.74	65.1%	1.17	75.0%	0.98	79.4%	1.14	75.3%	0.94	79.5%
Contracts (PT)	2.62	49.8%	1.69	65.4%	1.14	75.4%	0.96	79.6%	1.67	66.8%	1.46	70.2%
Contracts (RU)	1.98	58.2%	1.29	71.6%	0.85	80.5%	0.70	84.6%	1.18	75.4%	0.99	78.8%
Contracts (All)	2.26	56.6%	1.43	71.0%	0.97	79.5%	0.87	82.9%	1.41	71.7%	1.16	76.1%
Overall (EN)	2.28	55.5%	1.44	69.9%	0.93	79.5%	0.76	83.8%	1.32	71.9%	1.02	77.3%
Overall (EL)	2.02	59.4%	1.33	71.7%	0.92	79.5%	0.81	82.9%	1.04	77.5%	0.81	82.1%
Overall (DE)	2.53	52.1%	1.60	67.5%	1.04	77.5%	0.87	81.7%	1.27	73.4%	0.99	78.6%
Overall (FR)	1.92	61.6%	1.20	74.6%	0.78	82.6%	0.69	85.7%	1.09	76.8%	0.86	81.2%
Overall (ES)	2.12	57.9%	1.36	71.2%	0.92	79.6%	0.81	83.0%	1.28	73.1%	1.03	77.6%
Overall (NL)	2.52	52.4%	1.60	67.4%	1.06	77.1%	0.91	81.1%	1.37	72.0%	1.06	77.4%
Overall (IT)	2.20	56.6%	1.40	70.7%	0.94	79.3%	0.83	82.8%	1.30	72.8%	1.03	77.8%
Overall (PL)	2.41	54.3%	1.56	68.3%	1.04	77.6%	0.86	81.7%	1.15	75.9%	0.90	80.5%
Overall (PT)	2.37	54.4%	1.53	68.8%	1.05	77.7%	0.93	81.2%	1.47	69.9%	1.22	74.4%
Overall (RU)	1.98	58.2%	1.29	71.6%	0.85	80.5%	0.70	84.6%	1.18	75.4%	0.99	78.8%
Overall	2.37	54.9%	1.53	69.0%	1.03	77.9%	0.90	81.5%	1.23	74.0%	0.96	79.0%

Table 15: Masked-Language-Models Validation Performance Scores (Cross-Entropy Loss, Accuracy).

Towards Cross-Domain Transferability of Text Generation Models for Legal Text

Vinayshekhar Bannihatti Kumar* **Kasturi Bhattacharjee*** **Rashmi Gangadharaiah**
AWS AI Labs
{vinayshk, kastb, rgangad}@amazon.com

Abstract

Legalese can often be filled with verbose domain-specific jargon which can make it challenging to understand and use for non-experts. Creating succinct summaries of legal documents often makes it easier for user comprehension. However, obtaining labeled data for every domain of legal text is challenging, which makes cross-domain transferability of text generation models for legal text, an important area of research. In this paper, we explore the ability of existing state-of-the-art T5 & BART-based summarization models to transfer across legal domains. We leverage publicly available datasets across four domains for this task, one of which is a new resource for summarizing privacy policies, that we curate and release for academic research. Our experiments demonstrate the low cross-domain transferability of these models, while also highlighting the benefits of combining different domains. Further, we compare the effectiveness of standard metrics for this task and illustrate the vast differences in their performance.

1 Introduction

Legalese is often perceived to be an expert language containing jargon-filled text, which makes it difficult for non-experts to comprehend (Kumar et al., 2019; Bannihatti Kumar et al., 2020; Obar and Oeldorf-Hirsch, 2020). However, owing to recent regulations (Voigt and Von dem Bussche, 2017; Moukad, 1979) there is a shift in paradigm to make legal documents more accessible to non-domain experts. Summarizing such documents is a vital step in this direction. A few examples include summarization over legislative bills (Kornilova and Eidelman, 2019; Zhang et al., 2020; Narayan et al., 2021) and legal contracts like terms of service (Manor and Li, 2019a; Jain et al., 2021; Shukla et al., 2022). However, obtaining annotated data for every domain of legal text for this task is expensive and often infeasible. Thus, exploring the ability of text generation models to transfer across multiple legal domains is of importance, particularly for low resource domains for which knowledge transfer from domains with large amounts of annotated data could be beneficial. While there has been research on various tasks and aspects of legal text, such as summarization (Jain et al., 2021; Kornilova and Eidelman, 2019; Zhang et al., 2020; Narayan et al., 2021), question answering (Ravichander et al., 2019; Keymanesh et al., 2021) and title generation in privacy policies (Gopinath et al., 2020), transferability of generative models across legal domains has remained relatively understudied.

In this work, we explore the cross-domain transferability of state-of-the-art text generation models across *four* distinctly different legal domains. We use standard summarization metrics to measure their degree of transferability. Further, we compare the effectiveness of such metrics at capturing the summarization capability of these models, and demonstrate the differences thereof. Further, since summarization datasets are not available in the privacy policy domain, we curate and release an annotated dataset for further research.

Contributions of our work:

- We measure the extent of cross domain transferability of T5 & BART-based summarization models on 4 different legal domains. Our experiments demonstrate the advantages of a multi-domain model over a single-domain one.
- We create a dataset for privacy policy summarization to enable further research in this area[1].
- We illustrate the shortcomings of BERTScore (Zhang et al., 2019) and

* Equal contribution

[1] https://github.com/awslabs/summarization-privacy-policies

Proceedings of the Natural Legal Language Processing Workshop 2022, pages 111 - 118
December 8, 2022 ©2022 Association for Computational Linguistics

	Train	Dev	Test	Context # of chars			Summary # of chars		
				Min	Max	Avg	Min	Max	Avg
BillSum	15159	3032	3269	5004	19997	10319	65	4966	1193
JRC-Acquis (en)	2026	2242	328	50	888444	13603	6	2382	209
Legal contracts	369	36	41	44	3922	407	19	328	92
Privacy Policies	20000	2000	2000	6	9222	793	6	1689	64

Table 1: Dataset statistics for all datasets. We show the varying nature of each dataset with statistics on the number of characters in context and summary. As observed, the mean number of characters differs to a large extent across each dataset.

BARTScore (Yuan et al., 2021) on cross-domain transferability and demonstrate that traditional metrics like ROUGE-L & METEOR are better for such an assessment pertaining to the legal domain.

2 Datasets

In order to study cross-domain transferability of generative models, we select four summarization datasets consisting of legal text of varying domains, each of which is described below.

BillSum: This dataset (Kornilova and Eidelman, 2019) consists of US congressional bills collected over a 25 year time-period (103rd-115th sessions of US Congress) ranging from 1993-2018 & summarized by the respective legislative counsel.

JRC-Acquis (en): This dataset introduced by Steinberger et al. (2006) is composed of the contents, political objectives of treaties, legislation, declarations, etc. pertaining to the member states of the EU. We focus on the English subset of the corpus for this paper. The task here is to summarize the paragraphs of the documents using their titles.

Legal contracts: Curated by Manor and Li (2019b), this dataset is composed of unilateral legal contracts such as terms of service, terms of use and licensing agreements. Instead of summarizing the entire document as a whole, manually curated summaries of each section are provided.

Privacy Policies: Privacy policies are legal documents that disclose ways in which a company collects and manages their user data. Each section of the privacy policy discusses various facets of user data management. While there has been work done to *summarize sections* of privacy policies (Gopinath et al., 2020), there is no open sourced dataset available for this task.

Privacy Policies Dataset Creation: We leverage the ~1M English language privacy policy dataset (Amos et al., 2021) in order to **create & release** a dataset for section summarization. To that end, we sample a subset of 20K privacy policies at random, from which we randomly select 24K sections. The dataset created for section summarization consist of <Body, Title> pairs extracted from these sections. For more details, please refer to Appendix A.1.

The statistics of the train/dev/test split for these datasets is shown in Table 1. Table 4 (Appendix) contains examples from each dataset, thereby highlighting the domain differences between them.

3 Methodology & Experiments

We leverage pretrained seq2seq Transformer-based text generation models such as BART (Lewis et al., 2020) and T5 (Raffel et al., 2020) for our experiments. In order to measure cross-domain transferability of generative models for the four domains discussed in Section 2, we first conduct experiments in the ***single-domain*** setting, in which each seq2seq model is fine-tuned with the <context, summary> pairs from the training split of a *single* domain-specific dataset, and subsequently used to generate summaries for the test splits of each dataset, both in and out-of-domain. Cross-domain performance of these models helps determine their transferability across different domains.

Further, in order to compare with a scenario in which the text generation model learns from all domains and is thereby able to incorporate the domain differences during generation, we propose a ***multi-domain*** setting, in which we fine-tune the model with training data of all domains, and generate summaries for each of the four datasets. For more details on experimental settings, please refer to Appendix A.3. Standard metrics such as **ROUGE-L** (Lin, 2004), **METEOR** (Banerjee and Lavie, 2005), **BERTScore** (Zhang et al., 2019) and **BARTScore** (Yuan et al., 2021) are reported to measure model performance.

4 Results

In this section, we report quantitative (Table 3) and qualitative results (Table 2) of the single and multi-domain text generation models.

Single-domain: As is evident from the single domain results, cross-domain model performance is low for both BART-base & T5-base models, across all reported metrics. For instance, a BART-base

Model	Generated Summary	Reference Summary
BART-base *single-domain*, FT: **Legal contracts**, Test: **JRC-Acquis (en)**	the European Economic Community should have a journal of its own.	*Decision creating the 'Official Journal of the European Communities'*
BART-base *multi-domain*, FT: **all domains**, Test: **JRC-Acquis (en)**	58/578/EEC: Council Decision of 15 September 1958 on the creation of the Official Journal of the European Communities	
T5-base *single-domain*, FT: **JRC-Acquis (en)** Test: **Privacy Policies**	Non-members - We do not collect any Personal Data about you - however, we may automatically collect information about your visits, such as browsing patterns - to analyse, manage and develop	*WHAT DATA DO WE COLLECT AND HOW?*
T5-base *multi-domain*, FT: **all domains** Test: **Privacy Policies**	Personal Data we collect	

Table 2: Summaries generated by single & multi-domain T5 & BART based generative models. **FT** represents the data (domain) the model was *fine-tuned* on.

Model	Data for fine-tuning	Test Set	ROUGE-L	METEOR	BERTScore	BARTScore
		Single-domain				
BART-base	JRC-Acquis (en)	JRC-Acquis (en)	0.769	0.756	0.954	-1.771
		Legal contracts	0.099	0.077	0.830	-4.653
		BillSum	0.104	0.059	0.821	-3.855
		Privacy Policies	0.098	0.061	0.825	-6.138
	Legal contracts	Legal contracts	0.358	0.368	0.899	-3.266
		JRC-Acquis (en)	0.166	0.113	0.831	-4.967
		BillSum	0.065	0.036	0.820	-3.861
		Privacy Policies	0.116	0.085	0.833	-6.002
	BillSum	BillSum	0.343	*0.292*	0.883	-2.850
		JRC-Acquis (en)	0.21	0.308	0.839	-3.978
		Legal contracts	0.150	0.258	0.850	-3.900
		Privacy Policies	0.080	0.121	0.810	-5.480
	Privacy Policies	Privacy Policies	0.500	0.480	0.904	-4.140
		JRC-Acquis (en)	0.05	0.0264	0.788	-5.334
		Legal contracts	0.085	0.059	0.823	-4.410
		BillSum	0.020	0.009	0.778	-4.067
T5-base	JRC-Acquis (en)	JRC-Acquis (en)	0.756	0.756	0.955	-1.818
		Legal contracts	0.135	0.149	0.849	-4.077
		BillSum	0.161	0.102	0.842	-3.539
		Privacy Policies	0.133	0.116	0.829	-5.669
	Legal contracts	Legal contracts	0.277	0.307	0.885	-3.597
		JRC-Acquis (en)	0.210	0.165	0.839	-4.729
		BillSum	0.139	0.089	0.839	-3.651
		Privacy Policies	0.132	0.106	0.834	-5.893
	BillSum	BillSum	0.380	0.316	0.887	-2.752
		JRC-Acquis (en)	0.233	0.312	0.839	-3.954
		Legal contracts	0.159	0.262	0.856	-3.720
		Privacy Policies	0.09	0.131	0.817	-5.430
	Privacy Policies	Privacy Policies	0.456	0.450	0.897	-4.340
		JRC-Acquis (en)	0.113	0.054	0.794	-5.26
		Legal contracts	0.075	0.040	0.820	-4.510
		BillSum	0.062	0.020	0.800	-3.840
		Multi-domain				
BART-base	*All Domains Combined*	BillSum	**0.355**	**0.302**	**0.886**	**-2.817**
		JRC-Acquis (en)	**0.794**	**0.784**	**0.959**	**-1.628**
		Legal contracts	**0.387**	**0.396**	**0.902**	**-3.008**
		Privacy Policies	**0.513**	**0.503**	**0.907**	**-4.075**
T5-base	*All Domains Combined*	BillSum	**0.386**	**0.316**	**0.889**	**-2.743**
		JRC-Acquis (en)	**0.792**	**0.795**	**0.962**	**-1.603**
		Legal contracts	**0.351**	**0.388**	**0.898**	**-3.219**
		Privacy Policies	**0.497**	**0.484**	**0.903**	**-4.168**

Table 3: Model performance for single & multi-domain scenarios with **BART-base** & **T5-base** models across datasets.

model trained on **JRC-Acquis (en)** yields 0.769 ROUGE-L score for text of the *same domain*, while achieving a much lower ROUGE-L score of 0.104 on *a different domain* (**BillSum**). A similar behavior is observed for **T5-base** as well. Here, a T5-base model trained on **Privacy policy** is able to obtain a METEOR score of 0.45 on a test set of the same domain, while a model trained on **Legal contracts** achieves 0.106 METEOR score on the same Privacy policy test set. Thus text generation models are observed to yield low cross-domain transferability for legal text.

Multi-domain: We observe the multi-domain T5 & BART models to yield better performance across each domain, in comparison to the single-domain setting. For instance, the METEOR score for the *best single-domain T5-base* model for **Privacy Policy** test set is 0.45, while the multi-domain T5 model is able to achieve 0.484 on the same test set. Similarly, the multi-domain BART-base model yields a ROUGE-L score of 0.794 on the **JRC-Acquis (en)** dataset, for which the corresponding best single-domain model performance is 0.769. This illustrates that it helps the model to learn from the domain differences of these datasets.

Comparing summarization metrics: An interesting observation is that the percentage drop in performance between the best and worst performing models, reflected via BERTScore & BARTScore is significantly less as compared to that obtained using other metrics such as METEOR ROUGE-L, for 14/16 settings considered in this study. For instance, in Figures 1a & 1c, we consider, for each dataset, the best & the worst performing models

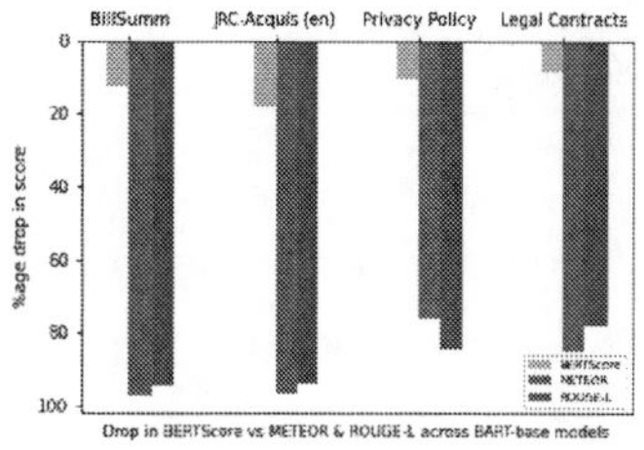

(a) BERTScore vs METEOR & ROUGE-L for BART models

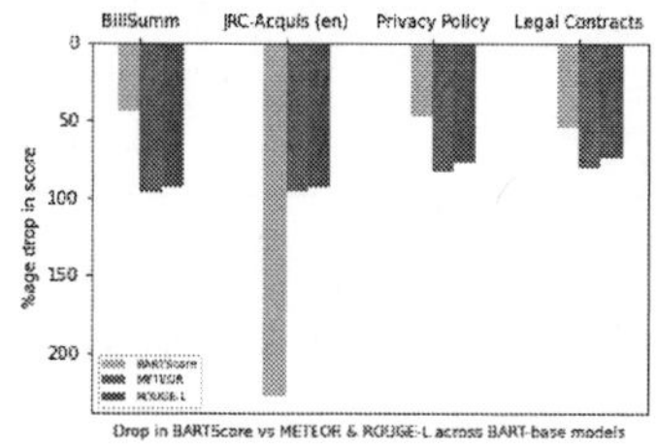

(b) BARTScore vs METEOR & ROUGE-L for BART models

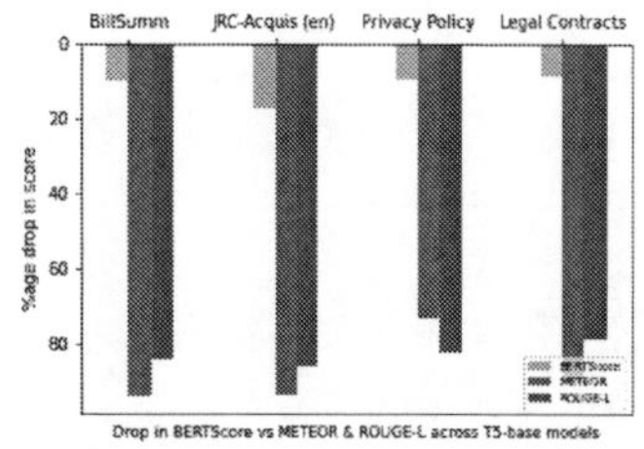

(c) BERTScore vs METEOR & ROUGE-L for T5 models

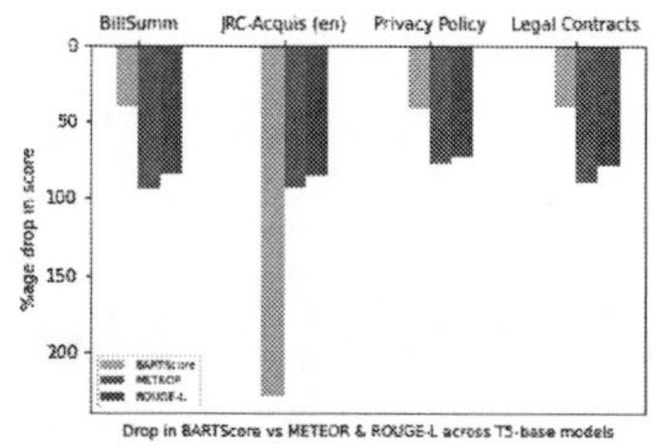

(d) BARTScore vs METEOR & ROUGE-L for T5 models

Figure 1: Percentage drop in BERTScore & BARTScore as compared to METEOR & ROUGE-L. Figures 1b & 1a provide a metrics comparison for the multi-domain model & the worst performing single-domain model w.r.t BARTScore & BertScore respectively. Similarly, Figures 1d & 1c illustrate the comparison for the corresponding T5-base counterparts.

based on BERTScore. For each pair of models, we plot the percentage drop in performance for BERTScore, and the corresponding METEOR & ROUGE-L scores. We observe that text overlap metrics like ROUGE-L and METEOR exhibit a significant drop in performance when compared to BERTScore. A similar trend is observed for BARTScore as well, which captures a lower drop in performance for 3 out of 4 datasets (Figures 1b & 1d). This illustrates that perhaps not all metrics are equally capable of capturing model performance adequately for summarization. Furthermore, upon manual investigation, we observe that the deterioration of quality of generated summaries is better reflected by ROUGE-L & METEOR, when compared to BERTScore and BARTScore.

Qualitative results Table 2 demonstrates model-generated summaries for a few of the single & multi-domain models. As is evident, the multi-domain models generate summaries that are closer to the reference, in each case.

5 Conclusion & Future Work

In this paper, we study the cross-domain transferability of neural text generation models across four different domains of legal text. We consider seq2seq model architectures such as BART & T5 and fine-tune them on datasets of specific domains. Based on standard generation metrics such as ROUGE, METEOR, BERTScore & BARTScore, we find such models to show a drop in performance for cross-domain settings. Further, our experiments demonstrate the benefits of combining different domains to train models for such tasks. Moreover, we observe some metrics to be more effective at capturing the differences in predicted and ground-truth summaries. We also curate & release a dataset on title generation for privacy policies for further research in this direction. In the future, we wish to explore text generation specific to legal text for low resource scenarios including zero and few-shot settings.

References

Ryan Amos, Gunes Acar, Eli Lucherini, Mihir Kshirsagar, Arvind Narayanan, and Jonathan Mayer. 2021. Privacy policies over time: Curation and analysis of a million-document dataset. In *Proceedings of the Web Conference 2021*, pages 2165–2176.

Satanjeev Banerjee and Alon Lavie. 2005. METEOR: An automatic metric for MT evaluation with improved correlation with human judgments. In *Proceedings of the ACL Workshop on Intrinsic and Extrinsic Evaluation Measures for Machine Translation and/or Summarization*, pages 65–72, Ann Arbor, Michigan. Association for Computational Linguistics.

Vinayshekhar Bannihatti Kumar, Roger Iyengar, Namita Nisal, Yuanyuan Feng, Hana Habib, Peter Story, Sushain Cherivirala, Margaret Hagan, Lorrie Cranor, Shomir Wilson, et al. 2020. Finding a choice in a haystack: Automatic extraction of opt-out statements from privacy policy text. In *Proceedings of The Web Conference 2020*, pages 1943–1954.

Abhijith Athreya Mysore Gopinath, Vinayshekhar Bannihatti Kumar, Shomir Wilson, and Norman Sadeh. 2020. Automatic section title generation to improve the readability of privacy policies.

Deepali Jain, Malaya Dutta Borah, and Anupam Biswas. 2021. Summarization of legal documents: Where are we now and the way forward. *Computer Science Review*, 40:100388.

Moniba Keymanesh, Micha Elsner, and Srinivasan Parthasarathy. 2021. Privacy policy question answering assistant: A query-guided extractive summarization approach. *arXiv preprint arXiv:2109.14638*.

Anastassia Kornilova and Vlad Eidelman. 2019. Billsum: A corpus for automatic summarization of us legislation. *arXiv preprint arXiv:1910.00523*.

Vinayshekhar Bannihatti Kumar, Abhilasha Ravichander, Peter Story, and Norman Sadeh. 2019. Quantifying the effect of in-domain distributed word representations: A study of privacy policies. In *AAAI Spring Symposium on Privacy-Enhancing Artificial Intelligence and Language Technologies*.

Mike Lewis, Yinhan Liu, Naman Goyal, Marjan Ghazvininejad, Abdelrahman Mohamed, Omer Levy, Veselin Stoyanov, and Luke Zettlemoyer. 2020. Bart: Denoising sequence-to-sequence pre-training for natural language generation, translation, and comprehension. In *Proceedings of the 58th Annual Meeting of the Association for Computational Linguistics*, pages 7871–7880.

Chin-Yew Lin. 2004. ROUGE: A package for automatic evaluation of summaries. In *Text Summarization Branches Out*, pages 74–81, Barcelona, Spain. Association for Computational Linguistics.

Laura Manor and Junyi Jessy Li. 2019a. Plain english summarization of contracts. *arXiv preprint arXiv:1906.00424*.

Laura Manor and Junyi Jessy Li. 2019b. Plain English summarization of contracts. In *Proceedings of the Natural Legal Language Processing Workshop 2019*, pages 1–11, Minneapolis, Minnesota. Association for Computational Linguistics.

Rosemary Moukad. 1979. New york's plain english law. *Fordham Urb. LJ*, 8:451.

Shashi Narayan, Yao Zhao, Joshua Maynez, Gonçalo Simões, Vitaly Nikolaev, and Ryan McDonald. 2021. Planning with learned entity prompts for abstractive summarization. *Transactions of the Association for Computational Linguistics*, 9:1475–1492.

Jonathan A Obar and Anne Oeldorf-Hirsch. 2020. The biggest lie on the internet: Ignoring the privacy policies and terms of service policies of social networking services. *Information, Communication & Society*, 23(1):128–147.

Colin Raffel, Noam Shazeer, Adam Roberts, Katherine Lee, Sharan Narang, Michael Matena, Yanqi Zhou, Wei Li, Peter J Liu, et al. 2020. Exploring the limits of transfer learning with a unified text-to-text transformer. *J. Mach. Learn. Res.*, 21(140):1–67.

Abhilasha Ravichander, Alan W Black, Shomir Wilson, Thomas Norton, and Norman Sadeh. 2019. Question answering for privacy policies: Combining computational and legal perspectives. *arXiv preprint arXiv:1911.00841*.

Bharti Shukla, Sonam Gupta, Arun Kumar Yadav, and Divakar Yadav. 2022. Text summarization of legal documents using reinforcement learning: A study. In *Intelligent Sustainable Systems*, pages 403–414. Springer.

Ralf Steinberger, Bruno Pouliquen, Anna Widiger, Camelia Ignat, Tomaz Erjavec, Dan Tufis, and Dániel Varga. 2006. The jrc-acquis: A multilingual aligned parallel corpus with 20+ languages. *arXiv preprint cs/0609058*.

Paul Voigt and Axel Von dem Bussche. 2017. The eu general data protection regulation (gdpr). *A Practical Guide, 1st Ed., Cham: Springer International Publishing*, 10(3152676):10–5555.

Weizhe Yuan, Graham Neubig, and Pengfei Liu. 2021. Bartscore: Evaluating generated text as text generation. *Advances in Neural Information Processing Systems*, 34:27263–27277.

Jingqing Zhang, Yao Zhao, Mohammad Saleh, and Peter Liu. 2020. Pegasus: Pre-training with extracted gap-sentences for abstractive summarization. In *International Conference on Machine Learning*, pages 11328–11339. PMLR.

Tianyi Zhang, Varsha Kishore, Felix Wu, Kilian Q Weinberger, and Yoav Artzi. 2019. Bertscore: Evaluating text generation with bert. *arXiv preprint arXiv:1904.09675*.

A Appendix

A.1 Privacy policy Dataset creation

In Algorithm 1 we describe the algorithm that we used for the creation of <Context, Summary> pairs in the case of privacy policies. Table 6 contains a few examples of the data. The data is further split into train/dev/test splits as specified in Table 1.

Algorithm 1 Algorithm for creation of privacy policy summarization corpus

```
N ← NumberOfPolicies
i ← 0
title ← ""
runningContent ← ""
samples ← []
while i < N do
    lines ← Policy_i
    if lines[0] is '#' or '**' then samples.append(<Body, Title>)
        title ← lines[i]
        runningContent ← ""
    else
        runningContent+ = lines[i]
    end if
end while
```

A.2 Data Sources & Examples

The specific sources for obtaining the datasets are as follows:

1. BillSum: We obtained the data from HuggingFace's Datasets library.

2. JRC-Acquis (en):The data was downloaded from this link.

3. Legal contracts: The data was downloaded from this link.

In Table 4, we show different samples from all the datasets considered in this paper. We can see from the samples below that the 4 domains considered in this paper vary widely from one another.

A.3 Experimental Details

BART-base & **T5-base** model checkpoints are initialized from HuggingFace for each of the experiments and fine-tuned using the provided script. For the single-domain experiments, we conduct Hyper-parameter optimization(HPO) using the dev set of the corresponding dataset. In case of the multi-domain experiments, we use a dev set built by combining the dev splits of each dataset for HPO. The following are the best hyper-parameters for each of the models.

- **T5 & BART-base Single-domain (JRC-Acquis (en)):**learning rate: 5e-05, batch size: 32, optimizer: Adam, number of epochs: 3.0

- **BART-base Single-domain (Legal contracts):**learning rate: 5e-05, batch size: 32, optimizer: Adam, number of epochs: 3.0

- **T5-base Single-domain (Legal contracts):**learning rate: 5e-05, batch size: 16, optimizer: Adam, number of epochs: 3.0

- **T5 & BART-base Single-domain (BillSum) & Single-domain (Privacy Policies):**learning rate: 5e-05, batch size: 12, optimizer: Adam, number of epochs: 3.0

- **BART-base Multi-domain:** learning rate: 8e-05, batch size: 64, optimizer: Adam, number of epochs: 5.0

- **T5-base Multi-domain:** learning rate: 8e-05, batch size: 16, optimizer: Adam, epsilon=1e-08, number of epochs: 5.0

A.4 Qualitative Examples

In Table 5 we show the different summaries that our model produces along with the reference summaries.

Domain	Context	Summary
BillSum	SECTION 1. SHORT TITLE.This Act may be cited as the "Taxpayer Transparency Act of 2013".. 2. REQUIREMENTS FOR PRINTED MATERIALS AND ADVERTISEMENTS BY FEDERAL AGENCIES.(a) Identification of Funding Sources.– Each communication funded a Federal agency for advertising or educational purposes shall state–(1) in the case of a printed communication, including mass mailings, signs, and billboards, that the communication is printed and published at taxpayer expense; and(2) in the case of a communication transmitted through radio, television, the Internet, or any means other than the means referred to in paragraph (1), that the communication is produced and disseminated at taxpayer expense..... (A) means any mailing or distribution of 499 or more newsletters, pamphlets, or other printed matter with substantially identical content, whether such matter is deposited singly or in bulk, or at the same time or different times; and(B) does not include any mailing–(i) in direct response to a communication from a person to whom the matter is mailed; or(ii) of a news release to the communications media.(e) Source of Funds.–The funds used by a Federal agency to carry this Act shall be derived from amounts made available to the agency advertising or other communications regarding the programs and of the agency.	Taxpayer Transparency Act of 2013 - Requires each communication funded by a federal agency for advertising or educational purposes to clearly state: (1) in the case of a printed communication, including mass mailings, signs, and billboards, that the communication is printed and published at taxpayer expense; and (2) in the case of a communication transmitted through radio, television, or the Internet, that the communication is produced and disseminated at taxpayer expense. Requires any such printed communication, including e-mails, to be of sufficient size to be clearly readable, to be set apart from the other contents of the communication, and to be printed with a reasonable degree of color contrast between the background and the printed statement. Exempts from such requirements: (1) information in or relating to a solicitation for offers for a federal contract or applications or submissions of a bid or proposal for a federal grant or other means of funding under a federal program; and (2) advertisements for employment opportunities, not including advertising materials developed for use in recruiting and retaining personnel for the Armed Forces.
JRC-Acquis (en)	2006/C 252/02) The Minister for Economic Affairs of the Kingdom of the Netherlands hereby gives notice that an application has been received for authorisation to prospect for hydrocarbons in block P1 as indicated on the map appended as Annex 3 to the Mining Regulation (Mijnbouwregeling) (Government Gazette (Staatscourant) 2002, No 245). With reference to Article 3(2) of Directive 94/22/EC of the European Parliament and of the Council of 30 May 1994 on the conditions for granting and using authorisations for the prospection, exploration and production of hydrocarbons and the publication required by Article 15 of the Mining Act (Mijnbouwwet) (Bulletin of Acts and Decrees (Staatsblad) 2002, No 542), the Minister for Economic Affairs hereby invites interested parties to submit an application for authorisation to prospect for hydrocarbons in block P1. The Minister for Economic Affairs is the competent authority for the granting of authorisations. The criteria, conditions and requirements referred to in Articles 5(1), 5(2) and 6(2) of the Directive are set out in the Mining Act (Bulletin of Acts and Decrees 2002, No 542). Applications may be submitted during the 13 weeks following the publication of this notice in the Official Journal of the European Union and should be sent to the Minister for Economic Affairs, for the attention of the Director for the Energy Market, Bezuidenhoutseweg 30, The Hague, Netherlands, and marked "personal". Applications submitted after the expiry of this period will not be considered. A decision on the applications will be taken not later than twelve months after this period has expired. Further information can be obtained from the following telephone number: (31-70) 379 72 98	Notice inviting applications for authorisation to prospect for hydrocarbons in block P1 of the Dutch continental shelf
Legal contracts	we may also automatically collect device specific information when you install access or use our services. this information may include information such as the hardware model operating system information app version app usage and debugging information browser information ip address and device identifiers.	the service may use tracking pixels web beacons browser fingerprinting and or device fingerprinting on users.
Privacy Policies	We take reasonable steps to ensure that personal information we process is accurate, complete, and current by using the most recent information provided to us.	Data Integrity

Table 4: Example of context and summary for the four datasets considered in this paper. For presentation purpose, we have reduced the size of context for BillSum.

Model	Generated Summary	Reference Summary
BART-base *single-domain* FT: **Legal contracts** Test: **JRC-Acquis (en)**	THE COMMISSION OF THE EUROPEAN COMMUNITIES, Having regard to the Treaty establishing the European Community, having regard to Council Regulation 90/425/EEC of 26 June 1990 concerning veterinary and zootechnical checks applicable in intra-Community trade.	98/168/EC: Commission Decision of 17 February 1998 amending Decision 93/70/EEC on codification for the message 'Animo' to include certain types of mammalian waste products (Text with EEA relevance)
BART-base *multi-domain* FT: **all domains** Test: **JRC-Acquis (en)**	98/766/EC: Commission Decision of 17 February 1998 amending Decision 93/70/EEC laying down the codes to be used for animals and animal products (Text with EEA relevance)	
T5-base *single-domain* FT: **JRC-Acquis (en)** Test: **Privacy Policies**	Complaints lodged in the summer of 2006 - Information Commissioner's Office - Data protection supervisory authority	Right to complain
T5-base *multi-domain* FT: **all domains** Test: **Privacy Policies**	Right to lodge a complaint	

Table 5: More Summaries generated by single & multi-domain T5 & BART based generative models. **FT** represents the data (domain) the model was fine-tuned on.

Context	Summary
We may share aggregated Non-Identifying Information and we may otherwise disclose Non-Identifying Information (including, without limitation, Hashed Information) to third parties. We do not share your Personal Information with third parties for those third parties' marketing purposes unless we first provide you with the opportunity to opt-in to or opt-out of such sharing. We may also share the information we have collected about you, including Personal Information, as disclosed at the time you provide your information, with your consent, as otherwise described in this Privacy Policy, or in the following circumstances	INFORMATION SHARING AND DISCLOSURE
You have the right at any time to access any Personal Data we hold about you, and where you feel the Personal Information that we hold is not correct, to request that the Personal Information is corrected.0 You also have the right to have your Personal Information deleted. All of the Personal Information, along with other data collected (as noted in the table above) is information that you can access, amend or delete by logging into your SOFTWARE112 Account. If you have any questions about accessing, correcting, amending, or deleting your information then you can contact us.	How can I Access, Amend, Correct and/or Delete my Personal Data?
Occasionally, at our discretion, we may include or offer third party products or services on our website. These third party sites have separate and independent privacy policies. We therefore have no responsibility or liability for the content and activities of these linked sites. Nonetheless, we seek to protect the integrity of our site and welcome any feedback about these sites.	Third party links
The information we collect from you will be used by Microsoft and its controlled subsidiaries and affiliates to enable the features you are using and provide the service(s) or carry out the transaction(s) you have requested or authorized.0 It may also be used to analyze and improve Microsoft products and services. In order to offer you a more consistent and personalized experience in your interactions with Microsoft, information collected through one Microsoft service may be combined with information obtained through other Microsoft services. We may also supplement the information we collect with information obtained from other companies. For example, we may use services from other companies that enable us to derive a general geographic area based on your IP address in order to customize certain services to your geographic area. Except as described in this statement, personal information you provide will not be transferred to third parties without your consent. We occasionally hire other companies to provide limited services on our behalf, such as packaging, sending and delivering purchases and other mailings, answering customer questions about products or services, processing event registration, or performing statistical analysis of our services. We will only provide those companies the personal information they need to deliver the service, and they are prohibited from using that information for any other purpose. Microsoft may access or disclose information about you, including the content of your communications, in order to: (a) comply with the law or respond to lawful requests or legal process; (b) protect the rights or property of Microsoft or our customers, including the enforcement of our agreements or policies governing your use of the services; or (c) act on a good faith belief that such access or disclosure is necessary to protect the personal safety of Microsoft employees, customers, or the public.0 We may also disclose personal information as part of a corporate transaction such as a merger or sale of assets. Information that is collected by or sent to Microsoft by WebPI may be stored and processed in the United States or any other country in which Microsoft or its affiliates, subsidiaries, or service providers maintain facilities. Microsoft abides by the safe harbor framework as set forth by the U.S. Department of Commerce regarding the collection, use, and retention of data from the European Union, the European Economic Area, and Switzerland.	Collection and Use of Your Information
You will find links to other websites on our websites to keep you really well informed. We do not have any influence upon the design and the content of these external websites.	Links to other websites
The advertisements diffused on our site are proposed by third companies. They may use data on users' visits to target content that may be of interest to them	Advertisements
Most of the content on this website is ours and subject to our copyright, but some of the content is owned by others. For instance where we link to other websites. You may: * use and enjoy the content for your own personal information purposes; and * share our posts on social media. If you want to use the content for any other purpose, please ask our permission first. You can contact us at info@thesouthafrican.com.	Content on this website

Table 6: Example of context and summary for the domain of privacy policies.

Parameter-Efficient Legal Domain Adaptation

Jonathan Li[1], **Rohan Bhambhoria**[1,2], **Xiaodan Zhu**[1,2]

[1] Ingenuity Labs, Queen's University
[2] Department of Electrical and Computer Engineering, Queen's University
{jxl, r.bhambhoria, xiaodan.zhu}queensu.ca

Abstract

Seeking legal advice is often expensive. Recent advancements in machine learning for solving complex problems can be leveraged to help make legal services more accessible to the public. However, real-life applications encounter significant challenges. State-of-the-art language models are growing increasingly large, making parameter-efficient learning increasingly important. Unfortunately, parameter-efficient methods perform poorly with small amounts of data (Gu et al., 2022), which are common in the legal domain (where data labelling costs are high). To address these challenges, we propose parameter-efficient legal domain adaptation, which uses vast unsupervised legal data from public legal forums to perform legal pre-training. This method exceeds or matches the fewshot performance of existing models such as LEGAL-BERT (Chalkidis et al., 2020) on various legal tasks while tuning only approximately 0.1% of model parameters. Additionally, we show that our method can achieve calibration comparable to existing methods across several tasks. To the best of our knowledge, this work is among the first to explore parameter-efficient methods of tuning language models in the legal domain.

1 Introduction

Seeking legal advice from lawyers can be expensive. However, a machine learning system that can help answer legal questions could greatly aid laypersons in making informed legal decisions. Existing legal forums, such as Legal Advice Reddit and Law Stack Exchange, are valuable data sources for various legal tasks. On one hand, they provide good sources of labelled data, such as mapping legal questions to their areas of law (for classification), as shown in Figure 1. On the other hand, they contain hundreds of thousands of legal questions that can be leveraged for domain adaptation. Furthermore, questions on these forums can serve as a starting point for tasks that do not have labels found directly in the dataset, such as classifying the severity of a legal question. In this paper, we show that this vast unlabeled corpus can improve performance on question classification, opening up the possibility of studying other tasks on these public legal forums.

Figure 1: Example classification task using legal questions from Legal Advice Subreddit (top) and Law Stack Exchange (bottom). Reddit data is generally more informal than Stack Exchange.

In the past few years, large language models have shown effectiveness in legal tasks (Chalkidis et al., 2022). A widespread method used to train these models is finetuning. Although finetuning is very effective, it is prohibitively expensive; training all the parameters requires large amounts of memory and requires a full copy of the language model to be saved for each task. Recently, prefix tuning (Li and Liang, 2021; Liu et al., 2022) has shown great promise by tuning under 1% of the parameters and still achieving comparable performance to finetuning. Unfortunately, prefix tuning performs poorly in low-data (i.e., fewshot) settings (Gu et al., 2022), which are common in the legal

Proceedings of the Natural Legal Language Processing Workshop 2022, pages 119 - 129
December 8, 2022 ©2022 Association for Computational Linguistics

domain. Conveniently, domain adaptation using large public datasets is an ideal setting for the legal domain with abundant unlabelled data (from public forums) and limited labelled data. To this end, we introduce prefix domain adaptation, which performs domain adaptation for prompt tuning to improve fewshot performance on various legal tasks.

Overall, our main contributions are as follows:

- We introduce prefix adaptation, a method of domain adaptation using a prompt-based learning approach.
- We show empirically that performance and calibration of prefix adaptation matches or exceeds LEGAL-BERT in fewshot settings while only tuning approximately 0.1% of the model parameters.
- We contribute two new datasets to facilitate different legal NLP tasks on the questions asked by laypersons, towards the ultimate objective of helping make legal services more accessible to the public.

2 Related Works

Forums-based Datasets Public forums have been used extensively as sources of data for machine learning. Sites like Stack Overflow and Quora have been used for duplicate question detection (Wang et al., 2020; Sharma et al., 2019). Additionally, many prior works have used posts from specific sub-communities (called a "subreddit") on Reddit for NLP tasks, likely due to the diversity of communities and large amount of data provided. Barnes et al. (2021) used a large number of internet memes from multiple meme-related subreddits to predict how likely a meme is to be popular. Other works, such as Basaldella et al. (2020), label posts from biomedical subreddits for biomedical entity linking. Similar to the legal judgement prediction task, Lourie et al. (2021) suggest using "crowdsourced data" from Reddit to perform ethical judgement prediction; that is, they use votes from the "r/AmITheAsshole" subreddit to classify who is "in the wrong" for a given real-life anecdote. We explore using data from Stack Exchange and Reddit, which has been vastly underexplored in previous works for the legal domain.

Full Domain Adaptation Previous works such as BioBERT (Lee et al., 2019) and SciBERT (Beltagy et al., 2019) have shown positive results while domain adapting models. In the industry, companies often use full domain adaptation for legal applications [1]. Chalkidis et al. (2020) introduce LEGAL-BERT, a BERT-like model domain adapted for legal tasks. They show improvements across various legal tasks by training on a domain-specific corpus. Zheng et al. (2021) also perform legal domain adapation, using the Harvard Law case corpus, showing better performance in the CaseHOLD multiple-choice question answering task. Unlike existing works, we perform domain adaptation parameter-efficiently, showing similar performance in a few-shot setting. We compare our approach against LEGAL-BERT as a strong baseline.

Parameter-efficient Learning Language models have scaled to over billions of parameters (He et al., 2021; Brown et al., 2020), making research memory and storage intensive. Recently, parameter-efficient training methods—techniques that focus on tuning a small percentage of the parameters in a neural network—have been a prominent research topic in natural language processing. More recently, prefix tuning (Li and Liang, 2021) has attracted much attention due to its simplicity, ease of implementation, and effectiveness. In this paper, we use P-Tuning v2 (Liu et al., 2022), which includes an implementation of prefix tuning.

Previously, Gu et al. (2022) explored improving prefix tuning's fewshot performance with pre-training by rewriting downstream tasks for a multiple choice answering task (in their "unified PPT"), and synthesizing multiple choice pre-training data (from OpenWebText). Unlike them, we focus on domain adaptation and not general pre-training. We show a much simpler method of prompt pre-training using the masked language modelling (MLM) task while preserving the format of downstream tasks. Ge et al. (2022) domain adapt continuous prompts (not prefix tuning) to improve performance with vision-transformer models for different image types (e.g., "clipart", "photo", or "product").

Zhang et al. (2021) domain adapt an adapter (Houlsby et al., 2019), which is another type of parameter-efficient training method where small neural networks put between layers of the large language model are trained. Vu et al. (2022) explored the transferability of prompts between tasks. They trained a general prompt for the "prefix LM"

[1] https://vectorinstitute.ai/2020/04/02/how-thomson-reuters-uses-nlp-to-enable-knowledge-workers-to-make-faster-and-more-accurate-business-decisions/

(Raffel et al., 2020) objective on the Colossal Clean Crawled Corpus (Raffel et al., 2020). They do not study the efficacy of their general-purpose prompt in fewshot scenarios. Though we use a similar unsupervised language modelling task (Devlin et al., 2019), we aim to train a domain adapted prompt and not a general-purpose prompt.

3 Background

Legal Forums Seeking legal advice from a lawyer can be incredibly expensive. However, public legal forums are incredibly accessible to laypersons to ask legal questions. One popular community is the Legal Advice Reddit community (2M+ members), where users can freely ask personal legal questions. Typically, the questions asked on the Legal Advice Subreddit are written informally and receive informal answers. Another forum is the Law Stack Exchange, a community for questions about the law. Questions are more formal than on Reddit. Additionally, users are not allowed to ask about a specific case and must ask about law more hypothetically, as specified in the rules.

In particular, data from the Legal Advice Subreddit is especially helpful in training machine learning models to help laypersons in law, as questions are in the format and language that regular people would write in (see Figure 1). We run experiments on Law Stack Exchange (LSE) for comprehensiveness, though we believe that the non-personal nature of LSE data makes it less valuable than Reddit data in helping laypersons.

Prefix Tuning As language models grow very large, storage and memory constraints make training impractical or very expensive. Deep prefix tuning addresses these issues by prepending continuous prompts to the transformer. These continuous prefix prompts, which are prepended to each attention layer in the model, and a task-specific linear head (such as a classification head) are trained.

More formally, for each attention layer L_i (as per Vaswani et al., 2017) in BERT's encoder, we append some trainable prefixes P_k (trained key prefix) and P_v (trained value prefix) with length n to the key and value matrices for some initial prompts:

$$\begin{aligned} L_i = \mathbf{Attn}(&xW_q^{(i)}, \\ &Cat(P_k^{(i)}, xW_k^{(i)}), \\ &Cat(P_v^{(i)}, xW_v^{(i)})) \end{aligned} \tag{1}$$

With $W^{(i)}_{\{q,k,v\}}$ representing the respective query, key, or value matrices for the attention at layer i, and x denoting the input to layer i. Here, we assume single-headed attention for simplicity. Here, the Cat function concatenates the two matrices along the dimension corresponding to the sequence length.

Note that in Equation 1 we do not need to left-pad any query values, as the shape of the query matrix does not need to match that of the key and value matrices.

Expected Calibration Error First suggested in Pakdaman Naeini et al. (2015) and later used for neural networks in Guo et al. (2017), expected calibration error (ECE) can determine how well a model is calibrated. In other words, ECE evaluates how closely a model's logit weights reflect the actual accuracy for that prediction. Calibration is important for two main reasons. First, having a properly calibrated model reduces misuse of the model; if output logits accurately reflect their real-world likelihood, then software systems using such models can better handle cases where the model is uncertain. Second, better calibration improves the interpretability of a model as we can better understand how confident a model is under different scenarios (Guo et al., 2017). Bhambhoria et al. (2022) used ECE in the legal domain, where it is especially important due the high-stakes nature of legal decision making.

4 Methods

Here we outline our approach and other baselines for comparison.

RoBERTA To establish a baseline, we train RoBERTa (Liu et al., 2019) for downstream tasks using full model tuning (referred to as "full finetuning"). In addition to the state of the art performance that RoBERTa achieves in many general NLP tasks, it has also shown very strong performance in legal tasks (Shaheen et al., 2020; Bhambhoria et al., 2022). Unlike some transformer models, RoBERTa has an encoder-only architecture, and is normally pre-trained on the masked language modelling task (Devlin et al., 2019). We evaluate the model on both of its size variants, RoBERTa-base (approximately 125M parameters) and RoBERTa-large (approximately 335M parameters).

LEGAL-BERT We evaluate the effectiveness of our approach against LEGAL-BERT, a fully

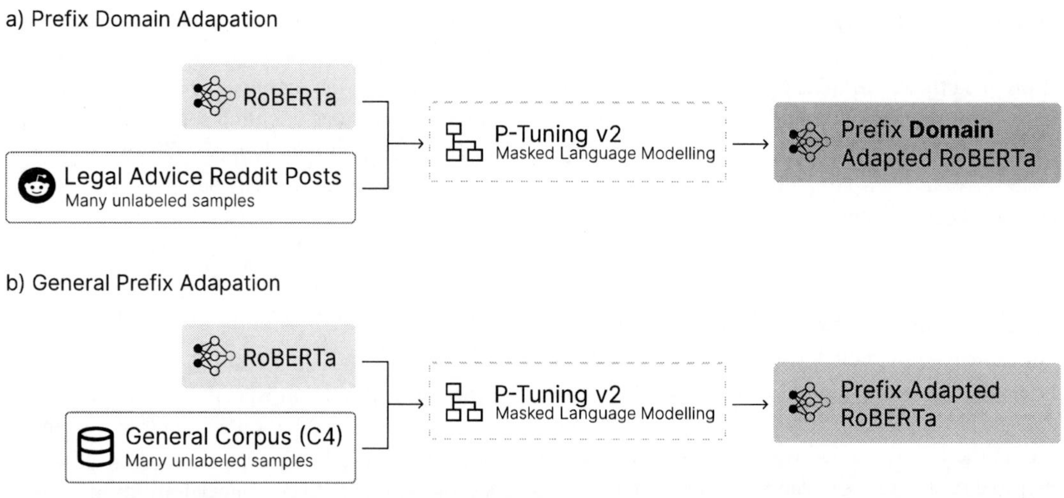

Figure 2: Training process for our methods, with colored boxes representing model weights, colored outlines representing datasets, and dotted outlines representing training method (in this case, P-Tuning v2). Notice that (a) prefix domain adapation and (b) prefix adaptation both use the same starting model and training method, but different datasets.

domain-adapted version of BERT for the legal domain (Chalkidis et al., 2020). In our experiments, we further perform full finetuning for each downstream task. The number of parameters in LEGAL-BERT (109M) is comparable to RoBERTa-base (125M), as used in our other experiments.

Full Domain Adaptation We also perform full domain adaptation by pre-training all model parameters using the masked language modelling (MLM) task with text from each dataset. Then, we train this fully domain adapted model using full-model tuning for each downstream task. This method is a strong baseline for comparison, as we tune all model parameters twice (MLM pre-training and downstream task) for each task, taking up many computational resources.

P-Tuning v2 We compare our approach against P-Tuning v2 (Liu et al., 2022), an "alternative to finetuning" that only optimizes a fractional percentage of parameters (0.1%-3%). It works by freezing the entire model, then appending some frozen prompts in each layer. That is, trainable prompts are added as prefixes to each layer, with only the key and value matrices of the self-attention mechanism trained. We use P-Tuning v2 as a baseline, being the original parameter-efficient training method that we base our study on.

Prefix Domain Adaptation Inspired by domain adaptation, we introduce *prefix domain adaptation*, which domain adapts a deep prompt (Li and Liang, 2021) to better initialize it for downstream tasks. As the domain adapted deep prompt is very small (approximately 0.1% the size of the base model), it is easy to store and distribute. Once trained, the deep prompt is used as a starting point for downstream tasks.

More specifically, we train a deep prompt, using prefix tuning as in Liu et al. (2022)[2], for the masked language modelling task (Devlin et al., 2019) on a large, domain-specific unsupervised corpus, as shown in Figure 2(a). Next, we use this pre-trained prompt and randomly initialize a task-specific head (such as a classification head for a classification task) for each downstream task. Finally, we train the resulting model for the downstream task, using the same prompt tuning approach from Liu et al. (2022). To the best of our knowledge, no prior works have trained a prefix prompt for a specific domain to better initialize it for downstream tasks using an unsupervised pre-training task (masked language modelling).

Formally, we can treat a prefix-tuned model as having a trained prefix P, and a trained task-specific head H. We group each downstream task into m domains in $\{ \mathcal{D}_1, \mathcal{D}_2, ..., \mathcal{D}_m \}$, such that there is some overlap between the tasks in each domain $\mathcal{D}_i$. For each domain $\mathcal{D}_i$, we use a domain-specific corpus, C_i, to train some prefix P_i for the masked language modelling task with prompt

[2] Same implementation as provided in Liu et al. (2022)

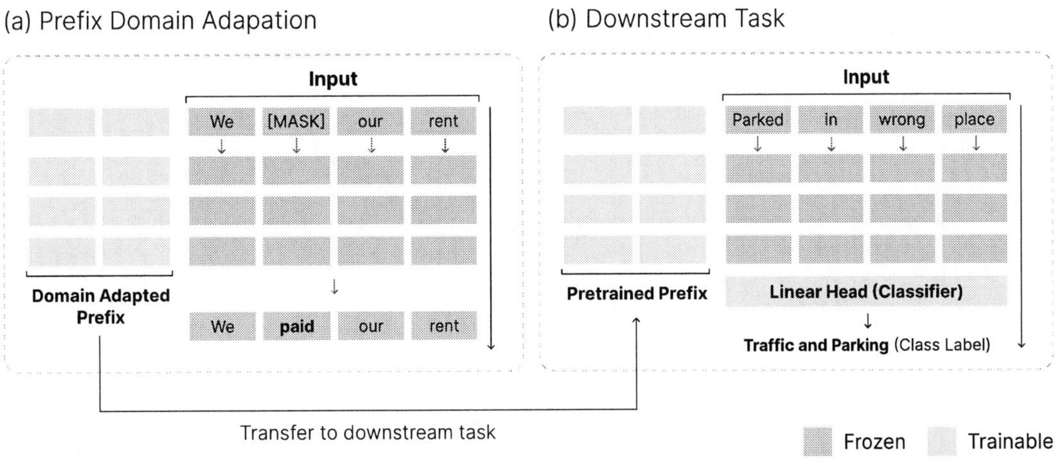

Figure 3: Toy example of how our framework works. (a) We pre-train a prefix on the unsupervised masked language modelling task. (b) We randomly initialize the classification head but preserve the prefix for downstream tasks. Green blocks represent trainable prompt embeddings or layers of the transformer, and blue blocks represent frozen embeddings or computations.

tuning (Figure 3(a)). Then, for each downstream task in $\mathcal{D}_i$, we use the deep prefix P_i to initialize the prompts, while randomly initializing the task-specific head H_i (Figure 3(b)).

Prefix Adaptation In addition to prefix domain adaptation, we conduct experiments using our approach in general settings, inspired by work done in Vu et al. (2022) and Gu et al. (2022). We name this more general approach *prefix adaptation*. That is, we test the performance of initializing a prompt with the masked language modelling task on a subset of the Colossal Clean Crawled Corpus (Raffel et al., 2020), instead of domain-specific texts (illustrated in Figure 2(b)). Formally, we use the same prefix domain adaptation approach as previously mentioned, but we group all tasks under one "General" domain $\mathcal{D}$, and thus only train one prefix P.

5 Datasets

We evaluate each of the approaches listed above on three different datasets.

Legal Advice Reddit We introduce a new dataset from the Legal Advice Reddit community (known as "/r/legaldvice"), sourcing the Reddit posts from the Pushshift Reddit dataset (Baumgartner et al., 2020) [3]. The dataset maps the text and title of each legal question posted into one of eleven classes, based on the original Reddit post's "flair" (i.e., tag). Questions are typically informal and use non-legal-specific language. Per the Legal Advice Reddit rules, posts must be about actual personal circumstances or situations. We limit the number of labels to the top eleven classes and remove the other samples from the dataset (more details in Appendix B). To prefix adapt the model for Reddit posts, we use samples from the Legal Advice sub-reddit that are not labelled or do not fall under the top eleven classes. We use the provided "flair" for each question for a legal area classification task (Soh et al., 2019), as illustrated in Figure 1.

European Court of Human Rights We use the European Court of Human Rights (ECHR) dataset (Chalkidis et al., 2019), which consists of a list of facts specific to a legal case, labelled with violated human rights articles (if any). Specifically, we evaluate our approach on the binary violation prediction task, where the task is to predict whether a given case violates any human rights articles given a list of facts. We undersample this relatively large dataset to simulate a fewshot learning environment. To prefix adapt the model for ECHR cases, we use the original corpus of unlabelled cases (similar to what was done in Chalkidis et al., 2020). As the average document length is 700 words (above BERT's maximum length limit), we truncate the text to 500 tokens, concatenating the title and facts of the case together.

Law Stack Exchange We also introduce a second dataset with data from the Law Stack Exchange

[3]https://huggingface.co/datasets/jonathanli/legal-advice-reddit

Dataset Name	N_{class}	Fewshot Sizes
ECHR	2	4, 8, 16, 32
Legal Advice Reddit	11	32, 64, 128, 256
Law Stack Exchange	16	32, 64, 128, 256

Table 1: Classification tasks evaluated in our experiments. N_{class} represents the number of classes, and "Fewshot Sizes" represents the various number of samples used (4 different fewshot sizes evaluated for each dataset).

(LSE)[4]. This dataset is composed of questions from the Law Stack Exchange, which is a community forum-based website containing questions with answers to legal questions. Unlike the Legal Advice Reddit dataset, the Law Stack Exchange dataset is generally more formal (shown in Figure 1), and questions are generally more theoretical or hypothetical. We link the questions with their associated tags (e.g., "copyright" or "criminal-law"), and perform the multi-label classification task. Though posts can have multiple tags, we use the questions with only one tag in the top 16 most frequent tags (excluding tags associated with countries). Similarly to the Legal Advice Reddit dataset, we use other unused questions from the Law Stack Exchange to prefix domain adapt the model.

6 Experimental Setup

We test our approaches under a fewshot setting, where prompt tuning is known to perform poorly (Gu et al., 2022). We use RoBERTa-base and RoBERTa-large (Liu et al., 2019) for our experiments. To simulate a fewshot learning scenario, we randomly undersample the train and validation sets for each dataset, ensuring that the distribution of train and validation data roughly matches. Additionally, we vary the amount of data undersampled to study how fewshot size affects performance. In these tasks, we use a validation size of 256 (much smaller than the original) to represent true fewshot learning better (Perez et al., 2021). Considering that fewshot learning is quite unstable, we ran all of our experiments five times, using the seeds $\{10, 20, 30, 40, 50\}$. We provide more training details in Appendix A.

There is often confusion around whether fewshot sizes represent the number of samples per class or

[4]https://huggingface.co/datasets/jonathanli/law-stack-exchange

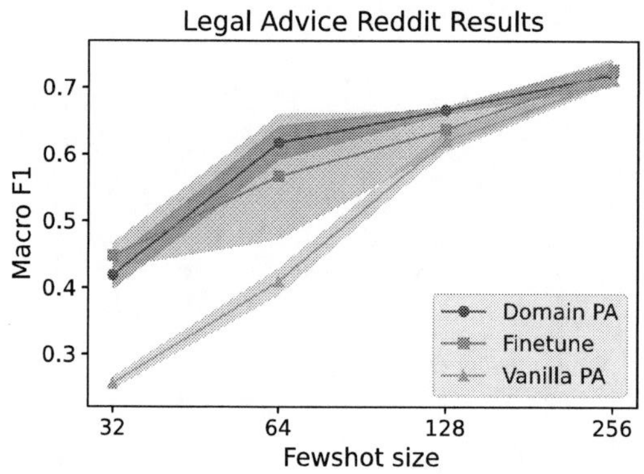

Figure 4: Various fewshot sizes and their performance (measured by macro F1). The shaded region represents the standard deviation across runs, while each point represents the mean performance across runs. Overall, our approach (prefix domain adaptation) matches the performance of full finetuning.

the total number of samples (Perez et al., 2021). In our results, the fewshot sizes we show are the exact number of training samples used (i.e., total training samples). The exact number of samples is listed in Table 1. To keep the number of samples per class roughly equivalent, we use fewer total samples for the ECHR task, which only has two classes.

7 Results and Discussion

We make a few observations on our results, shown in Table 2. We observe that our method, prefix domain adaptation, outperforms both regular prefix tuning and full finetuning in most tasks across fewshot sizes, despite training considerably fewer parameters. We find that prefix adaptation is comparable to full domain adaptation; in some settings (such as ECHR and some Reddit fewshot settings), prefix adaptation even outperforms full domain adaptation. We argue that prefix domain adaptation achieves better fewshot performance relative to regular prefix tuning because the pre-trained prompts are closer to an effective prompt after our domain adaptation step. This is similar to full domain adaptation, which improves performance on downstream tasks relative to a base model (Chalkidis et al., 2020) by making parameters closer to optimal parameters. Consistent with Gu et al. (2022), we find that regular prefix tuning falls behind full parameter tuning in fewshot settings.

Additionally, we find that LEGAL-BERT performs worse than other techniques on datasets with more informal language (such as the Reddit

	Legal Advice Reddit				Law Stack Exchange				European Court of Human Rights			
Fewshot Size	*32*	*64*	*128*	*256*	*32*	*64*	*128*	*256*	*4*	*8*	*16*	*32*
FT	$\mathbf{44.8_{1.9}}$	$56.7_{9.4}$	$63.8_{2.8}$	$72.7_{1.8}$	$19.5_{17.1}$	$29.0_{14.8}$	$58.8_{0.8}$	$67.4_{0.9}$	$53.7_{1.6}$	$60.1_{5.5}$	$66.5_{8.7}$	$66.3_{3.5}$
LEGAL-BERT + FT	$36.1_{2.9}$	$35.2_{16.1}$	$49.5_{3.7}$	$70.2_{1.7}$	$24.6_{13.1}$	$51.2_{0.9}$	$47.6_{24.9}$	$\mathbf{67.5_{0.2}}$	$59.3_{12.4}$	$55.8_{3.8}$	$61.1_{8.7}$	$67.6_{3.6}$
Domain Adapt + FT	$31.8_{16.4}$	$\mathbf{66.7_{3.3}}$	$66.6_{1.5}$	$\mathbf{75.8_{0.9}}$	$\mathbf{38.5_{0.4}}$	$\mathbf{53.2_{2.5}}$	$\mathbf{62.4_{1.1}}$	$66.6_{0.6}$	$47.6_{2.3}$	$51.2_{1.7}$	$47.9_{1.3}$	$56.7_{2.2}$
Prefix Domain Adapt	$41.9_{2.2}$	$61.7_{2.7}$	$\mathbf{66.6_{0.6}}$	$72.0_{1.9}$	$36.1_{0.9}$	$52.4_{1.7}$	$56.1_{0.8}$	$63.1_{1.7}$	$\mathbf{72.7_{4.6}}$	$70.9_{2.3}$	$\mathbf{75.1_{1.8}}$	$\mathbf{69.4_{2.0}}$
Prefix Adapt	$35.5_{2.1}$	$58.0_{6.4}$	$52.7_{21.4}$	$72.2_{0.5}$	$31.7_{1.2}$	$46.8_{2.5}$	$57.0_{0.8}$	$66.6_{0.5}$	$68.9_{6.4}$	$\mathbf{71.4_{1.4}}$	$75.0_{2.7}$	$66.3_{7.8}$
P-Tuning v2	$25.6_{1.0}$	$41.0_{2.1}$	$62.0_{1.6}$	$71.2_{0.6}$	$24.6_{2.2}$	$45.3_{2.0}$	$56.3_{0.7}$	$65.3_{0.6}$	$70.9_{2.6}$	$70.5_{3.6}$	$70.9_{2.3}$	$67.1_{0.9}$

Table 2: Classification results with RoBERTa-base (or similarly sized models), with fewshot size listed as italic numbers in the second row. Experiments run five times with different seeds, with subscripts representing the standard deviation of the five runs. **Bolded** results represent the best performance for the fewshot size, and underlined results represent second best. All methods are assumed to be initialized from RoBERTa-base, except for LEGAL-BERT from Chalkidis et al. (2020). "FT" represents fully finetuned for downstream tasks and "Domain Adapt" is full domain adaptation, with a line separating full-model (top) and parameter efficient (bottom) tuning methods.

dataset). LEGAL-BERT shows more instability across seeds (i.e., larger standard deviation) . As LEGAL-BERT-SC (the model we use) was only trained on very formal legal text, it did not see many colloquialisms or slang during training that are prevalent in informal text. For this reason, we do not think LEGAL-BERT would be effective as initialization for tasks involving legal questions asked by laypersons, which typically do not use incredibly formal legal language.

In contrast to other datasets, the ECHR dataset's train and test split have different distributions. In fewshot scenarios with very little data (i.e., 4-16 examples), we find that prefix tuning based approaches perform better than full finetuning; this suggests that prefix tuning approaches are more robust to changes in distribution (and possibly noise). We also note that BERT with truncation (maximum token length of 500) performs a lot better than initially reported in Chalkidis et al. (2019), who report an F1 worse than random guessing (macro F1 of 66.5 in ours, 17 in theirs). We believe this underperformance of finetuning BERT could be caused by a mistake in their training process.

In Figure 4, we show the trend of performance on Reddit data as the number of samples increases. Prefix domain adaptation is comparable to finetuning, consistently outperforming regular prefix tuning. As shown by the larger shaded area around the lines, the stability of finetuning is worse than prefix domain adaptation for this task. Performance gradually converges increases as more data is given to each method.

Larger models typically provide better performance on various tasks. Thus, we run experiments using RoBERTa-large (over 2x larger than RoBERTa-base) to see how our approach scales to larger models. As seen in Table 3, our approach is still comparable to or outperforms full finetuning with larger models. Impressively, in the fewshot sizes 32-128, prefix domain adaptation with RoBERTa-base is even comparable to full finetuning with RoBERTa-large. Additionally, we note that full domain adapation is more sensitive to learning rates in larger models, explaining weaker performance in fewshot sizes 32 and 64. Due to limitations in computational resources, we leave more extensive hyperparameter search as future work.

Fewshot Size	*32*	*64*	*128*	*256*
FT	$42.1_{5.7}$	$55.5_{5.4}$	$62.0_{3.5}$	$\mathbf{77.6_{1.0}}$
Domain Adapt + FT	$34.2_{7.3}$	$61.7_{5.6}$	$66.6_{8.7}$	$77.3_{1.3}$
Prefix Domain Adapt	$\mathbf{46.7_{2.1}}$	$\mathbf{63.5_{1.5}}$	$\mathbf{67.0_{1.7}}$	$72.2_{1.0}$
Prefix Adapt	$46.5_{3.4}$	$63.1_{2.5}$	$64.3_{1.8}$	$70.0_{1.9}$
P-Tuning v2	$46.7_{1.7}$	$59.0_{1.5}$	$65.6_{2.7}$	$69.2_{1.7}$

Table 3: Classification results on RoBERTa-large, evaluated on Reddit data. Note that we do not evaluate results with LEGAL-BERT because LEGAL-BERT models with comparable size to RoBERTA-large do not exist.

7.1 Calibration

While providing predictions to laypersons, it is vital that the distribution of the output logits accurately reflect the model's confidence. Thus, we use the expected calibration error (ECE) (Pakdaman Naeini et al., 2015) to measure the calibration of each model resulting from each method. We show that the calibration of our approach is better than finetuning across tasks, as seen in Table 4. Additionally, we observe that our approach is comparable to

	Reddit	LSE	ECHR
FT	$0.158_{0.012}$	$0.243_{0.015}$	$0.320_{0.037}$
LEGAL-BERT + FT	$0.454_{0.05}$	$\mathbf{0.165_{0.043}}$	$\underline{0.245_{0.042}}$
Domain Adapt + FT	$0.152_{0.004}$	$\underline{0.214_{0.01}}$	$0.320_{0.121}$
Prefix Domain Adapt	$\underline{0.133_{0.01}}$	$0.242_{0.023}$	$\mathbf{0.214_{0.032}}$
Prefix Adapt	$\mathbf{0.104_{0.021}}$	$0.24_{0.008}$	$0.266_{0.063}$
P-Tuning v2	$0.412_{0.019}$	$0.263_{0.009}$	$0.253_{0.050}$

Table 4: Calibration, measured by the top-1 expected calibration error (ECE). "Reddit" is the ECE on our Legal Advice Reddit dataset (fewshot size of 256), "ECHR" is ECE on European Court of Human Rights dataset (fewshot size of 32), and "LSE" is ECE on the Law Stack Exchange dataset (fewshot size of 256). Lower is better, with **bold** being the best and underline being second best.

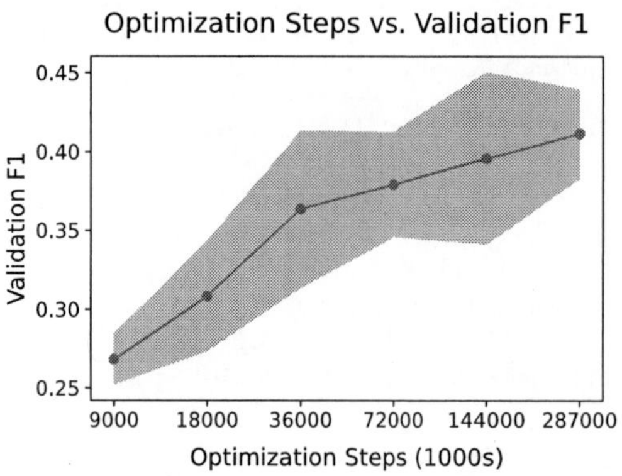

Figure 5: Performance of prefix domain adaptation after training the domain adapted prompt for a different number of training steps, performed on Reddit data with a fewshot size of 32 using RoBERTa-base. Shaded region represents standard deviation between five runs.

LEGAL-BERT across tasks. In the case where questions are well formulated (i.e., in the LSE dataset), we found that legal models are better calibrated. However, in Reddit data, which is central to helping laypersons with legal questions, we find that our approach is very competitive.

7.2 Sample Efficiency

We study the effect of training time (i.e., number of training steps) for the domain-adapted prompt on downstream performance. To analyze the effect of additional training steps on the domain adapted prefix's performance, we initialize models using pre-trained prefixes from specific steps and plot the performance (over five runs) in Figure 5. We find that more optimization steps during the prefix adaptation step lead to better downstream performance.

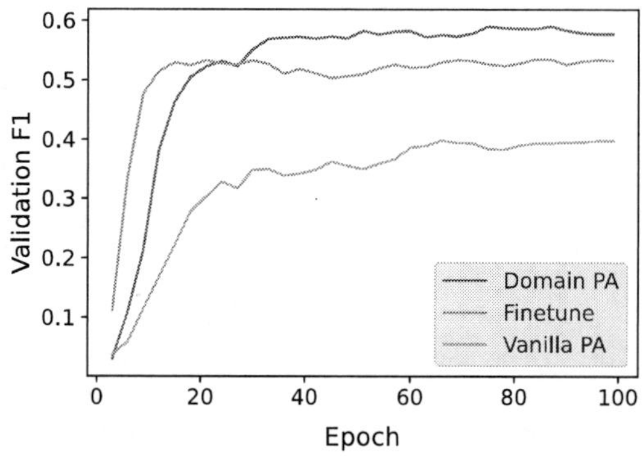

Figure 6: Convergence comparison of prefix domain adaptation ("Domain PA"), full finetuning ("Finetune"), and P-Tuning v2 on Reddit data, using a fewshot size of 64.

Intuitively, this makes sense as a longer training time means the prefix starts closer to an ideal one for a downstream task.

Though each optimization step is faster with regular prefix tuning (Gu et al., 2022), it converges slowly and thus is not necessarily faster than finetuning. As shown in Figure 6, our approach converges faster than regular prefix tuning. Again, we argue that this is expected as the prompts are closer to a desired solution when compared to regular prefix tuning, meaning fewer training steps are needed to reach an effective solution.

8 Conclusions

In this paper, we propose a novel training framework, *prefix domain adaptation*, aiming to domain adapt a prompt using a large corpus of domain-specific text. We show that our approach matches or outperforms LEGAL-BERT or related techniques in performance while training fewer (0.1%) parameters. With our technique, we improve few-shot performance and convergence time compared to other parameter-efficient methods. We believe this will make fewshot data more usable (and thus reduce data labelling costs) while using parameter-efficient methods to reduce computational and storage costs.

Additionally, we introduce two new datasets (Legal Advice Reddit and Law Stack Exchange) to lay foundations for future work in legal decision-making systems; as opposed to formal documents in ECHR, our two datasets are closer to legal questions asked by laypersons, helping to promote access to justice for all.

References

Kate Barnes, Tiernon Riesenmy, Minh Duc Trinh, Eli Lleshi, Nora Balogh, and Roland Molontay. 2021. Dank or not? analyzing and predicting the popularity of memes on reddit. *Applied Network Science*, 6(1):21.

Marco Basaldella, Fangyu Liu, Ehsan Shareghi, and Nigel Collier. 2020. COMETA: A corpus for medical entity linking in the social media. In *Proceedings of the 2020 Conference on Empirical Methods in Natural Language Processing (EMNLP)*, pages 3122–3137, Online. Association for Computational Linguistics.

Jason Baumgartner, Savvas Zannettou, Brian Keegan, Megan Squire, and Jeremy Blackburn. 2020. The pushshift reddit dataset.

Iz Beltagy, Kyle Lo, and Arman Cohan. 2019. SciBERT: A pretrained language model for scientific text. In *Proceedings of the 2019 Conference on Empirical Methods in Natural Language Processing and the 9th International Joint Conference on Natural Language Processing (EMNLP-IJCNLP)*, pages 3615–3620, Hong Kong, China. Association for Computational Linguistics.

Rohan Bhambhoria, Hui Liu, Samuel Dahan, and Xiaodan Zhu. 2022. Interpretable low-resource legal decision making. *Proceedings of the AAAI Conference on Artificial Intelligence*, 36(11):11819–11827.

Tom Brown, Benjamin Mann, Nick Ryder, Melanie Subbiah, Jared D Kaplan, Prafulla Dhariwal, Arvind Neelakantan, Pranav Shyam, Girish Sastry, Amanda Askell, Sandhini Agarwal, Ariel Herbert-Voss, Gretchen Krueger, Tom Henighan, Rewon Child, Aditya Ramesh, Daniel Ziegler, Jeffrey Wu, Clemens Winter, Chris Hesse, Mark Chen, Eric Sigler, Mateusz Litwin, Scott Gray, Benjamin Chess, Jack Clark, Christopher Berner, Sam McCandlish, Alec Radford, Ilya Sutskever, and Dario Amodei. 2020. Language models are few-shot learners. In *Advances in Neural Information Processing Systems*, volume 33, pages 1877–1901. Curran Associates, Inc.

Ilias Chalkidis, Ion Androutsopoulos, and Nikolaos Aletras. 2019. Neural legal judgment prediction in English. In *Proceedings of the 57th Annual Meeting of the Association for Computational Linguistics*, pages 4317–4323, Florence, Italy. Association for Computational Linguistics.

Ilias Chalkidis, Manos Fergadiotis, Prodromos Malakasiotis, Nikolaos Aletras, and Ion Androutsopoulos. 2020. LEGAL-BERT: The muppets straight out of law school. In *Findings of the Association for Computational Linguistics: EMNLP 2020*, pages 2898–2904, Online. Association for Computational Linguistics.

Ilias Chalkidis, Abhik Jana, Dirk Hartung, Michael Bommarito, Ion Androutsopoulos, Daniel Katz, and Nikolaos Aletras. 2022. LexGLUE: A benchmark dataset for legal language understanding in English. In *Proceedings of the 60th Annual Meeting of the Association for Computational Linguistics (Volume 1: Long Papers)*, pages 4310–4330, Dublin, Ireland. Association for Computational Linguistics.

Jacob Devlin, Ming-Wei Chang, Kenton Lee, and Kristina Toutanova. 2019. BERT: Pre-training of deep bidirectional transformers for language understanding. In *Proceedings of the 2019 Conference of the North American Chapter of the Association for Computational Linguistics: Human Language Technologies, Volume 1 (Long and Short Papers)*, pages 4171–4186, Minneapolis, Minnesota. Association for Computational Linguistics.

Chunjiang Ge, Rui Huang, Mixue Xie, Zihang Lai, Shiji Song, Shuang Li, and Gao Huang. 2022. Domain adaptation via prompt learning.

Yuxian Gu, Xu Han, Zhiyuan Liu, and Minlie Huang. 2022. PPT: Pre-trained prompt tuning for few-shot learning. In *Proceedings of the 60th Annual Meeting of the Association for Computational Linguistics (Volume 1: Long Papers)*, pages 8410–8423, Dublin, Ireland. Association for Computational Linguistics.

Chuan Guo, Geoff Pleiss, Yu Sun, and Kilian Q. Weinberger. 2017. On calibration of modern neural networks. In *Proceedings of the 34th International Conference on Machine Learning*, volume 70 of *Proceedings of Machine Learning Research*, pages 132–1330. PMLR.

Pengcheng He, Xiaodong Liu, Jianfeng Gao, and Weizhu Chen. 2021. Deberta: Decoding-enhanced bert with disentangled attention. In *International Conference on Learning Representations*.

Neil Houlsby, Andrei Giurgiu, Stanislaw Jastrzebski, Bruna Morrone, Quentin De Laroussilhe, Andrea Gesmundo, Mona Attariyan, and Sylvain Gelly. 2019. Parameter-efficient transfer learning for nlp. In *International Conference on Machine Learning*, pages 2790–2799. PMLR.

Jinhyuk Lee, Wonjin Yoon, Sungdong Kim, Donghyeon Kim, Sunkyu Kim, Chan Ho So, and Jaewoo Kang. 2019. BioBERT: a pre-trained biomedical language representation model for biomedical text mining. *Bioinformatics*.

Xiang Lisa Li and Percy Liang. 2021. Prefix-tuning: Optimizing continuous prompts for generation. In *Proceedings of the 59th Annual Meeting of the Association for Computational Linguistics and the 11th International Joint Conference on Natural Language Processing (Volume 1: Long Papers)*, pages 4582–4597, Online. Association for Computational Linguistics.

Xiao Liu, Kaixuan Ji, Yicheng Fu, Weng Tam, Zhengxiao Du, Zhilin Yang, and Jie Tang. 2022. P-tuning: Prompt tuning can be comparable to fine-tuning across scales and tasks. In *Proceedings of the 60th Annual Meeting of the Association for Computational Linguistics (Volume 2: Short Papers)*, pages 61–68, Dublin, Ireland. Association for Computational Linguistics.

Yinhan Liu, Myle Ott, Naman Goyal, Jingfei Du, Mandar Joshi, Danqi Chen, Omer Levy, Mike Lewis, Luke Zettlemoyer, and Veselin Stoyanov. 2019. Roberta: A robustly optimized bert pretraining approach.

Nicholas Lourie, Ronan Le Bras, and Yejin Choi. 2021. Scruples: A corpus of community ethical judgments on 32,000 real-life anecdotes. *Proceedings of the AAAI Conference on Artificial Intelligence*, 35(15):13470–13479.

Mahdi Pakdaman Naeini, Gregory Cooper, and Milos Hauskrecht. 2015. Obtaining well calibrated probabilities using bayesian binning. *Proceedings of the AAAI Conference on Artificial Intelligence*, 29(1).

Ethan Perez, Douwe Kiela, and Kyunghyun Cho. 2021. True few-shot learning with language models.

Colin Raffel, Noam Shazeer, Adam Roberts, Katherine Lee, Sharan Narang, Michael Matena, Yanqi Zhou, Wei Li, and Peter J. Liu. 2020. Exploring the limits of transfer learning with a unified text-to-text transformer. *Journal of Machine Learning Research*, 21(140):1–67.

Zein Shaheen, Gerhard Wohlgenannt, and Erwin Filtz. 2020. Large scale legal text classification using transformer models.

Lakshay Sharma, Laura Graesser, Nikita Nangia, and Utku Evci. 2019. Natural language understanding with the quora question pairs dataset.

Jerrold Soh, How Khang Lim, and Ian Ernst Chai. 2019. Legal area classification: A comparative study of text classifiers on Singapore Supreme Court judgments. In *Proceedings of the Natural Legal Language Processing Workshop 2019*, pages 67–77, Minneapolis, Minnesota. Association for Computational Linguistics.

Ashish Vaswani, Noam Shazeer, Niki Parmar, Jakob Uszkoreit, Llion Jones, Aidan N. Gomez, Lukasz Kaiser, and Illia Polosukhin. 2017. Attention is all you need.

Tu Vu, Brian Lester, Noah Constant, Rami Al-Rfou', and Daniel Cer. 2022. SPoT: Better frozen model adaptation through soft prompt transfer. In *Proceedings of the 60th Annual Meeting of the Association for Computational Linguistics (Volume 1: Long Papers)*, pages 5039–5059, Dublin, Ireland. Association for Computational Linguistics.

Liting Wang, Li Zhang, and Jing Jiang. 2020. Duplicate question detection with deep learning in stack overflow. *IEEE Access*, 8:25964–25975.

Rongsheng Zhang, Yinhe Zheng, Xiaoxi Mao, and Minlie Huang. 2021. Unsupervised domain adaptation with adapter.

Lucia Zheng, Neel Guha, Brandon R. Anderson, Peter Henderson, and Daniel E. Ho. 2021. When does pretraining help? assessing self-supervised learning for law and the casehold dataset of 53,000+ legal holdings. In *Proceedings of the Eighteenth International Conference on Artificial Intelligence and Law*, ICAIL '21, page 159–168, New York, NY, USA. Association for Computing Machinery.

Configuration	Learning Rates
RoBERTa-base PT	5e-2, 3e-2, 2e-2, 5e-3, 5e-4
RoBERTa-large PT	5e-2, 3e-2, 2e-2, 5e-3, 5e-4
RoBERTa-base FT	1e-3, 5e-4, 2e-4, 1e-4, 5e-5
RoBERTa-large FT	1e-4, 5e-5, 2e-5, 1e-5, 5e-6

Table 5: Learning rates searched for each configuration. The suffix "PT" means for prompt tuning based methods, and "FT" for finetuning based methods.

A Additional Training Details

We use the AdamW optimizer and a grid search of learning rates as in Table 5, mostly following Gu et al. (2022). For all of our experiments, we truncate the sequence to a length of 500 tokens (as opposed to 512 tokens) to allow space for a tuned deep prefix prompt. We report the calibration and general results using the checkpoint with the best validation macro F1, for each fewshot size and method.

Given that RoBERTa-base (~125M parameters) and RoBERTa-large (~355M parameters) can fit in a single NVIDIA 1080Ti GPU (using a smaller batch size), we do not perform any model or data parallelism. We use an effective batch size (i.e., factoring in gradient accumulation steps) of 32 for experiments on roberta-base, and due to memory constraints, an effective batch size of 24 for experiments on roberta-large. As the number of samples is low, we train for 100 epochs. However, while performing domain adaptation and prefix adaptation training steps, we train for 20 epochs as much more data as available (and therefore, more optimization steps are run in each epoch).

We use a prefix length of 8. Including the tuned linear head for classification, the largest number of parameters we tune for RoBERTa-base is 160K (varies slightly for each task depending on the number of classes), or ~0.13% of the model's parameters.

Dataset Name	N_{train}	N_{dev}	N_{test}	Avg. Words
ECHR	7100	2998	1380	2105_{2489}
Legal Advice Reddit	9887	9987	79136	145_{117}
Law Stack Exchange	638	319	1596	244_{217}

Table 6: Sizes of datasets. $N_{train,dev,test}$ represent sizes of the train, development, and test sets respectively.

B Data Details

For Reddit data we take the top 11 classes that are not countries. We concatenate the title of the Reddit post and body text together, then use this combination to train our models for the masked language modelling and flair classification task.

For Stack Exchange data, we take only the questions with a single tag, and again. The stack exchange data, taken from Internet Archive[5], includes the post body in an HTML form. As our base models were not trained on HTML formatted text, we convert the HTML to Markdown footnote to make it much more similar to human readable text.

For the ECHR dataset, we use the non-anonymized variant and concatenate the title of the case with each fact from the legal case. Additionally, we found that some documents had numbered facts (such as "**1.** <fact>"), while some documents were not numbered. We used a simple regular expression to remove this inconsistency which could possibly create biases in the model (e.g., if numbered facts were more likely to mean a violation).

In our domain adaptation experiments, we use all the data (i.e., including questions/posts that were previously filtered out because they didn't have top tags) for each dataset. We use the domain adapated checkpoint with the best validation cross-entropy loss for downstream tasks.

The sizes of each split are listed in Table 6. Test split sizes for the Reddit and Stack Exchange dataset are intentionally larger than the validation and training set to better simulate true fewshot learning, as per Perez et al. (2021).

[5]https://archive.org/download/stackexchange

Processing Long Legal Documents with Pre-trained Transformers: Modding LegalBERT and Longformer

Dimitris Mamakas[*] [†] **Petros Tsotsi**[*] [†]
Ion Androutsopoulos [†] **Ilias Chalkidis** [‡] [◇]
[†] Department of Informatics, Athens University of Economics and Business, Greece
‡ Department of Computer Science, University of Copenhagen, Denmark
[◇] Cognitiv+, Athens, Greece

Abstract

Pre-trained Transformers currently dominate most NLP tasks. They impose, however, limits on the maximum input length (512 sub-words in BERT), which are too restrictive in the legal domain. Even sparse-attention models, such as Longformer and BigBird, which increase the maximum input length to 4,096 sub-words, severely truncate texts in three of the six datasets of LexGLUE. Simpler linear classifiers with TF-IDF features can handle texts of any length, require far less resources to train and deploy, but are usually outperformed by pre-trained Transformers. We explore two directions to cope with long legal texts: (i) modifying a Longformer warm-started from LegalBERT to handle even longer texts (up to 8,192 sub-words), and (ii) modifying Legal-BERT to use TF-IDF representations. The first approach is the best in terms of performance, surpassing a hierarchical version of LegalBERT, which was the previous state of the art in LexGLUE. The second approach leads to computationally more efficient models at the expense of lower performance, but the resulting models still outperform overall a linear SVM with TF-IDF features in long legal document classification.

1 Introduction

Transformer-based models (Vaswani et al., 2017), like BERT (Devlin et al., 2019), RoBERTa (Liu et al., 2019), and their numerous offspring, currently dominate most natural language processing (NLP) tasks. These models are pre-trained on very large corpora using generic tasks (e.g., masked token prediction) that do not require human annotations, and are then fine-tuned (further trained) on typically much smaller task-specific datasets with manually annotated ground truth. The quadratic complexity of their attention mechanisms, however, imposes limits on the maximum input length

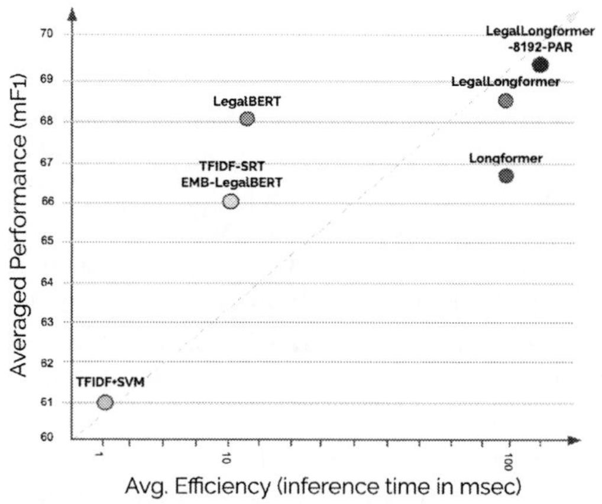

Figure 1: Comparison of examined models presented in Section 3, considering averaged down-stream performance and efficiency (inference time) in LexGLUE long document classification tasks (ECtHR, SCOTUS).

(512 sub-word tokens in BERT, RoBERTa), which are often too restrictive in the legal domain, where longer documents are common. The same restrictions apply to LegalBERT (Chalkidis et al., 2020), a BERT variant pre-trained on legal corpora.

Even the sparse-attention Longformer (Beltagy et al., 2020), a well-known Transformer that increases the maximum input to 4,096 sub-words, severely truncates texts in three of the six datasets (see Fig. 2) of the LexGLUE legal NLP benchmark (Chalkidis et al., 2022). On the other hand, simpler linear classifiers with TF-IDF features (Manning et al., 2008), which were very common before deep learning, can handle texts of any length, at least in text classification tasks, require far less resources to train and deploy, but are nowadays usually outperformed by pre-trained Transformers.

Motivated by these observations, we explore two directions to better cope with long legal texts: (i) we modify a Longformer warm-started from Legal-BERT to handle even longer texts (up to 8,192 sub-words), a resource-intensive direction that further increases the parameters and processing time

[*] Equal contribution.

Proceedings of the Natural Legal Language Processing Workshop 2022, pages 130 - 142
December 8, 2022 ©2022 Association for Computational Linguistics

of large sparse-attention Transformer models; and (ii) we modify LegalBERT to use TF-IDF representations, which allows processing longer texts without increasing the model sizes. The first approach is the best overall in terms of performance, surpassing a hierarchical version of LegalBERT (Chalkidis et al., 2021a), which was the previous state of the art in LexGLUE. The second direction leads to computationally more efficient models at the expense of lower performance, but still outperforms overall a linear Support Vector Machine (SVM) (Cortes and Vapnik, 1995) with TF-IDF features in long document classification.

2 Related Work

2.1 Long Document Processing

Transformer-based models consist of stacked Transformer blocks (Vaswani et al., 2017). Each block builds a revised embedding (vector representation) for each (sub-word) token of the input text, based on the embeddings of the previous block, starting from an initial embedding layer that provides an embedding per vocabulary token. For a block with a single attention head and an input n tokens long, generating a single revised token embedding involves computing a weighted sum (weighted by attention scores) over the n token embeddings of the previous block. Hence, $O(n^2)$ time is required to generate all the n revised token embeddings. With k attention heads, the complexity is $O(k \cdot n^2)$.

Sparse-attention variants of Transformers, like those used in Longformer (Beltagy et al., 2020), ETC (Ainslie et al., 2020), BigBird (Zaheer et al., 2020), generate each revised token embedding by attending (considering) only the previous block's embeddings for the current, the l previous, and the l next tokens in the input text, i.e., the weighted sum is now over only $2 \cdot l + 1$ (equal to 512 by default) token embeddings of the previous block. The complexity becomes $O(k \cdot n \cdot l)$, linear to n. To better capture long-distance dependencies, these models also use *global attention*. This involves either standard pseudo-tokens, such as the `[cls]` token at the beginning of each text, or additional pseudo-tokens, e.g., `[sep]` tokens placed at the end of each paragraph. In both cases, these special global tokens are attended by, and attend all other tokens, allowing information to flow across distant tokens, even when sparse attention is used.

We experiment with Longformer, a well-known and relatively simple sparse-attention Transformer, which can process texts up to 4,096 sub-words long. ETC and Big Bird use the same maximum input length and are very similar; one difference is that they employ additional pre-training objectives for the global tokens, whereas in Longformer the global tokens are not pre-trained. We also expand Longformer to process texts up to 8,192 sub-words long, and we consider an ETC-like global attention scheme with additional `[sep]` tokens.

Hierarchical Transformers, e.g., SMITH (Yang et al., 2020), use BERT (or other base models) to separately encode each paragraph or other segments of the input text that do not exceed the base model's maximum input length. The generated paragraph embeddings (e.g., the embeddings of `[cls]` tokens placed at the beginning of each paragraph) are then passed through additional stacked Transformer blocks, to allow interactions between the paragraph embeddings. The resulting context-aware paragraph embeddings can then be used to classify individual paragraphs or to classify the entire text (e.g., using the first paragraph embedding or by max-pooling over all paragraph embeddings).

In LexGLUE (Chalkidis et al., 2022) a similar hierarchical model (Chalkidis et al., 2021a) was used, with either generic BERT variants (e.g., BERT, RoBERTa, DeBERTa) or LegalBERT as the base model, in three of the benchmark's tasks (ECtHR Task A and B, SCOTUS) where the average text length was much higher than BERT's maximum length (Fig. 2). Unlike SMITH, the additional paragraph-level Transformer blocks were not pre-trained. We compare against this hierarchical variant of LegalBERT on LexGLUE.

Recurrent Transformers are another approach to handle long texts (Dai et al., 2019; Yang et al., 2019; Ding et al., 2021). We do not consider them here due to the latency that recurrency introduces.

Bag-of-Word (BoW) models typically represent each text as a (sparse) feature vector $\langle f_1, \ldots, f_{|V|} \rangle$, with one feature f_i per vocabulary word. TF-IDF features (Manning et al., 2008) are common. Given a text n words long, each feature f_i becomes:

$$f_i = TF_i \cdot IDF_i = \frac{c_i}{n} \cdot \log \frac{N}{1 + d_i},$$

where c_i is the frequency of the i-th vocabulary word in the text, N is the number of documents in a corpus (in text classification this is often the training set), and d_i counts the documents of the corpus

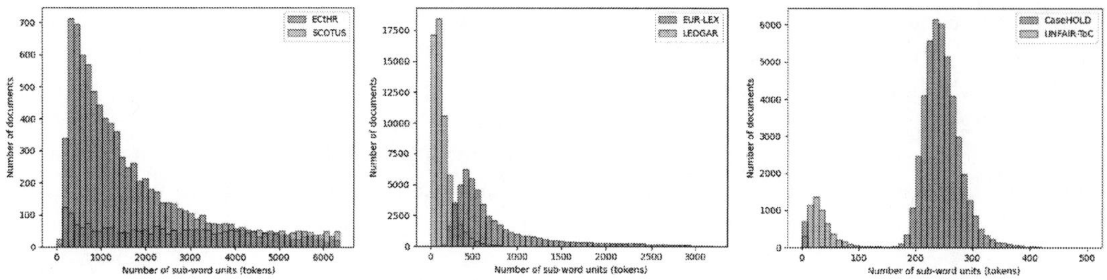

Figure 2: Distribution of input text length, measured in BERT sub-word tokens, across the six LexGLUE datasets. Copied with permission from Chalkidis et al. (2022).

that contain the i-th vocabulary word.[1] Averaging word embeddings (Jin et al., 2016; Brokos et al., 2016) with or without TF-IDF weighting, is also a BoW representation, but typically performs worse, since averaging leads to very noisy representations.

Such BoW representations discard word order, but are also insensitive to the length of the input text, in the sense that the feature vector always contains $|V|$ features. Combining TF-IDF feature vectors with linear classifiers leads to models that can handle texts of any length and require far less resources to train compared to modern Transformer-based models, at the expense of lower performance.

BoW-BERT: Our attempts to combine TF-IDF features with BERT were inspired by the work of Hessel and Schofield (2021), who reported that shuffling the words of each text during fine-tuning led to a degradation of less than 5 p.p. (F1 or accuracy) of BERT's performance in most GLUE tasks (Wang et al., 2018).[2] The resulting model, called BoW-BERT, can be seen as operating on BoW representations, in the sense that word order is lost. Hessel and Schofield (2021) also reported that BoW-BERT performed better than other BoW models on GLUE, including linear models with TF-IDF features. BoW-BERT's word shuffling, however, does not change the text length, hence it does not address BERT's maximum input length limit; IDF information is also not considered.

By contrast, we remove multiple occurrences of the same word from each text; to incorporate TF-IDF information, we order the remaining words by TF-IDF and/or we add a TF-IDF embedding layer, both discussed below.

[1]In 'sublinear' TF-IDF, a logarithm is also applied to TF.

[2]However, Hessel and Schofield (2021) also cite other work that found word shuffling to have a larger impact on pre-trained Transformers (and LSTMs) in other datasets and tasks. Sinha et al. (2021) and Abdou et al. (2022) investigated the effect of word shuffling on pre-trained Transformers in more detail, considering mostly word shuffling during pre-training.

2.2 Applications in Legal NLP

In the early days of Deep Learning for legal NLP, the community examined the use of the Hierarchical Attention Network (HAN) of Yang et al. (2016) or simpler variants (hierarchical BILSTMs) to encode long documents in applications of legal judgment prediction for Chinece (Zhong et al., 2018) or ECtHR (Chalkidis et al., 2019a) court cases, showcasing improvement over flat RNN-based models, such as stacked BILSTMs followed by a single-head attention layer (Xu et al., 2015). Hierarchical BILSTMs with self-attention were also employed by Chalkidis et al. (2018) for sequential sentence classification in order to identify obligations and prohibitions in contractual paragraphs.

Hierarchical variants of Transformers were initially proposed by Chalkidis et al. (2019a). In their work, document paragraphs are encoded via a shared BERT encoder to produce paragraph embeddings, which are then combined with max-pooling to form the final document embedding. This model outperformed strong RNN-based methods such as the Hierarchical Attention Network (HAN).

Later on, Chalkidis et al. (2021a) presented a new variant, where the paragraph embeddings are fed into additional stacked Transformer blocks, to allow cross-paragraph contextualization. This latter version has also been used in other legal NLP applications, by Niklaus et al. (2021, 2022) in judgment prediction of Swiss court cases, using XLM-R as the underlying encoder, and by Chalkidis et al. (2022) for the long document classification tasks of LexGLUE, using several alternative pre-trained Transformers, alongside Longformer. Xiao et al. (2021) released a Longformer pre-trained on Chinese legal corpora, which outperforms baselines in several legal NLP tasks. More recently, Dai et al. (2022) explored how tunable hyper-parameters of Hierarchical Transformers and Longformer, such as the size of the local window, affect downstream performance. In experiments on the ECtHR dataset, they found that fewer but larger local windows (paragraphs), e.g., 8×512, instead of 32×128, in Hierarchical Transformers improve performance.

Hierarchical Transformers are also used in the work of Malik et al. (2021) in legal judgment prediction of Indian court cases, where their best-performing model uses XLNet (Yang et al., 2019) as the underlying paragraph encoder followed by stacked BiGRUs. Moreover, hierarchical Transformers similar to those of Malik et al. have been also used by Kalamkar et al. (2022) for sequential legal sentence classification in order to segment Indian court cases into topical and coherent parts.

3 Models Considered

We discuss models Chalkidis et al. (2022) evaluated on LexGLUE as baselines, and models we introduce. The LexGLUE baselines also included RoBERTa (Liu et al., 2019), DeBERTa (He et al., 2021), BigBird (Zaheer et al., 2020), and CaseLaw-BERT (Zheng et al., 2021), which are not considered here. Chalkidis et al. (2022) found RoBERTa and DeBERTa to be better than BERT on LexGLUE, but worse than LegalBERT; no legally pre-trained variants of RoBERTa and DeBERTa are available. BigBird and CaseLaw-BERT were found to be overall slightly worse than Longformer and LegalBERT, respectively, on LexGLUE.

3.1 LexGLUE baselines

TFIDF-SVM is a linear SVM with TF-IDF features for the top-K most frequent word n-grams of the training set, where $n \in [1, 2, 3]$.[3]

LegalBERT (Chalkidis et al., 2020) is BERT pre-trained on English legal corpora (legislation, contracts, court cases). In the long document classification tasks (see Table 1), we deploy its hierarchical variant (Section 2) as in Chalkidis et al. (2022).

Longformer (Beltagy et al., 2020). This is the original Longformer, discussed in Section 2. It extends the maximum input length to 4,096 sub-word tokens. Like BERT and RoBERTa, Longformer uses absolute positional embeddings, i.e., there is a separate positional embedding for each token position up to the maximum input length. Longformer's positional embeddings were warm-started from the 512 positional embeddings of RoBERTa, cloning them 8 times (e.g., the embeddings of positions 513–1024 were initialized to the same RoBERTa positional embeddings as positions 1–512). All the other parameters of Longformer (and RoBERTa) are not sensitive to token positions and were warm-started from the corresponding RoBERTa parameters.[4] After warm-starting, Longformer was further pre-trained for 64k steps on generic corpora.

3.2 Extensions of LegalBERT

TFIDF-SRT-LegalBERT: This is LegalBERT, but we remove duplicate sub-words from the input text and sort the remaining ones by decreasing TF-IDF during fine-tuning. Removing duplicate words is an attempt to avoid exceeding the maximum input length. In ECtHR, for example, the average text length (in sub-words) drops from 1,619 to 1,120; in SCOTUS, from 5,953 to 1,636 (see Fig. 1). If the new form of the text still exceeds the maximum input length, we truncate it (keeping the first 512 tokens). Ordering sub-words by decreasing TF-IDF hopefully allows the model to learn to attend earlier sub-words (higher TF-IDF) more, utilizing BERT's positional embeddings as TF-IDF ranking encodings. This is a BoW model, since the original word order of the input text is lost.

TFIDF-SRT-EMB-LegalBERT: The same as the previous model, except that we add a TF-IDF embedding layer (Fig. 3). We bucketize the distribution of TF-IDF scores of the training set and assign a TF-IDF embedding to each bucket. During fine-tuning, we compute the TF-IDF score of each sub-word (before deduplication) and we add the corresponding TF-IDF bucket embedding to each token's input embedding when its positional embedding is also added. The TF-IDF bucket embeddings are initialized randomly and trained during fine-tuning. Hence, this model is informed both about TF-IDF token *ranking* (via word re-ordering) and TF-IDF *scores* (captured by TF-IDF embeddings). This is still a BoW model, since it ignores the original word order, like the previous model.

TFIDF-EMB-LegalBERT: The same as LegalBERT, but we add the TF-IDF layer of the previous model. Token deduplication and ordering by TF-IDF scores are not included. This allows us to study the contribution of the TF-IDF layer on its own by comparing to the original LegalBERT. The resulting model is aware of word-order via its positional

[3] $K \in [20k, 30k, 40k]$ is tuned per task on dev. data.

[4] E.g., the dense layers that produce the attention's query, key, value embeddings are the same for all token positions.

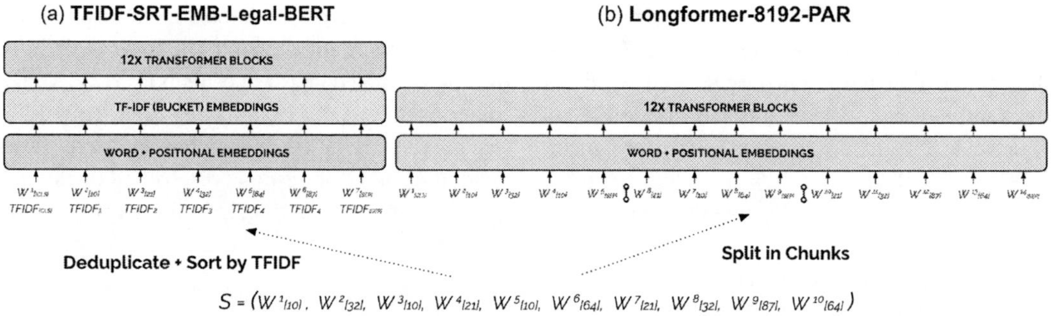

Figure 3: (a) TFIDF-SRT-EMB-LegalBERT, with sub-word token deduplication, re-ordering by TF-IDF, and TF-IDF embedding layer. (b) Longformer-8192-PAR extended to encode up to 8192 sub-word tokens, split into paragraphs separated by [sep] tokens. The original sequence (S) of sub-words (W) is shown in the bottom. Superscripts (W^p) denote positioning in each sequence. Subscripts ($W_{[id]}$) are the indices of the sub-words in the model's vocabulary. In both models, the resulting contextualized [cls] token embedding is fed to a linear classifier.

embeddings (like BERT and LegalBERT). For long texts, it addresses the maximum input length limitation via its hierarchical variant, which is similar to LegalBERT's (Chalkidis et al., 2022).

3.3 Extensions of Longformer

Longformer-8192: This is the same as the original Longformer (Beltagy et al., 2020), which was warm-started from RoBERTa (Section 3.1), but we extend the maximum input length to 8,192 sub-words. We warm-start the positional embeddings from those of Longformer, cloning them once (positions 4,097–8,192 get the same initial embeddings as positions 1–4,096). To keep the computational complexity under control, we decrease the local attention window size from 512 to 128 sub-words.[5] All parameters, including positional embeddings, are updated during fine-tuning, again as in the original Longformer. We did not perform any additional pre-training, however, beyond that of the original Longformer, lacking computing resources. All Longformer variants are aware of word order.

Longformer-8192-PAR: This is the same as the previous model, but we place a global token (Section 2), specifically a [sep] token, at the end of each paragraph (Fig. 3). By contrast, the original Longformer and Longformer-8192 use the single [cls] token at the beginning of the input text as a single global token for classification tasks.[6] As in the previous model, we decrease the local attention window size from 512 to 128 sub-words.

Our intuition was that using more global tokens, and synchronizing them with paragraph breaks would allow information to flow more easily across paragraphs, viewed as discourse segments. Previous work by Zaheer et al. (2020) also suggests that such ETC-like global attention layouts lead to better results. Again, all parameters are updated during fine-tuning, but we did not perform any additional pre-training to better adjust the model to the new global attention layout, lacking resources.

LegalLongformer: Similar to Longformer, but warm-started from LegalBERT. We clone the positional embeddings of LegalBERT eight times to cover positions 1–4,096 (instead of 1–512 in LegalBERT) and update them during fine-tuning. All other parameters are also warm-started from LegalBERT and are updated during fine-tuning. Following Beltagy et al. (2020), we warm-start the global attention parameters of LegalLongformer with the (local) attention parameters of LegalBERT. Again, no additional pre-training was performed.

LegalLongformer-8192: Similar to Longformer-8192, but again warm-started from LegalBERT. In this case, we clone the positional embeddings of LegalBERT 16 times to cover positions 1–8,192. Again, no additional pre-training was performed.

LegalLongformer-8192-PAR: The same as the previous model, but with global tokens at the end of each paragraph, as in Longformer-8192-PAR.

[5] Table 4 shows that despite this counter-measure, the expansion to 8,192 sub-words leads to almost 2× inference time and 30% increase in memory.

[6] Additional global tokens were used by Beltagy et al. (2020) in other tasks, e.g., question answering.

Dataset	Source	Text Length (Original/Unique)		Instances			Classes
		Average	Maximum	Train	Dev.	Test	
LONG DOCUMENT CLASSIFICATION TASKS							
ECtHR (Task A)	(Chalkidis et al., 2019a)	1.6k (1.1k)	35.4k (27.2k)	9,000	1,000	1,000	10+1
ECtHR (Task B)	(Chalkidis et al., 2021b)	1.6k (1.1k)	35.4k (27.2k)	9,000	1,000	1,000	10+1
SCOTUS	(Spaeth et al., 2020)	6.0k (1.6k)	88.6k (12.1k)	5,000	1,400	1,400	14
SHORT DOCUMENT CLASSIFICATION TASKS							
EUR-LEX*	(Chalkidis et al., 2021a)	1.1k (341)	140.1k (10k)	55,000	5,000	5,000	100
LEDGAR	(Tuggener et al., 2020)	113 (65)	1.2k (484)	60,000	10,000	10,000	100
UNFAIR-ToS	(Lippi et al., 2019)	33 (25)	441 (181)	5,532	2,275	1,607	8+1

Table 1: LexGLUE statistics. Lengths in sub-word tokens, before and after (in brackets) deduplication. *EUR-LEX is treated as a short document task in our work, since using only the first 512 tokens (what we do) has comparable performance with using the full texts (Chalkidis et al., 2019b). +1 denotes an extra class for no-label instances.

4 Experiments

4.1 Datasets

LexGLUE (Chalkidis et al., 2022) is a collection of six simplified English legal NLP datasets that are used to evaluate the performance of NLP methods across seven legal text understanding tasks. Inspired by GLUE (Wang et al., 2018) and SuperGLUE (Wang et al., 2019), LexGLUE was designed to push towards generic-pretrained models that can cope with multiple legal NLP tasks with limited extra training (fine tuning) for each one.

Here, we experiment with six of the seven tasks of LexGLUE, excluding CaseHOLD (Zheng et al., 2021), a multiple choice question answering task about holdings of US court cases. The other six tasks are all framed as text classification problems. While our work targets the long document classification tasks (ECtHR Tasks A and B, SCOTUS), we also experiment with tasks that involve short texts (EUR-LEX, LEDGAR, UNFAIR-ToS), for completeness. Table 1 lists the sources of the datasets we experiment with and provides key statistics. ECtHR Task A and B require deciding which articles of the European Convention of Human Rights were violated, or allegedly violated, respectively; both tasks use the same dataset in LexGLUE. SCOTUS requires classifying opinions of the US Supreme Court into issue areas (e.g., Criminal Procedure, Civil Rights). EUR-LEX requires labeling European laws with concepts from a European Union taxonomy. LEDGAR requires assigning topical categories to contract provisions. UNFAIR-ToS requires detecting unfair terms in terms of service. Consult Chalkidis et al. (2022) and the work cited in Table 1 for further information.

4.2 Evaluation measures

Following Chalkidis et al. (2022), for each task we report macro-F1 (m-F_1), which assigns equal importance to all classes, and micro-F1 (μ-F_1), which assigns more importance to frequent classes.

4.3 Experimental setup

Across all experiments, we use Adam (Kingma and Ba, 2015) with initial learning rate 3e-5. We train models up to 20 epochs using early stopping, monitoring μ-F_1 on the development data. We run all experiments with 5 different random seeds and report test results for the seeds with the best development scores. For the TF-IDF bucket embedding layer, we search in {16, 32, 64, 128} for the number of buckets that maximizes μ-F_1 on the development data, separately for each task.

4.4 Experimental results

Table 2 lists the test results of all models across the six tasks considered. Table 3 aggregates the test results over the three long-document classification tasks (ECtHR Tasks A and B, SCOTUS) we are mainly interested in (see also see Table 1). We use the harmonic mean over the scores of the three tasks, following Shavrina and Malykh (2021).

BoW models: The results of the two BoW variants of LegalBERT (TFIDF-SRT-LegalBERT, TFIDF-SRT-EMB-LegalBERT) in Table 2 are mixed. In the two ECtHR tasks and EUR-LEX, both models outperform the TFIDF-SVM baseline, a much simpler linear BoW model. Contrary, both models are outperformed by TFIDF-SVM in SCOTUS and LEDGAR. In UNFAIR-ToS, the three models perform overall on par. While the original word

Method	ECtHR (A)*		ECtHR (B)*		SCOTUS*		EUR-LEX		LEDGAR		UNFAIR-ToS	
	μ-F_1	m-F_1	μ-F_1	m-F_1	μ-F_1	m-F_1	μ-F_1	m-F_1	μ-F_1	m-F_1	μ-F_1	m-F_1
BoW models (word order lost)												
TFIDF-SVM	62.6	48.9	73.0	63.8	74.0	64.4	63.4	47.9	87.0	81.4	94.7	75.0
TFIDF-SRT-LegalBERT	69.8	62.8	78.5	71.9	73.4	61.8	69.6	53.7	86.9	80.8	95.3	80.6
TFIDF-SRT-EMB-LegalBERT	68.7	63.1	79.0	72.5	73.9	63.6	69.7	53.9	86.5	80.3	95.8	78.7
LegalBERT variants that retain word order												
LegalBERT	70.0	64.0	80.4	74.7	76.4	66.5	72.1	57.4	88.2	83.0	**96.0**	**83.0**
TFIDF-EMB-LegalBERT	70.0	61.9	79.4	73.5	74.9	64.7	71.6	56.9	88.7	83.4	95.9	82.1
Longformer variants (all retain word order)												
Longformer	69.9	64.7	79.4	71.7	72.9	64.0	71.6	**57.7**	88.2	83.0	95.5	80.9
Longformer-8192	70.9	62.1	79.2	73.9	73.7	63.6	(Not considered for short-document tasks.)					
Longformer-8192-PAR	70.8	62.3	79.0	73.1	73.9	66.0	>>					
LegalLongformer	**71.7**	63.6	80.5	**76.4**	76.6	66.9	72.2	56.5	**88.8**	**83.5**	95.7	80.6
LegalLongformer-8192	71.2	64.3	**81.4**	74.2	**77.5**	**67.3**	(Not considered for short-document tasks.)					
LegalLongformer-8192-PAR	71.4	**68.4**	79.6	73.9	76.2	66.3	>>					

Table 2: Test results across LexGLUE tasks considered. In starred tasks, we use the hierarchical variant of LegalBERT. We do not consider extended Longformers in short document classification tasks (last three; see also Table 1), which are included for completeness. Best scores per group are underlined, and best overall are in **bold**.

order is lost in all three models, TFIDF-SVM relies on n-grams up to 3 words long, which allows it to retain local word order in features that represent multi-word terms, like 'civil rights' or 'federal taxation' in the case of SCOTUS. We suspect that such multi-word terms are more important in SCOTUS and LEDGAR, which would explain the fact that TFIDF-SVM outperforms the other two BoW models in these tasks. Future work could add a TFIDF-SVM variant with only unigram features to check this hypothesis; there should be a large performance drop in the three tasks. One could also explore ways to use TF-IDF information about n-grams (not just unigrams) in the BoW variants of LegalBERT.

Switching to the aggregated results of the long document tasks of Table 3, we observe that both BoW variants of LegalBERT outperform TFIDF-SVM. Table 3 also shows that TFIDF-SRT-EMB-LegalBERT (which includes the TF-IDF embeddings layer) performs slightly better than TFIDF-SRT-LegalBERT in terms of m-F_1 (1 p.p. improvement), but there is almost no difference in μ-F_1, and the results of Table 2 show no clear winner between the two methods across tasks.

Method	μ-F_1	m-F_1
TFIDF-SVM	69.5	58.1
TFIDF-SRT-LegalBERT	73.7	65.2
TFIDF-SRT-EMB-LegalBERT	73.6	66.1
LegalBERT	75.4	68.1
TFIDF-EMB-LegalBERT	74.6	66.3
Longformer	73.9	66.6
Longformer-8192	74.4	66.1
Longformer-8192-PAR	74.4	66.8
LegalLongformer	76.1	68.6
LegalLongformer-8192	**76.5**	68.4
LegalLongformer-8192-PAR	75.6	**69.4**

Table 3: Test results aggregated (harmonic mean) over the long-document classification tasks (ECtHR Tasks A and B, SCOTUS) of LexGLUE. Best scores per group are underlined, and best overall are in **bold**.

LegalBERT variants that retain word order: Table 2 shows that adding the TF-IDF embeddings layer to LegalBERT (TF-IDF-EMB-LegalBERT), without word deduplication and retaining the original word order, leads to lower performance in 5 out of 6 tasks compared to the original LegalBERT; LEDGAR is the only exception, with small improvements. The aggregated results of Table 3 also show that TF-IDF-EMB-LegalBERT is worse than the original LegalBERT. We can only hypothesize that TF-IDF-EMB-LegalBERT is in most cases unable to learn how to use the additional information from the additive TF-IDF embeddings, which are added only during fine-tuning (they were not present during pre-training). This hypothesis is based on the positive (albeit small) impact of the TF-IDF embeddings layer on LEDGAR, the largest dataset with 60k training examples. All other datasets contain fewer than 10k training examples (Table 1), with the exception of EUR-LEX (55k), which does not support our hypothesis.

Given appropriate computing resources, one could further pre-train TFIDF-EMB-LegalBERT to help it learn how to exploit the newly introduced TF-IDF embeddings. The same applies to both BoW variants of LegalBERT, although in that case appropriate BoW pre-training objectives should be considered, since Masked Language Modeling (MLM) is not reasonable when the original word order is lost. Predicting the TF-IDF bucket id when masked, or predicting masked words given their TF-IDF bucket ids seem better alternatives.

Longformer variants: Comparing the original Longformer with Longformer-8192, a variant capable of processing even longer documents, the results are mixed (Table 2) across the 3 long document classification tasks (ECtHR Tasks A and B, SCOTUS), i.e., μ-F_1 is improved at the expense of m-F_1, or vice-versa. Aggregating the results (Table 3), we observe the very same trade-off (+0.5 p.p. in μ-F_1, -0.5 p.p. in m-F_1). Considering the additional global tokens in Longformer-8192-PAR, we have comparable results in ECtHR tasks and improved results in SCOTUS, the dataset with the longest documents in LexGLUE (Table 1). Aggregating the results (Table 3), we observe that the extra global tokens do not improve μ-F_1 further (74.4), but lead to the best m-F_1 (66.8) of all the Longformer variants that have not been pre-trained on legal corpora. Based on the aforementioned observations, we believe that the additional positional embeddings and adding more global tokens are in the right direction when seeking better long document performance with Longformer.

Moving on to Longformer variants warm-started from LegalBERT, Table 2 shows that LegalLongformer outperforms the original generic Longformer (Beltagy et al., 2020) in most cases, which highlights the importance of domain-specific models as already noted in the literature (Chalkidis et al., 2022; Zheng et al., 2021). We observe notable improvements in long document classification tasks (ECtHR A and B, SCOTUS), with approx. +2.0 p.p. in both μ-F_1 and m-F_1 in the aggregated results of Table 3. These results are impressive considering that LegalLongformer was warm-started from LegalBERT, but no additional pre-training was conducted; hence several parameters of the model (e.g., additional positional embeddings and global attention matrices) may be far from optimal. By contrast, the original Longformer was warm-started from RoBERTa and was pre-trained for 64k additional steps on generic long documents.

Considering the last two variants of LegalLongformer (-8192, -8192-PAR), the results are mixed (trade-off between μ-F_1 and m-F_1 in Table 2, as with the generic Longformer) and share the best aggregated results across all examined methods in long document classifications tasks (Table 3).

Based on the above, we believe that the proposed extensions (warm-start from a legally pre-trained model, additional positional embeddings, additional global tokens) are in the right direction, already producing better results compared to the generic Longformer, and state-of-the-art results in several LexGLUE tasks (ECtHR A&B and LEDGAR). Given appropriate resources, one could further pre-train LegalLongformer-8192-PAR for a limited number of steps (e.g., 64k) on long legal documents (e.g., the training subsets of ECtHR, and SCOTUS) to optimize the newly introduced parameters and expect further improvements.

4.5 Efficiency considerations

In Table 4, we present important information with respect to efficiency. As expected, TFIDF-SVM has the fewest parameters (200× fewer than LegalBERT variants) and is substantially faster and less memory-intensive compared to all other neural methods, while achieving state-of-the-art results in two tasks (SCOTUS and EUR-LEX, Table 2).

Our proposed BoW variants of LegalBERT are substantially less memory intensive; approx. 25% less GPU memory across the long document classification tasks (starred), and approx. 50% less GPU memory across others with much shortened texts compared to LegalBERT. The TF-IDF embeddings do not affect memory or inference time (storing and looking up TF-IDF embeddings are negligible).

Considering LegalLongformer, we observe an approx. 50% increase in the number of parameters and approx. 25% increase in GPU memory. With respect to inference time, there is a 10× increase compared to LegalBERT models in long document processing tasks, and larger in the other tasks with much shorter documents, which makes hierarchical Transformers a faster alternative.

Method	Params.	ECtHR*		SCOTUS*		EUR-LEX		LEDGAR		UNFAIR-ToS	
		Mem.	Time	Mem.	Time	Mem.	Time	Mem.	Time	Mem.	Time
BoW models (word order lost)											
TFIDF-SVM	0.5M	0.1	.001	0.1	.001	0.1	.001	0.1	.001	0.1	.001
TFIDF-SRT-LegalBERT	110M	0.9	.012	0.9	.012	0.9	.012	0.9	.007	0.9	.007
TFIDF-SRT-EMB-LegalBERT	110M	0.9	.012	0.9	.012	0.9	.012	0.9	.007	0.9	.007
LegalBERT variants that retain word order											
LegalBERT	110M	1.3	.014	1.3	.014	1.9	.012	1.9	.007	1.9	.007
TFIDF-EMB-LegalBERT	110M	1.3	.014	1.3	.014	1.9	.012	1.9	.007	1.9	.007
Longformer variants (all retain word order)											
LegalLongformer	148M	1.7	.164	1.7	.164	1.3	.033	1.3	.033	1.3	.033
LegalLongformer-8192	151M	2.2	.318	2.2	.318	(Not considered for short-document tasks.)					
LegalLongformer-8192-PAR	151M	2.2	.331	2.2	.331	>>					

Table 4: Model parameters, memory footprint (GBs/sample), and inference time (sec/sample). In starred tasks, we use the hierarchical variant of LegalBERT. For ECtHR Tasks A and B, the information of this table is identical.

Moving to the extensions of LegalLongformer that are able to encode longer documents (LegalLongformer8192) and use extra global tokens (LegalLongformer-8192-PAR), there is an approx. 30% increase in GPU memory compared to the standard Longformer (encoding up to 4,096 sub-words), and 2× increase in inference time. In other words, there is no free lunch when seeking performance improvements.

5 Conclusions and Future Work

Concluding, we presented BoW variants of LegalBERT, which remove duplicate words and consider TF-IDF scores by reordering the remaining words and/or by employing a TF-IDF embedding layer. These variants are more efficient than the original LegalBERT and still overall outperform a TF-IDF-based SVM in long legal document classification.

We also modified Longformer to handle even longer texts (up to 8,192 sub-words), use additional global tokens, and also showed the positive effect of warm-starting it from LegalBERT. Unlike the BoW models, this is a resource-intensive direction, with substantial improvements compared to the original Longformer (up to 4,096 sub-words, a single global token, warm-started from RoBERTa) in long legal document classification. The new LegalLongformer (and its variants) are the new state of the art in the long document tasks of LexGLUE.

In future work, we would like to further pre-train the proposed BoW variants of LegalBERT, LegalLongformer, and variants on legal corpora, to help them better optimize the newly introduced modifications (e.g., TF-IDF embeddings, additional positional embeddings, updated attention scheme with additional global tokens). We would also like to experiment with long documents from other domains (e.g., long business documents).

Acknowledgments

This research has been co-funded by the European Regional Development Fund of the European Union and Greek national funds through the Operational Program Competitiveness, Entrepreneurship and Innovation, under the call RESEARCH – CREATE – INNOVATE (T2EΔK-03849). This work is also partly funded by the Innovation Fund Denmark (IFD)[7] under File No. 0175-00011A.

References

Mostafa Abdou, Vinit Ravishankar, Artur Kulmizev, and Anders Søgaard. 2022. Word order does matter and shuffled language models know it. In *Proceedings of the 60th Annual Meeting of the Association for Computational Linguistics (Volume 1: Long Papers)*, pages 6907–6919, Dublin, Ireland.

Joshua Ainslie, Santiago Ontanon, Chris Alberti, Vaclav Cvicek, Zachary Fisher, Philip Pham, Anirudh Ravula, Sumit Sanghai, Qifan Wang, and Li Yang. 2020. ETC: Encoding long and structured inputs in transformers. In *Proceedings of the 2020 Conference on Empirical Methods in Natural Language Processing (EMNLP)*, pages 268–284, Online.

Iz Beltagy, Matthew E. Peters, and Arman Cohan. 2020. Longformer: The long-document transformer. *CoRR*, abs/2004.05150.

[7]https://innovationsfonden.dk/en

Georgios-Ioannis Brokos, Prodromos Malakasiotis, and Ion Androutsopoulos. 2016. Using centroids of word embeddings and word mover's distance for biomedical document retrieval in question answering. In *Proceedings of the 15th Workshop on Biomedical Natural Language Processing*, pages 114–118, Berlin, Germany. Association for Computational Linguistics.

Ilias Chalkidis, Ion Androutsopoulos, and Nikolaos Aletras. 2019a. Neural legal judgment prediction in English. In *Proceedings of the 57th Annual Meeting of the Association for Computational Linguistics*, pages 4317–4323, Florence, Italy. Association for Computational Linguistics.

Ilias Chalkidis, Ion Androutsopoulos, and Achilleas Michos. 2018. Obligation and prohibition extraction using hierarchical RNNs. In *Proceedings of the 56th Annual Meeting of the Association for Computational Linguistics (Volume 2: Short Papers)*, pages 254–259, Melbourne, Australia. Association for Computational Linguistics.

Ilias Chalkidis, Emmanouil Fergadiotis, Prodromos Malakasiotis, and Ion Androutsopoulos. 2019b. Large-scale multi-label text classification on EU legislation. In *Proceedings of the 57th Annual Meeting of the Association for Computational Linguistics*, pages 6314–6322, Florence, Italy. Association for Computational Linguistics.

Ilias Chalkidis, Manos Fergadiotis, Prodromos Malakasiotis, Nikolaos Aletras, and Ion Androutsopoulos. 2020. LEGAL-BERT: The muppets straight out of law school. In *Findings of the Association for Computational Linguistics: EMNLP 2020*, pages 2898–2904, Online.

Ilias Chalkidis, Manos Fergadiotis, Dimitrios Tsarapatsanis, Nikolaos Aletras, Ion Androutsopoulos, and Prodromos Malakasiotis. 2021a. Paragraph-level rationale extraction through regularization: A case study on European court of human rights cases. In *Proceedings of the 2021 Conference of the North American Chapter of the Association for Computational Linguistics: Human Language Technologies*, pages 226–241, Online. Association for Computational Linguistics.

Ilias Chalkidis, Manos Fergadiotis, Dimitrios Tsarapatsanis, Nikolaos Aletras, Ion Androutsopoulos, and Prodromos Malakasiotis. 2021b. Paragraph-level rationale extraction through regularization: A case study on european court of human rights cases. In *Proceedings of the Annual Conference of the North American Chapter of the Association for Computational Linguistics*, online.

Ilias Chalkidis, Abhik Jana, Dirk Hartung, Michael Bommarito, Ion Androutsopoulos, Daniel Martin Katz, and Nikolaos Aletras. 2022. Lexglue: A benchmark dataset for legal language understanding in english. In *Proceedings of the 60th Annual Meeting of the Association for Computational Linguistics*, pages 4310–4330, Dubln, Ireland.

Corinna Cortes and Vladimir Vapnik. 1995. Support-vector networks. *Maching Learning*, 20(3):273–297.

Xiang Dai, Ilias Chalkidis, Sune Darkner, and Desmond Elliott. 2022. Revisiting transformer-based models for long document classification. In *Findings of the Association for Computational Linguistics: EMNLP 2022*, Abu Dhabi, UAE. Association for Computational Linguistics.

Zihang Dai, Zhilin Yang, Yiming Yang, Jaime Carbonell, Quoc Le, and Ruslan Salakhutdinov. 2019. Transformer-XL: Attentive language models beyond a fixed-length context. In *Proceedings of the 57th Annual Meeting of the Association for Computational Linguistics*, pages 2978–2988, Florence, Italy.

Jacob Devlin, Ming-Wei Chang, Kenton Lee, and Kristina Toutanova. 2019. BERT: Pre-training of deep bidirectional transformers for language understanding. In *Proceedings of the 2019 Conference of the North American Chapter of the Association for Computational Linguistics: Human Language Technologies, Volume 1 (Long and Short Papers)*, pages 4171–4186, Minneapolis, Minnesota.

SiYu Ding, Junyuan Shang, Shuohuan Wang, Yu Sun, Hao Tian, Hua Wu, and Haifeng Wang. 2021. ERNIE-Doc: A retrospective long-document modeling Transformer. In *Proceedings of the 59th Annual Meeting of the Association for Computational Linguistics and the 11th International Joint Conference on Natural Language Processing (Volume 1: Long Papers)*, pages 2914–2927, Online.

Pengcheng He, Xiaodong Liu, Jianfeng Gao, and Weizhu Chen. 2021. DeBERTa: Decoding-enchanced BERT with disentangled attention. In *International Conference on Learning Representations*.

Jack Hessel and Alexandra Schofield. 2021. How effective is BERT without word ordering? implications for language understanding and data privacy. In *Proceedings of the 59th Annual Meeting of the Association for Computational Linguistics and the 11th International Joint Conference on Natural Language Processing (Volume 2: Short Papers)*, pages 204–211, Online.

Peng Jin, Yue Zhang, Xingyuan Chen, and Yunqing Xia. 2016. Bag-of-embeddings for text classification. In *Proceedings of the Twenty-Fifth International Joint Conference on Artificial Intelligence*, IJCAI'16, page 2824–2830. AAAI Press.

Prathamesh Kalamkar, Aman Tiwari, Astha Agarwal, Saurabh Karn, Smita Gupta, Vivek Raghavan, and Ashutosh Modi. 2022. Corpus for automatic structuring of legal documents. In *Proceedings of the Thirteenth Language Resources and Evaluation Conference*, pages 4420–4429, Marseille, France. European Language Resources Association.

D. P. Kingma and J. Ba. 2015. Adam: A method for stochastic optimization. In *Proceedings of the 5th International Conference on Learning Representations (ICLR)*, San Diego, CA, USA.

Marco Lippi, Przemysław Pałka, Giuseppe Contissa, Francesca Lagioia, Hans-Wolfgang Micklitz, Giovanni Sartor, and Paolo Torroni. 2019. CLAUDETTE: an automated detector of potentially unfair clauses in online terms of service. *Artificial Intelligence and Law*, pages 117–139.

Yinhan Liu, Myle Ott, Naman Goyal, Jingfei Du, Mandar Joshi, Danqi Chen, Omer Levy, Mike Lewis, Luke Zettlemoyer, and Veselin Stoyanov. 2019. RoBERTa: A robustly optimized BERT pretraining approach. *arXiv preprint arXiv:1907.11692*.

Vijit Malik, Rishabh Sanjay, Shubham Kumar Nigam, Kripabandhu Ghosh, Shouvik Kumar Guha, Arnab Bhattacharya, and Ashutosh Modi. 2021. ILDC for CJPE: Indian legal documents corpus for court judgment prediction and explanation. In *Proceedings of the 59th Annual Meeting of the Association for Computational Linguistics and the 11th International Joint Conference on Natural Language Processing (Volume 1: Long Papers)*, pages 4046–4062, Online. Association for Computational Linguistics.

Christopher D. Manning, Prabhakar Raghavan, and Hinrich Schütze. 2008. *Introduction to Information Retrieval*. Cambridge University Press, USA.

Joel Niklaus, Ilias Chalkidis, and Matthias Stürmer. 2021. Swiss-Court-Predict: A Multilingual Legal Judgment Prediction Benchmark. In *Proceedings of the 3rd Natural Legal Language Processing Workshop Workshop*, Online.

Joel Niklaus, Matthias Stürmer, and Ilias Chalkidis. 2022. An empirical study on cross-x transfer for legal judgment prediction. In *Proceedings of the 2nd Conference of the Asia-Pacific Chapter of the Association for Computational Linguistics (AACL-IJCNLP 2022)*, Online. Association for Computational Linguistics.

Tatiana Shavrina and Valentin Malykh. 2021. How not to lie with a benchmark: Rearranging NLP learderboards.

Koustuv Sinha, Robin Jia, Dieuwke Hupkes, Joelle Pineau, Adina Williams, and Douwe Kiela. 2021. Masked language modeling and the distributional hypothesis: Order word matters pre-training for little. In *Proceedings of the 2021 Conference on Empirical Methods in Natural Language Processing*, pages 2888–2913, Online and Punta Cana, Dominican Republic.

Harold J. Spaeth, Lee Epstein, Jeffrey A. Segal Andrew D. Martin, Theodore J. Ruger, and Sara C. Benesh. 2020. Supreme Court Database, Version 2020 Release 01. Washington University Law.

Don Tuggener, Pius von Däniken, Thomas Peetz, and Mark Cieliebak. 2020. LEDGAR: A large-scale multi-label corpus for text classification of legal provisions in contracts. In *Proceedings of the 12th Language Resources and Evaluation Conference*, pages 1235–1241, Marseille, France. European Language Resources Association.

Ashish Vaswani, Noam Shazeer, Niki Parmar, Jakob Uszkoreit, Llion Jones, Aidan N. Gomez, Lukasz Kaiser, and Illia Polosukhin. 2017. Attention is all you need. In *Proceedings of the 31st International Conference on Neural Information Processing Systems*, pages 6000–6010, Long Beach, California, USA.

Alex Wang, Yada Pruksachatkun, Nikita Nangia, Amanpreet Singh, Julian Michael, Felix Hill, Omer Levy, and Samuel Bowman. 2019. Superglue: A stickier benchmark for general-purpose language understanding systems. In *Advances in Neural Information Processing Systems*, volume 32. Curran Associates, Inc.

Alex Wang, Amanpreet Singh, Julian Michael, Felix Hill, Omer Levy, and Samuel Bowman. 2018. GLUE: A multi-task benchmark and analysis platform for natural language understanding. In *Proceedings of the 2018 EMNLP Workshop BlackboxNLP: Analyzing and Interpreting Neural Networks for NLP*, pages 353–355, Brussels, Belgium.

Chaojun Xiao, Xueyu Hu, Zhiyuan Liu, Cunchao Tu, and Maosong Sun. 2021. Lawformer: A pre-trained language model for chinese legal long documents. *AI Open*, 2:79–84.

Kelvin Xu, Jimmy Ba, Ryan Kiros, Kyunghyun Cho, Aaron Courville, Ruslan Salakhudinov, Rich Zemel, and Yoshua Bengio. 2015. Show, attend and tell: Neural image caption generation with visual attention. In *Proceedings of the 32nd International Conference on Machine Learning*, volume 37 of *Proceedings of Machine Learning Research*, pages 2048–2057, Lille, France. PMLR.

Liu Yang, Mingyang Zhang, Cheng Li, Michael Bendersky, and Marc Najork. 2020. Beyond 512 tokens: Siamese multi-depth transformer-based hierarchical encoder for long-form document matching. In *Proceedings of the 29th ACM International Conference on Information and Knowledge Management*, page 1725–1734, Virtual Event, Ireland.

Zhilin Yang, Zihang Dai, Yiming Yang, Jaime Carbonell, Ruslan Salakhutdinov, and Quoc V. Le. 2019. XLNet: Generalized autoregressive pretraining for language understanding. In *Proceedings of the 33rd International Conference on Neural Information Processing Systems*, Red Hook, NY, USA. Curran Associates Inc.

Zichao Yang, Diyi Yang, Chris Dyer, Xiaodong He, Alex Smola, and Eduard Hovy. 2016. Hierarchical attention networks for document classification. In

Proceedings of the 2016 Conference of the North American Chapter of the Association for Computational Linguistics: Human Language Technologies, pages 1480–1489, San Diego, California. Association for Computational Linguistics.

Manzil Zaheer, Guru Guruganesh, Kumar Avinava Dubey, Joshua Ainslie, Chris Alberti, Santiago Ontanon, Philip Pham, Anirudh Ravula, Qifan Wang, Li Yang, and Amr Ahmed. 2020. Big Bird: Transformers for longer sequences. In *Advances in Neural Information Processing Systems*, pages 17283–17297, online.

Lucia Zheng, Neel Guha, Brandon R. Anderson, Peter Henderson, and Daniel E. Ho. 2021. When does pretraining help? assessing self-supervised learning for law and the CaseHOLD dataset. In *International Conference on Artificial Intelligence and Law*.

Haoxi Zhong, Zhipeng Guo, Cunchao Tu, Chaojun Xiao, Zhiyuan Liu, and Maosong Sun. 2018. Legal judgment prediction via topological learning. In *Proceedings of the 2018 Conference on Empirical Methods in Natural Language Processing*, pages 3540–3549, Brussels, Belgium. Association for Computational Linguistics.

A Additional Material

In Figures 4–5, we show boxplots of the average text length (in sub-words) across LexGLUE datasets before and after word deduplication.

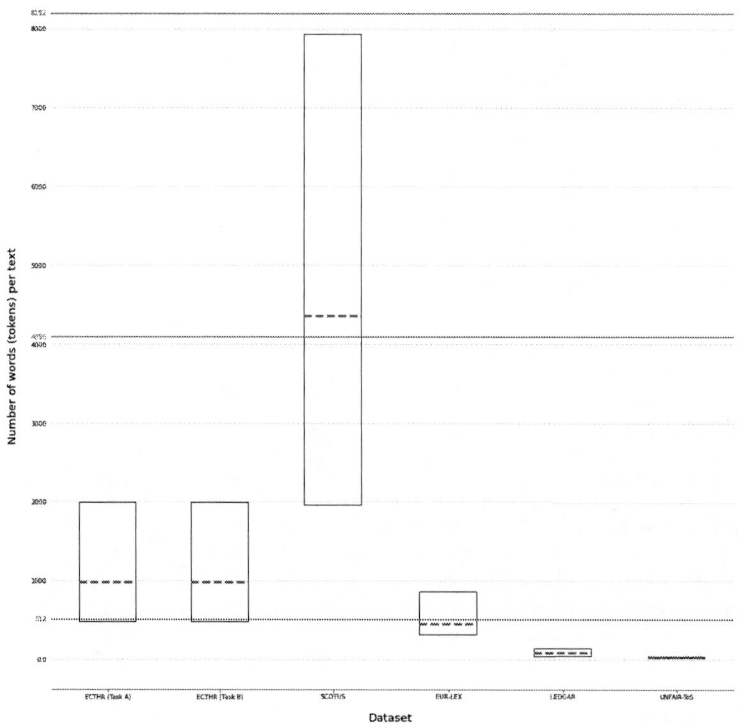

Figure 4: Average text length (in sub-words) across LexGLUE datasets before word deduplication.

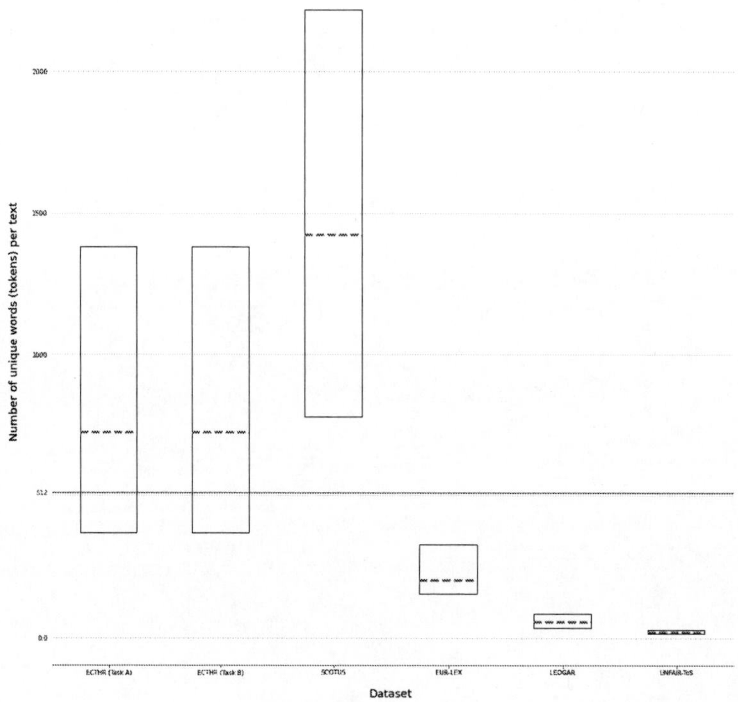

Figure 5: Average text length (in sub-words) across LexGLUE datasets after word deduplication.

Data-efficient End-to-end Information Extraction for Statistical Legal Analysis

Wonseok Hwang[a] **Saehee Eom**[a] **Hanuhl Lee**[a] **Hai Jin Park**[b] **Minjoon Seo**[a,c]
[a]LBox [b] Hanyang Univ. [c]KAIST
wonseok.hwang@lbox.kr saeheeeom99@lbox.kr leehanuhl@lbox.kr
haijinpark@hanyang.ac.kr minjoon@kaist.ac.kr

Abstract

Legal practitioners often face a vast amount of documents. Lawyers, for instance, search for appropriate precedents favorable to their clients, while the number of legal precedents is ever-growing. Although legal search engines can assist finding individual target documents and narrowing down the number of candidates, retrieved information is often presented as unstructured text and users have to examine each document thoroughly which could lead to information overloading. This also makes their statistical analysis challenging. Here, we present an end-to-end information extraction (IE) system for legal documents. By formulating IE as a generation task, our system can be easily applied to various tasks without domain-specific engineering effort. The experimental results of four IE tasks on Korean precedents shows that our IE system can achieve competent scores (-2.3 on average) compared to the rule-based baseline with as few as 50 training examples per task and higher score (+5.4 on average) with 200 examples. Finally, our statistical analysis on two case categories — drunk driving and fraud — with 35k precedents reveals the resulting structured information from our IE system faithfully reflects the macroscopic features of Korean legal system.

1 Introduction

Legal practitioners often need to analyze a vast number of documents while preparing legal cases. For instance, finding appropriate precedents from ever-growing court decisions on previous cases can be challenging due to its number, while they are critical for decision making on subsequent legal actions.

Although legal search engines based on both lexical and semantic similarity can dramatically decrease the burden, retrieved texts are still unstructured and require further reading. Furthermore, statistical analysis of legal documents is impossible without additional structuralization. Such statistical analysis from a vast amount of documents, if possible, may help decreasing implicit bias on judicial decision (Levinson et al., 2017).

However, structuralizng legal documents is very challenging due to their diversity as they reflect virtually all social phenomena. This makes building a comprehensive ontology and IE system very demanding. Instead of building a single perfect complex ontology and corresponding IE system, one can resort to building a task-specific IE system focusing on small number of relevant target information at each task. However, the number of required IE systems will quickly grow together with their development and maintenance cost due to the need of task-specific engineering. The cost from the task- and domain-specific engineering can be reduced if end-to-end systems based on generative models are employed but such systems are often unstable and require a large amount of training data.

In this study, we try to answer the following questions. (1) Is it possible to build an end-to-end (generative) neural system for legal information extraction showing high precision? If so, (2) how many training examples will be required? (3) What would be the best model architectures for this? (4) Would prompt-tuning be more efficient than fine-tuning? To answer these questions, we perform experiments using various language models with different model sizes and architectures on four IE tasks on Korean precedents. We show that the resulting end-to-end system (ISLA[1]) can achieve competent or better performance compared to the rule-based baseline with only 50 training examples per task. With 200 training examples, ISLA achieves up to +27% F_1 compared to the baseline. Using ISLA, we, for the first time, perform a large scale statistical analysis of "drunk driving" (24k samples) and "fraud" (11k samples) cases from Korean criminal trials. The results show that the

[1] END-TO-END INFORMATION EXTRACTOR FOR STATISTICAL LEGAL ANALYSIS

Proceedings of the Natural Legal Language Processing Workshop 2022, pages 143 - 152
December 8, 2022 ©2022 Association for Computational Linguistics

structured information by our IE system faithfully reflects the macroscopic features of the Korean legal system.

Our contribution can be summarized as below.

- We show that an end-to-end IE system for statistical legal analysis can achieve competent performance compared to the rule-based baseline with as few as 50 training examples.
- We also show the result of large-scale statistical legal analysis by structuralizing the data using our IE system on two criminal categories: "drunk driving" and "fraud".

2 Related Works

Many previous methods on legal IE tasks are based on tagging (classification) approach (Cardellino et al., 2017; Mistica et al., 2020; Hendrycks et al., 2021; Habernal et al., 2022; Chen et al., 2020; Pham et al., 2021; Hong et al., 2021; Yao et al., 2022). The brief description of individual works are presented in Appendix A.1. Compared to these studies, we map all IE tasks into a text-to-text format (Raffel et al., 2020). This end-to-end approach removes the burden of task- and domain-specific engineering and is known to show competent or better accuracy compared to tagging based method with enough amount of training examples (Hwang et al., 2021; Kim et al., 2021). Pires et al. (2022) also develop end-to-end IE system to extract information from four types of Portuguese legal documents. Compared to this study, we focus on building data-efficient end-to-end system combining both prompt- and fine-tuning methods. In this context, we investigate the effect of scaling model size, pre-training corpus, and training examples. Domain-wise, we focus on Korean precedents exclusively. Lastly, we show how end-to-end IE system can be applied for statistical legal analysis by analyzing 35k Korean precedents.

3 Tasks

We formulate all IE tasks as text generation where a model needs to generate the values of target fields. We prepare four IE tasks over Korean precedents, (1) three tasks from the facts and (2) one task from the rulings. Only the precedents from criminal trials of 1st level courts are used. In the facts IE tasks, a model needs to extract a subset of legally important information from the factual description of cases. We consider three case categories, (1) DRUNK DRIVING, (2) EMBEZZLEMENT, and (3) FRAUD. Tasks were selected to be composed of various difficulty levels. In DRUNK DRIVING, a model extracts "blood alcohol level", "travel distance", "type of the vechicle", and "previous criminal record on drunk driving". In EMBEZZLEMENT, a model needs to extract the loss from embezzlement. Finally, in FRAUD, a model needs to extract the loss from fraud, or from aiding and abetting fraud. Although similar to EMBEZZLEMENT, the facts from FRAUD cases show more diverse patterns which is reflected in their number of unique words (Table 2 in Appendix). In ruling IE task, a model extracts following five fields; (1) amount of fine; (2) imprisonment, (3) suspension of execution, (4) education, and (5) community service periods. Examples and data labeling process are shown in Appendix A.2.

4 Models

We use language models combined with task-specific prompts. For a given source text (facts or ruling) and corresponding task-specific prompt, a model generate the values of individual fields autoregressively. See Section A.3 for the details. For the comparison, we develop a rule-based baseline using regular expression. For each of the categories (DRUNK DRIVING, EMBEZZLEMENT, FRAUDand RULING-CRIMINAL), we read through diverse cases and manually identified suitable identification rules/patterns. See Section A.4.

5 Experiments

All experiments are performed on Nvidia A6000 GPU or RTX6000 using Transformers (Wolf et al., 2020) and OpenPrompt (Ding et al., 2021) libraries. We use `Precedent corpus` (150k Korean precedents) from LBox Open (Hwang et al., 2022) for the pre-training/domain-adaptation. See Section A.5 in Appendix for the details.

6 Results

In this section, we summarize our experimental result on four legal IE tasks with varying difficulties (Section 3). We examine 12 models while changing "model architecture", "model size", "the size of legal corpus for pre-training", or "the size of training dataset" (Table 1).

End-to-end models can show competent performance with 50 training examples. We first

Table 1: Comparison of various models. The F_1 scores of individual fields are shown; BAC (blood alcohol level), Dist (travel distance), Vehicle (type of the vehicle), Rec (previous criminal record on drunk driving), Loss, Loss-A (losses from aiding and abetting), Fine (amount of fine), Imp (imprisonment type and period), Susp (suspension of execution period), Educ (education period), Comm (community service period). The average scores over all tasks are shown in the 5th column (AVG). All scores are computed using the test sets that consists of 100 examples per task (total 400 examples).

Name	Size	Legal corpus size (tokens)	# of training examples (per task)	AVG	DRUNK DRIVING				EMBZ	FRAUD		RULING-CRIMINAL				
					BAC	Dist	Vehicle	Rec	Loss	Loss	Loss-A	Fine	Imp	Susp	Educ	Comm
GPT2-base (custom)	124M	0	50	73.0	96.9	83.7	87.6	85.7	60.1	35.9	0	80.7	93.4	98.9	92.6	60.0
mt5-small	300M	0	50	69.9	95.8	93.0	95.7	90.1	72.2	42.9	0	79.4	89.4	85.7	60.4	34.1
mt5-large	1.2B	0	50	74.5	98.0	96.4	94.7	93.6	87.5	64.8	0	84.7	82.1	96.7	68.1	27.0
LCUBE-base[§]	124M	259M	50	78.6	99.0	88.9	90.1	95.3	75.0	56.1	0	84.7	94.2	98.9	94.7	66.7
LCUBE-base (p)[†]	124M	259M	50	78.5	99.0	88.9	92.5	96.9	71.0	51.2	11.1	86.7	94.2	97.8	89.3	63.6
LCUBE-medium	354M	259M	50	78.6	98.0	90.7	93.6	94.2	73.9	58.4	0	84.7	91.9	98.9	75.6	82.8
LCUBE-medium (p)	354M	259M	50	79.5	98.5	91.3	93.0	96.4	78.3	59.0	0	86.7	92.6	98.9	92.9	66.7
mt5-small + d.a.	300M	259M	50	77.2	99.5	93.6	94.7	94.7	78.5	64.8	0	77.2	92.6	98.9	90.1	41.2
mt5-small + d.a. (p)	300M	259M	50	76.6	98.5	91.9	94.2	93.6	74.7	52.8	0	80.7	93.4	98.9	90.8	50.0
ISLA-50[‡]	1.2B	~1B*	50	80.5	99.5	94.7	95.8	90.0	90.0	69.0	10.0	88.9	94.2	98.9	89.7	45.7
ISLA-200	1.2B	~1B*	200	88.2	99.5	98.0	98.9	97.4	93.0	77.9	60.0	92.3	95.7	98.9	94.5	52.6
ISLA	1.2B	~1B*	–1,000*	93.1	99.5	97.4	99.5	99.0	91.7	80.3	69.6	95.5	95.7	98.9	98.2	92.3
Rule-based	-	-	-	82.8	98.0	87.6	71.8	92.5	71.8	50.9	45.5	88.5	97.2	98.9	98.2	92.3

§: Our custom GPT2 pre-trained with 150k precedent corpus (Hwang et al., 2022).
†: Prompt-tuning.
‡: Domain-adapted, and fine-tuned mt5-large with task-specific prompts for individual legal tasks. Our internal datasets were used.
*: Only the range is shown due to the confidential issue.

examine three language models GPT2-base, mt5-small, and mt5-large. GPT2-base model shows comparable or lower performance compared to the rule-based baseline on the most of tasks (1st vs final rows) whereas mt5-small and mt5-large shows comparable or better score (2nd, 3rd vs 13th rows). Notably the F_1 scores of FRAUD shows clear improvement upon model scaling and mt5-large (1.2B) exceeds the rule-base baseline. The low performance on "damages from aiding and abetting (Loss-A)", "education (Educ)", and "community service (Comm)" (1st–3rd rows) are due to lack of enough number of training examples for corresponding fields (Table 2, 1st row in Appendix).

Pre-training with Legal corpus is critical. The use of legal corpus greatly improves the accuracy across all tasks for both GPT2-base (+5.6 F_1 on average, 1st vs 4th rows, first column) and mt5-small (+7.3 F_1 on average, 2nd vs 8th rows). Notably, on Loss field of FRAUD task, GPT2-base shows +20.2 F_1 and mt5-small shows +21.9 F_1 (11th column) results highlighting the importance of pre-training with domain-specific corpus for IE tasks.

Prompt tuning does not show clear advantage. To investigate whether or not prompt-tuning can improve the model performance compared to fine-tuning approach, we perform control experiments with LCUBE-base (4th vs 5th rows), LCUBE-medium (6th vs 7th rows), and domain-adapted mt5-small (8th vs 9th rows) w/ or w/o fixing the parameters of the language models. Interestingly, under our experimental conditions, prompt-tuning does not show clear advantage over fine-tuning on generative IE tasks. Especially on FRAUD task, F_1 changed by -4.9 F_1 (LCUBE-base), +1.4 (LCUBE-medium), and -12.0 (domain adapted mt5-small).

Scaling model size, pre-training corpus, and training examples is beneficial. Since the domain-adapted mt5-small shows top performance on FRAUD and balanced performance over other tasks (8th row), we choose mt5 as a model architecture and perform scaling experiments. We first scale model (mt5-small → mt5-large) and perform the domain adaptation for 7 epochs with our internal precedent corpus (256M → ~1B tokens). The clear improvement over mt5-large (+6.0 F_1 on average, 3rd vs 10th rows) and the domain-adapted mt5-small (+3.3 F_1 on average, 8th vs 10th rows) are observed, showing the importance of scaling pre-training corpus and model size. Scaling training examples (50 → 200 examples) also leads to +7.7 F_1 on average (10th vs 11th rows). Notably, F_1 of Loss-A in FRAUD is increased by +50.0. Finally, we further collect the training examples up to ~1,000 and achieve 93.1 F_1 on average (12th row), an absolute +10.3 F_1 improvement over the baseline (final row).

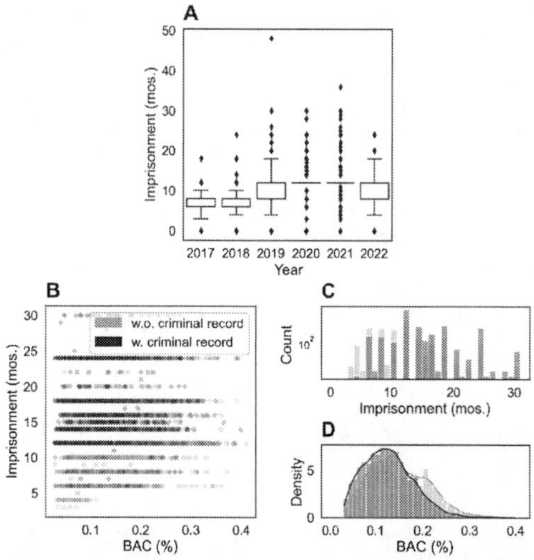

Figure 1: The result of statistical analysis of DRUNK DRIVING cases (A: 24k precedents, B–D: 5k precedents). (A) visualizes precedents from 2017 to 2022, and (B–D) visualizes precedents sentenced as suspension of execution or prison after 2019.

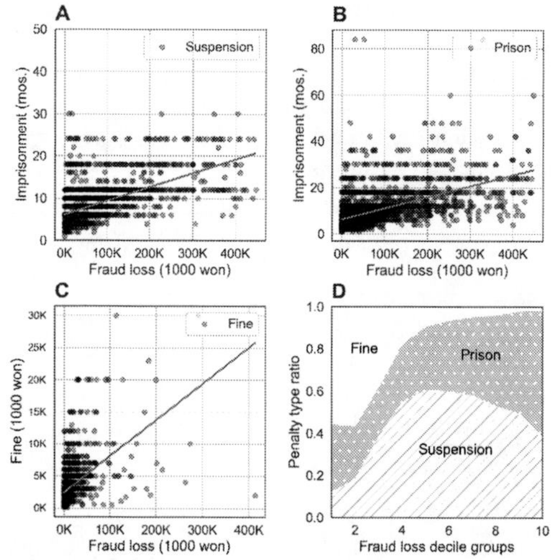

Figure 2: The result of statistical analysis of FRAUD cases (11k precedents). (A–D) visualizes each record sentenced suspension of execution, prison, and fine as black transparent dots. The regression lines are shown in red.

7 Analysis

In this section, we report the result of statistical legal analysis on two case categories, DRUNK DRIVING and FRAUD. Using ISLA, we first extract information from facts and rulings. For high precision, we control recall rate based on the model confidences that are computed by averaging the probabilities of the generated tokens (Appendix A.7). We analyze 24,230 confident cases out of 33,554 in DRUNK DRIVING task, and 10,898 confident cases from 15,106 in FRAUD task.

With the structured data in hand, we first analyze DRUNK DRIVING cases (Fig. 1). Two things are noticeable; (1) the average imprisonment period increases since 2019 (A); (2) the people with previous drunk driving record are sentenced longer imprisonment (B, C) regardless of their BACs (D). First result may be related to the fact that the Korean government has strengthened punishment on drunk driving since Jun 25, 2019 [2]. The second result may reflect the Article 148-2 (1) of the Road Traffic Act which subjects repeat offenders to aggravated punishment[3] (Table 3 in Appendix).

Next we analyze FRAUD cases. Fig. 2 shows the increases of imprisonment period and the amount of fine proportional to the loss[4]. Notably, the ratio of cases sentenced as fine decrease with the damages whereas the ratio of cases sentenced as suspension of execution increase initially but decreases with the damages, and the ratio of cases sentenced as prison becomes dominant [5].

8 Conclusion

We develop a data-efficient end-to-end IE system for legal statistical analysis. We show that the system can achieve competent performance with small number of examples and exceed the rule-based baseline by large margin upon scaling model size, pre-training corpus, and training examples. The statistical analysis on 35k precedents reveals the resulting structured data faithfully reflect the macroscopic features of the Korean legal system.

[2]Article 148-2 (1) of the Road Traffic Act (amended on December 24, 2018 and went into effect on June 25, 2019; https://elaw.klri.re.kr/kor_service/lawView.do?lang=ENG&hseq=50713)

[3]However, on Nov 25, 2021, Constitutional Court of Korea ruled that the corresponding part of Article 148-2 (1) of the Road Traffic Act (amended on Dec 24, 2018) is unconstitutional (Constitutional Court of Korea 2019Hun-Ba446, 2020Hun-Ka17, 2021Hun-Ba77 (consolidated) ruled on Nov 25, 2021; https://law.go.kr/LSW/detcInfoP.do?mode=1&detcSeq=170177

[4]The sentencing guideline for fraud recommends imprisonment proportional to the magnitude of the loss (https://sc.scourt.go.kr/sc/krsc/criterion/criterion_10/fraud_01.jsp).

[5]According to Article 62 (1) of the Criminal Act, suspension of sentence can be ruled only when the ruled imprisonment period/fine is not exceeding three years/5 million wons (https://elaw.klri.re.kr/kor_service/lawView.do?hseq=55948&lang=ENG)

Ethical considerations

We present the result of statistical analysis of two legal cases, (1) DRUNK DRIVING and (2) FRAUD. For high precision, we treat only the subset of the precedents in our database (24,230 out of 33,554 in DRUNK DRIVING, 10,898 out of 15,106 in FRAUD). Our database also consists of a smaller portion of data compared to the total Korean precedents, as accessing the entire precedents is practically not feasible in Korea due to their purchase cost(Hwang et al., 2022). This indicates that our result could emphasize certain properties of the data biasing the result. Another source of noise is that the model may produce erroneous results on $\sim$3% samples (Section 7). Thus, any legal decision based on our analysis should be taken carefully with explicit awareness of above two sources of noises.

References

Cristian Cardellino, Milagro Teruel, Laura Alonso Alemany, and Serena Villata. 2017. Legal NERC with ontologies, Wikipedia and curriculum learning. In *Proceedings of the 15th Conference of the European Chapter of the Association for Computational Linguistics: Volume 2, Short Papers*, pages 254–259, Valencia, Spain. Association for Computational Linguistics.

Yanguang Chen, Yuanyuan Sun, Zhihao Yang, and Hongfei Lin. 2020. Joint entity and relation extraction for legal documents with legal feature enhancement. In *Proceedings of the 28th International Conference on Computational Linguistics*, pages 1561–1571, Barcelona, Spain (Online). International Committee on Computational Linguistics.

Ning Ding, Shengding Hu, Weilin Zhao, Yulin Chen, Zhiyuan Liu, Hai-Tao Zheng, and Maosong Sun. 2021. Openprompt: An open-source framework for prompt-learning. *arXiv preprint arXiv:2111.01998*.

Ivan Habernal, Daniel Faber, Nicola Recchia, Sebastian Bretthauer, Iryna Gurevych, Christoph Burchard, et al. 2022. Mining legal arguments in court decisions. *arXiv preprint arXiv:2208.06178*.

Dan Hendrycks, Collin Burns, Anya Chen, and Spencer Ball. 2021. Cuad: An expert-annotated nlp dataset for legal contract review. *NeurIPS*.

Jenny Hong, Derek Chong, and Christopher Manning. 2021. Learning from limited labels for long legal dialogue. In *Proceedings of the Natural Legal Language Processing Workshop 2021*, pages 190–204, Punta Cana, Dominican Republic. Association for Computational Linguistics.

Wonseok Hwang, Dongjun Lee, Kyoungyeon Cho, Hanuhl Lee, and Minjoon Seo. 2022. A multi-task benchmark for korean legal language understanding and judgement prediction.

Wonseok Hwang, Hyunji Lee, Jinyeong Yim, Geewook Kim, and Minjoon Seo. 2021. Cost-effective end-to-end information extraction for semi-structured document images. In *Proceedings of the 2021 Conference on Empirical Methods in Natural Language Processing*, pages 3375–3383, Online and Punta Cana, Dominican Republic. Association for Computational Linguistics.

Geewook Kim, Teakgyu Hong, Moonbin Yim, Jinyoung Park, Jinyeong Yim, Wonseok Hwang, Sangdoo Yun, Dongyoon Han, and Seunghyun Park. 2021. Donut: Document understanding transformer without ocr. *arXiv preprint arXiv:2111.15664*.

Justin D. Levinson, Mark W. Bennett, and Koichi Hioki. 2017. Judging implicit bias: A national empirical study of judicial stereotypes. *69 Fla. L. Rev. 63*.

Meladel Mistica, Geordie Z. Zhang, Hui Chia, Kabir Manandhar Shrestha, Rohit Kumar Gupta, Saket Khandelwal, Jeannie Paterson, Timothy Baldwin, and Daniel Beck. 2020. Information extraction from legal documents: A study in the context of common law court judgements. In *Proceedings of the The 18th Annual Workshop of the Australasian Language Technology Association*, pages 98–103, Virtual Workshop. Australasian Language Technology Association.

Nhi Pham, Lachlan Pham, and Adam L. Meyers. 2021. Legal terminology extraction with the termolator. In *Proceedings of the Natural Legal Language Processing Workshop 2021*, pages 155–162, Punta Cana, Dominican Republic. Association for Computational Linguistics.

Ramon Pires, Fábio C. de Souza, Guilherme Rosa, Roberto A. Lotufo, and Rodrigo Nogueira. 2022. Sequence-to-sequence models for extracting information from registration and legal documents. In *Document Analysis Systems*, pages 83–95, Cham. Springer International Publishing.

Colin Raffel, Noam Shazeer, Adam Roberts, Katherine Lee, Sharan Narang, Michael Matena, Yanqi Zhou, Wei Li, and Peter J. Liu. 2020. Exploring the limits of transfer learning with a unified text-to-text transformer. *Journal of Machine Learning Research*, 21(140):1–67.

Mohammad Shoeybi, Mostofa Patwary, Raul Puri, Patrick LeGresley, Jared Casper, and Bryan Catanzaro. 2019. Megatron-lm: Training multi-billion parameter language models using model parallelism. *arXiv preprint arXiv:1909.08053*.

Maxim Tkachenko, Mikhail Malyuk, Andrey Holmanyuk, and Nikolai Liubimov. 2020-2022. Label Studio: Data labeling software. Open source software available from https://github.com/heartexlabs/label-studio.

Thomas Wolf, Lysandre Debut, Victor Sanh, Julien Chaumond, Clement Delangue, Anthony Moi, Pierric Cistac, Tim Rault, Rémi Louf, Morgan Funtowicz, Joe Davison, Sam Shleifer, Patrick von Platen, Clara Ma, Yacine Jernite, Julien Plu, Canwen Xu, Teven Le Scao, Sylvain Gugger, Mariama Drame, Quentin Lhoest, and Alexander M. Rush. 2020. Transformers: State-of-the-art natural language processing. In *EMNLP System Demonstrations*, Online. Association for Computational Linguistics.

Feng Yao, Chaojun Xiao, Xiaozhi Wang, Zhiyuan Liu, Lei Hou, Cunchao Tu, Juanzi Li, Yun Liu, Weixing Shen, and Maosong Sun. 2022. Leven: A large-scale chinese legal event detection dataset. *arXiv preprint arXiv:2203.08556*.

A Appendix

A.1 Previous studies on legal IE tasks: tagging-based approaches

Here we provide brief description of previous tagging methods on legal IE tasks. Cardellino et al. (2017) develops BIO-taggers for NER on legal documents. The model is trained with Wikipedia dataset and the result later maps into the legal ontology LKIF based on rules. Mistica et al. (2020) develops the classifier that tags the sentences from Australia precedents into three categories, fact, reasoning, and conclusion. Hendrycks et al. (2021) presents CUAD, a contract review dataset. In this task, a model needs to extract the span of text and classify in 41 label categories. Habernal et al. (2022) develop new argument minding dataset using European Court of Human Rights with new ontology rooted on legal argument research together with BIO-taggers. Chen et al. (2020) develops a triplet (entities and relation) extraction model on Chinese drug-related criminal judgment documents. Based on BERT encoding, they generate sequence of triplet vectors that are used to tag the position of entities and classify the relation between them. Pham et al. (2021) develops legal terminology extractor by modifying Termolator that relies on statistical properties of target and background corpora. Hong et al. (2021) develops the IE system that extract 11 features from the dialogue of California parole hearings via classification model. Yao et al. (2022) develops large-scale Chinese legal event detection dataset together with various baseline tagging models.

A.2 Datasets

A.2.1 Data preparation

We first build the ontologies for the individual tasks (target fields selection) and set-up labeling page using Label Studio (Tkachenko et al., 2020-2022). We place the source text (the facts or the rulings) on the left panel and the workspace on the right. As all tasks are formulated as text-generation, the workspace consists of simply a list of "the name of target field" and "text entry box". The annotators write (often copy and paste) the values of the target field appeared in the source text. We label 150 randomly selected precedents per each task and split them into 50 training and 100 test examples. After that, new examples are added to the training set. 20% of training examples are used as a validation set. All datasets were labeled under the guidance of a lawyer.

A.2.2 Examples

A.2.3 Drunk driving

- Facts: 【범죄전력】피고인은 2015. 11. 23. 광주지방법원 순천지원에서 도로교통법위반(음주운전)죄로 벌금 400만원의 약식명령을 발령받았다. 【범죄사실】피고인은 2021. 2. 25. 01:30경 여수시 B모텔 앞 도로에서부터 C에 있는 D 앞 도로에 이르기까지 약 20m 구간에서 혈중알코올농도 0.208%의 술에 취한 상태로 (차량번호 1 생략) 쏘나타 승용차를 운전하였다. 이로써 피고인은 음주운전 금지 규정을 2회 이상 위반하여 술에 취한 상태로 자동차를 운전하였다."
- Label:
  - BAC: 0.208%
  - Distance: 20m
  - Vehicle: 쏘나타 승용차
  - Criminal record: 1

A.2.4 Embezzlement

- Facts: 피고인은 피해자 B이 서울 성북구 C, D호에서 운영하는 E 주식회사에서 1993. 4. 1.경부터 2017. 1. 30.경까지 경리부장으로, 2017. 1. 31.경부터 2017. 10. 31.경까지 사내 이사로 각 근무하면서 임대관리 및 회계관리 등의 업무를 담당하였다. 피고인은 2009. 3. 10.경 위 E 사무실에서 15,596,670원에 대한 지출결의서를 작성하여 피해자의 결재를 득한 다음 같은 날 F은행 동소문로지점에서 위 지출결의서에 따른 예금인출을 하면서 예금청구서의 금액란을 위 지출결의서와 다르게 '19,596,670원'이라고 과다하게 기재한 후 피고인이 업무상 보관중인 E 주식회사 명의의 F은행 금융계좌(계좌번호 : G)에서 '19,596,670원'을 인출한 후 위 지출결의서와의 차액 4,000,000원을 피고인의 개인용도로 임의 사용하여 이를 횡령한 것을 비롯하여 그 무렵부터

2017. 10. 10.경까지 별지 범죄일람표 기재와 같이 총 51회에 걸쳐 합계 502,188,070원을 피해자를 위하여 업무상 보관하던 중 이를 횡령하였다.

- Label:
  - Loss: [502,188,070원]

A.2.5 FRAUD

- Facts: [2019고정1334] 피고인은 대구 동구 B에 있는 C공인중개사 사무소 직원으로 근무하는 사람이다. 피고인은 2018. 7. 3.경 위 공인중개사 사무소에서 대구 동구 D 원룸 건물주 E으로부터 원룸 세입자를 소개하여 달라는 부탁을 받고 피해자 F에게 '월세 나온게 있는데 월래 월 32만 원인데 계약서상 39만 원으로 적고 월세 39만 원을 내면 차액인 7만 원, 1년치 84만 원을 계약 당일 일시불로 지급하겠다'고 거짓말을 하였다. 그러나 사실 피고인은 피해자가 위 원룸 G호에 대한 월세 계약을 하더라도 대부업체 10여 곳으로부터 5,000만 원 상당의 채무가 있고 지급 능력이 되지 않아 이자도 납부하지 못하고 있어 피해자에게 1년분 월세 차액금 84만 원을 지급할 의사나 능력이 없었다. 그럼에도 불구하고 피고인은 위와 같이 피해자를 기망하여 이에 속은 피해자로부터 대구 동구 D건물 G호에 대한 부동산 월세 계약서를 작성하게 하고 건물주인 E 명의의 계좌로 2018. 7. 3. 실제 월세 32만 원을 초과한 7만 원을 더 많이 송금하게 하는 등 그때부터 같은 방법으로 2018. 8. 5. 7만 원, 2018. 9. 4. 7만 원, 2018. 10. 5. 7만 원, 2018. 11. 5. 7만 원, 2018. 12. 5. 7만 원 등 합계 42만원을 위 E 명의 계좌로 송금하게 하였다. [2019 고정 1335] 피고인은 2018. 9. 중순 일자불상경 대구 동구 H에 있는 I 음식점 안에서 피해자 J에게 '명절을 보내는 데 돈이 필요한데 카드를 빌려주면 2018. 10. 말일경까지 카드대금 변제를 하겠다'는 취지로 거짓말 하였다. 그러나 피고인은 피고인의 명의로 된 재산이 없고, 채무 5,000만 원이 있으나 채무변제도 하지 못하고 있고, 중개보조원으로 수입이 거의 없어서 사실상 피해자의 신용카드를 빌려 사용하더라도 그 대금을 지불할 의사나 능력이 없었다. 피고인은 위와 같이 피해자를 기망하여 이에 속은 피해자로부터 즉석에서 피해자 명의의 신한카드를 건네받아 2018. 9. 21.경 대구 동구 K에 있는 L당구장에서 당구게임 대금 15,000원을 결제한 것을 비롯하여 그 시경부터 2018. 10. 3.경까지 사이에 별지 범죄일람표 기재와 같이 도합 62회에 걸쳐 합계 1,926,934원 상당을 결제 하였으나 카드대금 결제일에 지급하지 않아 피해자로 하여금 그 대금을 대신 지급하게 하여 재산상 이익을 취득하였다.

- Label:
  - Loss: [42만원, 1,926,934원]

A.2.6 RULING-CRIMINAL

- Ruling: 피고인을 징역 1년 및 벌금 1,000,000원에 처한다. 피고인이 위 벌금을 납입하지 아니하는 경우 금 50,000원을 1일로 환산한 기간 피고인을 노역장에 유치한다. 다만, 이 판결 확정일로부터 2년간 위 징역형의 집행을 유예한다. 압수된 증 제1호 내지 제3호를 각 몰수한다.

- Label:
  - Fine: [벌금1,000,000원]
  - Imprisonment: [징역1년]
  - Suspension of execution: [2년]
  - Education: none
  - Community service: none

A.3 End-to-end IE system

We use decoder-only (GPT2) or encoder-decoder (mt5) language models. For a given source text (facts or ruling) and following task-specific prompt, the models generate the values of individual fields autoregressively. For instance, the output of the ruling task looks like "fine 10,000 won. imprisonment 6 months. suspension of execution 12 months. none. community service 40 hours." where the values of multiple fields are generated sequentially separated by "." delimiters. The prompts of individual tasks consists of soft tokens (trainable embeddings) initialized from simple declarative sentences like "Extract embezzled money.", "Write fine, imprisonment, and suspension of execution in sequence". We also perform prompt-tuning experiments where only the soft tokens are trained. All models are trained with cross-entropy loss from the generated tokens under multi-task setting. The examples are randomly sampled with equal ratio from individual tasks. All parameters are shared except the soft tokens. In addition to four IE tasks, a civil ruling IE task is included as an auxiliary task during the training. In this task, a model extracts "approved money" and "the ratio of litigation cost that plaintiffs' should pay" from the rulings and "claimed money" from the gist of claims. The same number of precedents with other tasks are labeled and used for the training.

A.4 Rule-based baseline

We develop a rule-based baseline using regular expression for comparison with the end-to-end approaches. For each of the categories (DRUNK DRIVING, EMBEZZLEMENT, FRAUDand RULING-CRIMINAL), we read through diverse cases and manually identified suitable identification rules/ patterns. In DRUNK DRIVING, as "blood alcohol level", "travel distance" and "previous criminal record on drunk driving" appear once each with expressions such as "%", "km" or "more than twice", these patterns were used to extract each of the information. Also,"type of the vehicle" was extracted by the pattern "(drunk)drove <vehicle><object marker>". In EMBEZZLEMENT, the embezzled money is extracted by (1) extracting all monetary values from facts and (2-a) if there is the word "total" preceding a monetary value, such amount of money was selected as the total amount of embezzled money. (2-b) Else, we selected the last appearing money. In FRAUD, the damages are extracted similarly to EMBEZZLEMENT cases except if "aid" appears in the sentence that includes last money, it is considered as loss from fraud aiding and abetting. In RULING-CRIMINAL, an amount of fine, imprisonment, suspension of execution, education, and community service periods are extracted by (1) selecting sentences including the indicators such as "fine", "imprisonment", "suspension of execution", "education", and "service" and (2) extracting numbers with corresponding units (won, years, months, hours, etc) from the same sentence.

A.5 Experimental details

All models are fine-tuned with batch size 8–16 with learning rate 0.0001 with maximum 100 epochs under multi-task setting (Section A.3). In the prompt-tuning experiments, learning rate is set to 1.0 with maximum epochs 250–300. GPT-2, LCUBE-base, and LCUBE-medium models are pre-trained from scratch using Megatron library (Shoeybi et al., 2019) using `Precedent corpus` (150k Korean precedents)from LBox Open (Hwang et al., 2022). To fine-tune mt5 models, `google/mt5-small/large` checkpoints are downloaded from Huggingface hub. For domain adaptation, mt5-small is pre-trained with word level span corruption objective for 22 epochs with the batch size 12. Also, ISLA is prepared by pre-training mt5-large starting from the official checkpoint for 7 epochs with batch size 24 using our internal legal corpus.

A.6 Metric

In all IE tasks, we calculate F_1 as followed. True positive if the target field (FLD) exists both in the ground truth (GT) and the prediction (PR) and their values are equal. False positive if either (1) the values are not equal, or (2) the FLD exsits only in PR. False negative if the value exists only in GT. True negative if FLD does not exist in both GT and PR.

A.7 Recall rates

We set the recall rates to be 84%, 81%, and 60% for RULING-CRIMINAL, DRUNK DRIVING, and FRAUD respectively. This results in 100%, 97%, and 97% precision on the our internal validation set.

A.8 Additional analysis

Table 2: Data statistics.

Name	Size	Legal corpus size	# of training examples	AVG	DRUNK DRIVING				EMBZ	FRAUD		RULING-CRIMINAL				
# of individual fields	-	-	50	-	50	50	50	49	49	48	2	19	39	22	10	5
# of individual fields	-	-	200	-	200	194	199	186	196	179	18	71	153	101	63	31
# of unique words	-	-	50	-	612				2,557	4,618		286				
# of unique words	-	-	200	-	1,821				6,928	11,712		664				

Table 3: The average imprisonment period w/ and w/o criminal records in DRUNK DRIVING cases.

Year	w/o criminal record	w/ criminal record
2017–2018	5.3 months	7.7 months
2019–2022	8.9 months	11.9 months

Semantic Segmentation of Legal Documents via Rhetorical Roles

Vijit Malik[1*] **Rishabh Sanjay**[1*] **Shouvik Kumar Guha**[2]
Angshuman Hazarika[3] **Shubham Nigam**[1] **Arnab Bhattacharya**[1]
Ashutosh Modi[1†]

[1]Indian Institute of Technology Kanpur (IIT-K)
[2]West Bengal National University of Juridical Sciences (WBNUJS)
[3]Indian Institute of Management Ranchi (IIM-R)

{vijitvm21,rishabh.lfs}@gmail.com shouvikkumarguha@nujs.edu
angshuman.hazarika@iimranchi.ac.in sknigam@cse.iitk.ac.in
arnabb@cse.iitk.ac.in ashutoshm@cse.iitk.ac.in

Abstract

Legal documents are unstructured, use legal jargon, and have considerable length, making them difficult to process automatically via conventional text processing techniques. A legal document processing system would benefit substantially if the documents could be segmented into coherent information units. This paper proposes a new corpus of legal documents annotated (with the help of legal experts) with a set of 13 semantically coherent units labels (referred to as Rhetorical Roles), e.g., facts, arguments, statute, issue, precedent, ruling, and ratio. We perform a thorough analysis of the corpus and the annotations. For automatically segmenting the legal documents, we experiment with the task of rhetorical role prediction: given a document, predict the text segments corresponding to various roles. Using the created corpus, we experiment extensively with various deep learning-based baseline models for the task. Further, we develop a multitask learning (MTL) based deep model with document rhetorical role label shift as an auxiliary task for segmenting a legal document. The proposed model shows superior performance over the existing models. We also experiment with model performance in the case of domain transfer and model distillation techniques to see the model performance in limited data conditions.

1 Introduction

The number of legal cases has been growing almost exponentially in populous countries like India. For example, as per the India's National Judicial Data Grid, there are about 41 million cases pending in India (National Judicial Data Grid, 2021). As per some of recent estimates by a retired Supreme Court of India Judge, it will take about 450 years to clear the backlog of cases (Katju, 2019). Technology could come to the rescue in dealing with the backlog, for example, if there were a technology (based on NLP techniques) that could help a legal practitioner to extract relevant information from legal documents then it could make the legal process more streamlined and efficient. However, legal documents are quite different from conventional documents used to train NLP systems (e.g., newspaper texts). Legal documents are typically long (tens of pages) (Malik et al., 2021), unstructured (Skylaki et al., 2021; Leitner et al., 2019), noisy (e.g., grammatical and spelling mistakes due to manual typing in courts) (Malik et al., 2021; Kapoor et al., 2022), and use different lexicon (legal jargon). The use of a specialized lexicon and different semantics of words makes pre-trained neural models (e.g., transformer-based models) ineffective (Chalkidis et al., 2020). The legal domain has several sub-domains (corresponding to different laws, e.g., criminal law, income tax law) within it. Although some of the fundamental legal principles are common, the overlap between different sub-domains is low; hence systems developed on one law (e.g., income tax law) may not directly work for another law (e.g., criminal law), so there is the problem of a domain shift (Bhattacharya et al., 2019; Malik et al., 2021; Kalamkar et al., 2022a; Kapoor et al., 2022).

In this paper, we target legal case proceedings in the form of judgment documents. To aid the processing of long legal documents, we propose a method of segmenting a legal document into coherent information units referred to as *Rhetorical Roles* (Saravanan et al., 2008; Bhattacharya et al., 2019). We propose a corpus of legal documents annotated with Rhetorical Roles (RRs). RRs could be useful for various legal applications. Legal documents are fairly long, and dividing these into rhetor-

*Equal Contributions
†Corresponding Author

Proceedings of the Natural Legal Language Processing Workshop 2022, pages 153 - 171
December 8, 2022

ical role units can help summarize documents effectively. In the task of legal judgment prediction, for example, using RRs, one could extract the relevant portions of the case that contributes towards the final decision. RRs could be useful for legal information extraction, e.g., it can help extract cases with similar facts. Similarly, prior cases similar to a given case could be retrieved by comparing different rhetorical role units. In this work, we make the following contributions:

1. We create a new corpus of legal documents annotated with rhetorical role labels. In contrast to previous work (8 RRs) (Bhattacharya et al., 2019), we create a more fine-grained set of 13 RRs. Further, we create the corpus on different legal domains (§3).
2. For automatically segmenting the legal documents, we experiment with the task of rhetorical role prediction: given a document, predict the text segments corresponding to various roles. Using the created corpus, we experiment with various deep text classification and baseline models for the task. We propose new multi-task learning (MTL) based deep model with document level rhetorical role shift as an auxiliary task for segmenting the document into rhetorical role units (§4). The proposed model performs better than the existing models for RR prediction. We further show that our method is robust against domain transfer to other legal sub-domains (§5). We release the corpus, model implementations and experiments code: `https://github.com/Exploration-Lab/Rhetorical-Roles`
3. Given that annotating legal documents with RR is a tedious process, we perform model distillation experiments with the proposed MTL model and attempt to leverage unlabeled data to enhance the performance (§5). We also show the use-case for RR prediction model.

2 Related Work

Legal text processing has been an active area of research in recent times. A number of datasets, applications, and tasks have been proposed. For example, Argument Mining (Wyner et al., 2010), Information Extraction and Retrieval (Tran et al., 2019), Event Extraction (Lagos et al., 2010), Prior Case Retrieval (Jackson et al., 2003), Summarization (Moens et al., 1999), and Case Prediction (Malik et al., 2021; Chalkidis et al., 2019; Strickson and De La Iglesia, 2020; Kapoor et al., 2022). Recently, there has been a rapid growth in the development of NLP and ML technologies for the Chinese legal system, inter alia, Chen et al. (2019); Hu et al. (2018); Jiang et al. (2018); Yang et al. (2019); Ye et al. (2018). Few works have focused on the creation of annotated corpora and the task of automatic rhetorical role labeling. Venturi (2012) developed a corpus, TEMIS of 504 sentences annotated both syntactically and semantically. The work of Wyner et al. (2013) focuses on the process of annotation and conducting inter-annotator studies. Savelka and Ashley (2018) conducted document segmentation of U.S. court documents using Conditional Random Fields (CRF) with handcrafted features to segment the documents into functional and issue-specific parts. Automatic labeling of rhetorical roles was first conducted in Saravanan et al. (2008), where CRFs were used to label seven rhetorical roles. Nejadgholi et al. (2017) developed a method for identification of factual and non-factual sentences using fastText. The automatic ML approaches and rule-based scripts for rhetorical role identification were compared in Walker et al. (2019). Kalamkar et al. (2022b) create a large corpus of RRs and propose transformer based baseline models for RR prediction. Our work comes close to work by Bhattacharya et al. (2019), where they use the BiLSTM-CRF model with sent2vec features to label rhetorical roles in Indian Supreme Court documents. In contrast, we develop a multi-task learning (MTL) based model for RR prediction that outperforms the system of Bhattacharya et al. (2019).

3 Rhetorical Roles Corpus

Corpus Acquisition: We focus on Indian legal documents in English; however, techniques we develop can be generalized to other legal systems. We consider legal judgments from the Supreme Court of India, High Courts, and Tribunal courts crawled from the website of IndianKanoon (`https://indiankanoon.org/`). We also scrape Competition Law documents from Indian Tribunal court cases (National Company Law Appellate Tribunal (NCLAT), COMPetition Appellate Tribunal (COMPAT), Competition Commission of India (CCI)). We focus on two domains of the Indian legal system: Competition Law (CL) (also called as Anti-Trust Law in the US and Anti-Monopoly law in China) and Income Tax (IT). CL deals with regulating the conduct of companies, particularly concerning competition. With the help of legal experts, we narrowed down the cases pertinent to CL and IT from the crawled corpus (also see Ethical Considerations in App. A).

Choice of CL and IT domains: India has a common law system where a decision may not be exactly as per the statutes, but the judiciary may come up with its interpretation and overrule existing precedents. This introduces a bit of subjectivity. One of the biggest problems faced during the task of identifying the rhetorical roles in a judgment is that the element of subjectivity involved in the judicial perception and interpretation of different rhetorical roles, ranging from the factual matrix (i.e., perception about facts, relevant facts and facts in an issue may vary) to the statutory applicability and interpretation to determine the fitness of a particular judicial precedent to the case at hand. In order to overcome this particular obstacle, we focus on specific legal domains (CL and IT) that display a relatively greater degree of consistency and objectivity in terms of judicial reliance on statutory provisions to reach decisions (Taxmann, 2021).

Corpus Statistics: We randomly selected a set of 50 documents each for CL and IT from the set of acquired documents ($\approx$ 1.6k for IT and $\approx$ 0.8k for CL). These 100 documents were annotated with 13 fine-grained RR labels (vs. 8 by Bhattacharya et al. (2019)) by a team of legal experts. Our corpus is double the size of the RR corpus of Bhattacharya et al. (2019). The CL documents have 13,328 sentences (avg. of 266 per document), and IT has a total of 7856 sentences (avg. of 157 per document). Label-wise distribution for IT and CL documents are provided in Appendix B.3. Annotating legal documents with RRs is a tedious as well as challenging task. Nevertheless, this is a growing corpus, and we plan to add more annotated documents. However, given the complexity of annotations, the RR labeling task also points towards looking for model distillation (§5) and zero-shot learning-based methods.

Annotation Setup: The annotation team (legal team) consisted of two law professors from prestigious law schools and six graduate-level law student researchers. Annotating just 100 documents took almost three months. Based on detailed discussions with the legal team, we initially arrived at the eight main rhetorical roles (facts, arguments, statues, dissent, precedent, ruling by lower court, ratio and ruling by present court) plus one 'none' label. During the annotation, roles were further refined, and the documents were finally annotated with 13 fine-grained labels since some of the main roles could be sub-divided into more fine-grained classes. The list of RRs is as follows (example sentences for each role is in Table 15 in the Appendix B.3):

- **Fact (FAC):** These are the facts specific to the case based on which the arguments have been made and judgment has been issued. In addition to Fact, we also have the fine-grained label **Issues (ISS)**. The issues which have been framed/accepted by the present court for adjudication.
- **Argument (ARG)**: The arguments in the case were divided in two more fine-grained sub-labels: **Argument Petitioner (ARG-P):** Arguments which have been put forward by the petitioner/appellant in the case before the present court and by the same party in lower courts (where it may have been petitioner/respondent). Also, **Argument Respondent (ARG-R):** Arguments which have been put forward by the respondent in the case before the present court and by the same party in lower courts (where it may have been petitioner/respondent)
- **Statute (STA):** The laws referred in the case.
- **Dissent (DIS):** Any dissenting opinion expressed by a judge in the present judgment/decision.
- **Precedent (PRE):** The precedents in the documents were divided into 3 finer labels, **Precedent Relied Upon (PRE-R):** The precedents which have been relied upon by the present court for adjudication. These may or may not have been raised by the advocates of the parties and amicus curiae. **Precedent Not Relied Upon (PRE-NR):** The precedents which have not been relied upon by the present court for adjudication. These may have been raised by the advocates of the parties and amicus curiae. **Precedent Overruled (PRE-O):** Any precedents (past cases) on the same issue which have been overruled through the current judgment.
- **Ruling By Lower Court (RLC):** Decisions of the lower courts which dealt with the same case.
- **Ratio Of The Decision (ROD):** The principle which has been established by the current

judgment/decision which can be used in future cases. Does not include the obiter dicta which is based on observations applicable to the specific case only.

- **Ruling By Present Court (RPC):** The decision of the court on the issues which have been framed/accepted by the present court for adjudication.
- **None (NON):** any other matter in the judgment which does not fall in any of the above-mentioned categories.

The dataset was annotated by six legal experts (graduate law student researchers), 3 annotated 50 CL documents, and the remaining 3 annotated 50 IT documents. We used Webanno (de Castilho et al., 2016) as the annotation framework. Each legal expert assigned one of the 13 Rhetorical roles to each document sentence. Note that we initially experimented with different levels of granularity (e.g., phrase level, paragraph level), and based on the pilot study, we decided to go for sentence-level annotations as it maintains the balance (from the perspective of topical coherence) between too short (having no labels) and too long (having too many labels) texts. Legal experts pointed out that a single sentence can sometimes represent multiple rhetorical roles (although this is not common). Each expert could also assign secondary and tertiary rhetorical roles to a single sentence to handle such scenarios (also App. B.4). As an example, suppose a sentence is a 'Fact' but could also be an 'Argument' according to the legal expert. In that case, the expert could assign the rhetorical roles 'Primary Fact' and 'Secondary Argument' to that sentence. We extended it to the tertiary level as well to handle rare cases.

Our corpus is different from the existing corpus (Bhattacharya et al., 2019). Firstly, we use 13 fine-grained RR labels and the size of the corpus is almost twice. Secondly, we focus on different legal sub-domains (IT and CL vs. Supreme Court Judgments). Lastly, we perform the primary, secondary, and tertiary levels of annotations since, according to legal experts, it is sometimes possible that a sentence might have multiple RR labels.

Adjudication and Data compilation: Annotating RR is not a trivial task, and annotators can have disagreements. We followed a majority voting strategy over primary labels to determine the gold labels. There were a few cases (≈ 5%) where all the three legal experts assigned a different role to the same sentence. We asked the law professors to finalize the primary label in such cases. If the law professors decided to go with a label completely different from the three annotated labels, we went with their verdict. However, such cases were not frequent (≈ 4% of adjudicated cases). In this paper, for RR prediction, we concentrate on the primary labels and leave explorations of secondary and tertiary labels for future work.

Label	IT	CL
AR	0.80	0.93
FAC	0.80	0.89
PR	0.70	0.86
STA	0.78	0.89
RLC	0.58	0.74
RPC	0.78	0.79
ROD	0.67	0.93
DIS	_	0.99
Macro F1	0.73	0.88

Table 1: Label-wise Inter-Annotator agreement (F1 Scores). Dissent label instance absent in IT.

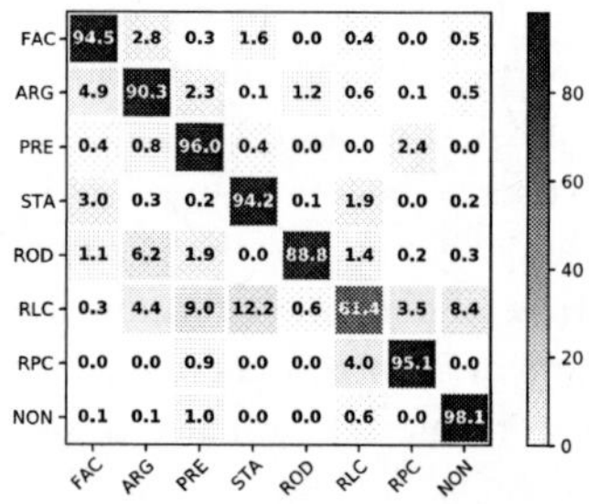

(a) IT

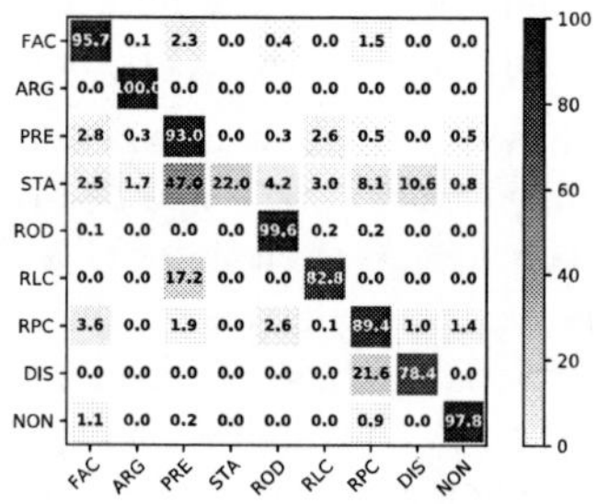

(b) CL

Figure 1: Confusion matrix between Annotators A_1 and A_3. Numbers represent % agreement. Dissent label instance is absent in IT.

Inter-annotator Agreements: The Fleiss kappa (Fleiss et al., 2013) between the annotators is 0.65 for the IT domain and 0.87 for the CL domain, indicating a substantial agreement between annotators. Additionally, as done in Bhattacharya et al. (2019) and Malik et al. (2021), we calculate the pair-wise inter-annotator F1 scores. To determine the agreement between the three annotators A_1, A_2, A_3 (each for IT and CL domain), we calculate the pairwise F1 scores (App. C) between annotators $(A_1, A_2), (A_2, A_3)$ and (A_3, A_1). We average these pairwise scores for each label and further average them out. We report the label-wise F1 and Macro F1 in Table 1. The table shows that the agreements between domains differ (0.73 for IT vs. 0.88 for CL). This is mainly due to (as pointed by law professors) the presence of more precedents and a greater number of statutory provisions in IT laws. These factors combine to produce more subjectivity (relative to CL) when it comes to interpreting and retracing judicial decisions. The confusion matrix between the annotators (A_1, A_3) is shown in Figure 1 (more details in App. B.5).

Analysis: Annotation of judgments to identify RR is a challenging task even for legal experts. Several factors contribute to this challenge. Annotators need to glean and combine information non-trivially (e.g., facts and arguments presented, the implicit setting, and the context under which the events described in the case happened) to arrive at the label. Moreover, the annotator only has access to the current document, which is a secondary account of what actually happened in the court. These limitations certainly make the task of the annotator more difficult and leave them with no choice other than to make certain educated guesses when it comes to understanding the various nuances, both ostensible and probable, of certain RR. It should, however, be noted that such variation need not occur for every RR since not all the roles are equally susceptible to it. A cumulative effect of the aforementioned factors can be observed in the results of the annotation. The analysis provided by the three annotators in the case of CL bears close resemblance with each other. On the other hand, in the case of IT, the analysis provided by Users 1 and 3 bears a greater resemblance with each other, compared to the resemblance between Users 1 and 2, or between Users 2 and 3. On a different note, it is also observed that the rhetorical role where the annotators have differed between themselves the most has been the point of Ruling made by the Lower Court, followed by the Ratio. This also ties in with the argument that all rhetorical roles are not equally susceptible to the variation caused by the varying levels of success achieved by the different annotators in retracing the judicial thought pattern (details and case studies in App. B.6).

Model	Dataset	F1
SBERT-Shift	IT	0.60
SBERT-Shift	CL	0.49
SBERT-Shift	IT+CL	0.47
BERT-SC	IT	0.66
BERT-SC	CL	0.64
BERT-SC	IT+CL	0.64

Table 2: Results for the auxillary task LSP

4 Rhetorical Roles Prediction

We would like to automate the process of segmenting a legal document, to develop ML models for the automation, we experiment with the task of Rhetorical Roles prediction.

Task Definition: Given a legal document, D, containing the sentences $[s_1, s_2, ...s_n]$, the task of rhetorical role prediction is to predict the label (or role) y_i for each sentence $s_i \in D$.

Baseline Models: For the first set of baseline models, the task is modeled as a single sentence prediction task, where given the sentence s, the model predicts the rhetorical role of the sentence. In this case, the context is ignored. We consider pre-trained BERT (Devlin et al., 2019) and LEGAL-BERT (Chalkidis et al., 2020) models for this. As another set of baseline models, we consider the task as a sequence labeling task, where the sequence of all the sentences in the document is given as input, and the model has to predict the RR label for each sentence. We used CRF with hand-crafted features (Bhattacharya et al., 2019) and BiLSTM network.

Label Shift Prediction: Rhetorical role labels do not change abruptly across sentences in a document, and the text tends to maintain topical coherence. Given the label y for a sentence s_i in the document, we hypothesize that the chances of shift (change) in the label for the next sentence s_{i+1} are low. We manually verified this using the training set and observed that on average in a document, if the label of sentence s_i is y, then 88% of the times the label of the next sentence s_{i+1} is same as y. Note that this is true only for consecutive sentences, but in general, label shift inertia fades as we try to predict beyond the second consecutive sentence. Since we are performing a sequence prediction task, this alone is not a good model for label prediction. Nevertheless, we think that this label shift inertia can provide a signal (via an auxiliary task) to the main sequence prediction model. Based on this observation, we define an auxiliary binary classification task: Label Shift Prediction (LSP), that aims to model the relationship between two sentences s_i and s_{i+1} and predict whether the labels y_i for s_i and y_{i+1} for s_{i+1} are different (shift occurs) or not. In particular, for each sentence pair $S = \{s_i, s_{i+1}\} \in D$, we define the label of LSP task, $Y = 1$ if $y_i \neq y_{i+1}$, otherwise $Y = 0$, here y_i is the rhetorical role for sentence s_i. Note that for the full model at the inference time, the true label of a sentence is not provided; hence predicting a shift in label makes more sense than performing a binary prediction that the next sentence has the same label or not. We model the LSP task via two different models:

SBERT-Shift: We model the label shift via a Siamese network. In particular, we use the pre-trained SBERT model (Reimers and Gurevych, 2019) to encode sentences s_i and s_{i+1} to get representations e_i and e_{i+1}. The combination of these representations ($e_i \oplus e_{i+1} \oplus (e_i - e_{i+1})$) is passed through a feed-forward network to predict the shift.

BERT-SC: We use the pre-trained BERT model and fine-tune it for the task of LSP. We model the input in the form of sentence semantic coherence task, $[CLS] \oplus s_i \oplus [SEP] \oplus s_{i+1} \oplus [SEP]$ to make the final prediction for shift. In general, the BERT-SC model performs better than SBERT-Shift (Table 2). Due to the superior performance of BERT-SC, we include it to provide label shift information to the final MTL model. The aim of our work is to predict RR, and we use label shift as auxiliary information even if it may not be predicted correctly at all times. As shown in results later, this limited information improves the performance.

Proposed Models: We propose two main models for the rhetorical role prediction: Label Shift Prediction based on BiLSTM-CRF and MTL models.

LSP-BiLSTM-CRF: Signal from label shift is used to aid the RR prediction in the LSP-BiLSTM-CRF model. The model consists of (Figure 2) a BiLSTM-CRF model with specialized input representation. Let the sentence embedding (from pre-trained BERT) corresponding to i^{th} sentence be b_i. Let, the representation of the label shift (the layer before the softmax layer in LSP model) between current sentence and previous sentence pair $\{s_{i-1}, s_i\}$ be $e_{i-1,i}$. Similarly for the next pair ($\{s_i, s_{i+1}\}$) we get $e_{i,i+1}$. The sentence representation for i^{th} sentence is given by $e_{i-1,i} \oplus b_i \oplus e_{i,i+1}$. This sentence representation goes as input to the BiLSTM-CRF model for RR prediction.

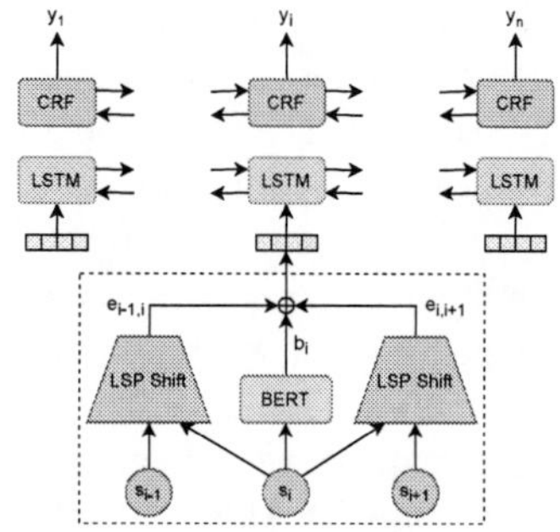

Figure 2: LSP-BiLSTM-CRF Model

MultiTask Learning (MTL): We use the framework of Multitask learning, where rhetorical role prediction is the main task and label shift prediction is the auxiliary task. Sharing representations between the main and related tasks helps in better generalization on the main task (Crawshaw, 2020). The intuition is that a label shift would help the rhetorical role component make the correct prediction based on the prospective shift. The MTL model (Figure 3) consists of two components: the shift detection component and the rhetorical role prediction component. The shift component predicts if a label shift occurs at i^{th} position. The output of the BiLSTM layer of shift component is concatenated with the BiLSTM output of the rhetorical role component. The concatenated output is passed to a CRF layer for the final prediction of the rhetorical role. The loss for the model is given by: $L = \lambda L_{shift} + (1 - \lambda) L_{RR}$, where, L_{shift} is the loss corresponding to label shift prediction and L_{RR} is the loss corresponding to rhetorical role prediction, and hyperparameter λ balances the importance of each of the task. If λ is set to zero, we are back with our baseline BiLSTM-CRF model. Since there are two components, we experimented with sending the same encodings of sentences to both the components ($E_1 = E_2$), as well as sending different encodings of the same sentence to both components ($E_1 \neq E_2$). The proposed model is very different from the previously proposed BiLSTM-CRF by Bhattacharya et al. (2019) that does not use any multitasking and label shift information.

5 Experiments, Results and Analysis

Due to the complexity of the task of RR prediction and to be comparable with the existing baseline systems, for experiments, we consider 7 main labels (FAC, ARG, PRE, ROD, RPC, RLC, and STA). We plan to explore all fine-grained RR label (13) pre-

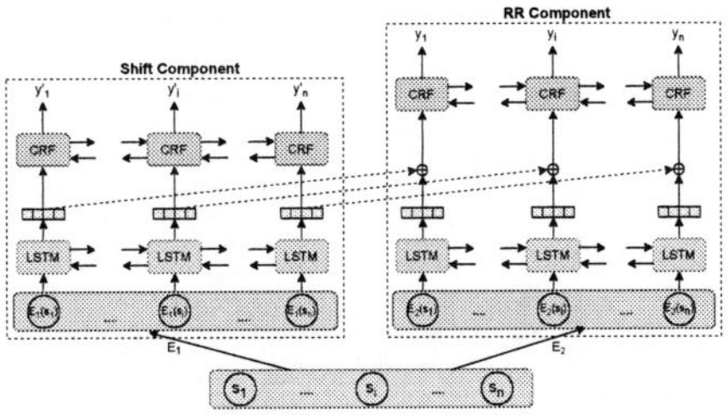

Figure 3: MTL architecture for Rhetorical Role Labelling and Shift Prediction.

dictions in the future. Based on recommendations by legal experts, we ignore sentences with NON (None) label (about 4% for IT and 0.5% for CL) (more details in App. D.1). Further, the IT domain did not have any instance of dissent (DIS) label, and CL has only three documents with very few DIS instances. Based on consultations with law experts, we discarded DIS sentences (more details in App. D.1). We randomly split (at document level) IT/CL into 80% train, 10% validation, and 10% test set. In contrast to Bhattacharya et al. (2019), we did not perform cross-validation for better comparison across different models. We also experiment with a combined dataset of IT and CL (IT+CL); the splits are made by combining individual train/val/test split of IT and CL. We experimented with a number of baseline models (Table 3, 4). In particular, we considered BiLSTM with sent2vec embeddings (Bhattacharya et al., 2019), non-contextual models (single sentence) like BERT (Devlin et al., 2019), LegalBERT (Chalkidis et al., 2020) and BERT-neighbour (we take both left and right neighboring sentences in addition to the sentence of interest). We also considered sentence-level sequence prediction models (contextual models): CRF model using handcrafted features provided by Bhattacharya et al. (2019), different variants of BiLSTM-CRF, one with handcrafted features, with sent2vec embeddings, with BERT embeddings, and with MLM embeddings. We finetuned BERT with Masked Language Modeling (MLM) objective on the train set to obtain MLM embeddings (CLS embedding) for each of the sentences (App. D has hyperparameters, training schedule, and compute settings). We use the Macro F1 metric for evaluation (App. C). We tuned the hyperparameter λ of the MTL loss function using the validation set. We trained the MTL model with $\lambda \in [0.1, 0.9]$ with strides of 0.1 (Figure 4). $\lambda = 0.6$ performs the best for the IT domain and performs competitively on the combined domains.

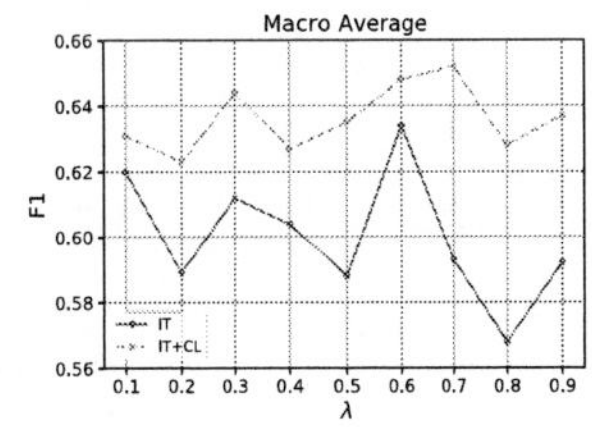

Figure 4: Variation of F1 score with λ on IT and IT+CL domain

Model	IT (F1)	CL (F1)
BERT	0.56	0.52
BERT-neighbor	0.53	0.51
LEGAL-BERT	0.55	0.53
CRF (Handcrafted)	0.55	0.52
BiLSTM (sent2vec)	0.55	0.54
BiLSTM-CRF (handcraft)	0.57	0.56
BiLSTM-CRF (sent2vec)	0.59	0.61
BiLSTM-CRF (BERT emb)	0.63	0.63
BiLSTM-CRF (MLM emb)	0.58	0.60
LSP (SBERT)	*0.64*	*0.63*
LSP (BERT-SC) •	*0.65*	*0.68*
MTL (MLM emb)	*0.67*	*0.67*
MTL (BERT-SC) ⋆ ⋄	***0.70***±*0.02*	***0.69***±*0.01*

Table 3: Results of baseline and proposed models on IT and CL. LSP and MTL refer to the LSP-BiLSTM-CRF and MTL-BiLSTM-CRF models respectively. • LSP result is significant with $p \leq 0.05$ in comparison to baseline (BiLSTM-CRF(sent2vec)). Similarly, MTL (BERT-SC) has significant result in comparison to baseline ($\diamond$, $p \leq 0.05$). MTL (BERT-SC) is significant w.r.t. LSP ($\star$, $p \leq 0.05$).

Results and Analysis: Among the baseline models (Table 3), we note that LEGAL-BERT performs slightly better on the CL domain but slightly worse on the IT domain when compared to pre-trained BERT. It might be attributed to that LEGAL-BERT (trained on EU legal documents, which also has European competition law) is not trained on Indian IT law documents. Using BERT embeddings with BiLSTM-CRF provides better results. Both the proposed approaches outperform the previous approaches by a substantial margin. The MTL approach (with $\lambda = 0.6$) provides the best results on both datasets with an average (over six runs) F1 score of 0.70 (standard deviation of 0.02) on the IT domain, an average F1 of $0.69(\pm 0.01)$ on CL domain, and an average F1 score of $0.71(\pm 0.01)$ for the combined domain. The MTL model shows variance across runs; hence we average the results. Other models were reasonably stable across runs.

We use the LSP shift component with BERT-SC as the encoder E_1 and the pre-trained BERT model as the encoder E_2 in our MTL architecture. We

Model	IT+CL (F1)
BiLSTM-CRF (sent2vec)	0.65
BiLSTM-CRF (BERT embs)	0.63
LSP-BiLSTM-CRF (BERT-SC)	0.67
MTL-BiLSTM-CRF (BERT-SC)	**0.70**±0.01

Table 4: Results of baseline and proposed models on combined dataset (IT+CL)

Label	IT	CL
AR	0.67±0.010	0.78±0.005
FAC	0.78±0.020	0.75±0.010
PR	0.69±0.005	0.62±0.005
STA	0.79±0.020	0.82±0.020
RLC	0.62±0.005	0.53±0.005
RPC	0.70±0.010	0.71±0.010
ROD	0.66±0.005	0.65±0.005
Macro F1	0.70±0.020	0.69±0.010

Table 5: Label-wise average (across 6 runs) F1 scores of MTL-BiLSTM-CRF (BERT-SC) model.

did not use SBERT since it was under-performing when compared to BERT-SC. We provide the label-wise F1 scores for the MTL model in Table 5. Note the high performance on the FAC label and low performance on the RLC label; this is similar to what we observe for annotators (Table 1). Also, the MTL model performs better on the AR label in the CL domain than the IT domain. An opposite trend can be observed for the RLC label. The contribution of the LSP task is evident from the superior performance. We conduct the ablation study of our MTL architecture from multiple aspects. Instead of using shift embeddings from BERT-SC as the encoder E_1, we use a BERT model fine-tuned upon the MLM task on the IT and CL domain. However, we obtain a comparatively lower score (see App. D). This observation yet again points towards the significance of the LSP in the task of rhetorical role prediction (results on other encoders in App. D). The results have two interesting observations: firstly, MTL model performance on IT cases comes close to the average inter-annotator agreement. In the case of CL, there is a gap. Secondly, for the model, the performance on the IT domain is better than the CL domain, but in the case of annotators opposite trend was observed. We do not know the exact reason for this, but the legal experts pointed out that this is possible because the selected documents might be restricted to specific sections of the IT law and model learned solely from these documents alone without any other external knowledge. However, annotators, having knowledge of the entire IT law, might have looked from a broader perspective.

Domain Transfer: In order to check the generalization capabilities of the MTL model compared to the baseline model, we conducted some domain transfer experiments. We experimented with a RR dataset of 50 documents (referred to as G) by Bhattacharya et al. (2019). G dataset comes from a different legal sub-domain (criminal and civil cases) with very less overlap with IT and CL. We tried different combinations of train and test datasets of IT, CL, and G. Note that G (criminal and civil cases) has very less overlap with IT and CL cases, so practically, it is a different domain. The results are in Table 6. We can observe that the MTL model generalizes better across the domains than the baseline model. Both the models perform better on the G_{test} when the combined (IT+CL)$_{\text{train}}$ set is used. This points towards better generalization.

Train Dataset	Test Dataset	BiLSTM-CRF (sent2vec)	MTL
G_{train}	G_{test}	0.55	**0.59**
G_{train}	CL_{test}	0.48 (12.78%)	**0.50** (15.25%)
G_{train}	IT_{test}	0.41 (25.45%)	**0.46** (22.03%)
G_{train}	(IT+CL)$_{\text{test}}$	0.42 (23.64%)	**0.48** (18.64%)
(IT+CL)$_{\text{train}}$	G_{test}	0.60	**0.63**

Table 6: Domain transfer experiments to compare the performance of MTL-BiLSTM-CRF with the baseline BiLSTM-CRF. The number in parenthesis denotes Δ_G : the % difference between the performance on G_{test} and the new domain.

Model distillation: RR annotation is a tedious process, however, there is an abundance of unlabelled legal documents. We experimented with semi-supervised techniques to leverage the unlabelled data. In particular, we tried a self-training based approach (Xie et al., 2020). The idea is to learn a teacher model θ_{tea} on the labelled data D_L. The teacher model is then used to generate hard labels on unlabeled sentences $s_u \in d_i$: $\hat{y}_i = f_{\theta_{tea}}(\hat{d}_i)\ \forall \hat{d}_i \in D_U$. Next, a student model θ_{stu} is learned on labeled and unlabeled sentences, with the loss function for student training given by: $L_{ST} = \frac{1}{|D_L|}\sum_{d_j \in D_L} L(f_{\theta_{stu}}(d_j), y_j) + \frac{\alpha_U}{D_U}\sum_{\hat{d}_i \in D_U} L(f_{\theta_{stu}}(\hat{d}_i), \hat{y}_i)$. Here, α_U is a weighing hyperparameter between the labelled and unlabelled data (details in App. D). The process can be iterated and the final distilled model is used for prediction. The results of model distillation are shown in Table 8 for two iterations (initializing the teacher model of the current iteration as the learned student model of the previous iteration; further iterations do not improve results). MTL model was run just once, due to variance it shows F1 of 0.68. The results improve for majority of labels with an increment of 0.11 F1 score for the RLC label in the first iteration. Also, the variance of F1 scores across labels decreases.

5.1 Application of Rhetorical Role to Judgment Prediction

To check the applicability of RR in downstream applications, as a use-case, we experimented with how RR could contribute towards judgment prediction (ethical concerns discussed later). We use the legal judgment corpus (ILDC) provided by Malik et al. (2021) and fine-tune a pre-trained BERT model on the train set of ILDC for the task of judgment prediction on the last 512 tokens of the documents. Malik et al. (2021) observed that training on the last 512 (also the max size of the input to BERT) tokens of a legal document give the best results; we use the same setting. We use this trained model directly for predicting the outcome on 84 IT/CL cases. We removed text corresponding to the final decisions (and extracted gold decisions) from these documents with the help of legal experts. In the first experiment, we use the last 512 tokens of IT/CL cases for prediction. To study the effect of RRs, in another experiment, we extract the sentences corresponding to gold ratio (ROD) and ruling (RPC) RR labels in IT/CL documents and use this as input to the BERT model. We consider these two RR only since, by definition, these sentences denote the principles and the decision of the court related to the issues in the proceedings. There were no ROD or RPC labels for some documents (16 out of 100 for both IT and CL); we removed these in both experiments. The results are shown in Table 7. Using the gold RR gives a boost to the F1 score. We also experimented with using predicted RR, and the performance was comparable to that of the BERT model.

To explore how predicted rhetorical roles would perform on judgment prediction task, we perform the following experiment. We use our best performing model MTL (BERT-SC), trained on the combined IT+CL domain to check the applicability of rhetorical roles for the task of Judgment Prediction. In the first step, we obtain the predicted rhetorical roles for each sentence in the documents. Next, we select the sentences labeled as ROD or RPC[1]. Third, we use a BERT base model fine-tuned on the last 512 tokens of each document in the ILDC corpus (Malik et al., 2021) and use it to predict the judgment of the test set documents, given only the predicted ROD and RPC sentences. We compare the results by the MTL model and BiLSTM-CRF baseline on performing judgment prediction with predicted rhetorical roles. Refer to Appendix Table 14 for the results. Since RR prediction for ROD and RPC is not perfect, improving it would greatly enhance the results as shown in Table 7.

[1]We select only these two labels since by definition, these sentences provide the necessary cues towards the judgment.

Model	IT+CL docs	F1
BERT-ILDC	last 512 tokens	0.55
BERT-ILDC	Gold ROD & RPC	**0.58**

Table 7: Judgment prediction using RR. The model using gold ROD and RPC is found to be statistically significant ($p \leq 0.05$).

Label	Base MTL	Dist. Iter 1	Dist. Iter 2
AR	0.62	0.70	**0.70**
FAC	0.74	**0.75**	0.73
PR	0.68	0.72	**0.74**
STA	0.76	**0.77**	0.75
RLC	0.59	**0.70**	0.70
RPC	0.67	0.63	**0.73**
ROD	0.68	0.66	**0.68**
Macro F1	0.68	0.71	**0.72**

Table 8: Model Distillation: F1 scores of MTL-BiLSTM-CRF (BERT-SC) model after two distillation iterations on the IT domain.

6 Conclusion

We introduce a new corpus annotated with rhetorical roles. We proposed a new MTL model that uses label shift information for predicting labels. We further showed via domain transfer experiments the generalizability of the model. Since RR are tedious to annotate, we showed the possibility of using model distillation techniques to improve the system. In the future, we plan to explore cross-domain transfer techniques to perform RR identification in legal documents in other Indian languages. Nevertheless, we plan to grow the corpus. We also plan to apply RR models for other legal tasks such as summarization and information extraction.

Acknowledgements

We would like to thank anonymous reviewers for their insightful comments. We would like to thank student research assistants Tridib Mandal, Chirag Mittal, Shefali Deshmukh, Shailja Beria, and Syamantak Sinha from West Bengal National University of Juridical Sciences (WBNUJS) for annotating the documents. This work would not have been possible without their help.

References

Paheli Bhattacharya, Shounak Paul, Kripabandhu Ghosh, Saptarshi Ghosh, and Adam Wyner. 2019. Identification of rhetorical roles of sentences in indian legal judgments. *CoRR*, abs/1911.05405.

Ilias Chalkidis, Ion Androutsopoulos, and Nikolaos Aletras. 2019. Neural legal judgment prediction in English. In *Proceedings of the 57th Annual Meeting of the Association for Computational Linguistics*, pages 4317–4323, Florence, Italy. Association for Computational Linguistics.

Ilias Chalkidis, Manos Fergadiotis, Prodromos Malakasiotis, Nikolaos Aletras, and Ion Androutsopoulos. 2020. LEGAL-BERT: The muppets straight out of law school. In *Findings of the Association for Computational Linguistics: EMNLP 2020*, pages 2898–2904, Online. Association for Computational Linguistics.

Huajie Chen, Deng Cai, Wei Dai, Zehui Dai, and Yadong Ding. 2019. Charge-based prison term prediction with deep gating network. In *Proceedings of the 2019 Conference on Empirical Methods in Natural Language Processing and the 9th International Joint Conference on Natural Language Processing (EMNLP-IJCNLP)*, pages 6362–6367, Hong Kong, China. Association for Computational Linguistics.

Michael Crawshaw. 2020. Multi-task learning with deep neural networks: A survey. *CoRR*, abs/2009.09796.

Richard Eckart de Castilho, Eva Mujdricza-Maydt, Seid Muhie Yimam, Silvana Hartmann, Iryna Gurevych, Anette Frank, and Chris Biemann. 2016. A web-based tool for the integrated annotation of semantic and syntactic structures. In *Proceedings of the Workshop on Language Technology Resources and Tools for Digital Humanities (LT4DH)*, pages 76–84.

Jacob Devlin, Ming-Wei Chang, Kenton Lee, and Kristina Toutanova. 2019. BERT: Pre-training of Deep Bidirectional Transformers for Language Understanding. In *Proceedings of the 2019 Conference of the North American Chapter of the Association for Computational Linguistics: Human Language Technologies, Volume 1 (Long and Short Papers)*, pages 4171–4186, Minneapolis, Minnesota. Association for Computational Linguistics.

Joseph L Fleiss, Bruce Levin, and Myunghee Cho Paik. 2013. *Statistical methods for rates and proportions*. john wiley & sons.

Zikun Hu, Xiang Li, Cunchao Tu, Zhiyuan Liu, and Maosong Sun. 2018. Few-shot charge prediction with discriminative legal attributes. In *Proceedings of the 27th International Conference on Computational Linguistics*, pages 487–498, Santa Fe, New Mexico, USA. Association for Computational Linguistics.

Peter Jackson, Khalid Al-Kofahi, Alex Tyrrell, and Arun Vachher. 2003. Information extraction from case law and retrieval of prior cases. *Artificial Intelligence*, 150(1-2):239–290.

Xin Jiang, Hai Ye, Zhunchen Luo, WenHan Chao, and Wenjia Ma. 2018. Interpretable rationale augmented charge prediction system. In *Proceedings of the 27th International Conference on Computational Linguistics: System Demonstrations*, pages 146–151, Santa Fe, New Mexico. Association for Computational Linguistics.

Prathamesh Kalamkar, Aman Tiwari, Astha Agarwal, Saurabh Karn, Smita Gupta, Vivek Raghavan, and Ashutosh Modi. 2022a. Corpus for automatic structuring of legal documents. In *Proceedings of the Language Resources and Evaluation Conference*, pages 4420–4429, Marseille, France. European Language Resources Association.

Prathamesh Kalamkar, Aman Tiwari, Astha Agarwal, Saurabh Karn, Smita Gupta, Vivek Raghavan, and Ashutosh Modi. 2022b. Corpus for automatic structuring of legal documents. In *Proceedings of the Thirteenth Language Resources and Evaluation Conference*, pages 4420–4429, Marseille, France. European Language Resources Association.

Arnav Kapoor, Mudit Dhawan, Anmol Goel, Arjun T H, Akshala Bhatnagar, Vibhu Agrawal, Amul Agrawal, Arnab Bhattacharya, Ponnurangam Kumaraguru, and Ashutosh Modi. 2022. HLDC: Hindi legal documents corpus. In *Findings of the Association for Computational Linguistics: ACL 2022*, pages 3521–3536, Dublin, Ireland. Association for Computational Linguistics.

Justice Markandey Katju. 2019. Backlog of cases crippling judiciary. `https://perma.cc/D8V4-L566`.

Nikolaos Lagos, Frederique Segond, Stefania Castellani, and Jacki O'Neill. 2010. Event extraction for legal case building and reasoning. In *International Conference on Intelligent Information Processing*, pages 92–101. Springer.

Elena Leitner, Georg Rehm, and Julian Moreno-Schneider. 2019. Fine-grained named entity recognition in legal documents. In *Semantic Systems. The Power of AI and Knowledge Graphs*, pages 272–287, Cham. Springer International Publishing.

Vijit Malik, Rishabh Sanjay, Shubham Kumar Nigam, Kripabandhu Ghosh, Shouvik Kumar Guha, Arnab Bhattacharya, and Ashutosh Modi. 2021. ILDC for CJPE: Indian legal documents corpus for court judgment prediction and explanation. In *Proceedings of the 59th Annual Meeting of the Association for Computational Linguistics and the 11th International Joint Conference on Natural Language Processing (Volume 1: Long Papers)*, pages 4046–4062, Online. Association for Computational Linguistics.

Marie-Francine Moens, Caroline Uyttendaele, and Jos Dumortier. 1999. Abstracting of legal cases: the potential of clustering based on the selection of representative objects. *Journal of the American Society for Information Science*, 50(2):151–161.

National Judicial Data Grid. 2021. National judicial data grid statistics. https://www.njdg.ecourts.gov.in/njdgnew/index.php.

Isar Nejadgholi, Renaud Bougueng, and Samuel Witherspoon. 2017. A semi-supervised training method for semantic search of legal facts in canadian immigration cases. In *JURIX*, pages 125–134.

Nils Reimers and Iryna Gurevych. 2019. Sentence-bert: Sentence embeddings using siamese bert-networks. *arXiv preprint arXiv:1908.10084*.

M Saravanan, Balaraman Ravindran, and S Raman. 2008. Automatic identification of rhetorical roles using conditional random fields for legal document summarization. In *Proceedings of the Third International Joint Conference on Natural Language Processing: Volume-I*.

Jaromir Savelka and Kevin D Ashley. 2018. Segmenting us court decisions into functional and issue specific parts. In *JURIX*, pages 111–120.

Stavroula Skylaki, Ali Oskooei, Omar Bari, Nadja Herger, and Zac Kriegman. 2021. Legal entity extraction using a pointer generator network. In *2021 International Conference on Data Mining Workshops (ICDMW)*, pages 653–658.

Benjamin Strickson and Beatriz De La Iglesia. 2020. Legal judgement prediction for uk courts. In *Proceedings of the 2020 The 3rd International Conference on Information Science and System*, pages 204–209.

Taxmann. 2021. Interpretation of statutes: Strict versus liberal construction. https://tinyurl.com/2p85h3xd.

Vu Tran, Minh Le Nguyen, and Ken Satoh. 2019. Building legal case retrieval systems with lexical matching and summarization using a pre-trained phrase scoring model. In *Proceedings of the Seventeenth International Conference on Artificial Intelligence and Law*, pages 275–282.

Giulia Venturi. 2012. Design and development of temis: a syntactically and semantically annotated corpus of italian legislative texts. In *Proceedings of the Workshop on Semantic Processing of Legal Texts (SPLeT 2012)*, pages 1–12.

Vern R Walker, Krishnan Pillaipakkamnatt, Alexandra M Davidson, Marysa Linares, and Domenick J Pesce. 2019. Automatic classification of rhetorical roles for sentences: Comparing rule-based scripts with machine learning. In *ASAIL@ ICAIL*.

Adam Wyner, Raquel Mochales-Palau, Marie-Francine Moens, and David Milward. 2010. Approaches to text mining arguments from legal cases. In *Semantic processing of legal texts*, pages 60–79. Springer.

Adam Z Wyner, Wim Peters, and Daniel Katz. 2013. A case study on legal case annotation. In *JURIX*, pages 165–174.

Qizhe Xie, Minh-Thang Luong, Eduard Hovy, and Quoc V Le. 2020. Self-training with noisy student improves imagenet classification. In *Proceedings of the IEEE/CVF Conference on Computer Vision and Pattern Recognition*, pages 10687–10698.

Wenmian Yang, Weijia Jia, Xiaojie Zhou, and Yutao Luo. 2019. Legal judgment prediction via multi-perspective bi-feedback network. In *Proceedings of the Twenty-Eighth International Joint Conference on Artificial Intelligence, IJCAI-19*, pages 4085–4091. International Joint Conferences on Artificial Intelligence Organization.

Hai Ye, Xin Jiang, Zhunchen Luo, and Wenhan Chao. 2018. Interpretable charge predictions for criminal cases: Learning to generate court views from fact descriptions. In *Proceedings of the 2018 Conference of the North American Chapter of the Association for Computational Linguistics: Human Language Technologies, Volume 1 (Long Papers)*, pages 1854–1864, New Orleans, Louisiana. Association for Computational Linguistics.

Appendix

A Ethical Considerations

The proposed corpus and methods do not have direct ethical consequences to the best of our knowledge. The corpus is created from publicly available data from a public resource: www.indiankanoon.org. The website allows free downloads, and no copyrights were violated. With the help of law professors, we designed a course project centered around RR annotations for the student annotators. The students **voluntarily** participated in the annotations as a part of the course project. Moreover, annotators were curious about learning about AI technologies and further contributing towards its progress. There was no compulsion to take part in the annotation activity.

The cases were selected randomly to avoid bias towards any entity, situation, or laws. Any meta-information related to individuals, organizations, and judges was removed so as to avoid any introduction of bias. For the application of corpus to judgment prediction task, we are not the first ones to do the task of judgment prediction. For the task, we took all the steps (names anonymization and removal of meta-information) as outlined in the already published work of Malik et al. (2021). The focus of this paper is rhetorical role prediction, and the task of judgment prediction is only a use-case. Moreover, in this paper we focus mainly on IT and CL cases where facts and scenarios are more objective and there are less biases compared to other types of cases (e.g., criminal and civil cases). As also described by Malik et al. (2021), we do not believe that the task could be fully automated, but rather it could augment the work of a judge or legal practitioner to expedite the legal process in highly populated countries.

Legal-NLP is a relatively new area; we have taken all the steps to avoid any direct and foreseeable ethical implications; however, a lot more exploration is required by the research community to understand implicit ethical implications. For this to happen, resources need to be created, and we are making initial steps and efforts towards it.

B Dataset and Annotations

B.1 Data Collection and Preprocessing

The IT and CL cases come from the Supreme Court of India, Bombay and Kolkata High Courts. For CL cases, we use the cases from the tribunals of NCLAT (National Company Law Appellate Tribunal)[2], CCI (Competition Commission of India)[3], COMPAT (Competition Appellate Tribunal)[4]. Since the IT laws are 50 years old and relatively dynamic, we stick to certain sections of IT domain only, whereas we use all the sections for CL domain. We restrict ourselves to the IT cases that are based on Section 147, Section 92C and Section 14A only to limit the subjectivity in cases. We randomly select 50 cases from IT and CL domain each to be annotated. We used regular expressions in Python to remove the auxillary information in the documents (For example: date, appellant and respondent names, judge names etc.) and filter out the main judgment of the document. We use the NLTK[5] sentence tokenizer to split the document into sentences. The annotators were asked to annotate these sentences with the rhetorical roles.

B.2 Annotators Details

With the help of law professors, we designed a course project centered around RR annotations for the student annotators. The students **voluntarily** participated in the annotations as a part of the course project. Moreover, annotators were curious about learning about AI technologies and further contributing towards its progress. There was no compulsion to take part in the annotation activity.

The 6 annotators come from an Indian Law University. Three of them specialize in Income Tax domain and the other three specialize in Competition Law domain.

B.3 Rhetorical Roles

We provide the definition of each of the Rhetorical Role in the main paper. Examples for each of the RR are given in Table 15. Figure 5 provides the number of sentences for each label in the IT and CL dataset. Note that representation of both the domains is similar with the exception of DIS label.

B.4 Secondary and Tertiary Annotation Labels

Legal experts pointed out that a single sentence can sometimes represent multiple rhetorical roles (although this is not common). Each expert could also assign secondary and tertiary rhetorical roles to a single sentence to handle such scenarios and

[2]https://nclat.nic.in/
[3]https://www.cci.gov.in/
[4]http://compatarchives.nclat.nic.in
[5]http://www.nltk.org/

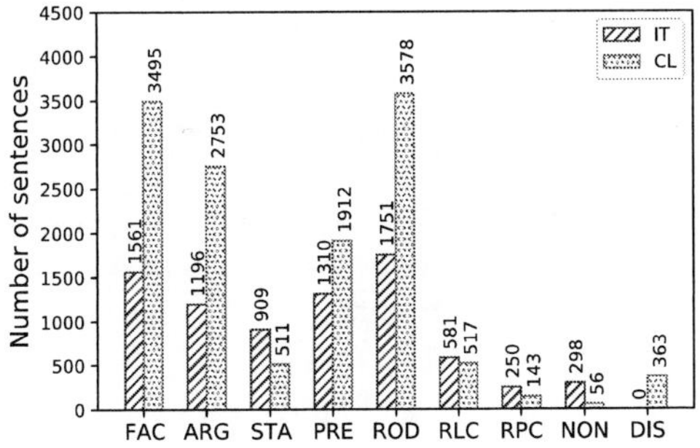

Figure 5: Distribution of RR labels in IT and CL documents.

motivate future research. On an average annotators assigned secondary role in 5-7% cases and assigned tertiary roles in 0.5-1% cases.

B.5 Inter-annotator Agreement

Fleiss Kappa between all (fine-grained) labels is 0.59 for IT and 0.87 for CL, indicating substantial agreement. We provide the inter-annotator agreement (averaged pairwise macro F1 between annotators) upon 13 fine-grained labels in Table 9. Also, we provide the pairwise confusion matrices of annotators (A_1, A_2) and (A_2, A_3) for both IT and CL domain in Figure 6.

Label	IT	CL
ARG-P	0.74	0.90
ARG-R	0.73	0.97
FAC	0.77	0.88
ISS	0.75	0.75
PRE-RU	0.67	0.86
PRE-NR	0.58	0.80
PRE-O	0.43	_
STA	0.78	0.89
RLC	0.58	0.74
RPC	0.75	0.74
ROD	0.64	0.93
DIS	_	0.98
NON	0.45	0.52
F1	*0.73*	*0.88*

Table 9: Label-wise inter-annotator agreement for all 13 fine-grained labels.

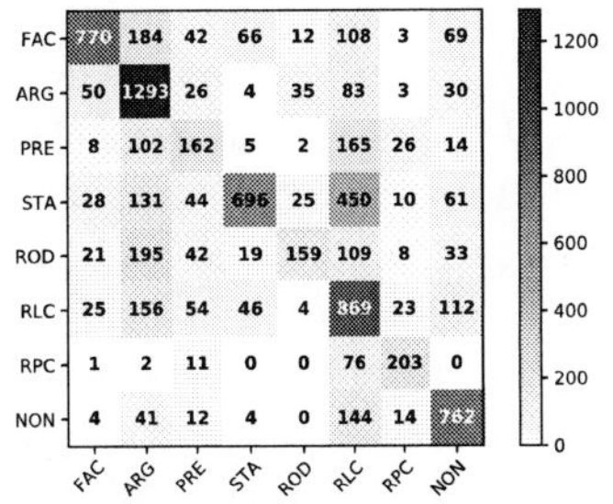

(a) Between annotators A_1 and A_2 for IT domain

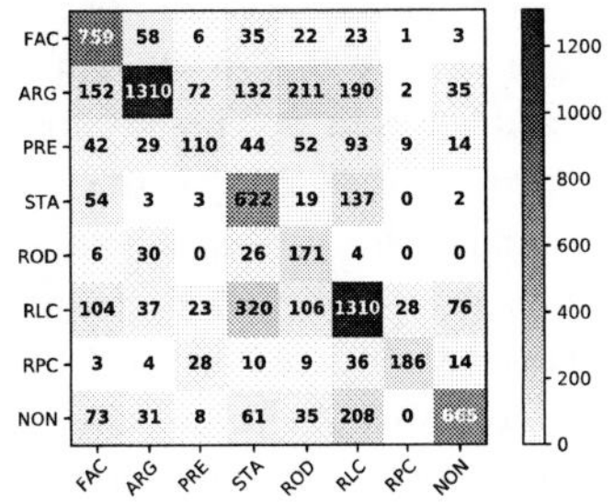

(b) Between annotators A_2 and A_3 for IT domain

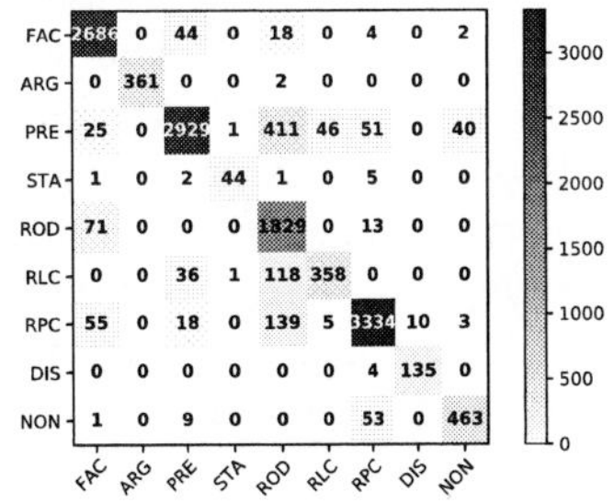

(c) Between annotators A_1 and A_2 for CL domain

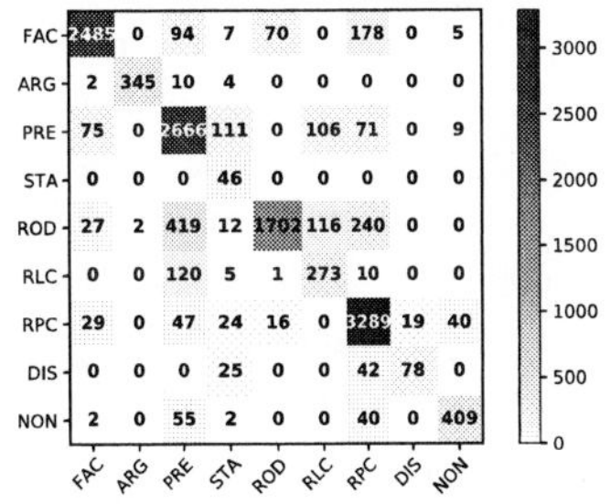

(d) Between annotators A_2 and A_3 for IT domain

Figure 6: Confusion matrix between Annotators for IT and CL domains.

B.6 Annotation Analysis

Annotation of judgments in order to identify and distinguish between the rhetorical roles played by its various parts is in itself a challenging task even for legal experts. We provide some qualitative examples of sentences and their corresponding rhetorical roles in Table 15 There are several factors involved in the exercise that requires the annotator to retrace the judicial decision making and recreate the impact left by the inputs available to the judge such as certain specific facts of the case, a particular piece of argument advanced by the lawyer representing one of the parties, or a judicial precedent from a higher court deemed applicable in the current case by the lawyer(s) or by the judge or by both. Moreover, the annotator only has access to the current document which is secondary account of what actually happened in the court. These limitations certainly makes the task of the annotator further difficult, and leaves them with no choice other than to make certain educated guesses when it comes to understanding the various nuances, both ostensible and probable, of certain rhetorical roles. It should, however, be noted that such variation need not occur for every rhetorical role, since not all the roles are equally susceptible to it –for instance, the facts of the case as laid down by the judge are more readily and objectively ascertainable by more than one annotator, whereas the boundaries between the issues framed by the judge and those deemed relevant as per the arguments advanced by the lawyers may blur more, especially because if the judge happens to agree with one of the lawyers and adopts their argument as part of the judicial reasoning itself. Similarly, it should also be noted that despite differing in their views of the nature and extent of rhetorical role played by a certain part of the judgment, the annotators may still agree with each other when it comes to identifying and segregating the final ruling made by the judge in that case –this phenomenon of having used two different routes to arrive at the same destination is not uncommon in the reenactment or ex-post-facto analysis of a judicial hearing and decision making process. A cumulative effect of the aforementioned factors can be observed in the results of the annotation. The analysis provided by the three annotators in case of competition law bear close resemblance with each other. On the other hand, in case of income tax law, the analysis provided by Users 1 and 3 bear greater resemblance with each other, compared to the resemblance between Users 1 and 2, or between Users 2 and 3. On a different note, it is also observed that the rhetorical role where the annotators have differed between themselves the most has been the point of Ruling made by the Lower Court, followed by the Ratio. This also ties in with the aforesaid argument that all rhetorical roles are not equally susceptible to the variation caused by the varying levels of success achieved by the different annotators in retracing the judicial thought pattern.

B.7 Annotation Case Studies

Along with law professors, we analyzed some of the case documents. Please refer to data files for the actual judgment.

In the case of CL cases, the best resemblance that has been achieved is in the case of SC_Competition Commission of India vs Fast Way Transmission Pvt Ltd and Ors 24012018 SC.txt, one would find that the judgment has been written in a manner as to provide specific indicators before every rhetorical role. For instance, before the Ruling by Lower Court starts, reference has been made that this is the opinion given the Competition Commission of India (the lower court in the relevant domain). Similarly, before Arguments made by Petitioner/Respondent, reference has been made that this is the argument made by the lawyer representing the petitioner/respondent. This judgment also provides a nice, consistent flow following the arrangement of the rhetorical roles in order. The relatively smaller size of the judgment also indicates a lower level of complexity (although there need not always be a consistent correlation between the two). On the other hand, if one considers the least resemblance achieved in the competition law domain, in the case of SC_Excel Crop Care Limited vs Competition Commission of India and Ors 08052017 SC(1).txt, one would find that such specific indicators are usually absent, thus leaving scope for individual discretion and interpretation, the judgment goes back and forth between certain rhetorical roles (Issue, Ruling by Lower Court, Ratio by Present Court, Argument by Petitioner/Respondent, Precedent Relied Upon), and the relatively bigger size also involves additional complexity and analysis, which make room for further nuances as described above.

Similarly, if one considers the best resemblance that has been achieved in the income tax domain, in the case of SC_2014_17.txt, one would find the case has involved fewer rhetorical roles, cut down on facts (mainly dealing with procedural issues on an appellate stage), and even among the rhetorical roles, it has focused on statutes and provisions thereof and the ratio and ruling. This has significantly reduced the possibility of the aforementioned richer jurisprudence, greater range of precedents, and resulting greater degree of subjective interpretation being at play. On the other hand, if one considers the least resemblance that has been achieved in the income tax domain, in the case of SC_2008_1597.txt, discusses Precedents to a greater detail including facts thereof, goes back and forth between certain rhetorical roles instead of maintaining a consistent order, and is not very clear about whether the judge is at times merely reiterating the arguments made by the lawyers, or is demonstrating their own view of such arguments. Collectively, these leave the scope for greater involvement of subjective interpretation of the aforesaid nuances.

Yet on an overall basis, the elements of subjectivity, personal discretionary interpretation, and arbitrariness have been minimized by the selection of the chosen domains, along with the methodology adopted for annotation, thus leading to the present success attained in identification of rhetorical roles and using the same for prior relevant case identification and prediction.

C Evaluation Metrics

We use the Macro F1 metric to evaluate the performance of models upon the task of Rhetorical Role labelling. Macro F1 is the mean of the label-wise F1 scores for each label. Given the true positives (TP), false positives (FP) and false negatives (FN), the F1 score for a single label is calculated as:

$$F1 = \frac{TP}{TP + \left(\frac{FP+FN}{2}\right)} \quad (1)$$

The pairwise inter-annotator agreement F1 between two annotators A and B is calculated by considering the annotations by annotator A as the true labels and the annotations by annotator B as the predicted labels.

We also calculate Fleiss Kappa[6] to measure the inter-annotator agreement.

D Model Training Details

All of our baseline experiments and training of Label shift prediction models (SBERT and BERT-SC) were conducted on Google Colab[7] and used the default single GPU Tesla P100-PCIE-16GB, provided by Colab. Our models were trained upon a single 11GB GeForce RTX 2080 TI. We used the SBERT model provided in the sentence-transformers library[8]. We use the Huggingface[9] implementations of BERT-base and LEGAL-BERT models. Refer to Table 10, 11 and 12 for dataset-wise results and hyperparameters for each model. We also provide the training time and number of parameters of each model in Table 13.

For SBERT-Shift, we kept the SBERT model as fixed and tuned the 3 linear layers on top. We used the Binary Crossentropy loss function with Adam Optimizer to tune the model upon the LSP task.

For BERT-SC, we fine-tuned the pre-trained BERT-base model upon the LSP task. We used the maximum sequence length of 256 tokens, a learning rate of $2e-5$ and kept the number of epochs as 5 during training. We used the same loss function and optimizer as the SBERT-Shift model.

D.1 Reduced Label Set

Due to the complexity of the task of RR prediction, we consider seven main labels (FAC, ARG, PRE, ROD, RPC, RLC, and STA) only. We plan to explore developing predictive models using fine-grained labels.

NON Label: We ignore sentences with NON (None) labels (about 4% for IT and 0.5% for CL). We believe that this was necessary since the inter-annotator agreement for the NON label in both IT and CL domains, has an F1 score as low as 0.45, implying that even the legal experts themselves do not agree whether a particular sentence has a NON label.

Dissent Label: Analysis of the annotated dataset reveals that the IT domain does not have any instance of dissent (DIS) label. There were only three documents (out of 50) in the CL domain having few instances of dissent label. Moreover, the instances of dissent label were present as a contiguous chunk of sentences at the end of the document. Hence, we discarded the sentences with dissent labels. Furthermore, law experts told us that the dissent phenomenon is rare; from a practical (application) point of view, these labels can be discarded.

[6] https://en.wikipedia.org/wiki/Fleiss%27_kappa

[7] https://colab.research.google.com/

[8] https://pypi.org/project/sentence-transformers/

[9] https://huggingface.co/

D.2 Single Sentence Classification Baselines

We train single sentence classification models for the task of rhetorical role labelling. We use BERT-base-uncased and Legal-BERT models and fine-tune them upon the sentence classification task. We also try a variant of using context sentences (left sentence and the right sentence) along with the current sentence to make classification, we call this method BERT-neighbor. We use CrossEntropyLoss as the criterion and Adam as the optimizer. We use a batch size of 32 with a learning rate of 2e-5 and fine-tune for 5 epochs for all our experiments. Refer to Tables 10 , 12 and 11 and for results and more information about the hyperparameters.

D.3 Sequence Classification Baselines

We experiment with Sequence Classification Baselines like CRF with handcrafted features, BiLSTM with sent2vec embeddings and different versions of BiLSTM-CRF in which we varied the input embeddings. We experimented with sent2vec embeddings fine-tuned on Supreme Court Cases of India (same as in (Bhattacharya et al., 2019)). We also tried with sentence embeddings obtained from the BERT-base model. In another experiment, we fine-tuned a pre-trained BERT model upon the task of Masked Language Modelling (MLM) on the unlabelled documents of IT and CL domain, and used this model to extract the sentence embeddings for the BiLSTM-CRF model.

We used the same implementation of BiLSTM-CRF from (Bhattacharya et al., 2019), with Adam optimizer and NLL loss function. Refer to Tables 10 , 12 and 11 for experiment-wise hyperparameters.

D.4 LSP-BiLSTM-CRF and MTL-BiLSTM-CRF models

In our proposed approach of LSP-BiLSTM-CRF, we experiment with two methods of generating shift embeddings, namely BERT-SC and SBERT-Shift. These embeddings were then used as input to train a BiLSTM-CRF with similar training schedules. Refer to Tables 10 , 12 and 11 for other hyperparameters.

For MTL models, we experimented with different encoders E_1 and E_2. We experimented with using Shift embeddings (or BERT embeddings of sentences obtained from pre-trained BERT model) from BERT-SC in both the components. However, the best performing model was the one in which we used shift embeddings for the shift component and BERT embeddings for the RR component. We used the NLL loss in both components of the MTL model weighted by the hyperparameter λ. We use the Adam Optimizer for training. We provide dataset-wise hyperparameters and results in Tables 10 , 12 and 11.

D.5 Hyperparameter λ

We tuned the hyperparameter λ of the MTL loss function upon the validation set. We trained the MTL model with $\lambda \in [0.1, 0.9]$ with strides of 0.1 and show the performance of our method on IT and IT+CL datasets in Figure 4. $\lambda = 0.6$ performs the best for the IT domain and also performs competitively on the combined domains.

D.6 Model Distillation

For model distillation experiments we trained the teacher model with same hyperparameters in Table 10 on the IT dataset. For the next two iteration of learning a student model, we used 48 unlabelled cases in each iteration. The weighing hyperparameter, α_U was kept as 0.3. In each iteration, the student model was trained with a batch size 16, a learning rate of 0.005 and for 300 epochs.

Model	Hyperparameters(E=Epochs), (LR=Learning rate), (BS=Batch Size), (Dim=Embedding dimension), (E1=Embedding dimension Shift), (E2=Embedding dimension RR), (H=Hidden dimension),	IT (Macro F1)
BERT	LR=2e-5, BS=32, E=5	0.56
BERT-neighbor	LR=2e-5, BS=32, E=5	0.53
Legal-BERT	LR=2e-5, BS=32, E=5	0.55
CRF(handcrafted)	LR=0.01, BS=40, Dim=172, E=300	0.55
BiLSTM(sent2vec)	LR=0.01, BS=40, Dim=200, H=100, E=300	0.55
BiLSTM-CRF(handcrafted)	LR=0.01, BS=40, Dim=172, H=86, E=300	0.57
BiLSTM-CRF(sent2vec)	LR=0.01, BS=40, Dim=200, H=100, E=300	0.59
BiLSTM-CRF(BERT emb)	LR=0.01, BS=40, Dim=768, H=384, E=300	0.63
BiLSTM-CRF(MLM emb)	LR=0.01, BS=40, Dim=768, H=384, E=300	0.58
LSP(SBERT)	LR=0.005, BS=40, Dim=2304, H=1152, E=300	0.64
LSP(BERT-SC)	LR=0.005, BS=40, Dim=2304, H=1152, E=300	0.65
MTL(MLM emb)	LR=0.005, BS=40, E1=2304, E2=768 , H=1152(Shift), H=384(RR), E=300	0.67
MTL(BERT-SC)	LR=0.005, BS=40, E1=2304, E2=768, H=1152(Shift), H=384(RR), E=300	0.70
MTL(BERT-SC)	LR=0.005, BS=40, E1=2304, E2=2304, H=1152(Shift), H=384(RR), E=300	0.68
MTL(BERT-SC)	LR=0.005, BS=40, E1=768, E2=768, H=1152(Shift), H=384(RR), E=300	0.64

Table 10: Hyperparameters and results on the IT dataset

Model	Hyperparameters(E=Epochs), (LR=Learning rate), (BS=Batch Size), (Dim=Embedding dimension), (E1=Embedding dimension Shift), (E2=Embedding dimension RR), (H=Hidden dimension),	IT+CL (Macro F1)
BiLSTM-CRF(sent2vec)	LR=0.01, BS=40, Dim=200, H=100, E=300	0.65
BiLSTM-CRF(BERT)	LR=0.01, BS=40, Dim=768, H=384, E=300	0.63
LSP-BiLSTM-CRF(BERT-SC)	LR=0.005, BS=20, Dim=2304, H=1152, E=300	0.67
MTL-BiLSTM-CRF(BERT-SC)	LR=0.005, BS=20, E1=2304, E2=768, H=1152(Shift), H=384(RR), E=300	0.70
MTL-BiLSTM-CRF(BERT-SC)	LR=0.005, BS=20, E1=2304, E2=2304, H=1152(Shift), H=384(RR), E=300	0.68
MTL-BiLSTM-CRF(BERT-SC)	LR=0.005, BS=20, E1=768, E2=768, H=1152(Shift), H=384(RR), E=300	0.65

Table 11: Hyperparameters and results on the combined (IT+CL) dataset

Model	Hyperparameters(E=Epochs), (LR=Learning rate), (BS=Batch Size), (Dim=Embedding dimension), (E1=Embedding dimension Shift), (E2=Embedding dimension RR), (H=Hidden dimension),	CL (Macro F1)
BERT	LR=2e-5, BS=32, E=5	0.52
BERT-neighbor	LR=2e-5, BS=32, E=5	0.51
Legal-BERT	LR=2e-5, BS=32, E=5	0.53
CRF(handcrafted)	LR=0.01, BS=40, Dim=172, E=300	0.52
BiLSTM(sent2vec)	LR=0.01, BS=40, Dim=200, H=100, E=300	0.54
BiLSTM-CRF(handcrafted)	LR=0.01, BS=40, Dim=172, H=86, E=300	0.56
BiLSTM-CRF(sent2vec)	LR=0.01, BS=40, Dim=200, H=100, E=300	0.61
BiLSTM-CRF(BERT emb)	LR=0.01, BS=40, Dim=768, H=384, E=300	0.63
BiLSTM-CRF(MLM emb)	LR=0.01, BS=40, Dim=768, H=384, E=300	0.60
LSP(SBERT)	LR=0.005, BS=40, Dim=2304, H=1152, E=300	0.63
LSP(BERT-SC)	LR=0.005, BS=40, Dim=2304, H=1152, E=300	0.68
MTL(MLM emb)	LR=0.005, BS=20, E1=2304, E2=768 , H=1152(Shift), H=384(RR), E=300	0.67
MTL(BERT-SC)	LR=0.005, BS=20, E1=2304, E2=768, H=1152(Shift), H=384(RR), E=300	0.69
MTL(BERT-SC)	LR=0.005, BS=20, E1=2304, E2=2304, H=1152(Shift), H=384(RR), E=300	0.67
MTL(BERT-SC)	LR=0.005, BS=20, E1=768, E2=768, H=1152(Shift), H=384(RR), E=300	0.64

Table 12: Hyperparameters and results on the CL dataset

Model	No of Parameters		Training Time(min)	
	IT	CL	IT	CL
BiLSTM(sent2vec)	240000	240000	15	30
BiLSTM-CRF(sent2vec)	240000	240000	15	30
BiLSTM-CRF(BERT emb)	3538944	3538944	30	50
BiLSTM-CRF(MLM emb)	3538944	3538944	30	50
LSP(SBERT)	31850496	31850496	90	250
LSP(BERT-SC)	31850496	31850496	90	250
MTL(MLM emb)	35411060	35411060	300	1200
MTL(BERT-SC)	35411060	35411060	300	1200

Table 13: Approx. number of parameters and computational budget of models.

Model	**IT+CL docs**	**F1**
BERT-ILDC	Predicted ROD & RPC using BiLSTM-CRF(sent2vec)	0.55
BERT-ILDC	Predicted ROD & RPC using MTL(BERT-SC)	0.56

Table 14: Judgment Prediction results using predicted ROD & RPC

Label	Sentence
Fact	It has also been alleged that the copies of the notices were also sent, inter alia, to the principal officer of the said company and also to the ladies as mentioned herein before, who has sold the immovable property in question.
Fact	For executing this contract, the assessee entered into various contracts -Offshore Supply contract and Offshore Service Contracts.
Ruling By Lower Court	But the words inland container depot were introduced in Section 2(12) of the Customs Act, 1962, which defines customs port.
Ruling By Lower Court	We may also mention here that the cost of superstructure was Rs. 2,22,000 as per the letter of the assessee dated 28-11-66 addressed to the ITO during the course of assessment proceedings.
Argument	Such opportunity can only be had by the disclosure of the materials to the court as also to the aggrieved party when a challenge is thrown to the very existence of the conditions precedent for initiation of the action.
Argument	In this connection, it was urged on behalf of the assessee(s) that, for the relevant assessment years in question, the Assessing Officer was required to obtain prior approval of the Joint Commissioner of Income Tax before issuance of notice under Section 148 of the Act.
Statute	In the meantime, applicant has to pay the additional amount of tax with interest without which the application for settlement would not be maintainable.
Statute	On the other hand, interest for defaults in payment of advance tax falls under section 234B, apart from sections 234A and 234C, in section F of Chapter XVII.
Ratio of the Decision	The State having received the money without right, and having retained and used it, is bound to make the party good, just as an individual would be under like circumstances.
Ratio of the Decision	Therefore, the Department is right in its contention that under the above situation there exists a Service PE in India (MSAS).
Ruling by Present Court	For these reasons, we hold that the Tribunal was wrong in reducing the penalty imposed on the assessee below the minimum prescribed under Section 271(1)(iii) of the Income-tax Act, 1961.
Ruling by Present Court	Hence, in the cases arising before 1.4.2002, losses pertaining to exempted income cannot be disallowed.
Precedent	Yet he none the less remains the owner of the thing, while all the others own nothing more than rights over it.
Precedent	I understand the Division Bench decision in Commissioner of Income-tax v. Anwar Ali, only in that context.
None	Leave granted.
None	There is one more way of answering this point.
Dissent	Therefore a constructive solution has to be found out.
Dissent	In the light of the Supreme Court decision in the case of CCI vs SAIL (supra) t his issue has to be examined.

Table 15: Example sentences for each label.

Privacy-Preserving Models for Legal Natural Language Processing

Ying Yin and **Ivan Habernal**
Trustworthy Human Language Technologies
Department of Computer Science, Technical University of Darmstadt
ivan.habernal@tu-darmstadt.de
www.trusthlt.org

Abstract

Pre-training large transformer models with in-domain data improves domain adaptation and helps gain performance on the domain-specific downstream tasks. However, sharing models pre-trained on potentially sensitive data is prone to adversarial privacy attacks. In this paper, we asked to which extent we can guarantee privacy of pre-training data and, at the same time, achieve better downstream performance on legal tasks without the need of additional labeled data. We extensively experiment with scalable self-supervised learning of transformer models under the formal paradigm of differential privacy and show that under specific training configurations we can improve downstream performance without sacrifying privacy protection for the in-domain data. Our main contribution is utilizing differential privacy for large-scale pre-training of transformer language models in the legal NLP domain, which, to the best of our knowledge, has not been addressed before.[1]

1 Introduction

Transformer-based models (Vaswani et al., 2017; Devlin et al., 2019) trained in a self-supervised fashion on a huge collection of freely accessible Web texts belong to the currently most successful techniques for almost any downstream NLP task across languages or domains. Their ability to 'learn' certain language properties (Rogers et al., 2020) and the need of having only a small amount of labeled data in the target domain for fine-tuning makes them superior to other approaches (Brown et al., 2020). Moreover, additional pre-training with unlabeled target-domain data typically boosts their performance further (Chalkidis et al., 2020).

However, when it comes to preserving private information contained in the original large unlabeled text data, transformer models tend 'remember' way too much. Carlini et al. (2020) show that it is possible to extract verbatim sensitive information from transformer models, such as names and addresses, even when such a piece of information had been 'seen' by the model during pre-training *only once*. Current transformer models thus represent a threat to privacy protection, which can have harmful consequences if such models trained on very sensitive data are published, as is the current trend in sharing pre-trained models.

In the legal domain, sensitive information, including names, addresses, dates of birth, are important part of many documents, such as court decisions. Especially in countries with the case-law system, court decisions make the largest fraction of legal texts. However, transformer models pre-trained on such corpora do not protect personal information by design, and ad-hoc solutions, e.g. whitening names in the original texts, are prone to errors and potential reconstruction attacks (Lison et al., 2021; Pilán et al., 2022).

Existing approaches to privacy-preserving deep learning have adapted differential privacy (DP) (Dwork and Roth, 2013), a rigorous mathematical treatment of privacy protection and loss. In particular, stochastic gradient descent with DP (DP-SGD) has been successfully applied to various NLP problems (Senge et al., 2022; Igamberdiev and Habernal, 2022), including transformer pre-training (Hoory et al., 2021; Anil et al., 2021). However, how well DP-regimes perform in the legal domain, pre-trained and fine-tuned across various downstream legal-NLP tasks, remains an open question.

This paper addresses the following three research questions. First, what are the best strategies for pre-training transformer models to be applied in the legal domain? Second, does DP-SGD training scale up to tens of gigabytes of pre-training data without ending up with an extremely big privacy budget? Finally, can large-scale privacy-

[1] https://github.com/trusthlt/privacy-legal-nlp-lm

Proceedings of the Natural Legal Language Processing Workshop 2022, pages 172 - 183
December 8, 2022

preserving transformers compete to their small-scale non-private alternatives?

2 Related work

Transformer models in legal NLP Large contextual LMs based on transformer architecture (Vaswani et al., 2017) are the state of the art in numerous NLP tasks. Domain adaptation aims to improve the model performance on downstream tasks in a specialized domain. A common approach is to pre-train BERT (Devlin et al., 2019) with a large collection of unlabeled in-domain texts. In the legal domain, Chalkidis et al. (2020) provide a systematic investigation of possible strategies for BERT adaptation and published their model as LEGAL-BERT. Their work shows that both training BERT form scratch or further pre-training the existing general BERT-BASE[2] model with legal corpora achieve comparable performance gains. Besides, broader hyper-parameter search has large impact on the downstream performance. Zheng et al. (2021) point out that despite the uniqueness of legal language, domain pre-training in the legal field rarely show significant performance gains probably due to the lack of appropriate benchmarks that are difficult enough to benefit from pre-training on law corpora. To address this issue, they release a new benchmark called CaseHOLD that gains up to 6.7% improvement on macro F1 by additional domain pre-training. In the legal field, the vast majority of benchmarks exhibit small performance gains after further pre-training BERT on law datasets (Elwany et al., 2019; Chalkidis et al., 2020). However, existing research on legal language models has not considered privacy of the textual datasets.

Privacy-preserving NLP with differential privacy Large machine learning models including transformer-based LMs can be prone to privacy attacks such as membership inference attack (Shokri et al., 2017; Hayes et al., 2019; Carlini et al., 2020), which means it is possible to predict whether or not a data record exists in the model's training dataset given only black-box query access to the model. It hinders the application of such models on numerous real-word tasks involving private user information. To mitigate this limitation, many recent studies devote to privacy-preserving algorithm for large NLP models.

Differential Privacy (DP) (Dwork et al., 2006; Dwork and Roth, 2013) has been taken as the gold-standard approach to ensure privacy for sensitive dataset. The main goal of privacy-preserving data analysis is to enable meaningful statistical analysis about the database while preventing leakage of individual information. The intuition behind DP is that an individual's data can't be revealed by a statistical release of the database regardless of whether or not the individual is present in the database, thus any individual shouldn't have significant influence on the statistical release. We formally introduce DP in Section 3.

Unlike works focusing of privatization of individual texts (Habernal, 2021, 2022; Igamberdiev et al., 2022), applying DP to training neural networks is typically done through differentially-private stochastic gradient descent (DP-SGD) (Abadi et al., 2016); see also (Yu et al., 2019) for a great explanation. Although DP pre-training of BERT has been shown to gain performance on a Medical Entity Extraction task (Hoory et al., 2021), how well it performs in the legal area still remains an open question.

2.1 Off-the-shelf strategies for training with differential privacy

DP-SGD training often suffers from big running time overhead that comes from the per-sample gradient clipping. Mainstream DL frameworks such as PyTorch and TensorFlow are designed to produce the reduced gradients over a batch that is sufficient for SGD but are unable to compute the per-sample gradients efficiently. A naive way to achieve this is to compute and clip the gradient of each sample in the batch one by one through a for-loop, which is implemented in PyVacy.[3] This approach completely loses parallelism and hence dramatically slows down the training speed. A more advanced method is to derive the per-sample gradient formula and compute it in a vectorized form. Opacus[4] implements this by replacing the matrix multiplication between the back-propagated gradients and the activations from the previous layer in the original PyTorch back-propagation with outer products via einsum function (Yousefpour et al., 2021). The activations and back-propagated gradients are captured through forward and backward hooks. A disadvantage of this method is that it cannot cur-

[2]BERT-BASE stands for 'bert-base-uncased' from `https://huggingface.co/bert-base-uncased`.

[3]`https://github.com/ChrisWaites/pyvacy`

[4]`https://github.com/pytorch/opacus`

rently support all kinds of neural network modules. In addition, it is restricted by quadratic memory consumption (Subramani et al., 2021).

3 Learning with differential privacy

This section formally introduces differential privacy and can be skipped by readers familiar with that topic.

3.1 Pure Differential Privacy (ε-DP)

Definition of ε-DP Given a real number $\varepsilon > 0$, a randomized mechanism (or algorithm) $\mathcal{M} : D \mapsto R$ satisfies ε-DP if for any two neighboring input datasets $d, d' \in D$ that differs in a single element and for any subset of outputs $S \subseteq R$ it holds that

$$\frac{\Pr[\mathcal{M}(d) \in S]}{\Pr[\mathcal{M}(d') \in S]} \leq \exp(\varepsilon), \quad (1)$$

where Pr stands for the probability distribution taken from the randomness of the mechanism, and ε refers to the privacy budget.

The value of ε upper-bounds the amount of influence any individual data has on the mechanism's outputs. Smaller ε value means stronger privacy guarantee. However, there is no conclusive answer to how small we should set ε to prevent information leakage in practice. The general consensus is that $\varepsilon \leq 1$ would indicate strong privacy protection, while $\varepsilon \geq 10$ possibly doesn't guarantee much privacy, although the value is application-specific.[5]

The above definition implies that the outputs of the mechanism should not differ much, with or without any specific data record. In this case, an adversary can't infer whether or not a record exists in the input dataset from the outputs of the mechanism, which prevents the extraction of individual training data from a pre-trained model.

The *sensitivity* of a mechanism $\mathcal{M}$ is the upper bound of the amount of output difference when it's input changes by one entry. Formally, the Global Sensitivity (GS) of $\mathcal{M}$ is given by

$$GS(\mathcal{M}) = \max_{d,d':|d|=|d'|\pm 1} |\mathcal{M}(d) - \mathcal{M}(d')|, \quad (2)$$

where d and d' are neighboring datasets. The "global" means this holds for any pair of neighboring datasets, as opposed to the "local" sensitivity with one of the datasets fixed. For example, sensitivity of the counting query that computes how many entries in a database is 1.

[5] https://programming-dp.com/

There are two important properties of DP: Sequential composition and post-processing.

- **Sequential Composition** For mechanisms $\mathcal{M}_1(d)$ satisfies ε_1-DP and $\mathcal{M}_2(d)$ satisfies ε_2-DP, the mechanism $\mathcal{M}(d) = (\mathcal{M}_1(d), \mathcal{M}_2(d))$ that releases both results satisfies $(\varepsilon_1 + \varepsilon_2)$-DP.
- **Post Processing** If a mechanism $\mathcal{M}(D)$ satisfies ε-DP, then after performing arbitrary function f on $\mathcal{M}(D)$, the mechanism $f(\mathcal{M}(D))$ still satisfies ε-DP.

These properties facilitate the design and analysis of a DP algorithm. The composability enables the track of privacy loss for algorithms that traverse the dataset multiple times, and the post processing property ensures that a DP algorithm is robust to privacy attack with auxiliary information. Moreover, advanced composition exists for approximate DP that provides tighter upper bound of privacy.

3.2 Appropriate Differential Privacy ((ε, δ)-DP)

Definition of (ε, δ)-DP Approximate DP relaxes the pure ε-DP requirement by introducing a "failure probability" δ. Similar to the definition of ε-DP, given real numbers $\varepsilon > 0$ and $\delta > 0$, we say a mechanism $\mathcal{M} : D \to R$ satisfies (ε, δ)-DP if for all adjacent inputs $d, d' \in D$ and all $S \subseteq R$, we have

$$\Pr[\mathcal{M}(d) \in S] \leq e^{\varepsilon} \Pr[\mathcal{M}(d') \in S] + \delta \quad (3)$$

The pure ε-DP is equivalent to $(\varepsilon, 0)$-DP. A non-zero item δ allows the mechanism fails to be ε-DP with probability δ. This sounds a bit scary, since under certain probability we get no guarantee of privacy at all and there is a risk of compromising the whole dataset. Therefore, the value of δ must be small enough, preferably less than one over the size of dataset (i.e. $\frac{1}{|D|}$) in order to deliver meaningful results. One of the biggest advantage of (ε, δ)-DP is that even with negligible δ, it can significantly reduce the sample complexity compared to the pure DP (Beimel et al., 2013; Steinke and Ullman, 2015; Bun et al., 2014). Roughly speaking, given the same size of dataset, (ε, δ)-DP can achieve higher statistical accuracy than ε-DP while preserving the privacy. Additionally, the (ε, δ)-DP mechanisms in practice usually don't fail catastrophically and release the whole dataset. Instead, they fail gracefully and still satisfy $c\varepsilon$-DP for some value c in the case of failure probability. For these reasons, approximate DP becomes popular in real applications.

The Gaussian Mechanism A Gaussian mechanism that satisfies (ε, δ)-DP can be obtained by injecting Gaussian noise as follows

$$\mathcal{M}_G(x, f, \varepsilon, \delta) = f(x) + \mathcal{N}(0, \frac{2S^2 \ln(\frac{1.25}{\delta})}{\varepsilon^2}). \quad (4)$$

3.3 Deep Learning with DP

In general, the goal of deep learning is to optimize the model parameters so that the output of the loss function is minimized. This optimization is usually achieved by Gradient Descent and its variants. Basically, the model are learned from the gradient of the loss outputs w.r.t. the model parameters. Take the mini-batch Stochastic Gradient Descent (SGD) as example, at each step t, a certain number of randomly selected training samples $\{\boldsymbol{x}_i \mid i \in \boldsymbol{B}_t, \boldsymbol{B}_t \subseteq \{1, ..., N\}\}$[6] are fed into the loss function $\mathcal{L}$ and the average of their output gradients are calculated as an estimate of the loss gradient w.r.t the model weights $\boldsymbol{\theta}$, which is then multiplied by the learning rate η for Gradient Descent. This can be formulated as follows: A DP algorithm has certain guarantee that it doesn't leak individual training examples. In the Gradient Descent algorithm, the only access to the training examples is occurred in the computation of the gradient. Therefore, one way to achieve DP is through introducing noise into the gradient before the update of model weights. If the access to the gradient calculated via training data remains DP, then the resulting model is DP according to the post-processing property. Based on this, Abadi et al. (2016) propose a sophisticated method that turns the mini-batch SGD algorithm into DP, named DP-SGD, which has become a dominant approach to privacy-preserving deep learning.

DP-SGD primarily modifies two places of the original SGD algorithm to ensure DP. One is to clip the per-example gradients so that the Euclidean-norm (L2-norm) of each individual gradient does not exceed a pre-defined upper bound C, which corresponds to a constraint for the sensitivity of gradient. The other one is to add scale-specific Gaussian noise $\mathcal{N}$ into the aggregated clipping gradient:

$$\boldsymbol{\theta}_t \leftarrow \boldsymbol{\theta}_{t-1} - \frac{\eta}{|\boldsymbol{B}_t|}\left(\sum_{\forall i \in \boldsymbol{B}_t} \text{clip}(\nabla_{\boldsymbol{\theta}_{t-1}} \mathcal{L}(\boldsymbol{\theta}_{t-1}, \boldsymbol{x}_i), C) + \mathcal{N}(0, \sigma^2 C^2 \boldsymbol{I})\right), \quad (5)$$

where σ refers to the a constant called "noise multiplier", higher σ produce stronger privacy guarantee. According to the definition of 4, the modified SGD is a Gaussian mechanism that satisfies (ε, δ)-DP. The choice of Gaussian noise is due to the high-dimensionality of the gradient. L2-norm can be applied to measure the sensitivity of a high-dimensional vector-valued function for Gaussian mechanism, which yields much lower sensitivity than Laplace mechanism that only allows the use of L1-Norm, thus much less noise needs to be added to the gradient. Moreover, Abadi et al. (2016) introduce the Moments Accountant for tighter estimation of the privacy cost. Despite its simplicity, DP-SGD brings successes in many deep learning fields.

4 Experimental setup and data

Our experiments aim to find a strategy where BERT can benefit from additional domain-specific DP pre-training. Moreover, we explore the trade-off between the privacy budget and model utility under the best setup we obtain.

Privacy-protecting scenario In our scenario, we assume that we publish a pre-trained or fine-tuned model, to which an adversary has a full access (Yu et al., 2019). The model can be pre-trained on (a) a public general dataset and (b) in-domain, potentially sensitive legal documents, and fine-tuned on (c) a public down-stream task. Our aim is to protect (b) from the adversary.

4.1 Pre-training BERT from scratch

BERT pre-training is a very expensive task, especially with DP. While further pre-training the existing BERT-BASE can take advantage of the already learned language features and greatly reduce the convergence time, the original generic vocabulary remains unchanged. A generic vocabulary might not match the specialized legal terminology and could lead to drastic splitting into sub-word units and reducing semantic expressiveness (Zheng et al., 2021; Habernal et al., 2022). To address this problem, pre-train BERT from scratch with a custom

[6] N is the total number of training examples.

legal tokenizer built on the legal corpus using the WordPiece algorithm (Wu et al., 2016).

In order to investigate the effect of domain vocabulary on model performance and also follow the setup in Hoory et al. (2021) that successfully introduce DP to the pre-training of medical BERT our pre-training from scratch can be roughly divided into three steps:

1. Generating a domain-specific tokenizer and vocabulary set based on the legal corpus.[7]
2. Pre-training BERT from scratch on the generic BookCorpus and Wikipedia dataset using the domain-specific tokenizer.
3. Further pre-training BERT with DP on the legal corpus.

In spite of that the first step also involves access to the legal corpus and may cause information leakage, there is no good solution to convert the WordPiece algorithm into DP with tight privacy bound. We leave this problem to future work. Currently, we only ensure privacy during the pre-training on the legal corpus. The second step only uses the general corpora and thereby has no privacy issue. We don't use the legal corpora at the beginning of the pre-training because the overhead to train DP BERT from scratch is too expensive. We call the model trained with the first two steps BERT-SC.

4.2 Further pre-training BERT-BASE

Continuing the pre-training of BERT-BASE with legal-domain corpora is an economical and effective way for domain transfer. We start with a small-scale pre-experimental corpus to quickly investigate the effectiveness of additional domain pre-training with different hyper-parameter settings. Afterward, we scale up the training on the full legal corpus and focus on the batch size and learning rate tuning. In order to avoid overfitting, 5% of the pre-training data is kept as a validation set, on which the sum loss of the MLM (masked language modeling) and NSP (next sentence prediction) objectives and their accuracy is evaluated at each checkpoint.

5 Downstream tasks and datasets

We experiment with two downstream benchmark datasets, Overruling and CaseHOLD, on which we fine-tune our pre-trained models.[8] Note that for the downstream tasks, we do not use differential private training.

The Overruling dataset (Zheng et al., 2021) corresponds to a binary classification task that predicts if a sentence has the meaning of voiding a legal decision made in a previous case, which is important to ensure the correctness and validity of legal agreements. The sentences in the dataset are sampled from the Casetext law corpus, where positive overruling examples are manually annotated by lawyers, and negative examples are automatically generated by randomly sampling the Casetext sentences because over 99% of them are non-overruling. The complete dataset contains 2400 items and the two classes are balanced. It is a relatively simple task that has already achieved state-of-the-art performance on BERT-BASE model, since the positive examples explicitly contain 'overrule' or words with similar meaning such as disapprove, decline, reject, etc., which makes them highly distinguishable from the negative ones.

The CaseHOLD (Case Holdings on Legal Decisions) is a multiple-choice QA task to select a correct holding statement among 5 potential answers that matches the given citing context from a judicial decision. Zheng et al. (2021) construct the dataset by extracting the legal citations and the accompanying holding statements from the corpus of U.S. CaseLaw and using them as questions and answers respectively. Here the cases contained in the CaseHOlD are removed from our legal pre-training corpus according to the case IDs they provide. Moreover, they search for propositions that are semantically similar to the corresponding answer from other extracted holding statements as the wrong answers according to the TF-IDF similarity between them, which makes the CaseHOLD a multiple-choice QA task. The labels of the correct answers are uniformly distributed within the 5 indices 0-4. Excluding some samples containing invalid labels, the full dataset we use has a total of 52,978 items. It is a challenging task and yields only a macro F1 of around 0.613 using the general BERT-BASE (Zheng et al., 2021). We use it to investigate whether a sufficiently difficult legal task benefits from additional domain pre-training in the private preserving scenario.

[7]Here we use `BertWordPieceTokenizer` from `https://github.com/huggingface/tokenizers`, we set the vocabulary size to 30,522 which is the same as with BERT-BASE.

[8]Hyperparameters for the downstream tasks are discussed in Appendix A.

6 Our approach to pre-training legal transformer models with DP

6.1 Datasets for pre-training

For the in-domain pre-training with differential privacy, we prepare a legal corpus consisting of 14GB legal texts that are collected from three different resources (see Table 1). Although these are public datasets, we treat them as if they were private, containing sensitive data whose leakage from the pre-trained models should be prevented. For compiling and caching the large-scale pre-training corpora, we leverage the HuggingFace Datasets library[9] based on Arrow, which allows fast lookup for big datasets by building a memory-mapped cache on disk.

Source	Documents	Size (GB)
Sigma Law[10]	39,155	1.2
LEDGAR[11]	≈ 300,000	0.2
Case Law[12]	≈ 28,300,000	12.6

Table 1: Details of the legal corpora for pre-training.

6.2 Scalable pre-training with DP

In section 2.1 we discussed the shortcomings of off-the-shelf DP-SGD implementations in mainstream frameworks. We carried out preliminary experiments and found that these shortcomings make DP-SGD pre-training infeasible due to 12 to 28-times longer runtime per epoch.

The training speed of DP-SGD can be significantly improved by vectorization, just-in-time (JIT) compilation and static graph optimization using JAX framework,[13] which is defined by JIT compilation and automatic differentiation built up on the XLA compiler (Subramani et al., 2021). The core transformation methods of main interest in JAX includes `grad`, `vmap`, `jit`, and it allows us to arbitrarily compose these operations. In the DP-SGD scenario, `grad` can automatically compute the gradients of the loss objective w.r.t. the model parameters, and combing `vmap` enables efficient computation of per-example gradients by vectorizing the gradient calculation along the batch dimension.

Furthermore, the DP-SGD step can be decorated by `jit` to leverage XLA compiler that has proven acceleration in BERT MLPerf submission. Although JAX shows great advantages over other mainstream DP frameworks and libraries on a wide variety of networks such as Convolutional Neural Network (CNN) and Long-Short Term Memory network (LSTM) in Subramani et al. (2021), how much speedup it can produce on large transformer-based LMs remains unknown.

To investigate this, we implementat a JAX version of DP BERT based on FlaxBert models,[14] which provides transformers with JAX/FLAX backend including BERT. We adapt its training step into DP by adding the per-sample gradients clipping before aggregation and introducing randomly sampled Gaussian noise to the reduced gradients. Moreover, we use the strategy of gradient accumulation to enable DP pre-training with arbitrarily large batch sizes. Specifically, a training step is split into many iterations such that each iteration handles a shard of examples that the GPU[15] memory can maximally hold, and the clipped per-example gradients are accumulated over iterations within a batch.

6.2.1 Finding optimal hyper-parameters

Our starting point to further pre-training with differential privacy is the uncased BERT-BASE model that contains 110M parameters. For the optimization, we use Adam with weight decay (AdamW, (Loshchilov and Hutter, 2019)) and a linear learning rate schedule, which consists of a warm-up phrase followed by a linear decay. The warm-up steps are set to roughly 5% of the total training steps with a lower bound of 25. In addition, we use the TensorFlow privacy library[16] based on Rényi DP (RDP) (Mironov, 2017; Mironov et al., 2019) for the track of privacy, which can be converted to a standard (ε, δ)-DP but provides a tighter composition for Gaussian mechanism than directly using (ε, δ)-DP. The method takes the noise multiplier σ as input and calculates the privacy budget ε for each step. Conversely, we obtain the desired ε by the binary search for an optimal noise multiplier that leads to a privacy budget close enough to the target ε in a proper range.

[9] https://huggingface.co/docs/datasets/
[10] https://osf.io/qvg8s/
[11] Tuggener et al. (2020)
[12] https://case.law
[13] https://github.com/google/jax
[14] https://huggingface.co/docs/transformers/model_doc/bert
[15] All the experiments are carried out on an NVIDIA A100 40GB.
[16] https://github.com/tensorflow/privacy

Model	Overruling	CaseHOLD
BERT-BASE	0.971	0.617
BERT-SC	0.975	0.618

Table 2: Baseline Macro-F_1 scores without any domain pre-training.

σ	ε	Overruling	CaseHOLD
BERT-BASE			
–	–	0.975	0.652
1e-5	∞	0.967	0.648
0.1	4e+5	0.971	0.616
0.5	3.726	0.969	0.613
BERT-SC			
–	–	0.969	0.647
1e-5	∞	0.967	0.645
0.1	4e+5	0.967	0.618
0.5	3.726	0.964	0.616

Table 3: Macro-F_1 scores for further small-scale pre-training of BERT-BASE and BERT-SC. σ="–" corresponds to the training without DP.

In our experiments, the gradient clipping norm and the weight decay are less significant factors, and we fix them to 1.0 and 0.5 accordingly. To study the influence of the batch size, we keep the privacy ε to 5, which is considered as a sweet point between a very strong privacy guarantee 1 and a weak guarantee 10. In order to avoid overfitting, 5% of the pre-training data is kept as a validation set, on which the sum loss of the MLM and NSP objectives and their accuracy is evaluated at each checkpoint.

7 Results and analysis

Baselines Our baseline results (Table 2) are reported from BERT-BASE and BERT-SC with tuned hyper-parameters with no privacy gurantees. BERT trained from scratch with a custom legal vocabulary (BERT-SC) slightly outperforms vanilla BERT-BASE.

Small-scale pre-training with DP We experimented with further pre-training of two baseline models on a small-scale 2.3GB legal sub-corpus. The goal was to efficiently explore the effect of several key hyper-parameters on DP training with a small amount of data. We trained for 29k steps at batch size 256.

Table 3 shows that while both baseline models after further pre-training without privacy achieve ~ 3% substantial performance gains on CaseHOLD, the results of DP pre-training is disappointing. The benefits of domain training for CaseHOLD task seem to disappear after adding even a small amount of noise ($\sigma = 0.1$). The results from $\sigma = 0.1$ and $\sigma = 0.5$ don't outperform the baseline or are even marginally worse than it. In addition, the legal tokenizer doesn't indicate an advantage over the general one. We conclude that small-scale DP pre-training barely brings any improvement and even hurts the performance. We decide to scale up the training and explore larger batch sizes.

7.1 Large-scale domain pre-training with DP

As the batch size is one of the most important parameter in DP training, we fix the target privacy budget ε as 5 and further pre-train BERT-BASE on the large-scale full legal corpus starting with the default parameters (see Table 4 in the Appendix). Then we explore the parameter space by gradually increasing the batch size up to ~ 1M and roughly tune the learning rate at the same time. Although we have significantly accelerated the DP training by JAX framework, large-scale DP pre-training is still quite expensive. Due to resource and time constraints, we do not perform a complete grid search but only experiment with the likely best learning rates at each batch size in our experience.

Gradient-SNR Following the work in Anil et al. (2021), we keep track of the gradient signal-to-noise ratio at each step during the DP pre-training of BERT. Figure 1 shows the impact of batch size and learning rate on the Gradient-SNR. In general, the SNR decreases with training and eventually converges to a small value. This is probably due to the fact that the magnitude of the gradient decreases constantly during the learning, whereas the magnitude of the noise remains basically the same, so the ratio of the two keeps shrinking until the gradients become stable. From the left subplot 1(a) we can see that a larger batch size leads to higher Gradient-SNRs. Moreover, the right subfigure (b) shows that an appropriate learning rate can also improve the Gradient-SNR for a certain batch size. However, a too large learning rate leads to dramatic oscillation of Gradient SNR, and the model may move away from the local optima and thus increase the training loss.

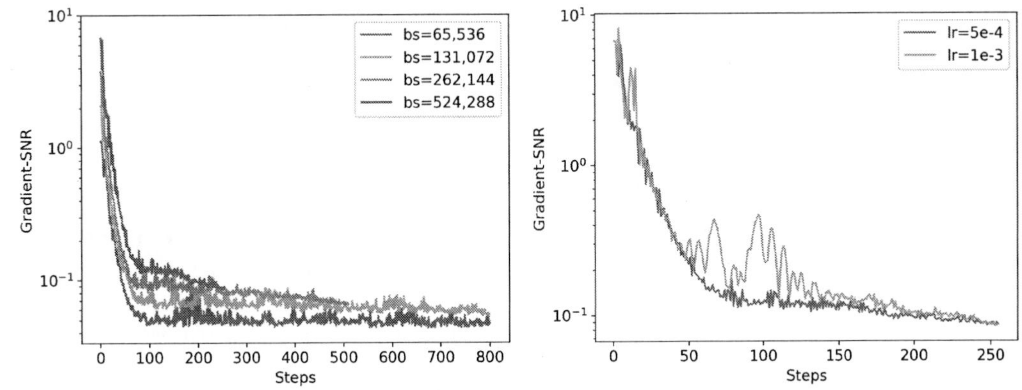

Figure 1: Gradient-SNR over steps for DP pre-training with same privacy budget and fixed epochs while varying the batch size (bs) or learning rate (lr). The left plot shows the trends of SNR at four different batch sizes. For smaller batch sizes, the SNRs after 800 steps are not presented, but they've basically converged to a small value as seen in the figure. Their initial learning rates are uniformly set as 5e-4. The right-hand figure draws the changes on SNR at batch size 524,288 using two different learning rates.

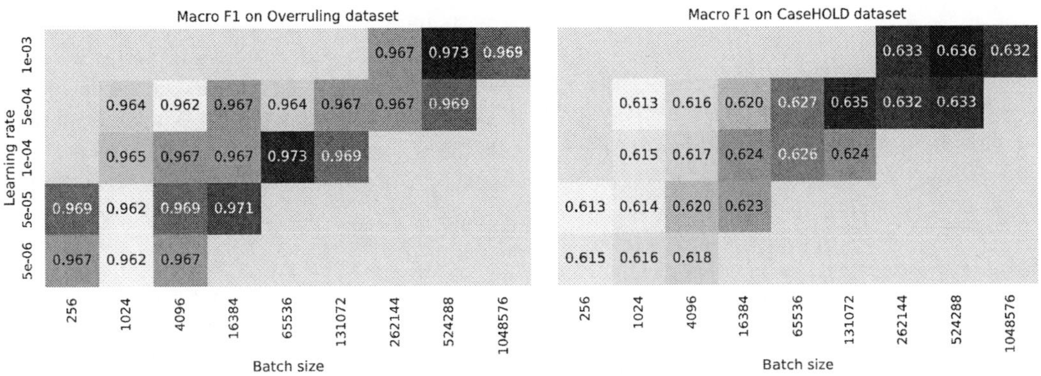

Figure 2: Downstream results obtained by tuning the batch size and learning rate of large-scale domain pre-training when fixing both the target privacy ε and training epochs to 5.

Results on downstream tasks In our experiments with fixed training epochs, the batch size and learning rate jointly influence the performance on CaseHOLD. As can be seen from the bottom subplot of Figure 2, training with unusually large batch sizes and high learning rates (upper right area) produces significantly better Macro F1 scores than using small batch sizes and low learning rates (bottom left area). By scaling up the batch size and tuning the learning rate accordingly, we achieve the best Macro F1 of 0.636 at batch size 524,288 and learning rate 1e-3. This **outperforms the baseline by almost 2%**.

As a summary, for a fixed training epoch setting, enlarging the batch size is not always beneficial and tuning the learning rate is crucial as well. However, according to our experiments, DP pre-training of BERT with a regular small batch size performs overall very poorly, and it starts to make performance gains on CaseHOLD when the batch size is stepped up to 4,096. We obtain a significant boost when increasing the batch size to 130K+. We conclude that scaling up the batch size and in-domain corpus is necessary to obtain good performance for DP pre-training of BERT in the legal field.

8 Discussion

Here we clarify some questions and comments raised by the reviewers.

Is the 2% improvement worth the effort? We believe so. Let's put our result into a broader context by having a closer look at results achieved by LEGAL-BERT (Chalkidis et al., 2020). On three downstream tasks, they gained similar improve-

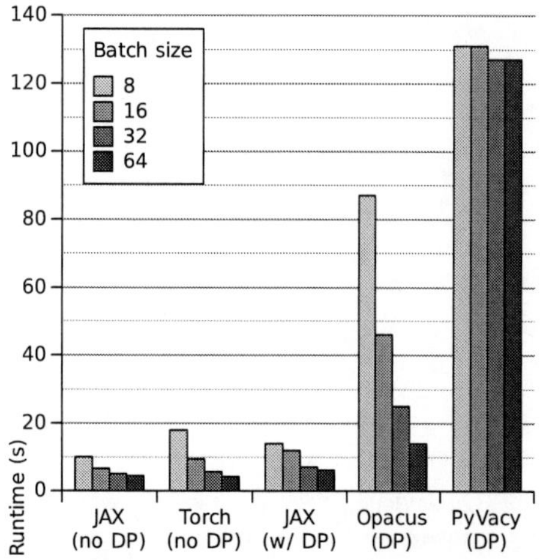

Figure 3: Runtimes (in seconds) per epoch for fine-tuning BERT on the Overruling binary classification task with different batch sizes and frameworks.

ments. First, *"in ECHR-CASES, we [...] observe small differences [...] in the performance on the binary classification task (0.8% improvement)."* Second, on NER they observed an *"increase in F1 on the contract header (1.8%) and dispute resolution (1.6%) subsets. In the lease details subset, we also observe an improvement (1.1%)."* Finally, on EURLEX57k, they observed *"a more substantial improvement in the more difficult multi-label task (2.5%) indicating that the LEGAL-BERT variations benefit from in-domain knowledge."* Moreover, our approach achieves similar gains under differential privacy guarantees.

How expensive is DP training? We experimentally evaluate the running performance of different frameworks on a binary classification task (Overruling) in both private and non-private cases. Figure 3 show the runtimes per epoch taken from the median over 20 epochs of training. In our experiments, Opacus is unable to support BERT's Embedding layer, although we use its official tutorial for training. This also prevents us to use it for the DP pre-training. We freeze its Embedding layer for the fine-tuning, which reduces nearly 22% training parameters compared to other methods. By doubling the batch size each time, 64 is the maximum batch size that the current GPU can support for JAX framework. Opacus uses a `BatchMemoryManager` to eliminate the limit of batch size similar to gradient accumulation, but the physical batch size it can achieve is actually much smaller than 64. This indicates that JAX has higher memory-efficiency than Opacus. The runtime of all the methods decreases significantly as the batch size grows except for PyVacy. In summary, due to the performance of JAX in the DP training, the 'extra costs' are negligible and allows us to upscale DP pre-training.

The title is misleading, the authors do not propose a privacy-preserving legal NLP model. If we take the definition of privacy through the lenses of differential privacy, then our pre-trained model is privacy-preserving; see, e.g., Yu et al. (2019) for a terminology clarification, or parallel works with the T5 language model (Ponomareva et al., 2022).

Why even do this? The scenario in which we want to protect privacy is the following. Say a company has huge amounts of in-house sensitive legal texts (e.g., contracts) which are valuable for pre-training a LM. This model is likely to be better performing on similar domains, so the company wants to offer an API or provide the model to other parties for further fine-tuning. Without DP, privacy of the pre-training data can be compromised (Pan et al., 2020; Carlini et al., 2020; Yu et al., 2019).

9 Conclusion

This paper shows that we can combine large-scale in-domain pretraining for a better downstream performance while protecting privacy of the entire pre-training corpus using formal guarantees of differential privacy. In particular, we implemented highly-scalable training of the BERT model with differentially-private stochastic gradient descent and pre-trained the model on $\approx$ 13 GB legal texts, using a decent $\varepsilon = 5$ privacy budget. The downstream results on the CaseHOLD benchmark show up to 2% improvements over baseline models with tuned hyper-parameters and models trained from scratch with a custom legal vocabulary. Our main contribution is utilizing differentially-private large-scale pre-training in the legal NLP domain. We believe that adapting formal privacy guarantees for training models might help overcome the difficulties of using large but potentially sensitive datasets in the legal domain.

Acknowledgements

The independent research group TrustHLT is supported by the Hessian Ministry of Higher Education, Research, Science and the Arts. We thank the anonymous reviewers for their useful feedback.

References

Martin Abadi, Andy Chu, Ian Goodfellow, H. Brendan McMahan, Ilya Mironov, Kunal Talwar, and Li Zhang. 2016. Deep Learning with Differential Privacy. In *Proceedings of the 2016 ACM SIGSAC Conference on Computer and Communications Security*, pages 308–318, Vienna, Austria. ACM.

Rohan Anil, Badih Ghazi, Vineet Gupta, Ravi Kumar, and Pasin Manurangsi. 2021. Large-Scale Differentially Private BERT. *arXiv preprint*, pages 1–12.

Jimmy Lei Ba, Jamie Ryan Kiros, and Geoffrey E Hinton. 2016. Layer normalization. In *NIPS 2016 Deep Learning Symposium*.

Amos Beimel, Kobbi Nissim, and Uri Stemmer. 2013. Private Learning and Sanitization: Pure vs. Approximate Differential Privacy. In *Approximation, Randomization, and Combinatorial Optimization. Algorithms and Techniques*, pages 363–378, Berlin, Heidelberg. Springer Berlin Heidelberg.

Tom B. Brown, Benjamin Mann, Nick Ryder, Melanie Subbiah, Jared Kaplan, Prafulla Dhariwal, Arvind Neelakantan, Pranav Shyam, Girish Sastry, Amanda Askell, Sandhini Agarwal, Ariel Herbert-Voss, Gretchen Krueger, Tom Henighan, Rewon Child, Aditya Ramesh, Daniel M. Ziegler, Jeffrey Wu, Clemens Winter, Christopher Hesse, Mark Chen, Eric Sigler, Mateusz Litwin, Scott Gray, Benjamin Chess, Jack Clark, Christopher Berner, Sam McCandlish, Alec Radford, Ilya Sutskever, and Dario Amodei. 2020. Language Models are Few-Shot Learners. *arXiv preprint*.

Mark Bun, Jonathan Ullman, and Salil Vadhan. 2014. Fingerprinting codes and the price of approximate differential privacy. In *Proceedings of the Forty-Sixth Annual ACM Symposium on Theory of Computing*, page 1–10, New York, New York. ACM.

Nicholas Carlini, Florian Tramer, Eric Wallace, Matthew Jagielski, Ariel Herbert-Voss, Katherine Lee, Adam Roberts, Tom Brown, Dawn Song, Ulfar Erlingsson, Alina Oprea, and Colin Raffel. 2020. Extracting Training Data from Large Language Models. *arXiv preprint*.

Ilias Chalkidis, Manos Fergadiotis, Prodromos Malakasiotis, Nikolaos Aletras, and Ion Androutsopoulos. 2020. LEGAL-BERT: The Muppets straight out of Law School. In *Findings of the Association for Computational Linguistics: EMNLP 2020*, pages 2898–2904, Online. Association for Computational Linguistics.

Jacob Devlin, Ming-Wei Chang, Kenton Lee, and Kristina Toutanova. 2019. BERT: Pre-training of Deep Bidirectional Transformers for Language Understanding. In *Proceedings of the 2019 Conference of the North American Chapter of the Association for Computational Linguistics: Human Language Technologies, Volume 1 (Long and Short Papers)*, pages 4171–4186, Minneapolis, Minnesota. Association for Computational Linguistics.

Cynthia Dwork, Frank McSherry, Kobbi Nissim, and Adam Smith. 2006. Calibrating noise to sensitivity in private data analysis. In *Theory of cryptography conference*, pages 265–284. Springer.

Cynthia Dwork and Aaron Roth. 2013. The Algorithmic Foundations of Differential Privacy. *Foundations and Trends® in Theoretical Computer Science*, 9(3-4):211–407.

Emad Elwany, Dave Moore, and Gaurav Oberoi. 2019. Bert goes to law school: Quantifying the competitive advantage of access to large legal corpora in contract understanding. In *Document Intelligence 2019 Workshop at NeurIPS*.

Ivan Habernal. 2021. When differential privacy meets NLP: The devil is in the detail. In *Proceedings of the 2021 Conference on Empirical Methods in Natural Language Processing*, pages 1522–1528, Punta Cana, Dominican Republic. Association for Computational Linguistics.

Ivan Habernal. 2022. How reparametrization trick broke differentially-private text representation learning. In *Proceedings of the 60th Annual Meeting of the Association for Computational Linguistics (Volume 2: Short Papers)*, pages 771–777, Dublin, Ireland. Association for Computational Linguistics.

Ivan Habernal, Daniel Faber, Nicola Recchia, Sebastian Bretthauer, Iryna Gurevych, Indra Spiecker genannt Döhmann, and Christoph Burchard. 2022. Mining Legal Arguments in Court Decisions. *arXiv preprint*.

Jamie Hayes, Luca Melis, George Danezis, and Emiliano De Cristofaro. 2019. Logan: Membership inference attacks against generative models. In *Proceedings on Privacy Enhancing Technologies (PoPETs)*, volume 2019, pages 133–152. De Gruyter.

Shlomo Hoory, Amir Feder, Avichai Tendler, Sofia Erell, Alon Peled-Cohen, Itay Laish, Hootan Nakhost, Uri Stemmer, Ayelet Benjamini, Avinatan Hassidim, and Yossi Matias. 2021. Learning and Evaluating a Differentially Private Pre-trained Language Model. In *Findings of the Association for Computational Linguistics: EMNLP 2021*, pages 1178–1189, Punta Cana, Dominican Republic. Association for Computational Linguistics.

Timour Igamberdiev, Thomas Arnold, and Ivan Habernal. 2022. DP-Rewrite: Towards Reproducibility and Transparency in Differentially Private Text Rewriting. In *Proceedings of the 29th International Conference on Computational Linguistics*, pages 2927–2933, Gyeongju, Republic of Korea. International Committee on Computational Linguistics.

Timour Igamberdiev and Ivan Habernal. 2022. Privacy-Preserving Graph Convolutional Networks for Text

Classification. In *Proceedings of the Language Resources and Evaluation Conference*, pages 338–350, Marseille, France. European Language Resources Association.

Pierre Lison, Ildikó Pilán, David Sánchez, Montserrat Batet, and Lilja Øvrelid. 2021. Anonymisation Models for Text Data: State of the Art, Challenges and Future Directions. In *Proceedings of the 59th Annual Meeting of the Association for Computational Linguistics and the International Joint Conference on Natural Language Processing (Volume 1: Long Papers)*, pages 4188–4203, Dublin, Ireland. Association for Computational Linguistics.

Ilya Loshchilov and Frank Hutter. 2019. Decoupled weight decay regularization. In *International Conference on Learning Representations*.

Ilya Mironov. 2017. Rényi differential privacy. In *2017 IEEE 30th Computer Security Foundations Symposium (CSF)*, pages 263–275. IEEE.

Ilya Mironov, Kunal Talwar, and Li Zhang. 2019. Rényi Differential Privacy of the Sampled Gaussian Mechanism. *arXiv preprint*.

Xudong Pan, Mi Zhang, Shouling Ji, and Min Yang. 2020. Privacy Risks of General-Purpose Language Models. In *2020 IEEE Symposium on Security and Privacy (SP)*, pages 1314–1331, San Francisco, USA. IEEE.

Ildikó Pilán, Pierre Lison, Lilja Øvrelid, Anthi Papadopoulou, David Sánchez, and Montserrat Batet. 2022. The text anonymization benchmark (TAB): A dedicated corpus and evaluation framework for text anonymization. *arXiv pre-print*.

Natalia Ponomareva, Jasmijn Bastings, and Sergei Vassilvitskii. 2022. Training Text-to-Text Transformers with Privacy Guarantees. In *Findings of the Association for Computational Linguistics: ACL 2022*, pages 2182–2193, Dublin, Ireland. Association for Computational Linguistics.

Anna Rogers, Olga Kovaleva, and Anna Rumshisky. 2020. A Primer in BERTology: What We Know About How BERT Works. *Transactions of the Association for Computational Linguistics*, 8:842–866.

Manuel Senge, Timour Igamberdier, and Ivan Habernal. 2022. One size does not fit all: Investigating strategies for differentially-private learning across NLP tasks. In *Proceedings of the 2022 Conference on Empirical Methods in Natural Language Processing*, Abu Dhabi, UAE. Association for Computational Linguistics.

Reza Shokri, Marco Stronati, Congzheng Song, and Vitaly Shmatikov. 2017. Membership inference attacks against machine learning models. In *2017 IEEE Symposium on Security and Privacy (SP)*, pages 3–18. IEEE.

Thomas Steinke and Jonathan Ullman. 2015. Between pure and approximate differential privacy. *arXiv preprint arXiv:1501.06095*.

Pranav Subramani, Nicholas Vadivelu, and Gautam Kamath. 2021. Enabling fast differentially private sgd via just-in-time compilation and vectorization. *Advances in Neural Information Processing Systems*, 34.

Don Tuggener, Pius vo von Däniken, Thomas Peetz, and Mark Cieliebak. 2020. LEDGAR: A Large-Scale Multi-label Corpus for Text Classification of Legal Provisions in Contracts. In *Proceedings of the 12th Language Resources and Evaluation Conference*, pages 1235–1241, Online. European Language Resources Association.

Ashish Vaswani, Noam Shazeer, Niki Parmar, Jakob Uszkoreit, Llion Jones, Aidan N. Gomez, Lukasz Kaiser, and Illia Polosukhin. 2017. Attention Is All You Need. In *Advances in Neural Information Processing Systems 30*, pages 5998—-6008, Long Beach, CA, USA. Curran Associates, Inc.

Yonghui Wu, Mike Schuster, Zhifeng Chen, Quoc V Le, Mohammad Norouzi, Wolfgang Macherey, Maxim Krikun, Yuan Cao, Qin Gao, Klaus Macherey, et al. 2016. Google's neural machine translation system: Bridging the gap between human and machine translation. *arXiv preprint arXiv:1609.08144*.

Ashkan Yousefpour, Igor Shilov, Alexandre Sablayrolles, Davide Testuggine, Karthik Prasad, Mani Malek, John Nguyen, Sayan Ghosh, Akash Bharadwaj, Jessica Zhao, et al. 2021. Opacus: User-friendly differential privacy library in PyTorch. *arXiv preprint arXiv:2109.12298*.

Lei Yu, Ling Liu, Calton Pu, Mehmet Emre Gursoy, and Stacey Truex. 2019. Differentially Private Model Publishing for Deep Learning. In *2019 IEEE Symposium on Security and Privacy (SP)*, pages 332–349, San Francisco, USA. IEEE.

Lucia Zheng, Neel Guha, Brandon R. Anderson, Peter Henderson, and Daniel E. Ho. 2021. When Does Pretraining Help? Assessing Self-Supervised Learning for Law and the CaseHOLD Dataset of 53,000+ Legal Holdings. In *Proceedings of the Eighteenth International Conference on Artificial Intelligence and Law*, pages 159–168, Sao Paulo, Brazil. ACM.

A Hyperparemeters for downstream tasks

As shown by Chalkidis et al. (2020) and Zheng et al. (2021), downstream hyper-parameters have a significant impact on the evaluation results and an enriched search range is necessary for the legal benchmarks. Therefore, instead of blindly following the recommended search range given by Devlin

	Learning Rate	Batch Size	Epochs
Devlin et al. (2019)	2e-5, 3e-5, 4e-5, 5e-5	16, 32	3, 4
First round	5e-6, 1e-5, 5e-5, 1e-4	8, 16, 32, 64, 128	max 10, early stop
Second round	7e-6, 2e-5, 3e-5, 7e-5	16 Overruling; 128 CaseHOLD	max 10, early stop
Final setup	1e-5, 3e-5, 5e-5, 7e-5	16 Overruling; 128 CaseHOLD	max 5, early stop

Table 4: Summary of the hyper-parameter search

ω	FP eval loss	MLM acc	NSP acc	F1 on Overruling	F1 on CaseHOLD
0.1	1.706	0.682	0.947	0.973	0.636
0.5	1.701	0.681	0.947	0.973	0.636
1.0	1.695	0.681	0.948	0.969	0.636

Table 5: Evaluation results for tuning the weight decay ω on the best setup (bs=524,288, lr=1e-3).

et al. (2019), we perform a broader search through two rounds of coarse- to fine-grained grid search. The details of the searched hyper-parameters are shown in Table 4. In the final setup, we fix the batch size as 16 for Overruling and 128 for CaseHOLD, and train for a maximum of 5 epochs. Furthermore, the downstream performances are relatively sensitive to the learning rate, we do a search over {1e-5, 3e-5, 5e-5, 7e-5} and the best macro-f1 scores are reported for each pre-trained model.

B Additional experiments with limited impact

B.1 Weight Decay ω

BERT uses layer normalization (Ba et al., 2016) that makes the output of a layer independent of the scale of its weights. As explained in Anil et al. (2021), the Frobenius norm of the layer weights tends to grow due to the noise introduced in the DP training, which reduces the norm of the gradients and thereby slows down the learning process under the layer normalization. To address this problem, they suggest using a much larger weight decay for Adam optimizer compared to the non-private training. Therefore, we experiment with several different weight decays on the best setup of batch size and learning rate. The results are outlined in Table 5. Different from the results in Anil et al. (2021), changing the weight decay causes almost no impact on the downstream performance and accuracy of MLM and NSP. One can only observe a negligible decline in loss as the weight decay increases. This is probably because our training starts from a well pre-trained base model, the weight update is more stable than training from scratch.

B.2 L2 Clipping Norm C

Recall that the two critical steps in DP-SGD are to clip the L2 norms of per-example gradients to C and to introduce randomly sampled Gaussian noise with standard deviation σC. Both steps involve the clipping norm C, thus it is likely to be an important hyper-parameter for DP training. We experiment with different values of C in $\{0.01, 0.1, 1.0, 10\}$ at batch size 1024 and σ 0.5. However, the MLM and NSP accuracy and downstream performance are almost unchanged when we drastically vary C. Hence, we consider that the L2 clipping norm may not be a key factor to DP pre-training and fix it to 1.0 in future experiments based on the common best results of two end tasks.

Named Entity Recognition in Indian court judgments

Prathamesh Kalamkar[1,2,*], **Astha Agarwal**[1,2,*], **Aman Tiwari**[1,2,*], **Smita Gupta**[3,*], **Saurabh Karn**[3,*], **Vivek Raghavan**[1]
[1]EkStep Foundation, [2]Thoughtworks Technologies India Pvt Ltd., [3]Agami
{prathamk, aman.tiwari, astha.agarwal}@thoughtworks.com,
{smita, saurabh}@agami.in, vivek@ekstep.org

Abstract

Identification of named entities from legal texts is an essential building block for developing other legal Artificial Intelligence applications. Named Entities in legal texts are slightly different and more fine-grained than commonly used named entities like Person, Organization, Location etc. In this paper, we introduce a new corpus of 46545 annotated legal named entities mapped to 14 legal entity types. The Baseline model for extracting legal named entities from judgment text is also developed. We publish the training, dev data and trained baseline model https://github.com/Legal-NLP-EkStep/legal_NER.

1 Introduction

Artificial Intelligence has the potential to increase access to justice and make various legal processes more efficient (Zhong et al., 2020). Populous countries such as India have a problem with high case pendency. As of March 2022, over 47 million cases are pending in Indian courts[1]. Hence, it becomes imperative to use AI to reduce the strain on the judicial system and reduce pendency. For developing legal AI applications, it is essential to have access to judicial data and open-source foundational AI building blocks like Named Entity Recognition (NER). A lot of Indian legal data is publicly available thanks to open data initiatives like National Judicial Data Grid (NJDG) and the Crime and Criminal Tracking Network and System (CCTNS).

NJDG provides non-exhaustive metadata of Indian court judgements like the names of petitioners, respondents, lawyers, judges, date, court etc. Extracting these entities from judgment text makes the information extraction exhaustive and reduces errors like misspellings compared to NJDG metadata. Helpful information like precedents and statutes are also not written in the NJDG metadata. Hence it is essential to extract from court judgment texts rather than just relying on the published NJDG metadata. Extracting named entities from the text also paves the foundation for more tasks like relation extraction, coreference resolution, knowledge graph creation etc.

In this paper, we have created a corpus of annotated judgment texts with 14 legal entities (details in §3). An example of annotated entities is shown in Figure 1.

We make the following contributions in this paper

- We create a corpus of 14444 Indian court judgment sentences and 2126 judgment preambles annotated with 14 legal named entities.
- We develop a transformer-based legal NER baseline model
- We create rule-based post-processing, which captures the document level context and coreference resolution for certain entities
- A representative sample of Indian high court and supreme court judgments having 11970 judgments across 29 Indian courts

2 Related Work

Named Entity Recognition (NER) is widely studied in literature ranging from statistical models (Borthwick et al., 1998),(Bikel et al., 1999),(McCallum and Li, 2003) to state-of-the-art deep neural nets (Li et al., 2020). The task complexity is also evolved over time from flat named entities to nested entities, from monolingual to multilingual NER.

Legal domain-specific entities are often used for more meaningful information extraction from legal texts. Pioneering work in legal NER by (Dozier et al., 2010) developed named entity recognition & resolution system on US legal texts using 5 legal named entities (judges, attorneys, companies,

* Authors contributed equally

[1]https://www.livelaw.in/pdf_upload/au595-426886.pdf

Proceedings of the Natural Legal Language Processing Workshop 2022, pages 184 - 193
December 8, 2022 ©2022 Association for Computational Linguistics

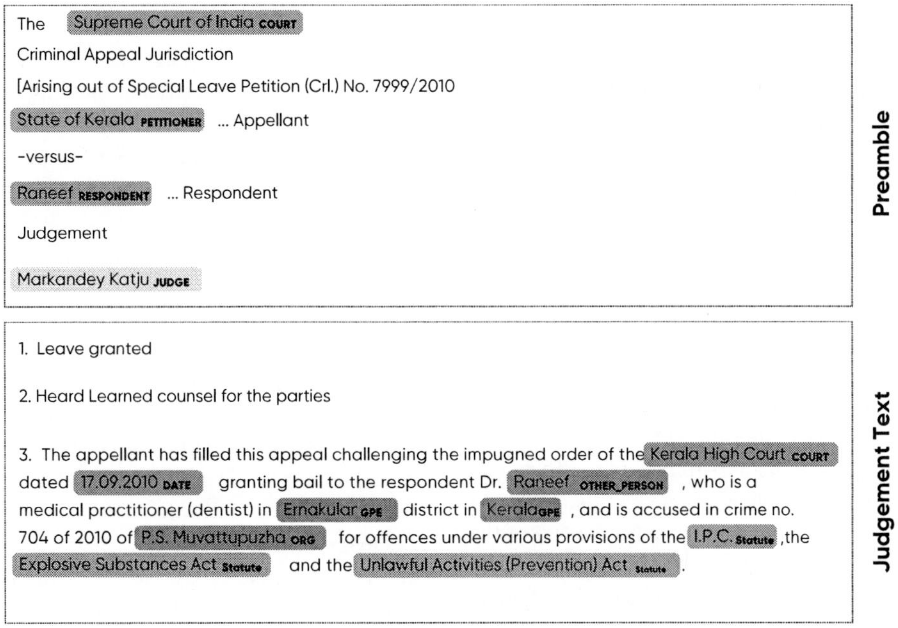

Figure 1: Legal Named Entities in a court judgment

jurisdictions, and courts). (Cardellino et al., 2017) created Named Entity Recognizer, Classifier and Linker by mapping LKIF ontology to YAGO ontology using Wikipedia data and various levels of abstraction of the legal ontology. Since the legal vocabulary and style of writing of legal text varies by language and geography, it is often necessary to create separate datasets and models. (Glaser et al., 2018) compared GermaNER (Benikova et al., 2015) and DBpedia Spotlight (Mendes et al., 2011; Daiber et al., 2013) NER systems on German legal contracts. (Leitner et al., 2020) created a German NER dataset with 19 fine-grained semantic classes. (Păiș et al., 2021) created a Romanian legal corpus called Legal NERo, which has 370 documents annotated with five entity classes and used legal domain word embeddings to build the NER system. (Luz de Araujo et al., 2018) created a corpus of legal documents from several Brazilian Courts called LeNER-Br, which is annotated with six entity classes. (Angelidis et al., 2018) created Named Entity Recognizer and Linker for Greek legislation with 254 annotated pieces of legislation. (Chalkidis et al., 2021) extracted contract elements extraction using LSTM encoders. NER using contextual dictionaries was applied to the French legal corpus of 94 court judgments with four entity classes by (Barriere and Fouret, 2019). As a part of Lynx, project (Schneider et al., 2020), a set of services, including NER, were developed to help create a legal domain knowledge graph and its use for the semantic analysis of legal documents.

Transition-based parsing for NER was proposed by (Lample et al., 2016) using stacked LSTM. NER task can be treated as graph-based dependency parsing (Yu et al., 2020) to provide a global view of the input using biaffine model. Recent advances in span representation have shown promising results for Named Entity Recognition (Ouchi et al., 2020). Span pretraining methods (Joshi et al., 2020) improve the span representation for pre-trained language models via span-level pretraining tasks. Infusing external knowledge for entity representation and linking (Yamada et al., 2020), (Wang et al., 2021) helps to better represent the knowledge in legal texts. (Ye et al., 2022) considered interrelation between spans by considering the neighbouring spans integrally to better model the entity boundary information.

Recently a lot of work has been done in the legal AI field in the Indian context. Structuring the court judgments (Kalamkar et al., 2022), legal statute identification (Paul et al., 2022a), judgment outcome prediction (Malik et al., 2021), judgment summarization (Shukla et al., 2022) provide AI building blocks. (Paul et al., 2022b) created InLegalBERT and InCaseLawBERT, which are further pre-trained versions of LegalBERT (Chalkidis et al., 2020) and CaseLawBERT (Zheng et al., 2021) respectively on Indian legal text.

3 Legal Named Entity Recognition Corpus

3.1 Legal Named Entities

A typical Indian court judgment can be split into two parts viz., preamble and judgment. The preamble of a judgment contains formatted metadata like names of parties, judges, lawyers, date, court etc. The text following the preamble till the end of the judgment is called "judgment". An example showing the preamble and judgment of a court judgment along with entities is shown in Figure 1. The preamble typically ends with keywords like JUDGMENT or ORDER etc. In case these keywords are not found, we treat the first occurrence of 2 consecutive sentences with a verb as the start of the judgment part. This is because the preamble typically contains formatted metadata and not grammatically complete sentences.

After discussion with legal experts about the useful information to be extracted from court judgments, we came up with a list of legal named entities which are described in Table 1. Some entities are extracted from the preamble, and some from the judgment text. Some entities are extracted from both the preamble and judgment, and their definitions may change depending on where they are extracted from.

Flat entities were considered for annotation i.e., "Bank of China" should be considered as an ORG entity and "China" should not be marked as GPE inside this entity. The detailed definitions with correctly and incorrectly marked examples can be found here[2].

3.2 Representative Sample of Indian High Court & Supreme Court judgments

Selecting a representative sample of court judgments text is vital to cover varieties of styles of writing judgments. Most cited judgements are likely to be more important for applying the NER model. But just taking the most cited judgments from a given court would produce bias in certain types of cases. Hence it is necessary to control case types as well. We created the following 8 types of cases (Tax, Criminal, Civil, Motor Vehicles, Land & Property, Industrial & Labour, Constitution and Financial) which cover most of the cases in Indian courts. Classification of each judgment into one of these 8 types is a complex task. We have used a naive approach to use keywords based on act names for assigning a judgment to a case type. E.g., If the judgment mentions the "income tax act" then most probably it belongs to the "Tax" category. We use IndianKanoon search engine[3] to get the most cited court judgments matching the key act names. The key act names for each of the case types are given in Table 2.

One IndianKanoon search query was created for each of the 8 case types and 29 courts (supreme court, 23 high courts, three tribunals and 2 district courts). The Topmost cited results from each query were combined and de-duplicated to produce the final corpus of judgments. We consider judgments in the English language only. Judgments obtained by this method from 1950 to 2017 were used for training data annotations, and judgments from 2018 to March 2022 were used for the test and dev data annotations. The representative sample dataset of 11970 judgments, along with search queries, the full text of the judgments and descriptive statistics, are published in our git repository[4]. We believe these representative judgments can be used for other future studies as well.

3.3 Data Annotation Process

The annotations for judgment text were done at a sentence level, i.e. separate individual judgment sentences were presented for annotation without the document-level context. However, annotators had the freedom to access the entire judgment text by clicking on the Indiankanoon URL shown below the text in case they needed more context. Complete preambles were presented for annotation.

3.3.1 Selecting Raw Text to Annotate

Legal named entities in a judgment text tend to be sparse, i.e., many of the sentences in a court judgment may not have any legal named entities. Hence is essential to identify entity-rich sen-

[2]https://storage.googleapis.com/indianlegalbert/OPEN_SOURCED_FILES/NER/NER_Definitions.pdf

[3]https://indiankanoon.org/

[4]https://github.com/Legal-NLP-EkStep/legal_NER/tree/main/representative_judgments_sample

Named Entity	Extract From	Description
COURT	Preamble, Judgment	Name of the court which has delivered the current judgement if extracted from the preamble. Name of any court mentioned if extracted from judgment sentences.
PETITIONER	Preamble, Judgment	Name of the petitioners/appellants/revisionist from current case
RESPONDENT	Preamble, Judgment	Name of the respondents/defendants/opposition from current case
JUDGE	Preamble, Judgment	Name of the judges from the current case if extracted from the preamble. Name of the judges of the current as well as previous cases if extracted from judgment sentences.
LAWYER	Preamble	Name of the lawyers from both the parties
DATE	Judgment	Any date mentioned in the judgment
ORG	Judgment	Name of organizations mentioned in text apart from the court.
GPE	Judgment	Geopolitical locations which include names of states, cities, villages
STATUTE	Judgment	Name of the act or law mentioned in the judgement
PROVISION	Judgment	Sections, sub-sections, articles, orders, rules under a statute
PRECEDENT	Judgment	All the past court cases referred to in the judgement as precedent. Precedent consists of party names + citation(optional) or case number (optional)
CASE_NUMBER	Judgment	All the other case numbers mentioned in the judgment (apart from precedent) where party names and citation is not provided
WITNESS	Judgment	Name of witnesses in current judgment
OTHER_PERSON	Judgment	Name of all the persons that are not included in petitioner, respondent, judge and witness

Table 1: Legal Named Entities Definitions

Case Type	Key Act keywords
Tax	tax act, excise act, customs act, goods and services act etc.
Criminal	IPC, penal code, criminal procedure etc.
Civil	civil procedure, family courts, marriage act, wakf act etc.
Motor Vehicles	motor vehicles act, mv act, imv act etc.
Land & Property	land acquisition act, succession act, rent control act etc.
Industrial & Labour	companies act, industrial disputes act, compensation act etc.
Constitution	constitution
Financial	negotiable instruments act, sarfaesi act, foreign exchange regulation act etc.

Table 2: Key Act Names for Each Case Type

tences for annotation rather than taking a random sample. We used the spacy pre-trained model (en_core_web_trf) (Montani et al., 2022) with custom rules to predict the legal named entities. Custom rules were used to map the Spacy-defined named entities to the legal named entities defined in this paper. E.g., An entity predicted by spacy as PERSON with the keyword "petitioner" nearby was marked as PETITIONER etc. We passed the representative sample judgment texts through this Spacy model with custom rules to get predicted noisy legal entities. Using these predicted legal entities, we selected the sentences that are entity-rich and that reduce the class imbalance across different entity types. We also added sentences without any predicted entities. Very short sentences and sentences with non-English characters were discarded. Preambles, where party names are written side by side on the same line, were also discarded.

3.3.2 Pre-annotations

The data annotation was done in 4 cycles. The preambles and sentences were pre-annotated in each cycle to reduce annotation effort.

For the first annotation cycle, the predicted legal entities obtained during the raw text selection process, as mentioned in 3.3.1, were reviewed and corrected. At the end of cycle 1, a machine learning model using Roberta+ transition-based parser architecture (explained in detail in §4) was trained using the labelled data obtained in cycle 1. This machine learning model was used to pre-annotate the cycle 2 data. Similarly, the machine learning model trained using cycle 1 and 2 data was used to pre-annotate cycle 3 data and so on.

3.3.3 Manual Reviews & Corrections

In each cycle, all of the pre-annotated preambles and sentences were carefully reviewed and corrected by humans. Roughly the same amount of preamble and sentences were annotated in each cycle. The team of 4 legal experts and 4 data scientists at OpenNyAI did the data annotation. Legal experts were law students from various law universities across India. We did not do duplicate annotations to maximize the number of annotated data. We used the Prodigy tool[5] for the annotations.

The corrected data obtained from the four annotation cycles was split into the train, dev and test datasets as per the time ranges mentioned in Table 3. We tried to keep the dev data distribution similar to the test data distribution. Test and dev data was carefully cross-reviewed twice to ensure data quality. The total count of entities, total number of preambles and judgment sentences in train, dev and test data are shown in Table 3. The counts of

	Train	Dev	Test
Time Range	1950 to 2017	2018 to 2022	2018 to 2022
Preambles	1560	125	441
Judgment sentences	9435	949	4060
Entities	29964	3216	13365

Table 3: Train & Test data counts

each legal named entity in training data are shown in Table 4.

[5]https://prodi.gy/

Entity	Judgment Count	Preamble Count
COURT	1293	1074
PETITIONER	464	2604
RESPONDENT	324	3538
JUDGE	567	1758
LAWYER	NA	3505
DATE	1885	NA
ORG	1441	NA
GPE	1398	NA
STATUTE	1804	NA
PROVISION	2384	NA
PRECEDENT	1351	NA
CASE_NUMBER	1040	NA
WITNESS	881	NA
OTHER_PERSON	2653	NA
Total	17485	12479

Table 4: Counts of Legal Entities for Training data in Preamble & Judgment

4 NER Baseline Model

The end goal behind this work is to enable the development of other legal AI applications that consume automatically detected legal named entities from judgment texts. Towards this goal, we experimented with some famous NER model architectures. A single model was trained to predict entities from both judgment sentences and the preamble. As transformer-based architectures have shown a lot of success in NER tasks (Li et al., 2020), we mainly experimented with them. We compared the performance of 2 NER architecture types when trained on our legal NER dataset. The first architecture type uses a transition-based dependency parser (Honnibal and Johnson, 2015) on top of the transformer model. The second architecture type uses a fine-tuning based approach which adds a single linear layer to the transformer model and fine-tunes the entire architecture on the NER task. Figure 2 shows the 2 NER architecture types.

We experimented with multiple transformer models for each of the architecture types. For transition-based parser architecture we experimented with the Roberta-base model (Liu et al., 2019), InLegalBERT (Paul et al., 2022b) using Spacy library. For the fine-tuning approach we experimented with Roberta-base, InLegalBERT, legalBERT (Chalkidis et al., 2020) using TNER library (Ushio and Camacho-Collados, 2021).

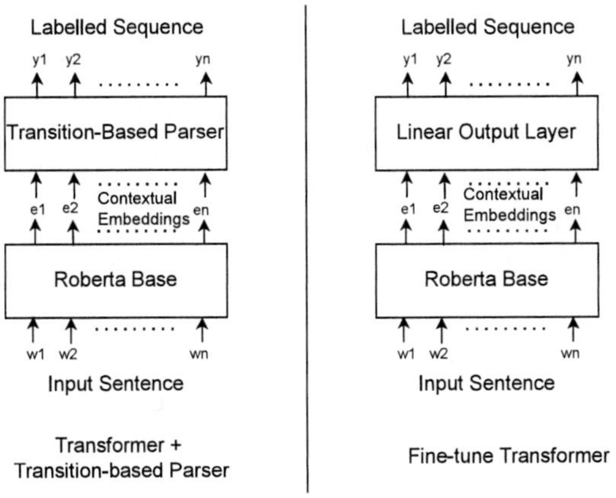

Figure 2: NER Architectures

Architecture Type	Trans. Model	P	R	F1
Transformer + Transition Based Parser	**Roberta-base**	**92.0**	**90.2**	**91.1**
	InLegal BERT	87.3	85.8	86.5
Fine Tune Transformer	Roberta-base	77.6	80.0	78.8
	InLegal BERT	77.7	84.6	81.0
	Legal BERT	75.4	79.5	77.5

Table 5: Model Performance on test data

The models are evaluated by using recall, precision and strict F1 scores on combined preamble and judgment sentences. The named entity is considered correct when both boundary and entity class are predicted correctly. Table 5 shows the performance of these experiments on the test data.

Performance of the best performing model (Roberta+ transition-based parser) on each of the entity classes on test data along with average character length is shown in Table 6. It also shows the Type match F1 score which was proposed in (Segura-Bedmar et al., 2013). Under the Type match evaluation scheme, some overlap between the tagged entity and the gold entity is required along with entity type match. In strict f1 calculation, the entities with correct entity type match and partial span overlap are considered incorrect. But in the Type match evaluation, such entities are considered the correct entity. Hence the Type match F1 score gives an indication of how much overlap exists between ground truth and prediction considering partial matches.

Entity	Count	Avg. Len.	F1	Type match F1
COURT	1231	25	95.4	97.2
PETITIONER	835	20	89.8	92.6
RESPONDENT	1125	34	83.0	91.8
JUDGE	580	15	95.4	96.5
LAWYER	1813	16	94.1	95.5
DATE	1111	11	91.9	98.7
ORG	920	18	86.4	90.2
GPE	711	8	85.7	90.9
STATUTE	971	17	96.0	97.6
PROVISION	1220	14	95.7	98.6
PRECEDENT	634	62	80.1	96.2
CASE_NUMBER	683	23	89.1	92.4
WITNESS	446	12	89.7	89.7
OTHER_PERSON	1085	12	93.8	95.2
Overall	**13365**	**20**	**91.1**	**94.9**

Table 6: Entity-wise performance of Roberta + Transition-based Parser model on test data

Parameter	Value
Transformer	Roberta-base
Optimizer	Adam with beta1 = 0.9, beta2 = 0.999, L2 = 0.01, initial learning rate = 0.00005
max training steps	40000
training batch size	256

Table 7: Key training procedure parameters

The trained Roberta+Transition-based Parser is made available as a Spacy pipeline in our git repository and hugging face model repository[6].

4.1 Training Procedure

Early stopping using dev data was used during training to select the best epoch for all the experiments. The details about the training procedure for Roberta + Transition-based parser using Spacy are available in the GitHub repository. NVIDIA Tesla V100 GPU was used to train the model and the training time was 12 hours. The key parameters used are mentioned in Table 7.

[6]https://huggingface.co/opennyaiorg/en_legal_ner_trf

4.2 Results Discussion

Adding a transition-based parser to the transformer architecture significantly improves the model's accuracy for this NER task, as seen in Table 5.

As seen from Table 6, the Roberta-base + transition-based parser NER model can extract shorter entities like WITNESS, PROVISION, STATUTE, LAWYER, COURT and JUDGE with excellent performance.

PRECEDENT has degraded performance as compared to other entities because the precedent names are usually very long (average entity length is 62 characters) and missing out on even a few characters makes the entire entity to be marked as incorrect. Because of this reason, there is a significant difference between strict F1 and Type match F1 for PRECEDENT. Manual inspection of errors in PRECEDENT prediction reveals that many a time, the prefixes of party names like "Mr.", "M/S", etc. are missed in the prediction while gold entities have them. E.g., the gold entity type is PRECEDENT with the text "Mr Amit Kumar Vs State of Maharashtra," and the predicted entity type is PRECEDENT with the text "Amit Kumar Vs State of Maharashtra". In strict F1 evaluation, this example is considered incorrect, while in Type match evaluation, this example is considered correct. One possible reason for the model not to include the prefixes in the PRECEDENT prediction could be that prefixes are not considered as a part of other entities like PETITIONER, RESPONDENT and ORG. So possibly, the model has also learned to omit the prefixes in PRECEDENT.

The average character length of RESPONDENT entities is considerably higher than that of PETITIONER entities. This difference is because, often, the respondents are posts or authorities rather than a person. E.g. "The Chief Engineer, Water Resource Organization, Chepauk, Chennai-5". In such cases, gold data marks the authority or post names along with the address as the corresponding entity, making them longer. The difference between strict F1 and Type match F1 for RESPONDENT shows that the model is missing in predicting a few characters in such long entities.

The overall accuracy of this model makes it very useful in practical legal AI applications.

5 Post-Processing of Named Entities

Since the annotators were asked to annotate individual sentences without document-level context, any trained NER model on this data will also focus only on the sentence-level information. While inferring the NER model on a complete judgment text, it is important to perform post-processing of extracted entities to capture document-level context. In particular, we create rules to perform the following tasks

- Reconciliation of the entities extracted from individual sentences of a judgment
- Coreference resolution of precedents
- Coreference resolution of statutes
- Assign statute to every provision

5.1 Reconciliation of the Extracted Entities

The same entity text can be tagged with different legal entity classes in separate sentences of the same judgment. E.g., In the preamble of a judgment, it is written that "Amit Kumar" is a petitioner. In the same judgement text, the judge later writes, "Four unidentified persons attacked Amit Kumar". NER model would mark "Amit Kumar" in the second mention as OTHER_PERSON because there is no information about Amit Kumar being a petitioner in this sentence. Marking this person's name as PETITIONER is more valuable than marking it as an OTHER_PERSON.

As part of entity reconciliation, entities predicted as OTHER_PERSON or ORG are matched with all the PETITIONER, RESPONDENT, JUDGE, LAWYER and WITNESS entities. If an exact match is found, then the entity type is overwritten with the matching entity type. In the previous example, all the extracted entities that match "Amit Kumar" would be overwritten with entity type PETITIONER.

5.2 Coreference Resolution of Precedents

The names of precedent cases are usually very long. Hence judges typically mention the complete name of a precedent case for the first mention and later use the name of the first party as a reference. E.g., "The constitution bench of this court in Gurbaksh Singh Sibbia and others Vs State of Punjab (1980) 2 SCC 565 dealt with the scope and ambit of anticipatory bail". Then, later on, the judge uses a reference to this case, like "The learned counsel for the petitioner placed reliance on Sibbia's case (supra)." The NER model identifies "Sibbia" as OTHER_PERSON in the second sentence. But here, "Sibbia" is a reference to the earlier extracted PRECEDENT entity "Gurbaksh Singh Sibbia and others Vs State of Punjab (1980) 2 SCC 565".

We first cluster all the extracted precedent entities within a judgment by matching the party names and citations. A precedent cluster contains all the precedent entities with matching party names or citations. Then we identify potential precedent referents as ORG or OTHER_PERSON entity followed by keywords "supra" or "'s case". We then search such referent entities in the extracted precedents' party names and find the closest matching preceding precedent. If the match is found, then we change the referent entity type to PRECEDENT. Referent entities are also added to the precedent cluster where the closest matching precedent belongs. Once all the matching precedent referents are assigned to precedent clusters, the longest entity in each cluster is marked as the cluster head. So in the example before, the entity type for "Sibbia" in the second sentence would be changed from OTHER_PERSON to PRECEDENT, and a precedent cluster would be created with the head as "Gurbaksh Singh Sibbia and others Vs State of Punjab (1980) 2 SCC 565" and the member as "Sibbia".

The information about precedents coreference can be accessed through output Spacy doc object property *doc.user_data['precedent_clusters'].*

5.3 Coreference Resolution of Statutes

Statute names can be long and are frequently mentioned in judgment text. Hence judges typically write the complete statute name at the beginning of the judgment and specify the referent for this statute for the remaining judgement. E.g., "The complaint was filed under the Companies Act, 1956 (for brevity, 'the Act') ...". Later on in the same judgment, the judge writes ", Section 5 of the Act defines ...". We write rules to identify such statute referents by searching for a STATUTE entity followed by keywords in parenthesis. Such statute referents are added to the statute cluster with its head as the complete statute name. All entities in a statute cluster refer to the same statute, which is the head of the cluster. Extracted statutes are also looked up against a list of famous acronyms (IPC, CrPC etc.), and if a match is found, then the corresponding full form is added to the statutes cluster. The information about statute coreference can be accessed through output Spacy doc object property *doc.user_data['statute_clusters'].*

5.4 Assign Statute to Every Provision

Every extracted provision should be associated with an extracted statute. Sometimes a provision and its corresponding statute are explicitly mentioned in the same sentence. E.g., "Section 420 of Indian Penal Code says ...". Sometimes, the provision-statute mapping is implicit where only the provision is mentioned, and the corresponding statute is understood from the context. E.g., "The section 420 says ...".

In case of explicit mentions, we assign the statute to the immediately preceding provision in the same sentence. All the remaining provisions are considered implicit provisions. We first search for all the implicit provisions if a unique explicit mapping exists in another sentence. E.g., if the judge writes an explicit mention like "Section 420 of Indian Penal Code" and there is no other explicit mention of Section 420 for any other statute in the entire judgment text, then all the implicit mentions of Section 420 are mapped to "Indian Penal Code". Suppose no explicit mention for a provision is found, or multiple explicit mentions are found for a provision. In that case, the statute extracted from the closest preceding sentence is assigned.

The assignment of the statute to provisions can be accessed via output Spacy doc object property *doc.user_data['provision_statute_pairs']*

6 Conclusion & Future Directions

In this paper, we proposed a new corpus of legal named entities using 14 legal entity types. We also proposed baseline models trained using this corpus along with post-processing of the extracted entities to capture document-level information. We have also released a representative sample of Indian court judgments which could be used in further studies. We believe this corpus will lay the foundation for further NLP tasks like relationship extraction, knowledge graph population etc. using Indian court judgments.

Acknowledgements

This work is part of the OpenNyAI mission, which is funded by EkStep and Agami. We thank all the law experts, student volunteers for contributing to data annotation.

References

Iosif Angelidis, Ilias Chalkidis, and Manolis Koubarakis. 2018. Named entity recognition, linking and generation for greek legislation. In *JURIX*, pages 1–10.

Valentin Barriere and Amaury Fouret. 2019. May i check again?—a simple but efficient way to generate and use contextual dictionaries for named entity recognition. application to french legal texts. In *Proceedings of the 22nd Nordic Conference on Computational Linguistics*, pages 327–332.

Darina Benikova, Seid Muhie, Yimam Prabhakaran, and Santhanam Chris Biemann. 2015. C.: Germaner: Free open german named entity recognition tool. In *In: Proc. GSCL-2015*. Citeseer.

Daniel M Bikel, Richard Schwartz, and Ralph M Weischedel. 1999. An algorithm that learns what's in a name. *Machine learning*, 34(1):211–231.

Andrew Borthwick, John Sterling, Eugene Agichtein, and Ralph Grishman. 1998. Nyu: Description of the mene named entity system as used in muc-7. In *Seventh Message Understanding Conference (MUC-7): Proceedings of a Conference Held in Fairfax, Virginia, April 29-May 1, 1998*.

Cristian Cardellino, Milagro Teruel, Laura Alonso Alemany, and Serena Villata. 2017. A low-cost, high-coverage legal named entity recognizer, classifier and linker. In *Proceedings of the 16th edition of the International Conference on Articial Intelligence and Law*, pages 9–18.

Ilias Chalkidis, Manos Fergadiotis, Prodromos Malakasiotis, Nikolaos Aletras, and Ion Androutsopoulos. 2020. LEGAL-BERT: The muppets straight out of law school. In *Findings of the Association for Computational Linguistics: EMNLP 2020*, pages 2898–2904, Online. Association for Computational Linguistics.

Ilias Chalkidis, Manos Fergadiotis, Prodromos Malakasiotis, and Ion Androutsopoulos. 2021. Neural contract element extraction revisited: Letters from sesame street. *arXiv preprint arXiv:2101.04355*.

Joachim Daiber, Max Jakob, Chris Hokamp, and Pablo N Mendes. 2013. Improving efficiency and accuracy in multilingual entity extraction. In *Proceedings of the 9th international conference on semantic systems*, pages 121–124.

Christopher Dozier, Ravikumar Kondadadi, Marc Light, Arun Vachher, Sriharsha Veeramachaneni, and Ramdev Wudali. 2010. Named entity recognition and resolution in legal text. In *Semantic Processing of Legal Texts*, pages 27–43. Springer.

Ingo Glaser, Bernhard Waltl, and Florian Matthes. 2018. Named entity recognition, extraction, and linking in german legal contracts. In *IRIS: Internationales Rechtsinformatik Symposium*, pages 325–334.

Matthew Honnibal and Mark Johnson. 2015. An improved non-monotonic transition system for dependency parsing. In *Proceedings of the 2015 conference on empirical methods in natural language processing*, pages 1373–1378.

Mandar Joshi, Danqi Chen, Yinhan Liu, Daniel S Weld, Luke Zettlemoyer, and Omer Levy. 2020. Spanbert: Improving pre-training by representing and predicting spans. *Transactions of the Association for Computational Linguistics*, 8:64–77.

Prathamesh Kalamkar, Aman Tiwari, Astha Agarwal, Saurabh Karn, Smita Gupta, Vivek Raghavan, and Ashutosh Modi. 2022. Corpus for automatic structuring of legal documents. In *Proceedings of the Language Resources and Evaluation Conference*, pages 4420–4429, Marseille, France. European Language Resources Association.

Guillaume Lample, Miguel Ballesteros, Sandeep Subramanian, Kazuya Kawakami, and Chris Dyer. 2016. Neural architectures for named entity recognition. In *Proceedings of the 2016 Conference of the North American Chapter of the Association for Computational Linguistics: Human Language Technologies*, pages 260–270.

Elena Leitner, Georg Rehm, and Julian Moreno Schneider. 2020. A dataset of german legal documents for named entity recognition. In *Proceedings of the 12th Language Resources and Evaluation Conference*, pages 4478–4485.

Jing Li, Aixin Sun, Jianglei Han, and Chenliang Li. 2020. A survey on deep learning for named entity recognition. *IEEE Transactions on Knowledge and Data Engineering*, 34(1):50–70.

Yinhan Liu, Myle Ott, Naman Goyal, Jingfei Du, Mandar Joshi, Danqi Chen, Omer Levy, Mike Lewis, Luke Zettlemoyer, and Veselin Stoyanov. 2019. Roberta: A robustly optimized bert pretraining approach. *arXiv preprint arXiv:1907.11692*.

Pedro Henrique Luz de Araujo, Teófilo E de Campos, Renato RR de Oliveira, Matheus Stauffer, Samuel Couto, and Paulo Bermejo. 2018. Lener-br: a dataset for named entity recognition in brazilian legal text. In *International Conference on Computational Processing of the Portuguese Language*, pages 313–323. Springer.

Vijit Malik, Rishabh Sanjay, Shubham Kumar Nigam, Kripabandhu Ghosh, Shouvik Kumar Guha, Arnab Bhattacharya, and Ashutosh Modi. 2021. Ildc for cjpe: Indian legal documents corpus for court judgment prediction and explanation. In *Proceedings of the 59th Annual Meeting of the Association for Computational Linguistics and the 11th International Joint Conference on Natural Language Processing (Volume 1: Long Papers)*, pages 4046–4062.

Andrew McCallum and Wei Li. 2003. Early results for named entity recognition with conditional random fields, feature induction and web-enhanced lexicons. In *Proceedings of the seventh conference on Natural language learning at HLT-NAACL 2003-Volume 4*, pages 188–191.

Pablo N Mendes, Max Jakob, Andrés García-Silva, and Christian Bizer. 2011. Dbpedia spotlight: shedding light on the web of documents. In *Proceedings of the 7th international conference on semantic systems*, pages 1–8.

Ines Montani, Matthew Honnibal, Matthew Honnibal, Sofie Van Landeghem, Adriane Boyd, Henning Peters, Paul O'leary McCann, Maxim Samsonov, Jim Geovedi, Jim O'Regan, Duygu Altinok, György Orosz, Søren Lind Kristiansen, Roman, Explosion Bot, Lj Miranda, Leander Fiedler, Daniël de Kok, Grégory Howard, Edward, Wannaphong Phatthiyaphaibun, Yohei Tamura, Sam Bozek, murat, Mark Amery, Ryn Daniels, Björn Böing, Pradeep Kumar Tippa, and Peter Baumgartner. 2022. explosion/spacy: v3.2.4: Workaround for Click/Typer issues.

Hiroki Ouchi, Jun Suzuki, Sosuke Kobayashi, Sho Yokoi, Tatsuki Kuribayashi, Ryuto Konno, and Kentaro Inui. 2020. Instance-based learning of span representations: A case study through named entity recognition. In *Proceedings of the 58th Annual Meeting of the Association for Computational Linguistics*, pages 6452–6459.

Vasile Păiș, Maria Mitrofan, Carol Luca Gasan, Vlad Coneschi, and Alexandru Ianov. 2021. Named entity recognition in the romanian legal domain. In *Proceedings of the Natural Legal Language Processing Workshop 2021*, pages 9–18.

Shounak Paul, Pawan Goyal, and Saptarshi Ghosh. 2022a. Lesicin: A heterogeneous graph-based approach for automatic legal statute identification from indian legal documents. In *Proceedings of the AAAI Conference on Artificial Intelligence*, volume 36, pages 11139–11146.

Shounak Paul, Arpan Mandal, Pawan Goyal, and Saptarshi Ghosh. 2022b. Pre-training transformers on indian legal text.

Julian Moreno Schneider, Georg Rehm, Elena Montiel-Ponsoda, Víctor Rodríguez Doncel, Artem Revenko, Sotirios Karampatakis, Maria Khvalchik, Christian Sageder, Jorge Gracia, and Filippo Maganza. 2020. Orchestrating nlp services for the legal domain. In *Proceedings of the 12th Language Resources and Evaluation Conference*, pages 2332–2340.

Isabel Segura-Bedmar, Paloma Martínez, and María Herrero-Zazo. 2013. SemEval-2013 task 9 : Extraction of drug-drug interactions from biomedical texts (DDIExtraction 2013). In *Second Joint Conference on Lexical and Computational Semantics (*SEM), Volume 2: Proceedings of the Seventh International Workshop on Semantic Evaluation (SemEval 2013)*, pages 341–350, Atlanta, Georgia, USA. Association for Computational Linguistics.

Abhay Shukla, Paheli Bhattacharya, Soham Poddar, Rajdeep Mukherjee, Kripabandhu Ghosh, Pawan Goyal, and Saptarshi Ghosh. 2022. Legal case document summarization: Extractive and abstractive methods and their evaluation. In *The 2nd Conference of the Asia-Pacific Chapter of the Association for Computational Linguistics and the 12th International Joint Conference on Natural Language Processing*.

Asahi Ushio and Jose Camacho-Collados. 2021. T-NER: An all-round python library for transformer-based named entity recognition. In *Proceedings of the 16th Conference of the European Chapter of the Association for Computational Linguistics: System Demonstrations*, pages 53–62, Online. Association for Computational Linguistics.

Xiaozhi Wang, Tianyu Gao, Zhaocheng Zhu, Zhengyan Zhang, Zhiyuan Liu, Juanzi Li, and Jian Tang. 2021. Kepler: A unified model for knowledge embedding and pre-trained language representation. *Transactions of the Association for Computational Linguistics*, 9:176–194.

Ikuya Yamada, Akari Asai, Hiroyuki Shindo, Hideaki Takeda, and Yuji Matsumoto. 2020. Luke: Deep contextualized entity representations with entity-aware self-attention. In *Proceedings of the 2020 Conference on Empirical Methods in Natural Language Processing (EMNLP)*, pages 6442–6454.

Deming Ye, Yankai Lin, Peng Li, and Maosong Sun. 2022. Packed levitated marker for entity and relation extraction. In *Proceedings of the 60th Annual Meeting of the Association for Computational Linguistics (Volume 1: Long Papers)*, pages 4904–4917.

Juntao Yu, Bernd Bohnet, and Massimo Poesio. 2020. Named entity recognition as dependency parsing. In *Proceedings of the 58th Annual Meeting of the Association for Computational Linguistics*, pages 6470–6476.

Lucia Zheng, Neel Guha, Brandon R Anderson, Peter Henderson, and Daniel E Ho. 2021. When does pretraining help? assessing self-supervised learning for law and the casehold dataset of 53,000+ legal holdings. In *Proceedings of the Eighteenth International Conference on Artificial Intelligence and Law*, pages 159–168.

Haoxi Zhong, Chaojun Xiao, Cunchao Tu, Tianyang Zhang, Zhiyuan Liu, and Maosong Sun. 2020. How does nlp benefit legal system: A summary of legal artificial intelligence. In *Proceedings of the 58th Annual Meeting of the Association for Computational Linguistics*, pages 5218–5230.

The Legal Argument Reasoning Task in Civil Procedure

Leonard Bongard and **Lena Held** and **Ivan Habernal**
Trustworthy Human Language Technologies
Department of Computer Science
Technical University of Darmstadt
leonard.bongard@stud.tu-darmstadt.de
{lena.held, ivan.habernal}@tu-darmstadt.de

Abstract

We present a new NLP task and dataset from the domain of the U.S. civil procedure. Each instance of the dataset consists of a general introduction to the case, a particular question, and a possible solution argument, accompanied by a detailed analysis of why the argument applies in that case. Since the dataset is based on a book aimed at law students, we believe that it represents a truly complex task for benchmarking modern legal language models. Our baseline evaluation shows that fine-tuning a legal transformer provides some advantage over random baseline models, but our analysis reveals that the actual ability to infer legal arguments remains a challenging open research question.

1 Introduction

Arguing a legal case is an essential skill that aspiring lawyers must master. This skill requires not only knowledge of the relevant area of law, but also advanced reasoning abilities, such as using analogy arguments or finding implicit contradictions. Despite recent significant contributions aimed at setting objective benchmarks for modern NLP models in various areas of legal language understanding (Chalkidis et al., 2022), there is still no complex task dealing with argument reasoning in legal matters.

In this paper, we propose a new task and provide a new benchmark dataset. We believe that a genuinely difficult task, coming from legal education, will help to demonstrate both the capabilities and the limitations of the current state-of-the-art legal transformation models, such as Legal-BERT (Chalkidis et al., 2020). In particular, we present a new, publicly available[1] legal corpus for binary text classification of U.S. civil procedure problems. The goal is to classify whether a solution to a given question is correct or incorrect. The data for the corpus is based on the *The Glannon Guide To Civil Procedure* by Joseph Glannon (Glannon, 2018), which is aimed at law students. The book allows for the study of basic U.S. civil procedure topics and also contains multiple-choice questions on civil procedure problems to test the reader.

With this newly created corpus, we also intend to investigate the performance of the different approaches and establish baselines and an error analysis. All source codes used to parse, extract and reformat the data and evaluate the solution methods can be found at https://github.com/trusthlt/legal-argument-reasoning-task.

[1] See the Data sheet in the appendix for details.

2 Related work

General QA and argument reasoning benchmarks Although the landscape of Question Answering (QA) corpora is vast, there are several categories and nuances which enable a more fine-grained division. For a better overview of the field, we refer the reader to a recent survey (Rogers et al., 2022). A possible distinction can be made on the basis of the target skill to be learned, among which commonsense reasoning is a more challenging one. In order to contribute to the learning of reasoning, a corpus must be designed in such a way that questions cannot be answered with a given context or linguistic cues alone. Several corpora take this into account by making their QA design "hard to answer" without additional context (Mostafazadeh et al., 2017; Huang et al., 2019). To further support the ability to reason, some datasets provide an explanation in addition to the typical format of context, question and answer (Jansen et al., 2016; Camburu et al., 2018; Lamm et al., 2021). Somewhat specific is the Argument Reasoning Comprehension Task by Habernal et al. (2018) in which the goal is to choose one of two contradicting warrants that connect a premise with the given

Proceedings of the Natural Legal Language Processing Workshop 2022, pages 194 - 207
December 8, 2022

claim. Apart from traditional commonsense reasoning which requires general knowledge and understanding (Talmor et al., 2019; Sap et al., 2019), there are also datasets in specialized fields like biomedical QA (Tsatsaronis et al., 2015) which target domain specific factoid knowledge.

Legal question answering and legal reasoning In legal NLP, the number of publicly available corpora is considerably smaller, especially in the areas of argumentation and reasoning. An early compilation of legal questions in a multiple-choice format is found in (Fawei et al., 2016). Each of the 100 questions taken from the United States Multistate Bar Examination is interpreted as an entailment task with one correct answer (entailment) and three incorrect answers (non-entailment). However, their evaluation shows that a mere similarity between theory (question) and hypothesis (answer) is insufficient to solve this task. A follow-up work extends the bar exam corpus with older exam practice questions and reformulates the task into an "Answer-Sentence-Selection" task instead of textual entailment (John et al., 2017). Additionally, 15 of the questions are annotated with an explanation. Pursuing a different approach, Holzenberger et al. (2020) try to answer natural language questions in the domain of tax law by encoding knowledge as a set of rules with the help of a prolog solver. Holzenberger and van Durme (2021) extend the previously introduced corpus and subdivide statutory reasoning into a sequence of smaller tasks. Although this logic-based approach facilitates the answering, instantiation from natural language is not a trivial task. Apart from resources in English, Zhong et al. (2020) compile a corpus for Legal QA in Chinese with knowledge-driven questions and case-analysis questions from the National Judicial Examination of China. They identify different types of reasoning needed to answer the questions and conclude that existing models lack reasoning ability, especially for knowledge-driven questions. Contests such as the COLIEE competition (Kano et al., 2019; Rabelo et al., 2022) also include legal question answering tasks in a format that requires retrieval of relevant articles and entailment. The corpus for these tasks is taken from Japanese Bar Exams and manually translated into English. Although there are several resources available that deal with legal question answering, only few of them target statutory law in the English language. There is also still a shortcoming of datasets dedicated to argumentative answers in Legal QA which we aim to complement with our work.

3 Dataset construction

We built the dataset based on the content of *The Glannon Guide To Civil Procedure* (Glannon, 2018). We collaborated with the author and the publisher[2] and negotiated a permission agreement under which the resulting dataset will be freely available to the research community.

The book contains 25 chapters with multiple choice questions. Each chapter deals with a specific topic and asks and answers several questions. The topic of a question is introduced beforehand in an introduction. Each question is followed by three to five answer candidates, where only one candidate is correct. The answer candidates can be considered as hypotheses. Choosing the correct answer requires examining if the various prerequisites of a hypothesis hold. Whether an answer is correct or incorrect is then discussed in the analysis afterward.

We parsed the book first fully automatically, as the structure allowed us to extract the components of each instance in the resulting dataset (introduction, question, answers, analysis). Anomalies in the structure, e.g., the same introduction for two questions, were caught by additional parsing rules. However, minor portions of the book had to be extracted manually, for instance the correctness of the answer candidate because the solution is addressed within the analysis' free text. The analysis is loosely designed as follows. Each paragraph deals with an answer candidate and classifies it as true or false. Therefore, we decided to further separate the analysis to isolate the relevant aspect for each answer. There were no keywords or structure artifacts indicating where to split the text. Furthermore, several inconsistencies regarding the structure exist. Thus, separating the analysis had to be done manually too. Two complete examples (one incorrect and one correct, labeled as 0 and 1, respectively) are shown in Appendix A.

Separating the analysis allows the creation of a binary classification task, which should be suitable for many application scenarios. The final legal argument reasoning task is defined as follows:

[2] Joe Terry, vice president of Aspen Publishing

Task Given a question with a possible correct answer and a short introduction to the topic of the question, identify if the answer candidate is correct or incorrect.

After parsing the book, each question and answer pair is ordered as follows: *1. Question; 2. Answer; 3. Solution; 4. Analysis; 5. Complete Analysis; 6. Introduction.*

Glannon (2018) intended to ask more difficult questions at the end of each chapter. We thus created a data split accordingly. The *rational data split* divides the first 80% of questions of each chapter into the train set, the following 10% of questions into the dev set, and the last 10% (which tend to be more difficult) into the test set.

The final dataset consists of 918 entries. To evaluate if there is any evidence that some answers were more likely to be the correct answer than others, a distance analysis using *Sentence-Bert*[3] (Reimers and Gurevych, 2019) was applied. This evaluation method was applied to the train-, dev- and test-set. The results indicate that there is little to no evidence that clues exist in the train and dev set. The test set shows an increased accuracy at guessing the correct answer, which is 9.88% more than the expected result of 24.5% (calculated average of guessing the correct answer of a question).

4 Baseline experiments

A first baseline evaluation of the task included classification through pre-trained transformer models. To evaluate the performance, the macro F_1 score is used. We chose Legal-BERT as the classification model because of its legal tech application domain (although the model was not pre-trained with American civil procedure data). We evaluated BERT (Devlin et al., 2019) as well as Legal-BERT (Chalkidis et al., 2020) with and without fine-tuning giving it the question, answer, and introduction on an instance as input. Another evaluation with these models included only the question and answer as input. For fine-tuning we experimented as suggested by Chalkidis et al. (2020) with the learning-rate, weight-decay and the dropout-rate. We finished training through early-stopping (patience was set to 3). The deep learning approach uses two techniques to bypass the maximum token limit problem.

[3]https://huggingface.co/sentence-transformers/all-mpnet-base-v2

Classifier	Accuracy	F_1
Random Baseline	50.33	46.74
Majority Baseline	80.52	44.21
Legal-BERT-Base		
— (q,a)	68.86	50.39
— SWS (q,e,a)	61.54	45.19
— SWC (q,e,a)	62.63	49.83
— Finetuned (q,a)	80.22	44.51
— Finetuned SWS (q,e,a)	81.31	63.03
— Finetuned SWC (q,e,a)	76.92	**65.73**
BERT-Base		
— Finetuned (q,a)	80.22	44.51
— Finetuned SWS (q,e,a)	71.43	50.71
— Finetuned SWC (q,e,a)	80.22	56.80

Table 1: Accuracy and macro F_1-score (in %) of transformer based models on the test set. To fit the complete question and introduction, the Sliding Window Simple (SWS) and Sliding Window Complex (SWC) are used.

Sliding Window Simple (SWS) separates the concatenated question and introduction into chunks. Each chunk is then classified, and the result is the average of the predicted outputs.

Sliding Window Complex (SWC) divides the introduction into multiple chunks, where each chunk contains the complete question and is padded up with the introduction. Each chunk is then classified where the result is the average of the predicted outputs.

Table 1 displays the best results out of 15 runs with different hyper-parameters. The fine-tuned Legal-BERT model performs best with the SWC approach and outperforms the best performing BERT model as well as the random baseline significantly. Furthermore, there is a notable difference between the performance of BERT and Legal-BERT using the SWS method.

5 Analysis and discussion

Understanding legal argumentation is not an easy task by any means. Therefore it is not surprising that the performance of the transformer model is struggling. *The Glannon Guide To Civil Procedure* is an educational book to help students learn civil procedure questions. Thus, even professionals have problems answering case law questions.

Question: 14. Additions and objections. In July 2006, a week before the three-year statute of limitations passes, Carson sues Herrera in federal court for breach of a contract to design a computer system for his store in Calpurnia, Illinois. In July 2007, he moves to amend his complaint to add a claim for violation of the state Consumer Protection Act, based on the same dispute. The Consumer Protection Act has a two-year statute of limitations.

Answer 1: The second claim would not be barred by the limitations period, as long as the judge grants the motion to amend.

Answer 2: The second claim would "relate back" to the date of the original filing of the case, and therefore would not be barred by the statute of limitations.

Answer 3: The second claim will be barred by the limitations period, because it will not "relate back" to the original filing under Rule 15.

Answer 4: *The amendment will be barred, even if it relates back to the filing of the original complaint.*

Figure 1: The fine-tuned Legal-BERT model predicts every possible answer of the corresponding question as correct. However, only answer 4 (italic) is correct.

A comparison to a human baseline would be beneficial to evaluate the overall performance of our model. We leave establishing the human upper bound for future work.

We did a brief error analysis by comparing the classification results between the fine-tuned BERT and Legal-BERT model. Out of 91 samples, the BERT model labels 6 of them as correct, while the Legal-BERT model labels 21 as correct. The BERT model predicted 3 of the 18 correct samples correctly, the Legal-BERT model predicted 9 of them correctly. 17 answers have divided model predictions. We read these samples for the error analysis, to understand the prediction. We assume that the legal language used in the data the Legal-BERT model is pretrained on, has an impact on the prediction results. This could be additionally indicated by the low amount of samples which are labeled as correct by the BERT model. We further noticed that some questions have multiple answers that the Legal-BERT model considers correct, even though the assertion of these answers differs. One example can be seen in Figure 1.

In an attempt to understand why the fine-tuned model has labeled all answers as correct we tried to follow the classification process through the usage of Captum, a Pytorch model interpretability library (Kokhlikyan et al., 2020). Captum is used to calculate the attribution of each word vector as input feature for the final prediction. However, as visualized in appendix C, a similar pattern for labeling each answer could not be found, despite the similarity of vocabulary between the answer possibilities. Inconsistencies like these reveal that the Legal-BERT model does not comprehensively reason about the answer.

Another explanation for the shortcomings of the evaluated models could be their inherent structure. In our dataset, concatenating the question, answer and introduction leads to 689 (646, 835) words or 3508 (3243, 4245) characters on average for the rational data split. Although the Sliding Window methods mitigate the token limits of BERT, a model that can deal with longer documents, like Longformer (Beltagy et al., 2020) or Big Bird (Zaheer et al., 2020) could prove to be more efficient. While a pretrained version of the Longformer architecture based on legal input exists in Chinese (Xiao et al., 2021), to the best of our knowledge there is no English equivalent available. The computationally expensive pretraining of such a model and testing it with our new dataset is left for future work.

Even more so, we have not included the most distinguishing property of our dataset in the experiments: the analysis. It is used to explain in human language why the answer to a question is correct or incorrect. As a possible future task, it would be interesting to see if this explanation could be used to boost the reasoning capabilities of a model.

6 Conclusion

We present a new challenging NLP task whose solution requires deeper knowledge and reasoning skills. We compare multiple transformer baselines and provide an error analysis showing that the correct prediction of the model for one instance does not prevent incorrect predictions for other relevant instances. We have obtained a license to share the dataset from the author of the original book and its publisher, and hope that it will help advance research in the complex field of legal argument reasoning.

Acknowledgements

We would like to thank John Glannon and Aspen Publishing for their support. The independent research group TrustHLT is supported by the Hessian Ministry of Higher Education, Research, Science and the Arts. This work has been partly funded by the German Research Foundation as part of the ECALP project (HA 8018/2-1).

References

Iz Beltagy, Matthew E. Peters, and Arman Cohan. 2020. Longformer: The Long-Document Transformer. *arXiv:2004.05150*.

Oana-Maria Camburu, Tim Rocktäschel, Thomas Lukasiewicz, and Phil Blunsom. 2018. e-SNLI: Natural Language Inference with Natural Language Explanations. In *Advances in Neural Information Processing Systems*, volume 31. Curran Associates, Inc.

Ilias Chalkidis, Manos Fergadiotis, Prodromos Malakasiotis, Nikolaos Aletras, and Ion Androutsopoulos. 2020. LEGAL-BERT: The Muppets straight out of Law School. In *Findings of the Association for Computational Linguistics: EMNLP 2020*, pages 2898–2904, Online. Association for Computational Linguistics.

Ilias Chalkidis, Abhik Jana, Dirk Hartung, Michael Bommarito, Ion Androutsopoulos, Daniel Katz, and Nikolaos Aletras. 2022. LexGLUE: A Benchmark Dataset for Legal Language Understanding in English. In *Proceedings of the 60th Annual Meeting of the Association for Computational Linguistics (Volume 1: Long Papers)*, pages 4310–4330, Dublin, Ireland. Association for Computational Linguistics.

Jacob Devlin, Ming-Wei Chang, Kenton Lee, and Kristina Toutanova. 2019. BERT: Pre-training of Deep Bidirectional Transformers for Language Understanding. In *Proceedings of the 2019 Conference of the North American Chapter of the Association for Computational Linguistics: Human Language Technologies, Volume 1 (Long and Short Papers)*, pages 4171–4186, Minneapolis, Minnesota. Association for Computational Linguistics.

Biralatei Fawei, Adam Wyner, and Jeff Pan. 2016. Passing a USA National Bar Exam: a First Corpus for Experimentation. In *Proceedings of the Tenth International Conference on Language Resources and Evaluation (LREC'16)*, pages 3373–3378, Portorož, Slovenia. European Language Resources Association (ELRA).

Timnit Gebru, Jamie Morgenstern, Briana Vecchione, Jennifer Wortman Vaughan, Hanna Wallach, Hal Daumé III, and Kate Crawford. 2021. Datasheets for Datasets. *Commun. ACM*, 64(12):86–92.

Joseph W Glannon. 2018. *The Glannon Guide To Civil Procedure: Learning Civil Procedure Through Multiple-Choice Questions and Analysis*, 4th edition. Aspen Publishing.

Ivan Habernal, Henning Wachsmuth, Iryna Gurevych, and Benno Stein. 2018. The Argument Reasoning Comprehension Task: Identification and Reconstruction of Implicit Warrants. In *Proceedings of the 2018 Conference of the North American Chapter of the Association for Computational Linguistics: Human Language Technologies, Volume 1 (Long Papers)*, pages 1930–1940, New Orleans, Louisiana. Association for Computational Linguistics.

Nils Holzenberger, Andrew Blair-Stanek, and Benjamin van Durme. 2020. A Dataset for Statutory Reasoning in Tax Law Entailment and Question Answering. In *Proceedings of the Natural Legal Language Processing Workshop 2020 co-located with the 26th ACM SIGKDD International Conference on Knowledge Discovery & Data Mining (KDD 2020)*.

Nils Holzenberger and Benjamin van Durme. 2021. Factoring Statutory Reasoning as Language Understanding Challenges. In *Proceedings of the 59th Annual Meeting of the Association for Computational Linguistics and the 11th International Joint Conference on Natural Language Processing (Volume 1: Long Papers)*, pages 2742–2758, Stroudsburg, PA, USA. Association for Computational Linguistics.

Lifu Huang, Ronan Le Bras, Chandra Bhagavatula, and Yejin Choi. 2019. Cosmos QA: Machine Reading Comprehension with Contextual Commonsense Reasoning. In *Proceedings of the 2019 Conference on Empirical Methods in Natural Language Processing and the 9th International Joint Conference on Natural Language Processing (EMNLP-IJCNLP)*, pages 2391–2401, Hong Kong, China. Association for Computational Linguistics.

Peter Jansen, Niranjan Balasubramanian, Mihai Surdeanu, and Peter Clark. 2016. What's in an Explanation? Characterizing Knowledge and Inference Requirements for Elementary Science Exams. In *Proceedings of COLING 2016, the 26th International Conference on Computational Linguistics: Technical Papers*, pages 2956–2965, Osaka, Japan. The COLING 2016 Organizing Committee.

Adebayo Kolawole John, Luigi Di Caro, and Guido Boella. 2017. Solving Bar Exam Questions with Deep Neural Networks. In *Proceedings of the Second Workshop on Automated Semantic Analysis of Information in Legal Texts: co-located with the 16th*

International Conference on Artificial Intelligence and Law.

Yoshinobu Kano, Mi-Young Kim, Masaharu Yoshioka, Yao Lu, Juliano Rabelo, Naoki Kiyota, Randy Goebel, and Ken Satoh. 2019. COLIEE-2018: Evaluation of the Competition on Legal Information Extraction and Entailment. In *New Frontiers in Artificial Intelligence*, volume 11717 of *Lecture Notes in Computer Science*, pages 177–192, Cham. Springer International Publishing.

Narine Kokhlikyan, Vivek Miglani, Miguel Martin, Edward Wang, Bilal Alsallakh, Jonathan Reynolds, Alexander Melnikov, Natalia Kliushkina, Carlos Araya, Siqi Yan, et al. 2020. Captum: A unified and generic model interpretability library for PyTorch. *arXiv preprint arXiv:2009.07896.*

Matthew Lamm, Jennimaria Palomaki, Chris Alberti, Daniel Andor, Eunsol Choi, Livio Baldini Soares, and Michael Collins. 2021. QED: A Framework and Dataset for Explanations in Question Answering. *Transactions of the Association for Computational Linguistics*, 9.

Nasrin Mostafazadeh, Michael Roth, Annie Louis, Nathanael Chambers, and James Allen. 2017. LSDSem 2017 Shared Task: The Story Cloze Test. In *Proceedings of the 2nd Workshop on Linking Models of Lexical, Sentential and Discourse-level Semantics*, pages 46–51, Valencia, Spain. Association for Computational Linguistics.

Juliano Rabelo, Randy Goebel, Mi-Young Kim, Yoshinobu Kano, Masaharu Yoshioka, and Ken Satoh. 2022. Overview and Discussion of the Competition on Legal Information Extraction/Entailment (COLIEE) 2021. *The Review of Socionetwork Strategies*, 16(1):111–133.

Nils Reimers and Iryna Gurevych. 2019. Sentence-BERT: Sentence Embeddings using Siamese BERT-Networks. In *Proceedings of the 2019 Conference on Empirical Methods in Natural Language Processing and the 9th International Joint Conference on Natural Language Processing (EMNLP-IJCNLP)*, pages 3982–3992, Hong Kong, China. Association for Computational Linguistics.

Anna Rogers, Matt Gardner, and Isabelle Augenstein. 2022. QA Dataset Explosion: A Taxonomy of NLP Resources for Question Answering and Reading Comprehension. *ACM Comput. Surv.*

Maarten Sap, Hannah Rashkin, Derek Chen, Ronan Le Bras, and Yejin Choi. 2019. Social IQa: Commonsense Reasoning about Social Interactions. In *Proceedings of the 2019 Conference on Empirical Methods in Natural Language Processing and the 9th International Joint Conference on Natural Language Processing (EMNLP-IJCNLP)*, pages 4463–4473, Hong Kong, China. Association for Computational Linguistics.

Alon Talmor, Jonathan Herzig, Nicholas Lourie, and Jonathan Berant. 2019. CommonsenseQA: A Question Answering Challenge Targeting Commonsense Knowledge. In *Proceedings of the 2019 Conference of the North American Chapter of the Association for Computational Linguistics: Human Language Technologies, Volume 1 (Long and Short Papers)*, pages 4149–4158, Minneapolis, Minnesota. Association for Computational Linguistics.

George Tsatsaronis, Georgios Balikas, Prodromos Malakasiotis, Ioannis Partalas, Matthias Zschunke, Michael R. Alvers, Dirk Weissenborn, Anastasia Krithara, Sergios Petridis, Dimitris Polychronopoulos, Yannis Almirantis, John Pavlopoulos, Nicolas Baskiotis, Patrick Gallinari, Thierry Artiéres, Axel-Cyrille Ngonga Ngomo, Norman Heino, Eric Gaussier, Liliana Barrio-Alvers, Michael Schroeder, Ion Androutsopoulos, and Georgios Paliouras. 2015. An overview of the BIOASQ large-scale biomedical semantic indexing and question answering competition. *BMC bioinformatics*, 16:138.

Chaojun Xiao, Xueyu Hu, Zhiyuan Liu, Cunchao Tu, and Maosong Sun. 2021. Lawformer: A Pre-trained Language Model forChinese Legal Long Documents. *AI Open*, 2:79–84.

Manzil Zaheer, Guru Guruganesh, Kumar Avinava Dubey, Joshua Ainslie, Chris Alberti, Santiago Ontanon, Philip Pham, Anirudh Ravula, Qifan Wang, Li Yang, and Amr Ahmed. 2020. Big Bird: Transformers for Longer Sequences. In *Advances in Neural Information Processing Systems*, volume 33, pages 17283–17297. Curran Associates, Inc.

Haoxi Zhong, Chaojun Xiao, Cunchao Tu, Tianyang Zhang, Zhiyuan Liu, and Maosong Sun. 2020. JEC-QA: A Legal-Domain Question Answering Dataset. *Proceedings of the AAAI Conference on Artificial Intelligence*, 34(05):9701–9708.

A Incorrect Example

Introduction My students always get confused about the relationship between removal to federal court and personal jurisdiction. Suppose that a defendant is sued in Arizona and believes that she is not subject to personal jurisdiction there. Naturally, she should object to personal jurisdiction. But suppose further that she isn't sure that her objection will carry the day; it's a close issue, as so many personal jurisdiction issues are under minimum contacts analysis. And suppose that her tactical judgment is that, if she must litigate in Arizona, she would rather litigate in federal court in Arizona. What should she do? One thing she could do is to move to dismiss in the Arizona state court. But that motion is not likely to be ruled on within thirty days, and if she's going to remove, she's got to do it within thirty days. So she could do one of two things: She could move to dismiss for lack of personal jurisdiction in the state court (assuming that the state rules allow her to do that) and then remove to federal court within the thirty-day period. Her motion would then be pending in federal court instead of state court, and the federal court would rule on it. Or she could remove the case before a response was due in state court, and then, after removal, raise her objection to personal jurisdiction by a Rule 12(b)(2) motion to dismiss or in her answer to the complaint in federal court. Either way, the point is that removal does not waive the defendant's right to object to personal jurisdiction. It simply changes the court in which the objection will be litigated. It is true that, after removal, the question will be whether the federal court has personal jurisdiction. But generally the scope of personal jurisdiction in the federal court will be the same as that of the state court, because the Federal Rules require the federal court in most cases to conform to state limits on personal jurisdiction. Fed. R. Civ. P. 4(k)(1)(A). I've stumped a multitude of students on this point. Consider the following two cases to clarify the point.

Question 7. A switch in time. Yasuda, from Oregon, sues Boyle, from Idaho, on a state law unfair competition claim, seeking $250,000 in damages. He sues in state court in Oregon. Ten days later (before an answer is due in state court), Boyle files a notice of removal in federal court. Five days after removing, Boyle answers the complaint, including in her answer an objection to personal jurisdiction. Boyle's objection to personal jurisdiction is

Answer not waived by removal, but will be denied because the federal courts have power to exercise broader personal jurisdiction than the state courts.

Solution 0

Analysis C is also wrong, because it suggests that, after removal, personal jurisdiction over Boyle will be tested by a different standard from that used in state court. In a diversity case, the reach of the federal court's personal jurisdiction is governed by Fed. R. Civ. P. 4(k)(1)(A), which provides that the defendant is subject to personal jurisdiction in the federal court if she "is subject to the jurisdiction of a court of general jurisdiction in the state where the district court is located." In other words, if the state courts of Oregon could exercise jurisdiction over Boyle, the Oregon federal court can; otherwise not.

Complete Analysis There are so many ways to go astray on this issue that I had to include five choices . . . and I could have made it seven! Surely the farthest astray is E. The fact that the court has subject matter jurisdiction over this diversity case does not mean that it has personal jurisdiction over Boyle. Though easily confused, the subject matter and personal jurisdiction analyses are separate; the court must have both subject matter jurisdiction over the case and personal jurisdiction over the defendant in order to proceed with the case. A reflects the faulty assumption that removal waives objections to personal jurisdiction. It doesn't; it simply changes the forum in which the personal jurisdiction question will be litigated. Boyle may remove the case, and then respond to it, raising his defenses and jurisdictional objections in federal court. And B is wrong, because Boyle removed the case before the answer was due in state court. It is true, under some states' procedural rules, that answering a complaint without including an objection to personal jurisdiction would waive it. But where a defendant removes before a response is due in state court, she does not waive any defenses by removal. She simply changes the forum in which such defenses will be raised. See Fed. R. Civ. P. 81(c)(1) (Federal Rules govern procedure after removal). C is also wrong, because it suggests that, after removal, personal jurisdiction over Boyle will be tested by a different standard from that used in state court. In a diversity case, the reach of the federal court's personal jurisdiction is governed by Fed. R. Civ. P. 4(k)(1)(A), which provides that the defendant is subject to personal jurisdiction in the federal court if she "is subject to the jurisdiction of a court of general jurisdiction in the state where the district court is located." In other words, if the state courts of Oregon could exercise jurisdiction over Boyle, the Oregon federal court can; otherwise not. D is the correct answer. Boyle has not waived his objection to personal jurisdiction. If the federal court lacks jurisdiction over Boyle, it should dismiss the case, even though it was properly removed. Now, another.

B Correct Example

Question 7. A switch in time. Yasuda, from Oregon, sues Boyle, from Idaho, on a state law unfair competition claim, seeking $250,000 in damages. He sues in state court in Oregon. Ten days later (before an answer is due in state court), Boyle files a notice of removal in federal court. Five days after removing, Boyle answers the complaint, including in her answer an objection to personal jurisdiction. Boyle's objection to personal jurisdiction is

Answer not waived by removal. The court should dismiss if there is no personal jurisdiction over Boyle in Oregon, even though the case was properly removed.

Solution 1

Analysis D is the correct answer. Boyle has not waived his objection to personal jurisdiction. If the federal court lacks jurisdiction over Boyle, it should dismiss the case, even though it was properly removed.

Complete Analysis There are so many ways to go astray on this issue [...]. *Same as in Appendix A.*

Introduction My students always get confused about the relationship between removal to federal court and personal jurisdiction. [...] *Same as in Appendix A.*

C Error Analyis

Legend: ■ Negative □ Neutral ■ Positive

True Label	Predicted Label	Attribution Label	Attribution Score	Word Importance
0	tensor([1]) (1.00)	1	-2.91	14 . addition ##s and objection ##s . in july 2006 , a week before the three - year statute of limitations passe ##s , cars ##on sue ##s her ##rera in federal court for breach of a contract to design a computer system for his store in cal ##pur ##nia , illinois . in july 2007 , he move ##s to amend his complaint to add a claim for violation of the state consumer protection act , based on the same dispute . the consumer protection act has a two - year statute of limitations . | 59 the second claim would not be barred by the limitations period , as long as the judge grants the motion to amend .
0	tensor([1]) (1.00)	1	-3.61	14 . addition ##s and objection ##s . in july 2006 , a week before the three - year statute of limitations passe ##s , cars ##on sue ##s her ##rera in federal court for breach of a contract to design a computer system for his store in cal ##pur ##nia , illinois . in july 2007 , he move ##s to amend his complaint to add a claim for violation of the state consumer protection act , based on the same dispute . the consumer protection act has a two - year statute of limitations . | 60 the second claim would [UNK] [UNK] relate back [UNK] [UNK] to the date of the original filing of the case , and therefore would not be barred by the statute of limitations .
0	tensor([1]) (1.00)	1	-1.71	14 . addition ##s and objection ##s . in july 2006 , a week before the three - year statute of limitations passe ##s , cars ##on sue ##s her ##rera in federal court for breach of a contract to design a computer system for his store in cal ##pur ##nia , illinois . in july 2007 , he move ##s to amend his complaint to add a claim for violation of the state consumer protection act , based on the same dispute . the consumer protection act has a two - year statute of limitations . | 61 the second claim will be barred by the limitations period , because it will not [UNK] [UNK] relate back [UNK] [UNK] to the original filing under rule 15 .
1	tensor([1]) (1.00)	1	-3.20	14 . addition ##s and objection ##s . in july 2006 , a week before the three - year statute of limitations passe ##s , cars ##on sue ##s her ##rera in federal court for breach of a contract to design a computer system for his store in cal ##pur ##nia , illinois . in july 2007 , he move ##s to amend his complaint to add a claim for violation of the state consumer protection act , based on the same dispute . the consumer protection act has a two - year statute of limitations . | 62 the amendment will be barred , even if it relates back to the filing of the original complaint .

Figure 2: Legal-BERT Model interpretability with Captum:

D Data sheet

The data sheet is provided following a template[4] for *Datasheets for datasets* (Gebru et al., 2021). We have answered the questions to the best of our knowledge, but we would like to note that we can only make reliable statements about our collection process of the data but not the original book.

Motivation

For what purpose was the dataset created? Was there a specific task in mind? Was there a specific gap that needed to be filled? Please provide a description.
The dataset was created to enable research on reasoning towards civil procedure legal arguments. The dataset was created intentionally with that task in mind, focusing on the content provided by the book *The Glannon Guide To Civil Procedure* containing civil procedure problems.

Who created this dataset (e.g., which team, research group) and on behalf of which entity (e.g., company, institution, organization)?
The dataset was created by Leonard Bongard, Lena Held, and Ivan Habernal (Technical University Darmstadt, Germany), based on a book by Joseph Glannon (Suffolk University, USA). The creators of the dataset had no influence on the creation and publication of the book. The correctness of the solutions lies solely with the author and publisher of the book.

Who funded the creation of the dataset? If there is an associated grant, please provide the name of the grantor and the grant name and number.
N/A

Any other comments?
None.

Composition

What do the instances that comprise the dataset represent (e.g., documents, photos, people, countries)? Are there multiple types of instances (e.g., movies, users, and ratings; people and interactions between them; nodes and edges)? Please provide a description.
The instances are civil procedure problems extracted from the book *The Glannon Guide To Civil Procedure*. Multiple topics of civil procedure are covered in the book and are represented through the instances.

How many instances are there in total (of each type, if appropriate)?
There are 918 instances in total. Each question-answer pair is treated as a separate instance.

Does the dataset contain all possible instances or is it a sample (not necessarily random) of instances from a larger set? If the dataset is a sample, then what is the larger set? Is the sample representative of the larger set (e.g., geographic coverage)? If so, please describe how this representativeness was validated/verified. If it is not representative of the larger set, please describe why not (e.g., to cover a more diverse range of instances, because instances were withheld or unavailable).
The dataset contains all possible instances.

What data does each instance consist of? "Raw" data (e.g., unprocessed text or images) or features? In either case, please provide a description.
Each instance consists of a question, a corresponding answer, a solution, an analysis of the specific answer, the complete analysis of the question, and a topic introduction. The data is not further processed.

Is there a label or target associated with each instance? If so, please provide a description.
The label is the correctness or incorrectness of the answer derived from the analysis in binary format (0 or 1).

Is any information missing from individual instances? If so, please provide a description, explaining why this information is missing (e.g., because it was unavailable). This does not include intentionally removed information, but might include, e.g., redacted text.
The book contains multiple choice questions that were parsed into a binary classification format. However, there exist answers like "None of the answers are correct" which are excluded in our

[4] https://www.overleaf.com/latex/templates/datasheet-for-dataset-template/jgqyyzyprxth

dataset. These answers cannot be used with our approach for reasoning.

Are relationships between individual instances made explicit (e.g., users' movie ratings, social network links)? If so, please describe how these relationships are made explicit.
No.

Are there recommended data splits (e.g., training, development/validation, testing)? If so, please provide a description of these splits, explaining the rationale behind them.
The author of the book intended to ask more difficult questions at the end of each chapter. Thus, we created a data split accordingly. The *rational data split* divides the first *80%* of questions of each chapter into the train set, the following *10%* of questions into the dev set, and the last *10%* into the test set.

Are there any errors, sources of noise, or redundancies in the dataset? If so, please provide a description.
Since each question has multiple possible answers and each answer is assigned to a separate instance, there are redundancies in the content of the question, the complete analysis, and the explanation. For each instance, the analysis is also contained in the complete analysis.

Is the dataset self-contained, or does it link to or otherwise rely on external resources (e.g., websites, tweets, other datasets)? If it links to or relies on external resources, a) are there guarantees that they will exist, and remain constant, over time; b) are there official archival versions of the complete dataset (i.e., including the external resources as they existed at the time the dataset was created); c) are there any restrictions (e.g., licenses, fees) associated with any of the external resources that might apply to a future user? Please provide descriptions of all external resources and any restrictions associated with them, as well as links or other access points, as appropriate.
The dataset is self-contained. However, answering the questions requires an understanding of US civil procedure, which may change over time.

Does the dataset contain data that might be considered confidential (e.g., data that is protected by legal privilege or by doctor-patient confidentiality, data that includes the content of individuals non-public communications)? If so, please provide a description.
No.

Does the dataset contain data that, if viewed directly, might be offensive, insulting, threatening, or might otherwise cause anxiety? If so, please describe why.
Some instances discuss civil procedure cases, which may discuss socially relevant issues like discrimination or racism.

Does the dataset relate to people? If not, you may skip the remaining questions in this section.
Unknown to the authors of the datasheet.

Does the dataset identify any subpopulations (e.g., by age, gender)? If so, please describe how these subpopulations are identified and provide a description of their respective distributions within the dataset.
No.

Is it possible to identify individuals (i.e., one or more natural persons), either directly or indirectly (i.e., in combination with other data) from the dataset? If so, please describe how.
It is possible to identify some individuals indirectly by the occurrence of a name in a precedent. By looking up the precedent in an external source, a natural person can be inferred. (e.g. Swift v. Tyson)

Does the dataset contain data that might be considered sensitive in any way (e.g., data that reveals racial or ethnic origins, sexual orientations, religious beliefs, political opinions or union memberships, or locations; financial or health data; biometric or genetic data; forms of government identification, such as social security numbers; criminal history)? If so, please provide a description.
No.

Any other comments? None.

Collection Process

How was the data associated with each instance acquired? Was the data directly observable (e.g., raw text, movie ratings), reported by subjects (e.g., survey responses), or indirectly inferred/derived from other data (e.g., part-of-speech tags, model-based guesses for age or language)? If data was reported by subjects or indirectly inferred/derived from other data, was the data validated/verified? If so, please describe how.
The data was directly observable as raw text, except for the labels and the specific analysis, which were annotated and extracted manually. The data was collected from *The Glannon Guide To Civil Procedure*.

What mechanisms or procedures were used to collect the data (e.g., hardware apparatus or sensor, manual human curation, software program, software API)? How were these mechanisms or procedures validated?
The data was gathered by automatically parsing the book *The Glannon Guide To Civil Procedure* through the python library *fitz*[5]. The separation could mostly be done through rule based parsing. Only the labels, and the specific analyses were annotated manually. Correctness of the data parsing method was validated manually.

If the dataset is a sample from a larger set, what was the sampling strategy (e.g., deterministic, probabilistic with specific sampling probabilities)?
N/A.

Who was involved in the data collection process (e.g., students, crowdworkers, contractors) and how were they compensated (e.g., how much were crowdworkers paid)?
Unknown to the authors of the datasheet.

Over what timeframe was the data collected? Does this timeframe match the creation timeframe of the data associated with the instances (e.g., recent crawl of old news articles)? If not, please describe the timeframe in which the data associated with the instances was created.
Unknown to the authors of the datasheet.

[5]https://github.com/pymupdf/PyMuPDF

Were any ethical review processes conducted (e.g., by an institutional review board)? If so, please provide a description of these review processes, including the outcomes, as well as a link or other access point to any supporting documentation.
Unknown to the authors of the datasheet.

Does the dataset relate to people? If not, you may skip the remaining questions in this section.
Unknown to the authors of the datasheet.

Did you collect the data from the individuals in question directly, or obtain it via third parties or other sources (e.g., websites)?
N/A.

Were the individuals in question notified about the data collection? If so, please describe (or show with screenshots or other information) how notice was provided, and provide a link or other access point to, or otherwise reproduce, the exact language of the notification itself.
Unknown to the authors of the datasheet.

Did the individuals in question consent to the collection and use of their data? If so, please describe (or show with screenshots or other information) how consent was requested and provided, and provide a link or other access point to, or otherwise reproduce, the exact language to which the individuals consented.
Unknown to the authors of the datasheet.

If consent was obtained, were the consenting individuals provided with a mechanism to revoke their consent in the future or for certain uses? If so, please provide a description, as well as a link or other access point to the mechanism (if appropriate).
Unknown to the authors of the datasheet.

Has an analysis of the potential impact of the dataset and its use on data subjects (e.g., a data protection impact analysis) been conducted? If so, please provide a description of this analysis, including the outcomes, as well as a link or other access point to any supporting documentation.
No.

Any other comments?

None.

Preprocessing/cleaning/labeling

Was any preprocessing/cleaning/labeling of the data done (e.g., discretization or bucketing, tokenization, part-of-speech tagging, SIFT feature extraction, removal of instances, processing of missing values)? If so, please provide a description. If not, you may skip the remainder of the questions in this section. Instances in which the correct answer refers to other answers (e.g. "Answer C and D are correct" were removed. For these instances, the solution label was adjusted such that the two answers were labeled as correct.

Was the "raw" data saved in addition to the preprocessed/cleaned/labeled data (e.g., to support unanticipated future uses)? If so, please provide a link or other access point to the "raw" data.
No.

Is the software used to preprocess/clean/label the instances available? If so, please provide a link or other access point. `https://github.com/trusthlt/legal-argument-reasoning-task`.

Any other comments?
None.

Uses

Has the dataset been used for any tasks already? If so, please provide a description.
No.

Is there a repository that links to any or all papers or systems that use the dataset? If so, please provide a link or other access point.
No.

What (other) tasks could the dataset be used for?
The dataset can be used for any NLP research related to civil procedure. For example, the provided answer analysis could allow natural language generation models to automatically generate an analysis.

Is there anything about the composition of the dataset or the way it was collected and preprocessed/cleaned/labeled that might impact future uses? For example, is there anything that a future user might need to know to avoid uses that could result in unfair treatment of individuals or groups (e.g., stereotyping, quality of service issues) or other undesirable harms (e.g., financial harms, legal risks) If so, please provide a description. Is there anything a future user could do to mitigate these undesirable harms?
There is no risk.

Are there tasks for which the dataset should not be used? If so, please provide a description.
We advocate using the dataset for tasks in the legal domain because the linguistic properties in Legal NLP may differ slightly from the general domain of argumentation and reasoning. Please also note the terms of use.

Any other comments?
None.

Distribution

Will the dataset be distributed to third parties outside of the entity (e.g., company, institution, organization) on behalf of which the dataset was created? If so, please provide a description.
Yes, the dataset will be available for non-commercial research purposes only for three years beginning July 1, 2022.

How will the dataset will be distributed (e.g., tarball on website, API, GitHub) Does the dataset have a digital object identifier (DOI)?
The dataset can be obtained by contacting ivan.habernal@tu-darmstadt.de. There is no DOI.

When will the dataset be distributed?
The dataset was first released at [to be updated upon paper acceptance and publication].

Will the dataset be distributed under a copyright or other intellectual property (IP) license, and/or under applicable terms of use (ToU)? If so, please describe this license and/or ToU, and provide a link or other access

point to, or otherwise reproduce, any relevant licensing terms or ToU, as well as any fees associated with these restrictions.
The parsed data copyright belongs to the author of the book *The Glannon Guide To Civil Procedure*. The corpus can only be used under the folowing conditions: 1. The dataset gathered is used only for the purpose of Natural Language Processing (NLP) experiments with the aim to enhance legal NLP models and show their current incapability of reasoning (and not, under any circumstances, for commercial purposes). 2. The dataset may not be distributed further and must be deleted after completing the experiments. 3. For each publication based on the dataset, credit will be given to the author of the book and the publisher.

Have any third parties imposed IP-based or other restrictions on the data associated with the instances? If so, please describe these restrictions, and provide a link or other access point to, or otherwise reproduce, any relevant licensing terms, as well as any fees associated with these restrictions.
No.

Do any export controls or other regulatory restrictions apply to the dataset or to individual instances? If so, please describe these restrictions, and provide a link or other access point to, or otherwise reproduce, any supporting documentation.
No.

Any other comments?
None.

Maintenance

Who will be supporting/hosting/maintaining the dataset?
Ivan Habernal is supporting/hosting the dataset.

How can the owner/curator/manager of the dataset be contacted (e.g., email address)?
ivan.habernal@tu-darmstadt.de

Is there an erratum? If so, please provide a link or other access point.
No.

Will the dataset be updated (e.g., to correct labeling errors, add new instances, delete instances)? If so, please describe how often, by whom, and how updates will be communicated to users (e.g., mailing list, GitHub)?
No substantial updates are planned, however, we will fix bugs if any are reported and communicate accordingly through the standard channels (e.g., GitHub, Twitter).

If the dataset relates to people, are there applicable limits on the retention of the data associated with the instances (e.g., were individuals in question told that their data would be retained for a fixed period of time and then deleted)? If so, please describe these limits and explain how they will be enforced.
No.

Will older versions of the dataset continue to be supported/hosted/maintained? If so, please describe how. If not, please describe how its obsolescence will be communicated to users.
No.

If others want to extend/augment/build on/contribute to the dataset, is there a mechanism for them to do so? If so, please provide a description. Will these contributions be validated/verified? If so, please describe how. If not, why not? Is there a process for communicating/distributing these contributions to other users? If so, please provide a description.
No.

Any other comments?
None.

Efficient Deep Learning-based Sentence Boundary Detection in Legal Text

Reshma Sheik and **Gokul T. Adethya** and **Dr. S. Jaya Nirmala**
Department of Computer Science and Engineering
National Institute of Technology, Tiruchirappalli, Tamil Nadu, India
rezmasheik@gmail.com

Abstract

A key component of the Natural Language Processing (NLP) pipeline is Sentence Boundary Detection (SBD). Erroneous SBD could affect other processing steps and reduce performance. A few criteria based on punctuation and capitalization are necessary to identify sentence borders in well-defined corpora. However, due to several grammatical ambiguities, the complex structure of legal data poses difficulties for SBD. In this paper, we have trained a neural network framework for identifying the end of the sentence in legal text. We used several state-of-the-art deep learning models, analyzed their performance, and identified that Convolutional Neural Network(CNN) outperformed other deep learning frameworks. We compared the results with rule-based, statistical, and transformer-based frameworks. The best neural network model outscored the popular rule-based framework with an improvement of 8% in the F1 score. Although domain-specific statistical models have slightly improved performance, the trained CNN is 80 times faster in run-time and doesn't require much feature engineering. Furthermore, after extensive pre-training, the transformer models fall short in overall performance compared to the best deep learning model.

1 Introduction

From linguistic theory, a sentence is a textual segment or span of one or more grammatically correct words representing a complete thought. Declarative statements, questions, exclamations, requests, commands, and suggestions can all be expressed in sentences. A grammatical subject and grammatical predicate are typically present in an expressive sentence. The person, place, or object (including abstract concepts) that the sentence is about is the grammatical subject, which is typically a noun phrase, and a verb phrase serves as the grammatical predicate(Savelka et al., 2017).

It is quite simple for a person to separate a given text into sentences. However, one realizes how difficult this task is when attempting to condense this segmentation into rules that a machine could follow. Many Natural Language Processing (NLP) applications, including part-of-speech taggers, named entity recognition, document indexing, and question-answering, use sentence boundary detection as a crucial pre-processing step. The pre-processing requirements depend on both the nature of the corpus and the NLP application. Thus SBD faces challenges when working with a specialized corpus like legal text because it offers issues distinguishing between citations, abbreviations, and law-specific keywords.

Existing SBD systems work well for generic corpora but pose serious issues when dealing with Legal Domain. The language, structure, and content are very different and more challenging to understand. When working with SBD, the fundamental presumptions used with the generic corpora are not always applicable. Legal documents typically consist of smaller components like paragraphs, sentences, etc. Sentences can be lengthy and contain intricate structures like lists. There is no standard formatting structure or style for legal documents, even those of the same category (such as statutes or judgments). A sentence segmentation system must resolve these issues to create pure sentences from the mixture of such diverse textual elements.

One main difficulty in SBD is to pinpoint potential boundary spots(e.g. "."). The uncertainty of the delimiter period "." symbol, which has multiple purposes in the legal domain, makes it challenging. It could denote the end of a sentence, an acronym, an initialism, a numerical number (Grefenstette and Tapanainen, 1994), or part of a citation in legal text. To determine if a punctuation character is actually a sentence end marker, a sentence boundary detection system must to resolve the issue of using ambiguous punctuation characters.

Proceedings of the Natural Legal Language Processing Workshop 2022, pages 208 - 217
December 8, 2022 ©2022 Association for Computational Linguistics

With this motivation of identifying the potential end-of-sentence marker, we build a deep-learning architectural framework using the context at the character level surrounding the period as input.

The main contribution of this paper is that we use a context window-based deep learning framework for sentence boundary detection in legal text. We compared various deep learning models, identified the best framework, and compared the models with the existing state-of-the-art rule-based and statistical models. We also compared the deep learning model with various transformer architectures like LEGAL-BERT(Chalkidis et al., 2020) and XL-Net(Yang et al., 2019).

The rest of the paper is organized as follows: Section 2 provides an existing literature summary of earlier studies about sentence boundary detection. Section 3 gives a brief description of the dataset and its associated pre-processing. We describe our methodologies and the suggested neural network architecture in Section 4. Section 5 covers results with evaluation techniques and performance comparisons. Finally, the paper concludes with some future steps in Section 6.

2 Related Work

Sentence Boundary Detection in a normal English text is regarded as an answered problem with robust methods. In the NLP literature, several methods for identifying sentence borders have been studied, encompassing algorithms and models ranging from rule-based, statistical, and machine learning-based models. Several techniques for recognizing sentence boundaries across various corpora are presented in the seminal paper(Read et al., 2012).

Decision tree algorithm, Support Vector Machines (SVM)(Gillick, 2009), Bayesian networks, and unsupervised methods like Punkt(Kiss and Strunk, 2006) are among the various algorithms for generic SBD. The identification of sentence boundaries in speech transcriptions is crucial for enhancing readability and supporting later language processing modules. In (Liu et al., 2005), prosodic and textual information sources are used to identify speech sentence boundaries, and (Donabauer et al., 2021) detect sentence boundaries and speaker changes in the unpunctuated text. Recently a well-known rule-based model called Pragmatic Sentence Boundary Disambiguation(pySBD)(Sadvilkar and Neumann, 2020) with more than 98 percent test coverage was developed as an open-source package. PySBD supports 22 languages and is robust in noisy text and domains. We have used pySBD as our baseline model for comparison. In general, these algorithms work well for processing text that adheres to the rules of normal English but operates poorly in other areas. To yield acceptable findings in fields like medical(Le et al., 2021), scientific(Miah et al., 2022), legal, and finance areas(Au et al., 2020), the algorithms used are heavily customized.

The main issues with current Legal SBD systems are a lack of compliance with known sentence patterns, sentence length, and the use of punctuation, particularly periods as non-sentence ending characters. Legal experts use "linguistic indications, structure, and semantic interpretations which interact with domain knowledge" (Wyner and Peters, 2011). (Savelka et al., 2017) examines the use of conditional random fields (CRF) models (Lafferty et al., 2001) for sentence boundary identification in legal documents since these models are frequently used for sequence modeling, or assigning labels for the items in the connected input sequence. Here they developed many CRF models using basic textual features. They employed an aggressive tokenization technique that divides the text into more tokens than normal. The tokens are represented using simple features like the length of the token, whether it is a digit or space, or is written in upper-case or lower-case, etc. A token's features are a combination of its characteristics and features obtained from nearby tokens. For the final model's training, these corresponding feature extractors were utilized, which led to an increase in the inference time of the models. Later (Sanchez, 2019) examined the same dataset with Punkt, CRF, and Bidirectional LSTM neural network architecture. They enhanced the performance of the Punkt model by training it with an updated abbreviation set based on the legal text domain. In neural network architecture, the sentence token is represented by a concatenation of word2vec(Mikolov et al., 2013) embeddings using a three-word window and eight features fed as input to the stacked BiLSTM network with a softmax layer as output. They concluded that this token classification architecture did not result in an SBD that was superior to the CRF model.

The issue of detecting sentence boundaries can be viewed as a classification problem. So our work is inspired by (Schweter and Ahmed, 2019) which

Decisions	#Docs	#Chars	#Tokens	#Sentences	#Average Tokens/Sentence
CC	20	984,756	367,740	8295	19.82
IP	20	932,133	343,831	7,262	21.42
BVA	20	474,478	170,166	3,727	20.73
SC	20	960,890	31,872	602	24.20
Total	80	3,352,257	1,237,414	26,052	21.54

Table 1: Statistics of the dataset

Delimiter	#Occurences	#Occurrence as EOS
.	45048	17835
:	1221	287
!	28	5
;	2453	18

Table 2: Delimiter and its occurences in the dataset

builds an end-to-end methodology independent of the effectiveness of any tokenization technique to make the classification. They developed a general-purpose framework for identifying the potential end-of-sentence markers that can be adapted to multi-lingual benchmarks for 12 distinct languages which work on zero-shot scenarios resulting in building a robust, language-independent SBD.

In addition to processing English legal texts, (Glaser et al., 2021) used CRF and neural network architectures to find the sentence boundaries in German legal documents. They produced and released a dataset of numerous German legal papers with annotations. However, none of the previous literature has applied transformer-based pre-trained language models for the SBD in the legal domain at the context level and used domain-specific transformer models like LEGAL-BERT.

3 Dataset

The algorithm was trained using a dataset (Savelka et al., 2017) of 80 court decisions in four different domains: Cyber Crime (CC), Intellectual Properties (IP), Board of Veterans (BVA), and the United States Supreme Court (SC). These decisions were put in four JSON files of 20 decisions each, along with the list of offsets that denotes the sentence boundaries. The complete dataset of 26052 annotated sentences is publicly available. [1] The summary of the statistics of the four decision sets is specified in Table 1.

The dataset composition of the delimiter occurrences is shown in Table 2. We focused on identifying the period as a potential end-of-sentence (EOS) marker even though the method of SBD can be used for various delimiters. This is because, compared to other delimiters in legal text, the period symbol frequently appears as the EOS markers (98.3%), and the dataset is insufficient to train deep learning models for other delimiters. Furthermore, only 40% of the period's occurrences in the dataset are identified as true boundary delimiters, making it challenging to classify.

3.1 Data Preprocessing

All models were trained using BVA, IP, and SC decisions and tested using CC decisions. The protocol outlined in (Sanchez, 2019) served as the foundation for the manual sentence demarcation for the test file. The sentence in the files was extracted using offset boundaries, and the start and end words were given the labels *BEGIN* and *END* based on the positions provided in the dataset. This annotation is required for comparison with the baseline frameworks. For the deep learning model architecture, the character level context window is taken and retained as input to the model after the period (delimiter) symbol has been located inside the files. For the transformer architecture, we extract the context at the sub-word level.

4 Model Architecture

The architecture of the deep learning framework is depicted in Fig. 1. This context window-based model architecture is used for training sequence classification neural network models. Once the file identifies the delimiter, the corresponding left and right contexts with efficient window size are

[1] https://github.com/jsavelka/sbd_adjudicatory_dec

Raw chunk	*Left Context*	*Delimiter*	*Right Context*	**Input Chunk**
12d 95. The r	12d 95	.	The r	12d 95 The r

Table 3: Example of the input

taken and fed as input to the embedding layer. The input embeddings from the embedding layer are provided to the deep learning model framework and bypassed to an optional attention layer. The last vector output from this framework is fed into the dense layer with sigmoid activation. Thus, this architecture serves as a binary classification model to determine if the period denotes the end of the sentence or not.

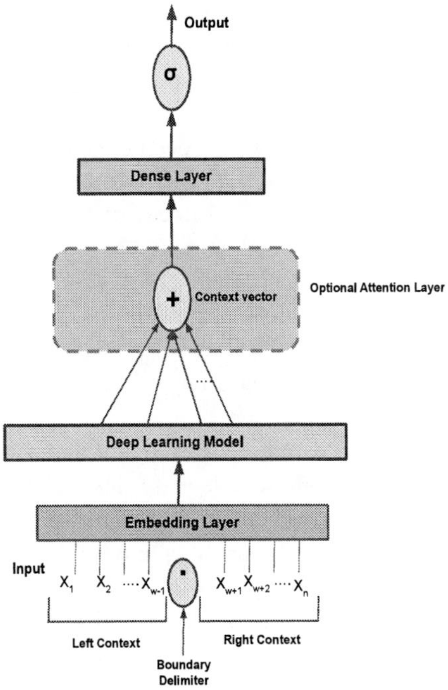

Figure 1: Model Architecture

4.1 Deep Learning Models

Here we used five different architectures of neural networks: Long Short Term Memory(LSTM)(Gers et al., 2000), Gated Recurrent Unit(GRU)(Chung et al., 2014), Bidirectional LSTM(BiLSTM), Bidirectional GRU(BiGRU), and Convolutional Neural Network(CNN). BiLSTM and BiGRU neural network models were also trained to incorporate the attention mechanisms(Bahdanau et al., 2014) to attend to and focus on key parts in input sentences. Each of these models captures information data at the character level. Given the context of surrounding characters, our models identify likely end-of-sentence markers. Our model takes the concatenation of this left and right context excluding the delimiter. This fixed-size context window is fed as input to the model. Table 3 shows an example of the input along with the retrieved left and right contexts.

4.1.1 LSTM

We employ a typical 128-embedding size LSTM network with a hidden size of 256. A dropout probability of 0.2 is used at the hidden layer. The final output vector from the LSTM is fed to the dense layer with a sigmoid activation to classify the output.

4.1.2 BiLSTM

To provide more effect to context, here we used a Bidirectional LSTM architecture that processes input text sequences in the forward and backward directions thus making input size to 512 when feeding to subsequent dense layer. Other factors used are comparable to the LSTM design.

4.1.3 BiLSTM with Attention

Attention weights are used to incorporate an attention mechanism into the BiLSTM architecture(Lin et al., 2017). In this model, soft alignment scores between each hidden state and the final hidden state of the LSTM will be computed using attention. Thus drawing out global dependencies between the inputs and output using the attention process.

4.1.4 GRU

GRU is a more condensed form of LSTM that uses fewer parameters as there is no explicit memory unit. The GRU uses 256 hidden states and an embedding size of 128. During the training process, We employ dropout with a probability of 0.2 after the hidden layer.

4.1.5 BiGRU

The design of this framework is identical to that of BiLSTM, using GRU in place of LSTM.

4.1.6 BiGRU with Attention

Adding attention to the BiGRU architecture enables the inputs to interact and determine who deserves more attention. These interactions and attention scores are combined to create the outputs.

4.1.7 CNN

We used a 1D convolution layer for the CNN architecture with six filters and a kernel size of five. The output of the convolution filter is concatenated to represent the context after being fed through a global max pooling layer. Before the prediction layer, we apply a 250-dimensional hidden layer with ReLU activation and a learning rate of 0.001. A dropout with a 0.2 probability is used during training.

4.2 Transformer Based Models

In contrast to the deep learning architectures discussed above, the transformer-based encoder model reads the input at the subword level as the models used here are pre-trained using sub-word level tokens as input. Six subwords on the left and right of the delimiter period are extracted and concatenated without the delimiter to provide input to the sequence classification model. In our experiments, we have used the pre-trained language models LEGAL-BERT and XLNet.

4.2.1 LEGAL-BERT

LEGAL-BERT(Chalkidis et al., 2020) is a family of BERT models designed to aid in legal NLP research. There are three options of LEGAL-BERT used in the paper for domain adaptation. They are (i) using the original BERT straight out of the box, (ii) adding extra pre-training on domain-specific corpora, and (iii) pre-train BERT from scratch on domain-specific corpora. Here in our experiments, we have used legal-bert-base-uncased, a model trained from scratch in the legal corpora with a number of output labels fixed as two.

4.2.2 XLNet

In the generalized autoregressive model known as XLNet(Yang et al., 2019), each subsequent token depends on every preceding token. XLNet is "generalized" because it uses a process known as "permutation language modeling" to capture bidirectional context. It overcomes the drawbacks of BERT while integrating the concepts of autoregressive models and bi-directional context modeling. We have used xlnet-base-cased models for our experiments.

4.3 Experimental Setup

We have used the Torch version '1.12.1+cu113' for implementation and the Hugging Face library [2] for fine-tuning the pre-trained language models. The deep learning models were trained for a maximum of 25 epochs, whereas the transformer models got trained for ten epochs. The optimal number of epochs and the model's training time per epoch are shown in Table 4. When compared to other models, it has been found that the transformer models require around 40 times more training time than CNN models. The training/validation loss, accuracy, and F1-score concerning the number of epochs for the CNN architecture are shown in Fig. 2, 3, and 4, respectively. In our tests, we experimented with a one-side context size ranging from 3 to 10 and observed that the context size of six characters produces a better result in deep learning models. The inefficiencies in the fixed-size context input are padded with extra token embedding(s). Since our models are trained on period as the only delimiter, including them in the input did not show any performance improvement. The addition of an extra input delimiter can be used for extending the same architecture to handle multiple delimiters(Schweter and Ahmed, 2019).

With a learning rate of $1e-3$ and a mini-batch size of 32, all models are trained using averaged stochastic gradient descent algorithm. The optimizer used is the Adam optimizer(Kingma and Ba, 2015) with binary cross entropy as a loss function. For pre-trained models, we used a learning rate of $5e-5$. The code used for experimenting with the models is publicly available. [3]

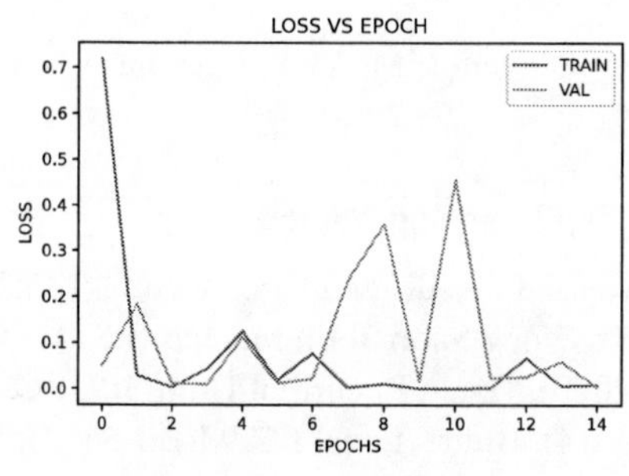

Figure 2: Loss vs Epoch

[2]https://huggingface.co/

[3]https://github.com/NLLP-ML/SBD

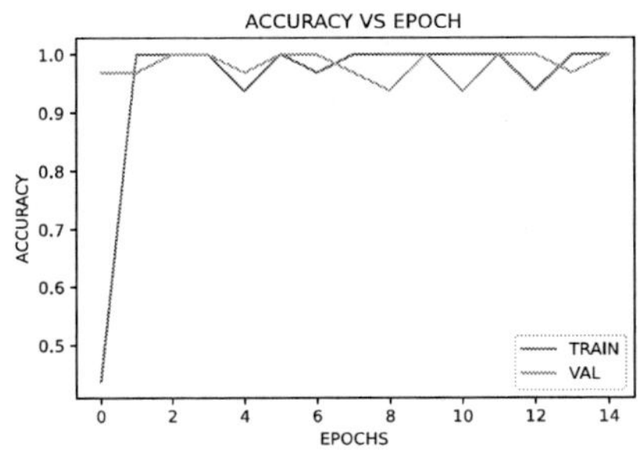

Figure 3: Accuracy vs Epoch

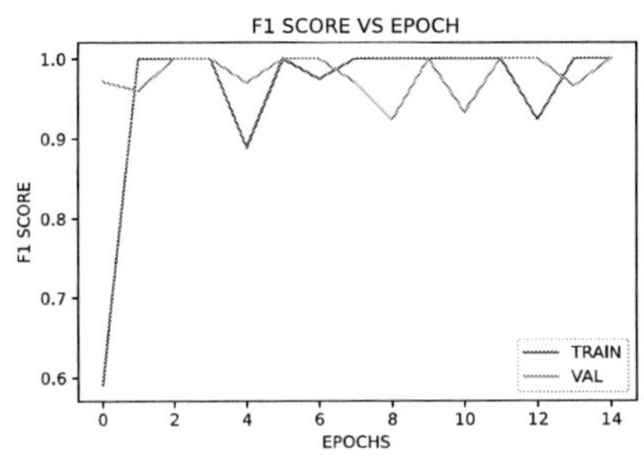

Figure 4: F1 Score vs Epoch

Model	#Epochs	Training time/ epoch (in sec)
LSTM	10	1.88
BiLSTM	10	2.87
BiLSTM + attn	10	2.98
GRU	15	1.86
BiGRU	10	2.86
BiGRU + attn	25	3.06
CNN	15	**1.78**
LEGAL-BERT	10	94.24
XLNet	4	106.61

Table 4: No: of epochs with average training time

Moreover, the number of trainable parameters is also higher for transformer-based models, as shown in Table 5. Thus it can be trained effectively with the help of GPU architectures. The CNN models are the best in model size and number of trainable parameters.

Model	Model size	# Parameters
LSTM	1.55 MB	4,08,449
BiLSTM	3.21 MB	8,03,969
BiLSTM + attn	3.21 MB	8,03,969
GRU	1.18 MB	3,09,633
BiGRU	2.31 MB	6,06,337
BiGRU + attn	2.31 MB	6,06,337
CNN	**116 kB**	**29,275**
LEGAL-BERT	418 MB	110M
XLNet	449 MB	110M

Table 5: Number of trainable parameters

5 Results and Discussion

We organize the results into three subsections. The first two sections focus on evaluation patterns used in our research to compare with the existing state-of-the-art models. In the first section, we compare the deep learning models against the baseline models based on offset boundaries. The second evaluation provides an inference time-based performance analysis of all the models. The final result section covers the performance assessment of the deep learning models to the architecture for the binary classification task.

5.1 Evaluation based on Offset Boundaries

Since the baseline models are evaluated based on offset boundaries, we post-process the results obtained from the deep learning architecture to label the words representing *BEGIN* and *END* tokens. Each document in the test set was sentence tokenized, and the model assigned the predicted labels for the test file.

Table 6 summarizes the results with other baseline models. We calculate the F1 score for each model at the *BEGIN* and *END* token levels. We used the state-of-the-art rule-based pySBD model and statistical Conditional Random Field(CRF) model as baselines. The result shows that the CNN model outperformed other neural network architectures and the pySBD framework. It is also observed that the statistical CRF has a slightly better F1 score than the CNN model. This might be due to

Comparison - Neural Network Models			
Model	*Begin*	*Last*	*Average F1-Score*
LSTM	0.809	0.862	0.8354
BiLSTM	0.805	0.853	0.8292
BiLSTM + attn	0.811	0.859	0.8347
GRU	0.809	0.859	0.8342
BiGRU	0.808	0.855	0.8316
BiGRU + attn	0.803	0.851	0.8267
CNN	0.822	0.871	**0.8464**
LEGAL-BERT	0.827	0.865	0.8462
XLNet	0.801	0.849	0.8247
Comparison - Other Models			
Model	*Begin*	*Last*	*Average F1-Score*
Rule-based pySBD	0.751	0.77	0.761
Statistical -CRF(Sanchez, 2019)	0.894	0.892	0.893

Table 6: Comparison at token level (F1- score)

the CRF models' ability to locate boundary delimiters other than periods in the legal text. However, its performance level depends on how inventively the features were created.

5.1.1 Error Analysis

The errors in SBD identified by the CNN and CRF models had many things in common. Both models found it challenging to identify the characters out of the sentence as in examples 1 and 2 in Table 7. As shown in example 3, the CRF models had difficulty in finding out the true boundary with the delimiter ":", but CNN doesn't have that ability making it weaker than CRF models. In example 4, the best-performed CNN model could not capture sentences with multiple periods, whereas the CRF models could correctly identify the boundaries. Most of the citations within sentences are not properly handled by the baseline CRF models and are considered as separate sentences (Sanchez, 2019) as shown in example 5.

5.2 Comparison based on Inference Time

The run-time of the models for the exact hardware specification is shown in Table 8. It is evident that the CNN model has the fastest inference time and that of CRF models, with inference time 84 times longer than CNN models. The transformer models LEGAL-BERT and XLNet have the highest inference times of 112 and 113 seconds, respectively.

5.3 Comparison based on the Model Architecture

The results of the context window-based deep learning models are shown in Table 9. Here the performance of nine deep learning frameworks to correctly identify the end of sentence boundary in the legal text was showcased based on accuracy, precision, recall, and F1 score. The table makes it clear that CNN performed the best among others. Employing an attention mechanism to the LSTM/GRU architecture doesn't help in improving performance. The outcomes of the transformer models were not improved even after intensive pretraining. We have also observed that domain-specific LEGAL-BERT performed better in the F1 score when compared to the generic XLNet model. In light of the model size and runtime, the CNN models performed well.

Overall, we found that CNN outperformed the pySBD model and produced the best results among the deep-learning models. The best neural network model outperformed the popular rule-based framework by 8% in terms of the F1 score. In contrast to statistical models, the deep learning model's inference time is 84 times shorter. It is also possible to parallelize the SBD task at runtime by using batch processing in the proposed neural network architecture. LEGAL-BERT performs very close to the CNN model in the F1 score. Despite having scores that are on par with the CNN model, the domain-specific LEGAL-BERT models might be difficult

Example 1	See, e.g., Cal. Family Code Ann. §760 (West 2004). **Sentence 1:** 4 See, e.g., Cal. **Sentence 2:** Family Code Ann. §760 (West 2004).
Example 2	In the first case, petitioner David Riley was stopped by a police officer for driving with expired registration tags. I A In the first case, petitioner David Riley was stopped by a police officer for driving with expired registration tags.
Example 3	Decided: November 26, 2002. **Sentence 1:** Decided: **Sentence 2:** November 26, 2002.
Example 4	Id., at 180. . . ." Id., at 180.
Example 5	Franklin also moved to dismiss eleven of the fourteen copyright infringement counts on the ground that Apple failed to comply with the procedural requirements for suit under 17 U. S. C. § § 410, 411. < 714 F. 2 d 1245 >. **Sentence 1:** Franklin also moved to dismiss eleven of the fourteen copyright infringement counts on the ground that Apple failed to comply with the procedural requirements for suit under 17 U. S. C. § § 410, 411. **Sentence 2:** < 714 F. 2 d 1245 >.

Table 7: Errors in SBD: The actual sentence in the text is marked in grey, while the predicted sentence is marked in red.

Model	Runtime(in sec)
LSTM	0.85
BiLSTM	1.75
BiLSTM + attn	1.71
GRU	0.62
BiGRU	1.19
BiGRU + attn	1.31
CNN	**0.16**
LEGAL-BERT	112.86
XLNet	113.07
pySBD	5.50
CRF	13.41

Table 8: Inference time of models

to implement because of their high memory requirements and slow speeds. The CNN models display impressive performance given the model size, training, and testing times. As a result, CNN with a small number of trainable parameters outperformed huge models.

6 Conclusion

This paper uses a context window-based deep learning model framework for efficient sentence boundary detection in legal text. We compared various deep learning models, including transformers, for analysis. We showed that CNN showed a better performance when compared to other deep learning models. This model also outperformed the popular rule-based pySBD framework. Even though the statistical model has a minor performance improvement, the trained CNN had a decent performance without the requirement of exhaustive feature engineering compared to domain-specific CRF models. Also, CNN is faster than the state-of-the-art CRF models by multiple folds compared to the running time. As a result, the Convolutional Neural Network is the model with the best performance.

In the future, we plan to broaden the scope of our architecture by including the different delimiters found in legal text. Also, we aim to chain multiple models together to improve the SBD performance. However, we could demonstrate that our model had an excellent performance and could thus be incorporated into NLP pipelines for various downstream legal tasks.

Limitations

The major limitation addressed in this paper is the choice of delimiter used in the deep learning architecture. Here we have only used the period "." as the potential end of sentence marker in the legal text. We could explore more sentence ending punctuation's like colons ":", exclamation "!", etc., to the architecture and thereby improve the results. In

Model	Accuracy	Precision	Recall	F1-Score
LSTM	0.968	0.974	0.953	0.963
BiLSTM	0.964	0.970	0.945	0.957
BiLSTM + attn	0.967	0.971	0.952	0.961
GRU	0.966	0.973	0.947	0.960
BiGRU	0.967	0.969	0.951	0.960
BiGRU + attn	0.964	0.955	0.954	0.955
CNN	**0.981**	0.976	0.978	**0.977**
Legal-BERT	0.979	0.975	0.977	0.976
XLNet	0.970	0.939	0.993	0.965

Table 9: Results of the classification performance of the models

contrast to the pre-trained transformers, which are trained using sub-word level embedding, we have analyzed the performance of deep learning models using character-level embedding. The requirement of considerable GPU resources is another limitation of transformer-based models. More training data is also necessary for deep learning models to produce better results. These limitations can be future opportunities to facilitate further research.

Ethics Statement

Our work contributes to implementing deep learning models for sentence boundary detection in legal text. The dataset used in this paper is publicly available for research, and we have appropriately cited it in the article. The code we implemented is made open to facilitate future research.

References

Willy Au, Bianca Chong, Abderrahim Ait Azzi, and Dialekti Valsamou-Stanislawski. 2020. Finsbd-2020: The 2nd shared task on sentence boundary detection in unstructured text in the financial domain. In *Proceedings of the Second Workshop on Financial Technology and Natural Language Processing*, pages 47–54.

Dzmitry Bahdanau, Kyunghyun Cho, and Yoshua Bengio. 2014. Neural machine translation by jointly learning to align and translate. *arXiv preprint arXiv:1409.0473*.

Ilias Chalkidis, Manos Fergadiotis, Prodromos Malakasiotis, Nikolaos Aletras, and Ion Androutsopoulos. 2020. Legal-bert: The muppets straight out of law school. *arXiv preprint arXiv:2010.02559*.

Junyoung Chung, Caglar Gulcehre, KyungHyun Cho, and Yoshua Bengio. 2014. Empirical evaluation of gated recurrent neural networks on sequence modeling. *arXiv preprint arXiv:1412.3555*.

Gregor Donabauer, Udo Kruschwitz, and David Corney. 2021. Making sense of subtitles: Sentence boundary detection and speaker change detection in unpunctuated texts. In *Companion Proceedings of the Web Conference 2021*, pages 357–362.

Felix A Gers, Jürgen Schmidhuber, and Fred Cummins. 2000. Learning to forget: Continual prediction with lstm. *Neural computation*, 12(10):2451–2471.

Dan Gillick. 2009. Sentence boundary detection and the problem with the us. In *Proceedings of Human Language Technologies: The 2009 Annual Conference of the North American Chapter of the Association for Computational Linguistics, Companion Volume: Short Papers*, pages 241–244.

Ingo Glaser, Sebastian Moser, and Florian Matthes. 2021. Sentence boundary detection in german legal documents. In *ICAART (2)*, pages 812–821.

Gregory Grefenstette and Pasi Tapanainen. 1994. What is a word, what is a sentence? problems of tokenization.

Diederik P. Kingma and Jimmy Ba. 2015. Adam: A method for stochastic optimization. In *3rd International Conference on Learning Representations, ICLR 2015, San Diego, CA, USA, May 7-9, 2015, Conference Track Proceedings*.

Tibor Kiss and Jan Strunk. 2006. Unsupervised multilingual sentence boundary detection. *Computational linguistics*, 32(4):485–525.

John Lafferty, Andrew McCallum, and Fernando CN Pereira. 2001. Conditional random fields: Probabilistic models for segmenting and labeling sequence data.

Daniel X Le, James G Mork, and Sameer Antani. 2021. Hybrid ensemble-rule algorithm for improved medline® sentence boundary detection. In *AMIA Annual Symposium Proceedings*, volume 2021, page 677. American Medical Informatics Association.

Zhouhan Lin, Minwei Feng, Cicero Nogueira dos Santos, Mo Yu, Bing Xiang, Bowen Zhou, and Yoshua Bengio. 2017. A structured self-attentive sentence embedding. *arXiv preprint arXiv:1703.03130*.

Yang Liu, Andreas Stolcke, Elizabeth Shriberg, and Mary Harper. 2005. Using conditional random fields for sentence boundary detection in speech. In *Proceedings of the 43rd Annual Meeting of the Association for Computational Linguistics (ACL'05)*, pages 451–458, Ann Arbor, Michigan. Association for Computational Linguistics.

Md Miah, Saef Ullah, Junaida Sulaiman, Talha Bin Sarwar, Ateeqa Naseer, Fasiha Ashraf, Kamal Zuhairi Zamli, and Rajan Jose. 2022. Sentence boundary extraction from scientific literature of electric double layer capacitor domain: Tools and techniques. *Applied Sciences*, 12(3):1352.

Tomas Mikolov, Kai Chen, Greg Corrado, and Jeffrey Dean. 2013. Efficient estimation of word representations in vector space. *arXiv preprint arXiv:1301.3781*.

Jonathon Read, Rebecca Dridan, Stephan Oepen, and Lars Jørgen Solberg. 2012. Sentence boundary detection: A long solved problem? In *Proceedings of COLING 2012: Posters*, pages 985–994.

Nipun Sadvilkar and Mark Neumann. 2020. Pysbd: Pragmatic sentence boundary disambiguation. *arXiv preprint arXiv:2010.09657*.

George Sanchez. 2019. Sentence boundary detection in legal text. In *Proceedings of the natural legal language processing workshop 2019*, pages 31–38.

Jaromir Savelka, Vern R Walker, Matthias Grabmair, and Kevin D Ashley. 2017. Sentence boundary detection in adjudicatory decisions in the united states. *Traitement automatique des langues*, 58:21.

Stefan Schweter and Sajawel Ahmed. 2019. Deep-eos: General-purpose neural networks for sentence boundary detection. In *KONVENS*.

Adam Wyner and Wim Peters. 2011. On rule extraction from regulations. In *Legal Knowledge and Information Systems*, pages 113–122. IOS Press.

Zhilin Yang, Zihang Dai, Yiming Yang, Jaime Carbonell, Russ R Salakhutdinov, and Quoc V Le. 2019. Xlnet: Generalized autoregressive pretraining for language understanding. *Advances in neural information processing systems*, 32.

Tracking Semantic Shifts in German Court Decisions with Diachronic Word Embeddings

Daniel Braun
University of Twente
Department of High-tech Business and Entrepreneurship
d.braun@utwente.nl

Abstract

Language and its usage change over time. While legal language is arguably more stable than everyday language, it is still subject to change. Sometimes it changes gradually and slowly, sometimes almost instantaneously, for example through legislative changes. This paper presents an application of diachronic word embeddings to track changes in the usage of language by German courts triggered by changing legislation, based on a corpus of more than 200,000 documents. The results show the swift and lasting effect that changes in legislation can have on the usage of language by courts and suggest that using time-restricted word embedding models could be beneficial for downstream NLP tasks.

1 Introduction

Languages change over time on different levels, from phonetic and spelling changes to lexical changes, semantic changes, and syntactic changes. Semantic shifts, i.e. changes to the meaning of words, have been researched for hundreds of years, and different taxonomies exist for their classification, e.g. by Bloomfield (1933). These changes are often happening slowly over the course of many years, like the word "dog", which used to refer to a specific breed and now refers to all breeds (Hollmann, 2009), or the word "broadcast" that in the early 20th century meant "casting out seeds" and now refers to transmitting a signal (Hamilton et al., 2016).

Arguably, the stability of language is higher and more important in legal documents than in most other contexts. Many legal terms, but also terms that are used more freely in everyday language, are well-defined in the context of legal proceedings, either by laws or years of legal precedent. However, language and its meaning and interpretation also change in the context of legal practice. Very prominent examples of that can be found in constitutions. In many western democracies, constitutions are very stable documents whose texts are hardly changed in decades or sometimes even centuries. Yet, as societies and culture change, the interpretation of these documents by politicians and judges changes as well. Since its implementation in 1949, the first sentence of the second paragraph of article 3 of the German constitution reads "Männer und Frauen sind gleichberechtigt" (Men and women have equal rights). However, it was not until 1977, that a wife would not need the approval of her husband anymore to get a job. A practice that, beyond any doubt, would be ruled unconstitutional today based on the very same sentence. The reasons why the use of language in legal practice can change are manifold, just like in everyday language.

A reason that is particular to the legal domain are changes in legislation that can lead to semantic shifts that are unseen in other domains in speed and thoroughness. By introducing a new law or changing an existing law, legislators have the power to almost instantaneously change the meaning of a word in legal practice. An example of such a quick shift is the German word "Rundfunkbeitrag". Before 2013, a "Rundfunkbeitrag" was a TV or radio report. However, in January 2013, the "Rundfunkbeitragsstaatsvertrag"(broadcast fee state contract) renamed the German public broadcasting license fee from "Rundfunkgebühr" to "Rundfunkbeitrag", giving the word a new meaning that quickly has become predominant in legal proceedings (see Section 5). In everyday language, however, the new "Rundfunkbeitrag" is still regularly referred to by its old name.

In recent years, diachronic distributional models, and especially diachronic word embeddings, have been successfully used in different contexts to track semantic changes and changes in language use (see Section 2). The basic idea behind this approach is to train separate word embedding models based on documents from different time periods and then analyse how the word vectors for chosen terms

Proceedings of the Natural Legal Language Processing Workshop 2022, pages 218 - 227
December 8, 2022 ©2022 Association for Computational Linguistics

change between the different models (and hence over time) in relation to other terms (Kutuzov et al., 2018).

This paper presents an application of diachronic word embeddings to the legal domain and specifically focuses on the analysis of semantic shifts introduced by legislative changes. We trained multiple word embedding models on different temporal subsets of a corpus of more than 200,000 decisions from German courts provided by Open Legal Data (Ostendorff et al., 2020), containing texts from the 1970s to 2020.

The results show that diachronic word embeddings can capture immediate and permanent changes in the language used by courts after relevant legislation comes into force. These significant semantic shifts indicate that it could be beneficial for prediction and classification tasks that are connected to words that have undergone such a shift, to use word embeddings that are temporally aligned with this shift, even if that reduces the overall available data.

2 Related Work

In 2018, Kutuzov et al. presented a comprehensive survey on works on diachronic word embeddings, including the work of Hamilton et al. (2016), Liao and Cheng (2016), Kutuzov et al. (2017), Rosin et al. (2017), and many others. Therefore, we will focus on works published after 2018.

Kutuzov et al. (2018) found that, as is the case often, most of the existing work focuses on the English language. One notable recent exception from that is the work by Walter et al. (2021), in which the authors analysed a corpus of German parliamentary proceedings spanning from 1867 to 2020. They were, for example, able to show an increase in antisemitic rhetoric in the years leading to the seizure of power by the national socialists.

The data sources that have been used to train diachronic word embeddings in recent years are diverse. Tsakalidis et al. (2021), for example, used a corpus of websites from the UK called DUKweb, Brandl and Lassner (2019) used two newspaper corpora in English and German, and many researchers use the Google Books corpus (Boukhaled et al., 2019; Vijayarani and Geetha, 2020; Yüksel et al., 2021).

While multiple works have been published training diachronic word embeddings on political data and debates, including the previously mentioned work by Walter et al. (2021), but also work from Rozado and Al-Gharbi (2022) an Indukaev (2021), there is very little work focusing on the legal domain, although the idea that training diachronic distributional models on legal language could provide valuable insights has been voiced before (Rice, 2019).

Year(s)	# sentences	Avg. sentences/doc
1970-1979	3,014	26.2
1980-1989	22,102	27.4
1990-1999	170,082	26.4
2000-2009	1,991,396	31.6
2010-2019	4,957,720	38.5
2020	158,705	59.1
1970-2020	7,303,019	36.2

Table 1: Number of sentences and average number of sentences per document per decade

Soni et al. (2021) were the first, and, as far as we are aware, so far the only ones, to specifically train diachronic word embeddings on court decisions. By training on decisions from US federal courts, they were able to identify decisions that are "on the leading edge of semantic change" and show that such decisions are cited more often. While Soni et al. (2021) focused on semantic change that originates from the decisions themselves and happens at a moderate pace, this paper focuses on semantic change that is introduced to the decisions from an external source, the legislation.

3 Data Set

This work is based on the corpus provided by Open Legal Data (Ostendorff et al., 2020). It consists of over 200,000 German court rulings, published between April 2022 and April 1970, by different German courts, ranging from the "Bundesverfassungsgericht" (federal constitutional court) to "Amtsgerichte" (district courts). For reasons of reproducibility, we used the latest stable dump from December 2020[1], which contains data from April 1970 to December 2020. The dump consists of 201,824 documents from 626 courts.

Figure 1 shows the temporal distribution of the documents and the number of courts that contributed documents in each year. Over time, more and more courts started to publish their decisions digitally and courts also increased the number of

[1] https://static.openlegaldata.io/dumps/de/2020-12-10/

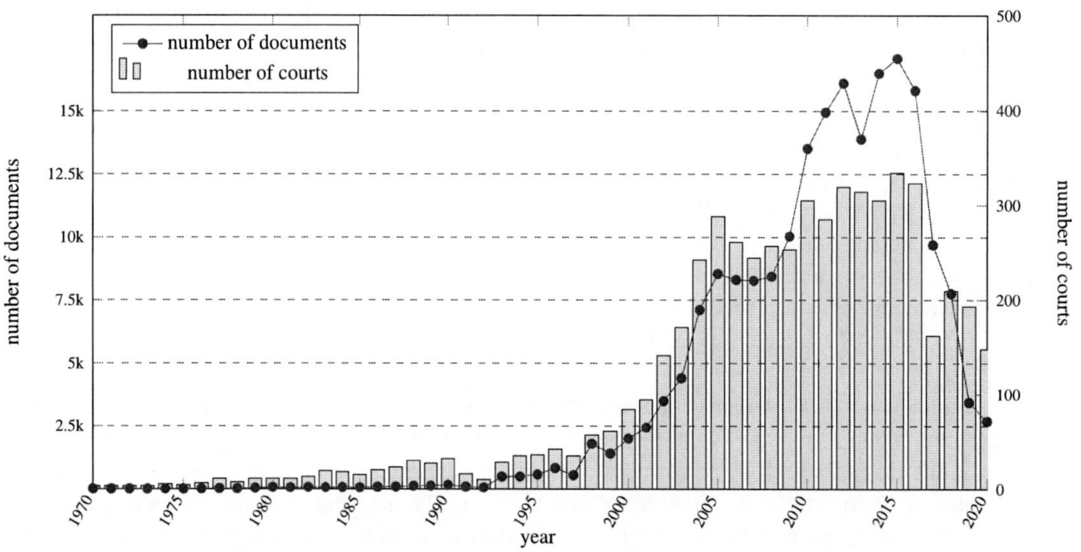

Figure 1: Number of documents per year and the number of courts these documents are from

decisions they published. Therefore, most of the documents in the data set are from recent years. And not only are there more decisions available from more recent years, but the average length of the documents also increased, as is shown in Table 1.

Such a temporal imbalance is very common in legal corpora and the results of this paper suggest, that diachronic word embeddings could help to mitigate the bias that is introduced by such an imbalanced corpus. However, since the available data before 2000 is very limited, with only three to 61 documents per year, we will focus on semantic shifts that happened after 2000.

4 Approach

In order to be able to identify the swift semantic shifts we expect to see based on changing legislation, we trained 51 word embedding models, one for each year from 1970 to 2020. That differentiates our approach from works like Hamilton et al. (2016) and Jatowt and Duh (2014), which focus on long-term shifts and therefore aggregate their data over decades. For reasons of comparability and in order to observe more long-term trends, we also trained five models, each of which is spanning a decade from the 1970s to the 2010s. Additionally, we also trained two larger models, one including all data before 2000 and one including all data from 2000 onwards. Lastly, we also trained a model based on all available data, i.e. data from the years 1970 to 2020, resulting in a total of 59 models.

4.1 Word Embeddings

We used the Python library gensim[2] in version 4.2.0 to train word embeddings with the Word2Vec algorithm (Mikolov et al., 2013). Before starting the training, the data has to be split into individual sentences and tokenized. We used the SoMaJo library (Proisl and Uhrig, 2016) for sentence splitting and tokenization because it has been shown to outperform other libraries on German legal texts (Braun, 2021; Schamel et al., 2022).

We used a window size of five and a vector size of 300 for the word embeddings. The initial learning rate was set to 0.025, the seed to 1, and all words that occurred in the data were included, independent of frequency.[3] Table 2 shows the sizes of the vocabularies for the models spanning a decade, showing a strong correlation between the vocabulary size and the number of sentences that were used to train the model.

4.2 Measuring Semantic Shifts

The algorithms that are used to train word embeddings are inherently stochastic, which means they will most likely return different vectors for the same words, even if they are run twice on the exact same data. Therefore, comparing the absolute values of

[2] `https://radimrehurek.com/gensim/`

[3] Parameters for the training: vector_size=300, window=5, alpha=0.025, min_count=1, sample=1e-3, seed=1, epochs=5, workers=4.

Year(s)	Vocabulary size
1970-1979	20,033
1980-1989	73,310
1990-1999	298,985
2000-2009	1,279,225
2010-2019	2,079,610
2020	204,645
1970-2020	3,322,051

Table 2: Size of the vocabularies of the different word embedding models

word embeddings from different models does not provide meaningful insights. Instead, we want to compare how the position of certain word vectors changes in relation to other word vectors. If, for example, in one model, based on older data, the vector of "to text" is closer to "advertising" than to "smartphone" and in another model, based on newer data, it moves away from "advertising" and closer to "smartphone", that indicates that the meaning of "to text" is shifting. The similarity of two word vectors can be measured with the cosine similarity. Another approach we use to investigate semantic shifts is looking at the closest neighbours of the word vector of a given word and how these change over time.

Lastly, in order to visualise the change of semantics over the decades in cases that are not related to new legislation, we follow the approach described by Hamilton et al. (2016): For each word that should be analysed, we calculate the union of the word's k nearest neighbours in each decade. We then mathematically align and map the different models into a shared two-dimensional system of coordinates, using Principle Component Analysis (PCA). We then plot the vector for the word that we want to analyse in each decade in this system of coordinates. As suggested by Hamilton et al. (2016) we only plot the most "modern" vector for the nearest neighbours, simplifying the plot.

5 Results

First, we will look at three examples of rapid semantic shifts that have been caused by changes in legislation (see Section 5.1). We selected three legislative changes which came into force between 2001 and 2013, in order to focus on time periods with sufficient data available. Afterwards, we will look at slower, more traditional patterns of semantic shift in which words change the context they are used in, based on broader societal changes (see Section 5.2). Finally, we will also take a brief look at changes on the level of the vocabulary (see Section 5.3).

5.1 Semantic Shifts caused by Legislation

With the introduction of the "Lebenspartnerschaftsgesetz" (Civil Partnership Act) in 2001 and subsequent changes, the meaning of the word "Lebenspartner" (life partner), as used by courts, shifted gradually from a somewhat vague personal relationship without any legal implications to the meaning of the word "Ehepartner" (spouse) and continued to move closer as the civil partnership received equal rights to the "traditional" marriage in more and more aspects.

Table 3 shows that in the model trained with data from before 2000, the most similar word to "Lebenspartner" is "Lebensgefährten", which can be seen as a synonym for "Lebenspartner" and also describes a personal relationship without any legal implications. After 2000, the most similar word is "Ehepartner" (spouse), even before "Lebenspartnerin", the female version of "Lebenspartner". This clearly indicates a semantic shift that also reflects the new legal implications connected with the word.

Figure 2 shows the cosine similarity between "Lebenspartner" and "Lebensgefährten" and "Ehepartner" for the aligned yearly models. It is notable that right in 2001 when the new legislation was implemented, the cosine similarity between "Lebenspartner" and "Ehepartner" rose significantly. And although there was a drop in the next year, from 2007 onwards, the cosine similarity between "Lebenspartner" and "Ehepartner" was constantly above the similarity of "Lebenspartner" and "Lebensgefährten".

In 2011, compulsory military service was suspended in Germany, ending 55 years of mandatory service and changing the "Wehrdienst" (military

Rank	1970 - 1999	2000 - 2020
1	lebensgefährten	ehepartner
2	reisepaß	lebenspartnerinnen
3	onkel	lebenspartnerschaft
4	vorgesetzen	ehegatten
5	freunden	lebenspartnern

Table 3: Five most similar words to the term "Lebenspartner" before and after 2000

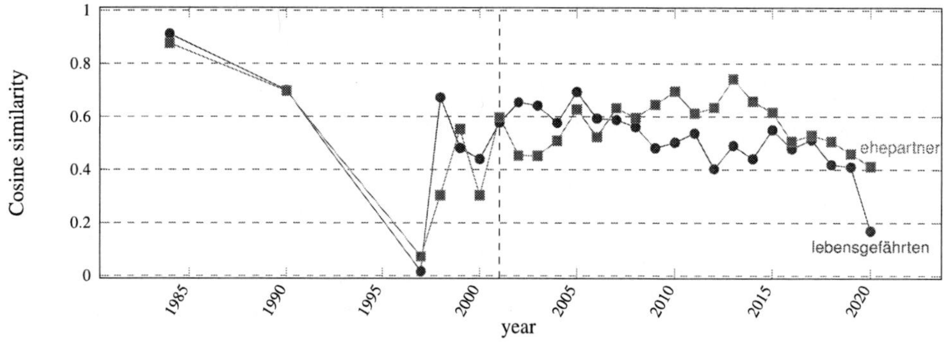

Figure 2: Cosine similarity between the word vector of "Lebenspartner" and "Lebensgefährten" and "Ehepartner" per year

service) from a mandatory to a voluntary service. This change in legislation is also well visible in the corpus of court documents. Before the mandatory service was suspended, the word "Wehrdienst" was closely related to the civilian substitute service ("Zivildienst", "Ersatzdienst"), as shown in Table 4. While "Militärdienst", a synonym for "Wehrdienst", remained the most similar word, the different words describing substitute service disappeared, indicating the shift of "Wehrdienst" from describing a mandatory service to describing a voluntary service.

On a more fine-grained level, an immediate effect is visible in the year 2011 in Figure 4, where the similarity between "Wehrdienst" and "Zivildienst" drops and continues to decline from there, until after 2019 the word is not even in the data anymore.

Rank	1970 - 1999	2000 - 2020
1	militärdienst	militärdienst
2	grundwehrdienst	islam
3	zivildienst	topographen
4	nationaldienst	lienhaushalt
5	ersatzdienst	christentum

Table 4: Five most similar words to the term "Wehrdienst" before and after 2000

In January 2013, the "Rundfunkbeitragsstaatsvertrag" (broadcast fee state contract) renamed the German public broadcasting license fee from "Rundfunkgebühr" to "Rundfunkbeitrag". Previously, a "Rundfunkbeitrag" would have been a TV or radio report. The new meaning of the word has been adopted very quickly in legal proceedings. Looking at the most similar words in Table 5 reveals an interesting pattern. Before 2000, all but one entry consist of dates, probably indicating that specific reports are referenced within the documents by the date they have been broadcasted. After 2000, there is a clear connection to the different other fees, as well as the old "Rundfunkgebühr".

On the yearly level, we can again see how the legislative change has immediate impact on the usage of the "Rundfunkbeitrag" and how it becomes more similar to "Rundfunkgebühr" in 2013.

Rank	1970 - 1999	2000 - 2020
1	07.09	rundfunkgebühr
2	22.12.1980	fremdenverkehrsbeitr.
3	11.8.	kammerbeitrag
4	25.05.1992	kurbeitrag
5	schürfwunde	rundfunkbeitrags-staatsvertrag

Table 5: Five most similar words to the term "Rundfunkbeitrag" before and after 2000

5.2 General Context Shifts

In addition to these specific and swift semantic shifts, that are introduced by legislative changes, we can also observe more "classical" semantic shifts in the data, for example, words that are used in different contexts over time. One word for which such a shift has been described often in literature is the word asylum (Hamilton et al., 2016; Wiedemann and Fedtke, 2021; Soni et al., 2021). In this corpus, the word "Asyl" (asylum, see Figure 5a) is after 2010 suddenly used very frequently in connection with "Österreich" (Austria) and other European countries, most likely because of refugees seeking asylum reaching Germany through these countries.

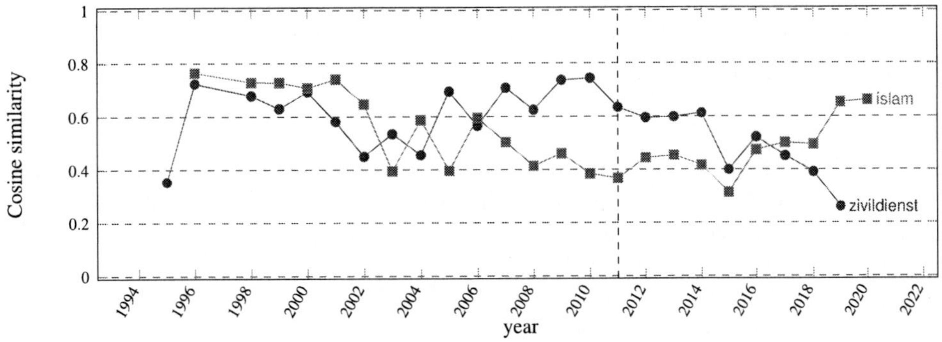

Figure 3: Cosine similarity between the word vector of "Wehrdienst" and "Zivildienst" and "Islam" per year

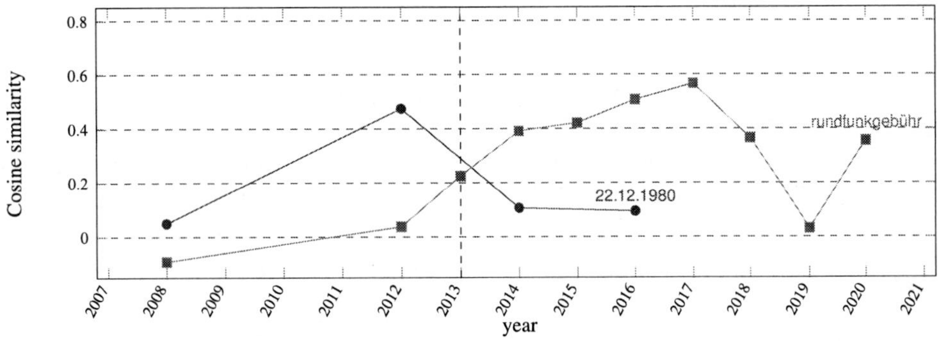

Figure 4: Cosine similarity between the word vector of "Rundfunkbeitrag" and "22.12.1980" and "Rundfunkgebühr" per year

Another shift can be observed for the word "Altlasten", as shown in Figure 5b. In the 1980s, the word was often used as a euphemism, in the sense of "legacy issues", to describe the fact that many of the leading figures in German society had already held their positions during the NS rule. Over time, the context in which the word is used, both in the corpus and in society, shifts to contaminated sites or polluted areas, a topic that gains more attention as environmental standards increase.

Other words for which the contexts they appear in have changed include "Freiheit" (freedom, see Figure 5c) and "Geschlecht" (sex and/or gender, see Figure 5d). In our current decade, freedom is in the corpus frequently used in the context of "Versammlungsfreiheit" (freedom of assembly), most likely connected to restrictions of this freedom as part of the measures against the COVID-19 pandemic. For "Geschlecht", German for both, sex and gender, we can see how it changes from a pure "technicality" (male or female) to a more complex interpretation including health and well-being.

5.3 Vocabulary Changes

Since the vocabularies of the 2000s and 2010s are significantly larger than the vocabularies of previous decades, many new words are found in the more recent models, that cannot be found in the older models. However, there is also a number of words and forms of spelling, that are only used in the documents pre-2000s. The German orthography reform in 1996 changed the spelling of numerous words, therefore, variants like "Prozeß" (process or in the legal context also lawsuit) or "wieviel" can only be found in models trained on data from earlier years. In addition, we can also observe words vanishing from the corpus because of changes in legislation, like the disappearance of the word "Zivildienst", mentioned in Section 5.1.

6 Discussion

The results of our analysis show that changes in legislation can cause almost instantaneous semantic changes in the language used by courts and that diachronic word embeddings can be used to track these semantic shifts.

For all instances discussed in the paper, the model that was trained on the complete corpus with data from 1970 to 2020 represented the same meaning as the post-2000 model, which was to be expected, given the temporal imbalance of the data. If we would want to work on historical decisions, or if a semantic shift would have happened only in 2020, the model trained on all data would most likely misinterpret the words for which a semantic shift has happened. That suggests that using diachronic word embeddings within downstream NLP tasks, like classification or outcome prediction, could be useful in cases where it is known that a word that is important in the context of the task has changed its meaning, e.g. through a change of the law or other significant events. In such cases, aligning the data with such events could help to improve performance, even if it means a reduced corpus for training.

6.1 Limitations

The imbalance of the corpus we used for this work limits the generalisability and reliability of the results:

- **Temporal imbalance:** With increasing digitization, the number of available decisions in the corpus also increases, therefore, the data for the 70s and 80s is very limited, affecting both, the comparability, as well as the quality of the word embedding models trained on the data. From 2020 alone, there are already more decisions available in the corpus than from the 70s and 80s combined.
- **Imbalance between courts and court levels:** The highest and higher courts have historically been among the first in Germany to publish their decisions (digitally), therefore, they are over-represented in the dataset, compared to their actual share in decisions made. There is also a difference in the availability of decisions from individual courts and regions, potentially biasing the results. The data from the 70s, for example, contains solely decisions from courts in North Rhine-Westphalia.

7 Conclusion

The paper presents an application of diachronic word embeddings to a data set of more than 200,000 German court rulings. 59 different embedding models have been trained, spanning different time spans from years to decades, in order to observe semantic shifts introduced by changes in legislation. The results show that these semantic shifts happen quickly and have a lasting influence on the language that is used by courts.

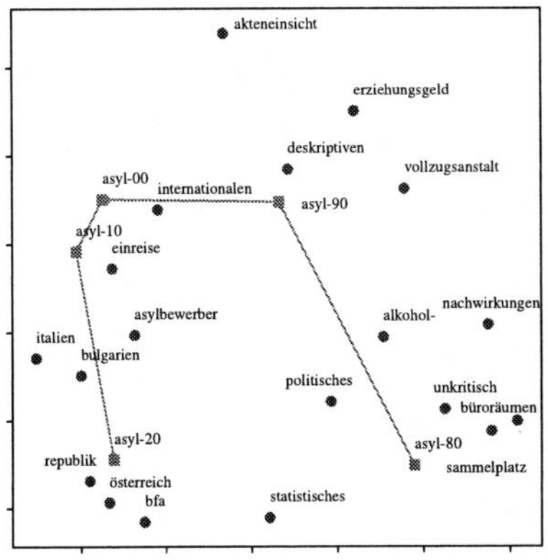

(a) Word "Asyl" (asylum)

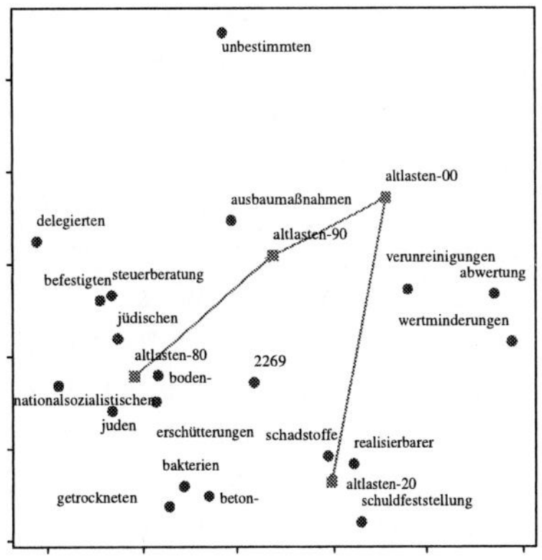

(b) Word "Altlasten"

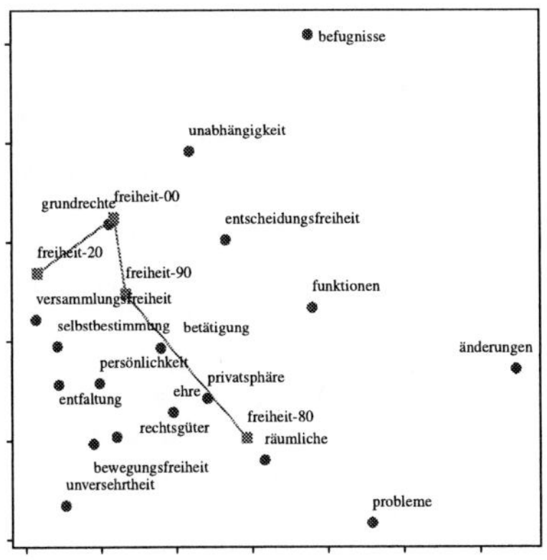

(c) Word "Freiheit" (freedom)

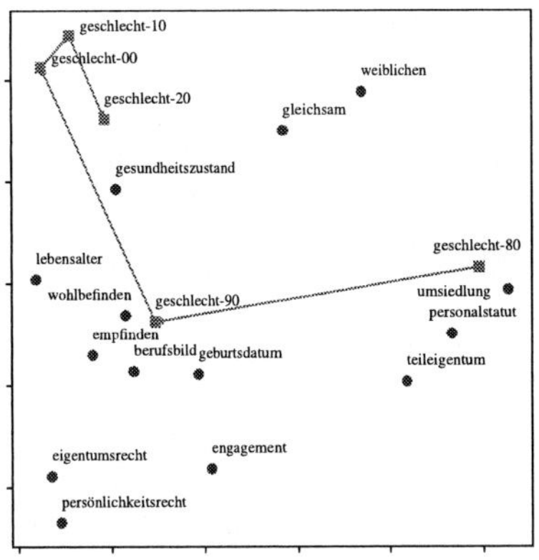

(d) Word "Geschlecht" (sex and/or gender)

Figure 5: Changing contexts in which words are used over time

For tasks, like classification or outcome prediction, that are directly connected to legal terms that have undergone such a semantic shift, it could therefore be beneficial to train word embeddings on a time-restricted dataset, to ensure correct interpretation of the terms in questions, even if that means reducing the available data for training.

In the future, it would be desirable to conduct a similar experiment with a temporally more balanced data set. Another interesting direction for future research would be to connect our findings on the usage of language by courts with the existing literature on semantic shifts in political debates and general language. One could hypothesise that changes in the language used by courts could be predicted by changes in the language used in political debates, which might precede them, and which in turn might be preceded by changes in the general use of language. Analysing whether such influences can be seen in diachronic word embeddings could help to develop models to predict when changed language use will start to have an influence on politics and law.

References

Leonard Bloomfield. 1933. *Language*. Allen & Unwin, New York.

Mohamed Amine Boukhaled, Benjamin Fagard, and Thierry Poibeau. 2019. Modelling the semantic change dynamics using diachronic word embedding. In *11th International Conference on Agents and Artificial Intelligence (NLPinAI Special Session)*.

Stephanie Brandl and David Lassner. 2019. Times are changing: Investigating the pace of language change in diachronic word embeddings. In *Proceedings of the 1st International Workshop on Computational Approaches to Historical Language Change*, pages 146–150, Florence, Italy. Association for Computational Linguistics.

Daniel Braun. 2021. *Automated Semantic Analysis, Legal Assessment, and Summarization of Standard Form Contracts*. Ph.d. thesis, Technische Universität München.

William L. Hamilton, Jure Leskovec, and Dan Jurafsky. 2016. Diachronic word embeddings reveal statistical laws of semantic change. In *Proceedings of the 54th Annual Meeting of the Association for Computational Linguistics (Volume 1: Long Papers)*, pages 1489–1501, Berlin, Germany. Association for Computational Linguistics.

Willem B. Hollmann. 2009. *English Language*, chapter Semantic change. Springer.

Andrey Indukaev. 2021. Studying ideational change in russian politics with topic models and word embeddings. In *The Palgrave Handbook of Digital Russia Studies*, pages 443–464. Palgrave Macmillan, Cham.

Adam Jatowt and Kevin Duh. 2014. A framework for analyzing semantic change of words across time. In *IEEE/ACM Joint Conference on Digital Libraries*, pages 229–238.

Andrey Kutuzov, Lilja Øvrelid, Terrence Szymanski, and Erik Velldal. 2018. Diachronic word embeddings and semantic shifts: a survey. In *Proceedings of the 27th International Conference on Computational Linguistics*, pages 1384–1397, Santa Fe, New Mexico, USA. Association for Computational Linguistics.

Andrey Kutuzov, Erik Velldal, and Lilja Øvrelid. 2017. Tracing armed conflicts with diachronic word embedding models. In *Proceedings of the Events and Stories in the News Workshop*, pages 31–36, Vancouver, Canada. Association for Computational Linguistics.

Xuanyi Liao and Guang Cheng. 2016. Analysing the semantic change based on word embedding. In *Natural Language Understanding and Intelligent Applications*, pages 213–223, Cham. Springer International Publishing.

Tomas Mikolov, Ilya Sutskever, Kai Chen, Greg S Corrado, and Jeff Dean. 2013. Distributed representations of words and phrases and their compositionality. In *Advances in Neural Information Processing Systems*, volume 26. Curran Associates, Inc.

Malte Ostendorff, Till Blume, and Saskia Ostendorff. 2020. Towards an open platform for legal information. In *Proceedings of the ACM/IEEE Joint Conference on Digital Libraries in 2020*, JCDL '20, page 385–388, New York, NY, USA. Association for Computing Machinery.

Thomas Proisl and Peter Uhrig. 2016. SoMaJo: State-of-the-art tokenization for German web and social media texts. In *Proceedings of the 10th Web as Corpus Workshop*, pages 57–62, Berlin. Association for Computational Linguistics.

Douglas Rice. 2019. Understanding legal meaning through word embeddings. *SSRN 3455747*.

Guy D. Rosin, Eytan Adar, and Kira Radinsky. 2017. Learning word relatedness over time. In *Proceedings of the 2017 Conference on Empirical Methods in Natural Language Processing*, pages 1168–1178, Copenhagen, Denmark. Association for Computational Linguistics.

David Rozado and Musa Al-Gharbi. 2022. Using word embeddings to probe sentiment associations of politically loaded terms in news and opinion articles from news media outlets. *Journal of Computational Social Science*, 5(1):427–448.

Tobias Schamel, Daniel Braun, and Florian Matthes. 2022. Structured extraction of terms and conditions from German and English online shops. In *Proceedings of The Fifth Workshop on e-Commerce and NLP (ECNLP 5)*, pages 181–190, Dublin, Ireland. Association for Computational Linguistics.

Sandeep Soni, Kristina Lerman, and Jacob Eisenstein. 2021. Follow the leader: Documents on the leading edge of semantic change get more citations. *Journal of the Association for Information Science and Technology*, 72(4):478–492.

Adam Tsakalidis, Pierpaolo Basile, Marya Bazzi, Mihai Cucuringu, and Barbara McGillivray. 2021. Dukweb, diachronic word representations from the uk web archive corpus. *Scientific Data*, 8(1):1–12.

J Vijayarani and TV Geetha. 2020. Knowledge-enhanced temporal word embedding for diachronic semantic change estimation. *Soft Computing*, 24(17):12901–12918.

Tobias Walter, Celina Kirschner, Steffen Eger, Goran Glavaš, Anne Lauscher, and Simone Paolo Ponzetto. 2021. Diachronic analysis of german parliamentary proceedings: Ideological shifts through the lens of political biases. In *2021 ACM/IEEE Joint Conference on Digital Libraries (JCDL)*, pages 51–60.

Gregor Wiedemann and Cornelia Fedtke. 2021. From frequency counts to contextualized word embeddings: The saussurean turn in automatic content analysis. In *Handbook of Computational Social Science, Volume 2*, pages 366–385. Routledge.

Arda Yüksel, Berke Uğurlu, and Aykut Koç. 2021. Semantic change detection with gaussian word embeddings. *IEEE/ACM Transactions on Audio, Speech, and Language Processing*, 29:3349–3361.

Should I disclose my dataset?
Caveats between reproducibility and individual data rights

Raysa M. Benatti
Institute of Computing
University of Campinas
Campinas, Brazil
raysa.benatti@gmail.com

Camila M. L. Villarroel
Law School of Ribeirão Preto
University of São Paulo
Ribeirão Preto, Brazil
cami.lima.v@gmail.com

Sandra Avila
Institute of Computing
University of Campinas
Campinas, Brazil
sandra@ic.unicamp.br

Esther L. Colombini
Institute of Computing
University of Campinas
Campinas, Brazil
esther@ic.unicamp.br

Fabiana C. Severi
Law School of Ribeirão Preto
University of São Paulo
Ribeirão Preto, Brazil
fabianaseveri@usp.br

Abstract

Natural language processing techniques have helped domain experts solve legal problems. Digital availability of court documents increases possibilities for researchers, who can access them as a source for building datasets — whose disclosure is aligned with good reproducibility practices in computational research. Large and digitized court systems, such as the Brazilian one, are prone to be explored in that sense. However, personal data protection laws impose restrictions on data exposure and state principles about which researchers should be mindful. Special caution must be taken in cases with human rights violations, such as gender discrimination, over which we elaborate as an example of interest. We present legal and ethical considerations on the issue, as well as guidelines for researchers dealing with this kind of data and deciding whether to disclose it.

1 Introduction

The increasing availability of data in digital formats, along with the means to process and interpret it, has boosted the interest in its versatile use. The enriched commercial value of personal data has justified the adoption of personal data protection laws aiming to protect individual and collective rights. Having such a legal structure — with a broader social recognition of implications associated with personal data usage — demands that data controllers be mindful about ethical issues and legal liabilities when dealing with this resource.

Research agents have been major controllers of data on individuals. While science has always relied on data, the societal switch to digital-intensive structures has changed much of their nature, amount, and availability. This context calls for specific approaches from researchers when balancing individual rights and scientific reproducibility — since disclosing datasets, while beneficial for research publicity, might expose information over which special considerations might apply.

Computational research based on data-intensive frameworks, such as machine learning, typically operates over collecting, processing, and interpreting large amounts of data; being used to awareness of resource sharing, the computing community tends to encourage reproducibility practices. In experimental contexts, that usually means disclosing descriptions of methods and results and codes, tools, and data.

Digital data can come from many sources. When derived from the realm of the social sciences it is often produced in text form, which motivates its use as input for natural language processing methods. Social scientists have relied on computational approaches to help answer some of their research questions; in the legal domain, court documents often provide rich material, which computational tools allow to be analyzed on improved scales.

Among the many inquiries that large-scale analysis of court documents could help address, we are particularly interested in gender-related ones. Examples include: (a) Which role do gender biases play in decisions regarding gender-based violence (GBV) legal cases? (b) How many cases are linked to the same victim? (c) How many police investigations make it to court? These are research questions for which natural language processing methods seem suitable.

Domain experts often identify demands for this research while exploring their own areas, creating communities around common issues. A large community of researchers and practitioners interested

Proceedings of the Natural Legal Language Processing Workshop 2022, pages 228 - 237
December 8, 2022

in how computational approaches can be used to address questions in the legal domain has emerged in Brazil; the country is one of the most litigious of the world in the court, having one lawyer for each batch of around 160 people[1], and approximately 80 million active legal cases[2].

With a substantial court system, large databases of documents issued by such courts, and an engaged research community in the field, Brazil emerges as a legal data hotspot — with many issues regarding data disclosure from state entities and researchers. The country issued its General Data Protection Act in 2018, based on European's General Data Protection Regulation, which expanded the debate on such issues.

Focus on GBV-related cases is justified not only by research and human rights significance but also due to the amount of delicate personal information they carry on the subjects involved, meaning that disclosing them without regard for legal and ethical principles could implicate severe harm. While focusing on this context, we stress that our considerations might apply to others.

A similar observation should be made for the location we chose to highlight. Focusing on the Brazilian context will benefit its large community of researchers and practitioners interested in the field. It may also provide useful insights from other legal settings — particularly civil law ones (e.g., continental Europe), in which Brazilian legal structures and fundamental statutes are heavily based.

Our main contributions are:

1. To bring ethical considerations on personal data disclosure by researchers;
2. To provide guidelines for researchers to help them decide on data disclosure;
3. To discuss how to preserve both reproducibilities of computational research and individual data rights.

We hope to help the community of interested researchers and practitioners understand the fundamentals of the Brazilian data protection legal system and its caveats.

This paper is organized as follows. Section 2 introduces research reproducibility concepts. It is followed by discussions on data disclosure and publicity in Section 3, where we present legal principles, practical issues, and ethical concerns on the matter. Risk assessment and mitigation measures are described in Section 4. Sections 3 and 4 also suggest guidelines of good practices for researchers. Finally, Section 5 summarizes approaches that could help researchers address concerns on disclosure of court documents and similar data.

2 Reproducibility

Reproducibility has been at the core of the debate on scientific integrity, being recognized as a critical quality of modern research (Goodman et al., 2016; Baker, 2016; Loscalzo, 2012). The concept is open enough to evoke debate on its meaning, and comprises different aspects of scientific soundness and accountability (Goodman et al., 2016; Drummond, 2009); however, there appears to be some consensus on the importance of community scrutiny for research quality assessment, for which reproducibility is essential.

Scrutiny, fraud prevention, and fraud detection are not the only motivation behind efforts toward reproducible research. Science is a collective endeavor of public interest; therefore, resource-sharing strengthens networks, creates research possibilities, and helps build connections inside and between communities — not only for science itself but also for practitioners and society as a whole.

This is especially true in empirical research, as is usually the case in computer science. In fact, many efforts have been made towards fostering a culture of openness of resources inside the computing-related community — from free and open source software initiatives[3][4] to open science guidelines and frameworks (Wilkinson et al., 2016; Peng, 2011; Sonnenburg et al., 2007). Peng (2011) describes a reproducibility spectrum for computer science research in which the gold standard would be attained by publishing linked and executable code and data along with results. In some fields, such as machine learning, the importance of empirical choices behind results that might support decision-making processes is such that it could justify one arguing that reproducibility is as important of a property as the research results themselves.

In this context, data sharing and quality assessment emerge as an object of concern as well (Gebru et al., 2021; De Schutter, 2010; Blockeel and Vanschoren, 2007). Data collecting, cleaning, labeling,

[1]Data from the Brazilian Bar Association (*Ordem dos Advogados do Brasil*).

[2]Data from the 2022 Brazil Justice Yearbook.

[3]`https://www.fsf.org`

[4]`https://opensource.org`

and/or processing are often part of the experimental pipeline in machine learning research, which justifies interest in making them available for peers and stakeholders. In some cases, however, the means and extent to which data should be shared are not trivial decisions.

When individual rights of the subjects regarded in the dataset might be at stake, sharing this data becomes a challenge since adjustments — or even the decision not to share — might be needed to avoid legal and/or ethical violations. Privacy, for instance, is one of the main concerns (Pröell et al., 2015). Some domains, such as health and clinic research, are notably prone to this issue. When faced with such a situation, researchers must take legal and ethical boundaries into account, assess the risks involved in disclosing the data, and weigh them against the benefits of reproducibility.

3 Issues on disclosing data provided by courts

Particularities on data sharing emerge in the context of research that uses computational approaches to court decisions. This section delves into some of them from the perspective of our research example: exploring natural language processing and other computational techniques over Brazilian court decisions in GBV-related cases. However, as mentioned in Section 1, our considerations might also be helpful for other contexts.

3.1 Publicity vs. Reproducibility

Brazilian court decisions are, by default, public documents. Publicity[5] of procedural acts issued by the justice system is such an important principle that it is stated in the country's federal constitution (articles 5 LX, 93 IX, and 93 X), which provides secrecy as an exception to be reserved for the protection of "intimacy" and "social interest". (Secrecy is discussed further in Section 3.2.) Codes of civil (articles 11 and 189) and criminal (article 792) procedures, which present bounding proceeding rules for legal cases, have similar statements.

The National Council of Justice (CNJ)[6], created in 2004 to supervise and manage the Brazilian justice system, provides more specific regulations on the matter. It declares that essential data regarding legal cases must be publicly accessible to "any person, regardless of previous enrollment or demonstration of interest" (Res. 121, article 1). The list of what is considered to be essential data includes (a) number, class, and theme; (b) name of parties and their lawyers; (c) procedural flow and updates; (d) full content of court decisions. Other documents, such as petitions and investigation reports, are restricted to lawyers, parties, and some official entities (articles 2 and 3). Again, cases that must remain in secrecy are preserved as exceptions.

Some provisions foster the use of digital documents in the justice system rather than physical ones, such as Federal Law 11419/2006 and regulation from the CNJ itself (Res. 215, articles 5 and 6). This scenario increases the availability of data for computational research purposes since it facilitates the extraction and processing of legal information. In the context of our research example and similar ones, it is then possible to scrape such documents and build datasets based on them — along with metadata, executable code, and research results, attaining a gold standard of scientific reproducibility. In that sense, we could acknowledge reproducibility as analogous to publicity, perceiving reproducibility as the public sector publicity principle applied to the science realm. Ultimately, they are both cultivated in the name of the public interest behind their related activities, which requires scrutiny, transparency, and community implication in their processes.

However, we recognize caveats. It does not follow from court decisions being publicly available by default that researchers could relinquish concerns when scraping and building datasets from these documents; our research example can illustrate that, as described in Sections 3.2, 3.3 and 4.

Despite the intersection between motivations supporting publicity and reproducibility, the justice system has different obligations and prerogatives than research institutions. When disclosing a court decision, the state complies with a legal duty to publicize and acts by itself; it claims the rights and responsibilities carried by such a publicization. If another person or entity — for instance, a researcher or research agency — extracts and discloses the same record, s/he creates another point of access, claiming responsibility over the content (even if unwittingly).

Another issue arises in that, in research settings, the data might not be shared on its own; instead, it is often made available in the context of an experimental pipeline, with annotation, modifications,

[5]Meaning, in this context, transparency or openness.

[6]https://www.cnj.jus.br

associated code, and/or results from models learned from them. In that case, disclosing the data is more than merely indexing it; it also publicizes it from a specific perspective. It makes sense that whoever is in charge of disclosing it is also legally and ethically responsible. Thus, when seeking reproducibility, researchers must account for that boundaries, being wary about emulating publicity-guided acts from the public administration.

3.2 The issue(s) of secrecy

Access to information is a fundamental right in a democratic environment. In Brazil, its legal and constitutional strengthening is linked to democratization processes in the 80s and later, after the country's military dictatorship. The right to information is a fundamental element of civic citizenship and scrutiny of executive, legislative, and judiciary spheres of power, protected by several national and international legal statements.

In addition to the default public status of court decisions, transparency propositions also apply to documents provided by public institutions in general (LAI[7], articles 2 and 3), and publicity is a vital principle of public administration (CF, article 37). Therefore, confidentiality[8] is an exception and must be justified by legal restrictions and/or particular circumstances — such as when national security is at risk (LAI, articles 3 III and 23).

In some cases, publicity and open access to information are restricted due to the need to protect other important rights or principles — notably intimacy and social interest (CF, article 5 LX). Intimacy, personal life, honor, and image are individual rights protected by the federal constitution (article 5 X) and other statements, such as the Access to Information Act (article 31). However, confidentiality must be well justified due to the (theoretically) quasi-paramount status of publicity-based principles in the Brazilian legal system.

When is secrecy justified? In Brazilian civil cases, the law states specific circumstances that warrant secrecy: (a) if needed to preserve matters of social or public interest; (b) in disputes on marriage, separation, divorce, civil union, parentage, alimony, or custody of children and adolescents; (c) in cases with data protected by the constitutional right to intimacy; (d) in arbitration cases (CPC, article 189). Interpretation of these statements is usually restrictive for the benefit of publicity.

In the criminal realm, secrecy is legally established in all crimes against sexual dignity (CP, article 234-B). The judge might also declare secrecy on a criminal case to avoid the victim's exposure to the media (CPP, article 201, 6th paragraph).

Besides legal restrictions, any party of a dispute has the right to request secrecy on the whole case or on specific documents, which might or not be granted by the judge — who also has the authority to revoke it, *ex officio* or by request (CNJ Res. 185, article 28).

This set of rules means that secrecy is established in many GBV-related lawsuits, since family law, civil disputes, and cases on sexual crimes are notably settings where gender-based abuse and biases are often brought to court. Therefore, when dealing with court decisions in this domain, one must be attentive to confidentiality boundaries that might restrain data disclosure.

Who can access these court decisions? When secrecy is established, court documents — including usually public ones such as decisions — are only accessible to parties and their lawyers (CNJ Res. 121, article 1)[9]. Secrecy is also a legal exception to the general rule of access to information (CNJ Res. 215, article 12 VII; LAI, article 22).

Courts might establish internal rules to deal with different degrees of secrecy — e.g., some cases might be totally unavailable except for allowed people, while others might have some documents publicized as long as information on parties is previously anonymized. However, such anonymization does not always happen as expected, especially in large courts where the systematization of documents is particularly challenging. In that case, decisions that are supposed to remain in total secrecy can end up publicly available. While courts are liable for the publicization, and it is not reasonable to expect researchers always to identify when that is the case, they should be aware of this possibility.

Guidelines of good practices Given the restrictions derived from secrecy in some legal cases, researchers might consider the following guidelines

[7]Legal abbreviations are described in A (Appendix).

[8]Although secrecy and confidentiality have the same meaning, we can interpret secrecy (a concept mainly used in the context of the justice system) as a type of confidentiality (that can apply to any document, data, or information).

[9]It is granted that they are also available to the justice system employees whose work is operationally essential for the case to be processed, e.g., the assigned judge.

of good practices for data disclosure when working with datasets made of court documents:

- If data is provided from secrecy cases, it **should not** be disclosed **unless** it is thoroughly anonymized and/or provided by demand only, with a deed of undertaking (details in Section 4);
- Otherwise, the researcher should check if other restrictions apply (Section 3.3).

We stress that having been able to access court decisions online does not guarantee that the case is not under secrecy. Deciding to disclose non-anonymized secret documents is a legal liability since it might violate privacy and intimacy rights, subjecting the liable person or entity to penalties.

3.3 Personal data restrictions

Court documents might carry publishing restrictions justified by reasons beyond secrecy, especially since personal data of people involved in legal cases are often disclosed in this material. Recent data protection laws, such as Brazil's General Data Protection Act (LGPD) and Europe's General Data Protection Regulation (GDPR), emerged in the context of increasing commercial usage of (more abundant than ever) personal data; thus, their main goal is to protect individuals from potentially abusive behavior perpetrated by profit-oriented agents. Legal restrictions on personal data usage are not the same for agents who do not fall under this category, such as public institutions and researchers; however, liabilities and ethical issues might still apply to them.

In Brazil, the concept of personal information precedes LGPD; the Access to Information Act defines it as "information regarding identified or identifiable natural person" (article 4 IV) and states restrictions on its processing[10] (article 31). Figure 1 shows a flowchart on whether personal information can be processed (open padlock); it applies to personal information whose production happened not earlier than 100 years ago — since, in that case, confidentiality no longer applies[11] (article 31, 1st paragraph, I).

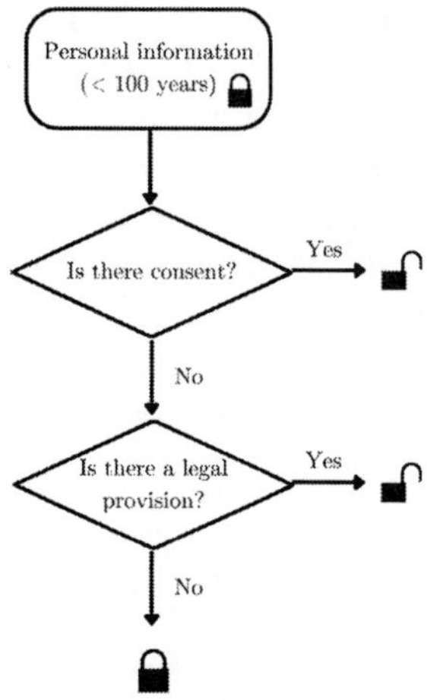

Figure 1: Flowchart of incidence of Access to Information Act restrictions (article 31) on personal information.

Personal information can be processed **if** there is explicit consent from the owner of its rights **or** if there is a legal provision to do so. In computational research settings, getting consent from all subjects involved is seldom feasible; therefore, if willing to abide by this statute, researchers might consider if their use case can be framed as a legally supported exception.

Usually, it can. The Act presents statistical and scientific research of "evident public or general interest" as a situation allowing personal information processing without the need for consent — as long as anonymization is guaranteed. Other exceptions include: (a) for medical treatment if the owner of rights is incapable of consenting; (b) to fulfill a court order; (c) if necessary for the defense of human rights; (d) to protect the public and general interest. We argue that scientific activity itself is a matter of public interest; therefore, not only could it be framed in hypothesis (d) (which would dismiss the need for data anonymization), it is redundant to require evidence of public interest to allow for information processing in this case.

In our study scenario, demanding anonymization also conflicts with what is stated by the LGPD — according to which it would be optional, although recommended. Figure 2 shows a flowchart for researchers willing to comply with this statute regarding processing personal data. Research settings entail a special application of the law (article 4 II (b)), being one of the situations in which personal data might be processed (article 7 IV) and conserved

[10]Processing (*tratamento*) refers to "any operation or set of operations which are performed on personal data or sets of personal data, whether or not by automated means" (GDPR, article 4(2)). It can mean use, storage, diffusion, destruction, alteration, collection, retrieval, extraction, and so forth. Thus, it might include any operation in a machine learning pipeline — collecting, cleaning, using as input for models, publishing.

[11]Lifting confidentiality after a maximum of 100 years allows for the use and interpretation of documents regarding their historical value since cultural heritage is a protected asset under the federal constitution (article 216).

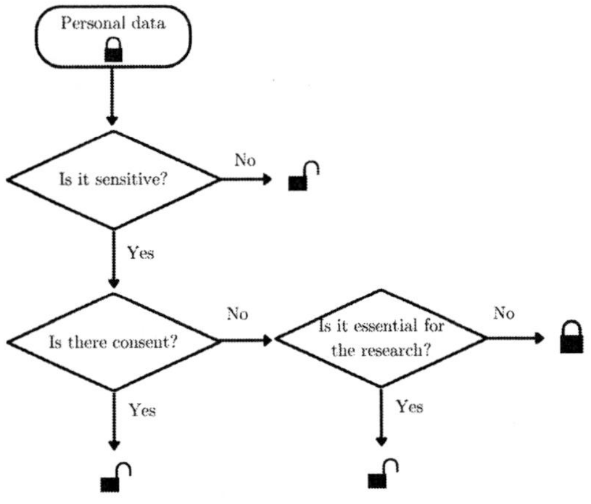

Figure 2: Flowchart of incidence of LGPD restrictions for researchers (articles 7 and 11) on personal data processing.

(article 16 II) as long as:

- Data is **not** sensitive **and** general principles of the law, as well as function, good faith and public interest, are preserved; **or**
- There is consent from the owner of rights; **or**
- The operation is essential for the research activity to be performed.

In any case, anonymization must be assured "whenever possible". Thus, it is not a duty, but a recommendation, not entailing punishment if not followed — which means that complying with it is an ethical deed of the researcher rather than a legal obligation.

Personal data is sensitive if it refers to racial or ethnic origin, political opinions, religious or philosophical beliefs, trade union membership, health or sex life, or personal genetic or biometric information — as stated in article 9(1) of GDPR, with a similar provision in Brazilian law. Sensitiveness of data implies special responsibilities for its processing; for researchers, processing of sensitive data can only occur if (a) there is consent from the owner of the rights or (b) the operation is **essential** for the activity.

Once a research project has been designed, and the need for using sensitive data in its context has been demonstrated, indispensability is established — therefore complying with legal provisions. There remains, however, the issue of whether full reproducibility is an imperative element of the scientific endeavor that would justify disclosing sensitive data to fulfill essential research activities. We argue that preserving sensitive data, while might diminish possibilities of replicability, does not hamper acceptable levels of reproducibility (Drummond, 2009); thus, when using this data, disclosing it only under mitigation guidelines (as described in Section 4) might be a fair trade-off between research publicity and protection of human rights. While the most usual metadata provided with court decisions (e.g., names of parties and their lawyers) are not sensitive, such documents might contain information that, when combined with identification of parties, becomes sensitive — even when not issued in cases under secrecy. This arises since court sentences must include a report on the case and the reasoning behind the verdict[12] — which could contain sensitive information on the subjects[13].

In other situations, while the legal case is not under secrecy nor displays strictly sensitive information, other forms of delicate information might appear in a court decision. For instance, in domestic violence cases, children and/or teenagers often witness the event and are either listened to in court or mentioned in case reports, therefore having their names (or other data) exposed in public documents. While there might not be an explicit legal restriction for researchers to fully disclose such records, doing so would raise ethical concerns.

4 Risk assessment and mitigation

When faced with the decision to disclose court documents used in research, one must confront risks against the benefits of science replicability since full disclosure might potentially harm and violate the rights of the subjects whose personal data is displayed. Risks can exist regardless of legal restrictions, given that records from courts typically carry a large amount of personal information of parties, witnesses, and other subjects related to the case, both in the document(s) text and metadata.

Making personal data available establishes as liable the person or entity in charge of the disclosure, who becomes a controller according to law (GDPR, article 4(7); LGPD, article 5 VI) (Schwait-

[12]These are required elements for any court sentence issued under Brazilian law, besides the verdict itself (CPC, article 489); other legal systems have similar provisions (Facchini Neto and Dall'Alba, 2022).

[13]As an example, if a domestic violence case is brought to court and issues on the sex life of the people involved are relevant for the circumstances, such issues will possibly be described in the decision report and/or motivation — thus exposing sensitive information on the identifiable subjects.

zer, 2021). As a controller, a researcher or research agency operates under distinct ethical guidelines than those of courts and law enforcement agencies — which, when disclosing personal data, are usually complying with a legal duty to transparency and publicity, as well as broader public interest principles. While carrying public interest on its own, science reproducibility is not a legal obligation (thus not dismissing liability in the same way that applies to state entities), and can be acceptably achieved with mitigation-mindful data availability when full disclosure is not allowed or advised.

Further, the legal system context represents a special circumstance for personal data disclosing due to implications regarding rights of access to justice, due process of law, and defense — which also relates to publicity and transparency. One would be unable to build a defense if not provided with complete information on the case, including data on parties and their lawyers, allegations, documents, and evidence. Transparency of court documents is generally a matter of state accountability. Imposing severe constraints against this kind of publicity could have noxious outcomes for democratic settings and is not the same as restricting personal data disclosure in scientific frameworks.

In that sense, although documents used in research might be publicly available in other sources (e.g., court websites), their disclosure by researchers can increase risks for the subjects involved, considering that: (a) it reunites the data in a single, cohesive source, often cleaner, and more structured than the original and combined with annotation and metadata, therefore making it easier for different groups of people to access it and make inferences from it; (b) public status of such documents in original sources might change over time, adding an extra layer of harm-related responsibility on the researcher who decides to disclose them.

In the context of GBV-related cases, risks of full personal data disclosure by researchers or research agencies include:

- Violation of privacy and intimacy rights of:
  - minors, in disagreement with their best interest and right to informational self-determination;
  - victims and witnesses, which might contribute to reinforcing their vulnerability against aggressors and their communities;
  - defendants, which might contribute to reinforcing penal populism actions and ideas at the cost of individual rights violations;
- Exposure of sensitive data, which might violate the civil rights of the subject(s);
- Exposure of confidential information;
- Exposure of any information that might jeopardize the safety or integrity of the subject(s) involved in a legal case.

In fact, such risks have been used to advocate for initiatives such as Bill 3333/20, whose main proposal is to establish "absolute secrecy" for personal information displayed in police reports and court documents in cases of domestic violence — which are currently public by default. If approved, alleged aggressors would be hindered from accessing personal data on the victim(s), thus impairing their right to defense. For researchers, this would add a class of documents in the secrecy-justified caution cluster.

Exposing sensitive and/or confidential data can increase the possibilities of rights restrictions, retaliation from a subject's community and institutions, and physical and mental suffering. Let us consider, for instance, the disclosure of the LGBTQ+ status of a subject implicated in a legal case: such a deed could have discrimination-related consequences such as the loss of a job, impairment of social and family ties, or threats to one's physical integrity.

Ease of access to data obtained from courts allows for inferences that would hardly be made otherwise — an exciting possibility for good-faith researchers and policymakers but also a caution-inspiring scenario. From a dataset of Brazilian court decisions with specific characteristics, for example, one could extract a map of precise addresses of victims, defendants, or plaintiffs (some of which could be minors or belong to other protected groups). An ill-motivated, technically capable agent could use that information to perpetrate physical, moral, emotional, or other kinds of harm to these people — and, while there are legal provisions to make perpetrators accountable, some damages might be beyond repair.

We note that the risks mentioned above do not constitute an exhaustive list; ideally, researchers should evaluate which issues might apply to their context and know their data enough to build a proper risk assessment in order to decide on the extent of data disclosure considering available resources and both ethical and legal restrictions.

When personal information is part of the data source in research, mitigating such risks is possible and advised. Risks are usually associated with data disclosure rather than their use itself. Personal data protection laws ordinarily do not distinguish use from disclosure for legal purposes, placing both operations under the concept of "processing" (see Note 10). However, discerning them is relevant in our context of interest.

While using court documents in research settings (e.g., as input for training models or to perform other quantitative and qualitative analyses) does not directly threaten or pose harm to subjects involved, disclosing them without taking prior mitigation actions might do. We identify three levels of personal data implication for our context:

1. **From secret cases**: Not to be disclosed without mitigation; disclosure without mitigation both legally and ethically inappropriate;
2. **From non-secret cases, with sensitive data**: Not illegal for researchers to disclose without mitigation if the disclosure is essential for research; disclosure without mitigation might be ethically debatable;
3. **From non-secret cases, without sensitive data**: Not illegal for researchers to disclose; disclosure without mitigation should ideally be preceded by an analysis of specific context and risk-benefit assessment.

Mitigation measures to protect personal data embedded in public court documents might include several actions from researchers and research agencies, who should evaluate the risks of data disclosure, benefits of full replicability, and availability of resources to perform mitigation. We stress two of them: (a) anonymization and (b) disclosure by demand with a deed of the undertaking.

Anonymization When personal data is anonymized, it is no longer considered personal data (LGPD, article 12; GDPR, recital 26) — therefore, none of the issues discussed in this work would apply, and documents containing them could be disclosed, *ab initio*, without legal nor ethical implications. To be considered fully anonymized, personal identification corresponding to the data must be untraceable and not reversible by reasonable efforts[14]; thus, pseudonymization — which allows for identification to be restored —, while allowed to comply with legal guidelines on data storage, is not enough to allow full disclosure.

There are, however, practical obstacles. Full anonymization is not always attainable since it might require massive manual efforts or the use of technically challenging tools, which do not necessarily guarantee complete accuracy. Some kinds of data are challenging to anonymize; computational research often deals with large amounts of documents and sensitive information is usually non-structurally embedded in the text, meaning that masking them pre-disclosure — or even identifying them — might not be possible. Deeper discussions on technical and juridical aspects of legal data anonymization can be found in the works of Csányi et al. (2021) and van Opijnen et al. (2017).

Regarding replicability, anonymization barely affects it unless the personal information is relevant for the analysis. In some cases, determining the relevance of personal information for experimental settings is overly demanding and/or outside of the scope of research, e.g., when black-box models learn from input documents. In those scenarios, approaches for model interpretability and/or explainability might be taken into consideration (Rudin, 2019a,b; Molnar, 2022). At any rate, if research results and code are duly published and the methodology is thoroughly explained, reproducibility should not be severely disturbed. Assuming that the documents used as the source are publicly available, anyone following the same procedures should be able to access them, therefore claiming their responsibility upon processing the data.

If mitigation is needed or advised, but adequate anonymization is not feasible, researchers should consider mitigation measures described next.

Disclosure by demand In this case, the person, group, or entity responsible for research provides a contact channel through which the data can be requested and sent by demand. Ideally, whoever requests the material should agree to a deed of undertaking bound by the good faith of parties, with clauses preventing inappropriate data processing and protecting the subjects' best interest. Traceability of data controllers is a major advantage of this method.

[14] What could be considered "reasonable" is open for debate and can vary depending on specifics of each case, as explained by Vokinger et al. (2020).

While being the safest option regarding personal data protection, we identify the following caveats: (a) it relies on assuming good faith of the researchers; (b) it constrains replicability, given that it adds extra layers of compromise, bureaucracy, and communication for interested parties.

Also, mitigation measures (a) and (b) could be combined, although this would require extra effort. Researchers can still decide not to make data available, therefore escaping from the burden of responsibility over the dataset disclosure and choosing privateness over publicity.

5 Possible paths

Both research reproducibility and data protection of subjects mentioned are essential values in democratic settings and must be preserved and encouraged. Good research practices and awareness of legal and ethical restrictions can help researchers and agencies decide whether — and to which extent — disclose their court documents datasets. While much of the responsibility for the form and availability of such documents relies on the courts, researchers also have liability over the content they choose to disclose. The following approaches could help them address it in the future.

Guidelines: While provisions for researchers should not be too strict, having more explicit guidelines or recommendations in place — provided by national authorities on data protection and other official entities — could help address some of the concerns;

Anonymization tools: Adequate anonymization of data is not trivial. While this burden does not rely solely on researchers, tools that help get past this task might encourage them to act in this sense;

Official data repositories: Much of current replicability practices rely on individual data repositories. Having official, institutional data repositories in place, backed up by research agencies and supplemented by somewhat automatic deeds of undertaking by parties, could be an option for data availability without compromising protection of individual data rights.

We expect that, with proper guidelines of good practices and tools, as well as engagement from the scientific community and state agencies, a fair balance can be achieved between the publicity that guides research and the protection of human rights and the informational self-determination of individuals.

Acknowledgements

R. Benatti is partially funded by CAPES/Brazil and FAEPEX/Unicamp. C. Villarroel is partially funded by FAPESP (São Paulo Research Foundation) 2017/26174-6. F. Severi is supported by the University of São Paulo's Law School of Ribeirão Preto. S. Avila is partially funded by CNPq/Brazil 315231/2020-3, FAPESP 2013/08293-7, 2020/09838-0, H.IAAC (Artificial Intelligence and Cognitive Architectures Hub), and Google LARA 2021. E. Colombini is partially funded by CNPq PQ-2 grant 315468/2021-1 and H.IAAC. The Recod.ai lab is supported by projects from FAPESP, CNPq, and CAPES. Finally, we are grateful for the reviewers of this work, who enriched it with their evaluation and comments.

References

Monya Baker. 2016. 1,500 scientists lift the lid on reproducibility. *Nature*, 533:452–454.

Hendrik Blockeel and Joaquin Vanschoren. 2007. Experiment Databases: Towards an Improved Experimental Methodology in Machine Learning. In *European Conference on Principles of Data Mining and Knowledge Discovery*, pages 6–17.

Gergely Márk Csányi, Dániel Nagy, Renátó Vági, János Pál Vadász, and Tamás Orosz. 2021. Challenges and open problems of legal document anonymization. *Symmetry*, 13(8).

Erik De Schutter. 2010. Data Publishing and Scientific Journals: The Future of the Scientific Paper in a World of Shared Data. *Neuroinformatics*, 8(3):151–153.

Chris Drummond. 2009. Replicability Is Not Reproducibility: Nor Is It Good Science. In *Proceedings of the Evaluation Methods for Machine Learning Workshop at the 26th ICML*.

Eugênio Facchini Neto and Felipe Camilo Dall'Alba. 2022. Nem concisas, nem prolixas: o novo estilo de sentenças na França e na Itália – a convergência dos extremos. *Revista de Informação Legislativa: RIL*, 59(234):35–60.

Timnit Gebru, Jamie Morgenstern, Briana Vecchione, Jennifer Wortman Vaughan, Hanna Wallach, Hal Daumé III, and Kate Crawford. 2021. Datasheets for Datasets. *Communications of the ACM*, 64(12):86–92.

Steven N. Goodman, Daniele Fanelli, and John P. A. Ioannidis. 2016. What does research reproducibility mean? *Science Translational Medicine*, 8(341):341ps12–341ps12.

Joseph Loscalzo. 2012. Irreproducible Experimental Results: Causes, (Mis)interpretations, and Consequences. *Circulation*, 125(10):1211–1214.

Christoph Molnar. 2022. *Interpretable Machine Learning: A Guide for Making Black Box Models Explainable*. Independently published.

Roger D. Peng. 2011. Reproducible Research in Computational Science. *Science*, 334(6060):1226–1227.

Stefan Pröell, Rudolf Mayer, and Andreas Rauber. 2015. Data Access and Reproducibility in Privacy Sensitive eScience Domains. In *2015 IEEE 11th International Conference on e-Science*, pages 255–258.

Cynthia Rudin. 2019a. Please Stop Doing "Explainable" ML. Talk at The Berkman Klein Center for Internet & Society.

Cynthia Rudin. 2019b. Stop explaining black box machine learning models for high stakes decisions and use interpretable models instead. *Nature Machine Intelligence*, 1:206–215.

Lenora Schwaitzer. 2021. LGPD e gestão documental no Poder Judiciário: aplicabilidade e impactos. Talk at the *Núcleo de Estudos em História e Memória, Escola Paulista da Magistratura* (Center of Studies in History and Memory, São Paulo School of Magistracy).

Sören Sonnenburg, Mikio L. Braun, Cheng Soon Ong, Samy Bengio, Leon Bottou, Geoffrey Holmes, Yann LeCun, Klaus-Robert Müller, Fernando Pereira, Carl Edward Rasmussen, Gunnar Rätsch, Bernhard Schölkopf, Alexander Smola, Pascal Vincent, Jason Weston, and Robert Williamson. 2007. The Need for Open Source Software in Machine Learning. *Journal of Machine Learning Research*, 8(81):2443–2466.

Marc van Opijnen, Ginevra Peruginelli, Eleni Kefali, and Monica Palmirani. 2017. On-Line Publication of Court Decisions in the EU: Report of the Policy Group of the Project 'Building on the European Case Law Identifier'. *SSRN Electronic Journal*.

Kerstin Vokinger, Daniel Stekhoven, and Michael Krauthammer. 2020. Lost in Anonymization — A Data Anonymization Reference Classification Merging Legal and Technical Considerations. *The Journal of Law, Medicine & Ethics*, 48:228–231.

Mark Wilkinson, Michel Dumontier, IJsbrand Jan Aalbersberg, Gaby Appleton, Myles Axton, Arie Baak, Niklas Blomberg, Jan-Willem Boiten, Luiz Olavo Bonino da Silva Santos, Philip Bourne, Jildau Bouwman, Anthony Brookes, Tim Clark, Merce Crosas, Ingrid Dillo, Olivier Dumon, Scott Edmunds, Chris Evelo, Richard Finkers, and Barend Mons. 2016. The FAIR Guiding Principles for scientific data management and stewardship. *Scientific Data*, 3.

A Appendix: List of legal statutes mentioned in this paper

In order of appearance:

1. CF (*Constituição Federal*): Brazilian Federal Constitution (1988);
2. CPC (*Código de Processo Civil*): Brazilian Code of Civil Procedures (Law n. 13105, March 16, 2015);
3. CPP (*Código de Processo Penal*): Brazilian Code of Criminal Procedures (Decree-Law n. 3689, October 3, 1941);
4. CNJ Res. 121: National Council of Justice, Resolution n. 121 (October 5, 2010);
5. Brazilian Law n. 11419/2006 (December 19, 2006);
6. CNJ Res. 215: National Council of Justice, Resolution n. 215 (December 16, 2015);
7. LAI (*Lei de Acesso à Informação*): Brazilian Access to Information Act (Law n. 12527, November 18, 2011);
8. CP (*Código Penal*): Brazilian Criminal Code (Decree-Law n. 2848, December 7, 1940);
9. CNJ Res. 185: National Council of Justice, Resolution n. 185 (December 18, 2013);
10. LGPD (*Lei Geral de Proteção de Dados*): Brazilian General Data Protection Act (Law n. 13709, August 14, 2018) – also available in English (unofficial translation);
11. GDPR: European General Data Protection Regulation (Regulation (EU) 2016/679 of the European Parliament and of the Council of 27 April 2016);
12. Bill 3333/20: Brazilian Chamber of Deputies, Bill (*Projeto de Lei*) n. 3333 (2020); author: deputy Ricardo José Magalhães Barros.

Attack on Unfair ToS Clause Detection: A Case Study using Universal Adversarial Triggers

Shanshan Xu and **Irina Broda** and **Rashid Haddad**
Marco Negrini and **Matthias Grabmair**
School of Computation, Information, and Technology; Technical University of Munich, Germany
{firstname.lastname}@tum.de

Abstract

Recent work has demonstrated that natural language processing techniques can support consumer protection by automatically detecting unfair clauses in the Terms of Service (ToS) Agreement. This work demonstrates that transformer-based ToS analysis systems are vulnerable to adversarial attacks. We conduct experiments attacking an unfair-clause detector with universal adversarial triggers. Experiments show that a minor perturbation of the text can considerably reduce the detection performance. Moreover, to measure the detectability of the triggers, we conduct a detailed human evaluation study by collecting both answer accuracy and response time from the participants. The results show that the naturalness of the triggers remains key to tricking readers.

1 Introduction

When using online platforms, users are asked to agree to the Terms of Service (ToS), which are often long and difficult to understand. According to (Obar and Oeldorf-Hirsch, 2020), it would take a user around 45 minutes on average to read a ToS properly. Most users accept the terms without reading them, including clauses which would be deemed unfair under consumer protection standards. Software applications that warn consumers about unfair clauses can support consumers' rights, and have been the subject of prior work (e.g., Lippi et al., 2019; Ruggeri et al., 2022). At the same time, their existence forms an incentive for drafters of ToS to formulate clauses with potentially unfair effects that bypass automated screening. In turn, developers of control systems seek to make their detectors robust against such 'adversarial attacks'. In this paper, we report on an experiment in discovering weaknesses of ToS analysis models.

Natural language processing (NLP) models for ToS analysis conduct binary classification of a given clause as fair/unfair. Previous studies have shown that state-of-the-art transformer-based classifiers are vulnerable to adversarial attacks (Belinkov and Bisk, 2017); even slight modifications to the input text (e.g., changing a few characters) can cause incorrect classifications (Ebrahimi et al., 2018). Numerous adversarial attack methods have been developed and demonstrate effective attack performance in various downstream NLP tasks such as sentiment analysis (Iyyer et al., 2018), question answering (Wang et al., 2020), machine-translation (Cheng et al., 2019) etc. One such method is the attack via a *universal adversarial trigger*, which is a sequence of tokens (words, sub-words, or characters) that can be injected into *any* text input from a dataset to mislead the victim model to a target prediction (see Table 1 for examples). These input-agnostic triggers, once generated, can be distributed to anyone, and do not need access to the victim model at the time of attack.

Adversarial attacks have, to the best of our knowledge, remained largely unaddressed in legal NLP. Our work extends the state of the art through the following contributions: (1) We conduct experiments attacking ToS unfair clause detectors trained on the public CLAUDETTE dataset with universal adversarial triggers. Our results show that a minor perturbation of the text can reduce the detection performance of transformer based models significantly. (2) We also use artifacts from the training data for universal trigger attacks. Our experiments demonstrate that such words can considerably reduce the victim model's accuracy, highlighting the potential threat of training data leakage. (3) We conduct a human evaluation study to measure the detectability of the generated triggers. The results show that suppressing sub tokens can make generated triggers more difficult to detect. [1]

[1] Our code is available at https://github.com/TUMLegalTech/ToS_attack_nllp22

Proceedings of the Natural Legal Language Processing Workshop 2022, pages 238 - 245
December 8, 2022

ToS Clause (red = trigger)	Model Detection
Pinterest isn't liable for damages that result from a may vote against non-material breach of any other applicable duty of care.	Unfair → Fair
The English courts will have jurisdiction over any claim arising from may vote against, or related to , any use of our services.	Unfair → Fair

Table 1: The universal adversarial trigger can be injected into *any* input from a dataset to mislead the victim model. By inserting the displayed trigger can cause the trained unfair ToS detector to flip its correct unfair predictions to fair.

2 Related Work

Adversarial Attacks in NLP: Most adversarial attack methods in NLP are white-box, where the attacker has full access to the victim model (including architectures, parameters, and training data). Prevalent white-box attacks include HotFlip (Ebrahimi et al., 2018), a gradient-based method that generates adversarial examples on discrete text structure; PWWS (Ren et al., 2019), an importance-based method that substitutes words of high saliency. By contrast, black-box attacks assume no knowledge of the victim model's architectures and parameters. Example techniques include the use of generative adversarial networks (GANs) (Zhao et al., 2018) and human-in-the-loop heuristics (Wallace et al., 2019b)

Universal Triggers: Wallace et al. (2019a) generate universal attack triggers by using gradient signals to guide a search over the word embedding space. They are input-agnostic, which makes them more threatening in real-world scenarios. Despite being successful in confusing classification systems, universal triggers are often unnatural and can easily be detected by human readers. Song et al. (2021) generate attack triggers that appear closer to natural text by using a pre-trained GAN. Training a GAN in the ToS domain from scratch requires large datasets and GPU resources. In this work we try to generate natural triggers by simply skipping all the subword and special tokens during the search process; and leave the development and evaluation of a ToS-GAN to future work.

3 Universal Trigger Generation

We assume a text input x and its target label y from the dataset $D = \{X, Y\}$, a trained victim classifier model f that predicts $f(x) = \hat{y}$. While in a *non-universal* targeted attack the focus is on flipping the prediction of a single text input x, our goal is to find an input-agnostic trigger t consisting of a sequence of tokens $\{w_1, w_2, \ldots, w_i\}$ such that when concatenating t with any input x from X, the victim model incorrectly predicts $f(x;t) = \tilde{y}$, where $\tilde{y} \neq \hat{y}$. Specifically, we use the following objective function:

$$\arg\min_{t} \mathbb{E}_{x\sim X}[\mathcal{L}(\tilde{y}, f(x;t))] \tag{1}$$

To solve the above objective function, we follow the approach of Wallace et al. (2019a) by utilizing the HotFlip method (Ebrahimi et al., 2018) at the token level: First, we initiate the trigger t with a sequence of i placeholder tokens (i.e., 'the'); then we compute the gradient of (1) w.r.t the trigger. Since tokens are discrete, we approximate the loss function around the current token embedding using the first-order Taylor expansion

$$\arg\min_{e'_i \in \mathcal{V}} \left[e'_i - e_{adv_i}\right]^T \nabla_{e_{adv_i}} \mathcal{L} \tag{2}$$

where $\mathcal{V}$ is the set of all token embeddings over the entire vocabulary and e_{adv_i} represent the embedding of the current trigger token.

We update the embedding for every trigger token e_{adv_i} to minimize (2). This can be efficiently computed through d-dimensional dot products, with d corresponding to the dimension of the token embeddings. For constructing the entire updated trigger, we then use beam search to evaluate the top i token candidates from (2) for each token position in the trigger t. As variable parameters, we run experiments with triggers of different lengths [3, 5, 8] and insert positions [begin, middle, end] in the input text.

4 Experiments

4.1 Dataset and the Victim Model

The CLAUDETTE dataset (Lippi et al., 2019; Ruggeri et al., 2022) consists of 100 ToS contracts (20,417 clauses) of online platforms. A clause is deemed as unfair if it creates an unacceptable imbalance in the parties' rights and obligations, i.e., harms the user's rights or minimizes the online service's obligations. Each clause was labelled by legal experts. [2]

Following Lippi et al. 2019, we discard sentences shorter than 5 words. In order to avoid an information leak between training and testing sentences by virtue of them stemming from the same document of contracts, we split the 100 contracts randomly into 40:40:20 for training, development and testing. Table 2 in Appendix A shows the detailed statistics of each split. Notably, the CLAUDETTE has a very imbalanced class ratio of 9:1 (fair:unfair).

For the victim model, we finetune an instance of LEGAL-BERT (nlpaueb/legal-bert-base-uncased) (Chalkidis et al., 2020) on the CLAUDETTE training set. Please refer to Appendix B for details on model finetuning. It achieves overall macro F1 of 88.9%, 97.7% F1 for class fair, and 80.1% for class unfair.

4.2 Attack Results

In the following we focus on the attack scenario *fairwashing*: targeted attacks that flip *unfair* predictions to *fair*. We apply the universal attack trigger algorithm on the development set and report the attack performance on the test set. The generated triggers can considerably degrade the victim model's performance. For instance, inserting the trigger of token length 8 "##purchased another opponent shall testify unless actuarial opponent" in the middle of the sentence can decrease the model's accuracy from 80.1% to 16.9%. However, we observe that triggers often contain special tokens or subwords, such as '[SEP]' or '##purchased', which makes them easily detectable for human readers. Inspired by Wang, 2022, we facilitate the generation of natural triggers by simply skipping all subwords and special tokens during the search (hereafter we denote this approach as mode 'no_subword' for simplicity). Although slightly less effective than the original triggers (Table 4 in Appendix C), the no_subword triggers are less likely to be detected by human readers (See our human evaluation study

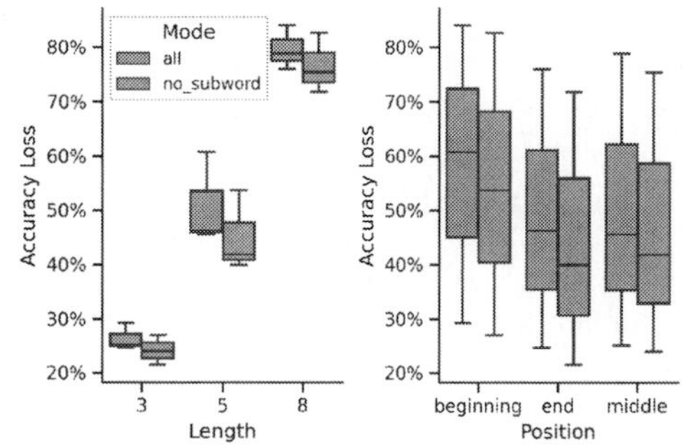

Figure 1: Accuracy loss of the victim model's detection performance when attacked by universal triggers of different insert positions and lengths. For completeness, we report the full attack results in Appendix C

in Section 6).

We also run experiments to study the impact of trigger length, insert position, and mode (with/without subwords) on the attack's effectiveness. Figure 1 shows that increasing the token length improves attack effectiveness by a noticeable margin. The victim model's accuracy degrades by 25% to 60% using three words and by 80% to 13% with eight words. The result also indicates the victim model's sensitivity to the insert position of the triggers. These results are consistent with previous studies (Wallace et al., 2019b; Wang, 2022): Triggers are more effective when inserted at the beginning of the clause, which may be due to the transformer-based model paying more attention to the terms at the beginning of the text. These results hold across both modes. Between the modes, a higher effectiveness is consistently observed for 'all' compared with 'no_subword'. This is in line with 'no_subword' generating triggers from a subset of potential trigger tokens of 'all' mode.

5 Data Artifacts as Universal Triggers

A growing number of works have raised awareness that deep neural models may exploit spurious artifacts in the dataset and take erroneous shortcuts (McCoy et al., 2019; Xu and Markert, 2022). In this section, we experiment with using dataset artifacts as universal triggers to explore the feasibility of generating universal triggers without access to the victim model's gradient signals. Following Gururangan et al. (2018), Wallace et al. (2019a) identified the dataset artifacts as words with high pointwise mutual information (PMI) (Church and Hanks, 1990) with each label. Since the Claudette dataset has a heavily imbalanced label distribu-

[2] To measure the inter-annotation agreement, Lippi et al. (2019) have an additional test set containing 10 contracts labelled by two distinct experts, which achieve a high inner-annotator agreement with standard Cohen κ= 0.871. For details on the annotation process and the legal rational of unfair contractual clauses, please refer the original CLAUDETTE paper.

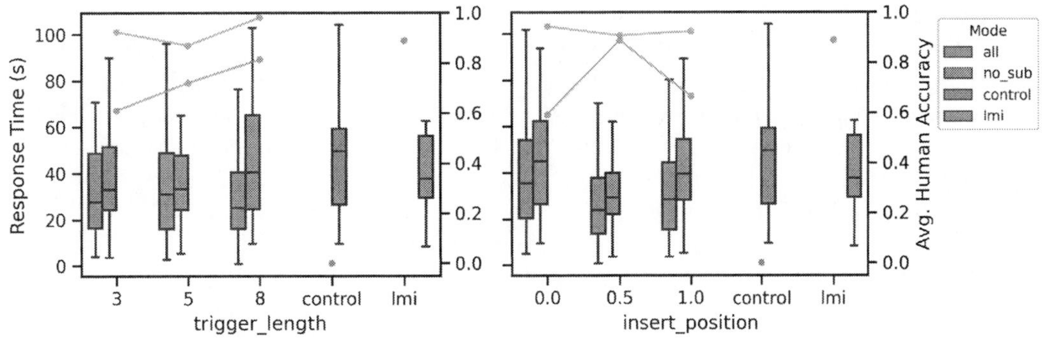

Figure 2: Human response time (box plots) and detection accuracy (line plots) for triggers of different insert positions and lengths. *Control* stands for the question where no trigger is inserted. *LMI* represents an LMI trigger of length eight inserted in the middle of the sentence. The insert positions are the following. 0.0 : beginning, 0.5 : middle, 1.0 : end.

tion, in order to prevent picking up very sparse tokens, in this work, we use local mutual information (LMI) (Schuster et al., 2019), a re-weighted version of PMI. We observe that high LMI ranked words are successful triggers. We use the 8 highest LMI words and PMI words with label fairness as triggers (hereafter LMI trigger and PMI trigger respectively, please refer to Appendix E for the list of words used); and insert them to the unfair clauses at different token positions. The LMI trigger is able to reduce the victim model's classification accuracy from 80% to around 60%; while the PMI trigger can only reduce the performance to around 76% (see Figure 3 in Appendix E). Although less successful than the universal adversarial triggers, the LMI triggers are natural and less detectable than 'all' mode triggers according to our human evaluation studies. Critically, LMI triggers are extracted by simply analyzing the training data and do not require access to the victim model. The attack effectiveness of LMI trigger highlights the potential threat of training data leakage in the NLP application.

6 Human Evaluation Study

We perform a human evaluation to study the impact of token length, insert position and mode on the triggers' detectability [3]. The task is to identify which sentence out of four candidate sentences from ToS contracts was modified. We include one question with no modified sentence as the control. In a previous study, Song et al. 2021 directly asked the human participants to rate whether the generated triggers were natural or not. However, the rating of naturalness is very abstract and varies between individuals. Inspired by studies on the detection process in psychological studies (Pandya and Macy, 1995; Yap and Balota, 2007), we assume response time (i.e., the length of time taken for a human to detect a trigger) can act as a proxy for the naturalness. To measure the human detectability of triggers, we hence collect the answer accuracy as well as the response time from the participants.

19 participants of different ages, English abilities, and legal experience were recruited from the personal network of the authors. Figure (2) demonstrates that it is consistently easier for participants to detect 'all' mode triggers than 'no_subword' mode triggers. Participants were on average 19% faster in detecting that a sentence inserted by 'all' than 'no_subword' triggers; and they find 'all' triggers with 21% higher accuracy on average. We include the LMI trigger of token length eight in the study and find its detectability is in between the 'no_subword' and 'all' triggers of the same length. The intuitive notion that participants are better at finding longer triggers generally holds with regard to detection accuracy. Nevertheless, we cannot observe a trend in the response time change, which may be due to our small sample size. Regarding the insert position, participants are the fastest in detecting triggers inserted in the middle. Further, we notice that special tokens and subwords make triggers more obvious. Qualitative, informal reports from participants indicate that 'spelling error' stuck out in a legal context. All triggers containing these tokens can be detected with more than 90%

[3] We report the details of the web application used and full instructions for the human subjects in Appendix D

accuracy, which include two 'all' triggers of length three (containing special token [SEP] or combination of subtokens '##assignabilityconsult'); and one 'no_subword' triggers inserted at position 5 (includes a bound stem 'concul'). This likely explains why these two data points do not conform to the general trend of detection accuracy.

7 Conclusion

We attacked ToS unfair clause detectors with universal adversarial triggers generated by a gradient-based algorithm as well as by simply analyzing the training data. The effectiveness of the triggers exposes the vulnerability of the transformer-based classification model, and highlights the potential threat of training data leakage. We also conducted a human evaluation to study the detectability of the triggers. The results show that the triggers are less likely to be detected if they do not include subtokens. Future work can explore ways to generate more natural triggers in the legal domain, which may even deceive readers with a formal education in law.

Limitations

Wallace et al. (2019a) reduce the detection accuracy to 1% while we can only manage to degrade it to 10%. This might be due to the imbalanced label distribution and comparatively small size of the CLAUDETTE dataset. Our human evaluation is an initial exploration with only 19 participants. Future work will focus on using crowdsourcing techniques for large survey data collection. Furthermore, we generate the 'no_subword' triggers by skipping all the tokens preceded by the double hashtag '##'. This enables us to avoid derivational morphemes and inflection suffixes but fails to exclude bound stems such as 'consul', which makes some triggers obvious to human readers. Future work can explore better ways to generate natural triggers.

Ethics Statement

The study presented here works exclusively with the publicly available CLAUDETTE dataset, which consists of the Terms of Service (ToS) Agreements of various online platforms. The techniques described in this paper are prone to misuse. However, we design this study to draw public attention to the vulnerability of the transformer-based classification model. We hope our work will help accelerate progress in detecting and defending adversarial attacks. We finetuned the victim model and generated all the triggers on Google Colab. Our models adapted pretrained language models and we did not engage in any training of such large models from scratch. We did not track computation hours.

References

Yonatan Belinkov and Yonatan Bisk. 2017. Synthetic and natural noise both break neural machine translation. *arXiv preprint arXiv:1711.02173*.

Ilias Chalkidis, Manos Fergadiotis, Prodromos Malakasiotis, Nikolaos Aletras, and Ion Androutsopoulos. 2020. LEGAL-BERT: The muppets straight out of law school. In *Findings of the Association for Computational Linguistics: EMNLP 2020*, pages 2898–2904, Online. Association for Computational Linguistics.

Yong Cheng, Lu Jiang, and Wolfgang Macherey. 2019. Robust neural machine translation with doubly adversarial inputs. In *Proceedings of the 57th Annual Meeting of the Association for Computational Linguistics*, pages 4324–4333, Florence, Italy. Association for Computational Linguistics.

Kenneth Church and Patrick Hanks. 1990. Word association norms, mutual information, and lexicography. *Computational linguistics*, 16(1):22–29.

Javid Ebrahimi, Anyi Rao, Daniel Lowd, and Dejing Dou. 2018. HotFlip: White-box adversarial examples for text classification. In *Proceedings of the 56th Annual Meeting of the Association for Computational Linguistics (Volume 2: Short Papers)*, pages 31–36, Melbourne, Australia. Association for Computational Linguistics.

Miguel Grinberg. 2018. *Flask web development: developing web applications with python.* " O'Reilly Media, Inc.".

Suchin Gururangan, Swabha Swayamdipta, Omer Levy, Roy Schwartz, Samuel Bowman, and Noah A. Smith. 2018. Annotation artifacts in natural language inference data. In *Proceedings of the 2018 Conference of the North American Chapter of the Association for Computational Linguistics: Human Language Technologies, Volume 2 (Short Papers)*, pages 107–112, New Orleans, Louisiana. Association for Computational Linguistics.

Mohit Iyyer, John Wieting, Kevin Gimpel, and Luke Zettlemoyer. 2018. Adversarial example generation with syntactically controlled paraphrase networks. In *Proceedings of the 2018 Conference of the North American Chapter of the Association for Computational Linguistics: Human Language Technologies, Volume 1 (Long Papers)*, pages 1875–1885, New Orleans, Louisiana. Association for Computational Linguistics.

Marco Lippi, Przemysław Pałka, Giuseppe Contissa, Francesca Lagioia, Hans-Wolfgang Micklitz, Giovanni Sartor, and Paolo Torroni. 2019. Claudette: an automated detector of potentially unfair clauses in online terms of service. *Artificial Intelligence and Law*, 27(2):117–139.

Tom McCoy, Ellie Pavlick, and Tal Linzen. 2019. Right for the wrong reasons: Diagnosing syntactic heuristics in natural language inference. In *Proceedings of the 57th Annual Meeting of the Association for Computational Linguistics*, pages 3428–3448, Florence, Italy. Association for Computational Linguistics.

Jonathan A Obar and Anne Oeldorf-Hirsch. 2020. The biggest lie on the internet: Ignoring the privacy policies and terms of service policies of social networking services. *Information, Communication & Society*, 23(1):128–147.

Abhijit S Pandya and Robert B Macy. 1995. *Pattern recognition with neural networks in C++*. CRC press.

Shuhuai Ren, Yihe Deng, Kun He, and Wanxiang Che. 2019. Generating natural language adversarial examples through probability weighted word saliency. In *Proceedings of the 57th Annual Meeting of the Association for Computational Linguistics*, pages 1085–1097, Florence, Italy. Association for Computational Linguistics.

Federico Ruggeri, Francesca Lagioia, Marco Lippi, and Paolo Torroni. 2022. Detecting and explaining unfairness in consumer contracts through memory networks. *Artificial Intelligence and Law*, 30(1):59–92.

Tal Schuster, Darsh Shah, Yun Jie Serene Yeo, Daniel Roberto Filizzola Ortiz, Enrico Santus, and Regina Barzilay. 2019. Towards debiasing fact verification models. In *Proceedings of the 2019 Conference on Empirical Methods in Natural Language Processing and the 9th International Joint Conference on Natural Language Processing (EMNLP-IJCNLP)*, pages 3419–3425.

Liwei Song, Xinwei Yu, Hsuan-Tung Peng, and Karthik Narasimhan. 2021. Universal adversarial attacks with natural triggers for text classification. In *Proceedings of the 2021 Conference of the North American Chapter of the Association for Computational Linguistics: Human Language Technologies*, pages 3724–3733, Online. Association for Computational Linguistics.

Eric Wallace, Shi Feng, Nikhil Kandpal, Matt Gardner, and Sameer Singh. 2019a. Universal adversarial triggers for attacking and analyzing NLP. In *Proceedings of the 2019 Conference on Empirical Methods in Natural Language Processing and the 9th International Joint Conference on Natural Language Processing (EMNLP-IJCNLP)*, pages 2153–2162, Hong Kong, China. Association for Computational Linguistics.

Eric Wallace, Pedro Rodriguez, Shi Feng, Ikuya Yamada, and Jordan Boyd-Graber. 2019b. Trick me if you can: Human-in-the-loop generation of adversarial examples for question answering. *Transactions of the Association for Computational Linguistics*, 7:387–401.

Boxin Wang, Hengzhi Pei, Boyuan Pan, Qian Chen, Shuohang Wang, and Bo Li. 2020. T3: Tree-autoencoder constrained adversarial text generation for targeted attack. In *Proceedings of the 2020 Conference on Empirical Methods in Natural Language Processing (EMNLP)*, pages 6134–6150, Online. Association for Computational Linguistics.

Yumeng Wang. 2022. Global triggers for attacking and analyzing ranking models. Master's thesis, Hannover: Gottfried Wilhelm Leibniz Universität.

Thomas Wolf, Lysandre Debut, Victor Sanh, Julien Chaumond, Clement Delangue, Anthony Moi, Pierric Cistac, Tim Rault, Rémi Louf, Morgan Funtowicz, et al. 2019. Huggingface's transformers: State-of-the-art natural language processing. *arXiv preprint arXiv:1910.03771*.

Shanshan Xu and Katja Markert. 2022. The chinese causative-passive homonymy disambiguation: an adversarial dataset for nli and a probing task. In *Proceedings of the 13th Language Resources and Evaluation Conference*, Marseille, France. European Language Resources Association.

Melvin J Yap and David A Balota. 2007. Additive and interactive effects on response time distributions in visual word recognition. *Journal of Experimental Psychology: Learning, Memory, and Cognition*, 33(2):274.

Zhengli Zhao, Dheeru Dua, and Sameer Singh. 2018. Generating natural adversarial examples. In *International Conference on Learning Representations*.

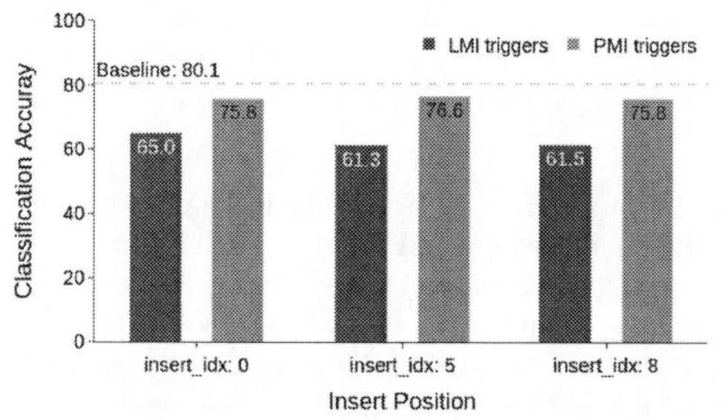

Figure 3: Attack performance of LMI trigger and PMI trigger of the different insert position.

split	# sentences	% fair label	% unfair label
train	8354	89.5%	10.5%
dev	8279	89.1%	10.9%
test	3784	89.3%	10.7%

Table 2: Statistics of the train, dev and test split of the CLAUDETTE dataset.

A Dataset Statistics

Table 2 displays the statics of the CLAUDETTE dataset.

B Finetuning the Victim Model

We used LEGAL-BERT (nlpaueb/legal-bert-base-uncased) with a sequence classification head on top from the transformers library (Wolf et al., 2019); and finetuned it on the CLAUDETTE training set. The model is fine-tuned with 5 epochs, a learning rate of 1e-5. We determine the best learning rate using grid search on the development set and use early stopping based on the development set F1 score.

C Additional Experimental Results

Table 3 demonstrates the attack results on *fair* clauses. Restricted to limited GPU resources, we generated only triggers of eight tokens which are inserted at the beginning of the sentence.

Table 4 displays the attack on *unfair* clauses with triggers of different lengths [3,5,8], insert position [begin, middle, end] and mode [original, no_subword].

D Instruction for the human evaluation study

The application is written in Python using Flask (Grinberg, 2018) and was hosted on an AWS EC2 instance. It included a landing page with a short instructions. Figure 4 is a screenshot of the web application. Following is the instruction on the landing page for the human evaluation study:

"Background information

When using online platforms, users are asked to agree to the Terms of Service (ToS). ToS documents tend to be long and difficult to understand. As a result, most users accept the terms without reading them, including clauses which would be deemed unfair under consumer protection standards. Therefore, applications that can support consumers in detecting unfair clauses would be useful. Nevertheless, studies have shown that such applications are vulnerable to adversarial attacks; even slight modifications to the input text, like inserting a few words into the text, can cause incorrect classifications. In this study, we ask you to help us detect the malicious modifications in the text.

Task instruction

You will be shown an excerpt of four sentences from a ToS contract. The task is to identify which sentence is modified. Please feel free to contact us if you have any questions. Many thanks for taking part in the study."

E LMI and PMI triggers

Figure 3 demonstrates the attack performance of LMI and PMI triggers. The 8 highest LMI ranked words that used as LMI trigger are ['information', 'payment', 'must', 'provide', 'person', 'license', 'rights', 'please']. The PMI trigger words are: ['berlin', 'attribution', 'addressing', 'android', 'sources', 'organiser', 'pc', 'unreasonable']

Trigger	Length	Position	Mode	Accuracy	Δ
Baseline	-	-	-	97.7	
not liable whenever	3	beginning	no_sub	69.8	-28.5%
terminate our convening practices if	5	beginning	no_sub	47.6	-51.2%
agree tankage bound through cloud terms 2016 laws	8	beginning	no_sub	9.0	-90.0%

Table 3: Performance of Universal Triggers on Fair Clauses

Trigger	Length	Position	Mode	Accu.	Δ
Baseline	-	-	-	80.1	
witness should testify	3	beginning	no_sub	58.4	-27.0%
may vote against	3	middle	no_sub	60.8	-24.1%
witness testified without	3	end	no_sub	62.9	-21.5%
interrelat order refusing priority where	5	beginning	no_sub	37.1	-53.7%
consul must produce his attorney	5	middle	no_sub	46.6	-41.9%
privilege to authenticate testimony groot	5	end	no_sub	48.1	-39.9%
testimony allows contracts opposing person tuber testify where	8	beginning	no_sub	13.9	-82.7%
compute another opponent shall testify unless lockbox opponent	8	middle	no_sub	19.7	-75.4%
another witness seems thus admissible scope testify usc	8	end	no_sub	22.6	-71.8%
admissible in evidence	3	beginning	all	56.7	-29.3%
##assignabilityconsult assigned	3	middle	all	59.9	-25.2%
[SEP] expert testimony	3	end	all	60.2	-24.8%
evid allowed equit testify where	5	beginning	all	31.4	-67%
[SEP] give precedence before priority	5	middle	all	43.6	-45.6%
368 hearsay witnesses may exclude	5	end	all	43.1	-46.2%
inference forbid 2028 opposing person may testify where	8	beginning	all	12.8	-84.0%
##purchased another opponent shall testify unless actuarial opponent	8	middle	all	16.9	-78.9%
assist [SEP] witness normally justifies cross admissibilitywillingness	8	end	all	19.2	-76.0%

Table 4: Performance of Universal Triggers on Unfair Label

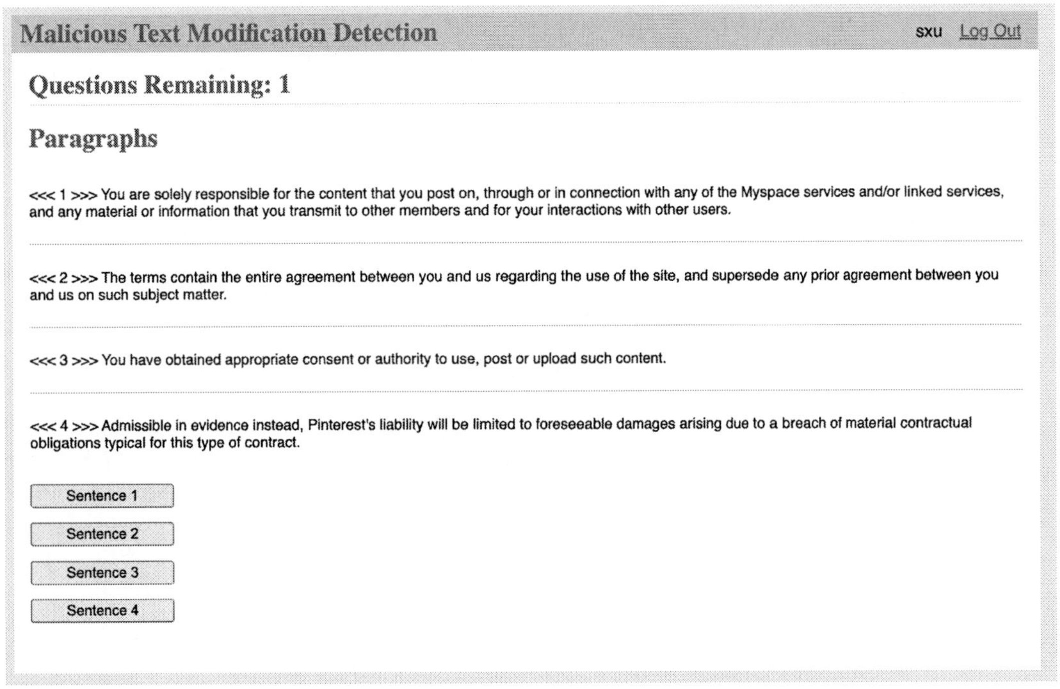

Figure 4: Screenshot of the web application for human evaluation

E-NER — An Annotated Named Entity Recognition Corpus of Legal Text

Ting Wai Terence Au[1], **Vasileios Lampos**[1] and **Ingemar J. Cox**[1,2]

[1] Centre for Artificial Intelligence, Department of Computer Science, University College London, UK

[2] Department of Computer Science, University of Copenhagen, Denmark

{ting.au.19, v.lampos}@ucl.ac.uk, ingemar@ieee.org

Abstract

Identifying named entities such as a person, location or organization, in documents can highlight key information to readers. Training Named Entity Recognition (NER) models requires an annotated data set, which can be a time-consuming labour-intensive task. Nevertheless, there are publicly available NER data sets for general English. Recently there has been interest in developing NER for legal text. However, prior work and experimental results reported here indicate that there is a significant degradation in performance when NER methods trained on a general English data set are applied to legal text. We describe a publicly available legal NER data set, called E-NER, based on legal company filings available from the US Securities and Exchange Commission's EDGAR data set. Training a number of different NER algorithms on the general English CoNLL-2003 corpus but testing on our test collection confirmed significant degradations in accuracy, as measured by the F1-score, of between 29.4% and 60.4%, compared to training and testing on the E-NER collection.

1 Introduction

Named Entity Recognition (NER) aims to identify names of specific objects in the world (mostly nouns with few exceptions), such as the name of a person, location and organization, which indicate possibly important phrases that readers should pay attention to. NER has been used in a variety of downstream tasks such as question answering (Mollá et al., 2006), document de-identification (Stubbs et al., 2015; Catelli et al., 2020), relation extraction (Miwa and Bansal, 2016), and machine translation (Babych and Hartley, 2003). Consequently, there has been considerable work on NER using general language corpora (Yadav and Bethard, 2018; Li et al., 2020a) and a variety of test collections are available. Previous work has examined domain-specific NER, e.g. in finance (Alvarado et al., 2015; Alexander and de Vries, 2021; Zhang and Zhang, 2022), biomedical (Zhou et al., 2004; Wang et al., 2018), online user-generated content (Tran et al., 2015; Li et al., 2014), and legal (Luz de Araujo et al., 2018) applications, and found that the performance of domain-specific NER systems was poor if trained on general language corpora. Constructing test collections for specialist domains can be a time consuming task requiring manual annotation of a corpus. To reduce this effort there has been considerable recent interest in transfer learning, such as pre-trained language models (Brown et al., 2020; Howard and Ruder, 2018). Nevertheless, there remains a need for specialist test collections whether for training or fine-tuning.

Legal text is one specialist domain where NER is of interest, due to its usefulness in assisting other legal tasks such as record linkage (Dozier et al., 2010), court case linkage (Kříž et al., 2014), contract analysis (Chalkidis et al., 2017), prediction of judicial decisions (Aletras et al., 2016), credit risk assessment (Alvarado et al., 2015), and question-answering systems (Jayakumar et al., 2020). However, despite increasing interest in this sub-domain, there is no publicly available corpus for the evaluation of NER methods for legal applications.

This paper describes E-NER, an annotated NER collection of legal documents,[1] based on publicly available legal company filings in the United States Securities and Exchange Commissions' EDGAR database. Overall, we deployed four NER models to compare classification performance when (i) trained and tested on general English, (ii) trained on general English and tested on E-NER, and (iii) trained and tested on E-NER. The results support insights from earlier work, i.e. we observed significant performance degradation when trained on general English but tested on legal text. Our experiments justify the utility of a domain-specific (legal)

[1] E-NER data set, github.com/terenceau2/E-NER-Dataset

Proceedings of the Natural Legal Language Processing Workshop 2022, pages 246 - 255
December 8, 2022

NER corpus.

2 Related work

The primary contribution of this paper is a legal-English test collection for NER. We do not propose a new algorithm for NER and consequently restrict our description of NER methods to those used in our experimental work.

Hidden Markov models (HMM) (Rabiner and Juang, 1986) can be used to label sequences. Bikel et al. (1997) demonstrated the application of HMM to NER. Conditional Random Fields (CRF) (Lafferty et al., 2001) is another sequence labelling model which improves on HMM, by relaxing the stationarity and the output independence assumptions. McCallum and Li (2003) and Sobhana et al. (2010) demonstrated the application of CRF to NER.

In more recent years, pre-trained language models (Qiu et al., 2020) and prompt-based learning (Liu et al., 2022) have demonstrated superior performance. Bidirectional Encoder Representations from Transformers (BERT) (Devlin et al., 2019) is a pre-trained language model which is based on transformers (Vaswani et al., 2017). BERT pre-trains on a large corpus of non annotated text, performing self-supervised tasks, namely masked word prediction and next sentence pairing. BERT can facilitate transfer learning: the model parameters from the pre-training step are used during the fine-tuning step, in order for the model to learn downstream tasks such as NER (Souza et al., 2019; Hakala and Pyysalo, 2019; Li et al., 2020b).

There exist publicly available annotated NER data sets for general English text, such as CoNLL-2003 (Sang and De Meulder, 2003), WNUT17 (Derczynski et al., 2017), and the Wikipedia gold standard corpus (Balasuriya et al., 2009), as well as for other languages (Neudecker, 2016; Sang and De Meulder, 2003; Santos et al., 2006; Ševčíková et al., 2007). For legal domain-specific data sets, non annotated legal text is abundant, as detailed in Pontrandolfo (2012). For example, the pre-training of Legal-BERT (Chalkidis et al., 2020) is performed on a corpus of non annotated documents consisting of legislation, court cases, and contracts from the UK, US, and the European Union. However, the fine-tuning of Legal-BERT is based on an annotated data set CONTRACTS-NER that is not publicly available. Alvarado et al. (2015) annotated 8 filings from the US SEC EDGAR data set, the source of documents for our data set. The primary distinction between their work and ours is the size of the data set, 54K tokens in their data set vs. 400K tokens in ours. Furthermore, Alvarado et al. (2015) was focused on NER in the financial (credit risk) rather than legal domain.

Păiș et al. (2021) published a Romanian NER data set consisting of 370 legal documents, and Trias et al. (2021) created a data set consisting of header sections of court cases text (the header section will declare the parties involved in a court case). Finally, we also note that the EDGAR database has been used by Loukas et al. (2022) to create an annotated data set, called FiNER, which contains over 1.1 million sentences. However, this data set is tagged with eXtensive Business Reporting Language (XBRL) tags, and it is used for numeric entity recognition.

3 EDGAR-NER (E-NER) data set

We first describe the source documents that constitute the EDGAR-NER (E-NER) data set. We then enumerate the named entity classes, which slightly extend those used by CoNLL-2003 (CoNLL),[2] which is widely used in the NER community.

Financial entities, such as companies, individuals, and funds, that are registered with the United States Securities and Exchange Commission (US SEC) are required by law to submit financial filings to the Electronic Data Gathering, Analysis, and Retrieval system (EDGAR). All filings in the EDGAR data set are publicly available. There is a wide variety of different filings some of which contain almost no text, e.g. Form 3 (Initial statement of beneficial ownership of securities) or Form 4 (Statement of changes in beneficial ownership of securities). We have arbitrarily chosen the year 2010 and downloaded 52 documents.

The 52 EDGAR documents consisted of a variety of different filings. We only selected filings that contain content in the form of sentences, such as Form 10-Q, which are company quarterly reports, or Form 8-K, which are used by companies to announce major events relevant to their shareholders. The 52 documents consist of 24 different types of forms. Please see Appendix A for details.

The filings were downloaded using the index file[3] provided by EDGAR, in the form of HTML

[2]CoNLL-2003, clips.uantwerpen.be/conll2003/ner/

[3]This is available at sec.gov/os/accessing-edgar-data.

text. Each document was pre-processed using the Python package "Beautiful Soup" to extract sentences. We remove:

• the SEC filing header, where the filer fills in the information in a designated space. This is indicated by the HTML tag `<SEC-HEADER>`.

• graphical elements, such as company logos or scanned photos. This is indicated by `<TYPE>GRAPHIC`.

• tables with no sentences in them. Tables are indicated by the HTML tag `TABLE`.

• page titles and page numbers.

• figures and plots.

• any XBRL (eXtensible Business Reporting Language) instance.

An illustration of what elements we removed or kept in an example filing is shown in Appendix B. After preprocessing the 52 documents, we split the document into sentences by identifying the line breaks in the document, and using the sentence tokenizer from the Python NLTK package. In total, we identified 11,696 sentences that required annotation.

Annotation of the collection was performed by the first author. Note that we did attempt to outsource the annotation to a commercial crowdsourcing platform. We provided instructions, including the definitions of the named entity classes and the tagging guidelines. Each document was assigned to 3 crowd workers to independently label so as to ensure the correctness of the labels. However, we found that there were significant discrepancies in the labels provided. While we acknowledge that this variation may have been due to our instructions being poor, it is our opinion that the task has a significant difficulty for a non-expert.

The CoNLL-2003 data set defines 4 classes of named entities (and the class "Outside" for non-named entities)[4] as enumerated in Table 1. For our data set we annotated the filings with 7 named entity classes as shown in Table 1. We note that there is no consensus on the appropriate labeling of named entities for the legal domain, with various authors (Dozier et al., 2010; Cardellino et al., 2017; Leitner et al., 2019) proposing related but different classifications. Our class labels were chosen in consultation with a legal company (Clifford Chance LLP). Note, however, that for the experimental results reported in Section 4, we used the same categories as CoNLL-2003, merging and matching categories as shown in Table 1. E-NER follows the same file format conventions as CoNLL.

[4]See cnts.ua.ac.be/conll2003/ner/annotation.txt

CoNLL	E-NER
Location	Location
Person	Person
Organization	Business
	Goverment
	Court
Miscellaneous	Legislation/Act
	Miscellaneous

Table 1: Named entities used in the CoNLL and E-NER data sets and their pairing in the two classficiation frameworks

Table 2 provides a statistical comparison between the E-NER and CoNLL-2003 data sets. We see that while the number of tokens in the E-NER data set exceeds that of CoNLL (by combining the training, validation, and test sets), the number of NE phrases is considerably smaller (8,821 for E-NER, compared to 35,088 CoNLL combined). We also observe that the CoNLL data set has considerably more sentences (22,136 vs. 11,696) and that these sentences are much shorter (13.7 words vs. 34.5 words per sentence). The number of tokens constituting a NE is also shorter in CoNLL (1.45 vs. 2.68).

4 Experiments

To verify the need for a legal NER collection, we evaluated the performance of four NER methods by (i) training and testing on a general English collection (CoNLL), (ii) training on general English, but testing on our legal collection (E-NER), and (iii) training and testing on our E-NER collection.

The CoNLL collection is subdivided into train, validation, and test partitions, as indicated in Table 2. When training and testing using E-NER, we performed k-fold cross-validation. Since the size of the train and test data sets in CoNLL-2003 has a ratio of approximately 4:1, we chose $k = 5$. We report the micro-F1 score.

Data set	Tokens	Sentences	Avg. words / sentence	NE phrases	Avg. tokens / NE
CoNLL train	204,563	14,986	13.7	23,498	1.45
CoNLL val.	51,578	3,466	14.9	5,942	1.45
CoNLL test	46,666	3,684	12.7	5,648	1.44
E-NER	403,673	11,696	34.5	8,821	2.68

Table 2: Basic statistics of the CoNLL and E-NER data sets

4.1 CoNLL-2003 workshop baseline model

The baseline model records all the NE phrases in the training set. During testing, phrases are matched against these learned NE phrases and labeled accordingly (i.e. there is no generalisation). If a phrase in the dictionary has multiple NE classes associated to it, the one with the highest frequency is used.

4.2 Hidden Markov Model

Our HMM implementation follows the same approach as proposed by Morwal et al. (2012). The NE tags are treated as the hidden states, and the tokens are treated as the observations.

4.3 Conditional Random Fields

Our CRF implementation is similar to the one proposed by McCallum and Li (2003). However, we did not use lexicons or other reference corpora to assist our CRF models to identify names of countries, companies, and surnames. Our choice of feature functions is hand-crafted, and consists of (i) the current word, (ii) the first and last 2 letters of the current word, (iii) the capitalization of the word, and (iv) the above 3 features for the word to the left and to the right of the current word.

Model	G to G	G to L	L to L
Baseline	.596	.136	.491
HMM	.622	.148	.401
CRF	.820	.216	.902
BERT	.905	.611	.961

Table 3: F1-scores of different models when trained (or fine-tuned) and tested on different data sets. In the column headers, the first entry is the training data set (or data set to fine-tune on), and the second is the test data set. **G** denotes a general data set for NER (here CoNLL), and **L** denotes a legal data set (here E-NER). For the column **L to L**, we perform 5-fold cross-validation.

4.4 BERT

We used a pre-trained version of BERT.[5] In our experiments, we fine-tuned BERT using Hugging Face's transformer package.[6]

4.5 Results

In Table 3, we present the F1-score for the aforementioned NER models when we train and test them on different data sets. In the columns, the first entry in the brackets shows the data set used for training (or fine-tuning), and the second entry shows the test data sets.

When we train and test the models on the CoNLL corpus, F1-scores range from 59.6% to 90.5%. However, when we train on CoNLL and test on E-NER, F1-scores degrade significantly, ranging from 13.6% to 61.1%. When training and testing using the E-NER collection the F1-scores range from 49.1% to 96.1% which consistutes a significant improvement over training using the CoNLL data set. Interestingly, we observe that the dictionary baseline and HMM models perform similarly or worse on legal text compared to their performance on general English. Conversely, for the more advanced CRF and BERT models, performance on legal text exceeds that for general English. It is unclear whether this is principally due to differences in the models, or differences in the test collections. Nevertheless, experimental results support earlier work indicating degradation in performance when NER methods are trained on general English but applied to the legal domain.

5 Conclusions and future work

This paper describes the publicly available E-NER data set, derived from company filings from the US SEC EDGAR data set. The collection contains over 400,000 tokens, and as such, is of similar size to the CoNLL-2003 collection. However, the number

[5]BERT, huggingface.co/bert-base-uncased

[6]Available at github.com/huggingface/transformers/tree/main/examples/pytorch/token-classification.

of NE phrases (almost 9,000) is only about 25% of the number of NE phrases in the CoNLL corpus. In part, this reflects the statistical differences between general and legal English, where we observed that the sentence length for legal English (34.5 words) is much larger than for general English (13.7), and that the token length of a NE in legal text is longer (2.68 tokens compared to 1.45). In addition, the fact that E-NER encompasses only 52 documents from EDGAR might also contribute to this discrepancy.

Our experimental results compared the performance of four NER methods when trained and tested on combinations of general and legal English. Our results reaffirm that for legal NER in-domain performance is significantly degraded when training without using specific in-domain data.

There is a number of potential future research directions. First, there is a variety of legal specialities, e.g. finance, civil litigation, and criminal law. Further work is needed to investigate how NER models perform in various legal sub-domains – how diverge and large should annotated corpora be for legal NER? To this end, we plan to create annotated datasets for other types of legal documents, such as court proceedings or contracts. In addition, the evaluation of NER models using state-of-the-art methods and language models in legal NLP might unveil more informative results and drive potential methodological improvements.

Acknowledgements

T.W.T.A. and I.J.C. would like to thank Clifford Chance LLP for the financial support and for providing guidance with respect to requirements from the legal community.

References

Nikolaos Aletras, Dimitrios Tsarapatsanis, Daniel Preoţiuc-Pietro, and Vasileios Lampos. 2016. Predicting judicial decisions of the European Court of Human Rights: A natural language processing perspective. *PeerJ Computer Science*, 2:e93.

Daria Alexander and Arjen P de Vries. 2021. "This research is funded by...": Named Entity Recognition of Financial Information in Research Papers. In *Proceedings of the 11th International Workshop on Bibliometric-enhanced Information Retrieval*, pages 102–110.

Julio Cesar Salinas Alvarado, Karin Verspoor, and Timothy Baldwin. 2015. Domain adaption of Named Entity Recognition to support credit risk assessment. In *Proceedings of the Australasian Language Technology Association Workshop*, pages 84–90.

Bogdan Babych and Anthony Hartley. 2003. Improving machine translation quality with automatic named entity recognition. In *Proceedings of the 7th International EAMT workshop on MT and other language technology tools, Improving MT through other language technology tools, Resource and tools for building MT at EACL 2003*.

Dominic Balasuriya, Nicky Ringland, Joel Nothman, Tara Murphy, and James R Curran. 2009. Named entity recognition in Wikipedia. In *Proceedings of the 2009 workshop on the people's web meets NLP: Collaboratively constructed semantic resources (People's Web)*, pages 10–18.

Daniel M Bikel, Scott Miller, Richard Schwartz, and Ralph Weischedel. 1997. Nymble: a high-performance learning name-finder. In *Fifth Conference on Applied Natural Language Processing*, pages 194–201.

Tom Brown, Benjamin Mann, Nick Ryder, Melanie Subbiah, Jared D Kaplan, Prafulla Dhariwal, Arvind Neelakantan, Pranav Shyam, Girish Sastry, Amanda Askell, et al. 2020. Language models are few-shot learners. In *NeurIPS*, volume 33, pages 1877–1901.

Cristian Cardellino, Milagro Teruel, Laura Alonso Alemany, and Serena Villata. 2017. A low-cost, high-coverage legal named entity recognizer, classifier and linker. In *Proceedings of the 16th edition of the International Conference on Articial Intelligence and Law*, pages 9–18.

Rosario Catelli, Francesco Gargiulo, Valentina Casola, Giuseppe De Pietro, Hamido Fujita, and Massimo Esposito. 2020. Crosslingual named entity recognition for clinical de-identification applied to a COVID-19 Italian data set. *Applied Soft Computing*, 97:106779.

Ilias Chalkidis, Ion Androutsopoulos, and Achilleas Michos. 2017. Extracting contract elements. In *Proceedings of the 16th edition of the International Conference on Articial Intelligence and Law*, pages 19–28.

Ilias Chalkidis, Manos Fergadiotis, Prodromos Malakasiotis, Nikolaos Aletras, and Ion Androutsopoulos. 2020. LEGAL-BERT: The Muppets straight out of Law School. In *Findings of the Association for Computational Linguistics: EMNLP 2020*, pages 2898–2904.

Leon Derczynski, Eric Nichols, Marieke van Erp, and Nut Limsopatham. 2017. Results of the WNUT2017 shared task on novel and emerging entity recognition. In *Proceedings of the 3rd Workshop on Noisy User-generated Text*, pages 140–147.

Jacob Devlin, Ming-Wei Chang, Kenton Lee, and Kristina Toutanova. 2019. BERT: Pre-training of deep bidirectional transformers for language understanding. In *Proceedings of the 2019 Conference of the North American Chapter of the Association for Computational Linguistics: Human Language Technologies, Volume 1 (Long and Short Papers)*, pages 4171–4186.

Christopher Dozier, Ravikumar Kondadadi, Marc Light, Arun Vachher, Sriharsha Veeramachaneni, and Ramdev Wudali. 2010. *Named Entity Recognition and Resolution in Legal Text*, pages 27–43. Springer.

Kai Hakala and Sampo Pyysalo. 2019. Biomedical named entity recognition with multilingual BERT. In *Proceedings of the 5th workshop on BioNLP open shared tasks*, pages 56–61.

Jeremy Howard and Sebastian Ruder. 2018. Universal Language Model Fine-tuning for Text Classification. In *Proceedings of the 56th Annual Meeting of the Association for Computational Linguistics (Volume 1: Long Papers)*, pages 328–339.

Hariharan Jayakumar, Madhav Sankar Krishnakumar, Vishal Veda Vyas Peddagopu, and Rajeswari Sridhar. 2020. RNN based question answer generation and ranking for financial documents using financial NER. *Sādhanā*, 45(1):1–10.

Vincent Kríž, Barbora Hladká, Jan Dědek, and Martin Nečaský. 2014. Statistical recognition of references in Czech court decisions. In *Mexican International Conference on Artificial Intelligence*, pages 51–61.

John D. Lafferty, Andrew McCallum, and Fernando C. N. Pereira. 2001. Conditional Random Fields: Probabilistic Models for Segmenting and Labeling Sequence Data. In *Proceedings of the 18th International Conference on Machine Learning*, pages 282—-289.

Elena Leitner, Georg Rehm, and Julian Moreno-Schneider. 2019. Fine-grained named entity recognition in legal documents. In *International Conference on Semantic Systems*, pages 272–287.

Chenliang Li, Aixin Sun, Jianshu Weng, and Qi He. 2014. Tweet segmentation and its application to named entity recognition. *IEEE Transactions on Knowledge and Data Engineering*, 27(2):558–570.

Jing Li, Aixin Sun, Jianglei Han, and Chenliang Li. 2020a. A survey on deep learning for named entity recognition. *IEEE Transactions on Knowledge and Data Engineering*, 34(1):50–70.

Xiangyang Li, Huan Zhang, and Xiao-Hua Zhou. 2020b. Chinese clinical named entity recognition with variant neural structures based on BERT methods. *Journal of Biomedical Informatics*, 107:103422.

Pengfei Liu, Weizhe Yuan, Jinlan Fu, Zhengbao Jiang, Hiroaki Hayashi, and Graham Neubig. 2022. Pre-Train, Prompt, and Predict: A Systematic Survey of Prompting Methods in Natural Language Processing. *ACM Computing Surveys*. In Press.

Lefteris Loukas, Manos Fergadiotis, Ilias Chalkidis, Eirini Spyropoulou, Prodromos Malakasiotis, Ion Androutsopoulos, and Georgios Paliouras. 2022. FiNER: Financial numeric entity recognition for XBRL tagging. In *Proceedings of the 60th Annual Meeting of the Association for Computational Linguistics (Volume 1: Long Papers)*, pages 4419–4431.

Pedro Henrique Luz de Araujo, Teófilo E de Campos, Renato RR de Oliveira, Matheus Stauffer, Samuel Couto, and Paulo Bermejo. 2018. LeNER-Br: a rabiner for named entity recognition in Brazilian legal text. In *International Conference on Computational Processing of the Portuguese Language*, pages 313–323.

Andrew McCallum and Wei Li. 2003. Early results for Named Entity Recognition with Conditional Random Fields, Feature Induction and Web-Enhanced Lexicons. In *Proceedings of the Seventh Conference on Natural Language Learning at HLT-NAACL 2003*, pages 188–191.

Makoto Miwa and Mohit Bansal. 2016. End-to-End Relation Extraction using LSTMs on Sequences and Tree Structures. In *Proceedings of the 54th Annual Meeting of the Association for Computational Linguistics (Volume 1: Long Papers)*, pages 1105–1116.

Diego Mollá, Menno Van Zaanen, and Daniel Smith. 2006. Named entity recognition for question answering. In *Proceedings of the Australasian Language Technology Workshop*, pages 51–58.

Sudha Morwal, Nusrat Jahan, and Deepti Chopra. 2012. Named Entity Recognition using Hidden Markov Model (HMM). *International Journal on Natural Language Computing (IJNLC)*, 1(4):15–23.

Clemens Neudecker. 2016. An open corpus for named entity recognition in historic newspapers. In *Proceedings of the 10th International Conference on Language Resources and Evaluation (LREC'16)*, pages 4348–4352.

Gianluca Pontrandolfo. 2012. Legal corpora: An overview. Technical report, University of Trieste.

Vasile Păiş, Maria Mitrofan, Carol Luca Gasan, Vlad Coneschi, and Alexandru Ianov. 2021. Named entity recognition in the Romanian legal domain. In *Proceedings of the Natural Legal Language Processing Workshop 2021*, pages 9–18.

Xipeng Qiu, Tianxiang Sun, Yige Xu, Yunfan Shao, Ning Dai, and Xuanjing Huang. 2020. Pre-trained models for natural language processing: A survey. *Science China Technological Sciences*, 63(10):1872–1897.

Lawrence Rabiner and Biinghwang Juang. 1986. An introduction to hidden Markov models. *IEEE ASSP Magazine*, 3(1):4–16.

Erik Tjong Kim Sang and Fien De Meulder. 2003. Introduction to the CoNLL-2003 Shared Task: Language-Independent Named Entity Recognition. In *Proceedings of the Seventh Conference on Natural Language Learning at HLT-NAACL 2003*, pages 142–147.

Diana Santos, Nuno Seco, Nuno Cardoso, and Rui Vilela. 2006. HAREM: An advanced NER evaluation contest for Portuguese. In *Proceedings of the 5th International Conference on Language Resources and Evaluation*, pages 1986–1991.

Magda Ševčíková, Zdeněk Žabokrtský, and Oldřich Krůza. 2007. Named entities in Czech: annotating data and developing NE tagger. In *International Conference on Text, Speech and Dialogue*, pages 188–195.

N Sobhana, Pabitra Mitra, and SK Ghosh. 2010. Conditional random field based named entity recognition in geological text. *International Journal of Computer Applications*, 1(3):143–147.

Fábio Souza, Rodrigo Nogueira, and Roberto Lotufo. 2019. Portuguese named entity recognition using BERT-CRF. *arXiv preprint arXiv:1909.10649*.

Amber Stubbs, Christopher Kotfila, and Özlem Uzuner. 2015. Automated systems for the de-identification of longitudinal clinical narratives: Overview of 2014 i2b2/UTHealth shared task Track 1. *Journal of Biomedical Informatics*, 58:S11–S19.

Van Cuong Tran, Dosam Hwang, and Jason J Jung. 2015. Semi-supervised approach based on co-occurrence coefficient for named entity recognition on Twitter. In *2015 2nd National Foundation for Science and Technology Development Conference on Information and Computer Science (NICS)*, pages 141–146.

Fernando Trias, Hongming Wang, Sylvain Jaume, and Stratos Idreos. 2021. Named entity recognition in historic legal text: A transformer and state machine ensemble method. In *Proceedings of the Natural Legal Language Processing Workshop 2021*, pages 172–179.

Ashish Vaswani, Noam Shazeer, Niki Parmar, Jakob Uszkoreit, Llion Jones, Aidan N Gomez, Łukasz Kaiser, and Illia Polosukhin. 2017. Attention is all you need. In *NeurIPS*, volume 30.

Xu Wang, Chen Yang, and Renchu Guan. 2018. A comparative study for biomedical named entity recognition. *International Journal of Machine Learning and Cybernetics*, 9(3):373–382.

Vikas Yadav and Steven Bethard. 2018. A survey on recent advances in named entity recognition from deep learning models. In *Proceedings of the 27th International Conference on Computational Linguistics*, pages 2145–2158.

Yuzhe Zhang and Hong Zhang. 2022. FinBERT-MRC: financial named entity recognition using BERT under the machine reading comprehension paradigm. *arXiv preprint arXiv:2205.15485*.

Guodong Zhou, Jie Zhang, Jian Su, Dan Shen, and ChewLim Tan. 2004. Recognizing names in biomedical texts: a machine learning approach. *Bioinformatics*, 20(7):1178–1190.

A Tables

Form types	Count	Form types	Count
497K	6	DEFA14A	1
8-K	6	N-CSR	1
10-Q	5	POSASR	1
425	4	PRE 14C	1
N-Q	3	SC 13D	1
11-K	3	SC 13DA	1
424B3	3	S-3	1
CORRESP	2	S-4	1
DEF 14A	2	S-8	1
10-K	2	10-KA	1
40-17G	2	424B5	1
497	2	40-APPA	1

Table 4: Type of forms in the E-NER data set

B Example filing

An example filing in the E-NER data set, in the form of the HTML and its rendered version, is shown in Figure 1 and 2. Figure 3 shows an image element in this filing, which we remove during preprocessing. This filing's CIK number is 0001045487. The accession number is 000119312511147903. The URL to this filing is sec.gov/Archives/edgar/data/1045487/0001193125 11147903.

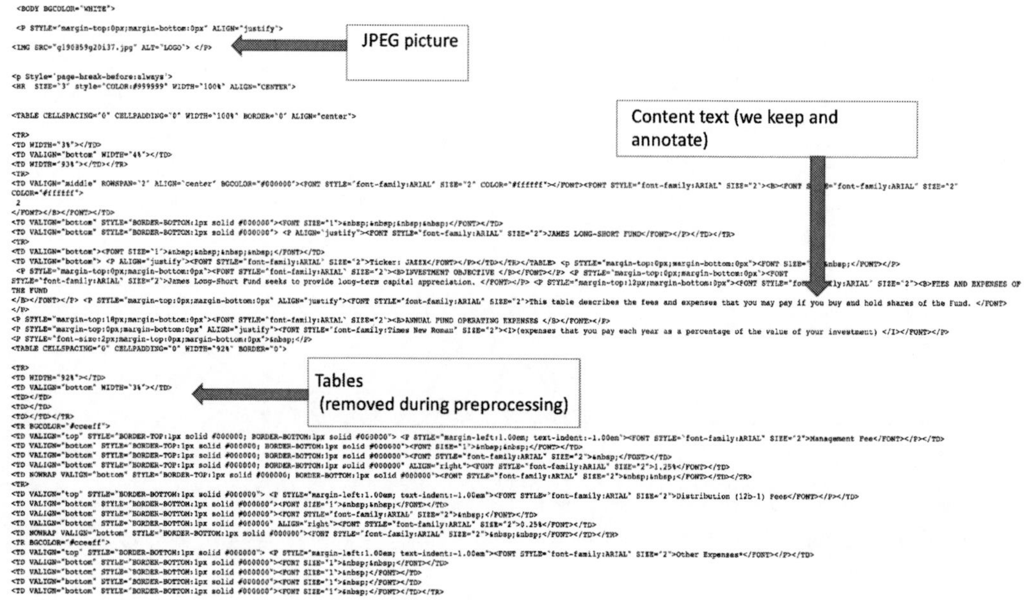

Figure 1: Raw HTML of an example filing, downloaded from the EDGAR database.

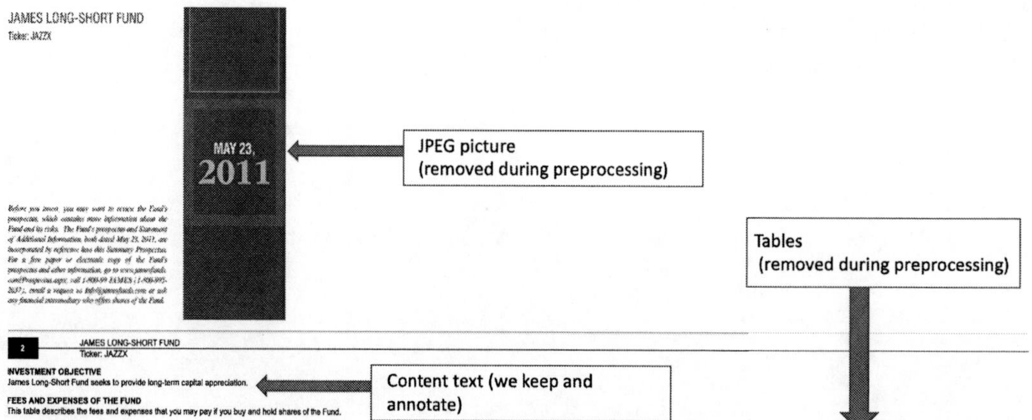

Figure 2: The rendered version of the filing.

Figure 3: Raw HTML of an example filing, where one of the documents uploaded is an image.

Detecting Relevant Differences Between Similar Legal Texts

Xiang Li[*], **Jiaxun Gao**[*], **Diana Inkpen,** and **Wolfgang Alschner**
University of Ottawa
{xli355,jgao081,diana.inkpen,wolfgang.alschner}@uottawa.ca

Abstract

Given two similar legal texts, is it useful to be able to focus only on the parts that contain relevant differences. However, because of variation in linguistic structure and terminology, it is not easy to identify true semantic differences. An accurate difference detection model between similar legal texts is therefore in demand, in order to increase the efficiency of legal research and document analysis. In this paper, we automatically label a training dataset of sentence pairs using an existing legal resource of international investment treaties that were already manually annotated with metadata. Then we propose models based on state-of-the-art deep learning techniques for the novel task of detecting relevant differences. In addition to providing solutions for this task, we include models for automatically producing metadata for the treaties that do not have it.

1 Introduction

Legal documents typical use standardized forms and structures ("boilerplate language"). Moreover, within a given domain, legal documents often follow model texts and templates resulting in shared norms, principles and dispute resolution mechanisms. However, faced with high-similarity texts, what matters most to lawyers are often textual differences. Where does a contract deviate from an industry standard? How does a law differ from an international model law? And when are these differences legally relevant rather than just stylistic?

Our work seeks to detect such relevant differences between otherwise similar legal texts. It uses international investment treaties as a case study. Table 1 and table 2 provide examples to show what we mean by "relevant" differences. Both of these two sentence pairs have cosine similarity scores around 0.97 when applying LegalBERT (Chalkidis et al., 2020a) to represent them as dense vectors.

Sentence 1
The right of each contracting party to establish its own domestic labour standards and to adopt or modify accordingly its labour legislation each contracting party shall strive to ensure that its legislation provide for labour standards consistent with the internationally recognised labour rights set forth in paragraph 6 of article 1 and shall strive to improve those standards in that light.
Sentence 2
Recognising the right of each contracting party to establish its own levels of domestic environmental protection and environmental development policies and priorities and to adopt or modify accordingly its environmental legislation each contracting party shall strive to ensure that its legislation provide for high levels of environmental protection and shall strive to continue to improve this legislation.
Similarity Score: 0.9734

Table 1: Example of *relevant* difference

Sentence 1
Contracting party shall promptly respond to specific questions and provide upon request information to the other contracting party on matters referred to in paragraph 1 of this article.
Sentence 2
Each contracting party shall upon request by the other contracting party promptly respond to specific questions and provide that other contracting party with information on matters set out in paragraph 1.
Similarity Score: 0.9746

Table 2: Example of *stylistic* difference (not semantically relevant)

However, the sentences in table 1 refer to different subjects even though they share a very similar structure: one deals with labour standards; the other talks about environmental protection. This is an example of a relevant difference which would catch the attention of legal researchers. On the contrary, the sentences in table 2 are similar representations with the same legal meaning and are thus not of interest to legal researchers; we call them stylistic differences. Sentences in table 3 differ completely in semantics and structure. However, due to their highly overlapping vocabulary, they would be extracted as similar sentences. The examples are articles from the Electronic Database of Investment

[*]These authors contributed equally to this work.

Proceedings of the Natural Legal Language Processing Workshop 2022, pages 256 - 264
December 8, 2022 ©2022 Association for Computational Linguistics

Sentence 1
Case of reinvestment of returns from the investments these reinvestments and their returns will enjoy the same protection as the initial investments.
Sentence 2
Each contracting party shall accord at all times fair and equitable treatment to investments of investors of the other contracting party.
Similarity Score: 0.8416

Table 3: Example of *irrelevant* difference (not relevant in sentence structure)

Treaties (EDIT) (Alschner et al., 2020), a resource that we will use in this work, as described later, in section 4.

Traditional measures, such as cosine similarity between TF-IDF (term frequency / inverse document frequency) vectors to represent sentences, fail to capture semantic information crucial for separating stylistic and semantic similarity. The variety of the expressions in these texts can easily mislead word-based approaches to provide similarity scores that are too low. At the same time, small but relevant differences can be easily overlooked if state-of-the-art sentence embedding models are applied directly.

In this paper, we address these challenges by proposing a text difference detection model which is trained on international legal treaties to indicate relevant differences between otherwise similar articles.

2 Related Work

There is a growing body of research on Natural Language Processing and Machine Learning techniques for legal applications. The applications that focus on legal text processing can be divided by the type of text: court judgements and related types of texts on one side, and contracts, treaties, or statutes on the other side.

The tasks addressed vary, from information retrieval from large amounts of legal text, to legal text summarization, legal named entity extraction, court judgement prediction, and more. Pre-trained neural language models were developed for English texts, such as LegalBERT (Chalkidis et al., 2020a), as well as for a few other languages (Masala et al., 2021) (Douka et al., 2021).

Common shared legal text mining tasks are exemplified by SemEval-2023 Task 6 LegalEval: Understanding Legal Text [1] which has three subtasks: predicting the rhetorical roles of sentences (such as preamble, fact, ratio, arguments, etc.), legal named entity extraction, and court judgement prediction with explanation. Similarly, the Artificial Intelligence for Legal Assistance (AILA 2021) shared task at FIRE 2021 [2] included a rhetorical role labelling task continued from previous editions, and legal judgement summarization task. (Parikh et al., 2021). Finally, the Competition on Legal Information Extraction/Entailment (COLIEE 2022) [3] included tasks relating to case law and statutory law such as a legal case retrieval task, a legal case entailment task, a Question Answering system based on relevant statutes from a database of Japanese civil code statutes and entailment of a yes/no answer from the retrieved civil code statutes. The solutions used to solve these tasks involved classical information retrieval methods, while a few applied deep learning methods for retrieval (Rabelo et al., 2022).

Specifically relating to statutory law type documents, such as contracts, laws and treaties, there is a growing interest to automatically identify similarities between documents. Use-cases include identifying where national laws implement international laws (Nanda et al., 2019). In addition, researchers have attempted to assess to what extent legal texts copied from each other or from model agreements (Ash and Marian, 2019) (Allee and Elsig, 2019).

While these studies provide insights into document similarity, most legal scholars are interested not in how similar documents are but where and how similar documents differ, as discussed in (Alschner, 2018). Standard text difference detection algorithms (such as diff in linux/unix) are not able to detect which differences are relevant from a semantic point of view and which are not.

Therefore, our task is different from the tasks addressed in related work or in the shared tasks. We are also using a dataset of legal texts that has not been exploited before by computational methods.

3 Definitions

3.1 Document Hierarchy and Structure categories of Articles

A treaty is a highly standardized legal document. It is composed of articles that divide the treaty into "structure categories" such as Preamble, Defini-

[1] https://sites.google.com/view/legaleval/

[2] https://sites.google.com/view/aila-2021

[3] https://sites.ualberta.ca/ rabelo/COLIEE2022/

tions, Exceptions or Final Provisions. Within each of these structure categories, articles can be further classified according to their content. We call these subcategories "content categories". Each article can have multiple content categories but can only belong to exactly one structure category. The structure categories and the content categories together form a tree-like hierarchy of article categories.

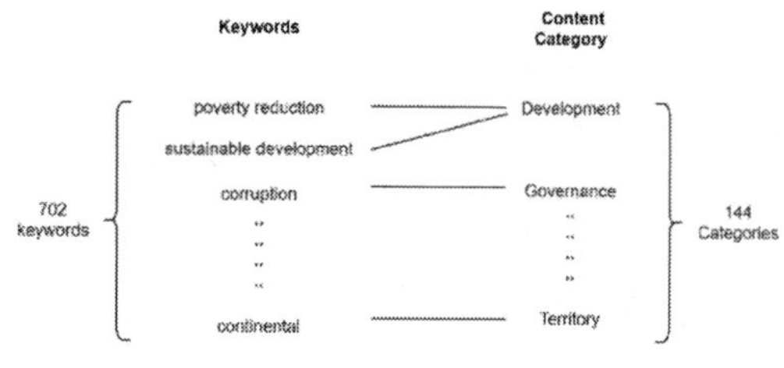

Figure 1: Example of keyword mapping

3.2 Keyword Mapping and Content Categories of Articles

In the EDIT database, articles were manually classified into structure categories. Keywords were then used to map articles to different content categories such as Sustainable Development, Governance, or Environmental Protection. Articles can match with multiple keywords. In that case, all corresponding content categories are assigned to an article.

3.3 Relevant Difference

A relevant difference is an abstract concept that is not the same as differences that are very obvious or too trivial. A relevant difference should be more substantial than a simple replacement of synonymous words (a "stylistic difference"), but less than a difference in structure categories (involving unrelated clauses). For the purpose of this project, sentences within the same structure category but within different content categories are considered relevant differences.

4 Data

The data used in the paper origins from the Electronic Database of Investment Treaties (EDIT) (Alschner et al., 2020), which is a new comprehensive full-text database of international investment agreements (IIAs). It contains 3,786 international treaties. In EDIT, all articles with an article title have their structure category labeled through a manual assignment by experts. 71 different structure categories exist in the dataset. In addition, articles in the treaties were further classified into 144 content categories according to 702 different keywords.

For the task we address in this paper, we need sentence pairs with high similarity to be classified into exhibiting a relevant, stylistic, or irrelevant difference. Instead of asking human judges to label pairs of texts, we use the existing EDIT metadata to construct the labels we need for our training and test data. We first extracted sentence pairs with high similarity scores evenly from within each structure category. We then used the keyword-category mapping from figure 1 to automatically label a dataset of sentence pairs for our task. For each two highly similar sentences (with similarity score bigger than 0.965 and less than 0.98)[4], we label them as only displaying a stylistic difference if both of them share a same set of content categories (according to the keywords they contain). In contrast, if the proportion of overlapping categories is less than one third of the sentence pair's content category union, we consider that one sentence discusses a subject or topic that is distinct from the other and that these two sentences thus have relevant differences. Moreover, we also introduced less similar sentences (with a score less than 0.85)[5] as examples of sentences having irrelevant differences. Via this method, we obtained a dataset with 12,968 sentence (article) pairs. 8,430 of them are sentences that have the same content categories and therefore are labelled as having only stylistic differences (no semantic or legal differences). 2,096 of the sentence pairs are labelled as containing relevant differences which would be the ones of interest to a legal researcher. We also introduced 2,442 sentence pairs which are less similar from each other and labeled as having irrelevant differences. This is done to better simulate common application scenarios[6]. We use this dataset of sentence pairs to train our automatic methods for detecting relevant differences. First, we keep aside 20% of the dataset

[4]Note that these values were chosen in order to produce candidate pairs; they do not affect the labels that will be assigned to them.

[5]This value is selected by observation of the experimental results.

[6]In real-world situations, this kind of irrelevant difference appears pretty commonly when trying to identify similar sentences. We incorporated this irrelevant data in the training process so that the model can better identify them and the final accuracy.

for testing the models that we will train. Figure 2 shows the distribution of the three classes in our dataset.

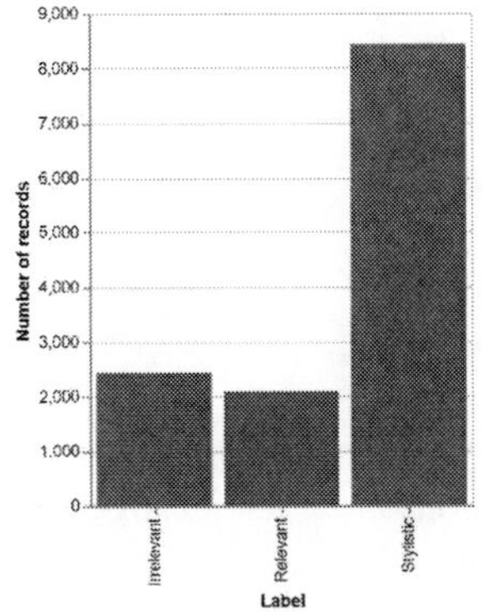

Figure 2: Distribution of labels in the constructed dataset for relevant differences detection

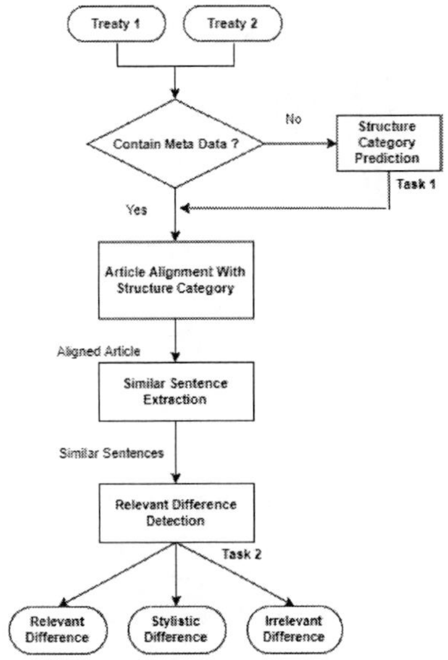

Figure 3: Workflow of relevant difference detection

5 Tasks

The main task of this paper is to distinguish relevant differences from stylistic or irrelevant differences between similar texts, in order to facilitate legal research. This means to ignore differences that are too small and uninteresting from a semantic point of view. At the same time, sentences that are very different are not of interest since they are easy to identify (such sentences were not included in our dataset). To achieve our goal, a few preprocessing tasks (explained below) were be performed in order to build a dataset of similar sentences labeled for relevant differences, to allow us to train the models and evaluate them. Figure 3 shows our workflow.

5.1 Structure Category Prediction

Given two treaties, the first step is to verify whether they contain article meta data. This meta data was manually assigned and is used to match similar articles. As mentioned in section 4, EDIT contains labels for the structure categories for most of the articles. However, there are still 1,052 articles without any meta data. These articles do not contain article title texts and could therefore not be categorized by the experts. As a result, not all the treaties contain structure categories for articles. In this circumstance, an additional classification of articles based on their structure category is required for the unlabeled articles before further analysis on relevant differences can be conducted. As a secondary task, we thus assess the feasibility of assigning structure categories automatically. This will be especially useful when new treaties will be added to EDIT, to avoid the need for more manual annotation.

5.2 Detecting Relevant Differences

After the topic classification, all articles are now labeled with structure categories. An alignment can be constructed between articles that share the same structure category. Similar sentences (having similarity score larger than 0.9) from the aligned articles are extracted and send to further automatic processing for the relevant differences detection. As mentioned above, our models will predict one of three classes: stylistic difference, relevant difference, and irrelevant difference.

6 Methods

6.1 Methods for Structure Category Prediction

6.1.1 Dataset Preprocessing

From all 3,786 legal treaties in EDIT, we extracted 27,530 articles having structure category label as training dataset for topic prediction and 6,883 articles as a separate test dataset. These articles are uniquely labelled with 71 different structure categories (manually entered in EDIT, as mentioned). Inspection on category distribution shows that the training dataset is highly imbalanced. Therefore, we replaced all categories which contain fewer than

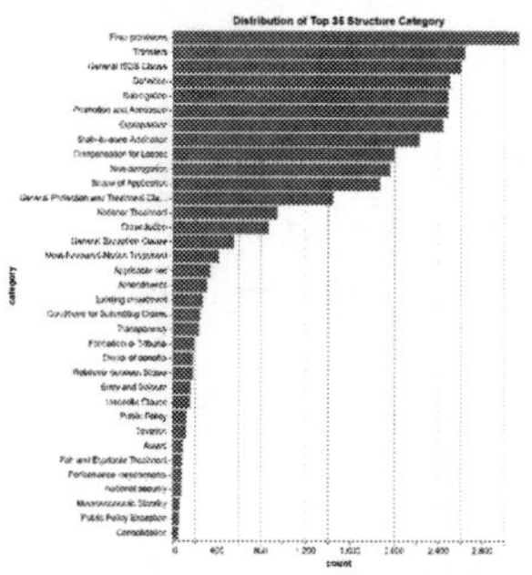

Figure 4: Structure categories Distribution (top 35)

5 articles with the label "other". This is applied to reduce the number of categories and to avoid overfitting. After the category replacement, 61 structure categories remained. See Figure 4 for examples of the most frequent categories. We also applied pre-processing steps such as lower-case conversion, stop words removal and lemmatization before further exploration.

6.1.2 Models

Baseline Models: To provide a point of reference for advanced models based on deep learning, we firstly trained a SVM model for the structure category prediction, as a baseline. A 100-dimension TF-IDF vectorization was applied on the corpus after preprocessing pipeline. We finally derived a 27,530 $\times$ 100 sparse matrix with 582844 non-zero elements as feature space and trained a linear-kernel SVM on it. For another model, we employed averaged word vectors (word2vec pretrained on the Google News corpus, with 300 dimensions) over the words composing the sentence as features. For this dense feature space, we applied an RBF-kernel SVM as the classifier.

BERT-based Models: For a state-of-the-art model for our task of topic classification, we designed a BERT-based model (Devlin et al., 2019) to predict the structure category from existing labeled articles via constructing auxiliary sentences and incorporating context knowledge (as explained below).

Our proposed model consists of three parts, also illustrated in figure 5:

1. The first input layer part aims to construct input sequence from given data.The WordPiece tokenization is applied to convert the input article into tokens and adds the [CLS] and [SEP] token as separator. The position embeddings, word embeddings and segmentation embeddings for each token are then summed up to yield the final input representations.

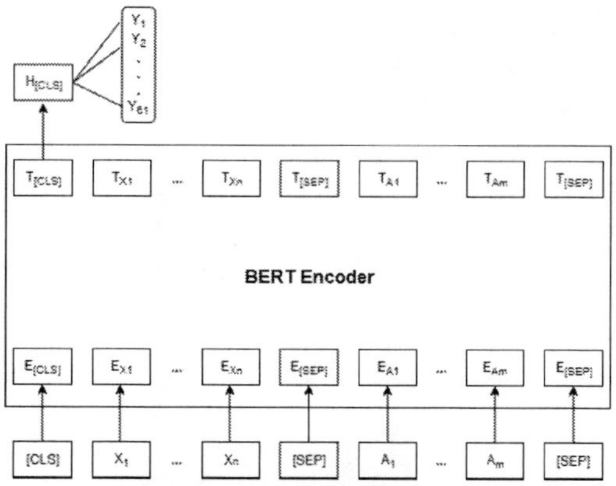

Figure 5: Structure of the proposed model for topic classification

2. The second BERT encoder part consists of 12 Transformer blocks and 12 self-attention heads by taking as input a sequence and outputting its representations.

3. The third output layer is composed by a simple softmax classifier taking the input from vector embedding of token [CLS].

For this task, inspired by the standard structure of legal treaties, we set the input sequence of our model as a combination of the article to be predicted and its succeeding article in the original treaty, to provide context. The article having the last position in a treaty will be transmitted twice if it is chosen as input. To allow comparisons with other BERT-based classification models whose input only consists of a simple text sequence, we experimented with the construction of input in both ways, with two models, as illustrated in figure 6:

- **BERT-base-S** for single input sequence with article to be predicted.

- **BERT-base-A** for input sequence contains article to be predicted along with auxiliary succeeding article.

Considering the length of articles, we set the input size to 512. Deducting the 3 tokens occupied by [CLS] and [SEP], only at most 509 tokens are reserved for input articles. When the sum of the target article of size n and the auxiliary article of size m exceeds 509, we choose to keep the article

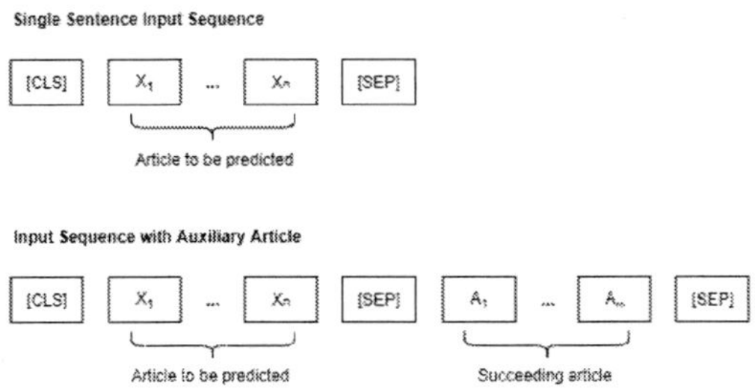

Figure 6: Two ways for input construction

to be predicted and only shorten succeeding the auxiliary article to size $(509 - n)$.

The output layer is a softmax classifier on the top of BERT encoder which maps the 768-dimension vector $H_{[CLS]}$ into the conditional probability distributions:

$$P(y_i|H_{[CLS]}, \theta) = softmax(W^T H_{[CLS]})$$

$$= \frac{exp(W^T H_{[CLS]}[i])}{\sum_{j=1}^{61} exp(W^T H_{[CLS]}[j])} \quad (1)$$

over all labels $y = \{y_1, y_2, ..., y_{61}\}$ where θ is the set of all trainable parameters and $W \in \mathbf{R}^{768 \times 61}$ is the weight matrix of the classifier.

We take $\hat{y} = argmax(P(y_i|H_{[CLS]}, \theta))$ as the predicted result and calculate the loss based on the cross-entropy function.

6.2 Methods for Relevant Difference Detection

6.2.1 Data Preprocessing

During the experiments, we found that BERT models, especially LegalBERT, are very sensitive to minor changes in articles. Even different notations appearing in sentences will lead to a lower similarity score and label two identical articles as different. Therefore, before further exploration, we first cleaned the dataset and removed misleading notations such as indices before treaties.

Another important step in our data preprocessing pipeline is categorical keyword removal. We replaced 85% tokens which are contained in the category keyword list with <MASK>. This procedure is motivated by the following observations: the correlation between the keyword contained in the sentence and the article category is high; this indicates that if we keep the keyword in the dataset, the model will be very likely to overfit. Moreover, if the categorical keywords have not been filtered out, the model will focus on the existing keywords and lose the generality to perform well on unseen categories. The threshold value 85% was chosen empirically and was inspired by BERT pre-training.

Dataset	Train Acc	Test Acc
keywords 85% removed	0.87	0.85
keywords 100% removed	0.74	0.71
keywords all kept	0.91	0.78

Table 4: Keyword removed vs Keyword kept

To demonstrate the above hypothesis, we experimented with three datasets, one with all keywords being kept, one with 85% keywords removed, and another one with all keywords being removed. We trained a CNN model for 10 epochs with FastText embeddings on the three datasets and obtained different results. Table 4 shows that keeping all keywords in the sentences can harm the generality of the network. Removing all the keywords will lead the model toward underfitting. As a result, keeping 15% of the categorical keywords achieved the best results among the three datasets. Therefore, we use this dataset in the following experiments.

The following is the summary of the preprocessing steps that we used for this task:

- Converting to lower case
- Remove indices before treaties
- Remove stop words and punctuation marks
- Convert word numbers to numeric form
- Correct wrong spelling
- Remove the identified category keyword on a small portion of training data

In the above procedure, the FastText library was used for word embeddings, word2number[7] was used for the conversion from word numbers to numeric value and a spell checker was applied on the dataset to correct all typos.

6.2.2 Models

Before the modeling, a train-test split was performed. We trained all our models on 80% of the data and the other 20% of the data was left for testing purposes. We used accuracy, precision, recall, and the F1-score as evaluation metrics to assess the performance of each classifier. We evaluated two

[7]https://pypi.org/project/word2number/

classical machine learning models and five deep learning methods, including three BERT-based classifiers, to detect relevant differences based on sentence pairs.

In all the models described below, we combined two sentences by a <SEP> token and fed the concatenated tokens to the model.

Baseline Methods: We used Mutinomial Naive Bayes and XGBoost decision tree as baseline classifiers. We included the document length, word counts, and n-gram TF-IDF representations as statistical features. The performance of the above classical approaches will be reported in section 7.

Deep Learning Approaches:

- **CNN_FastText**: A convolutional model with pretrained embedding was set up for the deep learning baseline. We used the 300-dimensional embedding layer provided by FastText[8] as sentence representation.
- **BiLSTM_FastText**: A bidirectional Long Short-Term Memory (LSTM) model was trained and evaluated on the dataset. Due to the nature of our task, the whole article is required before the inference, so we applied BiLSTM to incorporate the context from both directions.
- **BERT (bert-base)**: We also fine-tuned and evaluated the BERT-base model using pretrained transformer embedding layers provided by Huggingface [9]. To fine-tune the pretrained BERT model for classification, we applied dropout on the <CLS> token and the token was fed to a softmax function. We selected batchsize = 16, learning rate = 1e-6 and dropout = 0.5.
- **legalBERT**: LegalBERT (Chalkidis et al., 2020b) is a version of the BERT-base model that has been specifically trained on legal documents. The embedding representation was trained on 12 GB of diverse English legal text from several fields (e.g., legislation, court cases, contracts). The model was designed to be able to classify legal documents and to extract information from them.
- **RoBERTa**: RoBERTa (Liu et al., 2019) is a highly optimized version of BERT. The pretrained model from Huggingface [10] was fine-tuned on our dataset. The performance comparison between RoBERTa and other transformer-based models will be presented in the next section.

[8]https://fasttext.cc/docs/en/english-vectors.html

[9]https://huggingface.co/bert-base-uncased

7 Results and Discussion

7.1 Results for Structure category Prediction

Model	Prec.	Recall	F1	Acc.
NB_TF-IDF	0.912	0.825	0.849	0.809
SVM_TF-IDF	0.927	0.911	0.917	0.911
SVM_W2V	0.941	0.915	0.927	0.920
BERT-base-S	0.971	0.944	0.957	0.955
BERT-base-A	**0.974**	**0.953**	**0.963**	**0.962**

Table 5: Evaluation results of structure category prediction on the articles from the test data.

Table 5 shows the results on the test data described in section 6.1.1, for two baseline text classification models and for two BERT based models. The best results (marked in bold font) are achieved by our enhanced context-dependent model. These experimental results support our idea that context knowledge provided by the succeeding article helps the prediction of structure category. Another notable fact is that, in this task, all experimented models have precision score higher than recall. This is because the prediction of structure categories is actually a classification with 61 labels. Labels with few articles are less often predicted and hence have lower recall.

7.2 Results for Relevant Difference Detection

Model	Prec.	Recall	F1	Acc.
Multinomial NB	0.621	0.705	0.594	0.592
XGBoost	0.744	0.761	0.754	0.734
CNN_FastText	0.843	0.867	0.858	0.875
BiLSTM_FastText	0.826	0.845	0.835	0.837
BERTbase	0.885	0.911	0.886	0.938
legalBERT	0.864	0.904	0.868	0.913
RoBERTa	**0.940**	**0.956**	**0.939**	**0.960**

Table 6: Evaluation results of different classifiers on the pairs of articles from our test data

Table 6 shows the results on the test data described in section 6.2.1, for two classical machine learning algorithms, as baselines, and the performance of five deep learning algorithms. We can see

[10]https://huggingface.co/roberta-base

that the RoBERTa model achieved the best performance (marked in bold font) among all classifiers. The LegalBERT model is lagging behind despite of being a domain-specific model. The limited performance of LegalBERT was noted in related work (Geng et al., 2021).

We conducted a comprehensive error analysis on the RoBERTa model's output. Among all sentence pairs that have been misclassified, 60% of them are stylistic differences falsely predicted as relevant differences.

Sentence 1
Contracting party shall encourage investments made in its territory by investors of the other contracting party and shall accept such investments in accordance with its laws and regulations.
Sentence 2
Each contracting party shall in its territory promote investments by investors of the other contracting party and admit such investments in accordance with its laws and regulations.

Table 7: Example of stylistic difference misclassified as relevant difference

Table 7 shows such a typical example. Both sentences are in the structure category of "Admission" with minor differences, but they have been classified as having a relevant difference. The possible cause of this misclassification is that the term "encourage" (in the first sentence) might be treated as a keyword mapping to different content categories, and our embedding representation tends to capture this keyword and thus makes our model biased.

To verify this assumption, we performed the same error analysis on the dataset without replacing any keyword as <MASK>, as a result, the proportion of misclassified stylistic difference will increase from 60% to 87%. This increase of false positive rate also verifies the effectiveness of the category keyword removal when constructing the dataset, as mentioned in section 6.2.1.

8 Limitations

We limited our experiments to articles from legal treaties, though our techniques could be applied on any kind of legal texts or even wider, to any similar texts in general language or specific domains. Though a significant barrier on experimenting with other kinds of texts is the lack of annotated data for training supervised classifiers. In our current experiments, we were able to use the already existing manual annotations in EDIT to produce training data of text pairs without the need for new manual work.

Another limitation is caused by the imbalance of the dataset for the structure category prediction. None of existing re-sampling methods seems appropriate to be applied on legal articles, as their structure is highly standardized. Domain-specific re-sampling methods could be further investigated.

9 Conclusion and Future Work

In this paper, we presented several deep leaning based models for the novel task of detecting semantically relevant differences between similar legal texts. In addition, we proposed an enhanced model that uses contextual information for the secondary task of predicting metadata (structure categories). We exploited a valuable legal resource that was not used before for computational analysis of this kind. We are making available our code on GitHub and our datasets with training/test splits for reproducibility purposes[11].

We achieved very good results with the deep learning models that we considered as promising for our tasks, but there are other deep learning models that could be tried in future work.

Another direction of future research is to apply text entailment methods on the articles with relevant differences, to see if one entails the other. This could mean that one treaty was derived from the other one. We could apply this over multiple treaties to trace back the historical evolution of treaty writing. In case the entailment goes in both directions, one article entails the second one and the reverse holds too, this could be another filter to add on top of our best model for detecting relevant differences.

References

Todd L. Allee and Manfred Elsig. 2019. Are the contents of international treaties copied and pasted? evidence from preferential trade agreements. *International Studies Quarterly*.

Wolfgang Alschner. 2018. *Sense and Similarity: Automating Legal Text Comparison*. Edward Elgar.

Wolfgang Alschner, Manfred Elsig, and Rodrigo Polanco. 2020. Introducing the electronic database of investment treaties (edit): The genesis of a new

[11]Code available at: https://github.com/coollx/Relevant-Difference-Detector-for-Legal-Text

database and its use. *World Trade Review*, 20:73 – 94.

Elliott Ash and Omri Y. Marian. 2019. The making of international tax law: Empirical evidence from natural language processing. *InfoSciRN: Natural Language Processing (Sub-Topic)*.

Ilias Chalkidis, Manos Fergadiotis, Prodromos Malakasiotis, Nikolaos Aletras, and Ion Androutsopoulos. 2020a. Legal-bert: The muppets straight out of law school. pages 2898–2904.

Ilias Chalkidis, Manos Fergadiotis, Prodromos Malakasiotis, Nikolaos Aletras, and Ion Androutsopoulos. 2020b. LEGAL-BERT: The muppets straight out of law school. In *Findings of the Association for Computational Linguistics: EMNLP 2020*, pages 2898–2904, Online. Association for Computational Linguistics.

Jacob Devlin, Ming-Wei Chang, Kenton Lee, and Kristina Toutanova. 2019. BERT: Pre-training of deep bidirectional transformers for language understanding. In *Proceedings of the 2019 Conference of the North American Chapter of the Association for Computational Linguistics: Human Language Technologies, Volume 1 (Long and Short Papers)*, pages 4171–4186, Minneapolis, Minnesota. Association for Computational Linguistics.

Stella Douka, Hadi Abdine, Michalis Vazirgiannis, Rajaa El Hamdani, and David Restrepo Amariles. 2021. JuriBERT: A masked-language model adaptation for French legal text. In *Proceedings of the Natural Legal Language Processing Workshop 2021*, pages 95–101, Punta Cana, Dominican Republic. Association for Computational Linguistics.

Sakbo Geng, Rémi Lebret, and Karl Aberer. 2021. Legal transformer models may not always help. *ArXiv*, abs/2109.06862.

Yinhan Liu, Myle Ott, Naman Goyal, Jingfei Du, Mandar Joshi, Danqi Chen, Omer Levy, Mike Lewis, Luke Zettlemoyer, and Veselin Stoyanov. 2019. Roberta: A robustly optimized bert pretraining approach. Cite arxiv:1907.11692.

Mihai Masala, Radu Cristian Alexandru Iacob, Ana Sabina Uban, Marina Cidota, Horia Velicu, Traian Rebedea, and Marius Popescu. 2021. jurBERT: A Romanian BERT model for legal judgement prediction. In *Proceedings of the Natural Legal Language Processing Workshop 2021*, pages 86–94, Punta Cana, Dominican Republic. Association for Computational Linguistics.

Rohan Nanda, Giovanni Siragusa, Luigi Caro, Guido Boella, Lorenzo Grossio, Marco Gerbaudo, and Francesco Costamagna. 2019. Unsupervised and supervised text similarity systems for automated identification of national implementing measures of european directives. *Artificial Intelligence and Law*, 27(2):199–225.

Vedant Parikh, Upal Bhattacharya, Parth Mehta, Ayan Bandyopadhyay, Paheli Bhattacharya, Kripa Ghosh, Saptarshi Ghosh, Arindam Pal, Arnab Bhattacharya, and Prasenjit Majumder. 2021. Aila 2021: Shared task on artificial intelligence for legal assistance. In *Forum for Information Retrieval Evaluation*, FIRE 2021, page 12–15, New York, NY, USA. Association for Computing Machinery.

Juliano Rabelo, Randy Goebel, mi-young Kim, Yoshinobu Kano, Masaharu Yoshioka, and Ken Satoh. 2022. Overview and discussion of the competition on legal information extraction/entailment (coliee) 2021. *The Review of Socionetwork Strategies*, 16.

Legal and Political Stance Detection of SCOTUS Language

Noah Bergam
Columbia University
New York, NY
njb2154@columbia.edu

Emily Allaway
Columbia University
New York, NY
eallaway@cs.columbia.edu

Kathleen McKeown
Columbia University
New York, NY
kathy@cs.columbia.edu

Abstract

We analyze publicly available US Supreme Court documents using automated stance detection. In the first phase of our work, we investigate the extent to which the Court's public-facing language is political. We propose and calculate two distinct ideology metrics of SCOTUS justices using oral argument transcripts. We then compare these language-based metrics to existing social scientific measures of the ideology of the Supreme Court and the public. Through this cross-disciplinary analysis, we find that justices who are more responsive to public opinion tend to express their ideology during oral arguments. This observation provides a new kind of evidence in favor of the attitudinal change hypothesis of Supreme Court justice behavior. As a natural extension of this political stance detection, we propose the more specialized task of *legal* stance detection with our new dataset `SC-stance`, which matches written opinions to legal questions. We find competitive performance on this dataset using language adapters trained on legal documents.

1 Introduction

The relationship between the Supreme Court of the United States (SCOTUS) and American public opinion is complicated. Some scholars debate normative questions as to whether the Court's power of judicial review ought to obey democratic principles[1] (Bassok and Dotan, 2013). Others investigate how SCOTUS behaves in relation to the public and why (Katz et al., 2017) . Prior work in the field of American political science has consistently demonstrated an association between the partisan ideology of the Court, as expressed through its decisions, and that of the public, as recorded through poll data (Casillas et al., 2011; Mishler and Sheehan, 1996, e.g.,). However, more recent work, particularly in light of the 2022 Dobbs v. Jackson decision, suggests a departure from this general pattern (Jessee et al., 2022). This change in institutional behavior has profound social significance which calls for academic attention. This paper heeds that call by providing a new analytical perspective on SCOTUS' democratic tendencies.

Despite extensive research confirming SCOTUS' general responsiveness to public opinion, the underlying reasoning for this relationship is disputed. One hypothesis centers on *strategic behavior*: it posits that the Court consciously acts in accordance with the public will in order to protect its Constitutionally fragile claim to the power of judicial review (Hammond et al., 2005). Alternatively, the *attitudinal change hypothesis* contends that broader socio-political forces such as news media present confounding factors that influence both the justices and the public (Norpoth et al., 1994).

In this paper, we gain new insight into these hypotheses by applying automated stance detection to a newly assembled corpus of Supreme Court written opinions and oral arguments. Stance detection (i.e., automatically identifying the position of an author towards a given target statement) allows us to evaluate the implications of a justice's language. We use stance detection and related techniques to build two different textual indicators of ideology which we call *issue-specific stance* (ISS) and *holistic political stance* (HPS) respectively. We compare these indicators to existing social scientific metrics related to general public opinion (i.e. the Stimson Policy Mood; Stimson, 2018), Supreme Court justice ideology (i.e. the Martin-Quinn score; Martin and Quinn, 2002), and Supreme Court case salience (i.e. the Clark case salience; Clark et al., 2015).

In addition, we build a supervised stance detection dataset, `SC-stance`, over a subset of Supreme Court written opinions. Our dataset matches the text of the written opinion to a corresponding le-

[1]Famously dubbed the "counter-majoritarian difficulty" by political scientist Alexander Bickel in 1962, this problem has been said to lie at the heart of American Constitutional scholarship (Friedman, 1998)

Proceedings of the Natural Legal Language Processing Workshop 2022, pages 265 - 275
December 8, 2022 ©2022 Association for Computational Linguistics

$D_1 =$	*Once the Court starts looking to the currents of public opinion regarding a particular judgment, it enters a truly bottomless pit from which there is simply no extracting itself.* (Rehnquist, 1992)
$D_2 =$	*Will this institution survive the stench that this creates in the public perception that the Constitution and its reading are just political acts?* (Sotomayor, 2022)
$T =$	*The Supreme Court ought to make decisions with the public opinion in mind.*
	stance(D_1, T) = con **stance(D_2, T) = pro**

Table 1: A relevant, sophisticated example of stance detection.

gal question (i.e., the target) posed on a legal educational website[2]. We present baselines on this dataset using tf-idf features, two language models for the legal domain (Chalkidis et al., 2020; Zheng et al., 2021), and a new method which involves augmenting BERT (Devlin et al., 2018) with an adapter (Pfeiffer et al., 2020a) pre-trained for the legal domain. We find performance gains both with this new method and from masking named entities in the training data.

The main contributions of this work are as follows. **(1)** Using stance detection, we formulate two distinct ideology metrics (i.e. *holistic political stance* and *issue-specific stance*) for SCOTUS justices serving from 1955 to 2020. We find that justices who are responsive to public opinion tend to use language which correlates ideologically with their voting behavior. This provides new evidence in favor of the attitudinal change hypothesis. **(2)** We release a new dataset, `SC-stance`, which matches written opinion text to relevant legal questions. It is the first *legal stance detection* dataset as far as the authors are aware. **(3)** We set baselines on our new dataset and find two ways to potentially improve performance: using a law-specific language adapter, and removing named entities during training.

The repository of relevant code is publicly available through the following link: https://github.com/njbergam/scotus-public-stance.

2 Related Work

Supreme Court and Public Opinion There is extensive academic work analyzing the Supreme Court's relationship with public opinion. In some cases, facts about the Supreme Court are gauged using a public opinion-related proxy. For instance, Segal and Cover (1989) developed an ideology score of justices based on newspaper editorials written at the time of their appointment while Epstein and Segal (2000) and Clark et al. (2015) used front-page news articles in order to quantify the political salience of Supreme Court cases. Other projects take a more direct look at the correlation between SCOTUS decisions and public opinion metrics. Casillas et al. (2011) uses a two-step least-squares regression approach in order to trace the public's influence on Court voting patterns, while Kastellec et al. (2010) looks at the relationship between state-level public opinion polls and Senator votes for SCOTUS justice nominations.

A common thread in many prior studies is the focus on Court voting behavior or its reception in the public eye. In contrast, our work investigates how SCOTUS presents its politics through its *language*. This approach takes advantage of the fact that the corpus of official SCOTUS language is publicly available, relatively small, and well-structured.

Previous work in various fields demonstrates that there are concrete differences between the language used by people of different political ideologies. In psycholinguistics, Robinson et al. (2017) suggests that the language of liberals tends to emphasize mental concepts, while that of conservatives uses more references to the body. NLP research has further investigated this concept through political ideology detection on two datasets (Iyyer et al., 2014, e.g.,): Convote (i.e. Congressional dialogue labeled with the political affiliation of the speaker) (Thomas et al., 2006a), and the Ideological Books Corpus (i.e. sentences from political articles and books annotated for political cues) (Sim et al., 2013).

Legal Artifical Intelligence The legal domain presents a unique challenge for NLP due to the precision, structure, and everyday importance of legal language (Dale, 2019). Furthermore, legal language is interesting in terms of its intersection with political discourse[3], a much more well-studied

[2] `Oyez.org`

[3] This intersection can be problematic. The Code of Conduct for US Judges states: "A Judge Should Refrain from Political Activity" (Courts, 2019) and presents restrictions on language, e.g. no public endorsement of political candidates.

genre in NLP. In this work, we investigate that very intersection by leveraging existing stance and political ideology detection datasets in the context of legal language.

There are two major types of legal AI models (Zhong et al., 2020): rule-based methods, which are mostly supported by legal AI practitioners in industry, and embedding-based methods, which seem to garner the most attention from researchers in academia. The latter body of work has recently focused on adapting pre-trained language models (e.g., BERT) to the legal domain, either through law-specific pre-training, fine-tuning, or a combination of both (Chalkidis et al., 2020; Zheng et al., 2021). Due to the general accessibility of many legal documents around the world, a wide variety of legal NLP datasets are now available, six of which were recently consolidated into the LexGLUE benchmark (Chalkidis et al., 2021). Our dataset, `SC-stance`, provides a test of legal understanding which is not currently captured by existing datasets. Rather than evaluating the relevance between legal statements or documents, `SC-stance` goes a step further and tests the relative stance.

Stance Detection The task of stance detection is to determine the stance (e.g., `Pro`, `Con`, or `Neutral`) of a text on a target (e.g., 'abortion') (Mohammad et al., 2016) (see Table 1 for an illustration). In many works on stance detection, the topic is a noun-phrase (e.g., 'legalization of abortion') and texts are relatively short, such as posts from debate forums (Abbott et al., 2016; Walker et al., 2012; Hasan and Ng, 2014, e.g.,), and comments on news articles (Krejzl et al., 2017; Allaway and McKeown, 2020). Stance detection on Twitter towards political targets is particularly popular (Sobhani et al., 2017; Li et al., 2021; Cignarella et al., 2020; Lai et al., 2020; Taulé et al., 2017). Despite this interest, there is a lack of labeled stance data in the legal domain. Our dataset `SC-stance` not only fills this gap, it also challenges stance detection systems with complex targets (i.e., full sentences) and long documents (i.e., thousands of words).

3 Evaluating Political Stance

3.1 Methods

In the first phase of our work, we track how Supreme Court justices express political leanings in their public-facing language. We focus on two particular corpora: the set of written opinions (1789-2020), and the set of oral argument transcripts (1955-2020). The former was obtained through a Kaggle database (Fiddler, 2020) which used the Harvard CaseLaw Project's[4] API to collect full text files of 33,490 Supreme Court written opinions.The latter was scraped from the Oyez Project (Urofsky, 2001), a multimedia archive of SCOTUS data. We collected over 3.8 million lines of dialogue

Metric	Dataset	Model	$F1$	Acc.
ISS	VAST	Baseline	58.2	-
		Ours	62.8	63.4
HPS	Convote	Baseline	-	70.2
		Ours	75.3	76.3

Table 2: Performance of the stance detection classifiers. The baseline for VAST is a BERT-based model (Allaway and McKeown, 2020) and for Convote it is an RNN (Iyyer et al., 2014).

3.1.1 Linguistic Ideology Metrics

Stance detection allows us to represent the political polarity of judicial language through our two new ideology metrics: issue-specific stance (ISS) and holistic political stance (HPS). Both measure a speaker's ideology along the classic liberal-conservative spectrum (Stimson, 2012). However, they arrive at their answers very differently. The ISS evaluates a speaker's stance relative to a set of representative topics, while the HPS seeks to classify the political affiliation of the speaker directly. Both metrics are built on top of transformer-based text classification algorithms. Although the ISS and HPS are calculated by statement, it is understood that each requires large representative samples of a speaker's statements in to provide some insight into their overall ideology.

Issue-specific stance (ISS) To obtain a speaker's ISS, we gauge a speaker's stance on various liberal and conservative political statements. We adapt these statements from the Pew Political Typology Quiz (Center, 2021), which uses a variety of questions to evaluate ideology on a continuous scale from "Progressive Left" to "Faith and Flag Conservative." Based on how much the given text agrees or disagrees with each of the liberal and conservative statements (which are paraphrased for simplicity), we construct a score which is meant to gauge ideology.

[4]https://case.law/

If a higher score indicates a conservative leaning (this is, of course, an arbitrary choice), then we can frame the ISS calculation for a specific text t as follows. Given a set of targets which align roughly with liberal ideals S_L, a conservative counterpart S_C, and a stance model which maps to some signed interval $[-1, 1]$ we calculate ISS as follows:

$$\text{ISS}_{S_L,S_C}(t) = \sum_{l \in S_C} s(l,t) - \sum_{c \in S_L} s(c,t)$$

We formulate the above stance model as giving a continuous output. In practice, this amounts to adding the softmax probability of the predicted class, signed according to the ideology of the statement.

Holistic political stance (HPS) This metric seeks to immediately classify whether a given piece of language expresses more conservative or liberal ideology overall. As such, the underlying detector is not trained to detect stance relative to a specific topic; rather, it is trained to predict the ideology of the speaker. This framework may help provide a a broader psychological perspective on the underlying ideology of someone's language. For instance, suppose Robinson et al. (2017) is correct that liberals and conservatives generally express metaphors differently. Then HPS may pick up on that implicit ideological cue if it noticed such a pattern in its training data. In contrast, ISS is, by design, better at picking up on explicit cues such as the affirmation of a liberal or conservative belief. Additionally, HPS is simple to calculate (i.e., it is the confidence output of a binary ideology classifier). Unlike ISS, it does not require the parameters of liberal and conservative targets. This inherent simplicity also makes the HPS algorithm run faster.

3.1.2 Calculating HPS and ISS

ISS and HPS rely on pre-trained stance and ideology classification models, respectively. This means they require different datasets for training. For the ISS metric, we train a model using the Varied Stance Topics (VAST) dataset (Allaway and McKeown, 2020), which covers a large range of mostly political topics with broad themes like climate change and immigration. For the HPS metric, we train a classifier using the Convote dataset (Thomas et al., 2006b), which maps statements spoken by Congressional representatives to their partisan affiliation. We formulate both of these as binary stance classification tasks for the sake of simplicity.

Our classifiers use RoBERTa (Liu et al., 2019) without fine-tuning. As shown in Table 2, we achieve higher accuracy than the existing baselines in the original papers for each datset

To obtain the ISS or HPS score of a justice in a particular time period, we first collect the set of statements which contain some sort of emotion, with the intuition that this would increase the likelihood that the statement contains an opinion (as opposed to boilerplate legal language). To do this, we collect statements which feature a word from the NRC Emotion Lexicon (Mohammad and Turney, 2013). Then, for each justice, we collect a representative sample of statements per year and take the average score over all of these statements, to get the HPS of that particular year. In our experiments in the next section, we took sample sizes on the order of 10^3 per year per judge due to the time constraints of processing the text.

3.1.3 Baseline Metrics

We compare our linguistic ideology metrics to three existing metrics in the quantitative political sciences. These will serve as important baselines since they help us contextualize and evaluate our own metrics. These metrics have been calculated in previous research and are available through online databases.

Martin-Quinn scores[5] are dynamic ideal-point estimations of justices' political ideologies (Martin and Quinn, 2002). This metric, calculated on a yearly basis, uses a latent variable model where a justice's voting behavior is the observed variable.

The Stimson Policy Mood [6] gauges the general political leanings of the public through longitudinal surveys, which ask questions on a variety of issues over repeated time points (Stimson, 2018).

The Clark case salience[7] metric uses front page newspaper articles in The New York Times, The Washington Post, and The L.A. Times to quantify how relevant different Supreme Court cases are in the public eye (Clark et al., 2015).

3.2 Results

The first round of our analysis centers on the relationship between our linguistic ideology metrics and existing measures of Supreme Court behavior.

[5] mqscores.lsa.umich.edu/

[6] stimson.web.unc.edu/data/

[7] dataverse.harvard.edu/dataset.xhtml...

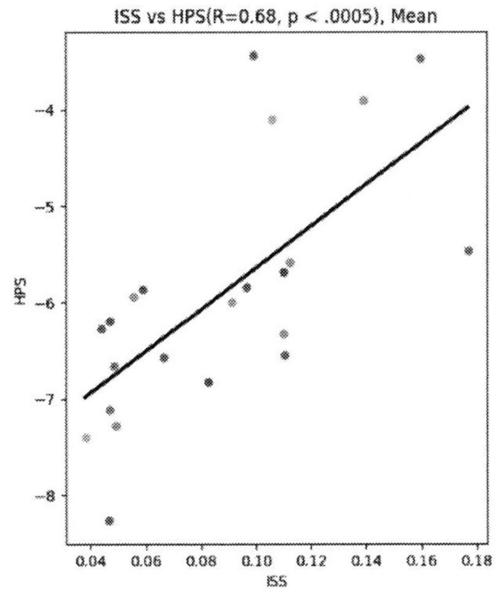

Figure 1: A strong correlation ($R = 0.68, p < 0.0005$) between the holistic and the issue-specific stance scores. Each data point represents a justice's mean score over their tenure (the significance drops to $p < 0.0001$ when we consider their median score).

ISS and HPS correlate. We first undertake a simple methodological audit and compare the issue-specific and holistic political stance scores across 23 justices who served from 1955 to 2020. We find that the two correlate quite strongly (Fig 1), despite the fact that the underlying stance detectors were formulated and trained in very different ways (§3.1). This suggests that the detectors are measuring the same signal and provides evidence that there is in fact a political signal in the dialogues of justices. This is not only important for our analysis, but it is also surprising in its own right given the officially apolitical stance of the Supreme Court (Courts, 2019).

Insight on the Attitudinal Change Hypothesis. Next, we looked at our metrics (ISS and HPS) in relation to the Martin-Quinn score. Importantly, we partition the justices based on their general responsiveness to public opinion. We measure this responsiveness by gauging the correlation between yearly Martin-Quinn scores (i.e., estimating justices' ideology) and the Stimson policy mood (i.e., estimating public opinion), by justice. We say that justices are "responsive" if this correlation is significant with $p < 0.05$.

We found that justices who are more responsive to the public opinion, compared to their counterparts, exhibit a much greater correlation between the ideology of their language, as measured by ISS and HPS and that of their voting decisions (Fig 2). This pattern is particularly noticeable with the HPS score. Additionally, this pattern intensifies when we looked purely at justices who have served past 1990.

This result offers new support for the *attitudinal change hypothesis*, which explains the correlation between Supreme Court decisions and public opinion by arguing that "the same social forces that shape the mass public also influence Supreme Court justices" (Casillas et al., 2011).

Our results support the *attitudinal change hypothesis* for two reasons. Firstly, note that a major underlying assumption of attitudinal change is that "individual attitudes are assumed to be the primary determinants of behavior" (Mishler and Sheehan, 1996). Thus, if justices are responsive to public opinion because of their attitudes, then these attitudes would affect both voting behavior and language. This is precisely what we observe when we find a correlation between Martin-Quinn scores and HPS for responsive justices.

Furthermore, the *strategic behavior hypothesis* does not have as much explanatory power for our results. HPS, by design, is sensitive to speech patterns that mirror those of Congresspeople. Considering the norms of the Court, it is more likely that such quasi-political behavior stems from latent, ideological influences rather than strategic behavior. If anything, strategic behavior would explain a correlation between ISS (i.e. explicit ideological expression) and MQ, which we did not observe.

Case salience and political language. We also consider political undertones of written opinions. We analyzed the relationship between the *magnitude* of the HPS of the written opinion text (a measure of its general political signal) and the Clark Case salience (i.e., public relevance) of the corresponding case. We found that the correlation was almost always slightly negative and only statistically significant for a handful of years (Fig 3).

This seemingly negative result actually parallels previous findings. In particular, Casillas et al. (2011) argue that public opinion may (counterintuitively) hold less of an influence on salient cases as opposed to non-salient cases, since non-salient cases are simply more frequent. If the use of political language in a ruling can be seen as response to public opinion — which would seem to be the case under either of the leading hypotheses of Supreme Court behavior — then our result supports the the-

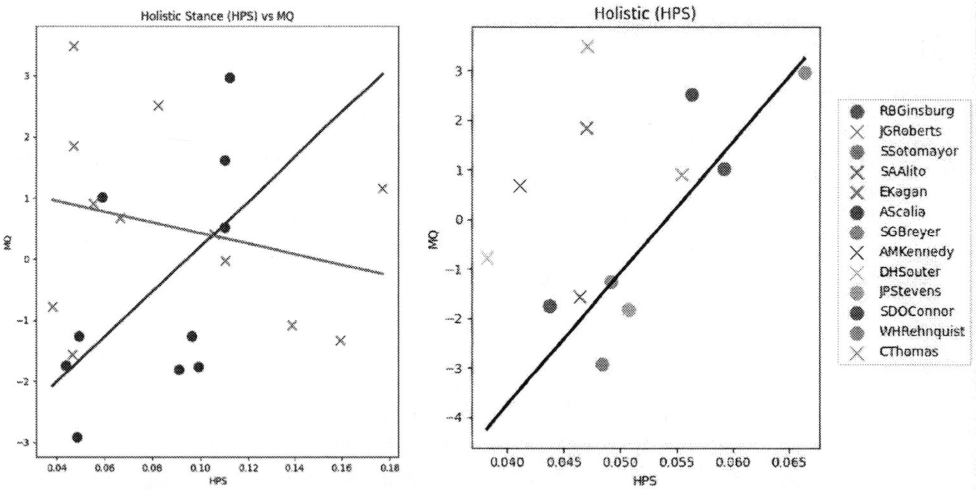

Figure 2: Mean holistic political stance versus mean Martin-Quinn score, by justice. In both figures, circles represent justices whose MQ scores correlate significantly with the Stimson policy mood over their tenure as justices. The left graph shows justices from 1955 to 2020, while the right shows and labels justices only after 1990. HPS was obtained using random sampling, with $n = 2000$ statements per year in the left graph and $n = 1000$ statements per year on the right.

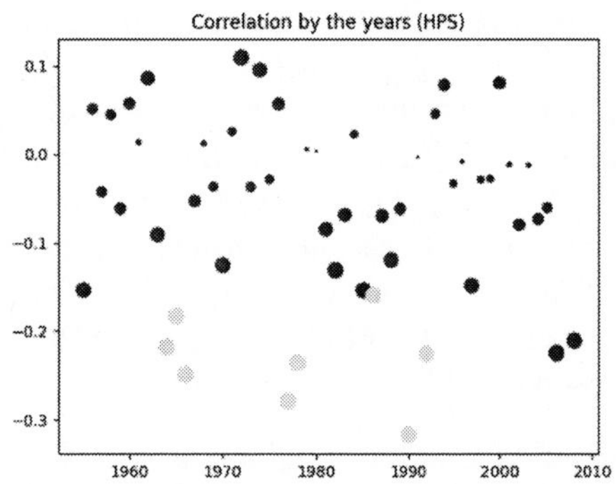

Figure 3: Correlation between confidence of the HPS score and the Clark case salience over all Supreme Court written opinions from 1955 to 2008. Yellow denotes a statistically significant correlation.

ory of an inverse relationship between salience and politicality.

4 SC-stance dataset

4.1 Methods

We describe the collection and characteristics of our new stance dataset, `SC-stance`, as well as the methods we apply to it.

Our dataset `SC-stance` was drawn from three sources: a dataset of full-text Supreme Court opinions through 2020 (Fiddler, 2020), the Washington University Supreme Court Database (Spaeth et al., 2014), and the Oyez website (Urofsky, 2001). We started by collecting written opinions which had non-neutral holdings, as encoded in the SC Database. We then automatically matched these opinion texts to the key legal question on the Oyez website to obtain text-target pairs. Since the questions on Oyez are always phrased such that an affirmative answer is in favor of the petitioner, we used the Winning Party label[8] from the Supreme Court Database, as well as the opinion type given in the Kaggle dataset (i.e. majority, concurring, dissenting, etc.) to infer the stance that a given written opinion takes towards the legal question (e.g. if the winning party was the respondent, and the opinion type was dissenting, then the opinion affirms the legal question).

The final dataset has 2708 labeled instances (1179 labeled `pro`, 930 labeled `con`). The average length of a target (i.e., the legal question) is 35 tokens and the average length of a text (i.e., the Supreme Court written opinion) is 5330 tokens. We show an example datapoint in Table 3.

In addition to providing a legal stance detection task, our dataset could provide an interesting passage retrieval task. Most other legal information retrieval datasets map documents to other docu-

[8] scdb.wustl.edu/documentation.php?var=partyWinning

Case: School District of Abington Township v. Schempp (ID 1962-148), Majority Opinion.
Target: Did the Pennsylvania law requiring public school students to participate in classroom religious exercises violate the religious freedom of students as protected by the First and Fourteenth Amendments?
Text: Once again we are called upon to consider the scope of the provision of the First Amendment to the United States Constitution which declares that "Congress shall make no law respecting an establishment of religion, or prohibiting the free exercise thereof" [...] In light of the history of the First Amendment and of our cases interpreting and applying its requirements, we hold that the practices at issue and the laws requiring them are unconstitutional under the Establishment Clause, as applied to the States through the Fourteenth Amendment. [...]
Label: pro (text affirms the target)

Table 3: An example data point from SC-stance, in which we highlight the relevant portion of the text which confirms the stance.

ments (e.g., the German Dataset for Legal Information Retrieval (Wrzalik and Krechel, 2021)) or to static questions which are unchanged between documents (e.g., the Contract Understanding Atticus Dataset (Hendrycks et al., 2021)). The closest counterpart to our dataset, to the best of our knowledge, is the Belgian Statutory Article Retrieval Dataset, a French language dataset that maps legal questions written by laypeople to Belgian law articles (Louis et al., 2021).

4.1.1 Models for Stance Detection

In comparing models, we are most interested in which ones learn the most informative *features* from the text. The final layer is, in almost all cases, a single layer feed-forward network (Fig 4).

Legal Adapter Inspired by the concept that "legalese" could potentially be treated as a unique language, we use a *language adapter* to transfer a BERT-based stance detection model from its training data's domain to the SC-stance dataset. It is important to note that Supreme Court opinion language is relatively clear and concise compared to the more pure legalese of contracts or securities filings. While it may seem conceptually extreme to treat SCOTUS filings as a separate language, it is experimentally interesting as it sheds light on

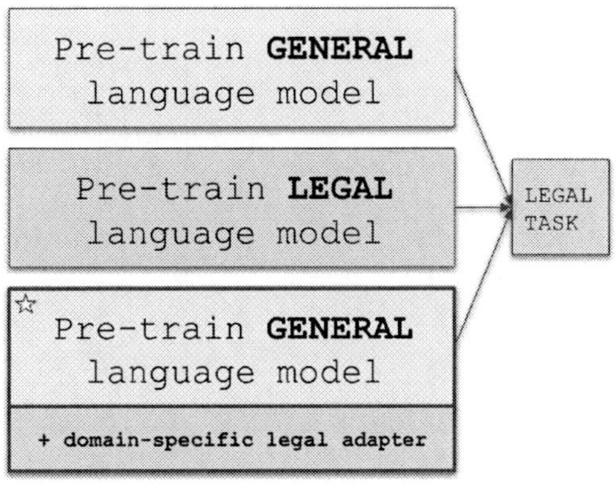

Figure 4: Three methods of tackling a legal NLP task using a large language model (the third being our new method which leverages language adapters). This paradigm generalizes to other domain-specific applications such as medicine or finance.

whether a dedicated adaptation for legal language allows for a more effective automated reading of legal stance.

Adapters have been used to enable efficient multilingual transfer for language models. An adapter module is a set of weights (i.e., feed-forward layers) inserted into each attention block of a transformer and trained using masked language modeling (MLM). Adapters were originally designed as an alternative to fine-tuning (Houlsby et al., 2019) and have since become a popular method of cross-lingual domain transfer (Pfeiffer et al., 2020b; Vidoni et al., 2020, e.g.). One intuitive benefit of this approach over pre-training an entire language model is that only unlabeled data is needed to train the adapter and training is more parameter efficient, since the adapter has comparatively few parameters.

Baselines We compare our new method to a number of baselines, the simplest being the tf-idf vectorization of each of the target and document. On these simple features, we compare logistic regression (LR) and multilayer perceptron (MLP) as final layers; we find that the latter performs significantly better with $p < 0.02$[9], so we proceed to use MLP as the classification layer in our BERT-based models.

We experiment with BERT (Devlin et al., 2018), a popular transformer-based encoder pre-trained with masked language modeling and next sentence prediction. We also investigate two variants, which

[9]We use an approximate randomization test.

	Binary		3-class	
	Original	**w/ NER-mask**	**Original**	**w/ NER-mask**
Majority	39.6	-	20.4	-
tf-idf (LR)	41.4	43.2	26.5	29.6
tf-idf (MLP)	50.0	49.8	32.0	31.5
BERT	50.4	47.1	36.9	35.1
CaseLaw-BERT	47.6	49.2	38.3	40.3
Legal-BERT	52.8	53.0	**47.4**	41.7
Legal Adapter	**55.6**	**53.4**	41.4	**42.2**

Table 4: F-1 scores on the `SCS-written` dataset, using an 80-20 train-test split.

differ largely in terms of their training corpus. One is Legal-BERT (Chalkidis et al., 2020), which is pre-trained on an English legal corpus and uses a sub-word vocabulary built from scratch. The other is CaseLaw-BERT (Zheng et al., 2021), which is pre-trained on the Harvard Law case corpus.

4.1.2 Experimental Details

We evaluated our stance models on `SC-stance` in two settings: binary classification (i.e., labels {pro, con}) and 3-class classification (i.e., {pro, con, neutral}). Since `SC-stance` does not have any neutral labeled instances, following Allaway and McKeown (2020) we randomly pair opinions with unrelated questions to augment the dataset. For the adapter, we follow Pfeiffer et al. (2020a) and train a legal language adapter using MLM for $230k$ epochs with a learning rate of 10^{-4} and a batch size of 16. As unlabeled data we use over 8.8 million sentences from case law documents, made available through SigmaLaw (de Silva, 2019). In all experiments the `SC-stance` dataset is split 80/20 for training and testing. Importantly, we consider the case in which the training set has all named entities (with the notable exception of laws) masked during the training phase[10] and revealed during testing. This is referred to as the *NER-mask* setting in Table 4. For BERT and its variants, we append the legal question followed by a '`[SEP]`' token and the written opinion, and we truncate past the 512 token limit, with the understanding that most written opinions, despite their length, express their stance early on.

[10]We masked named entities using the Python spacy library's 'en_core_web_sm' model. The mask was the named entity type: for instance, "October 10" would become "[DATE] [DATE]".

4.2 Results

Overall, we found that the legal adapter is competitive with the leading legal language models, achieving the highest F-1 score (55.6) on the binary classification task[11]. In the 3-class setting, it was only outperformed by Legal-BERT.

We found that Legal-BERT consistently outperforms BERT and CaseLaw-BERT ($p < 0.09$ for the 3-class setting), which corroborates the experiments of Legal-BERT's creators (Chalkidis et al., 2020). We also found that, while the BERT-based features consistently outperformed the "classical" counterparts, the tf-idf model with an MLP classification layer had strong performance on the binary classification task.

We found mixed results with the NER mask setting, in that it led to both gradual increases (e.g. tf-idf with logistic regression, CaseLaw-BERT) as well as considerable drops in performance (e.g. legal adapter binary, Legal-BERT the 3-class setting). Intuitively, the NER mask should remove spurious signals for the classifier, since the relationship between the target and topic should almost never be related to the entities (i.e. proper nouns), but instead the relationships between entities.

We believe this hypothetical advantage is what led to certain score increases. However, the flipside is that there may be instability introduced when the model is presented with proper nouns in the test setting, after having had them removed during training. We noticed that BERT was more susceptible to this instability, which may be attributable to its less specialized vocabulary or understanding of legal grammar. These weaknesses of domain shift may increase the model's susceptibility to spurious signals.

[11]Due to the small size of the dataset, we were unable to mark these differences as statistically significant.

5 Conclusion

Using state-of-the-art NLP techniques, we gain new insight into a longstanding political science problem: the Supreme Court's relationship with public opinion. In our analysis of the language of Supreme Court justices, we leverage existing metrics of SCOTUS behavior as well as stance detection datasets regarding political ideology. Notably, we find a new source of evidence for the attitudinal change hypothesis of the Supreme Court, and we experiment with a competitive new model for legal language domain adaptation.

This research sheds light on how stance detection allows us to interrogate the implicit opinions of static documents. This is a powerful use case of NLP for the social sciences, in that it allows for a large-scale, critical analysis of large bodies of text. Of course, there is a long way to go in the field of stance detection, both generally and in specific linguistic domains such as the law. Our contribution of `SC-stance` feeds into this goal, by providing semantically rich targets and a mix of legal and lay language. We emphasize this latter feature, in that quality textual understanding – for human and AI alike – is marked by a thorough comprehension of both colloquial and technical language formulation.

Limitations

Our stance detection analysis of Supreme Court language is a proof-of-concept experiment with considerable potential for expansion. For instance, one could obtain a much richer understanding of Supreme Court ideology using a flavor of stance detection which analyzes targets relevant to issues of *jurisprudence* (e.g. judicial activism, originalism) rather than common politics.

There is also room for expansion in terms of our use and formulation of certain metrics. For instance, we chose not to investigate "public opinion" through text data, partly because the concept has no clear-cut representative corpus, and sampling from the web or the news could present selection biases. However, this problem could be resolved with a narrower view of public opinion such as, say, the news media. The inherent benefit to having a text-based metric of public opinion is that it is more easily comparable to text-based metrics of Supreme Court ideology. Furthermore, it may be enlightening to track the partisanship of justices' language using ideal point estimation (i.e., the words are the observed variable, the ideology is the hidden variable), rather than direct measurement of the justice stance year after year (Bafumi et al., 2005).

In terms of processing the `SC-stance` dataset, future work should look into how to work with the long written opinions using BERT-based methods which have a token limit. There is also clear potential to expand the `SC-stance` dataset. This could be done through strategic web-scraping of certiorari petitions, which often contain the relevant legal questions of (what eventually becomes) a Supreme Court case. If this challenge of locating the petitions, scraping the relevant text, and matching to the relevant case can be met, then the `SC-stance` dataset could in principle grow by orders of magnitude, which would make it an even more promising ground for experimentation.

Ethics Statement

Our investigation of the Supreme Court is an academic exploration of a political subject. By employing stance detection, we mean to uncover large-scale patterns in the text which may not be obvious to a single reader or scholar. This should not take away from the pursuit of engaging with text directly. After all, by transforming text into statistics, we lose many dimensions of its complexity in order to zero in on specific attributes. It is important to acknowledge this methodological complexity as quantitative social sciences research continues to engage with NLP-driven metadata.

Acknowledgements

The authors thank Hayley Cohen, Suresh Naidu, and the anonymous reviewers at NLLP for their comments. We thank Ariella Lang for organizing the Laidlaw Scholars Program which provided funding and support for this project. We also recognize the Columbia NLP Group for providing computing resources which made these experiments possible.

References

Rob Abbott, Brian Ecker, Pranav Anand, and Marilyn A. Walker. 2016. Internet argument corpus 2.0: An sql schema for dialogic social media and the corpora to go with it. In *LREC*.

Emily Allaway and Kathleen McKeown. 2020. Zero-Shot Stance Detection: A Dataset and Model using Generalized Topic Representations. In *Proceedings of the 2020 Conference on Empirical Methods in*

Natural Language Processing (EMNLP), pages 8913–8931, Online. Association for Computational Linguistics.

Joseph Bafumi, Andrew Gelman, David K Park, and Noah Kaplan. 2005. Practical issues in implementing and understanding bayesian ideal point estimation. *Political Analysis*, 13(2):171–187.

Or Bassok and Yoav Dotan. 2013. Solving the countermajoritarian difficulty? *International journal of constitutional law*, 11(1):13–33.

Christopher J Casillas, Peter K Enns, and Patrick C Wohlfarth. 2011. How public opinion constrains the us supreme court. *American Journal of Political Science*, 55(1):74–88.

Pew Research Center. 2021. Political Typology Quiz — pewresearch.org. `https://www.pewresearch.org/politics/quiz/political-typology/`.

Ilias Chalkidis, Manos Fergadiotis, Prodromos Malakasiotis, Nikolaos Aletras, and Ion Androutsopoulos. 2020. Legal-bert: The muppets straight out of law school. *arXiv preprint arXiv:2010.02559*.

Ilias Chalkidis, Abhik Jana, Dirk Hartung, Michael Bommarito, Ion Androutsopoulos, Daniel Martin Katz, and Nikolaos Aletras. 2021. Lexglue: A benchmark dataset for legal language understanding in english. *arXiv preprint arXiv:2110.00976*.

Alessandra Teresa Cignarella, Mirko Lai, Cristina Bosco, Viviana Patti, and Paolo Rosso. 2020. SardiStance @ EVALITA2020: Overview of the Task on Stance Detection in Italian Tweets. In *EVALITA*.

Tom S Clark, Jeffrey R Lax, and Douglas Rice. 2015. Measuring the political salience of supreme court cases. *Journal of Law and Courts*, 3(1):37–65.

United States Courts. 2019. Code of Conduct for United States Judges — uscourts.gov. `https://www.uscourts.gov/judges-judgeships/code-conduct-united-states-judges#f`. [Accessed 01-Oct-2022].

Robert Dale. 2019. Law and word order: Nlp in legal tech. *Natural Language Engineering*, 25(1):211–217.

Nisansa de Silva. 2019. SigmaLaw - Large Legal Text Corpus and Word Embeddings — osf.io. `https://osf.io/qvg8s/`.

Jacob Devlin, Ming-Wei Chang, Kenton Lee, and Kristina Toutanova. 2018. Bert: Pre-training of deep bidirectional transformers for language understanding. *arXiv preprint arXiv:1810.04805*.

Lee Epstein and Jeffrey A Segal. 2000. Measuring issue salience. *American Journal of Political Science*, pages 66–83.

Garrett Fiddler. 2020. Scotus opinions. Full text and metadata of all opinions written by SCOTUS justices through 2020, `https://www.kaggle.com/datasets/gqfiddler/scotus-opinions`.

Barry Friedman. 1998. The history of the countermajoritarian difficulty, part one: The road to judicial supremacy. *NYUL Rev.*, 73:333.

Thomas H Hammond, Chris W Bonneau, and Reginald S Sheehan. 2005. *Strategic behavior and policy choice on the US Supreme Court*. Stanford University Press.

Kazi Saidul Hasan and Vincent Ng. 2014. Why are you taking this stance? identifying and classifying reasons in ideological debates. In *EMNLP*.

Dan Hendrycks, Collin Burns, Anya Chen, and Spencer Ball. 2021. Cuad: An expert-annotated nlp dataset for legal contract review. *arXiv preprint arXiv:2103.06268*.

Neil Houlsby, Andrei Giurgiu, Stanislaw Jastrzebski, Bruna Morrone, Quentin De Laroussilhe, Andrea Gesmundo, Mona Attariyan, and Sylvain Gelly. 2019. Parameter-efficient transfer learning for nlp. In *International Conference on Machine Learning*, pages 2790–2799. PMLR.

Mohit Iyyer, Peter Enns, Jordan Boyd-Graber, and Philip Resnik. 2014. Political ideology detection using recursive neural networks. In *Proceedings of the 52nd Annual Meeting of the Association for Computational Linguistics (Volume 1: Long Papers)*, pages 1113–1122.

Stephen Jessee, Neil Malhotra, and Maya Sen. 2022. A decade-long longitudinal survey shows that the supreme court is now much more conservative than the public. *Proceedings of the National Academy of Sciences*, 119(24):e2120284119.

Jonathan P Kastellec, Jeffrey R Lax, and Justin H Phillips. 2010. Public opinion and senate confirmation of supreme court nominees. *The Journal of Politics*, 72(3):767–784.

Daniel Martin Katz, Michael J Bommarito, and Josh Blackman. 2017. A general approach for predicting the behavior of the supreme court of the united states. *PloS one*, 12(4):e0174698.

Peter Krejzl, Barbora Hourová, and Josef Steinberger. 2017. Stance detection in online discussions. *ArXiv*, abs/1701.00504.

Mirko Lai, Alessandra Teresa Cignarella, D. I. H. Farías, Cristina Bosco, V. Patti, and P. Rosso. 2020. Multilingual stance detection in social media political debates. *Comput. Speech Lang.*, 63:101075.

Yingjie Li, Tiberiu Sosea, Aditya Sawant, Ajith Jayaraman Nair, Diana Inkpen, and Cornelia Caragea. 2021. P-Stance: A Large Dataset for Stance Detection in Political Domain. In *FINDINGS*.

Yinhan Liu, Myle Ott, Naman Goyal, Jingfei Du, Mandar Joshi, Danqi Chen, Omer Levy, Mike Lewis, Luke Zettlemoyer, and Veselin Stoyanov. 2019. Roberta: A robustly optimized bert pretraining approach. *arXiv preprint arXiv:1907.11692*.

Antoine Louis, Gerasimos Spanakis, and Gijs Van Dijck. 2021. A statutory article retrieval dataset in french. *arXiv preprint arXiv:2108.11792*.

Andrew D Martin and Kevin M Quinn. 2002. Dynamic ideal point estimation via markov chain monte carlo for the us supreme court, 1953–1999. *Political analysis*, 10(2):134–153.

William Mishler and Reginald S Sheehan. 1996. Public opinion, the attitudinal model, and supreme court decision making: A micro-analytic perspective. *The Journal of Politics*, 58(1):169–200.

Saif M. Mohammad, Svetlana Kiritchenko, Parinaz Sobhani, Xiao-Dan Zhu, and Colin Cherry. 2016. Semeval-2016 task 6: Detecting stance in tweets. In *SemEval@NAACL-HLT*.

Saif M Mohammad and Peter D Turney. 2013. Nrc emotion lexicon. *National Research Council, Canada*, 2:234.

Helmut Norpoth, Jeffrey A Segal, William Mishler, and Reginald S Sheehan. 1994. Popular influence on supreme court decisions. *American Political Science Review*, 88(3):711–724.

Jonas Pfeiffer, Andreas Rücklé, Clifton Poth, Aishwarya Kamath, Ivan Vulić, Sebastian Ruder, Kyunghyun Cho, and Iryna Gurevych. 2020a. Adapterhub: A framework for adapting transformers. *arXiv preprint arXiv:2007.07779*.

Jonas Pfeiffer, Ivan Vulić, Iryna Gurevych, and Sebastian Ruder. 2020b. Mad-x: An adapter-based framework for multi-task cross-lingual transfer. *arXiv preprint arXiv:2005.00052*.

Michael D Robinson, Ryan L Boyd, Adam K Fetterman, and Michelle R Persich. 2017. The mind versus the body in political (and nonpolitical) discourse: Linguistic evidence for an ideological signature in us politics. *Journal of Language and Social Psychology*, 36(4):438–461.

Jeffrey A Segal and Albert D Cover. 1989. Ideological values and the votes of us supreme court justices. *American Political Science Review*, 83(2):557–565.

Yanchuan Sim, Brice DL Acree, Justin H Gross, and Noah A Smith. 2013. Measuring ideological proportions in political speeches. In *Proceedings of the 2013 conference on empirical methods in natural language processing*, pages 91–101.

Parinaz Sobhani, Diana Inkpen, and Xiaodan Zhu. 2017. A dataset for multi-target stance detection. In *Proceedings of the 15th Conference of the European Chapter of the Association for Computational Linguistics: Volume 2, Short Papers*, pages 551–557, Valencia, Spain. Association for Computational Linguistics.

Harold Spaeth, Lee Epstein, Ted Ruger, Keith Whittington, Jeffrey Segal, and Andrew D Martin. 2014. Supreme court database code book. *URL: http://scdb. wustl. edu*.

James A Stimson. 2012. On the meaning & measurement of mood. *Daedalus*, 141(4):23–34.

James A Stimson. 2018. *Public opinion in America: Moods, cycles, and swings*. Routledge.

Mariona Taulé, Maria Antònia Martí, Francisco M. Rangel Pardo, Paolo Rosso, Cristina Bosco, and Viviana Patti. 2017. Overview of the Task on Stance and Gender Detection in Tweets on Catalan Independence. In *IberEval@SEPLN*.

Matt Thomas, Bo Pang, and Lillian Lee. 2006a. Get out the vote: Determining support or opposition from congressional floor-debate transcripts. In *Proceedings of the 2006 Conference on Empirical Methods in Natural Language Processing*, pages 327–335, Sydney, Australia. Association for Computational Linguistics.

Matt Thomas, Bo Pang, and Lillian Lee. 2006b. Get out the vote: Determining support or opposition from Congressional floor-debate transcripts. In *Proceedings of EMNLP*, pages 327–335.

Melvin I Urofsky. 2001. The oyez project: Us supreme court multimedia database. *The Journal of American History*, 88(2):753.

Marko Vidoni, Ivan Vulić, and Goran Glavaš. 2020. Orthogonal language and task adapters in zero-shot cross-lingual transfer. *arXiv preprint arXiv:2012.06460*.

Marilyn A. Walker, Jean E. Fox Tree, Pranav Anand, Rob Abbott, and Joseph King. 2012. A corpus for research on deliberation and debate. In *LREC*.

Marco Wrzalik and Dirk Krechel. 2021. Gerdalir: A german dataset for legal information retrieval. In *Proceedings of the Natural Legal Language Processing Workshop 2021*, pages 123–128.

Lucia Zheng, Neel Guha, Brandon R Anderson, Peter Henderson, and Daniel E Ho. 2021. When does pretraining help? assessing self-supervised learning for law and the casehold dataset of 53,000+ legal holdings. In *Proceedings of the Eighteenth International Conference on Artificial Intelligence and Law*, pages 159–168.

Haoxi Zhong, Chaojun Xiao, Cunchao Tu, Tianyang Zhang, Zhiyuan Liu, and Maosong Sun. 2020. How does nlp benefit legal system: A summary of legal artificial intelligence. *arXiv preprint arXiv:2004.12158*.

Graph-based Keyword Planning for Legal Clause Generation from Topics

Sagar Joshi*, **Sumanth Balaji***
IIIT Hyderabad
{sagar.joshi,sumanth.balaji}@research.iiit.ac.in

Aparna Garimella
Adobe Research
garimell@adobe.com

Vasudeva Varma
IIIT Hyderabad
vv@iiit.ac.in

Abstract

Generating domain-specific content such as legal clauses based on minimal user-provided information can be of significant benefit in automating legal contract generation. In this paper, we propose a controllable graph-based mechanism that can generate legal clauses using only the topic or type of the legal clauses. Our pipeline consists of two stages involving a graph-based planner followed by a clause generator. The planner outlines the content of a legal clause as a sequence of keywords in the order of generic to more specific clause information based on the input topic using a controllable graph-based mechanism. The generation stage takes in a given plan and generates a clause. The pipeline consists of a graph-based planner followed by text generation. We illustrate the effectiveness of our proposed two-stage approach on a broad set of clause topics in contracts.

1 Introduction

Contracts are essential discourse units that frequent in several day-to-day business workflows, especially between companies and governmental organizations. The fundamental units of discourse in contracts consist of "clauses" that are paragraphs of text that outline the terms and conditions of various types or *topics* (e.g., *severability*, *benefits*) (Table 1). Legal clauses can be characterized by their high inter-sentence similarity, and topic-specific content (Simonson et al., 2019). For example, Zhong et al. (2020) showed that the sentences in legal corpora are almost 20% similar to each other. Drafting contracts by legal counsel is a manual process of taking a skeletal set of clauses and adding or modifying them for the contract goal. Given their highly domain-specific content and unique linguistic structure, contract drafters in legal counsel can significantly benefit from applying Natural Language Processing (NLP) techniques to aid contract creation (Zhong et al., 2020).

In case any provision herein or obligation hereunder or any Note or other Credit Document shall be invalid, illegal, or unenforceable in any jurisdiction, the validity, legality and enforceability of the remaining provisions or obligations, or of such provision or obligation in any other jurisdiction, shall not in any way be affected or impaired thereby.

Table 1: An example *severability* clause from a legal contract.

There have been recent advances in Transformer-based (Vaswani et al., 2017) methods for text generation in varied flavors, such as prompt-based causal generation (Radford et al., 2019), conditional generation based on control codes (Keskar et al., 2019), and retrieval-augmented generation based on queries (Lewis et al., 2020b). However, these methods are primarily studied in generic NLP domains, and legal text generation remains largely unexplored. The only previous work that addressed the task of legal text generation is CLAUSEREC (Aggarwal et al., 2021), in which a Transformer-based decoder is trained to generate missing legal clauses in a given contract document, conditioned on the clause topic and the content in the contract. However, Aggarwal et al. (2021) noted that the clauses generated by CLAUSEREC suffer from low linguistic variations within topics, thus resulting in content that is thematically relevant but missing a few nuances. In general, we believe conditioning text generation on only the high-level clause topics or the contract content may not capture the subtleties present in legal clauses, hence call for an iterative approach to learn the clause-specific content in a top-down manner.

We find inspiration in the content planning paradigm for story generation (McIntyre and Lapata, 2010; Yao et al., 2018; Chen et al., 2021) in which an intermediate plan (e.g., a set of keywords) is used to generate final stories. In this paper, we study legal text generation, and propose a two-staged pipeline (Figure 1) to generate le-

*Both the authors have equal contribution to this work.

Proceedings of the Natural Legal Language Processing Workshop 2022, pages 276 - 286
December 8, 2022 ©2022 Association for Computational Linguistics

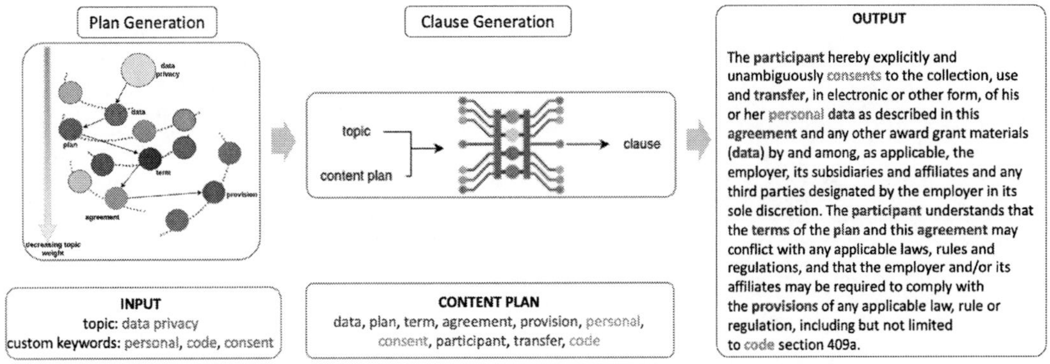

Figure 1: The proposed 2-stage clause generation pipeline: User specifies the input topic (*data privacy*) along with a set of keywords for customization (*personal, code, consent*). The first stage involves generating a customized content plan, including the custom keywords (green) along with other plan keywords derived purely from a graph walk (purple). In the second stage, a clause generator interpolates through the keywords in the plan to produce a coherent, meaningful legal clause for the given topic.

gal clauses from topics iteratively using keywords. Specifically, the first module of our pipeline comprises of a graph-based planner that takes in a topic (and an optional set of keywords) and produces an ordered content plan consisting of keywords, with those more generic to the topic ranked higher, and those more specific to a clause ranked lower. Note that unlike (Aggarwal et al., 2021), which aimed to generate missing clauses given a contract, we focus on generating legal clauses only based on a given topic and an optional set of keywords. We approximate the generated content plan to the user intent, which will be translated into a legal clause. In the second stage, the plan is used as a control mechanism, and a Transformer-based language model is trained to generate legal clauses conditioned on the topic and the plan.[1]

Following are the main contributions of this paper: **(1)** We propose a novel two-staged pipeline for legal clause generation, comprising a content planner that generates a keyword-based plan, and a content generator that generates legal clauses conditioned on the clause topics and keyword plans. Our proposed content planner consists of a simple, lightweight graph-based mechanism that performs a graph walk using the input topic to generate a plan consisting of generic to specific keywords. The plan can be customized by specifying a few control keywords, bringing controllability to the generation. **(2)** We compare our approach with several conditional and causal text generation baselines, and illustrate strong empirical results for legal clause generation. **(3)** We also show that our approach can be generalized well to a diverse range of clause topics, thus indicating the extensibility of our approach for legal text generation. We believe our work takes one step further in the area of automatic clause generation for AI-aided drafting of legal documents.

[1]The code for this work can be found here: `https://github.com/sagarsj42/legal_clause_gen_from_topic_keywords`

2 Graph-based Planning for Clause Generation

Our proposed approach aims to generate legal clauses to aid legal counsel in contract drafting. To do so, it takes as input a clause topic (e.g., *data privacy*) along with a few keywords for customization (*personal*, *code*, *consent*), and generates more keywords in order to obtain a customized content plan as illustrated in Figure 1. This keyword-based plan, which we consider an approximation to user-specified keywords per their preferences, is then used to generate a meaningful legal clause.

2.1 Dataset creation

Ranked keyword extraction per topic. For every clause topic t from the set of all clause topics T, we extract an ordered set of keywords $K^t = \{k_1^t, k_2^t, \ldots, k_{m_1}^t\}$ representing the topic using an off-the-shelf keyword extractor. Each extracted keyword is a single, comprehensible word unit occurring in a clause. The ordered set of keywords under a topic represents the salient words under that topic, approximately ranked based on their prominence. In the ranked order, the words more generic to the topic (perceived to carry more

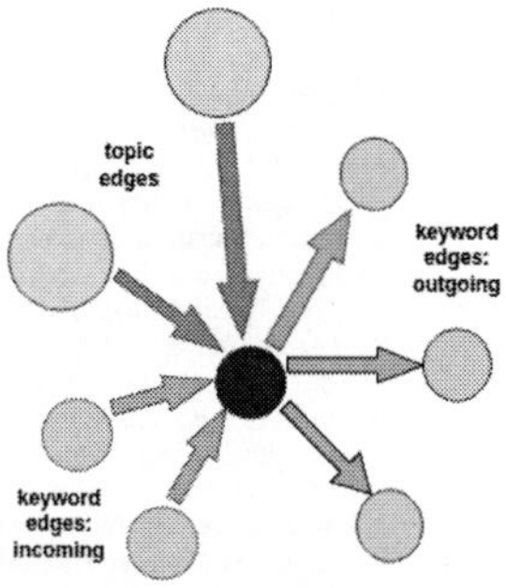

Figure 2: View of the types of node connections in the directed graph G.

Algorithm 1 Graph construction

Require: Topics T, keywords K, reference plans $R = \bigcup_{t \in T} R^t$

Initialize graph G with nodes $N \leftarrow T \cup K$
Edges $e(n_1, n_2) \leftarrow 0 \ \forall (n_1, n_2) \in N$
for topic $t \in T$ **do**
  Topic frequency, $f \leftarrow len(R^t)$
  for reference plan $r^t \in R^t$ **do**
    for step $s \leftarrow 1$ *to* n **do**
      Step value, $v = 1/(s \cdot f)$
      $e(t, r^t_s) \leftarrow e(t, r^t_s) + v$
      $e(r^t_{s-1}, r^t_s) \leftarrow e(r^t_{s-1}, r^t_s) + v$
    end for
  end for
end for
return G

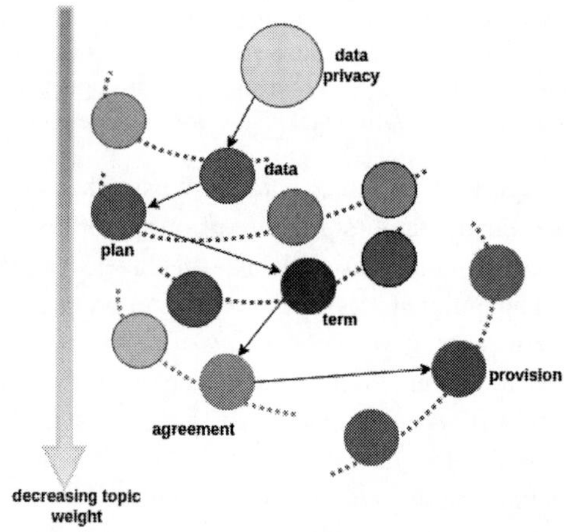

Figure 3: Illustration of the first 5 stages of freeform plan generation, i.e., without using custom keywords for control. Given input topic: *data privacy*.

information about the topic's generic form[2]) are ranked higher. The ones less generic to the topic but more specific to individual clauses (perceived to be more characteristic of an individual clause) are ranked lower. The keywords are lemmatized using a WordNet-based lemmatizer.

Reference keyword plans for clauses. Each clause is represented by a reference keyword plan which consists of a ranked list of keywords corresponding to the topic of that clause. For every clause in a topic, we check for the existence of each ranked topic keyword and sequentially add them as plan keywords, thus preparing a ranked plan of keywords appearing in the clause. Applying for all the topics, we have a dataset of clause-keyword plans $D^t = (C^t, R^t)$ for each topic t in the dataset. C^t represents the set of clauses $\{c^t_1, c^t_2, ..., c^t_{m2}\}$ under the topic, and R^t represents the set of corresponding reference keyword plans for the clauses, with the plan for a clause c being a ranked list of keywords, $r^c = [r^c_i]^{i=n}_{i=1}$ (where r^c_i represents keyword selected for each stage i).

2.2 Graph construction

A single, directed graph G is constructed to capture the keyword plan information from all the topics in a unified representation as illustrated in Algorithm 1. The graph G is initialized with the set of nodes $N = T \cup K$ consisting of all the topics T and an accumulated set of keywords from the topics, $K = \bigcup_{t \in T} K^t$. Each node in the graph has incoming connections from relevant topic nodes along with incoming and outgoing connections to keyword nodes, as shown in Figure 2.

Edges weights between every pair of topic-keyword and keyword-keyword nodes are calculated based on their occurrence in the train set as demonstrated in the algorithm. In this process, we walk through the reference plan for each clause under all the topics in the train set. A topic-keyword edge (t, r^t_s) is added for the occurrence of a keyword in a reference plan as a stage s of the plan. Similarly, a keyword-keyword edge $e(r^t_{s-1}, r^t_s)$ is added for the occurrence of consecutively occurring keywords r_{s-1} and r^t_s in the plan. Every occurrence of such topic-keyword or keyword-keyword pair adds an incremental weight to the corresponding edge. The weight given to each occurrence v is normalized by (1) no. of clauses f under that topic and (2) the stage value s at which the occurrence occurs. (1) accounts for the substantial imbalance in the clause type frequencies for the topics in the dataset, while (2) gives lesser importance to the keywords present at lower stages of the plan, thus statistically recording the generic to specific order within the edges of the graph.

[2]By topic's generic form, we refer to the clause content that most commonly occurs across clauses under that topic, being characteristic to that topic.

Algorithm 2 Plan generation

```
Require: Graph G, topic t, stepwise thresholds TH, optional custom keywords q_c
Initialize: Plan q ← []; Current node, cn ← t
for step s ← 1 to n do
    Neighbors of current node, N ← Neighbors(G, cn)
    # candidates to score, l ← len(N)
    Neighbor scores, S ← Zeros(l)
    for i ← 1 to l do
        cand ← Neighbors[i]
        S[i] ← G.edge_score(t, cand) + G.edge_score(cn, cand)
    end for
    SORT(N) by S, in descending order
    Top candidates, TC ← N[: TH[i]]
    if ∃k ∈ q_c s.t. k ∈ TC then
        cn ← k
        q_c ← q_c − k
    else
        cn ← GET_RANDOM(TC)
    end if
    APPEND(q, cn)
end for
return q
```

2.3 Plan generation

Plan generation. Once we have the graph G, a plan q is generated at inference time by walking on the graph using the given input topic t as the starting point as shown in Algorithm 2. The provided input can also contain additional keywords q_c to be included in the plan, based on which the generated plan q can be customized.

A walk down the graph starts from the topic node t while selecting a keyword k from the best neighbors of each node. The selected neighbor then acts as the node for the next stage from which subsequent selection is to be made. This proceeds till we complete n stages of plan generation. For an appropriate selection, all neighbors of the current node cn are scored and ranked before making a selection. The window size for selecting a neighbor from the top-ranked ones at each stage is specified by the thresholds TH. For ranking the neighbors, each candidate $cand$ is scored based on the sum of their edge scores to the topic $G.edge\_score(t, cand)$ and the current node $G.edge\_score(cn, cand)$, thus facilitating the selection of keywords relevant to the topic and the current node context. At every stage, if the list of top-ranked candidates contains one of the custom keywords q_c, we directly select the custom keyword and remove it from q_c to avoid further repetition of that word in the plan. The generated plan can thus be given as:

$$q = [q_s]_{s=1}^{s=n} \tag{1}$$

2.4 Clause generation

Model training. We train a language model $LM(\theta)$ for generating a clause c by conditioning on a reference plan r^c and topic t, where θ are the parameters of LM. In this, we minimize the negative log-likelihood of the probability of c as given by the model:

$$L_{gen} = \sum_{t \in T} \sum_{c \in C^t} -log[p(c \mid r^c, t, \theta)] \tag{2}$$

This trained model can be used for generating a clause from a custom-generated plan q. Since the model has seen a large number of reference plans and their corresponding clauses, the model is expected to generate the right c for a q given by the planner.

Inferencing clauses from custom plans. At inference, we use the constructed graph G and the language model $LM(\theta)$. We expect a minimal input t indicating the topic of the clause to be generated along with an optional set of keywords q_{k_c} for customization. We run the plan generation algorithm based on this information to obtain a custom plan q as demonstrated in Algorithm 2. The customizability in plan generation can be exploited through an iterative plan-and-generate process involving iterative modifications to the plan before achieving a user-desired state of the clause. Appendix B illustrates such an example flow of plan modification followed by subsequent clause generation to enable an end user to achieve the clause in desired state.

3 Experiments

3.1 Dataset

We use the LEDGAR (Tuggener et al., 2020) dataset for our experiments. The cleaned version of this dataset consists of 60,540 contracts extracted from the EDGAR (Loukas et al., 2021) database containing 846,274 clauses (or "provisions") from 12,608 topics (or "labels"). We first create splits of the dataset at the contract level to ensure no data leakage in evaluation by making train, dev, and test sets made in a proportion of 85:5:10. We discard those clauses which belong to more than one topic in the subsequent experiments. From the train set contracts, we select those clause topics with a minimum clause frequency of 100, resulting in 387,210 clauses from 939 topics for training. We use these selected topics for identifying applicable clauses in the dev and test splits.

3.2 Keyword extraction and graph construction

We use the YAKE (Campos et al., 2020) keyword extractor for extracting keywords. Using YAKE allows us to extract a ranked order of keywords based on their prominence. The quality of ranked keywords given by the simpler statistical algorithm in YAKE was found to align with the notion of generic to specific information flow. To approximate the generic to specific order of keywords, we concatenate all the clauses under a topic and extract up to 200 (m_1) keywords per topic (K^t). These extracted keywords in ranked order represent each clause (c_i^t) as a reference plan of keywords (r^{c_i}) in which we limit the number of keywords per clause to 10 (n). The dataset of clause-plans ($\bigcup_{t \in T} D^t$) thus obtained is used to construct the graph (G) which consists of 267,893 edges ($e(.,.)$) and 46,953 nodes (N) - with a sparsity of 99.99% enabling it to be used as a lightweight mechanism for control.

3.3 Experimental settings

We experiment with pretrained GPT-2 (Radford et al., 2019) and BART (Lewis et al., 2020a) models for clause generation. Both models are trained on a batch size of 32 for 15 epochs. The learning rate schedule follows an initial warm-up till $1e-05$ for $1/4th$ of the total training steps, followed by linear decay. AdamW (Loshchilov and Hutter, 2019) optimization with a weight decay of 0.01 is used. The maximum generation length of the clause is kept to 700 tokens.

GPT-2 is trained in the usual causal generation paradigm in which we supply the topic concatenated with the plan as the prompt based on which the model generates a clause. For BART, conditional generation is employed in which a topic-plan concatenated input is supplied to the encoder, conditioning on which the model is trained to output a relevant clause.

3.4 Baselines

We consider the following baselines to evaluate the effectiveness of our plan-based approach for clause generation.

- **Prompt2Clause:** We consider the first 10 words of a clause as the prompt (plan) and finetune a GPT-2 model for clause generation following the usual causal generation paradigm.
- **Top2Clause:** We train a BART model to generate a clause solely conditioned on the topic of the clause.
- **RandKwd2Clause:** Keyword order is randomized in the plan, and supplied with the topic for BART-based conditional generation.
- **Plan2Clause-Retrieval:** We use the reference plans to retrieve from a TF-IDF-based index of clauses in the train dataset.

4 Results

4.1 Plan generation

	mean	median
rank	26.70	9.5
# neighbors	385.62	327

Table 2: Ranking generated plans based on references for estimation of plan quality generation.

To estimate the generated plans' quality, we walk the graph as shown in Algorithm 2. However, we use a reference plan to determine the rank given to the expected keyword at every stage of the plan. We take aggregated mean and median values of the ranks given at each stage across all the plans and compare them against the corresponding number of neighbor nodes encountered for ranking. As seen in Table 2, the graph walk gave a median rank of 9.5 against 327 neighbors. This shows the effectiveness of a simple, lightweight graph-based modeling for generating clause plans.

4.2 Clause generation

Experiment	BLEU	R-1	R-2	R-L
Prompt2Clause	20.2	19.68	12.56	16.1
Top2Clause	33.38	43.32	24.14	33.74
RandKwds2Clause	28.4	51.18	32.11	40.74
Plan2Clause-Retrieval	40.74	48.34	29.57	38.73
Plan2Clause-GPT2	39.18	48.24	29.73	39.25
Plan2Clause-BART	**48.98**	**58.99**	**37.95**	**46.11**

Table 3: Results of clause generation from plans.

We compare the baselines outlined in Section 3.4 against results based on our finetuned GPT-2 (Plan2Clause-GPT2) and BART (Plan2Clause-BART) models in Table 3. We use BLEU (Papineni et al., 2002) and ROUGE (Lin, 2004) metrics to evaluate the quality of clause generation based on the reference plans by comparing them against the reference (expected) clauses.

The BART-based generative model outperforms all the baselines consistently. The significantly lesser performance of the GPT-2-based approach showcases the merit in conditional over causal generation for this problem. The difference in performance can also be observed in the Prompt2Clause (causal) and the Top2Clause (conditional) baselines. Plan2Clause-Retrieval turns out to be reasonably competitive, indicating the effectiveness of the proposed method for keyword planning and the potential advantage due to the similar nature of clauses. The importance of an ordered plan can be gauged from the poorer performance of the RandKwds2Clause baseline.

Although CLAUSEREC is a pre-existing literature in the generation of legal clauses, it works on a contract-level problem of recommending a new clause to an incomplete contract in contrast to our clause-level problem. The significant difference in the input and nature of the problem hinders a direct comparison between the two approaches. However, our work merits in demonstrating extensibility (refer Section 5.1) over clause topics compared to the previous work which was limited to a selected set of 5 high-frequency topics.

5 Analysis

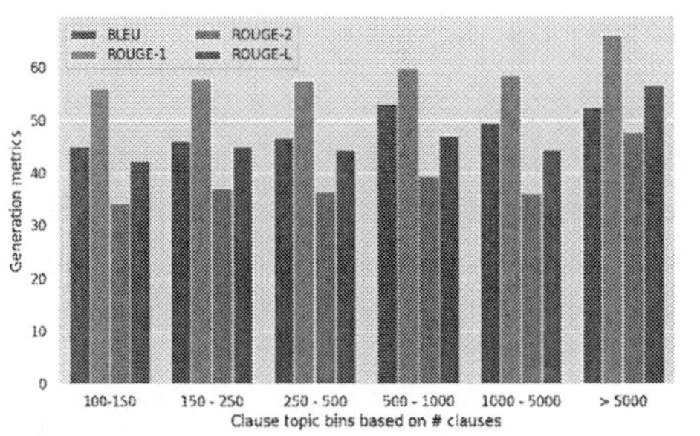

Figure 4: Illustration of the robustness of pipeline to clause topics of various frequencies.

5.1 Robustness across clause topic frequencies

Table 5 shows statistics of the distribution of clause topics in the dataset for different bins based on their frequencies.

As can be seen, a significant variation exists in the nature of clause topics: a large number of clause topics with fewer clauses per topic coexist with a small number of clause topics with a very high number of clauses. We inspected the generation performance across multiple bins of clause frequencies to analyze the difference in generation quality. As seen in Figure 4, there is only a small difference in the performance of the lowest frequency bin compared to the highest. This is despite the number of clauses under the lowest frequency topics being almost 2 orders of magnitude lesser than the highest frequency ones. This shows no significant bias towards the clause topics with a very high number of clauses, and the model can handle a diverse range of topics well. These observations demonstrate the extensibility of our approach to handle newer topics with fewer clauses per topic.

5.2 Comparison with sequential keyword order

We also ablate our proposed generic to specific order of keywords against a natural, sequential order for the planning and generation stages. Much of the existing literature uses a sequential content plan as the conditional prior for generation. This is natural, since the models typically work by generating the content sequentially based on the keyword information, which intends to plan a 'story' in that order.

5.2.1 Planning

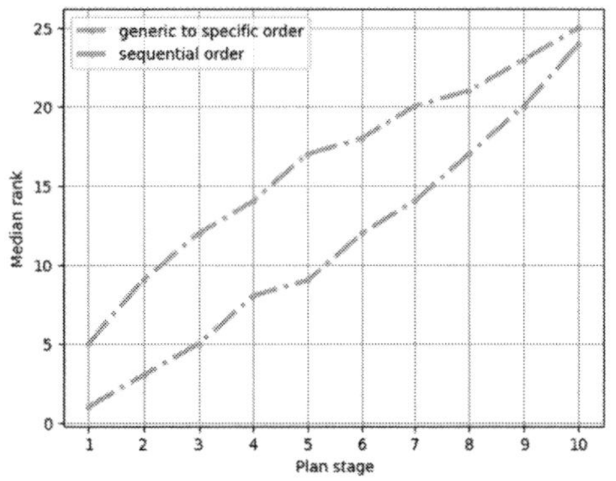

Figure 5: Comparison of stage-wise median ranks given to plans generated by generic to specific ordered keywords versus sequential keywords (the lower the better).

Figure 5 shows the median ranks given to the plans generated by our graph-based approach to each stage of the 10-stage plan. For generating plans with the sequential keywords approach, the first top 10 keywords from every clause were extracted to prepare the dataset $D^t \forall t \in T$, following which the same procedure was followed for graph generation and planning.

As can be observed from the figure, the proposed approach guided by topic-level information for keyword extraction performs better than the approach based on keyword extraction at a clause level for the initial stages of the plan. The lower ranks given in the initial stages of planning highlight the predictive components in both the approaches. There are only a few possibilities for topic-generic content keywords for the proposed generic to specific approach. In the sequential approach, the initial lower ranks bring out the predictable nature of initial phrases in a legal clause. As we move to later stages, the gap between the two approaches decreases as the ranks increase. This demonstrates the loss of predictability as we move on to increase the no. of plan keywords.

5.2.2 Generation

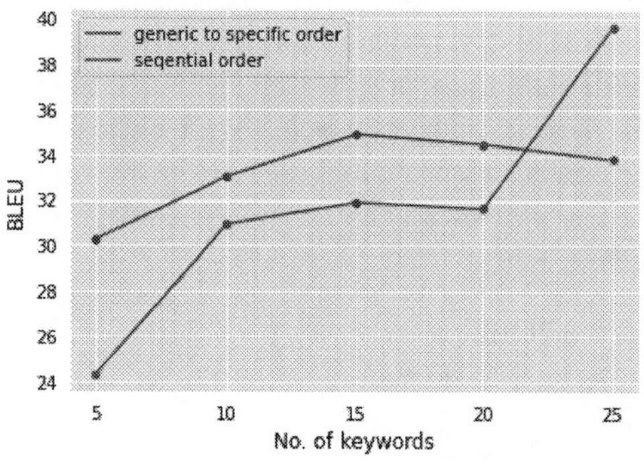

Figure 6: Ablation analysis based on the number of keywords for clause generation & comparison of the proposed content plan order against the traditional sequential keyword order.

In order to study the impact of the no. of keywords provided for generation, we conducted an ablation analysis by repeating our experiments for clause generation on a BART-base model for 10 epochs each, keeping the rest of the hyperparameters the same. The no. of keywords was changed from 5 to 25 in step of 5 for conducting these experiments.

To contrast our method with the sequential keyword order, we repeated the ablation experiments for the same number of keywords while considering the content plan as a sequential order of keywords in the clause. We measured the performance across these studies using BLEU and have illustrated the results in Figure 6.

For our proposed keyword order, we found the generation performance to initially increase with an increase in the number of keywords but later follow a decreasing trend. As we increase the number of keywords for generation, the number of keywords specific to a clause increases. This could help initially since the generative model gets more context for generation. However, adding too many clause-specific keywords away from the topic confounds the model by supplying too much information. Another factor that could play here is the increased noisiness in keywords as we move down the ranked hierarchy, where the keywords keep getting less indicative of the content.

However, when providing the keywords sequentially, the performance followed a continuously increasing trend. The increase seems natural since the generative model has to only fill in a lesser amount of content in the already provided natural order of keywords as we keep providing more keywords. So the task of generation for the model keeps getting easier. However, the sequential order performs markedly poorly against our approach for the initial stages before crossing over to higher scores, as shown in Figure 6. This shows the merit of our approach for clause generation based on minimal keyword information, helping the system to reach the desired clause quickly - without asking for a more significant number of keywords. It is important to appreciate the practicality aspect here since we may not expect an end user to keep providing input to the extent that the basis of the motive lying in automated clause generation gets moot.

5.3 Generation quality

We show a few examples of clauses generated from reference plans in Table 4. The generation quality observed, backed by the aggregated quantitative results showcases the clause generation model's efficacy in generating appropriate clauses from their corresponding plans.

The generated clauses succeed in conveying the same intent as the actual clause while also being strikingly similar in their lexical content. The clauses seem to capture the nuances in legal writing very well, and also change based on the topic and context of the content being generated. The generated clauses naturally fail to add any entity-specific information (such as the clause shown under the topic *brokers*) since the approach does not account for taking in these inputs from the user. Future work can explore incorporating such information from the user to generate entity-specific clauses. Considering contract-specific reference information (such as "section 2.2(b)" in the generated clause under the topic *advances* as opposed to "section 2.3(b)") can be yet another scope for future work. Many of the differences between the actual and generated clause content involved phrases implying similar intent, such as "explicitly and

Topic	advances
Plan	advance, amount, section, revolving, rate, accordance, outstanding, interest, principal, subject
Generated	Subject to section 2.2(b), the principal amount outstanding under the revolving line shall accrue interest at a floating per annum rate equal to the prime rate plus the applicable margin, which interest shall be payable monthly in accordance with the terms of this agreement.
Actual	Subject to section 2.3(b), the principal amount of advances outstanding under the revolving line shall accrue interest at a floating per annum rate equal to the prime rate, which interest shall be payable monthly in accordance with section 2.3(d) below.

Topic	brokers
Plan	broker, connection, commission, fee, agreement, finder, transaction, contemplated, brokerage, entitled
Generated	No broker, finder or investment banker is entitled to any brokerage, finders or other fee or commission in connection with the transactions contemplated by this agreement based upon arrangements made by or on behalf of buyer.
Actual	Except for Raymond James Financial, Inc. and Oppenheimer & Co. Inc., no broker, finder or investment banker is entitled to any brokerage, finder's or other fee or commission in connection with the transactions contemplated by this agreement or any other transaction agreement based upon arrangements made by or on behalf of strand.

Topic	data privacy
Plan	data, company, plan, personal, transfer, participation, administering, consent, purpose, managing
Generated	The grantee hereby explicitly and unambiguously consents to the collection, use and transfer, in electronic or other form, of his or her personal data as described in this agreement and any other award grant materials (data) by and among, as applicable, the employer, the company and any parent or subsidiary for the exclusive purpose of implementing, administering and managing the grantees participation in the plan.
Actual	The grantee hereby voluntarily consents to the collection, use and transfer, in electronic or other form, of the grantees personal data as described in this agreement and any other award grant materials by and among, as applicable, the company and any subsidiary or affiliate for the exclusive purpose of implementing, administering and managing the grantees participation in the plan.

Topic	withholdings
Plan	withholding, tax, applicable, payment, agreement, pursuant, subject, made, income, employment
Generated	All payments made pursuant to this agreement shall be subject to withholding of applicable income and employment taxes.
Actual	All payments made pursuant to this agreement will be subject to withholding of applicable income, employment and excise taxes.

Topic	limitation of liability
Plan	damage, party, consequential, indirect, punitive, incidental, notwithstanding, foregoing, entitled
Generated	The collateral trustee shall not be liable for any action taken or omitted to be taken by it hereunder or under any other secured debt document, except for its own gross negligence or willful misconduct.
Actual	The collateral trustee will not be responsible or liable for any action taken or omitted to be taken by it hereunder or under any other security document, except for its own gross negligence or willful misconduct as determined by a final order of a court of competent jurisdiction.

Table 4: Example clauses generated by the best performing BART model given a topic with the corresponding plans and actual (reference) clauses.

unabiguously" versus "voluntarily" for the example under *data privacy*. Most of the shorter length clauses showed good lexical overlap with the actual (e.g. *withholdings*) with hallucination observed in some content (e.g. *limitation of liability*).

Besides entity and contract-specific information, future work can also handle allowing phrase-level control in clauses, where the user can ask for explicit phrases to be included, or not to be included in the clause along with specification of a few custom keywords for reference. The challenge here would lie in detecting the appropriateness of position for placement of that phrase within the clause.

5.4 Controllable, iterative plan-to-clause workflow

We demonstrate the controllability in clause generation with an example flow of iterative clause customization in Appendix B. We found the generated clauses to suitably vary content based on simple addition and removal of necessary keywords which can encourage approaches for developing efficient tools in legal clause drafting.

Consider an end user to be acquainted with drafting legal contracts - for instance lawyers. An iterative flow involving content planning followed by clause generation allows the user to keep deleting and adding keywords to the plan for driving down towards a desired state of the clause. The idea is to allow an end-user to generate a legal clause by the specification of minimal information such that the final generated state of the clause can be used with minimal edits necessary. A keyword-based information control facilitates this simplicity compared to control based on latent space representation.

An interesting problem we believe future work

could look at is ensuring only necessary phrasal changes are made between two successive stages of clause generation in the iterative pipeline shown in Figure 7, thus making the control more precise. For instance, the addition of the keyword "law" to the plan in the third stage of generation makes changes to the clause like changing "governmental authority" to "arbitrator", increasing the verbosity of the clause and a slight change of meaning w.r.t. company's shares of common stock. Explainability and more nuanced control in this process would make clause generation more precise.

6 Conclusion

We propose a plan-based approach for generating legal clauses inspired by content planning techniques in story generation. The pipeline involves customizable content plan generation based on the clause topic and optional control keywords using a simple, lightweight graph followed by clause generation. The content plan represents its corresponding clause as an ordered list of generic to specific keywords. Our approach achieves promising results for clause generation across the broad range of clause topics in the dataset, indicating the extensibility of our approach. We also show the merit of our proposed order in generating clauses with lesser keyword information. While we discuss a use case for controllability in clause generation possible through our pipeline, the generation of clause content shows substantial changes for minor changes in the plan. Future work can look at increasing the preciseness of control involved by changing only the content of a clause as necessitated by a change in the input plan. The customization of clause content can be further drilled down to inclusion of entity-specific and contract-specific information.

7 Limitations

While we evaluate the generation of clauses by using regular generation-based metrics (BLEU & ROUGE), establishing results based on human evaluations would have provided substantial qualitative backing for the empirically strong results. However, the understanding and evaluation of clauses would require strong domain knowledge in legal clauses, and any evaluation from a layperson would not help in gauging the quality. Due to the practical difficulties in involving domain-specific experts to evaluate a substantial number of clauses to make a judgment, we relied on the quantitative metrics and some qualitative analysis performed randomly on a select set of clauses.

Controllable content generation has been popularly demonstrated by the CTRL (Keskar et al., 2019) architecture that shows fine capabilities in controlling the content based on the specification of control keywords appended before the prompt for a generation. Although it would have been interesting to study the performance of this model fine-tuned for clause generation, we were limited by sufficient computational resources to carry out the experiment on this model, and on the larger variants of models (BART, GPT-2) we currently have used.

References

Vinay Aggarwal, Aparna Garimella, Balaji Vasan Srinivasan, Anandhavelu N, and Rajiv Jain. 2021. ClauseRec: A clause recommendation framework for AI-aided contract authoring. In *Proceedings of the 2021 Conference on Empirical Methods in Natural Language Processing*, pages 8770–8776, Online and Punta Cana, Dominican Republic. Association for Computational Linguistics.

Ricardo Campos, Vítor Mangaravite, Arian Pasquali, Alípio Jorge, Célia Nunes, and Adam Jatowt. 2020. Yake! keyword extraction from single documents using multiple local features. *Inf. Sci.*, 509(C):257–289.

Hong Chen, Raphael Shu, Hiroya Takamura, and Hideki Nakayama. 2021. Graphplan: Story generation by planning with event graph.

Nitish Shirish Keskar, Bryan McCann, Lav R. Varshney, Caiming Xiong, and Richard Socher. 2019. Ctrl: A conditional transformer language model for controllable generation.

Mike Lewis, Yinhan Liu, Naman Goyal, Marjan Ghazvininejad, Abdelrahman Mohamed, Omer Levy, Veselin Stoyanov, and Luke Zettlemoyer. 2020a. BART: Denoising sequence-to-sequence pre-training for natural language generation, translation, and comprehension. In *Proceedings of the 58th Annual Meeting of the Association for Computational Linguistics*, pages 7871–7880, Online. Association for Computational Linguistics.

Patrick Lewis, Ethan Perez, Aleksandra Piktus, Fabio Petroni, Vladimir Karpukhin, Naman Goyal, Heinrich Küttler, Mike Lewis, Wen-tau Yih, Tim Rocktäschel, Sebastian Riedel, and Douwe Kiela. 2020b. Retrieval-augmented generation for knowledge-intensive nlp tasks. In *Proceedings of the 34th International Conference on Neural Information Processing Systems*, NIPS'20, Red Hook, NY, USA. Curran Associates Inc.

Chin-Yew Lin. 2004. ROUGE: A package for automatic evaluation of summaries. In *Text Summarization Branches Out*, pages 74–81, Barcelona, Spain. Association for Computational Linguistics.

Ilya Loshchilov and Frank Hutter. 2019. Decoupled weight decay regularization. In *ICLR*.

Lefteris Loukas, Manos Fergadiotis, Ion Androutsopoulos, and Prodromos Malakasiotis. 2021. EDGAR-CORPUS: Billions of tokens make the world go round. In *Proceedings of the Third Workshop on Economics and Natural Language Processing*, pages 13–18, Punta Cana, Dominican Republic. Association for Computational Linguistics.

Neil McIntyre and Mirella Lapata. 2010. Plot induction and evolutionary search for story generation. In *Proceedings of the 48th Annual Meeting of the Association for Computational Linguistics*, pages 1562–1572, Uppsala, Sweden. Association for Computational Linguistics.

Kishore Papineni, Salim Roukos, Todd Ward, and Wei-Jing Zhu. 2002. Bleu: a method for automatic evaluation of machine translation. In *Proceedings of the 40th Annual Meeting of the Association for Computational Linguistics*, pages 311–318, Philadelphia, Pennsylvania, USA. Association for Computational Linguistics.

Alec Radford, Jeff Wu, Rewon Child, David Luan, Dario Amodei, and Ilya Sutskever. 2019. Language models are unsupervised multitask learners.

D. Simonson, Daniel P. Broderick, and Jonathan Herr. 2019. The extent of repetition in contract language. *Proceedings of the Natural Legal Language Processing Workshop 2019*.

Don Tuggener, Pius von Däniken, Thomas Peetz, and Mark Cieliebak. 2020. LEDGAR: A large-scale multi-label corpus for text classification of legal provisions in contracts. In *Proceedings of the Twelfth Language Resources and Evaluation Conference*, pages 1235–1241, Marseille, France. European Language Resources Association.

Ashish Vaswani, Noam Shazeer, Niki Parmar, Jakob Uszkoreit, Llion Jones, Aidan N. Gomez, Łukasz Kaiser, and Illia Polosukhin. 2017. Attention is all you need. In *Proceedings of the 31st International Conference on Neural Information Processing Systems*, NIPS'17, page 6000–6010, Red Hook, NY, USA. Curran Associates Inc.

Lili Yao, Nanyun Peng, Ralph Weischedel, Kevin Knight, Dongyan Zhao, and Rui Yan. 2018. Plan-and-write: Towards better automatic storytelling.

Haoxi Zhong, Chaojun Xiao, Cunchao Tu, Tianyang Zhang, Zhiyuan Liu, and Maosong Sun. 2020. How does nlp benefit legal system: A summary of legal artificial intelligence.

A Frequency distribution of clause topics in the dataset

Aggregated statistics of bins of clause topics based on their frequencies are given in Table 5. By the frequency of a clause topic, we mean the number of clauses under that topic.

range	# topics	mean	std.	median
100-150	309	120.5	14.2	118.0
150-250	233	192.1	29.2	186.0
250-500	230	344.3	65.5	332.0
500-1k	102	660.7	119.2	643.5
1k-5k	62	1901.9	912.2	1483.5
>5k	5	8205.2	1304.7	7853.0
Overall	939	412.4	764.5	210.0

Table 5: Distribution of clause topics in the dataset w.r.t. the number of clauses under each topic. The values of mean, median, and std indicate the corresponding values of the number of clauses under a topic in that bin range. The topic *governing laws* had the highest number of clauses at 10,636.

B Iterative planning and generation: Example use case

Figure 7 shows an example use case of the customized plan to clause generation.

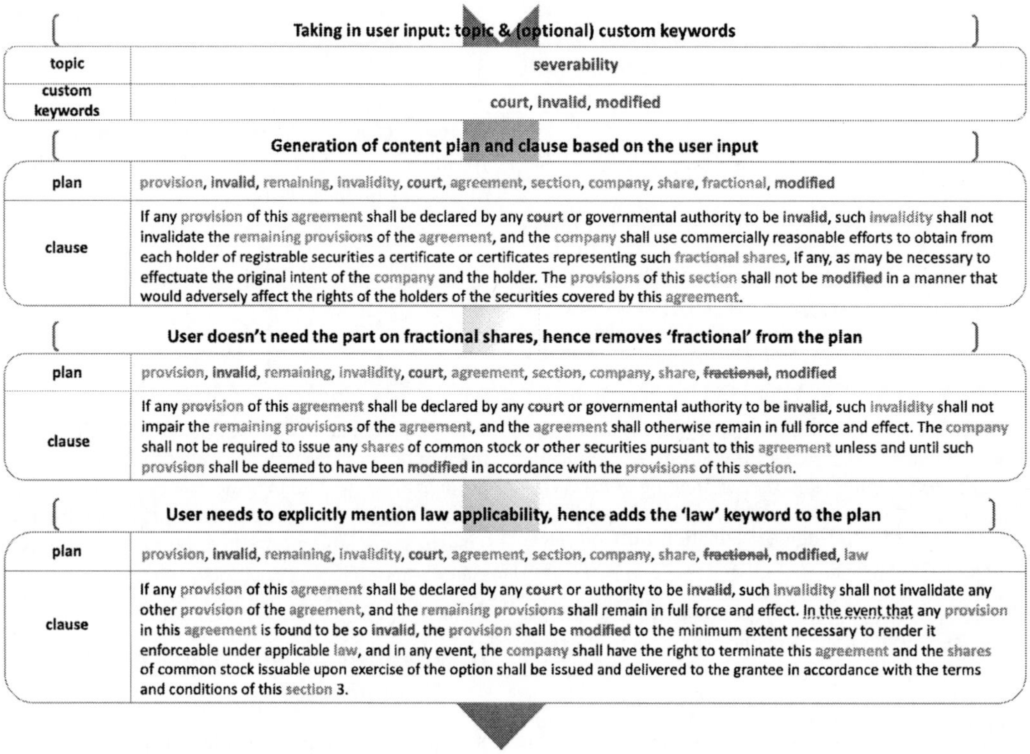

Figure 7: Example flow where an end user generates a clause for the clause topic *severability* by specifying a few additional keywords at the start. In subsequent stages, the user removes and adds keywords from the generated plan to directly control the clause content.

Automatic Classification of Legal Violations in Cookie Banner Texts

Marieke van Hofslot
Utrecht University
Information and Computing Sciences
m.t.vanhofslot@students.uu.nl

Almila Akdag Salah
Utrecht University
Information and Computing Sciences
a.a.akdag@uu.nl

Albert Gatt
Utrecht University
Information and Computing Sciences
a.gatt@uu.nl

Cristiana Santos
Utrecht University
Faculty of Law
c.teixeirasantos@uu.nl

Abstract

Cookie banners are designed to request consent from website visitors for their personal data. Recent research suggest that a high percentage of cookie banners violate legal regulations as defined by the General Data Protection Regulation (GDPR) and the ePrivacy Directive. In this paper, we focus on language used in these cookie banners, and whether these violations can be automatically detected, or not. We make use of a small cookie banner dataset that is annotated by five experts for legal violations and test it with state of the art classification models, namely BERT, LEGAL-BERT, BART in a zero-shot setting and BERT with LIWC embeddings. Our results show that none of the models outperform the others in all classes, but in general, BERT and LEGAL-BERT provide the highest accuracy results (70%-97%). However, they are influenced by the small size and the unbalanced distributions in the dataset.

1 Introduction

Cookie banners are a part of everyday life for EU-based users while browsing the Web. To comply with the General Data Protection Regulation (GDPR) (EU, 2018) and the ePrivacy Directive (ePD-09), website operators have to inform EU users and ask for their consent for the processing of their personal data for 'unnecessary purposes', i.e. data that is not needed for the website to function, such as user-targeted advertising (Article 29 Working Party, 2012). Accordingly, EU users have to navigate through a cookie banner and decide on whether to consent to their personal information being collected via cookies or other tracking technologies that the site embeds. A consent request needs to be unambiguous, clear, concise, and informative, and consent needs to be freely given (Articles 4(11) and 7(2) (EU, 2018)).

Research has found that 89% of cookie banners violate applicable laws (Santos et al., 2021; Soe et al., 2020; Nouwens et al., 2020). The legal study by (Santos et al., 2021) focused on processing purposes of cookie banners and confirmed that 89% of the cookie banners violated at least one legal requirement applied to the text of the stated purposes; they further detected the use of vagueness, framing, misleading wording, and technical jargon. Utz et al. (2019) noted that the text to explain the purpose of data collection was typically expressed in generic terms, and use of technical jargon was not understandable properly by the average data subject. Studies furthermore confirmed that the prevalence of "affirmative" options and positive framing could nudge users toward consenting to tracking (Hausner and Gertz, 2021; Kampanos and Shahandashti, 2021).

The *language* used in cookie banners is often formulated in a way that can confuse and impact users' privacy decisions, steering them to accept consent to tracking. Regulators, policymakers and scholars (CNIL, 2022; Gray et al., 2018; Article 29 Working Party, 2018; European Data Protection Board, 2020, 2022; Chatellier et al., 2019), confirm that certain textual strategies such as the use of motivational language and humor (European Data Protection Board, 2022; Frobrukerrådet, 2018), shame (Mathur et al., 2019), guilt (Brignull, 2010), blame (Chatellier et al., 2019), fear (Bongard-Blanchy et al., 2021) or uncertainty (European Data Protection Board, 2020) influence users' online decisions. Such textual expressions can violate the legal requirements for consent. Consent, if not obtained in compliance with the GDPR, provides invalid grounds for data processing, rendering the processing activity illegal (Article 6(1)(a) GDPR)).

There is a need to identify such textual violations and develop tools that can automatically de-

Proceedings of the Natural Legal Language Processing Workshop 2022, pages 287 - 295
December 8, 2022 ©2022 Association for Computational Linguistics

tect such textual *dark patterns* (Mathur et al., 2019) in order to provide proof of such practices (and legal evidence) to support the legal proceedings of enforcement authorities in their auditing efforts. Regulators are presently overwhelmed by the novelty and sheer scale at which such patterns are being deployed online. However, only a few studies have investigated automatic detection of legal violations in cookie banner text. Bollinger et al. (2022) used feature extraction and ensembles of decision trees for their cookie purpose classifier with which they developed a browser extension to remove cookies according to user preferences. Khandelwal et al. (2022) used a fine-tuned BERT Base-Cased model to discover and force cookie settings to disable all non-essential cookies.

These studies focus on enhancing the usability of websites for the users. In this paper, we focus on automatic detection of legal violations in cookie banner texts. We work with a dataset that is annotated by five experts for such violations, and test the performance of four state of the art deep neural network models, BERT, BERT with LIWC, LEGAL-BERT and BART in a zero-shot setting. Our aim is to understand if large, pretrained language models can be used with little or no finetuning for auditing purposes by policymakers or consumer protection organisations. To that end, we document the shortcomings of the models to provide insight on the problems and challenges of such a classification task. Our results suggest that no model outperforms all the others in all classification tasks, suggesting a need for more data annotation in this domain, as well as signalling a potential for models which are specifically trained or fine-tuned on the task at hand.

Annotation class	Classification labels
Consent options presence	Reject option No reject option
Framing	Negative framing Positive framing No framing
Misleading language	Deception Misleading language Prolixity Vagueness No Misleading language
Purpose	Purpose mentioned No purpose mentioned
Technical jargon	Technical jargon No technical jargon

Table 1: Annotation categories and classes

2 Methodology

In this section we first describe the dataset, discuss the annotation and classification based on manual labels. Lastly, we describe the classification models we have used.

2.1 Dataset

In Santos et al. (2021), cookie banner texts were manually annotated according to the GDPR legal requirements and their corresponding violations. The resulting dataset consists of 407 cookie banner text segments. The texts are in English, and have an average of 3.59 sentences and 49.77 words. The most common content words (i.e. 'cookies', 'website', 'policy', etc.) are very specific to the context of cookie banners.

Annotation classes and classification labels. These are based on the annotation guidelines used by the five experts for the study in Santos et al. (2021), where a given annotation *class* has one or more corresponding *labels*. The original dataset annotated texts segment-wise. In contrast, the goal of the present work was to label the cookie banner as a whole, to indicate whether it contains one or more instances of language that falls under any of these labels. The labels assigned to each cookie banner are thus determined by the presence of the labels in their text segments, in the original data. Thus, some segments might belong to more than one class and label.

Due to data sparseness, some classes in the original guidelines by Santos et al. (2021) were omitted, leaving five classes in total: *Consent options presence*, *Misleading language*, *Framing*, *Purpose* and *Technical jargon* (see Table 1).

2.2 Models

In this paper, we compare the performance of the following models, as measured by their classification accuracy:

BERT (Devlin et al., 2019) is a widely-used

Transformer-based model, which serves as the basis for a variety of text classification tasks, including topic classification, and sentiment analysis. The major advantage of BERT is that it was pretrained on a large corpus, allowing it to be fine-tuned on a downstream task with a relatively small data set. We encode each cookie banner text segment into a fixed-sized vector using its BERT embedding, using this as input to a classification layer fine-tuned on the training and validation data.

BERT with LIWC features. Linguistic Inquiry and Word Count (LIWC) (Pennebaker et al., 2001) is a dictionary-based text analysis tool with linguistic, psychological and topical categories. LIWC calculates the percentage of words from the cookie banner text that fall into each category and creates a vector of all these percentages. We concatenate BERT embeddings with a LIWC vector representing all 80 categories used by LIWC. The remaining architecture is the same with BERT. For classes like *framing*, *misleading language* and *technical jargon*, we expect that LIWC will increase the performance of the model, since these features reflect the more stylistic aspects of the text.

LEGAL-BERT. LEGAL-BERT are a family of BERT models that have been pre-trained on diverse English legal text from several fields, including European legislation (EURLEX[1]), UK legislation [2], and various courts from Europe and the US[3]. Since the general LEGAL-BERT model performs better than BERT on domain-specific tasks (Chalkidis et al., 2020), we use the general LEGAL-BERT as a comparison for the BERT model. While cookie banners are not themselves legal texts, they do explain legally relevant provisions; hence, we include this model to address the utility of a domain-specific BERT model in the general legal domain.

BART in ZS-setting. Zero-shot (ZS) classification in NLP has been used to classify text on which a model is not specifically trained (Sarkar et al., 2021; Yin et al., 2019a; Ye et al., 2020). Here, we use the pre-trained BART-Large MNLI model (Lewis et al., 2019) as an out-of-the-box zero-shot text classifier, similar to (Yin et al., 2019b). To do this, we reframe the classification task as a Natural Language Inference task (NLI), where the goal is to determine whether two texts, a premise and a hypothesis, are in a relation of entailment, contradiction, or are neutral. Here, the cookie banner text is the premise and the corresponding labels are hypotheses. We use the model to estimate the probability of each label for every cookie banner text segment. The label with the highest probability is selected.

Training details and hyperparameters. For simplicity, a separate model was trained for each class. For the fine-tuned models based on BERT and BERT-LEGAL, we use a classification layer of size 768, followed by a ReLU layer, to determine the most probable label for each class. For BERT and BERT+LIWC features, we use BERT Base-cased. Since Base-Cased is not available for LEGAL-BERT, we use LEGAL-BERT Base-uncased. For the BERT-like models, the learning rate is set as 1e-6, the model is trained by using cross-entropy loss and the Adam optimizer. The training was set for 12 epochs. For reporting our results, we used a 2-fold (50/50) cross-validation setup. As our dataset is small and the class distributions are not balanced, we preferred a stratified split. Since BART is used in a zero shot-setting, cross-validation is not applicable for this model, and the results are reported accordingly. All of the models were run on a laptop with AMD Ryzen 7 5700U processor (1.80 GHz) and 16 GB DDR 4 RAM.

3 Results and Discussion

Table 2 shows the performance of these models in terms of classification accuracy, computed as a proportion of correctly labelled instances per class. We provide F1-scores for all classes in Table 3.

Accuracy performance differs for each class. Overall, we do not have a model that outperforms all the others for all classes. The best accuracy performance for each class differs.

Technical jargon: LEGAL-BERT gives the best result with 81.3%, although the difference between the models is only a few percent, BERT + LIWC's result being the lowest with 74.95%. In general F1 scores are high for the majority labels and not the minority labels, but this is especially the case

[1]Publicly available from http://eur-lex.europa.eu/

[2]Publicly available from http://www.legislation.gov.uk

[3]Cases from the European Court of Justice (ECJ), also available from EURLEX, cases from HUDOC, the repository of the European Court of Human Rights (ECHR) (http://hudoc.echr.coe.int/eng), cases from various courts across the USA, see https://case.law and US contracts from EDGAR, the database of US Securities and Exchange Commission (SECOM) (https://www.sec.gov/edgar.shtml).

Class	BERT CV	BERT+LIWC CV	LEGAL-BERT CV	BART-ZS
Consent options presence	90.7 (±0.95)	89.7 (±0.95)	85.3 (±0.55)	**91.65**
Framing	**67.4 (±0.15)**	60.7 (±1.60)	65.9 (±0.15)	58.23
Misleading language	**65.2 (±2.85)**	60.2 (±3.50)	65.1 (±0.40)	54.30
Purpose	91.9 (±0.20)	90.0 (±0.75)	**93.4 (±0.25)**	76.90
Technical jargon	79.2 (±1.65)	74.95 (±2.55)	**81.3 (±0.45)**	78.87

Table 2: Comparison of cross-validation accuracies (mean and std) with best score per class/row in bold.

Class	Label	BERT CV	BERT+LIWC CV	LEGAL-BERT CV	Test set occurr. Fold 1	 Fold 2	BART-ZS
Consent opt. presence	Other	0.95 (±0.01)	0.94 (±0.00)	0.92 (±0.00)	172	172	0.95
	Reject option	0.62 (±0.05)	0.61 (±0.08)	0.13 (±0.13)	32	31	0.68
Framing	No framing	0.75 (±0.01)	0.71 (±0.02)	0.76 (±0.00)	120	119	0.73
	Positive	0.58 (±0.04)	0.45 (±0.01)	0.46 (±0.01)	76	76	0.17
	Negative	0.00 (±0.00)	0.00 (±0.00)	0.00 (±0.00)	8	8	0.13
Misleading language	None	0.82 (±0.00)	0.78 (±0.02)	0.79 (±0.00)	134	133	0.71
	Vagueness	0.21 (±0.03)	0.17 (±0.01)	0.00 (±0.00)	34	34	0.16
	Decept. lang.	0.08 (±0.08)	0.27 (±0.09)	0.00 (±0.00)	26	25	0.04
	Prolixity	0.00 (±0.00)	0.00 (±0.00)	0.00 (±0.00)	10	11	0.00
Purpose	Yes	0.95 (±0.00)	0.94 (±0.00)	0.96 (±0.00)	164	164	0.87
	None	0.75 (±0.00)	0.69 (±0.03)	0.81 (±0.00)	40	39	0.00
Technical jargon	None	0.88 (±0.01)	0.85 (±0.02)	0.90 (±0.01)	166	165	0.88
	Yes	0.13 (±0.13)	0.16 (±0.04)	0.08 (±0.03)	38	38	0.09

Table 3: Cross validation F1-scores (mean and std) for all models per class label

for LEGAL-BERT with only 0.08 F1 score for the minority label.

Consent options presence: The accuracy is high for all models, but the highest score is from BART with 91.65%.

Purpose: The highest accuracy comes from LEGAL-BERT with 93.4%, where BERT is close with 91.9% and BERT-LIWC still high with 90.0%. In general, this class suffers the least from the overfitting to the majority label, and has overall higher F1 scores for both labels. BART performs the worst with 76.9%, and has the lowest F1 scores.

Misleading language and *Framing*: these labels have the lowest accuracy out of the five classes, with accuracy percentages dropping to 60% for some models. We also observe the lowest occurrences in these classes, with very low or null F1 scores. Given that these are the classes with more than two labels and rely on stylistic aspects of the text, these results are not surprising.

Misleading language: BERT and LEGAL-BERT have close scores with 65.2% and 65.1%. However LEGAL-BERT has a lower std. The Prolixity label has null F1 scores for all models.

Framing: LEGAL-BERT produces the highest accuracy score for Framing with 65.9%. The Negative Framing label has null F1 scores for all models except BART.

Model comparison: To compare the classification results of models, we used pairwise McNemar tests, see Table 4. Overall, BERT and LEGAL-BERT models achieved relatively good and similar accuracy scores across all classes. However, LEGAL-BERT's F1 scores are lower then BERT for minority classes. Comparing the two models with McNemar test we observe that they perform significantly differently for Consent options class.

Observations: When we sample instances where the models fail to classify one of the five classes correctly, we see the shortcomings of each model better (see Appendix for a list of examples, and how they are classified by each

Class	BERT / BERT+LIWC	BERT / LEGAL-BERT	BERT+LIWC / LEGAL-BERT	BERT / BART-ZS	LEGAL-BERT / BART-ZS	BERT+LIWC / BART-ZS
Consent opt. presence	.585	.000**	.011*	.716	.007*	.396
Framing	.010*	.617	.069	.011*	.028*	.533
Misleading language	.013*	1.000	.012*	.002*	.002*	.097
Purpose	.134	.238	.013*	.000**	.000**	.000**
Technical jargon	.033*	.108	.000**	1.000	.419	.208

Table 4: P-values of McNemar's test on all model combinations. $^*p < .05$, $^{**}p < .001$

model). In most classes, BERT and LEGAL-BERT seem to wrongly over-classify the majority label. BERT+LIWC only does this with *"Framing"* and performs well on all other classes. LEGAL-BERT fails in the class *"Framing"*, where it classifies an instance of *"No framing"* as *"Positive framing"*. Overall, BART does not perform well, but contrary to the BERT models, the incorrect classifications are not due to choosing the majority class.

Occurrence distribution: Studying the classes and their corresponding misclassifications and the F1 scores, we observe that the data distribution affects the accuracy. Classification labels that have a low amount of occurrences in the data are almost always wrongly classified, even after the application of a stratified split for training and validation (see Table 3). This means that more data should be collected and annotated for these classes. Furthermore, fine-tuning of the models during training is needed, a common solution here is adding weights to the minority classes.

Implications: The challenges of automatic classification of cookie banners are due to purposefully confusing wording, lack of classified data by experts, and the shortness of cookie banners themselves. The obtained results show that using use a state of the art classification model off the shelf or with minimal fine-tuning will not yield reliable results for auditing or helping policymakers.

4 Conclusion and Future work

In this paper, we used a cookie banner dataset previously annotated by five experts that detected legal violations. We test state of the art deep learning models such as BERT, LEGAL-BERT and BART for automatic classification of such violations in this dataset. We also combined a dictionary based approach, i.e. LIWC embeddings with BERT, and checked if this improves performance or not.

Our approach aimed to give more insight into automatic detection of legal violations of cookie banners texts by comparing frequently used models. Our results suggest that there is not one model that outperforms all the others for all classes that need to be detected. In general, BERT and LEGAL-BERT work well for all classes; however, a closer look reveals that these models are also affected by the skewed data distribution for certain classes. In contrast, BART performs worst for most of the classes, but is not affected by the small size of the data set, and by class imbalance.

We further add to the limited amount of studies on automatic detection of textual legal violations of cookie banners and laying a foundation for further research on this topic. Since the language and style of the cookie banners change rapidly, we need robust algorithms that can adapt to changes both in the legal domain and in the manner of adoption of new regulations by website operators. Hence, it is crucial to develop an efficient annotation pipeline to speed up human-in-the-loop annotation and automatic classification. Our initial tests give insight into which model performs well for which challenges, and can be used further to build such a pipeline in the future.

5 Ethical implications and limitations

In this paper, we rely on large, pretrained language models for classification, fine-tuning them on a small, manually labelled dataset.

One limitation of this approach is the limited size of the manually labelled data. While accuracy and F1 figures may suggest reasonable performance on certain classes, we cannot consider such results as final, or as indicating that the models we use are sufficiently robust to be deployed in real-world settings. Rather, the results provide a picture of what current language models can achieve in a relatively under-explored domain, and provide directions for future work. As noted in the concluding section, one important direction is to curate larger and more diverse training data for the task of cookie banner classification.

References

Article 29 Working Party. 2012. Opinion 04/2012 on cookie consent exemption (WP 194). Technical report. https://ec.europa.eu/justice/article-29/documentation/opinion-recommendation/files/2012/wp194_en.pdf.

Article 29 Working Party. 2018. Guidelines on transparency under regulation 2016/679, (wp260). Technical report.

Dino Bollinger, Karel Kubicek, Carlos Cotrini, and David Basin. 2022. Automating cookie consent and gdpr violation detection. In *31st USENIX Security Symposium (USENIX Security 22)*. USENIX Association.

Kerstin Bongard-Blanchy, Arianna Rossi, Salvador Rivas, Sophie Doublet, Vincent Koenig, and Gabriele Lenzini. 2021. "i am definitely manipulated, even when i am aware of it. it's ridiculous!" - dark patterns from the end-user perspective. *Proceedings of ACM DIS Conference on Designing Interactive Systems*.

Harry Brignull. 2010. Dark patterns. https://www.darkpatterns.org.

Ilias Chalkidis, Manos Fergadiotis, Prodromos Malakasiotis, Nikolaos Aletras, and Ion Androutsopoulos. 2020. Legal-bert: The muppets straight out of law school. *arXiv preprint arXiv:2010.02559*.

Régis Chatellier, Geoffrey Delcroix, Estelle Hary, and Camille Girard-Chanudet. 2019. Shaping choices in the digital world. https://linc.cnil.fr/sites/default/files/atoms/files/cnil_ip_report_06_shaping_choices_in_the_digital_world.pdf.

CNIL. 2022. Deliberation of the restricted committee No. SAN-2021-024 of 31 December 2021 concerning FACEBOOK IRELAND LIMITED. https://www.cnil.fr/sites/default/files/atoms/files/deliberation_of_the_restricted_committee_no._san-2021-024_of_31_december_2021_concerning_facebook_ireland_limited.pdf.

Jacob Devlin, Ming-Wei Chang, Kenton Lee, and Kristina Toutanova. 2019. Bert: Pre-training of deep bidirectional transformers for language understanding. *Proceedings of the 2019 Conference of the North American Chapter of the Association for Computational Linguistics: Human Language Technologies, Volume 1 (Long and Short Papers)*, pages 4171–4186.

ePD-09. Directive 2009/136/ec of the european parliament and of the council of 25 november 2009 amending directive 2002/22/ec.

European Union EU. 2018. General data protection regulation.

European Data Protection Board. 2020. Guidelines 05/2020 on consent under regulation 2016/679. Technical report. https://edpb.europa.eu/sites/edpb/files/files/file1/edpb_guidelines_202005_consent_en.pdf.

European Data Protection Board. 2022. Guidelines 3/2022 on Dark patterns in social media platform interfaces: How to recognise and avoid them Version 1.0 Adopted on 14 March 2022. https://edpb.europa.eu/system/files/2022-03/edpb_03-2022_guidelines_on_dark_patterns_in_social_media_platform_interfaces_en.pdf.

Frobrukerrådet. 2018. Deceived by design: How tech companies use dark patterns to discourage us from exercising our rights to privacy. https://www.forbrukerradet.no/undersokelse/no-undersokelsekategori/deceived-by-design.

Colin M Gray, Yubo Kou, Bryan Battles, Joseph Hoggatt, and Austin L Toombs. 2018. The dark (patterns) side of ux design. In *Proceedings of the 2018 CHI Conference on Human Factors in Computing Systems*, pages 1–14.

Philip Hausner and Michael Gertz. 2021. Dark patterns in the interaction with cookie banners. *arXiv preprint arXiv:2103.14956*.

Georgios Kampanos and Siamak F. Shahandashti. 2021. Accept all: The landscape of cookie banners in greece and the uk.

Rishabh Khandelwal, Asmit Nayak, Hamza Harkous, and Kassem Fawaz. 2022. Cookieenforcer: Automated cookie notice analysis and enforcement. *arXiv preprint arXiv:2204.04221*.

Mike Lewis, Yinhan Liu, Naman Goyal, Marjan Ghazvininejad, Abdelrahman Mohamed, Omer Levy, Ves Stoyanov, and Luke Zettlemoyer. 2019. Bart: Denoising sequence-to-sequence pre-training for natural language generation, translation, and comprehension. *arXiv preprint arXiv:1910.13461*.

Arunesh Mathur, Gunes Acar, Michael J Friedman, Eli Lucherini, Jonathan Mayer, Marshini Chetty, and Arvind Narayanan. 2019. Dark patterns at scale: Findings from a crawl of 11k shopping websites.

Proceedings of the ACM on Human-Computer Interaction, 3(CSCW):1–32.

Midas Nouwens, Ilaria Liccardi, Michael Veale, David Karger, and Lalana Kagal. 2020. Dark patterns after the gdpr: Scraping consent pop-ups and demonstrating their influence. In *Proceedings of the 2020 CHI conference on human factors in computing systems*, pages 1–13.

James W Pennebaker, Martha E Francis, and Roger J Booth. 2001. Linguistic inquiry and word count: Liwc 2001. *Mahway: Lawrence Erlbaum Associates*, 71(2001):2001.

Cristiana Santos, Arianna Rossi, Lorena Sanchez Chamorro, Kerstin Bongard-Blanchy, and Ruba Abu-Salma. 2021. Cookie banners, what's the purpose? analyzing cookie banner text through a legal lens. In *Proceedings of the 20th Workshop on Workshop on Privacy in the Electronic Society*, pages 187–194.

Rajdeep Sarkar, Atul Kr Ojha, Jay Megaro, John Mariano, Vall Herard, and John Philip McCrae. 2021. Few-shot and zero-shot approaches to legal text classification: A case study in the financial sector. In *Proceedings of the Natural Legal Language Processing Workshop 2021*, pages 102–106.

Than Htut Soe, Oda Elise Nordberg, Frode Guribye, and Marija Slavkovik. 2020. Circumvention by design-dark patterns in cookie consent for online news outlets. In *Proceedings of the 11th Nordic Conference on Human-Computer Interaction: Shaping Experiences, Shaping Society*, pages 1–12.

Christine Utz, Martin Degeling, Sascha Fahl, Florian Schaub, and Thorsten Holz. 2019. (un)informed consent: Studying gdpr consent notices in the field. In *Proceedings of the 2019 acm sigsac conference on computer and communications security*, pages 973–990.

Zhiquan Ye, Yuxia Geng, Jiaoyan Chen, Jingmin Chen, Xiaoxiao Xu, Suhang Zheng, Feng Wang, Jun Zhang, and Huajun Chen. 2020. Zero-shot text classification via reinforced self-training. In *Proceedings of the 58th Annual Meeting of the Association for Computational Linguistics*, pages 3014–3024.

Wenpeng Yin, Jamaal Hay, and Dan Roth. 2019a. Benchmarking zero-shot text classification: Datasets, evaluation and entailment approach. *arXiv preprint arXiv:1909.00161*.

Wenpeng Yin, Jamaal Hay, and Dan Roth. 2019b. Benchmarking zero-shot text classification: Datasets, evaluation and entailment approach. *CoRR*, abs/1909.00161.

Appendix

Classification examples We provide some examples of (in)correct classifications of certain classes for all models, see Table 5. The corresponding cookie banner text segments are as follows:

1. In order to give you a better service our website uses cookies. By continuing to browse the site you are agreeing to our use of cookies. Further information. Yes, I agree.

2. This website or its third-party tools use cookies, which are necessary to its functioning and required to achieve the purposes illustrated in the cookie policy. If you want to know more or withdraw your consent to all or some of the cookies, please refer to the cookie policy. By closing this banner, scrolling this page, clicking a link or continuing to browse otherwise, you agree to the use of cookies.

3. We use cookies on this site to enhance your user experience Please read our Cookie policy for more info about our use of cookies and how you can disable them. By clicking the "I accept" button, you consent to the use of these cookies. More info I accept I do not accept.

4. This website uses cookies to enable you to place orders and to give you the best browsing experience possible. By continuing to browse you are agreeing to our use of cookies. Full details can be found here.

5. By using this site you agree to store cookies for the best site experience. More info Sure!

Banner text	Ground truth	BERT	BERT+LIWC	LEGAL-BERT	BART
1	**No framing**	No framing	No framing	Positive framing	No framing
2	**Negative framing**	No framing	No framing	No framing	Positive framing
3	**Positive framing**	No framing	No framing	No framing	Positive framing
1	**Vagueness**	No mislead. lang.	Vagueness	No mislead. lang.	Vagueness
3	**No mislead. lang.**	No mislead. lang.	No mislead. lang.	No mislead. lang.	Vagueness
4	**Deceptive lang.**	No mislead. ang.	No mislead. lang.	No mislead. lang.	Deceptive lang.
2	**Techn. jargon**	No techn. jargon	Techn. jargon	No techn. jargon	No techn. jargon
3	**No techn. jargon**	No techn. jargon	No techn. jargon	No techn. jargon	No techn. jargon
3	**Purpose ment.**	Purpose ment.	Purpose ment.	Purpose ment.	Purpose ment.
5	**No purpose ment.**	Purpose ment.	No purpose ment.	Purpose ment.	Purpose ment.
2	**No reject opt.**	No reject opt.	No reject opt.	No reject opt.	No reject opt.
3	**Reject opt.**	Reject opt.	Reject opt.	Reject opt.	No reject opt.

Table 5: Example cookie banner text segments and their corresponding classification for each model

Text Simplification for Legal Domain: Insights and Challenges

Aparna Garimella[1*], Abhilasha Sancheti[1,2*], Vinay Aggarwal[3†], Ananya Ganesh[4†], Niyati Chhaya[1], Nandakishore Kambhatla[1]
[1]Adobe Research [2]University of Maryland [3]Google [4]University of Colorado Boulder
{garimell,sancheti,nchhaya,nandakam}@adobe.com,
sancheti@umd.edu, vinayagg@google.com, ananya.ganesh@colorado.edu

Abstract

Legal documents such as contracts contain complex and domain-specific jargons, long and nested sentences, and often present with several details that may be difficult to understand for laypeople without domain expertise. In this paper, we explore the problem of text simplification (TS) in legal domain. The main challenge to this is the lack of availability of complex-simple parallel datasets for the legal domain. We investigate some of the existing datasets, methods, and metrics in the TS literature for simplifying legal texts, and perform human evaluation to analyze the gaps.[1] We present some of the challenges involved, and outline a few open questions that need to be addressed for future research in this direction.

1 Introduction

Contracts are legal documents used in several business workflows. They consist of paragraphs of text (*clauses*) outlining the terms and conditions for the involved parties. Prior to signing a contract, the parties need to understand the clauses, to ensure that they are aware of what they are agreeing to.

Contract clauses are usually very long, domain-specific, and contain several complex phrases (Table 1). Table 2 shows a linguistic comparison of legal language from SEC[2] contract clauses (Tuggener et al., 2020) and simple English Wikipedia (Coster and Kauchak, 2011); the average number of tokens in legal clauses is 129.73, while that in Simple Wikipedia (Coster and Kauchak, 2011) is 18.16, and similarly, the average sentence length of the former is 3.5 times that of the latter. Readability metrics such as Flesch Kincaid (FK) (Kincaid et al., 1975) and Automatic Readability Index (ARI) (Senter and Smith, 1967), and the tree depth of the syntactic parse trees of legal sentences, also indicate that legal language is much more complex compared to simple language in Wikipedia, and may be particularly difficult to read for laypeople without much legal background (our target readers). Further, obtaining legal aid to help interpret and review such language may be expensive for such readers. We believe natural language processing (NLP) techniques for text simplification (TS) can be of particular utility to aid legal document understanding for laypeople without much legal knowledge, who are the target readers for this work.

In the event that the Landlord shall deem it necessary or be required by any governmental authority to alter, repair, remove, reconstruct or improve any part of the demised premises or of the building in which the demised premises are located (unless the same result from Tenant's act, neglect, default or mode of operation in which event Tenant shall make all such repairs, alterations and improvements), then the same shall be made by the Landlord with reasonable dispatch, however, such obligation of Tenant shall not extend to maintenance, repairs or replacements necessitated by the intentional wrongdoing or gross negligence of Landlord.

Table 1: Legal sentence from an SEC contract legal clause.

DATA	# TOKENS	SENT. LEN.	FK	ARI	PARSE DEPTH
Clauses	129.73	62.52	29.89	35.05	10.79
SimpleWiki	18.16	17.98	11.72	13.11	5.72

Table 2: Legal language vs. simple English Wikipedia.

The objective of TS is to provide simpler translations for complex input texts. TS is performed at different levels. Lexical simplification aims to replace complex words in a given text with simpler alternatives with equivalent meaning (Gooding and Kochmar, 2019; Qiang et al., 2020). Syntactic simplification typically involves splitting long sentences in shorter ones (Niklaus et al., 2019a,b). (Zhu et al., 2010; Wubben et al., 2012; Martin et al., 2020) use seq2seq-based supervised methods for TS, owing to the availability of parallel datasets (Xu et al., 2015; Niklaus et al., 2019b). There have also been recent advancements in unsupervised TS without the need for parallel datasets (Surya et al., 2019; Laban et al., 2021). However, we believe they may not be readily suited to legal TS, due to the extremely complex nature of legal text as op-

*Equal contribution.
†Work done while at Adobe Research.
[1]The model outputs and human ratings are available at https://bit.ly/3U3ddI1.
[2]Securities and Exchange Commission contracts.

Proceedings of the Natural Legal Language Processing Workshop 2022, pages 296 - 304
December 8, 2022 ©2022 Association for Computational Linguistics

posed to the complex text seen in general news or Wikipedia-like datasets. While prior works on challenges in TS (Xu et al., 2015; Štajner, 2021) focus on the quality of the TS datasets and evaluation metrics, we focus on the generalizability of existing TS systems to legal domain, and challenges in using existing evaluation metrics for legal TS.

In this paper, we aim to address two main research questions. **(1)** How do existing simplification methods perform (in the absence of legal parallel datasets) on the task of legal TS? We specifically examine three types of simplification, namely lexical TS, sentence splitting, and end-to-end TS (split-and-rephrase). **(2)** What are the challenges, if any, in using existing automatic evaluation metrics for legal TS? To this end, we investigate three state-of-the-art (SoTA) unsupervised TS methods in the legal domain (§2.1): *(a)* a BERT-based method for lexical simplification (Qiang et al., 2020), *(b)* a rule-based discourse-aware sentence splitting framework (Niklaus et al., 2019a), and *(c)* a reward-based simplification method that learns to balance fluency, salience, and simplicity of output translations (Laban et al., 2021). We also investigate sequence-to-sequence-based supervised methods (Lewis et al., 2020) trained on three recently released parallel datasets for TS (§2.2). To address the second question, we use several reference-free automatic metrics in the TS literature for simplicity, meaning preservation, and fluency on the model outputs, and conduct human studies to analyze their effectiveness. Finally, we outline some of the challenges in adapting existing methods and metrics to the legal domain, and present a few preliminary research questions that need to be addressed for furthering the research in the space of legal TS.

2 Text Simplification for Legal Domain

We use several unsupervised and supervised methods. We briefly describe them below (please refer to Appendix B for further details).

2.1 Unsupervised Text Simplification

Lexical simplification (LS) aims to replace complex words in a given sentence with simpler words with equivalent meaning to make the resulting text more readable. We use a recent SoTA unsupervised LS method BERT-LS[3] (Qiang et al., 2020) that uses the pre-trained Transformer language model BERT (Devlin et al., 2019) to find simplification candidates for given complex words. Given a complex word w in a sequence S, a new sequence S' is constructed with w masked. The original and new sequences are concatenated and fed into BERT to obtain the probability distribution of the vocabulary $p(\cdot|S, S'\backslash\{w\})$ corresponding to the masked word. The top 10 words from $p(\cdot|S, S'\backslash\{w\})$ are selected as simplification candidates, excluding any morphological derivations. The candidates are ranked based on features such as BERT prediction probability, semantic similarity with complex word, and the candidate with the highest average rank is selected as the replacement. We associate complexity of a word with its commonness in a large corpus (Biran et al., 2011; Glavaš and Štajner, 2015), and identify complex words based on their frequency ($<$10K) in normal Wikipedia (Coster and Kauchak, 2011). Further details are provided in Appendix B.

Sentence splitting involves the segmentation of a sentence into two or more shorter sentences that can be better processed by NLP systems. We use DisSim, a discourse-aware syntactic TS framework, that breaks down a complex source sentence into a set of minimal propositions (Niklaus et al., 2019a).[4] Specifically, given a source sentence, it applies recursive transformations based on a set of 35 hand-crafted grammar rules based on syntactic and lexical patterns to split and rephrase the input sentence into structurally simplified sentences, and establish a semantic hierarchy among them.

Sentence simplification. We use a recent SoTA reward-based text simplification method KeepIt-Simple (KiS) (Laban et al., 2021) that uses a generative model GPT-2 (Radford et al., 2019) to transform a complex sentence into a simpler version, while balancing rewards for fluency, salience, and simplicity using reference-free scorers in a reinforcement learning setup.[5] For fluency, perplexity is used from GPT-2; for simplicity, the Fleish-Kincaid Grade Level (FKGL) (Kincaid et al., 1975) and word frequency in a large corpus are used; and for saliency, a coverage model that uses the generated text to answer fill-in-the-blank questions about the input is used. (Laban et al., 2020). While this work can handle paragraphs as unit of text, we use it for sentence simplification, as legal sentences are much longer than typical sentences. Please refer to (Laban et al., 2021) for further details.

[3] https://github.com/qiang2100/BERT-LS

[4] https://github.com/Lambda-3/DiscourseSimplification

[5] https://github.com/tingofurro/keep_it_simple

Model	Readability			Simplicity	Meaning Preservation			Hallucination		Fluency
	FK ↓	Smog ↓	ARI ↓	Depth ↓	BS ↑	Cov ↑	Blanc ↑	Entail ↑	% Unseen ↓	Ppl ↓
Legal sent	41.59	29.19	50.14	13.12	**1.00**	**0.94**	**0.59**	**99.46**	-	41.92
BERT-LS	41.09	28.38	49.46	12.85	0.98	0.78	0.51	96.76	**0.11**	43.29
DisSim	18.69	18.55	20.83	6.42	0.92	0.89	0.54	94.59	0.25	688.12
MWS	**14.71**	17.52	**15.96**	**5.92**	0.93	0.84	0.50	96.76	0.19	601.04
KiS	14.98	**15.87**	19.35	7.83	0.85	0.45	0.14	10.27	0.23	**32.91**
SBM-Wiki	20.42	20.81	23.01	8.67	0.97	0.89	0.53	91.89	0.14	69.19
SBM-Cont	19.88	20.48	22.37	8.70	0.97	0.89	0.54	91.35	0.13	73.26
Correl	0.16/0.29	0.08/0.36	0.20/0.29	0.10/0.22	0.76/0.75	0.05/0.08	0.27/0.24	-0.08/0.72	-/-	0.34/0.00

Table 3: Results from automatic metrics with **best** and worst values in each column. Correlation between automatic metrics and human ratings are reported for each annotator (A1/A2) in the last row. Correlation for hallucination (fluency) aspect is computed with 1-Entail (1/ppl) and inverse of simplicity with readability and depth measures.

2.2 Supervised Text Simplification

We use BART, a denoising autoencoder for pre-training sequence-to-sequence models, for supervised TS (Lewis et al., 2020). It pre-trains a model combining bidirectional and auto-regressive Transformers, with pre-training tasks to corrupt text with noising functions and learning to reconstruct the original text. We fine-tune BART on three complex-simple datasets, one for sentence splitting, and two for split-and-rephrase task.[6]

MiniWikiSplit (MWS) is a sentence splitting corpus consisting of 203K complex-simple sentence pairs from Wikipedia edit histories (Niklaus et al., 2019b). It was created by running DisSim (Niklaus et al., 2019a) over the complex input sentences from WikiSplit corpus (Botha et al., 2018) and filtering for grammatically incorrect sentences based on a set of dependency parse and part of speech tags.

For the task of split-and-rephrase, Zhang et al. (2020) proposed two benchmark datasets consisting of 500 complex-simple sentence pairs with significantly more diverse syntax in the Wikipedia and legal contracts domain. The data was collected by asking Amazon Mechanical Turk workers to split and rephrase the given complex sentences. We refer to them as **Small-But-Mighty (SBM)**.

3 Experiments

We train the KiS model on 67K legal text sentences selected randomly from LEDGAR dataset that do not occur in the test data (further implementation details in Appendix B). For evaluation, we use the LEDGAR dataset (Tuggener et al., 2020) consisting of Securities and Exchange Commission (SEC) contracts. We use 5K sentences randomly sampled from 100 most frequently occurring legal clauses in LEDGAR. Details on the types of clauses and sentence statistics are provided in Appendix A.

Metrics. We evaluate the legal sentences and model outputs on meaning preservation, syntactic simplicity, fluency, hallucination, and readability measures. For readability, we use Flesch Kincaid (**FK**) (Kincaid et al., 1975), **SMOG** (Mc Laughlin, 1969), and Automatic Readability Index (**ARI**) (Senter and Smith, 1967) to estimate the minimum age required to understand the given text. We compute syntactic simplicity as the average depth of dependency parse trees of the sentences. For meaning preservation, we use BertScore (**BS**) (Zhang et al., 2019) which is a similarity score for each token in the input sentence with each token in the simplified sentence, Coverage (**Cov**) (Laban et al., 2020) which is the accuracy of filling-in the masked tokens in the masked input sentence using the simplified sentence, and **BLANC** (Vasilyev et al., 2020). We measure hallucination as: (1) % of outputs entailed by the input (**Entail**) computed using SoTA RoBERTa-based (Liu et al., 2019) textual entailment model trained on MNLI (Williams et al., 2018), and (2) % of entities (found using spaCy library) in the output not present in the input (**%Unseen**) (Nan et al., 2021). We compute Fluency (**Ppl**) using perplexity score from GPT-2.

4 Results

Results are shown in Table 3. BERT-LS only replaces complex words (if they exist) in the legal sentences; thus it does not achieve much in terms of readability and syntactic simplicity. Since it retains rest other information, it has good meaning preservation and hallucination scores. However, the coverage scores drop, possibly due to

[6]Most of the existing TS datasets (Narayan et al., 2017; Botha et al., 2018; Niklaus et al., 2019b; Zhang et al., 2020; Kim et al., 2021) are for the task of split-and-rephrase; thus we study the splitting and split-and-rephrase tasks.

Model	Translation
Legal sentences	In the event that the Landlord shall deem it necessary or be required by any governmental authority to alter, repair, remove, reconstruct or improve any part of the demised premises or of the building in which the demised premises are located (unless the same result from Tenant's act, neglect, default or mode of operation in which event Tenant shall make all such repairs, alterations and improvements), then the same shall be made by the Landlord with reasonable dispatch, however, such obligation of Tenant shall not extend to maintenance, repairs or replacements necessitated by the intentional wrongdoing or gross negligence of Landlord.
BERT-LS	In the event that the **owner** shall **find** it necessary or be required by any governmental authority to alter, repair, remove, rebuild or improve any part of the deceased premises or of the building in which the **deceased** premises are located (unless the same result from owner's act, neglect, default or mode of operation in which event owner shall make all such repairs, alterations and improvements), then the same shall be made by the owner with reasonable care, however, such obligation of owner shall not extend to maintenance, repairs or replacements caused by the intentional mistake or gross indifference of owner.
DisSim	This is however. This is in the event. The Landlord shall deem it necessary. The Landlord shall be required by any governmental authority to alter, repair, remove, reconstruct or improve any part of the demised premises or of the building in which the demised premises are located (unless the same result from Tenant's act, neglect, default or mode of operation in which event Tenant shall make all such repairs, alterations and improvements). This was with reasonable dispatch. The same shall be made by the Landlord. Such obligation of Tenant shall not extend to maintenance, repairs or replacements. Maintenance, repairs or replacements were necessitated by the intentional wrongdoing or gross negligence of Landlord.
MWS	Such obligation of Tenant shall not extend to maintenance, repairs or replacements necessitated by the intentional wrongdoing or gross negligence of Landlord. In the event that the Landlord shall deem it necessary or be required by any governmental authority to alter, repair, remove, reconstruct or improve any part of the demised premises or of the building. This was however. The same result from Tenant's act shall make all such repairs, alterations and improvements. Tenant's act is neglect, default or mode of operation in which event Tenant.
KiS	The Landlord shall deem it necessary or be required by any governmental authority, to alter, repair, or improve, any part of the demised premises, in which he or she is to retain as a condition of his or her employment. This notice will be sent to Tenant via e-mail, to inform her of the changes that are to be made to the structure of the service. When the service is offered, the holder will advise him or her of his or her choice.
SBM-Wiki	In the event that the Landlord shall deem it necessary or be required by any governmental authority to alter, repair, remove, reconstruct or improve any part of the demised premises or of the building in which the Demised premises are located (unless the same result from Tenant's act, neglect, default or mode of operation in which event Tenant shall make all such repairs, alterations and improvements), then the same shall be made by Landlord with reasonable dispatch. Such obligation of Tenant may not extend to maintenance, repairs or replacements necessitated by the intentional wrongdoing or gross negligence of Landlord.
SBM-Contracts	In the event that the Landlord shall deem it necessary or be required by any governmental authority to alter, repair, remove, reconstruct or improve any part of the demised premises or of the building in which the Demised premises are located. Such obligation of Tenant shall not extend to maintenance, repairs or replacements necessitated by the intentional wrongdoing or gross negligence of Landlord. This is unless the same result from Tenant's act, neglect, default or mode of operation. In this case, then the same shall be made by the Landlords with reasonable dispatch. This shall be in the event Tenant makes all such repairs, alterations and improvements.

Table 4: Example model outputs. Phrases that may be factually inconsistent with the input sentence are highlighted in red Phrases or sentences that are not grammatical or fluent are highlighted in blue.

the lexical replacements being less legal-like, thus making it difficult to reconstruct the original sentence while using this metric. Perplexity increases slightly, perhaps due to some not very meaningful replacements. A few examples illustrating this are provided in Table 8 (Appendix D).

Both the unsupervised and supervised sentence splitting methods (DisSim, MWS) result in significantly better readability scores and dependency depth, indicating splitting of longer legal sentences. Their meaning preservation and entailment scores are also high. However, they have very high perplexity scores, due to the abrupt sentence breaks.

KiS achieves good readability and fluency scores; however, meaning preservation and entailment scores decrease significantly, also indicated by the generation of a few factually inconsistent phrases in the output (Table 4). This may be due to unsupervised nature of generation and the particularly complex nature of legal text as opposed to general news-like text. It is interesting that BART model trained on both SMB-Wiki (out-of-domain) and SMB-Contracts (in-domain) result in similar meaning preservation and entailment scores, where the out-of-domain effect is not seen. On closer examination, we note that in most cases, they just copy the sentences from input, with occasional sentence splitting or phrase deletions, that sometimes results in not very grammatical sentences and increased perplexity. A few qualitative examples are shown in Table 4.

Human evaluation. Due to the domain-specific nature of legal texts, we conduct human studies with two legal experts (A1 and A2) on Upwork. Since legal experts will be able to better comprehend legal text, we choose them for our human evaluation as opposed to laypeople (who form our target group of readers for legal TS). We provide them 150 sentences randomly selected from the test data along with corresponding model outputs, and instruct to rate the legal sentences for simplicity, and model outputs for simplicity, meaning preservation, fluency, and hallucinations on a scale of 1 (very complex, low meaning preservation, least fluent, or less hallucinated) to 5 (simple, high meaning preservation, most fluent, or highly hallucinated).[7] The task description and guideline are provided in Appendix C.

[7]For simplicity, we instruct them to rate the examples as per how they would explain to their clients (laypeople).

Model	Simp.↑	MP↑	Hall.↓	Flu.↑
Legal sentences	2.62/2.26	-	-	-
BERT-LS	2.77/3.14	4.94/4.66	**1.00**/1.21	**4.75**/**4.74**
DisSim	2.24/2.69	**4.95**/**4.93**	1.10/1.58	3.52/3.10
MWS	2.70/2.93	4.71/4.45	1.49/1.70	3.94/3.23
KiS	2.07/**3.82**	1.30/1.31	4.24/4.68	1.16/3.23
SBM-Cont	**2.79**/2.86	4.92/4.75	1.57/**1.07**	4.67/4.50
α(A1, A2)	-0.06	0.90	0.70	0.41

Table 5: Human ratings (A1/A2) with **best** and worst values in each column, with Krippendorff α between the ratings.

Table 5 shows the ratings from the annotators. It is very interesting to note that the inter-rater agreement using Krippendorff's α (Krippendorff, 1970) between their ratings for simplicity is -0.06, indicating disagreement between the way they perceive simplicity of legal text. However, they have high agreement for meaning preservation and hallucinations, possibly due to their good understanding of legal text, and a moderate agreement for fluency. From a few simplifications (Table 7 in Appendix C) the annotators provided (as per their selection process), we note that A1 simplifies colloquially , and sometimes chooses to exclude some details that may not concern an average layperson. Whereas, A2's language is less colloquial, with most of the details included, in a simpler language (with considerable paraphrasing, fewer nestings, and fewer legal jargons). We suspect this disagreement may be due to the legal experts' varying notions of simplicity in the manner in which they explain legal contract clauses to their clients;[8] further studies are needed to examine the simplicity of model outputs from laypeople's perspective—simplification datasets need to be curated based on whether the target audience prefers all the details or the most important content, colloquial or more formal simplifications, to develop TS models for legal domain.

Overall, both the annotators rate the KiS model poorly in terms of meaning preservation and hallucination; in terms of simplicity, A2 rates KiS highest, while A1 rates it lowest, possibly due to the amount of hallucinations in the outputs.

Correlation with automatic metrics. Table 3 (last row) shows the Pearson correlation coefficients of human ratings with automatic metrics for the 150 legal sentences and their model outputs. Since lower values are better for depth and readability metrics, we compute the correlation of inverse of human ratings with them. Tree depth and readability have weak (A1) to moderate (A2) correlations with annotators' simplicity ratings, indicating that these may not be appropriate metrics to measure simplicity of legal texts (Tanprasert and Kauchak, 2021). While splitting methods such as DisSim and MWS are rated well for readability and depth using the automatic metrics, the annotators rate them lower for simplicity (Table 5), as these methods do not rephrase complex phrases into simpler ones. For meaning preservation, BertScore has good correlation with both the annotators' ratings; however, coverage and Blanc metrics have weak correlations, indicating that they may not fully capture the meaning preservation in legal texts. For hallucination, entailment score captures to a significant degree any factually inconsistent information (A2), though A1's ratings indicate no correlation. Similarly for fluency, A1's ratings are moderately correlated with the inverse of perplexity, while A2's ratings show no correlation. Further investigation is needed to concretely understand these metrics before using them for this task.

5 Conclusions

While legal text is complex and domain-specific, thus making it a very interesting domain for TS, it is still in a nascent stage in NLP literature. We investigate and compare some of SoTA methods for lexical simplification, sentence splitting, and seq2seq sentence simplification, either unsupervised, or trained on closely related parallel datasets, using automatic metrics and human ratings. We conclude that lexical simplification methods will benefit from having a legal lexicon as they still sometimes generate replacements that do not fit the legal context. Seq2seq methods perform only surface-level transformations by either directly copying input sentences, or deleting a few phrases to make the sentences shorter, without much paraphrasing. While sentence splitting methods make the long nested sentences much shorter, they do so by sacrificing fluency. Reward-based generation method achieves transformations to an extent, but does so at the cost of meaning preservation. Legal TS can be particularly challenging, as even expert annotators have varied views of how to simplify legal sentences for laypeople. Understanding whether every detail is needed to be conveyed or providing a high-level overview suffices can aid in curating parallel datasets for furthering research in this space.

[8]Note that the clients of these legal experts form our target group of readers, and not the legal experts themselves.

6 Ethical statement

We are committed to ethical practices and protecting the anonymity and privacy of individuals who have contributed. We ensure that the privacy of the annotators is protected. For annotations, $\$15 - 20$/hr was paid per task.

References

Or Biran, Samuel Brody, and Noémie Elhadad. 2011. Putting it simply: a context-aware approach to lexical simplification. In *Proceedings of the 49th Annual Meeting of the Association for Computational Linguistics: Human Language Technologies*, pages 496–501, Portland, Oregon, USA.

Jan A. Botha, Manaal Faruqui, John Alex, Jason Baldridge, and Dipanjan Das. 2018. Learning to split and rephrase from Wikipedia edit history. In *Proceedings of the 2018 Conference on Empirical Methods in Natural Language Processing*, pages 732–737, Brussels, Belgium.

William Coster and David Kauchak. 2011. Simple English Wikipedia: A new text simplification task. In *Proceedings of the 49th Annual Meeting of the Association for Computational Linguistics: Human Language Technologies*, pages 665–669, Portland, Oregon, USA.

Jacob Devlin, Ming-Wei Chang, Kenton Lee, and Kristina Toutanova. 2019. BERT: Pre-training of deep bidirectional transformers for language understanding. In *Proceedings of the 2019 Conference of the North American Chapter of the Association for Computational Linguistics: Human Language Technologies, Volume 1 (Long and Short Papers)*, pages 4171–4186, Minneapolis, Minnesota.

Goran Glavaš and Sanja Štajner. 2015. Simplifying lexical simplification: Do we need simplified corpora? In *Proceedings of the 53rd Annual Meeting of the Association for Computational Linguistics and the 7th International Joint Conference on Natural Language Processing (Volume 2: Short Papers)*, pages 63–68, Beijing, China.

Sian Gooding and Ekaterina Kochmar. 2019. Recursive context-aware lexical simplification. In *Proceedings of the 2019 Conference on Empirical Methods in Natural Language Processing and the 9th International Joint Conference on Natural Language Processing (EMNLP-IJCNLP)*, pages 4853–4863, Hong Kong, China. Association for Computational Linguistics.

Joongwon Kim, Mounica Maddela, Reno Kriz, Wei Xu, and Chris Callison-Burch. 2021. BiSECT: Learning to split and rephrase sentences with bitexts. In *Proceedings of the 2021 Conference on Empirical Methods in Natural Language Processing*, pages 6193–6209, Online and Punta Cana, Dominican Republic.

J Peter Kincaid, Robert P Fishburne Jr, Richard L Rogers, and Brad S Chissom. 1975. Derivation of new readability formulas (automated readability index, fog count and flesch reading ease formula) for navy enlisted personnel. Technical report, Naval Technical Training Command Millington TN Research Branch.

Klaus Krippendorff. 1970. Estimating the reliability, systematic error and random error of interval data. *Educational and Psychological Measurement*, 30(1):61–70.

Philippe Laban, Andrew Hsi, John Canny, and Marti A. Hearst. 2020. The summary loop: Learning to write abstractive summaries without examples. In *Proceedings of the 58th Annual Meeting of the Association for Computational Linguistics*, pages 5135–5150, Online.

Philippe Laban, Tobias Schnabel, Paul Bennett, and Marti A. Hearst. 2021. Keep it simple: Unsupervised simplification of multi-paragraph text. In *Proceedings of the 59th Annual Meeting of the Association for Computational Linguistics and the 11th International Joint Conference on Natural Language Processing (Volume 1: Long Papers)*, pages 6365–6378, Online.

Mike Lewis, Yinhan Liu, Naman Goyal, Marjan Ghazvininejad, Abdelrahman Mohamed, Omer Levy, Veselin Stoyanov, and Luke Zettlemoyer. 2020. BART: Denoising sequence-to-sequence pre-training for natural language generation, translation, and comprehension. In *Proceedings of the 58th Annual Meeting of the Association for Computational Linguistics*, pages 7871–7880, Online.

Yinhan Liu, Myle Ott, Naman Goyal, Jingfei Du, Mandar Joshi, Danqi Chen, Omer Levy, Mike Lewis, Luke Zettlemoyer, and Veselin Stoyanov. 2019. Roberta: A robustly optimized bert pretraining approach. *arXiv preprint arXiv:1907.11692*.

Louis Martin, Éric de la Clergerie, Benoît Sagot, and Antoine Bordes. 2020. Controllable sentence simplification. In *Proceedings of the Twelfth Language Resources and Evaluation Conference*, pages 4689–4698, Marseille, France.

G Harry Mc Laughlin. 1969. Smog grading-a new readability formula. *Journal of reading*, 12(8):639–646.

Feng Nan, Ramesh Nallapati, Zhiguo Wang, Cicero Nogueira dos Santos, Henghui Zhu, Dejiao Zhang, Kathleen McKeown, and Bing Xiang. 2021. Entity-level factual consistency of abstractive text summarization. In *Proceedings of the 16th Conference of the European Chapter of the Association for Computational Linguistics: Main Volume*, pages 2727–2733, Online.

Shashi Narayan, Claire Gardent, Shay B. Cohen, and Anastasia Shimorina. 2017. Split and rephrase. In *Proceedings of the 2017 Conference on Empirical*

Methods in Natural Language Processing, pages 606–616, Copenhagen, Denmark. Association for Computational Linguistics.

Christina Niklaus, Matthias Cetto, André Freitas, and Siegfried Handschuh. 2019a. DisSim: A discourse-aware syntactic text simplification framework for English and German. In *Proceedings of the 12th International Conference on Natural Language Generation*, pages 504–507, Tokyo, Japan. Association for Computational Linguistics.

Christina Niklaus, André Freitas, and Siegfried Handschuh. 2019b. MinWikiSplit: A sentence splitting corpus with minimal propositions. In *Proceedings of the 12th International Conference on Natural Language Generation*, pages 118–123, Tokyo, Japan. Association for Computational Linguistics.

Jipeng Qiang, Yun Li, Zhu Yi, Yunhao Yuan, and Xindong Wu. 2020. Lexical simplification with pretrained encoders. *Thirty-Fourth AAAI Conference on Artificial Intelligence*, page 8649–8656.

Alec Radford, Jeffrey Wu, Rewon Child, David Luan, Dario Amodei, Ilya Sutskever, et al. 2019. Language models are unsupervised multitask learners. *OpenAI blog*, 1(8):9.

RJ Senter and Edgar A Smith. 1967. Automated readability index. Technical report, Cincinnati Univ OH.

Sanja Štajner. 2021. Automatic text simplification for social good: Progress and challenges. *Findings of the Association for Computational Linguistics: ACL-IJCNLP 2021*, pages 2637–2652.

Sai Surya, Abhijit Mishra, Anirban Laha, Parag Jain, and Karthik Sankaranarayanan. 2019. Unsupervised neural text simplification. In *Proceedings of the 57th Annual Meeting of the Association for Computational Linguistics*, pages 2058–2068.

Teerapaun Tanprasert and David Kauchak. 2021. Flesch-kincaid is not a text simplification evaluation metric. In *Proceedings of the 1st Workshop on Natural Language Generation, Evaluation, and Metrics (GEM 2021)*, pages 1–14, Online.

Don Tuggener, Pius von Däniken, Thomas Peetz, and Mark Cieliebak. 2020. Ledgar: a large-scale multi-label corpus for text classification of legal provisions in contracts. In *12th Language Resources and Evaluation Conference (LREC) 2020*, pages 1228–1234. European Language Resources Association.

Oleg Vasilyev, Vedant Dharnidharka, and John Bohannon. 2020. Fill in the blanc: Human-free quality estimation of document summaries. *arXiv preprint arXiv:2002.09836*.

Adina Williams, Nikita Nangia, and Samuel R Bowman. 2018. The multi-genre nli corpus.

Thomas Wolf, Lysandre Debut, Victor Sanh, Julien Chaumond, Clement Delangue, Anthony Moi, Pierric Cistac, Tim Rault, Rémi Louf, Morgan Funtowicz, et al. 2019. Huggingface's transformers: State-of-the-art natural language processing. *arXiv preprint arXiv:1910.03771*.

Sander Wubben, Antal van den Bosch, and Emiel Krahmer. 2012. Sentence simplification by monolingual machine translation. In *Proceedings of the 50th Annual Meeting of the Association for Computational Linguistics (Volume 1: Long Papers)*, pages 1015–1024.

Wei Xu, Chris Callison-Burch, and Courtney Napoles. 2015. Problems in current text simplification research: New data can help. *Transactions of the Association for Computational Linguistics*, 3:283–297.

Li Zhang, Huaiyu Zhu, Siddhartha Brahma, and Yunyao Li. 2020. Small but mighty: New benchmarks for split and rephrase. In *Proceedings of the 2020 Conference on Empirical Methods in Natural Language Processing (EMNLP)*, pages 1198–1205, Online. Association for Computational Linguistics.

Tianyi Zhang, Varsha Kishore, Felix Wu, Kilian Q Weinberger, and Yoav Artzi. 2019. Bertscore: Evaluating text generation with bert. *arXiv preprint arXiv:1904.09675*.

Zhemin Zhu, Delphine Bernhard, and Iryna Gurevych. 2010. A monolingual tree-based translation model for sentence simplification. In *Proceedings of the 23rd International Conference on Computational Linguistics (Coling 2010)*, pages 1353–1361.

A Dataset Statistics

We use 5K sentences randomly sampled from 100 most frequently occurring legal clause types from SEC contracts from the LEDGAR dataset (Tuggener et al., 2020) for evaluation. Some of these clause types include *amendments, base salary, benefits, duties, employment, entire agreements, expenses, governing laws, notices, positions, severability, terms, vacations, waivers*, and so on.

B Implementation Details

BERT-LS. BERT-LS requires identification of complex words in a sentence; we identify complex words in a given test sentence based on their frequency (< 10K) in normal Wikipedia (Coster and Kauchak, 2011) which is essentially the unsimplified text from Wikipedia. Its vocabulary is of size 594K tokens. In the test sentences, we consider a token potentially complex (or specific to legal domain) if it is less likely seen in normal Wikipedia

In this project, you are given a few sentences. For each sentence, there are at most 6 translations obtained using automatic AI models or human translations. Your task is to rate the sentence along with the translations on their simplicity. In addition, for each of the translations, you are required to rate the content preserved in them, their fluency, and any hallucinations that may have been introduced in them.
Simplicity: This refers to how simple of plain English-like the given sentence or translation is. When we say simplicity, we are referring to how plain English-like a given translation is looking. For pointers on plain English versions of SEC contracts, this resource gives very nice examples in Chapter 6: `https://www.sec.gov/pdf/handbook.pdf`. 1: very complex; 5: very simple and easily understandable for laypeople without much legal background.
Content preserved in a translation: This refers to the amount of information from the given sentence that is retained in the translation. 1: Almost every detail is missed; 5: Every detail is covered in the translation.
Fluency of a translation: Fluency refers to how natural and grammatical a sentence/translation is. **Example of fluent sentence**: In addition, it is impractical to make such a law. **Example of non-fluent sentence:** It is unfair to release a law only point to the genetic disorder. 1: Not fluent or unnatural or grammatically incorrect translation; 5: Very fluent, natural, and grammatically correct translation.
Hallucination in a translation: The refers to the degree of incorrect or redundant information included in the translation compared to given sentence. 1: No redundant or incorrect information is present in the translation, every detail in it is taken from the given sentence; 5: Lot of redundant or incorrect information present in the translation compared to given sentence.

Table 6: Instructions for human studies.

(frequency $< 10K$)[9]. This results in a total of $2,708$ complex tokens, which include *misconduct*, *acquisitions*, and *obligors*.

DisSim outputs a graph-like structure of the input. To get a sentence from the graph-like structure, we traverse it from left to right and construct an output using the leaf nodes. If DisSim fails to generate any graphs, we copy the input as output without any transformations. It uses a set of hand-crafted transformation rules to recursively transform an input sentence into a two-layered hierarchical representation in the form of core sentences and accompanying contexts that are linked via rhetorical relations (such as list, elaboration). For further details on the specific rule, we refer the readers to Niklaus et al. (2019a). We train the KiS model on 67K legal text sentences selected randomly from LEDGAR dataset that do not occur in the test data. We train the KiS model using the same GPT-2 medium checkpoint and other hyperparameters as in (Laban et al., 2021). We use huggingface's transformers library (Wolf et al., 2019) to fine-tune BART models for 3 epochs using Adam optimizer with batch size of 8 and maximum sequence length of 256.

C Human Evaluations

Table 6 shows the instructions used to guide the Upwork annotators for rating the legal sentences and model outputs for their simplicity, meaning preservation, hallucinations, and fluency. We conducted interviews by first giving a few legal sentences from SEC contracts and instructing them to explain the information conveyed in them in easy-to-understand language. Based on further discussions, we selected two annotators for this task. The two annotators are paid \$15 and \$20 per hour respectively. Table 7 shows a few simplifications that the annotators provided during the interviews.

D Qualitative Results

[9]We use 10K as threshold based on manual observation of resulting words. The maximum frequency of any token in Wikipedia is 173M.

Legal sentence	**Annotator-1**	**Annotator-2**
In the event that the Landlord shall deem it necessary or be required by any governmental authority to alter, repair, remove, reconstruct or improve any part of the demised premises or of the building in which the demised premises are located (unless the same result from Tenant's act, neglect, default or mode of operation in which event Tenant shall make all such repairs, alterations and improvements), then the same shall be made by the Landlord with reasonable dispatch, however, such obligation of Tenant shall not extend to maintenance, repairs or replacements necessitated by the intentional wrongdoing or gross negligence of Landlord.	The landlord will repair, remove, reconstruct or improve the leased property if it is required by any governmental authority. However, the landlord is not entitled to do so if it is the tenant's fault. The Landlord will make the repairs or replacements as soon as possible. Also, it is not the tenant's duty to maintain or repair the property if the damages were caused by the Landlord's negligence.	Where the landlord feels necessary or where it is required by any government authority to repair, remove or reconstruct any part or the building which is used by a Tenant under lease agreement. The landlord will make reasonable efforts to repair or reconstruct such part or building leased. As an exception, where such damage to the leased part or building is the result from the Tenant's act, default or mode of operating the area in such case the Tenant will make all such repairs. This obligation of Tenant will not extend to repairs if such damage is the result of intention carelessness on the part of the landlord.
Any termination of Executive's employment by the Company without Cause (and not due to Executive's death or Permanent Disability) shall be made by the provision of at least fourteen (14) days' prior written notice to Executive in accordance with Section 4.2 ; provided , however , that the Company may, in its sole discretion, elect to pay Executive for all or any part of the notice period in lieu of providing prior written notice, calculated based on the annualized rate of Executive's Effective Base Salary at the time of termination.	A written notice of fourteen days must be given by the company to the employee if the employee is terminated without any cause and not due to death. However, the company can pay an employee for the notice period as per their annual base salary.	As per Section 4.2, for terminating the Executive without cause (and not due to Executive's Death or Permanent Disability) the Company will provide a prior written notice of 14 days to the Executive. In this case, the Company at its own discretion can choose to pay to the Executive all or any part of the amount against such notice period. The calculation of such amount will be based on annual base salary of the Executive at the time of termination.

Table 7: Sample simplifications from legal experts.

LEGAL SENTENCE	**Lexical Simplification** (BERT-LS)	BERTSCORE	COVERAGE
The Stockholder hereby ratifies and confirms all that such irrevocable proxy may lawfully do or cause to be done by virtue hereof.	The company now **agrees** and agrees all that such **a** proxy may **illegally** do or cause to be done by virtue of.	0.92	0.18
There are no strikes, lockouts or other material labor disputes or grievances against the Borrower or any of its Subsidiaries, or, to the Borrower's knowledge, threatened against or affecting the Borrower or any of its Subsidiaries, and no significant unfair labor practice charges or grievances are pending against the Borrower or any of its Subsidiaries, or, to the Borrower's knowledge, threatened against any of them before any Governmental Authority.	There are no strikes, **strikes** or other material labor disputes or **claims** against the company or any of its **branches**, or, to the **company's** knowledge, threatened against or affecting the **company** or any of its **branches**, and no significant unfair labor practice charges or **claims** are pending against the **company** or any of its **branches**, or, to the **company's** knowledge, threatened against any of them before any Governmental Authority.	0.95	0.38

Table 8: Example BERT-LS outputs for lexical simplification to illustrate low coverage cases.

Legal Named Entity Recognition with Multi-Task Domain Adaptation

Răzvan-Alexandru Smădu[1], **Ion-Robert Dinică**[1], **Andrei-Marius Avram**[1], **Dumitru-Clementin Cercel**[1], **Florin Pop**[1,2], **Mihaela-Claudia Cercel**[3]

[1]University Politehnica of Bucharest, Faculty of Automatic Control and Computers
[2]National Institute for Research & Development in Informatics - ICI Bucharest, Romania
[3]First District Court of Buftea

{razvan.smadu,ion_robert.dinica}@stud.acs.upb.ro
{andrei_marius.avram}@stud.acs.upb.ro
{dumitru.cercel,florin.pop}@upb.ro

Abstract

Named Entity Recognition (NER) is a well-explored area from Information Retrieval and Natural Language Processing with an extensive research community. Despite that, few languages, such as English and German, are well-resourced, whereas many other languages, such as Romanian, have scarce resources, especially in domain-specific applications. In this work, we address the NER problem in the legal domain from both Romanian and German languages and evaluate the performance of our proposed method based on domain adaptation. We employ multi-task learning to jointly train a neural network on two legal and general domains and perform adaptation among them. The results show that domain adaptation increase performances by a small amount, under 1%, while considerable improvements are in the recall metric.

1 Introduction

Legal is one of the domains where NER plays a central role, especially in document processing, where it is used for identifying key elements like the court name, the name of the parties in a case, or the case number (Skylaki et al., 2020). In recent years, interest has grown in the research community for performing various tasks on legal documents, known as LegalAI (Zhong et al., 2020).

One direct application of these extracted named entities is document organization and search. However, they can be further incorporated into other systems like document anonymization, judgement prediction, or case summarization, offering additional insights to legal professionals (Zhong et al., 2020; Bansal et al., 2019).

Although still considered under-resourced, Romanian is one of the languages that has seen a recent expansion with the introduction of two Bidirectional Encoder Representation from Transformers (BERTs) (Devlin et al., 2019) trained on Romanian text (Dumitrescu et al., 2020; Masala et al., 2020), three named entity corpora (Dumitrescu and Avram, 2020; Păiș et al., 2021b; Mitrofan and Tufiş, 2018), over three hundred hours of publicly-available transcribed speech (Georgescu et al., 2020; Wang et al., 2021), and a benchmark that tracks the progress of various Romanian NLP tasks (Dumitrescu et al., 2021). In addition, domain adaptation research showed that we could perform knowledge transfer between datasets using effective methods in both supervised (Yue et al., 2021) and unsupervised (Ganin and Lempitsky, 2015) settings.

In this work, we want to take advantage of these recent developments and explore the area of domain adaptation with a task discriminator on the Romanian language. On a more granular level, we experiment with domain adaptation from the general to the legal domain, using the Romanian Named Entity Corpus (RONEC) (Dumitrescu and Avram, 2020) as a reference and Romanian Legal NER corpus (LegalNERo) (Păiș et al., 2021b) as a target.

Our proposed neural architecture employs multiple components. A pre-trained BERT layer generates the feature representation. Long Short-Term Memory (LSTM) (Hochreiter and Schmidhuber, 1997) is utilized in bidirectional configuration to capture both left-to-right and right-to-left dependencies. Conditional Random Fields (CRFs) (Lafferty et al., 2001) generate the predictions based on the conditional probability of the sequence. We employ multi-task learning (Changpinyo et al., 2018) to train the model on legal and general domains jointly, and on top of that, we apply domain adaptation as described by Ganin and Lempitsky (2015), but in a supervised setting.

Furthermore, to explore the robustness of our approach in another but better-resourced language, we apply the same methodology to German and investigate domain adaptation from GermEval 2014 (Benikova et al., 2014) to German Legal NER

Proceedings of the Natural Legal Language Processing Workshop 2022, pages 305 - 321
December 8, 2022

(German LER) (Leitner et al., 2020). Ultimately, we evaluate our approach through visualizations and analysis of the predictions.

We summarize the contributions as follows:

- We propose a multi-task domain adversarial model that is jointly trained on two domains, namely general and legal;
- We evaluate the performances of our approach, the quality of the predictions, and propose a way of visualizing the embedding space of the named entities;
- To the best of our knowledge, we are the first to experiment with domain adaptation in the legal NER.

2 Related Work

Named Entity Recognition. In the supervised setting, Lample et al. (2016) introduced LSTM-based neural architectures that do not rely on domain-specific resources or hand-crafted features. Both character-level and word-level representations passed through LSTM and CRF layers proved effective in NER.

Since Transformers (Vaswani et al., 2017) became popular in NLP, BERT-based approaches were evaluated on NER tasks, proving the effectiveness of the contextualized word embeddings and transformer word representations (Souza et al., 2019; Dai et al., 2019; Jiang et al., 2019; Liu et al., 2020; Syed and Chung, 2021). These methods combine the previous neural components (i.e., LSTM, BERT, and CRF) with deep learning techniques such as transfer learning (Weiss et al., 2016), active learning (Cohn et al., 1996), and domain adaptation. Pointer Generator Networks (See et al., 2017) were also employed in NER by Skylaki et al. (2020), showing that the proposed method achieves better results when compared to BERT-based and LSTM-based models.

Often, NER is jointly addressed along with relation extraction (Feldman and Rosenfeld, 2006; Nasar et al., 2021). While NER is usually solved using recurrent neural networks, relation extraction can be handled using convolutional (Zheng et al., 2017) and feed-forward layers (Bekoulis et al., 2018; Bhatia et al., 2019; Shi and Lin, 2019).

To generate labels for new types of entities and relation extraction in automated systems, distant supervision (Mintz et al., 2009) is utilized based on a dataset of entities. Improvements rely on introducing a reinforcement learning module in the tagger that selects clean data for the model architecture during training (Yang et al., 2018).

NER tasks can become challenging when entities are nested; often, they address flat NER. Generally, classical approaches do not consider nesting and treat this task as dependency parsing (Yu et al., 2020). The method relies on embeddings generated via BERT for word-based embeddings and convolutional layers for char-based embeddings. Feed-forward layers and a biaffine model (Dozat and Manning, 2017) predict the entity spans.

Legal NER. Previously, classical machine learning techniques such as Support Vector Machines, Naive Bayes, and ontologies were utilized to detect named entities from legal documents (Dozier et al., 2010; Bruckschen et al., 2010; Cardellino et al., 2017; Glaser et al., 2018). New datasets started to emerge in the legal domain since legal is one of the domains that received little attention (Leitner et al., 2019). Methods based on domain-specific embeddings and LSTMs combined with CRFs were utilized in multiple languages, such as English (Chalkidis et al., 2019), German (Leitner et al., 2020), Romanian (Păiș et al., 2021a), and Portuguese (Luz de Araujo et al., 2018). Barriere and Fouret (2019) employed a two-learning-step approach that first trains a model on the NER task, which then creates features for training a second neural network model. This approach was evaluated on French legal documents, showing a significant reduction in the F1-score error.

Domain Adaptation. The domain adaptation setting aims to reduce the domain gap between the source and target data distributions. This technique takes advantage of the knowledge of well-resourced domains and transfers it to downstream tasks with fewer resources. Jia and Zhang (2020) approached the cross-domain NER via multi-task learning and a variation of the LSTM cell. Their approach evaluated on few-shot datasets showed significant improvements over other multi-task learning methods. In the cross-domain setting, Liu et al. (2021) tested multiple model architectures based on BERT, LSTM, and CRFs. Their experiments suggested that domain-adaptive pre-training can enhance both span-level and token-level performances.

Various transfer learning and fine-tuning techniques, such as parameter initialization and multi-

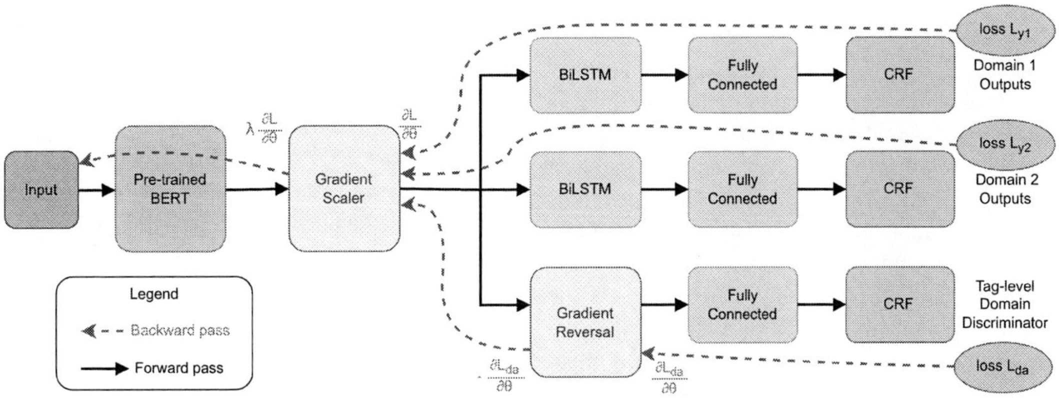

Figure 1: The proposed model architecture.

task learning, can be employed to reduce the training overhead of neural architectures (Lin and Lu, 2018). Bekoulis et al. (2018) enhanced the LSTM-CRF architecture by adding adversarial training through adversarial perturbation in the embedding space. Virtual Adversarial Training (VAT) (Miyato et al., 2019) was combined with the LSTM-CRF model in both supervised and semi-supervised settings. In the minimization objective, they introduced the Kullback-Leibler divergence computed between estimated labels of original and adversarial examples (Chen et al., 2020). VAT significantly improved performance over baseline models.

A language discriminator is added in the multi-lingual setting to perform adversarial learning (Chen et al., 2021). The goal of the discriminator is to force the feature encoder to learn language-invariant features. Moreover, domain adaptation was achieved using latent semantic association such that the same concepts from different domains should be semantically similar (Guo et al., 2009).

3 Approach

3.1 Neural Network Architecture

Inspired by the previously mentioned works, we based our neural network architecture on a domain adaptation technique via multi-task learning. We consider a two-domain model, which jointly trains, in a supervised fashion, on two datasets from domains characterized by a domain shift. Figure 1 presents the complete model architecture.

Each domain is associated with a branch in the model architecture while sharing the feature encoder. We utilize contextualized BERT embeddings to generate the feature space. Two branches and a domain discriminator process the BERT's output. The transformer model is pre-trained on the language of the datasets we use and follows a fine-tuning approach during training, such that we do not change too much the embedding space, but it is still subject to domain adaptation.

Implementation-wise, we introduce a gradient scaler layer that scales down the gradients during back-propagation by a factor γ, similar to a learning rate. We apply a scheduler that increases this learning rate over time:

$$\gamma^* = \frac{1}{1 + e^{\gamma(-2p+1)}} \tag{1}$$

where γ^* is the learning rate at the current progress rate $p \in [0, 1]$, and e is Euler's number. Our intuition is that at the beginning of the training, we want to avoid affecting the pre-trained Transformer model's weights since the higher-level layers are not trained, and we enable fine-tuning after some training steps.

Each domain branch comprises a BiLSTM (Bidirectional LSTM), followed by a fully connected layer and a CRF output layer. We use BiLSTMs since these are more resilient to gradient vanishing (Hochreiter and Schmidhuber, 1997) while capturing feature dependencies from both left-to-right and right-to-left directions, and CRFs to model the conditional probability distribution of the input sequence. Lastly, we introduce a discriminative branch linked to the shared embedding encoder via a gradient reversal layer (Ganin and Lempitsky, 2015), having a linear layer followed by CRF. The motivation for the usage of domain adaptation is presented in Section 3.3.

3.2 Conditional Random Field

CRFs (Lafferty et al., 2001) are discriminative models based on undirected graphs, modelling the conditioned probability of labels obeying the Markov property relative to the dependency graph, given the input (i.e., $P(y|X)$) (Sutton and McCallum, 2012). The input of the CRF is a sequence of features of the input sequence $X = (x_1, x_2, ..., x_n)$, being output by the last fully connected layer. The output sequence of the CRF is a label y from the set of all possible classes K. For each pair of input sequence labels, its score is defined as:

$$s(X, y) = \sum_{i=0}^{n} A_{y_i, y_{i+1}} + \sum_{i=1}^{n} P_{i, y_i} \quad (2)$$

where A is the transition score matrix of size $K \times K$, and P are the output scores generated by the last fully connected layer of size $n \times K$. Probability of the sequence y is defined as a softmax over all scores:

$$p(y|X) = \frac{\exp(s(X, y))}{\sum_{y' \in Y_X} \exp(s(X, y'))} \quad (3)$$

with Y_X being the set of all possible tag sequences for a sequence X. Compared with the softmax activation function, the CRF can handle sequential dependencies.

To determine the predictions of the input sequence, we run the Viterbi algorithm (Forney, 1973), which extracts the tags y^* with the maximum score:

$$y^* = \arg \max_{y' \in Y_X} s(X, y') \quad (4)$$

The optimization process is based on maximizing the likelihood:

$$\log p(y|X) = s(X, y) - log(\sum_{y' \in Y_X} \exp(s(X, y'))) \quad (5)$$

It allows us to combine CRFs with neural network models, where the loss function is the negative log-likelihood (i.e., $L_{CRF} = -\log p(y|X)$), which is optimized using gradient-based methods.

3.3 Optimization in Domain Adaptation Setting

One of the most influential works is in the unsupervised domain adaptation setting (Ganin and Lempitsky, 2015), which aims to reduce the domain shift by introducing a domain discriminator. Similar to how Generative Adversarial Networks (Goodfellow et al., 2014) work, the domain discriminator learns indistinguishable feature representations between different domains. Therefore, it minimizes the loss function concerning the labels while maximizing the error rate of the domain discriminator. This minimax game is formalized as follows:

$$\hat{\theta}_f, \hat{\theta}_y = \arg \min_{\theta_f, \theta_y} L(\theta_f, \theta_y, \hat{\theta}_d) \quad (6)$$

$$\hat{\theta}_d = \arg \max_{\theta_d} L(\hat{\theta}_f, \hat{\theta}_y, \theta_d) \quad (7)$$

where L is the loss function, θ_f are the parameters of the feature generator, θ_y are the parameters of the label predictor, and θ_d are the parameters of the domain discriminator. The variables with a hat are fixed during optimization. The empirical loss function is the difference between the prediction loss L_y and domain adaptation loss L_d:

$$L = L_y - \lambda L_{da} \quad (8)$$

where λ is a hyperparameter that controls the level of domain adaptation during training. This optimization problem is implemented by linking the discriminator to the feature extractor via a gradient reversal layer that negates the gradient during back-propagation while solving:

$$L = L_y + \lambda L_{da} \quad (9)$$

In this paper, we utilize the domain adaptation at the tag level, meaning that the discriminator learns specific feature representations based on the context of each tag. Therefore, we use a CRF layer to model the sequence of constant values among the same domain (for example, a sequence of 1s for the first domain and 2s for the second domain). This also motivates why we use a gradient scaler after the BERT layer.

When performing the feed-forward step, a batch containing examples from both domains is passed through the model. First, we utilize the samples from the first domain and accumulate gradients computed for the loss associated with the first domain L_{y_1} and domain discriminator L_{da_1}. Then, we pass the examples from the second domain and accumulate the gradients for the second domain output L_{y_2} and the domain discriminator L_{da_2}. Next, we perform gradient updates and repeat the training procedure for all batches in the training set. See Figure 1 for how the gradients are propagated throughout the network.

We minimize the negative log-likelihood loss for each branch, computed as described in Section 3.2. The total loss is formalized below:

$$L_{total} = L_{y_1} + L_{y_2} - \lambda(L_{da_1} + L_{da_2}) \quad (10)$$

We vary λ according to the same Equation (1) but scaled by a constant α. Hence, we enable more domain adaptation over time at a progress rate p:

$$\lambda_p = \alpha \left(\frac{2}{1 + e^{-\beta p}} - 1 \right) \quad (11)$$

where α defines the upper boundary of the function, and β controls the widening of the sigmoid function.

During training, we observed that the adversarial loss starts to increase after a period of training. At the same time, the discriminator performs poorly (that means the discriminator becomes unable to distinguish among features). Subsequently, this also hinders the performance on the other tasks, and limiting domain adaptation proved to yield better results. Another observation we made is that by negating the loss term of the domain discriminator, instead of using $+L_{da}$ (further referenced as ADAL), we utilize $-L_{da}$ during optimization (further referenced as SDAL). The performances considerably improved when compared with classical domain adaptation.

4 Experiments

4.1 Datasets

We evaluate our approach on datasets from general and legal domains, Romanian and German, respectively. We utilize the splits provided; where these were not provided, we randomly split the datasets into train/test/validation, using 80%-20%-20% ratios.

RONEC (Named Entity Corpus for the Romanian language) (Dumitrescu and Avram, 2020)[1] is an open-source dataset, currently at version 2.0, containing 0.5M tokens within 12,330 annotated sentences extracted from newspapers. The total number of entities annotated in the RONEC v2.0 corpus is 80,283 from 15 distinct classes, inspired by the OntoNotes5 (Weischedeld et al., 2013) and ACE (Doddington et al., 2004) datasets. The dataset is available under CoNLL-U format[2], using the BIO annotation schema (Lample et al., 2016). The second version was annotated by `termene.ro`[3]. The dataset is split into 9,000 sentences for training, 1,330 sentences for validation, and 2,000 for testing. The entity classes are roughly evenly balanced among the splits. This dataset also has version 1.0 available but was not utilized during experiments.

LegalNERo (Păiș et al., 2021a)[4] is a named entity corpus proposed for the Romanian language by researchers from the Romanian Institute of Artificial Intelligence. This dataset was annotated by five human annotators and consists of 370 documents extracted from the MARCELL-RO corpus (Tufiș et al., 2020). The dataset contains 8,284 sentences and a total of 13,614 entities. The entity classes considered in this dataset are the following: Person, Location, Organization, Time, and Legal Ref. The dataset is available in the CoNLL-U Plus format, annotated using the BIO schema.

GermEval 2014 (Benikova et al., 2014)[5] is a dataset proposed at the KONVENS workshop that introduces an extended set of tags compared with previous works. In summary, it contains 31,300 annotated sentences, consisting of a total of 590,000 tokens and 41,124 entities from four main classes (person, location, organization, and other), as well as derivations and parts of named entities for each of the main classes (there are 12 classes in total). The dataset is divided into three sets: 24,000 sentences for training, 2,200 sentences for validation, and 5,100 sentences for testing, all being provided in the CoNLL-U format, following the BIO schema.

LER (Legal Entity Recognition) (Leitner et al., 2019)[6] contains 750 court decisions from Germany, which were published on an online portal (i.e., "Rechtsprechung im Internet"; in eng. "Jurisprudence on the Internet"). The dataset has 66,723 sentences, which consists of 53,632 annotated named entities. This dataset is available in the CoNNL-U format, using the BIO annotation schema. The dataset consists of seven categories for the named entities (i.e., person, location, organization, legal norm, case-by-case regulation, court decision, and legal literature), divided into 19 fine-

[1] `https://github.com/dumitrescustefan/ronec`

[2] `https://universaldependencies.org/format.html`

[3] `https://termene.ro`

[4] `https://zenodo.org/record/4772095`

[5] `https://sites.google.com/site/germeval2014ner/`

[6] `https://github.com/elenanereiss/Legal-Entity-Recognition`

grained classes.

4.2 Data Preprocessing

Extracting named entities from documents can be cast to a tagging problem. Each word follows the BIO schema (Lample et al., 2016) (i.e., the beginning of entities are labelled with B, inside tokens are labelled with I, and outside of entities are annotated with O). The labels are numerically encoded such that each label indicate the BIO tag and its class.

In this work, we employ Transformer representations, and we utilize the pre-trained BERT tokenizer (Sennrich et al., 2016) on the language we train the model to generate the input tokens. Since the goal is to keep a small enough vocabulary, some words are split among multiple tokens. In this case, we consider a `NULL` tag that indicates the token is an inside subword (for example, when using BERT tokenizer, these tokens start with `'##'`). Each sample consists of a sentence. If the sentence length after tokenization is longer than the maximum sequence length for BERT, then we split the sentence into multiple examples.

4.3 BERT Embedding Representation

We use the language-specific pre-trained BERT model since we deal with multiple languages. For the Romanian language, we use the pre-trained Romanian BERT model (Dumitrescu et al., 2020), which was trained on three corpora, namely OPUS (Tiedemann, 2012), OSCAR (Suárez et al., 2019), and Romanian Wikipedia, in total representing 15.2GB of processed data. We employed the cased base model. For the German language, we utilized the German BERT model (Chan et al., 2020), which was pre-trained on four datasets (i.e., the German version of OPUS, OSCAR, and Wikipedia, at which it is added the Open Legal Data (Ostendorff et al., 2020) – a dataset for legal domain), worth over 150GB of data. We used the cased base model in our experiments since some words (such as nouns) are spelt with capital letters at the beginning of the words.

4.4 Baselines

We compare our approach with simplified versions of the proposed architecture, considered baseline. They consist of a BERT transformer, a BiLSTM layer, a fully connected layer, and a CRF layer for generating the probability distribution for the tokens. We trained this architecture on all four datasets and followed the same training procedure as the proposed method. During training, we set the BERT model to be fine-tuned to improve the embedding generation on the downstream task.

4.5 Experimental Setup

We trained all models on TPUv3-8[7] provided by Kaggle[8] for free. We used a batch size between 4 and 16 per TPU, and trained the baseline models for at most 10 epochs. The learning rate was varied using a linearly decreasing scheduler, with the warm-up proportion set to 1%. The maximum learning rate was set to 0.002, and the minimum value was attained at the last epoch. In all cases, we used a gradient scaler value of 1e-5. To reduce overfitting, we utilized the AdamW optimizer (Loshchilov and Hutter, 2019) with a weight decay of 1e-5. In addition, we employ gradient clipping of magnitudes greater than 2.0. For tokenizer, we set the maximum sequence length to 200. For domain adaptation setup, similar hyperparameters were employed. In addition, we set the maximum epoch to be 20 while keeping the best-performing checkpoint for evaluation, and the domain adaptation hyperparameter α was set to 0.1. In contrast, β was set to 10.

4.6 Evaluation Metrics

We assess the performance of the models in terms of negative log-likelihood computed as described in Section 3.2, and F1-score at the entity level (Yadav and Bethard, 2018; Dumitrescu et al., 2020) from four metrics: Entity Type, Partial, Exact, and Strict, computed as follows[9]:

$$P = \frac{Correct}{Correct + Incorrect + Partial + Spurius} \quad (12)$$

$$R = \frac{Correct}{Correct + Incorrect + Partial + Missing} \quad (13)$$

$$F1 = \frac{2PR}{P + R} \quad (14)$$

where $Correct$ represents correctly predicted entities; $Incorrect$ are the incorrectly predicted labels by the system; $Partial$ are the partially correct detected annotations; $Missing$ are the golden labels not detected by the model; $Spurius$ are the entities detected by the model, but they are not in the gold set.

[7]https://cloud.google.com/tpu

[8]https://www.kaggle.com/

[9]https://www.davidsbatista.net/blog/2018/05/09/Named_Entity_Evaluation/

5 Results

This section presents results on baseline models and domain adaptation. We present the precision, recall, and F1-scores at the entity level (strict measures). In the end, we provide t-SNE (van der Maaten and Hinton, 2008) visualizations of the embedding space on the feature space along with the limitations of the current approach. In Appendix A, we present more detailed results.

5.1 Baselines

For the baseline models, we present the results in Table 1. Results are obtained in the following configurations: RONEC - LegalNERo, and GermEval 2014 - LER. We present the negative log-likelihood averaged per token (NLL) as absolute values (the lower, the better) and F1-scores as percentages (the higher, the better). The German LER model achieves the highest F1-scores and the lowest NLL absolute value (0.0676) since this is the largest dataset we used. On the other side of the spectrum, the model trained on LegalNERo achieves the smallest F1-scores, with only 80.3%, being at the same time the smallest dataset. On RONEC, we observed higher scores for Entity Type and F1-Partial, meaning that the models partially identified entities in the text, while the exact boundaries and, in some cases, the types of the entities were misidentified. However, on this dataset, the model achieves the highest NLL score. On the GermEval 2014 dataset, the model reaches the best score when identifying partial entities. In contrast, the smallest score is achieved when determining the exact match of the boundaries and entity types.

Dataset	NLL	Ent. Type	F1-Partial	F1-Exact	F1-Strict
RONEC	0.1121	90.51	91.22	89.52	87.51
LegalNERo	0.0900	86.69	85.21	81.07	80.30
GermEval 2014	0.0684	84.60	88.40	84.22	82.62
LER	0.0676	96.18	93.76	90.37	89.86

Table 1: Baseline results obtained on all datasets.

All models achieve over 85% in F1-score in partially identifying entities while ignoring their type. At the same time, we observe that the performances drop by almost 5% when the model has to identify the exact boundaries and entity type. In general, we observe the following patterns inspecting the outputs of the baseline models:

- In the case of nested entities, the models predict the inside entities but not the whole one;
- The precision is lower compared with recall, meaning that the models predict non-existing entities, while those that correspond to ground truth are correctly identified and classified;
- Some classes are repeatedly misclassified (for example, on LegalNERo, organizations are predicted as persons, or in RONEC, events are predicted as organizations);
- Invalid boundaries, as observed earlier by the drop of 5% in strict metric compared with the partial metric.

5.2 Domain Adaptation on Different Domains

Applying domain adaptation, we experimented with two configurations: first, in which we add the domain adaptation loss $+L_{da}$, and second, in which we subtract the domain adaptation loss $-L_{da}$.

Table 2 presents the results of the ADAL scenario. We observe the performances are similar to the baseline models, meaning that even if we perform domain adaptation, the input space's new latent structure does not help improve performances. In general, the results are slightly lower, by at most 3% in F1-score. In the case of LegalNERo, we see an improvement of 1% in strict and exact metrics. In almost all cases, the evaluation NLL score is larger than the baseline values, the exception being LER.

Dataset	NLL	Ent. Type	F1-Partial	F1-Exact	F1-Strict
RONEC	0.1561	88.14	89.49	87.45	84.51
LegalNERo	0.1239	86.58	85.79	82.05	81.24
GermEval 2014	0.0739	83.77	88.21	87.13	81.96
LER	0.0245	94.45	93.54	90.62	89.15

Table 2: Domain adaptation trained using ADAL.

On SDAL (see Table 3), we notice improvements of up to 3% along almost all datasets, except for LegalNERo, where the performance drops by 5%. We note that the highest score obtained on LER is 92.2%, GermEval 2014 is 85.57%, and RONEC is 87.10%. Compared with ADAL, these scores are higher by up to 4% in the case of the generic datasets.

Dataset	NLL	Ent. Type	F1-Partial	F1-Exact	F1-Strict
RONEC	0.1084	90.17	90.86	89.13	87.10
LegalNERo	0.0910	81.21	79.95	76.39	75.68
GermEval 2014	0.0666	86.91	90.66	89.87	85.57
LER	0.0168	96.27	95.27	93.07	92.30

Table 3: Domain adaptation trained using SDAL.

5.3 In-Dataset Domain Adaptation

We analyze the effects of applying domain adaptation inside the same dataset. In other words, we utilize the same train set for both domains while keeping different domain tags. The intuition is to enforce a feature representation that is more robust against small variations in the latent space due to the random initialization of both branches. Table 4 shows the results on all four datasets.

Dataset	NLL	Ent. Type	F1-Partial	F1-Exact	F1-Strict
RONEC	**0.2558**	88.39	90.07	88.42	85.59
RONEC	0.2620	**89.65**	**90.62**	**88.99**	**86.82**
LegalNERo	0.1498	84.86	77.67	66.05	63.46
LegalNERo	**0.1435**	**89.15**	**88.86**	**85.93**	**85.17**
GermEval 2014	0.1073	**85.31**	89.76	88.86	83.79
GermEval 2014	**0.1090**	85.08	**90.23**	**89.49**	**83.94**
LER	0.0208	95.59	93.96	91.05	90.40
LER	**0.0203**	**95.70**	**93.99**	**91.16**	**90.59**

Table 4: Domain adaptation on the same datasets: RONEC - RONEC, LegalNERo - LegalNERo, GermEval 2014 - GermEval 2014, and LER - LER.

We observe that almost consistently, one of the two task heads performs better than the other. In the case of LegalNERo, there is a considerable difference in performances between the two heads while keeping similar NNL scores. This indicates that small changes in per-tag measurements may have larger impacts on sequential measurements. Moreover, these results improve upon the baseline results, by a small margin, under 1%, on all datasets except RONEC, on which we observe performance degradation by at most 1%. In addition, we observe higher NLL scores, except on the LER dataset.

5.4 Effects of Domain Adaptation on the Feature Space

We generate t-SNE representations in the latent space of the model, outputted by the Transformer layer. The visualizations are generated at perplexity set to 30. We compare these representations between datasets and assess how well the model adapted to the changes in the data distributions.

Figure 2 shows the scenario on the Romanian datasets. The pre-trained BERT outputs are generated using the non-fine-tuned version of the pre-trained BERT model in the Romanian language. We observe that the pre-trained BERT outputs on RONEC are sparse and tend to form two blobs (i.e., a large one on the left and a smaller one on the right). On the LegalNERo dataset, the data points tend to cluster and not follow the same distribution as RONEC.

In the case of the German datasets (see Figure 3), we observe similar behaviors as on the Romanian datasets. The pre-trained BERT model on the German language outputs entities generates a latent space in which examples from the GermEval 2014 dataset are close to LER while tending to cluster into groups of points from the same dataset. This phenomenon is emphasized when domain adaptation is employed. In both ADAL and SDAL, there is a separation between datasets.

When analyzing ADAL, we can see that the data tend to form clusters and separation between examples from the two datasets. In the SDAL training scenario, we observe at a smaller degree the tendency of clustering. We can see that both datasets are separated, but the data points are not cluttering into some spots. Considering the performance differences, we may hypothesize that the feature predictor prefers sparser representations to compact ones.

Having linearly separable classes is the desired objective since this representation is much easier to be classified by the simpler classifiers. We cannot assume this is the case (i.e., linear separation) due to how t-SNE works. From these visualizations, we can deduce that combining both gradient reversal and gradient scaler layers are an effective way of shaping the latent space, if set appropriately.

Therefore, from this empirical observation, the sign of the domain adaptation loss term does influence the latent representation, more specifically, when considering the sparsity of the data. When we add the loss term and perform the optimization step in domain adaptation, we aim to minimize that term so that the domain classifier is trained like a regular neural network. At the same time, we maximize the loss function in the latent representation to generate similar feature distributions. In our experiments, we see the opposite in the multi-task learning setup. The feature representation at the entity level tends to become separable and cluttered together. It is desired in the context of a label classifier since we want different features that are easily predictable for each class.

5.5 Limitations

Our proposed method has some limitations, especially during training. As previously mentioned, a more significant domain adaptation on the BERT architecture yields poor performances. This motivated us to introduce a gradient scaler layer and

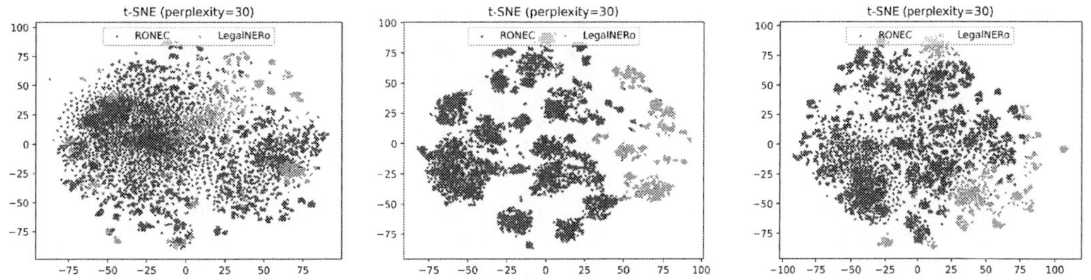

(a) Pre-trained BERT outputs (b) ADAL training (c) SDAL training

Figure 2: t-SNE visualizations of the embedding space on Romanian datasets for the baseline, ADAL, and SDAL.

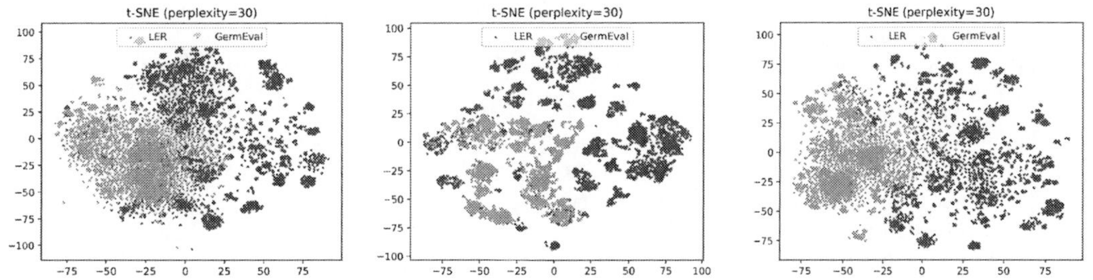

(a) Pre-trained BERT outputs (b) ADAL training (c) SDAL training

Figure 3: t-SNE visualizations of the embedding space on German datasets for the baseline, ADAL, and SDAL.

the hyperparameter schedulers, thus reducing this effect. On the other hand, we analyzed the models' predictions and observed that some boundaries are incorrectly determined, thus affecting the scores. For example, in the Romanian language, the entity "Sanctității Sale Papa Francisc" (eng., "His Holiness Pope Francisc") is split into two entities (see Appendix A.5). Our method does not detect some entities on all datasets in a different context. Also, the model does not capture this variety in the dataset, which overfits this scenario. More discussions on limitations can be seen in the case study from Appendix A.4.

6 Conclusions and Future Work

We proposed a method based on multi-task domain adaptation in a cross-domain setting. The model architecture is based on contextualized word embeddings generated using BERT, LSTM, fully connected, and CRF layers. We evaluated our approach on two languages (i.e., Romanian and German) from two domains (i.e., general and legal). We observed minimal improvements in the German dataset while reducing performance on the Romanian legal dataset. More research should be conducted in this direction.

For future work, we strive to investigate the performance degradation further and analyze the effects of domain adaptation on the embedding space via t-SNE visualizations. In addition, we want to evaluate a cross-lingual setting, considering the cross-language BERT pre-trained model and performing domain adaptation between the same domain but different languages.

References

Neha Bansal, Arun Sharma, and R. K. Singh. 2019. A review on the application of deep learning in legal domain. In *Artificial Intelligence Applications and Innovations*, pages 374–381, Cham. Springer International Publishing.

Valentin Barriere and Amaury Fouret. 2019. May I check again? — a simple but efficient way to generate and use contextual dictionaries for named entity recognition. application to French legal texts. In *Proceedings of the 22nd Nordic Conference on Computational Linguistics*, pages 327–332, Turku, Finland. Linköping University Electronic Press.

Giannis Bekoulis, Johannes Deleu, Thomas Demeester, and Chris Develder. 2018. Adversarial training for multi-context joint entity and relation extraction. In *Proceedings of the 2018 Conference on Empirical Methods in Natural Language Processing*, pages 2830–2836.

Darina Benikova, Chris Biemann, Max Kisselew, and Sebastian Pado. 2014. Germeval 2014 named entity recognition shared task: companion paper. In *Proceedings of the KONVENS GermEval Shared Task on Named Entity Recognition*.

Parminder Bhatia, Busra Celikkaya, Mohammed Khalilia, and Selvan Senthivel. 2019. Comprehend medical: a named entity recognition and relationship extraction web service. In *2019 18th IEEE International Conference On Machine Learning And Applications (ICMLA)*, pages 1844–1851. IEEE.

Mırian Bruckschen, Caio Northfleet, DM Silva, Paulo Bridi, Roger Granada, Renata Vieira, Prasad Rao, and Tomas Sander. 2010. Named entity recognition in the legal domain for ontology population. In *Proceedings of the 3rd Workshop on Semantic Processing of Legal Texts*.

Cristian Cardellino, Milagro Teruel, Laura Alonso Alemany, and Serena Villata. 2017. A low-cost, high-coverage legal named entity recognizer, classifier and linker. In *Proceedings of the 16th edition of the International Conference on Articial Intelligence and Law*, pages 9–18.

Ilias Chalkidis, Manos Fergadiotis, Prodromos Malakasiotis, and Ion Androutsopoulos. 2019. Neural contract element extraction revisited. In *Workshop on Document Intelligence at NeurIPS 2019*.

Branden Chan, Stefan Schweter, and Timo Möller. 2020. German's next language model. In *Proceedings of the 28th International Conference on Computational Linguistics*, pages 6788–6796, Barcelona, Spain (Online). International Committee on Computational Linguistics.

Soravit Changpinyo, Hexiang Hu, and Fei Sha. 2018. Multi-task learning for sequence tagging: An empirical study. In *Proceedings of the 27th International Conference on Computational Linguistics*, pages 2965–2977, Santa Fe, New Mexico, USA. Association for Computational Linguistics.

Luoxin Chen, Weitong Ruan, Xinyue Liu, and Jianhua Lu. 2020. Seqvat: Virtual adversarial training for semi-supervised sequence labeling. In *Proceedings of the 58th Annual Meeting of the Association for Computational Linguistics*, pages 8801–8811.

Weile Chen, Huiqiang Jiang, Qianhui Wu, Börje Karlsson, and Yi Guan. 2021. AdvPicker: Effectively Leveraging Unlabeled Data via Adversarial Discriminator for Cross-Lingual NER. In *Proceedings of the 59th Annual Meeting of the Association for Computational Linguistics and the 11th International Joint Conference on Natural Language Processing (Volume 1: Long Papers)*, pages 743–753, Online. Association for Computational Linguistics.

David A Cohn, Zoubin Ghahramani, and Michael I Jordan. 1996. Active learning with statistical models. *Journal of artificial intelligence research*, 4:129–145.

Zhenjin Dai, Xutao Wang, Pin Ni, Yuming Li, Gangmin Li, and Xuming Bai. 2019. Named entity recognition using bert bilstm crf for chinese electronic health records. In *2019 12th international congress on image and signal processing, biomedical engineering and informatics (cisp-bmei)*, pages 1–5. IEEE.

Jacob Devlin, Ming-Wei Chang, Kenton Lee, and Kristina Toutanova. 2019. BERT: Pre-training of deep bidirectional transformers for language understanding. In *Proceedings of the 2019 Conference of the North American Chapter of the Association for Computational Linguistics: Human Language Technologies, Volume 1 (Long and Short Papers)*, pages 4171–4186, Minneapolis, Minnesota. Association for Computational Linguistics.

George R Doddington, Alexis Mitchell, Mark A Przybocki, Lance A Ramshaw, Stephanie M Strassel, and Ralph M Weischedel. 2004. The automatic content extraction (ace) program-tasks, data, and evaluation. In *Lrec*, volume 2, pages 837–840. Lisbon.

Timothy Dozat and Christopher D. Manning. 2017. Deep biaffine attention for neural dependency parsing. In *5th International Conference on Learning Representations, ICLR 2017, Toulon, France, April 24-26, 2017, Conference Track Proceedings*. OpenReview.net.

Christopher Dozier, Ravikumar Kondadadi, Marc Light, Arun Vachher, Sriharsha Veeramachaneni, and Ramdev Wudali. 2010. Named entity recognition and resolution in legal text. In *Semantic Processing of Legal Texts*, pages 27–43. Springer.

Stefan Dumitrescu, Andrei-Marius Avram, and Sampo Pyysalo. 2020. The birth of romanian bert. In *Proceedings of the 2020 Conference on Empirical Methods in Natural Language Processing: Findings*, pages 4324–4328.

Stefan Daniel Dumitrescu and Andrei-Marius Avram. 2020. Introducing ronec-the romanian named entity corpus. In *Proceedings of the 12th Language Resources and Evaluation Conference*, pages 4436–4443.

Stefan Daniel Dumitrescu, Petru Rebeja, Beata Lorincz, Mihaela Gaman, Andrei Avram, Mihai Ilie, Andrei Pruteanu, Adriana Stan, Lorena Rosia, Cristina Iacobescu, Luciana Morogan, George Dima, Gabriel Marchidan, Traian Rebedea, Madalina Chitez, Dani Yogatama, Sebastian Ruder, Radu Tudor Ionescu, Razvan Pascanu, and Viorica Patraucean. 2021. Liro: Benchmark and leaderboard for romanian language tasks. In *Thirty-fifth Conference on Neural Information Processing Systems Datasets and Benchmarks Track (Round 1)*.

Ronen Feldman and Benjamin Rosenfeld. 2006. Boosting unsupervised relation extraction by using NER. In *Proceedings of the 2006 Conference on Empirical Methods in Natural Language Processing*, pages 473–481, Sydney, Australia. Association for Computational Linguistics.

G.D. Forney. 1973. The viterbi algorithm. *Proceedings of the IEEE*, 61(3):268–278.

Yaroslav Ganin and Victor S. Lempitsky. 2015. Unsupervised domain adaptation by backpropagation. In *Proceedings of the 32nd International Conference on Machine Learning, ICML 2015, Lille, France, 6-11 July 2015*, volume 37 of *JMLR Workshop and Conference Proceedings*, pages 1180–1189. JMLR.org.

Alexandru-Lucian Georgescu, Horia Cucu, Andi Buzo, and Corneliu Burileanu. 2020. Rsc: A romanian read speech corpus for automatic speech recognition. In *Proceedings of The 12th Language Resources and Evaluation Conference*, pages 6606–6612.

Ingo Glaser, Bernhard Waltl, and Florian Matthes. 2018. Named entity recognition, extraction, and linking in german legal contracts. In *IRIS: Internationales Rechtsinformatik Symposium*, pages 325–334.

Ian Goodfellow, Jean Pouget-Abadie, Mehdi Mirza, Bing Xu, David Warde-Farley, Sherjil Ozair, Aaron Courville, and Yoshua Bengio. 2014. Generative adversarial nets. *Advances in neural information processing systems*, 27.

Honglei Guo, Huijia Zhu, Zhili Guo, Xiaoxun Zhang, Xian Wu, and Zhong Su. 2009. Domain adaptation with latent semantic association for named entity recognition. In *Proceedings of Human Language Technologies: The 2009 Annual Conference of the North American Chapter of the Association for Computational Linguistics*, pages 281–289.

Christian Hänig, Stefan Thomas, and Stefan Bordag. 2014. Modular classifier ensemble architecture for named entity recognition on low resource systems.

Sepp Hochreiter and Jürgen Schmidhuber. 1997. Long short-term memory. *Neural Comput.*, 9(8):1735–1780.

Chen Jia and Yue Zhang. 2020. Multi-cell compositional lstm for ner domain adaptation. In *Proceedings of the 58th Annual Meeting of the Association for Computational Linguistics*, pages 5906–5917.

Shaohua Jiang, Shan Zhao, Kai Hou, Yang Liu, Li Zhang, et al. 2019. A bert-bilstm-crf model for chinese electronic medical records named entity recognition. In *2019 12th International Conference on Intelligent Computation Technology and Automation (ICICTA)*, pages 166–169. IEEE.

John D. Lafferty, Andrew McCallum, and Fernando C. N. Pereira. 2001. Conditional random fields: Probabilistic models for segmenting and labeling sequence data. In *Proceedings of the Eighteenth International Conference on Machine Learning*, ICML '01, page 282–289, San Francisco, CA, USA. Morgan Kaufmann Publishers Inc.

Guillaume Lample, Miguel Ballesteros, Sandeep Subramanian, Kazuya Kawakami, and Chris Dyer. 2016. Neural architectures for named entity recognition. In *Proceedings of the 2016 Conference of the North American Chapter of the Association for Computational Linguistics: Human Language Technologies*, pages 260–270, San Diego, California. Association for Computational Linguistics.

Elena Leitner, Georg Rehm, and Julian Moreno-Schneider. 2019. Fine-grained Named Entity Recognition in Legal Documents. In *Semantic Systems. The Power of AI and Knowledge Graphs. Proceedings of the 15th International Conference (SEMANTiCS 2019)*, number 11702 in Lecture Notes in Computer Science, pages 272–287, Karlsruhe, Germany. Springer. 10/11 September 2019.

Elena Leitner, Georg Rehm, and Julian Moreno Schneider. 2020. A dataset of german legal documents for named entity recognition. In *Proceedings of the 12th Language Resources and Evaluation Conference*, pages 4478–4485.

Bill Yuchen Lin and Wei Lu. 2018. Neural adaptation layers for cross-domain named entity recognition. In *Proceedings of the 2018 Conference on Empirical Methods in Natural Language Processing*, pages 2012–2022, Brussels, Belgium. Association for Computational Linguistics.

Mingyi Liu, Zhiying Tu, Zhongjie Wang, and Xiaofei Xu. 2020. Ltp: a new active learning strategy for bert-crf based named entity recognition. *arXiv preprint arXiv:2001.02524*.

Zihan Liu, Yan Xu, Tiezheng Yu, Wenliang Dai, Ziwei Ji, Samuel Cahyawijaya, Andrea Madotto, and Pascale Fung. 2021. Crossner: Evaluating cross-domain named entity recognition. In *AAAI*.

Ilya Loshchilov and Frank Hutter. 2019. Decoupled weight decay regularization. In *7th International Conference on Learning Representations, ICLR 2019, New Orleans, LA, USA, May 6-9, 2019*. OpenReview.net.

Pedro Henrique Luz de Araujo, Teófilo E de Campos, Renato RR de Oliveira, Matheus Stauffer, Samuel Couto, and Paulo Bermejo. 2018. Lener-br: a dataset for named entity recognition in brazilian legal text. In *International Conference on Computational Processing of the Portuguese Language*, pages 313–323. Springer.

Mihai Masala, Stefan Ruseti, and Mihai Dascalu. 2020. Robert–a romanian bert model. In *Proceedings of the 28th International Conference on Computational Linguistics*, pages 6626–6637.

Mike Mintz, Steven Bills, Rion Snow, and Dan Jurafsky. 2009. Distant supervision for relation extraction without labeled data. In *Proceedings of the Joint Conference of the 47th Annual Meeting of the ACL and the 4th International Joint Conference on Natural Language Processing of the AFNLP*, pages 1003–1011.

Maria Mitrofan and Dan Tufiş. 2018. Bioro: The biomedical corpus for the romanian language. In *Proceedings of the Eleventh International Conference on Language Resources and Evaluation (LREC 2018)*.

Takeru Miyato, Shin-Ichi Maeda, Masanori Koyama, and Shin Ishii. 2019. Virtual adversarial training: A regularization method for supervised and semi-supervised learning. *IEEE Transactions on Pattern Analysis and Machine Intelligence*, 41(8):1979–1993.

Zara Nasar, Syed Waqar Jaffry, and Muhammad Kamran Malik. 2021. Named entity recognition and relation extraction: State-of-the-art. *ACM Comput. Surv.*, 54(1).

Malte Ostendorff, Till Blume, and Saskia Ostendorff. 2020. Towards an open platform for legal information. In *Proceedings of the ACM/IEEE Joint Conference on Digital Libraries in 2020*, pages 385–388.

Vasile Păiș, Maria Mitrofan, Carol Luca Gasan, Vlad Coneschi, and Alexandru Ianov. 2021a. Named entity recognition in the Romanian legal domain. In *Proceedings of the Natural Legal Language Processing Workshop 2021*, pages 9–18, Punta Cana, Dominican Republic. Association for Computational Linguistics.

Vasile Păiș, Maria Mitrofan, Carol Luca Gasan, Alexandru Ianov, Corvin Ghiță, Vlad Silviu Coneschi, and Andrei Onuț. 2021b. Romanian Named Entity Recognition in the Legal domain (LegalNERo).

Abigail See, Peter J. Liu, and Christopher D. Manning. 2017. Get to the point: Summarization with pointer-generator networks. In *Proceedings of the 55th Annual Meeting of the Association for Computational Linguistics (Volume 1: Long Papers)*, pages 1073–1083, Vancouver, Canada. Association for Computational Linguistics.

Rico Sennrich, Barry Haddow, and Alexandra Birch. 2016. Neural machine translation of rare words with subword units. In *Proceedings of the 54th Annual Meeting of the Association for Computational Linguistics (Volume 1: Long Papers)*, pages 1715–1725, Berlin, Germany. Association for Computational Linguistics.

Peng Shi and Jimmy Lin. 2019. Simple bert models for relation extraction and semantic role labeling. *arXiv preprint arXiv:1904.05255*.

Stavroula Skylaki, Ali Oskooei, Omar Bari, Nadja Herger, and Zac Kriegman. 2020. Named entity recognition in the legal domain using a pointer generator network. *CoRR*, abs/2012.09936.

Fábio Souza, Rodrigo Nogueira, and Roberto Lotufo. 2019. Portuguese named entity recognition using bert-crf. *arXiv preprint arXiv:1909.10649*.

Pedro Javier Ortiz Suárez, Benoît Sagot, and Laurent Romary. 2019. Asynchronous pipeline for processing huge corpora on medium to low resource infrastructures. In *7th Workshop on the Challenges in the Management of Large Corpora (CMLC-7)*. Leibniz-Institut für Deutsche Sprache.

Charles Sutton and Andrew McCallum. 2012. An introduction to conditional random fields. *Found. Trends Mach. Learn.*, 4(4):267–373.

Muzamil Hussain Syed and Sun-Tae Chung. 2021. Menuner: Domain-adapted bert based ner approach for a domain with limited dataset and its application to food menu domain. *Applied Sciences*, 11(13).

Jörg Tiedemann. 2012. Parallel data, tools and interfaces in OPUS. In *Proceedings of the Eighth International Conference on Language Resources and Evaluation (LREC'12)*, pages 2214–2218, Istanbul, Turkey. European Language Resources Association (ELRA).

Dan Tufiș, Maria Mitrofan, Vasile Păiș, Radu Ion, and Andrei Coman. 2020. Collection and annotation of the Romanian legal corpus. In *Proceedings of the Twelfth Language Resources and Evaluation Conference*, pages 2773–2777, Marseille, France. European Language Resources Association.

Laurens van der Maaten and Geoffrey Hinton. 2008. Visualizing data using t-sne. *Journal of Machine Learning Research*, 9:2579–2605.

Ashish Vaswani, Noam Shazeer, Niki Parmar, Jakob Uszkoreit, Llion Jones, Aidan N Gomez, Łukasz Kaiser, and Illia Polosukhin. 2017. Attention is all you need. In *Advances in neural information processing systems*, pages 5998–6008.

Changhan Wang, Morgane Riviere, Ann Lee, Anne Wu, Chaitanya Talnikar, Daniel Haziza, Mary Williamson, Juan Pino, and Emmanuel Dupoux. 2021. VoxPopuli: A large-scale multilingual speech corpus for representation learning, semi-supervised learning and interpretation. In *Proceedings of the 59th Annual Meeting of the Association for Computational Linguistics and the 11th International Joint Conference on Natural Language Processing (Volume 1: Long Papers)*, pages 993–1003, Online. Association for Computational Linguistics.

Ralph Weischedeld, Martha Palmerd, Mitchell Marcusd, Eduard Hovyd, Sameer Pradhand, Lance Ramshawd, Nianwen Xued, Ann Taylord, Jeff Kaufmand, Michelle Franchinid, Mohammed El-Bachoutid, Robert Belvind, and Ann Houston. 2013. OntoNotes Release 5.0 LDC2013T19. Web Download. Philadelphia. Linguistic Data Consortium.

Karl Weiss, Taghi M Khoshgoftaar, and DingDing Wang. 2016. A survey of transfer learning. *Journal of Big data*, 3(1):1–40.

Vikas Yadav and Steven Bethard. 2018. A survey on recent advances in named entity recognition from deep learning models. In *Proceedings of the 27th International Conference on Computational Linguistics*, pages 2145–2158, Santa Fe, New Mexico, USA. Association for Computational Linguistics.

Yaosheng Yang, Wenliang Chen, Zhenghua Li, Zhengqiu He, and Min Zhang. 2018. Distantly supervised NER with partial annotation learning and reinforcement learning. In *Proceedings of the 27th International Conference on Computational Linguistics*, pages 2159–2169, Santa Fe, New Mexico, USA. Association for Computational Linguistics.

Juntao Yu, Bernd Bohnet, and Massimo Poesio. 2020. Named entity recognition as dependency parsing. In *Proceedings of the 58th Annual Meeting of the Association for Computational Linguistics*, pages 6470–6476, Online. Association for Computational Linguistics.

Xiangyu Yue, Zangwei Zheng, Shanghang Zhang, Yang Gao, Trevor Darrell, Kurt Keutzer, and Alberto Sangiovanni Vincentelli. 2021. Prototypical cross-domain self-supervised learning for few-shot unsupervised domain adaptation. In *Proceedings of the IEEE/CVF Conference on Computer Vision and Pattern Recognition*, pages 13834–13844.

Suncong Zheng, Yuexing Hao, Dongyuan Lu, Hongyun Bao, Jiaming Xu, Hongwei Hao, and Bo Xu. 2017. Joint entity and relation extraction based on a hybrid neural network. *Neurocomputing*, 257:59–66. Machine Learning and Signal Processing for Big Multimedia Analysis.

Haoxi Zhong, Chaojun Xiao, Cunchao Tu, Tianyang Zhang, Zhiyuan Liu, and Maosong Sun. 2020. How does nlp benefit legal system: A summary of legal artificial intelligence. In *Proceedings of the 58th Annual Meeting of the Association for Computational Linguistics*, pages 5218–5230.

A Appendix

A.1 Entity-Level Performance of the Domain Adaptation Model

The entity-level performance, in terms of strict metrics for precision, recall, and F1-score, are presented in Tables 5, 6, 7, and 8, for both Romanian and German languages, on the general and legal domains.

Entity	Without DA			With DA		
Type	P	R	F1	P	R	F1
DATETIME	55.56	91.01	69.00	46.72	90.07	61.53
EVENT	7.73	55.81	13.58	4.95	49.12	9.00
FACILITY	9.55	69.14	16.78	7.41	73.71	13.47
GPE	58.08	92.94	71.49	49.71	93.40	64.88
LANGUAGE	5.45	87.67	10.26	3.88	87.67	7.44
LOC	17.67	67.46	28.01	13.59	69.05	22.72
MONEY	14.74	87.05	25.21	10.48	83.48	18.62
NAT_REL_POL	38.35	89.76	53.74	30.21	89.24	45.14
NUMERIC	50.22	95.28	65.77	41.44	95.20	57.74
ORDINAL	17.96	80.92	29.39	13.97	85.53	24.02
ORG	40.43	70.44	51.38	38.26	80.69	51.90
PERIOD	12.05	77.11	20.85	9.22	81.00	16.56
PERSON	75.69	89.74	82.12	69.23	90.20	78.34
QUANTITY	17.19	93.90	29.06	12.73	93.90	22.42
WORK_OF_ART	10.96	54.65	18.26	9.04	60.37	15.72

Table 5: Entity-level performance on the RONEC dataset.

Entity	Without DA			With DA		
Type	P	R	F1	P	R	F1
LEGAL	58.87	83.83	69.17	50.86	80.60	62.37
LOC	46.28	76.57	57.69	41.79	85.30	56.10
ORG	66.13	87.59	75.36	59.88	86.89	70.90
PER	29.37	94.27	44.78	18.17	69.81	28.83
TIME	54.57	90.53	68.09	47.39	91.98	62.55

Table 6: Entity-level performance on the LegalNERo dataset.

Entity	Without DA			With DA		
Type	P	R	F1	P	R	F1
LOC	69.04	90.97	78.50	70.08	90.33	78.92
LOCderiv	44.32	93.23	60.08	45.97	94.47	61.84
LOCpart	9.34	63.30	16.27	10.30	66.97	17.85
ORG	55.35	80.52	65.60	56.07	79.77	65.85
ORGderiv	0.46	37.50	0.91	0.32	25.00	0.64
ORGpart	17.61	81.40	28.96	17.70	77.91	28.85
OTH	37.86	64.73	47.78	40.18	67.56	50.39
OTHderiv	3.24	56.41	6.13	4.02	66.67	7.59
OTHpart	3.11	50.00	5.85	2.48	38.10	4.66
PER	69.77	94.69	80.34	70.80	94.75	81.04
PERderiv	0.77	45.45	1.51	0.32	18.18	0.64
PERpart	2.81	43.18	5.28	3.74	54.55	7.00

Table 7: Entity-level performance on the GermEval 2014 dataset.

Entity	Without DA			With DA		
Type	P	R	F1	P	R	F1
AN	4.09	78.26	7.78	6.21	82.61	11.55
EUN	37.84	86.56	52.66	45.91	86.21	59.91
GRT	60.17	98.02	74.57	68.83	98.33	80.98
GS	88.19	98.16	92.91	91.10	97.97	94.41
INN	48.19	90.37	62.86	57.72	91.41	70.76
LD	39.34	97.85	56.12	48.58	97.85	64.92
LDS	6.21	70.00	11.41	9.63	77.50	17.13
LIT	51.27	88.42	64.91	58.22	87.02	69.76
MRK	8.28	76.00	14.93	10.77	68.63	18.62
ORG	30.24	82.05	44.19	37.70	81.55	51.56
PER	42.03	93.96	58.08	51.74	94.26	66.81
RR	20.60	98.20	34.06	27.27	97.30	42.60
RS	82.50	95.20	88.40	85.38	94.31	89.62
ST	22.43	95.31	36.31	28.54	91.41	43.49
STR	5.42	85.71	10.19	7.74	85.71	14.20
UN	32.92	90.21	48.24	40.74	88.94	55.88
VO	22.30	87.94	35.58	29.38	87.94	44.05
VS	16.70	73.55	27.22	21.14	68.00	32.26
VT	52.70	91.36	66.85	60.20	89.52	71.99

Table 8: Entity-level performance on the German LER dataset.

A.2 Comparison with Existing Works

We compare our approach in terms of the strict exact score on each dataset. On the LegalNERo dataset, we extracted the results for the best model (Păiș et al., 2021a) achieving the reported score on the test set. Their approach is similar to ours in that both methods utilize BiLSTM and CRF layers in the architecture. The main difference is that our approach uses BERT embeddings, while Păiș et al. (2021a) generated MARCELL embeddings and employed gazetteers. On RONEC, we considered the results reported for Romanian BERT cased and uncased (Dumitrescu et al., 2020), from their GitHub page[10]. We considered this because our architecture utilizes these pre-trained models as components for embedding generation.

On the German LER dataset, we considered the results for BiLSTM-CRF (Benikova et al., 2014), which utilizes pre-trained embeddings on the German language, and the previously mentioned architecture for predictions. In the end, on the GermEval 2014 dataset, we considered the winning team (Hänig et al., 2014) at the GermEval 2014 competition, which utilizes only the CRF model.

Table 9 showcases the results. We observe that our approach obtains comparable results on LegalNERo; on RONEC and German LER, the differ-

[10]https://github.com/dumitrescustefan/ronec/tree/master/evaluate

Method	LegalNERo	RONEC	LER	GermEval 2014
MARCELL+BiLSTM+CRF (Păiș et al., 2021a)	85.34	-	-	-
romanian-bert-cased (Dumitrescu et al., 2020)	-	91.9	-	-
romanian-bert-uncased (Dumitrescu et al., 2020)	-	95.2	-	-
BiLSTM-CRF (Benikova et al., 2014)	-	-	95.46	-
CRF (Hänig et al., 2014)	-	-	-	79.08
Our method	85.17	87.5	92.30	85.75

Table 9: Comparison with existing works. All scores are F1-strict scores, in percentages (%).

ence between 4% and 8%, and on the GermEval 2014 dataset, our method performs better than a CRF model by 6%.

A.3 Embedding Space Visualization

We analyze the embedding space by employing t-SNE representations on the embedding space generated with the pre-trained BERT models (before fine-tuning). Since some named entities may have more than one word or token, we average embeddings to generate a meaningful representation. Formally, given the set of token embeddings w_i^j, each token of the Transformer's input has the following embedding representation e^j:

$$e^j = \frac{1}{N^j} \sum_{i=1}^{N^j} w_i^j \tag{15}$$

where N_j represents the length of the jth named entity.

In this space, we apply t-SNE to generate the visualizations on the test set of each dataset we utilized in this work, the perplexity being set to 30. Figure 4 shows the plots on the Romanian language, while Figure 5 presents the visualizations on the German language. We observe that tokens from the same class cluster together in both languages. In addition, we can observe that LegalNERo is the sparsest dataset, with classes in general well separated. On the other hand, we see the data's tendency to cluster together on the LER dataset, but compared to the general domain, it is a less linearly separable dataset. However, the models trained on this dataset obtained better results due to model over-parametrization. We see linearly separable clusters in the t-SNE representations on the general domains, with some scattered points.

A.4 Case Study

We present examples of the outputs produced by the domain adaptation model in Table 10 from Appendix A.5.

In the case of the Romanian language, we see that the boundaries are not well recognized, such as in *"Trezoreria Statului"* (eng. "State Treasury"), where only *"Trezoreria"* is marked as an organization. In other cases, such as *"Băncii Naționale a României,"* (eng. "of the Romanian National Bank"), the comma is included in the entity. Other limitations rely on the misclassification of entity type, identifying entities that are not annotated in the ground truth, such as locations, dates, and organizations (although these can be considered entities in other contexts or can be subject to the difficulty for annotating datasets and ambiguity of words), and not identifying entities if are used in different contexts in the same sentence (for example, words that possess an indefinite/definite article; e.g., in the RONEC dataset, we have *"persoane fizice"* (eng. "natural persons") with both words annotated or only *"persoane"* (eng. "persons")). The model does not capture this variety in the dataset, which overfits this scenario. As presented in the Subsection 5.1, some entities are misclassified with other similar types, such as an event with an organization, when they present acronyms (for example, *"USFL"* - United States Football League and *"NFL"* - National Football League) and can be used interchangeably.

In the case of the German language, the model predicts the wrong boundaries rather than identifying the entity class (this is also supported by the higher partial metric than the strict and exact metrics). One such example can be seen in Table 10 on the GermEval 2014 dataset, where *"Przemyslaw II. von Großpolen"* (which is a name, where *"von Großpolen"* means "from Greater Poland" in English) is identified as two entities, namely the primary name *"Przemyslaw II."* and the location *"Großpolen"* which is from the name. Another limitation, which is not present in the Romanian dataset, is the identification of long entities. For example, *"Stellungnahme des Wissenschaftlichen Beirats beim Bundesministerium der Finanzen aus*

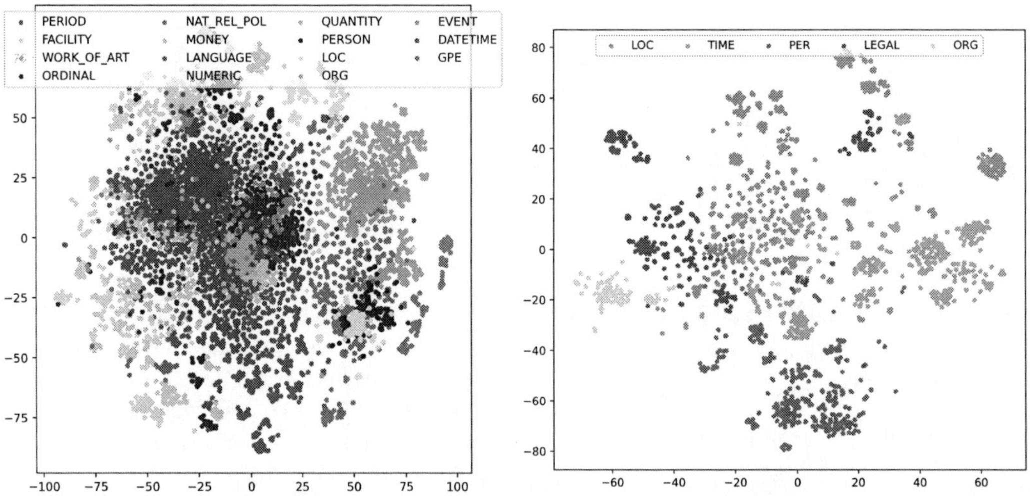

(a) RONEC dataset

(b) LegalNERo dataset

Figure 4: t-SNE visualizations of the embedding space on Romanian datasets.

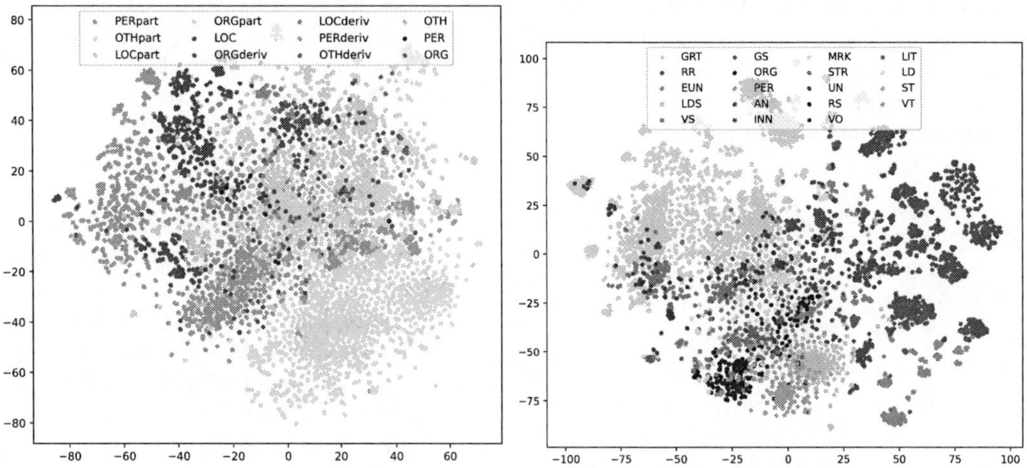

(a) GermEval 2014 dataset

(b) German LER dataset

Figure 5: t-SNE visualizations of the embedding space on German datasets.

dem Jahr 2010, Reform der Grundsteuer, S. 6" (eng., "Statement of the Scientific Advisory Board at the Federal Ministry of Finance from 2010, reform of the property tax, P. 6") which is not identified by our system. Finally, the last limitation is that the model does not identify the correct entity types. It can be viewed in Table 10, under the LER dataset, where *"A"* is a placeholder for a person, and *"X"* is a placeholder for a city. These were identified as company and location, respectively, just from the context. In this instance, we shall recall that LER has 19 fine-grained classes, some corresponding to coarse-grained, higher-level classes.

A.5 Example of Predictions for the Domain Adaptation Model

	LegalNERo
GT.	Punerea în circulaţie a monedelor de circulaţie, cu tema Vizita Apostolică a Sanctităţii Sale Papa Francisc **PER** în România **LOC**, se va face prin sucursalele regionale Bucureşti **LOC**, Cluj **LOC**, Iaşi **LOC** şi Timiş **LOC** ale Băncii Naţionale a României **ORG**, cu ocazia efectuării plăţilor în numerar către instituţiile de credit / Trezoreria Statului **ORG**.
Pred.	Punerea în circulaţie a monedelor de circulaţie, cu tema Vizita Apostolică a Sanctităţii Sale Papa **PER** Francisc **PER** în România **LOC**, se va face prin sucursalele regionale Bucureşti **LOC**, Cluj **LOC**, Iaşi **LOC** şi Timiş **LOC** ale Băncii Naţionale a României **ORG**, cu ocazia efectuării plăţilor în numerar către instituţiile de credit / Trezoreria Statului. **ORG**
	RONEC
GT.	Această regulă , reglementată în prezent la art. 83 **NUMERIC** alin. (3 **NUMERIC**) din Codul de procedură fiscală, republicat în M.O. nr. 863 **NUMERIC** / 26.09.2005 **DATETIME**, a generat unele efecte în sensul că în practică au existat numeroase situaţii în care suma impozitului datorat depăşea suma venitului (de exemplu există foarte mulţi acţionari **PERSON** persoane fizice **PERSON** cu dividende sub un leu nou **MONEY**).
Pred.	Această regulă , reglementată în prezent la art. 83 **NUMERIC** alin. (3 **NUMERIC**) din Codul de procedură fiscală, republicat în M.O. nr. 863 **NUMERIC** / 26.09.2005 **DATETIME**, a generat unele efecte în sensul că în practică au existat numeroase situaţii în care suma impozitului datorat depăşea suma venitului (de exemplu există foarte mulţi acţionari **PERSON** persoane fizice cu dividende sub un leu nou).
	GermEval 2014
GT.	Mit Herzog Przemysław II. **PER** von Großpolen **LOC** schloss Mestwin **PER** am 15. Februar 1282 im Vertrag von Kempen **LOC** eine „donatio inter vivos“ (Geschenk unter Lebenden) und vermachte ihm sein Herzogtum.
Pred.	Mit Herzog Przemysław II. von Großpolen **PER** schloss Mestwin **PER** am 15. Februar 1282 im Vertrag von Kempen **LOC** eine „donatio inter vivos“ (Geschenk unter Lebenden) und vermachte ihm sein Herzogtum.
	LER
GT.	Sie hatte in den Streitjahren bei der A **PER** mit Sitz in X **ST** (Österreich **LD**) Reisevorleistungen zur Durchführung von in der Bundesrepublik Deutschland **LD** (Deutschland **LD**) ausgeführten Radtouren bezogen.
Pred.	Sie hatte in den Streitjahren bei der A **UN** mit Sitz in X **ST** (Österreich **LD**) Reisevorleistungen zur Durchführung von in der Bundesrepublik Deutschland **LD** (Deutschland **LD**) ausgeführten Radtouren bezogen.

Table 10: Examples of ground truth (GT.) labels and predictions (Pred.) for the domain adaptation models. We selected the examples that have wrong predictions. Best viewed in color.

Computing and Exploiting Document Structure to Improve Unsupervised Extractive Summarization of Legal Case Decisions

Yang Zhong
University of Pittsburgh
Pittsburgh, PA, USA
yaz118@pitt.edu

Diane Litman
University of Pittsburgh
Pittsburgh, PA, USA
dlitman@pitt.edu

Abstract

Though many algorithms can be used to automatically summarize legal case decisions, most fail to incorporate domain knowledge about how important sentences in a legal decision relate to a representation of its document structure. For example, analysis of a legal case summarization dataset demonstrates that sentences serving different types of argumentative roles in the decision appear in different sections of the document. In this work, we propose an unsupervised graph-based ranking model that uses a reweighting algorithm to exploit properties of the document structure of legal case decisions. We also explore the impact of using different methods to compute the document structure. Results on the Canadian Legal Case Law dataset show that our proposed method outperforms several strong baselines.

1 Introduction

Single document summarization aims at rephrasing a long text into a shorter version while preserving the important information (Nenkova and McKeown, 2011). While recent years have witnessed a blooming of abstractive summarization models that can generate fluent and coherent new wordings (Rush et al., 2015; Zhang et al., 2020b; Lewis et al., 2020), abstractive summaries often contain hallucinated facts (Kryscinski et al., 2019). In contrast, extractive summarization models directly select sentences/phrases from the source document to form a summary. In certain domains such as the law or science (Bhattacharya et al., 2019; Dong et al., 2021), using exact wordings may be needed.

In this work, we focus on *extractive summarization of legal case decisions*. Different from texts in the news domain, case texts tend to be longer (e.g., in Canadian legal case decisions (Xu et al., 2021) there are on average 3.9k words, while standard news articles (Nallapati et al., 2016) range from 400 - 800 words) and also have more complicated document structures (e.g., legal cases are likely to be split into sections while news articles are not). In contrast to scientific domains, which also have long and structured texts, large training sets of case decisions and reference summaries are generally not freely available given the restrictions of the legal field. A currently used case dataset has less than 30k training examples (Xu et al., 2021), which is ten times less than scientific datasets such as arXiv and PubMed (Cohan et al., 2018). Thus, for the legal domain, it is not surprising that *unsupervised* extractive summarization methods are of interest. Unfortunately, when researchers (Saravanan et al., 2006; Bhattacharya et al., 2019) have attempted to directly apply standard unsupervised models to legal data, they have obtained mediocre results.

However, most such attempts have failed to utilize the *document structure of legal texts*. In case law, important sentences about the issues versus the decisions of the court occur in different places in the document structure. In contrast, summarization algorithms typically flatten any structure during initial processing (i.e., they concatenate sentences from different sections/paragraphs of a document to form a sentence list), or select sentences using structural biases from other domains (e.g., the importance of leading sentences in news (Zheng and Lapata, 2019)). As shown in Figure 1, while LexRank correctly extracts the legal issue from the beginning of the source text, it incorrectly extracts several redundant sentences (i.e., *[20], [21]* and [22] which talk about similar content) as well as ignores a large part of the article (e.g., no sentences are extracted from the last section of the original case: *RECAPITULATION OF CALCULATION OF DAMAGES*). In contrast, the human summary focuses on sentences related to the argument of the legal decision (e.g., what are the issues, reasoning and conclusions of this court case?), which tend to be spread across the document structure.

Recently, the HipoRank model was proposed

Proceedings of the Natural Legal Language Processing Workshop 2022, pages 322 - 337
December 8, 2022

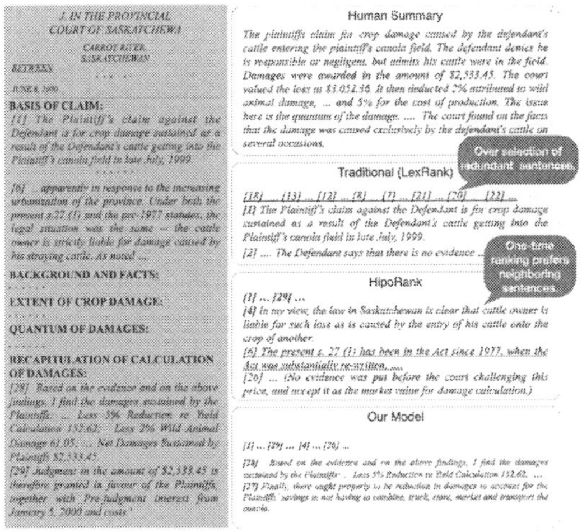

Figure 1: An example case law document-summary pair (ID: 3_2000canlii19612) and different summarization system outputs, where sentences are annotated with *argumentative* Issue, Reason, and Conclusion labels. Our method better extracts argumentative sentences from the source document by exploiting its structure.

to exploit discourse structure patterns during unsupervised extractive summarization (Dong et al., 2021). However, the model was designed for long scientific articles, and the experiments were based on data where the articles were already split into document sections. For case decisions, document structures are generally either missing or only implicitly conveyed by text formatting. For example, in Figure 1, document sections are conveyed by bolding in the source HTML file. Moreover, algorithms such as PACSUM and HipoRank compute sentence centrality just once and greedily select the top-k candidates as the extractive summary. Such a greedy selection algorithm fails to match the distribution of the argumentative sentences that ultimately appear in human case law summaries.

To address these limitations, we investigate the utility of different methods for automatically segmenting the sentences of legal case decisions into the sections of a document structure. We posit that incorporating *better views of document structure* could bring improvements in summarization quality when discourse-aware methods such as HipoRank are applied to legal case decisions. We also propose a novel *reweighting algorithm* to improve how HipoRank selects sentences when creating extractive summaries of legal decisions. The algorithm takes the history of already selected summary sentences into account, and gradually updates the importance score of a sentence. We posit that reweighting will decrease the selection of redundant sentences as well as increase the selection of argumentative sentences from less-represented document segments (e.g., in the middle).

We evaluate our proposed method[1] for summarizing legal decisions using an annotated Canadian case summarization dataset (CanLII) (Xu et al., 2021). Based on the belief that *argumentative sentences* will capture the important sentences to summarize in a legal decision (Xu et al., 2021; Elaraby and Litman, 2022), a portion of the CanLLI dataset comes with gold-standard sentence-level labels identifying which sentences are related to the issue/reasoning/conclusion of the court's decision in both source and summary documents. We use these labels to additionally propose a metric that can better evaluate the quality of the generated summary from a legal expert's perspective. Empirical results show that our method improves performance over previous unsupervised models (Zheng and Lapata, 2019; Dong et al., 2021; Erkan and Radev, 2004) in automatic evaluation.

2 Related Work

Supervised Extractive Summarization Using Discourse Information Graph-based methods have been exploited for extractive summarization tasks to better model the inter-sentence relations based on document structure. Xu et al. (2020) applied a GCN layer to aggregate information from the document's discourse graph based on RST trees and dependencies. More recently, HiStruct+ (Ruan et al., 2022) and HEGEL (Zhang et al., 2020a) started to incorporate the hierarchical structure and topic structure of scientific articles into supervised model training, respectively. However, HiSruct+ relied on the relatively fixed and explicit document structure of scientific articles[2], while HEGEL relied on a large training set to identify the topic distributions. *Our work uses an unsupervised extractive summarization approach in a lower-resource setting, as well as studies the effects of computing different types of document structures.* We leave the exploration of the aforementioned supervised approaches on legal domain texts for future work.

[1]Our code is available at `https://github.com/cs329yangzhong/DocumentStructureLegalSum`

[2]Section titles following a shared pattern (introduction, method ... and conclusion) are encoded to provide structural information. However, in our dataset, sectioning is often missing or not meaningful (e.g., titles such as "section 1").

Unsupervised Extractive Summarization Traditional extractive summarization methods are mostly unsupervised (Radev et al., 2000; Yin and Pei, 2015; Hirao et al., 2013), where a large portion apply the graph-based algorithms (Salton et al., 1997; Steinberger and Jezek, 2004; Erkan and Radev, 2004) or are based on term frequencies such as n-gram overlaps (Nenkova et al., 2005) to rank the sentences' importance. More recently, pretrained transformer-based models (Devlin et al., 2019; Lewis et al., 2020; Zhang et al., 2020b) have provided better sentence representations. For instance, Zheng and Lapata (2019) built directed unsupervised graph-based models on news articles using BERT-based sentence representations and achieved comparable performance to supervised models on multiple benchmarks. Dong et al. (2021) augmented the document graph of Zheng and Lapata (2019) with sentence position and section hierarchy to reflect the document structure of scientific articles. *Different from these two works which are based on assumptions of news and scientific article structures, our method uses reweighting to better utilize the document structure of legal cases.*

Extractive Summarization of Legal Texts Despite the success of supervised neural network models in news and scientific article summarization (Zhang et al., 2020b; Lewis et al., 2020; Zaheer et al., 2020), they face challenges in legal document summarization given the longer texts, distinct document structure, and limited training data (Bhattacharya et al., 2019). Instead, prior work has tackled legal extractive summarization by applying domain independent unsupervised algorithms (Luhn, 1958; Erkan and Radev, 2004; Saravanan et al., 2006), or designing domain specific supervised approaches (Saravanan et al., 2006; Polsley et al., 2016; Zhong et al., 2019). One recent work (Bhattacharya et al., 2021) frames the task as Integer Linear Programming and demonstrates the importance of in-domain structure and legal knowledge. In another line of research, Xu et al. (2021) propose a sentence classification task with the hope of exploiting the court decision's *argument structure* by making explicit its issues, conclusions, and reasons (i.e., argument triples). *Our work is unsupervised and implicitly reveals the relations between argument triples to generate better summaries.*

Case length (avg. # words)	3,971
Summary length (avg. # words)	266
Training set (# case/summary pairs)	27,241
Testing set (# case/summary pairs)	1,049

Table 1: Dataset statistics of CanLII.

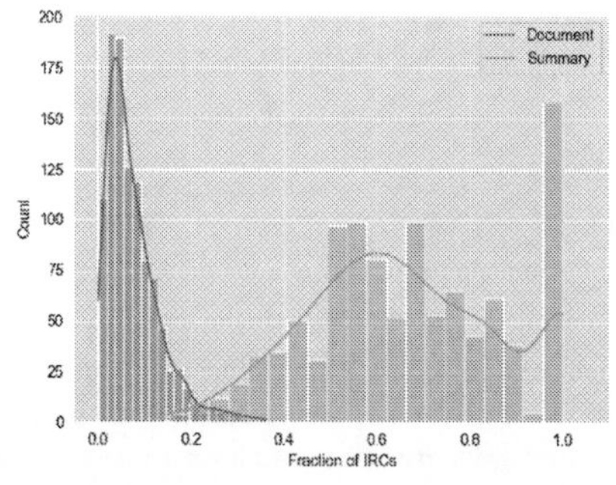

Figure 2: Fraction of sentences annotated as argumentative (using the IRC scheme) in the case documents versus in the summaries of the CanLII test set. Though only a small fraction of sentences in the original document are annotated as IRCs, IRCs are a large fraction of the human-written summaries.

3 Case Decision Summarization Dataset

Recent work has introduced a number of legal document summarization or salient information identification tasks with associated datasets, e.g., for bill summarization (Kornilova and Eidelman, 2019) and for case sentence argumentive classification (Xu et al., 2021) and rhetorical role prediction (Malik et al., 2022). Similarly to Xu et al. (2021), we use the **CanLII** (Canadian Legal Information Institute) dataset of legal case decisions and summaries[3]. Full corpus statistics are provided in Table 1, while an example case/summary pair from the test set is provided in Figure 6 in Appendix D.

Xu et al. (2021) only used a small portion of this dataset for their work in argumentative classification. Conjecturing that explicitly identifying the decision's argumentative components would be crucial in case summarization, they annotated 1,049 case and human-written summary pairs curated from the full dataset. In particular, they recruited legal experts to annotate the document on the sentence level, adopting an **IRC scheme** (see Figure 6 in Appendix D) which classifies individual sen-

[3]The data was obtained through an agreement with the Canadian Legal Information Institute (CanLII) (`https://www.canlii.org/en/`).

tences into one of four categories: **Issue** (legal question addressed in the case), **Conclusion** (court's decisions for the corresponding issue), **Reason** (text snippets explaining why the court made such conclusion) and **Non_IRC** (none of the above). The distributions of the IRC labels in the cases and summaries are shown in Figure 2 and illustrate that argumentative sentences do indeed play an important role in human summaries. We utilized the unannotated 27,241 pairs to train a supervised model baseline and the 1049 annotated pairs as our test set. While none of our summarization methods use the IRC annotations, they are used during testing as the basis of a domain-specific evaluation metric.

4 Method and Models

We propose a reweighting model that employs a graph-based ranking algorithm to exploit the structures encoded in long legal case decisions.

4.1 Discourse-Aware Backbone Model

The HipoRank (Hierarchical and Positional Ranking) model recently developed by Dong et al. (2021) constructs a directed graph for document representation using document section and sentence hierarchies. HipoRank computes the centrality score of each sentence as

$$c(s_i^I) = \mu_1 c_{inter}(s_i^I) + c_{intra}(s_i^I) \qquad (1)$$

where s_i^I refers to the i-th sentence in I-th section. μ_1 is a tunable hyper-paramter, $c_{inter}(s_i^I)$ computes the sentence's similarity to other section representations and $c_{intra}(s_i^I)$ computes the average similarity of the current sentence with all others in the same section. HipoRank then selects the top-K ranked sentences as the summary. More details of the algorithm are provided in Appendix A. Directly applying HipoRank to our data yielded multiple challenges (e.g., redundant neighboring sentences (recall Figure 1) as well as too many sentences from the ends of the article were selected).

4.2 Multiple Views of Document Structure

Before creating a HipoRank document graph, the document must be split into sections and sentences. The scientific datasets previously used with HipoRank were already split (Dong et al., 2021). We investigate *the summarization impact of using different approaches to automatically compute linear sections of the document structure*. Figure 3 shows different structures for the same case.

Original Document Structure This approach extracts the structure by processing the *HTML files*. We use a heuristic to mark the section names with an italic and bold format as the boundaries and segment the documents into multiple continuous sections. It is worth noting that 297 of the 1049 test case documents do not come with explicit section splits, thus we treat them as whole text spans[4].

Topic Segment View Meanwhile, we also explore using a traditional, *domain-independent linear text segmentation* algorithm. We use C99 (Choi, 2000) but with advanced sentence representation from SBERT (Reimers and Gurevych, 2019) to group neighboring sentences into topic blocks.

Thematic Stage View Early studies found that legal documents tend to have well-defined, *domain-dependent thematic structures* (Farzindar and Lapalme, 2004) or rhetorical roles (Saravanan et al., 2008). Following work that extracts stage views in conversations (introductions $\rightarrow$ problem exploration $\rightarrow$ problem solving $\rightarrow$ wrap up) (Chen and Yang, 2020), we extract thematic stages through a Hidden Markov Model (HMM). A fixed order of stages is imposed and only consecutive transitions are allowed between neighboring stages. We again represent the sentences using SBERT (Reimers and Gurevych, 2019) and set the number of stages as 5, including the starting Decision Data, Introduction, Context, Judicial Analysis, and Conclusion, as introduced by Farzindar and Lapalme (2004).

CanLII Header Removing Preliminary analysis demonstrated that the raw CanLII documents fail to distinguish the less important headers at the beginning (i.e., the descriptive text before the main content, for example, the content above the grey splitting line and BASIS OF CLAIM in Figure 1). Generated summaries also tend to cover a large portion of such information. We thus propose a legal case decision preprocessing procedure following certain heuristics[5] to remove those headers, and demonstrate the improved summarization quality (for all views of document structure) in Section 6.

4.3 Reweighting the Centrality Score

The HipoRank document graph will not change once built, and the important sentences are greedily

[4]The Original Structure method processed HTML source files and split sentences using a legal sentence splitter (`https://github.com/jsavelka/luima_sbd`). The Topic and Thematic views used non-HTML data preprocessed by Xu et al. (2021), but used the same sentence splitter.

[5]See Appendix D.3 for details.

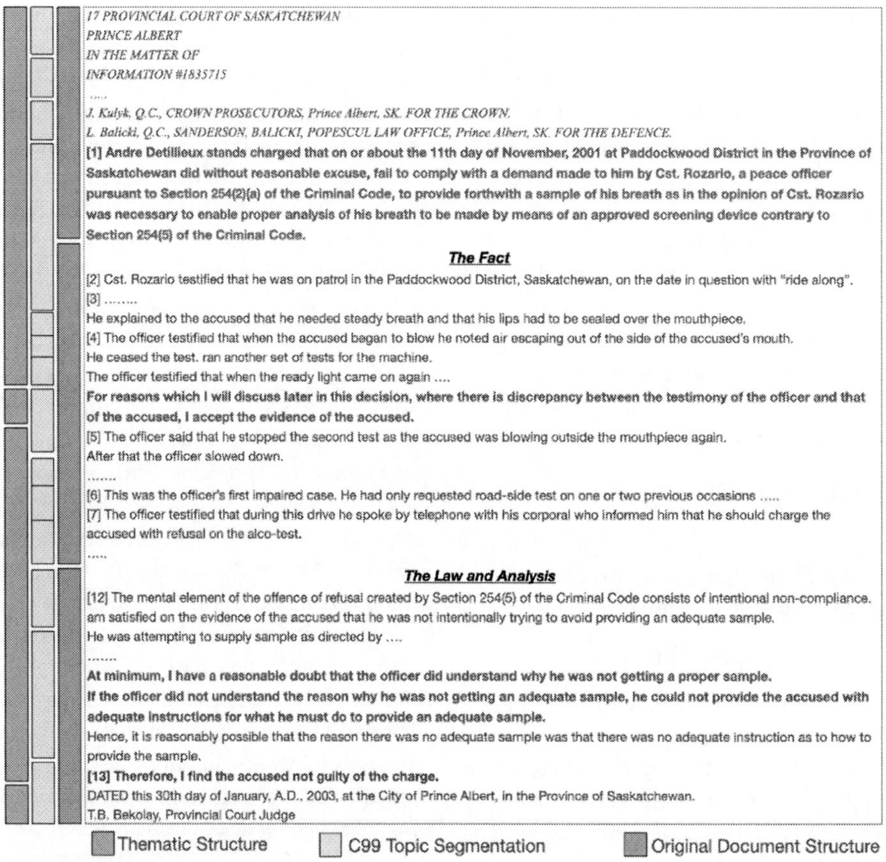

Figure 3: Different document structure views of a legal case decision (ID: c_2003skpc17) from our CANLLI test set. Original case sentences are annotated with Issue, Reason, and Conclusion labels. On the left side, the green, yellow and blue boxes refer to thematic stage, topic segmentation and the original document structure, respectively. The boxes mean the corresponding sentences on the right hand side are grouped into the same segments. For instance, for the first blue box, the original article is split by the italicized and bolded section name of "The Fact".

selected based on the aggregated centrality scores. This may introduce redundancies in selecting similar sentences and ignore the contents in the middle of the source case decisions that are more important once the argumentative sentences at the beginning and end are taken into account. We propose a novel reweighting approach that can tackle this problem. A prior attempt (Tao et al., 2021) on multi-round selection looked at the local similarity between selected sentences. They iteratively recompute the sentence to sentence similarities between the selected summary sentences and recompute the final sentence centrality scores after each sentence selection. Instead, we are focusing on modeling the relationship between the selected sentence and the other candidate sentences. Their method is also not directly applicable to longer text due to the n^2 time complexity of computation given large numbers of sentences (on average 205 sentences for CanLII dataset).

Our approach can be divided into two phases, as shown in Algorithm 1. In the first phase, we assume that important argumentative sentences at the two ends of the document can be easily detected (as shown in Figures 1 and 3, legal case documents generally start by introducing the issues and end with conclusions). A quantitative analysis of the top-5 selected sentences in CanLII in fact provides an 80% coverage of issue or conclusion sentences. We thus set up a threshold to pick the first k sentences based on the original document graphs. Afterward, we gradually downweight the sentence's centrality score using the location of the latest selected sentence, that is, we set a penalty score for sentences that are placed as a neighbor of the current sentence selected for the summary. Our

Algorithm 1 Reweighting Algorithm

Require: computed centrality score $c(s_i^I)$ for all sentence s, $c_{intra}(d)$ for different section d 's embedding, and a threshold g for phase transition and maximum summary length max_{len}.
$Summ \leftarrow []$
PHASE 1
while $len(Summ) \leq g * max_{len}$ **do**
$Summ.append(topK(\{c(s_i^I)\})$
end while

PHASE 2
while $len(Summ) \leq max_{len}$ **do**
$c(s_i^I) \leftarrow c(s_i^I) - sim(c_{intra}(I), c_{intra}(J)) * \mu_2$ ▷ J is the section index of last selected sentence, μ_2 is a hyperparameter
$Summ.append(top - 1(c(s_i^I)))$
end while
Return Summ

rationale is that reasoning sentences are more likely to be located in different sections in the middle that are not shared with issues and conclusions.

5 Experimental Setup

For supervised models, we split the training data in an 80:20 ratio for training and validation. For unsupervised models, we tune the hyperparameters on the validation set. Model training details can be found in Appendix B.

Upper Bound Oracles Based on Figure 2, we create a domain-dependent **IRC_Oracle** model where test sentences manually annotated with the IRC labels are concatenated to form the summary. Following Nallapati et al. (2017), we also report results for **EXT_Oracle**, a domain-independent summarizer which greedily selects sentences from the original document based on the ROUGE-L scores compared to the abstractive human summary.

Extractive Baselines For unsupervised models, we compare with LSA (Steinberger and Jezek, 2004), LexRank (Erkan and Radev, 2004), TextRank (Barrios et al., 2016), and PACSUM (Zheng and Lapata, 2019). We also include HipoRank (Dong et al., 2021) with document views. For supervised methods, we compare with BERT_EXT (Liu and Lapata, 2019). Although not our focus, abstractive baselines are in Appendix D.4.

Automic Evaluation Metrics We report ROUGE-1 (R-1), ROUGE-2 (R-2), and ROUGE-L (R-L) F1 scores, as well as BERTScore (BS) (Zhang et al., 2020c). We also propose metrics to measure the recall value of the annotated IRC types in the test set, which exploits the structure of case documents. More details are in Section 6.2.

6 Results

In this section, we aim to deal with three research questions: **RQ1**. How well do the extractive baselines including the HipoRank backbone deal with legal documents? **RQ2**. How well do the different views of document structures perform with the HipoRank backbone? **RQ3**. Can the reweighting algorithm help select important argumentative sentences and improve summary quality?

6.1 Automatic Summarization Evaluation

Table 2 compares our methods with prior extractive models. See Appendix D.1 for example summaries.

RQ1. Table 2 shows that there is still a gap between oracle models (rows 1 and 2) and current extractive baselines. There are around 20 points differences on R-1, R-2, and R-L. Among the baselines, the supervised model works best only for R-1 and R-L. Unsupervised methods obtain the highest BS (row 4) and R-2 (row 5), possibly due to the higher coverage of n-grams benefitting from longer extracted summaries (row 3 model generated summaries have an average length of 250; row 4-6 models generate on average 400-word summaries; row 7 and 8 models have a limit of 220 words). Without reweighting, the HipoRank backbone never outperforms the best extractive baseline. However, if only unsupervised baselines are considered, HipoRank in row 12 does show the best performance for 3 of the 4 evaluation metrics.

RQ2. To examine the effects of the document views in Section 4.2, we split the document into different types of linear segments and then used HipoRank to generate summaries. Recall that HipoRank is the only model to exploit document structure, and as noted for RQ1, with the right structure could obtain the best unsupervised R-1, R-L, and BS baseline scores. When naively constructing different document structures from the CanLII dataset without header removal, using NLP algorithms (rows 9 - 10) versus just using the HTML formatting (row 8) generally degraded results. However, when we experimented with a modified version of the input documents (rows 11-13) where the headers were filtered through heuristics before computing the

ID	Model	R-1	R-2	R-L	BS
	Oracles				
1	IRC	58.04	36.02	55.28	87.94
2	EXT (ROUGE-L, F1)	59.38	38.77	56.94	87.85
	Extractive baselines (no document structure)				
supervised					
3	BERT_EXT	*43.44*	17.84	*40.36*	84.47
unsupervised					
4	LSA	37.22	17.82	34.87	***<u>84.48</u>***
5	LexRank	37.90	*<u>18.17</u>*	35.62	84.32
6	TextRank	36.70	16.19	34.00	83.51
7	PACSUM	40.01	15.68	37.37	83.52
	HipoRank backbone (with different computed document structures)				
8	Original Structure	41.61	17.13	38.73	83.55
9	C99-topic	41.33	16.48	38.45	83.53
10	HMM-stage	40.71	15.64	37.93	83.57
11	Original Structure w/o header	42.58	18.01	39.63	83.62
12	C99-topic w/o header	<u>43.25</u>	18.02	<u>40.25</u>	***<u>84.48</u>***
13	HMM-stage w/o header	42.64	17.38	39.76	83.57
	Ours (HipoRank backbone + Reweighting Algorithm)				
14	Original Structure w/o header	43.14	18.46	40.23	84.20
15	C99-topic w/o header	**43.90**	**18.67**	**41.00**	84.34
16	HMM-stage w/o header	43.28	17.80	40.40	84.22

Table 2: The automatic evaluation results on the CanLII test set. **Bold** represents the best non-oracle score, *italic* the best baseline/backbone score, and <u>underline</u> the best unsupervised baseline/backbone score.

document structure, the scores in rows 11-13 were higher (or in one case the same) than the comparable scores in rows 8-10. Also, without headers, the C99 topic segmentation algorithm (row 12) now outperforms the use of HTML (row 11) (obtaining an average improvement of 0.5 points across ROUGE and 0.8 for BS), suggesting that better structures can improve summarization. As shown in Table 3 (and earlier in Figure 3), C99 creates many small sections (average number of sentences per section is 3.39 with standard deviation of 0.67). We hypothesize that this encourages the selection of sentences from more fine-grained segments. In contrast, the other two methods create lengthy sections (average of more than 50 sentences) with a large standard deviation (135.40 for original structure without headers). In sum, with improvements in automatic metrics, we find that document structures play an important role in summarizing cases.

Model	avg. # secs	avg. # sents per sec
with header		
Original Structure	4.83 (6.44)	83.82 (118.78)
C99-topic	63.47 (70.34)	3.38 (0.71)
HMM-stage	4.00(0.83)	54.32 (64.80)
without header		
Original Structure	3.67 (5.51)	102.99 (135.40)
C99-topic	59.74 (69.91)	3.39 (0.67)
HMM-stage	3.16 (1.08)	70.19 (119.39)

Table 3: Statistics about the average number of sections (avg. # secs) and average number of sentences per section (avg. # sents per sec) across the documents with different computed document structures (standard deviation in parenthesis).

RQ3. The final block of Table 2 presents the reweighting results (using the "w/o header" version of the CanLLI documents as they performed best in the prior block). By downweighting sentences that appear under the same section as previously selected ones, we observe an F1 improvement of 0.65, 0.65, and 0.75 on R-1, R-2, and R-L, respectively, on the previously best-performing topic segmented document (row 12 versus 15). Row 15 in fact has the best non-oracle results for all ROUGE scores. This observation regarding the value of reweighting also holds for the original structure (row 11 vs. 14) and the HMM-stage segments (row 13 vs. 16).

Finally, to better understand the behavior of different enhancements to the HipoRank backbone model, Figure 4 visualizes the positions of IRC sentences in the original article that are selected by a particular summarization method. Plot (a) shows that the human-annotated IRC sentences in the summary tend to span across the source documents, with issues appearing in the beginning and conclusions in the end. Plot (b) shows that although HipoRank using the original document structure can successfully pick middle section sentences, the darkest band at the starting positions shows that the model still heavily relies on the inductive bias to pick the beginning sentences. Plot (c) shows that removing the headers reduces the starting sentence bias. Finally, plot (d) shows that reweighting reduces the number of sentences appearing on both ends. Further analyses on the complete automatic evaluation results[6] suggest that the improvements come from higher recall values.

6.2 Argumentative Sentence Coverage

Taking advantage of the sentence-level IRC annotations, we propose recall metrics to better measure the summary quality from a legal argumentation perspective (**RQ3**). We compute the recall of "IRC" sentences extracted from the original case as source IRC coverage (src. IRC). We similarly compute the coverage of IRC sentences in the human-written summaries as target IRC coverage (tgt. IRC) and all sentences as target sentence coverage (trg. cov.). To do so we apply the oracle summarizer (Section 5) to map the generated extractive summaries to the human-written abstractive summaries.

We report these values for the IRC oracle, an unsupervised (LexRank) and supervised (BERT_EXT) baseline, the discourse-aware HipoRank with the original structure, and our best reweighting model using C99-topic segmentation. Table 4 shows that our model obtains the highest target IRC recall and coverage, suggesting that the summaries are more similar to the references with respect to the decision's argumentation. Another unsupervised model, LexRank, obtains the highest source IRC, but its off-the-shelf package requires a fixed sentence ratio selected from the source. This produced longer summaries than other approaches and thus captured more IRCs in the source.

Model	src. IRC	tgt. IRC	trg. cov.
Oracle			
IRC	1 (0.00)	0.918 (0.18)	0.820 (0.25)
Baselines			
BERT_EXT	0.804 (0.27)	0.846 (0.23)	0.833 (0.23)
LexRank	**0.912** (0.19)	0.811 (0.26)	0.800 (0.27)
HipoRank	0.800 (0.25)	0.851 (0.24)	0.844 (0.22)
Ours	0.823 (0.26)	**0.866** (0.20)	**0.850** (0.21)

Table 4: Average recall of IRC sentences matched in the original case (src. IRC), gold summary (tgt. IRC), as well as target sentences coverage (trg. cov.) for each document (standard deviation in parenthesis).

6.3 Human Evaluation Discussion

As a first step towards human evaluation, we tried to extend the HipoRank setup in Dong et al. (2021) and designed a human evaluation protocol as follows. We asked human judges[7] to read the human-written reference summary and presented extracted sentences from different summarization systems. The judges were asked to evaluate a system-extracted sentence according to two criteria: (1) *Content Coverage* - whether the presented sentence contained content from the human summary, and (2) *Importance* - whether the presented sentence was important for a goal-oriented reader even if it was not in the human summary[8]. The sentence selection was anonymized and randomly shuffled. We used the same sampling strategy in Dong et al. (2021) to pick ten reference summaries where the system outputs were neutral (i.e., had similar R-2 scores compared to the human reference). However, initial annotation on a small set by a legal expert demonstrated that the selected sentences may not reflect the model's capability. Most sampled system outputs had low ROUGE-2 F1 scores compared to the reference (normally below 10% while the average model performance is 17%), and the human evaluator reported that some

[6] See Appendix C for ROUGE precision and recall.

[7] All judges should be native English speakers who are at least pursuing a JD degree in law school and have experience in understanding case law.

[8] Here we assumed the goal-oriented reader as the lawyers or law students seeking information from the case.

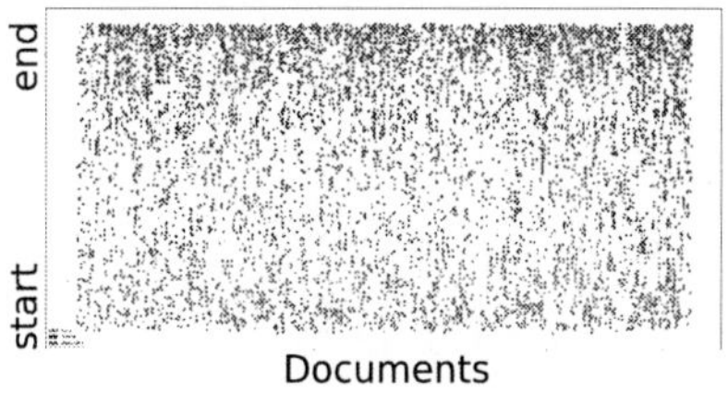

(a) IRC Oracles

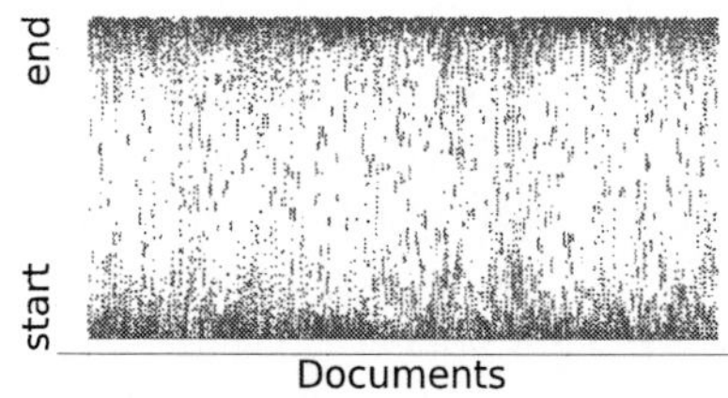

(b) HipoRank with headers

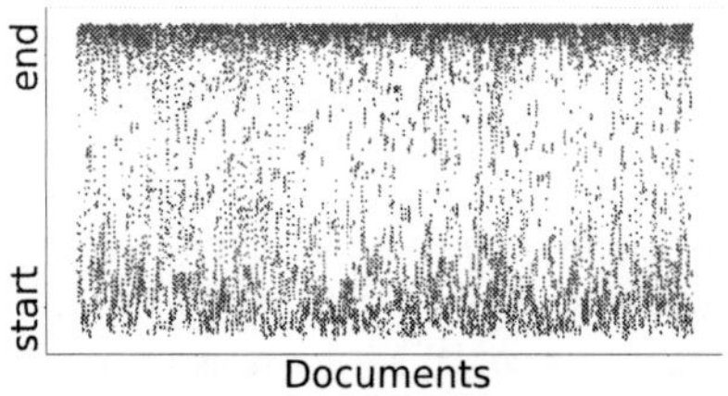

(c) HipoRank without headers

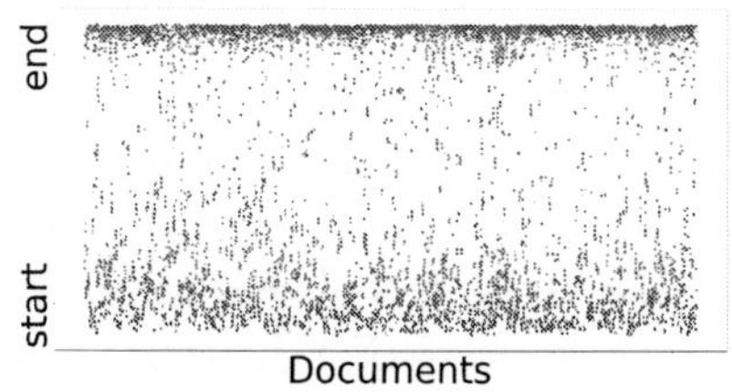

(d) HipoRank without headers and with reweighting

Figure 4: Sentence positions in source cases for extractive summaries generated by different models using the original document structure on the test set. For (b) (c) (d), documents on the x-axis are sorted in the same order. For IRC Oracles, Issue, Reasoning and Conclusion sentences are colored accordingly.

of the selected sentences were not meaningful. We thus propose that a more careful sampling technique will be required for legal annotation tasks such as ours.

To further guide our future work, we also reviewed how prior legal domain research has performed human evaluations when automatically summarizing legal documents (Polsley et al., 2016; Zhong et al., 2019; Salaün et al., 2022). Due to the burden of reading lengthy original documents, as in our human evaluation, most prior work evaluated summary quality using reference summaries rather than source documents. In addition, legal evaluations have typically been small-scale (5-20 summaries) due to the need to have evaluators with particular types of expertise (e.g., law graduate students or law professors), which was a similar constraint in our exploratory human evaluation. Researchers have also designed new types of legally-relevant evaluation questions that evaluate the summary for task-specific properties that go beyond more typical properties such as grammar, readability, and style. In our case, we would like legal experts to assess IRC coverage in the future.

7 Conclusion

We presented an unsupervised graph-based model for the summarization of long legal case decisions. Our proposed approach incorporated diverse views of the document structure of legal cases and utilized a reweighting scheme to better select argumentative sentences. Our exploration of document structure demonstrates how using different types of document structure impacts summarization performance. Moreover, a document structure inspired reweighting scheme yields performance gain on the CanLII case dataset.

Ethical Considerations

The utilization of the generated summary results of legal documents remains important. Current extractive methods avoid the problem of generating hallucinated information (Kryscinski et al., 2020; Maynez et al., 2020), which has been observed in abstractive methods that use large-scale pre-trained language models. The extracted sentences, however, may not capture the important contents of the legal documents. Meanwhile, CanLII has taken measures to limit the disclosure of defendants' identities (such as blocking search indexing). Thus, using the dataset may need to be taken good care of and avoid impacting those efforts.

Acknowledgement

We thank the Pitt AI Fairness and Law group, the Pitt PETAL group, and the anonymous reviewers for their valuable feedback. This research is supported by the National Science Foundation under Grant IIS-2040490 and a gift from Amazon.

Limitations

The dataset we used has a relatively small scale (1K) test set. Meanwhile, the automatic evaluation metrics may fall short compared to human evaluations, thus unfaithfully representing the final quality of generated summaries. Although lightweight, there is still a large performance gap between our unsupervised method and both the extractive oracles as well as abstractive models (Appendix D.4), especially given the small-scale training data. There are more graph-based methods to aggregate information from the built graphs and we would like to explore and include more graph-based methods but selected the most relevant one in this work. Moreover, our proposed reweighting paradigm heavily relied on observations about the structure of legal cases. Many other legal document types, such as bills and statutes, have inherently distinct structures. Our results also show the importance of finding the correct structure and weights, which can vary depending on the corpus. This will require more advanced methods to find the correct structure and weights for a dataset.

References

Federico Barrios, Federico López, Luis Argerich, and Rosa Wachenchauzer. 2016. Variations of the similarity function of textrank for automated summarization. *CoRR*, abs/1602.03606.

P. B. Baxendale. 1958. Machine-made index for technical literature—an experiment. *IBM Journal of Research and Development*, 2(4):354–361.

Iz Beltagy, Matthew E. Peters, and Arman Cohan. 2020. Longformer: The long-document transformer. *arXiv:2004.05150*.

Paheli Bhattacharya, Kaustubh Hiware, Subham Rajgaria, Nilay Pochhi, Kripabandhu Ghosh, and Saptarshi Ghosh. 2019. A comparative study of summarization algorithms applied to legal case judgments. In *Advances in Information Retrieval*, pages 413–428, Cham. Springer International Publishing.

Paheli Bhattacharya, Soham Poddar, Koustav Rudra, Kripabandhu Ghosh, and Saptarshi Ghosh. 2021. Incorporating domain knowledge for extractive summarization of legal case documents. In *Proceedings of the Eighteenth International Conference on Artificial Intelligence and Law*, pages 22–31.

Ilias Chalkidis, Manos Fergadiotis, Prodromos Malakasiotis, Nikolaos Aletras, and Ion Androutsopoulos. 2020. LEGAL-BERT: The muppets straight out of law school. In *Findings of the Association for Computational Linguistics: EMNLP 2020*, pages 2898–2904, Online. Association for Computational Linguistics.

Jiaao Chen and Diyi Yang. 2020. Multi-view sequence-to-sequence models with conversational structure for abstractive dialogue summarization. In *Proceedings of the 2020 Conference on Empirical Methods in Natural Language Processing (EMNLP)*, pages 4106–4118, Online. Association for Computational Linguistics.

Freddy Y. Y. Choi. 2000. Advances in domain independent linear text segmentation. In *1st Meeting of the North American Chapter of the Association for Computational Linguistics*.

Arman Cohan, Franck Dernoncourt, Doo Soon Kim, Trung Bui, Seokhwan Kim, Walter Chang, and Nazli Goharian. 2018. A discourse-aware attention model for abstractive summarization of long documents. In *Proceedings of the 2018 Conference of the North American Chapter of the Association for Computational Linguistics: Human Language Technologies, Volume 2 (Short Papers)*, pages 615–621, New Orleans, Louisiana. Association for Computational Linguistics.

Jacob Devlin, Ming-Wei Chang, Kenton Lee, and Kristina Toutanova. 2019. BERT: Pre-training of deep bidirectional transformers for language understanding. In *Proceedings of the 2019 Conference of the North American Chapter of the Association for Computational Linguistics: Human Language Technologies*, pages 4171–4186.

Yue Dong, Andrei Mircea, and Jackie Chi Kit Cheung. 2021. Discourse-aware unsupervised summarization for long scientific documents. In *Proceedings of the 16th Conference of the European Chapter of the Association for Computational Linguistics: Main Volume*, pages 1089–1102, Online. Association for Computational Linguistics.

Mohamed Elaraby and Diane Litman. 2022. ArgLegalSumm: Improving abstractive summarization of legal documents with argument mining. In *Proceedings of the 29th International Conference on Computational Linguistics*, pages 6187–6194, Gyeongju, Republic of Korea. International Committee on Computational Linguistics.

Günes Erkan and Dragomir R Radev. 2004. Lexrank: Graph-based lexical centrality as salience in text summarization. *Journal of artificial intelligence research*, 22:457–479.

Atefeh Farzindar and Guy Lapalme. 2004. Legal text summarization by exploration of the thematic structure and argumentative roles. In *Text Summarization Branches Out*, pages 27–34, Barcelona, Spain. Association for Computational Linguistics.

Tsutomu Hirao, Yasuhisa Yoshida, Masaaki Nishino, Norihito Yasuda, and Masaaki Nagata. 2013. Single-document summarization as a tree knapsack problem. In *Proceedings of the 2013 Conference on Empirical Methods in Natural Language Processing*, pages 1515–1520, Seattle, Washington, USA. Association for Computational Linguistics.

Anastassia Kornilova and Vladimir Eidelman. 2019. BillSum: A corpus for automatic summarization of US legislation. In *Proceedings of the 2nd Workshop on New Frontiers in Summarization*, pages 48–56, Hong Kong, China. Association for Computational Linguistics.

Wojciech Kryscinski, Nitish Shirish Keskar, Bryan McCann, Caiming Xiong, and Richard Socher. 2019. Neural text summarization: A critical evaluation. In *Proceedings of the 2019 Conference on Empirical Methods in Natural Language Processing and the 9th International Joint Conference on Natural Language Processing (EMNLP-IJCNLP)*, pages 540–551, Hong Kong, China. Association for Computational Linguistics.

Wojciech Kryscinski, Bryan McCann, Caiming Xiong, and Richard Socher. 2020. Evaluating the factual consistency of abstractive text summarization. In *Proceedings of the 2020 Conference on Empirical Methods in Natural Language Processing (EMNLP)*, pages 9332–9346, Online. Association for Computational Linguistics.

Mike Lewis, Yinhan Liu, Naman Goyal, Marjan Ghazvininejad, Abdelrahman Mohamed, Omer Levy, Veselin Stoyanov, and Luke Zettlemoyer. 2020. BART: Denoising sequence-to-sequence pre-training for natural language generation, translation, and comprehension. In *Proceedings of the 58th Annual Meeting of the Association for Computational Linguistics*, pages 7871–7880.

Yang Liu and Mirella Lapata. 2019. Text summarization with pretrained encoders. In *Proceedings of the 2019 Conference on Empirical Methods in Natural Language Processing and the 9th International Joint Conference on Natural Language Processing (EMNLP-IJCNLP)*, pages 3730–3740, Hong Kong, China. Association for Computational Linguistics.

H. P. Luhn. 1958. The automatic creation of literature abstracts. *IBM Journal of Research and Development*, 2(2):159–165.

Vijit Malik, Rishabh Sanjay, Shouvik Kumar Guha, Shubham Kumar Nigam, Angshuman Hazarika, Arnab Bhattacharya, and Ashutosh Modi. 2022. Semantic segmentation of legal documents via rhetorical roles. *AAAI*.

Joshua Maynez, Shashi Narayan, Bernd Bohnet, and Ryan McDonald. 2020. On faithfulness and factuality in abstractive summarization. In *Proceedings of the 58th Annual Meeting of the Association for Computational Linguistics*, pages 1906–1919, Online. Association for Computational Linguistics.

Ramesh Nallapati, Feifei Zhai, and Bowen Zhou. 2017. Summarunner: A recurrent neural network based sequence model for extractive summarization of documents. In *Thirty-First AAAI Conference on Artificial Intelligence*.

Ramesh Nallapati, Bowen Zhou, Cicero dos Santos, Çağlar Gulçehre, and Bing Xiang. 2016. Abstractive text summarization using sequence-to-sequence RNNs and beyond. In *Proceedings of The 20th SIGNLL Conference on Computational Natural Language Learning*, pages 280–290, Berlin, Germany. Association for Computational Linguistics.

Ani Nenkova and Kathleen McKeown. 2011. Automatic summarization. *Foundations and Trends® in Information Retrieval*, 5(2–3):103–233.

Ani Nenkova, Lucy Vanderwende, and Lucy Vanderwende. 2005. The impact of frequency on summarization.

Seth Polsley, Pooja Jhunjhunwala, and Ruihong Huang. 2016. CaseSummarizer: A system for automated summarization of legal texts. In *Proceedings of COLING 2016, the 26th International Conference on Computational Linguistics: System Demonstrations*, pages 258–262, Osaka, Japan. The COLING 2016 Organizing Committee.

Dragomir R. Radev, Hongyan Jing, and Malgorzata Budzikowska. 2000. Centroid-based summarization of multiple documents: sentence extraction, utility-based evaluation, and user studies. In *NAACL-ANLP 2000 Workshop: Automatic Summarization*.

Nils Reimers and Iryna Gurevych. 2019. Sentence-BERT: Sentence embeddings using Siamese BERT-networks. In *Proceedings of the 2019 Conference on Empirical Methods in Natural Language Processing and the 9th International Joint Conference on Natural Language Processing (EMNLP-IJCNLP)*, pages 3982–3992, Hong Kong, China. Association for Computational Linguistics.

Qian Ruan, Malte Ostendorff, and Georg Rehm. 2022. HiStruct+: Improving extractive text summarization with hierarchical structure information. In *Findings of the Association for Computational Linguistics: ACL 2022*, pages 1292–1308, Dublin, Ireland. Association for Computational Linguistics.

Alexander M. Rush, Sumit Chopra, and Jason Weston. 2015. A neural attention model for abstractive sentence summarization. In *Proceedings of the 2015 Conference on Empirical Methods in Natural Language Processing*, pages 379–389, Lisbon, Portugal. Association for Computational Linguistics.

Olivier Salaün, Aurore Troussel, Sylvain Longhais, Hannes Westermann, Philippe Langlais, and Karim Benyekhlef. 2022. Conditional abstractive summarization of court decisions for laymen and insights from human evaluation. In *35th International Conference on Legal Knowledge and Information System.*

Gerard Salton, Amit Singhal, Mandar Mitra, and Chris Buckley. 1997. Automatic text structuring and summarization. *Information Processing Management*, 33(2):193–207. Methods and Tools for the Automatic Construction of Hypertext.

M. Saravanan, B. Ravindran, and S. Raman. 2006. Improving legal document summarization using graphical models. In *Proceedings of the 2006 Conference on Legal Knowledge and Information Systems: JURIX 2006: The Nineteenth Annual Conference*, page 51–60. IOS Press.

M. Saravanan, B. Ravindran, and S. Raman. 2008. Automatic identification of rhetorical roles using conditional random fields for legal document summarization. In *Proceedings of the Third International Joint Conference on Natural Language Processing: Volume-I.*

Josef Steinberger and Karel Jezek. 2004. Using latent semantic analysis in text summarization and summary evaluation. volume 4, pages 93–100. ISIM.

Dehao Tao, Yingzhu Xiong, Jin He, Yongfeng Huang, et al. 2021. An unsupervised extractive summarization method based on multi-round computation. *arXiv preprint arXiv:2112.03203.*

Simone Teufel. 1997. Sentence extraction as a classification task. In *Intelligent Scalable Text Summarization.*

Huihui Xu, Jaromir Savelka, and Kevin Ashley. 2021. Accounting for sentence position and legal domain sentence embedding in learning to classify case sentences. In *Legal Knowledge and Information System.*

Jiacheng Xu, Zhe Gan, Yu Cheng, and Jingjing Liu. 2020. Discourse-aware neural extractive text summarization. In *Proceedings of the 58th Annual Meeting of the Association for Computational Linguistics*, pages 5021–5031, Online. Association for Computational Linguistics.

Wenpeng Yin and Yulong Pei. 2015. Optimizing sentence modeling and selection for document summarization. In *Proceedings of the 24th International Conference on Artificial Intelligence*, IJCAI'15, page 1383–1389. AAAI Press.

Manzil Zaheer, Guru Guruganesh, Kumar Avinava Dubey, Joshua Ainslie, Chris Alberti, Santiago Ontanon, Philip Pham, Anirudh Ravula, Qifan Wang, Li Yang, et al. 2020. Big bird: Transformers for longer sequences. *Advances in Neural Information Processing Systems*, 33.

Haopeng Zhang, Xiao Liu, and Jiawei Zhang. 2020a. Hegel: Hypergraph transformer for long document summarization. In *Proceedings of the 2022 Conference on Empirical Methods in Natural Language Processing (EMNLP).*

Jingqing Zhang, Yao Zhao, Mohammad Saleh, and Peter Liu. 2020b. Pegasus: Pre-training with extracted gap-sentences for abstractive summarization. In *International Conference on Machine Learning*, pages 11328–11339. PMLR.

Tianyi Zhang, Varsha Kishore*, Felix Wu*, Kilian Q. Weinberger, and Yoav Artzi. 2020c. Bertscore: Evaluating text generation with bert. In *International Conference on Learning Representations.*

Hao Zheng and Mirella Lapata. 2019. Sentence centrality revisited for unsupervised summarization. In *Proceedings of the 57th Annual Meeting of the Association for Computational Linguistics*, pages 6236–6247, Florence, Italy. Association for Computational Linguistics.

Linwu Zhong, Ziyi Zhong, Zinian Zhao, Siyuan Wang, Kevin D. Ashley, and Matthias Grabmair. 2019. Automatic summarization of legal decisions using iterative masking of predictive sentences. In *Proceedings of the Seventeenth International Conference on Artificial Intelligence and Law*, ICAIL '19, page 163–172, New York, NY, USA. Association for Computing Machinery.

A The HipoRank Algorithm

In this section, we provide a detailed recap of the HipoRank algorithm (Dong et al., 2021). Our approach mainly modifies the obtained document graphs by building a *section-section* graph and changes the final summary selection algorithms.

A.1 Hierarchical Document Graph Creation

The document is first split into its sections, then into sentences. Two levels of connections are allowed in the built hierarchical graph: intra-sectional connections and inter-sectional connections. Following the original paper, we display a toy example of these two types of connections in Figure 5.

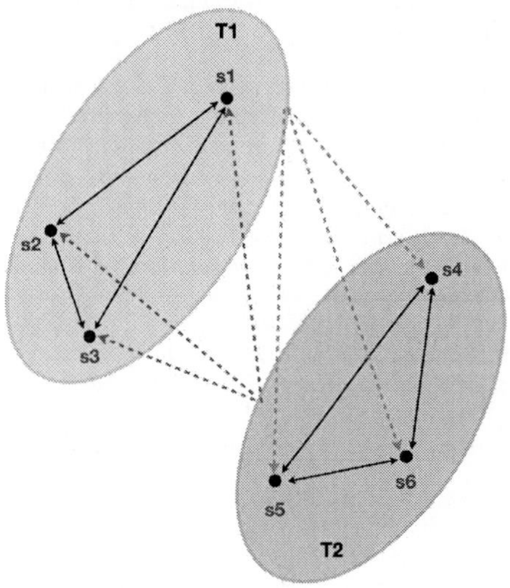

Figure 5: (Reproduced from (Dong et al., 2021)) An example of a hierarchical document graph constructed by HipoRank approach on a toy document, which contains two sections {T1, T2}, each containing three sentences for a total of six sentences {s1, . . . , s6}. In the graph, each double-headed arrow represents two edges with opposite directions. The solid and dashed arrows indicate intra-section and inter-section connections respectively.

Intra-sectional connections are designed to measure a sentence's importance score inside its section. The authors built a fully-connected subgraph over all sentences in the same section, allowing for *sentence-sentence* edges, which are measured by a weighted version of the similarities of sentence embeddings.

Inter-sectional connections "aim to model the global importance of a sentence with respect to other topics/sections in the document", according to Dong et al. (2021). To reduce the expensive computation of all sentence-sentence connections spanning across a document, HipoRank's authors introduce section nodes on top of sentence nodes, and only allow for *sentence-section* edges to model the global information.

A.2 Asymmetric Edge Weighting by Boundary Functions

In order to compute the weight of an edge, HipoRank measures the similarity of sentence-sentence pairs by computing the cosine similarity of encoded sentence embeddings. Similarly, for sentence-section pairs, it averages the sentences' representations in the same section, uses it as the section vector, and further computes the cosine similarity. Taking two discourse hypotheses of long scientific documents into account ((1) important sentences are near the boundaries (start or end) of a text (Baxendale, 1958) and (2) sections near the text boundaries (start or end) are more important (Teufel, 1997)), the authors of HipoRank capture this asymmetry by making their hierarchical graph directed and inject asymmetric edge weighting over intra-section and inter-section connections. We refer to the original paper for more detailed setups and algorithm details.

A.3 Importance Computation and Summary Generation

We talk about the importance computation approach and summary generation details in §4.1.

B Training Details and Hyperparameters

All of our experiments are conducted on Quadro RTX 5000 GPUs, each of which has 16 GB RAM. For the extractive oracle baseline, we use the python package of rouge[9] to compute the ROUGE-L scores for sentence scoring.

Document Segmentation We provide details of segmentation methods mentioned in §4.2 below. For sentence encoding, we use the sentence_transformer library[10], and the checkpoint of "bert-base-nli-stsb-mean-tokens" for sentence representations. For the HMM stage segmentation, we train a GaussianHMM model

[9] `https://pypi.org/project/rouge/`

[10] `https://www.sbert.net/`

with hmmlearn[11], setting the number of the components at 5 and train the model for 50 iterations on the validation set. For C99 algorithm, we use an implementation[12] shared from Chen and Yang (2020) in their original paper. We set the window size of 4 and std_coefficient as 1. All data processing scripts are publicly available in a combined package in https://github.com/cs329yangzhong/DocumentStructureLegalSum.

Supervised Model We build our BERT_EXT, the extractive model, on top of the official code base of the work of Liu and Lapata (2019)[13]. Since many original documents' lengths go beyond the 512 token limits, we break the full document into different chunks and train the model to extract the top-3 sentences. For hyperparameters, we use 4 GPUs, set the learning rate of 2e-3, and save the best checkpoints at every 5,000 steps. We set the batch size as 3,000, the maximum training step at 100,000, and warm-up steps at 10,000.

Unsupervised Models We use off-the-shelf packages for most traditional models. We use LSA[14], TextRank[15], and LexRank[16] accordingly.

For PACSUM model, we follow the re-implementation[17] of (Dong et al., 2021) and keep the hyperparameters fixed with the original setup. BERT-based sentence embeddings are extracted using the fine-tuned BERT model released from the original paper (Zheng and Lapata, 2019). We also experimented with LEGAL-BERT (Chalkidis et al., 2020) in the early stages of our research but found it degraded performance on the baselines.

For HipoRank, we use the publicly available code base[18]. We experimented with various hyperparameter settings on the validation set but we find that the original hyperparamters used in the original paper for PubMed dataset seem to be the most stable and produce the best results. ($\lambda_1 = 0.0$, $\lambda_2 = 1.0$, $\alpha = 1.0$, with $\mu_1 = 0.5$.)

[11] https://hmmlearn.readthedocs.io/en/latest/

[12] https://github.com/GT-SALT/Multi-View-Seq2Seq/blob/master/data/C99.py

[13] https://github.com/nlpyang/PreSumm

[14] https://github.com/luisfredgs/LSA-Text-Summarization

[15] https://github.com/summanlp/textrank

[16] https://github.com/crabcamp/lexrank

[17] https://github.com/mirandrom/HipoRank

[18] https://github.com/mirandrom/HipoRank

We build our reweighting model on top of the HipoRank dataset. We search the threshold g (for phase transition between phases 1 and 2) between [0.3, 0.5, and 0.7], finding that 0.5 is the best for the CanLII dataset.

C The Effects of Reweighting Algorithm

We study the effects of our reweighting algorithm by comparing different models' performances on the input documents with original structures. As shown in Table 5, with a minor sacrifice of precision, the recall values are greatly improved with the reweighting algorithm, thus resulting in the final improvements of F1 scores.

D Examples

D.1 Summary Generation Results

We show the reference, best baseline, and our model's output on the C99-topic view of the without header version of documents in Table 6.

D.2 IRC Annotation

We show the IRC annotation of both a case and its human summary in Figure 6.

D.3 Document Cleaning Heuristics

The heuristics for filtering the headers from cases are provided below for replication purposes; we also provide the code[19] to process the CanLII data (although it requires that the data must first be obtained through an agreement with the Canadian Legal Information Institute).

1. Cut the document until the sentence begins with "Introduction".
2. Cut the document until the sentence starts with an ordered number such as (1), [1].
3. Remove rows until the judge's name or case date appeared.

D.4 Comparing to Abstractive Summarization

For supervised abstractive baselines, we experiment with BART (Lewis et al., 2020) and Longformer-Encoder-Decoder (LED) (Beltagy et al., 2020). The latter model can process longer input documents up to 16k tokens. The results in Table 7 show that there still exists a gap between the extractive and abstractive models.

[19] https://github.com/cs329yangzhong/DocumentStructureLegalSum

Document Structures	ROUGE-1			ROUGE-2			ROUGE-L		
	P	R	F1	P	R	F1	P	R	F1
w/o header	45.24	47.39	42.58	19.23	20.12	18.01	42.25	43.95	39.63
w/o header + Reweighting	44.13	49.80	43.14	18.97	21.35	18.46	41.29	46.26	40.23

Table 5: The Precision (P), Recall (R) and F1 of ROUGE-1/2/L scores for the inputs with original document structures, with and without reweighting algorithm. We find that the reweighting algorithm improves the recall, suggesting that more argumentative sentences in the references are covered.

Model	Summary
Reference	FIAT: The defendants, Sims, Garbriel and Dumurs, bring separate motions, pursuant to Queen's Bench Rule 41(a), for severance of the claims against them or for an order staying the claims against them until the plaintiffs' claim against the primary defendant, Walbaum have been heard and decided. ǁ HELD: 1) ǁ The Court will look at all of the circumstances in deciding whether to grant an application for severance. ǁ In this case the plaintiffs should not be precluded from adducing evidence related to Walbaum's dealings with each of the applicants or required to segregate the evidence into two, three or four separate trials. ǁ Given the likelihood that the applicants will be required to attend portions of the trial in respect of the Walbaum Group in any event, severance would not necessarily result in a significant saving of time and expense. ǁ 2) The plain- -tiffs acknowledge that only relatively small portion of trial time (perhaps less than 1 day) will pertain to the claims against any one of the Sims, Gabriel or Dumurs. ǁ It wou- -ld be unfair to require all of the applicants to participate in all of the trial when very little of it will be relevant to them. ǁ Specific dates and times should be set aside for the plaintiff to call evidence with respect to its claims against each applicant group. ǁ The applicants should be relieved from attending the trial at any other time.
HipoRank	QUEEN'S BENCH FOR SASKATCHEWAN ǁ 2007 SKQB 296 ǁ Judicial Centre: Regina ǁ DUN-RITE PLUMBING & HEATING LTD. ǁ (d) Robert Dumur ǁ 593340 Saskatchewan Ltd., carrying on ǁ business as Dumur Industries (herein "the Dumurs") ǁ [2] The Sims, Gab- -riel and the Dumurs bring separate motions, pursuant to Queen's Bench Rule 41(a) for severance of the claims against them or for orders staying the claims until the plaintiffs' claims against the Walbaum Group have been heard and decided. ǁ ANALYSIS ǁ [12] T applications are brought pursuant to Queen's Bench Rule 41 which states: ǁ 41 (1) Where the joinder of multiple claims or parties in the same action may unduly complicate or delay the trial, or cause undue prejudice to a party, the court may: ǁ (a) order separate trials; ǁ [21] It will also be left to the trial judge (or the pre-trial management judge) to designate specific days on which defence evidence may be adduced during the trial and argument presented with respect to each claim. ǁ All defendants other than those comprising the Walbaum Group shall be relieved from attending the trial on any date not designated by counsel for the plaintiffs or designated by the trial judge for adducing defence evidence and presenting argument. ǁ [22] Costs will be in the cause. ǁ D.P. Ball
Ours	FIAT BALL J. ǁ August 14, 2007 ǁ [1] The plaintiff brings this action against nine defendants (the claim against the defendant Albert Fazakas has been discontinued) who can be separated into four groups: ǁ All-Rite Plumbing Heating Ltd. ǁ [18] Although choeunsel for the plaintiffs asserts that the evidence against all of the defendants can be adduced in no more than two and one-half days, given the number and complexity of the claims against the Walbaum Group this estimate seems very unrealistic. ǁ [19] The plaintiffs acknowledge that only relatively small portion of trial time (perhaps less than one day) will pertain to the claims against any one of the Sims, Gabriel or the Dumurs. ǁ It would be unfair to require all of the applicants to participate in all of the trial when very little of it will be relevant to them. ǁ The applicants should be relieved from attending the trial at any other time. ǁ The plaintiffs shall not call evidence in respect of those claims on any other date without leave of the court. ǁ All defendants other than those comprising the Walbaum Group shall be relieved from attending the trial on any date not designated by counsel for the plaintiffs or designated by the trial judge for adducing defence evidence and presenting argument.

Table 6: Generated summaries for a CanLII case decision (ID: 2_2007skqb296), we use special symbol "ǁ" to mark the sentence boundaries.

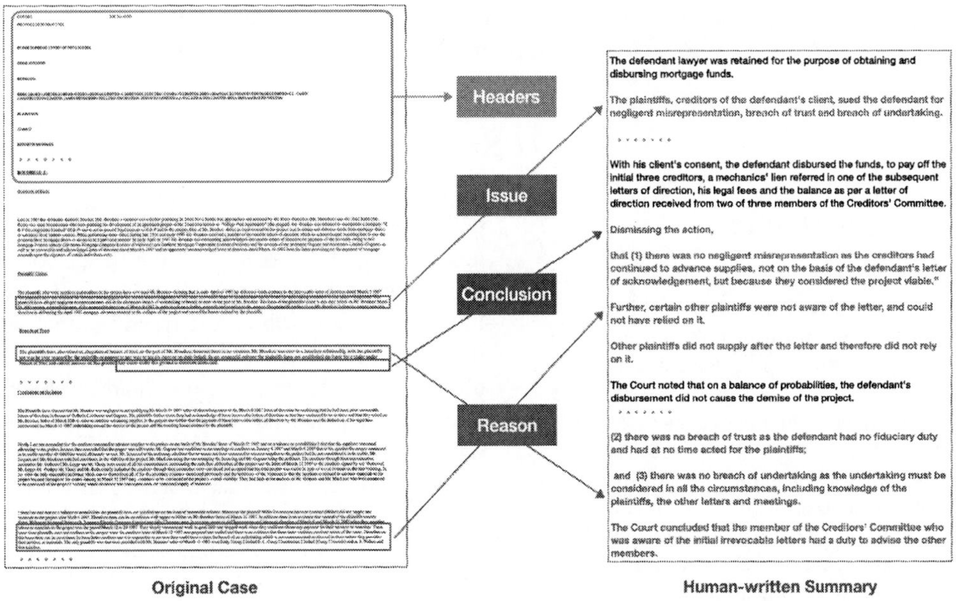

Figure 6: An example of the annotated Issue, Reason, and Conclusion sentences in CanLII dataset's case and summary pair (ID: 1991canlii4370). A portion of the beginning sentences in the case are not as important as the main document, including the meta-data of the case such as the participants' names, time, locations, etc. Thus, we treated them as headers and filtered them out using a heuristic introduced in Appendix D.3.

ID	Model	CanLII R1/R2/RL	CanLII BS
	Oracles		
1	IRC	58.04/36.02/55.28	87.94
2	EXT	59.38/38.77/56.94	87.85
	Supervised Extractive		
3	BERT_extractor	43.44/17.84/40.36	84.47
	Supervised Abtractive		
4	BART	50.50/25.58/46.82	87.25
5	LED	53.72/28.75/ 50.17	87.55

Table 7: The automatic evaluation results on the CanLII test set with supervised abstractive models.

AraLegal-BERT: A pretrained language model for Arabic Legal text

Muhammad AL-Qurishi, Sarah AlQaseemi and **Riad Soussi**
Elm Company, Research Department, Riyadh 12382, Saudi Arabia

Abstract

The effectiveness of the bidirectional encoder representations from transformers (BERT) model for multiple linguistic tasks is well documented. However, its potential for a narrow and specific domain, such as legal, has not been fully explored. In this study, we examine the use of BERT in the Arabic legal domain and customize this language model for several downstream tasks using different domain-relevant training and test datasets to train BERT from scratch. We introduce AraLegal-BERT, a bidirectional encoder transformer-based model that has been thoroughly tested and carefully optimized with the goal of amplifying the impact of natural language processing-driven solutions on jurisprudence, legal documents, and legal practice. We fine-tuned AraLegal-BERT and evaluated it against three BERT variants for the Arabic language in three natural language understanding tasks. The results showed that the base version of AraLegal-BERT achieved better accuracy than the typical and original BERT model concerning legal texts.

1 Introduction

The impressive performance of bidirectional encoder representations from transformers (BERT) (Devlin et al., 2018) inspired numerous authors to try and improve the original BERT. Such follow-up research progresses in several directions, including the development of specific solutions for various thematic domains. This is necessary because the vocabulary used in some fields significantly differs from the language used for everyday purposes and may contain the specific meanings of certain phrases or atypical relationships between contextual elements. This problem can be partially resolved through domain-specific adjustments to the training process. A good example of this approach is demonstrated in (Chalkidis et al., 2020), who created Legal-BERT specifically for mining legal text in English, improving the output of the standard transformer algorithm in this domain. Another form of the BERT concept was successfully adapted by (Beltagy et al., 2019; Lee et al., 2020), who created models that were pretrained on a compilation of scientific and biomedical data from various fields, achieving significantly better performance on scientifically related natural language processing (NLP) tasks. These examples show that BERT is currently far from a finished model and that its effectiveness could be further enhanced, at least for relatively narrowly defined tasks.

For the Arabic language, several BERT-based models have consistently demonstrated superior performance on numerous linguistic tasks requiring semantic understanding, outperforming all benchmarks on public datasets such as the Arabic NER corpus (ANERcorp) or the Arabic Reading Comprehension Dataset (ARCD), such as the works presented by (Antoun et al., 2020; Abdul-Mageed et al., 2020) and mBERT by Google (Devlin et al., 2018). This is largely a consequence of the efficient transfer learning inherent in this model, involving a high computational cost because this approach requires huge collections of training examples, followed by fine-tuning for specific downstream tasks. A significant advantage of BERT is that the training phase can be skipped because a pretrained version of the model can be used and trained further. However, (Chalkidis et al., 2020; Beltagy et al., 2019; Lee et al., 2020) has shown that a generic approach to pretraining does not work well when BERT must be used in a domain with highly specific terminology, such as legal, science, or medicine. There are two possible responses to this issue: continue specializing in a pretrained model or train a model from scratch with relevant materials from the domain. In this study, we built a language model from scratch based on the original BERT (Devlin et al., 2018), which is specific to Arabic legal texts. The aim was to improve the performance on most state-

Proceedings of the Natural Legal Language Processing Workshop 2022, pages 338 - 344
December 8, 2022

of-the-art language understanding and processing tasks, especially related to Arabic legal texts. We believe that the specific nature of legal documents and terminology needs to be considered because it affects the way sentences and paragraphs are constructed in this field. The extent of formal and semantic differences is such that some authors describe the linguistic content used for legal matters as almost a language of its own (Zhang et al., 2022; Silveira et al., 2021).

By focusing on a single domain, the Arabic legal text, this study attempts to reveal means of adapting an NLP model to fit any thematic domain. Based on our experiments, we can confirm that pretraining BERT with examples from the Arabic legal domain from scratch provides a better foundation for working with documents containing Arabic legal vocabulary than using the vanilla version of the algorithm. We introduce AraLegal-BERT, a transformer-based model that has been thoroughly tested and carefully optimized with the goal of amplifying the impact of NLP-driven solutions on jurisprudence, legal documents, and legal practice. We fine-tuned AraLegal-BERT and evaluated it against three BERT variants for Arabic in three natural language understanding (NLU) tasks. The results show that the base version of AraLegal-BERT achieved better accuracy than the general and original version of the BERT model, in regard to legal text. AraLegal-BERT is a particularly efficient model that can keep up with the output of computationally intensive models while producing its findings faster and using far fewer resources. Consequently, the base version of the model was observed to have the ability to achieve comparable accuracy to larger versions of the large general and original version of the BERT model when they were trained with domain-relevant examples similar to those used to test our model.

2 Related work

In a very short time, the transformer (Vaswani et al., 2017) architecture has become the gold standard for machine learning methods in the field of linguistics (Wolf et al., 2020; Su et al., 2022). The unprecedented success of BERT combined with its flexibility has led to a proliferation of tools based on it, built with a more narrowly defined vocabulary (Young et al., 2018; Brown et al., 2020). AraBERT (Antoun et al., 2020; Abdul-Mageed et al., 2020) is an example of such specialization and could have considerable practical value, given the number of Arabic speakers worldwide. Because the model is trained for some of the most common NLP tasks and has proven effective across regional variations in morphology and syntax, this language model has the potential to become a standard tool for analyzing Arabic text. The pretraining and fine-tuning procedures described in this work may not be optimal; however, the output of the localized model clearly indicated that the initial approach was correct. With further refinement, the model can become sufficiently reliable for a wide range of real-world applications. However, these models are based on data, most of which were collected from Modern Standard Arabic terms, and these language models may fail when the language switches to colloquial dialects (Abdelali et al., 2021). In addition, the performance of these language models can be affected when dealing with a language for a specific domain with special terms, such as scientific, medical, and legal terms (Yeung, 2019).

The majority of domain-specific BERT models are related to scientific or medical texts, and legal texts; however, the texts are all in English (Beltagy et al., 2019; Lee et al., 2020; Chalkidis et al., 2020). In a study by (Alsentzer et al., 2019), the main area of interest was clinical practice; therefore, the authors developed two different variants by pretraining basic BERT and BIOBERT with examples from this domain, with positive results in both cases. Another interesting related project was conducted by (Beltagy et al., 2019), resulting in the creation of SCIBERT, a whole branch of variations optimized for use with scientific documents. In this case, two different optimization strategies, including additional training and training from scratch using documents comprising scientific terminology, were tested, with both approaches yielding measurable improvements. A study by (Chalkidis et al., 2020) involved pretraining transformer models for English legal text by comparing three possible approaches to adapt BERT to thematic content niches: 1) using the vanilla model without any modifications, 2) introducing pretraining with datasets that contain examples from the target domain in addition to the standard training, and 3) using only domain-relevant samples to train BERT from scratch.

Essentially, all the adaptations of the standard BERT model that involve fine-tuning use the same approach to select hyperparameters as outlined in the original BERT formulation, without even questioning it. Another research gap is observed regarding the possibility of using shallow models to perform domain-specific tasks. The impressive generalizability of deep models with several layers could be argued as wasted when the model operates in a narrowly defined field where linguistic rules are more streamlined and vocabulary volume more limited. Despite BERT being the most successful deep learning model for various tasks related to the legal sphere, there have been no published attempts to develop a unique variation for this type of content, especially in Arabic, inspiring this study. Therefore, this is the first study to build a BERT-based language model for legal texts in Arabic.

3 AraLegal-BERT: Transformer Model Pretrained with Arabic Legal Text

To optimize BERT to work with Arabic legal documents, we followed the same procedures in the original BERT model (Devlin et al., 2018); however, for the Arabic language, we followed the same procedure in AraBERT (Antoun et al., 2020).

3.1 Dataset

Due to the relative scarcity of publicly available resources containing legal text in Arabic, the training dataset had to be manually collected from numerous sources and included several regional variations. All the collected documents were in the Arabic language and related to different subfields of legal practice, such as legislative documents, judicial documents, contracts and legal agreements, Islamic rules, and Fiqh. All data were collected from public sources, and the final size of the dataset was 4.5 GB. The final size of the training set after removing duplicates was approximately 13.7 million sentences. Table 1 lists the dataset used in this study.

3.2 AraLegal-BERT

This version of the model was created by following the original pretraining process with additional steps involving textual material from the Arabic legal domain. The authors of the original BERT model indicated that 100,000 steps would be sufficient; however, in our implementation, the model was trained with up to half a million steps to determine the impact of extended pretraining with narrowly focused data samples on the performance of various linguistic tasks. The pretraining of the BERT base model (Devlin et al., 2018) with general content involves significantly more steps; therefore, the model tends to be the most proficient, with a vocabulary containing approximately 30,000 words, found in everyday speech. With extended training using domain-focused examples, this tendency was presumed to have the ability to be partially reversed with a positive impact on model accuracy.

Before we started the training, the data was preprocessed, and in this phase, we followed the same procedure as in (Antoun et al., 2020). To account for the uniqueness of Arabic prefixes, subword segmentation was performed to separate all tokens into prefixes, stems, and suffixes, as explained in (Abdelali et al., 2016). This resulted in a vocabulary of approximately 64,000 words used to pretrain the model and create AraLegal-BERT. Subsequently, we trained our model using the masked language modeling (MLM) task, where 15% of the words in an entire input sequence were used as tokens because 80% of them were masked, 10% were replaced with a random token, and only 10% were left in their natural state. This procedure allows the algorithms to derive conclusions based on whole words and not just linguistic elements; this procedure is better suited for the Arabic language.

4 Experimental procedure

4.1 Pretraining stage

AraLegal-BERT was trained for approximately 50 epochs, involving a total of half a million steps, which is similar to the original BERT pretraining procedure. We trained our model at the Elm Research Center using NVIDIA DGX1 with eight GPUs. The batch size was set to 8 per GPU; therefore, the total training batch size (w. parallel, distributed & accumulation) was 512. The maximum sequence length was 512 tokens, and the learning rate ranged from $1e-5$ to $5e-5$.

4.2 Fine-tuning

The authors of BERT (Devlin et al., 2018) proposed an approach for determining the optimal parameters for fine-tuning based on a search within a limited range. In this concept, the learning rate, training duration, size of the training stack, and dropout rate are either fixed or can be one of a few possible discreet values. Although no particular reason was provided for this approach, it has been widely replicated in studies dealing with BERT derivatives (Wehnert et al., 2022; Rogers et al., 2020).

Table 1: Dataset used to train AraLegal-BERT

Type	Sample Size	Desc
Books	6K	Master and PhD theses, research papers, magazines, dictionaries and Fiqh books
Cases	336K	Legal Cases in KSA and Gulf countries which consists of copy rights, design rights, facts and appealing
Terms and laws	3K	Laws and regulations in KSA and Gulf countries
others	5K	Reports and studies, academic courses, forms, reports, contracts

Because these parameters do not always produce the best results, and their use can still leave a model undertrained, an alternative strategy was adopted to choose the upper limit of training epochs that tracks the loss of validation and terminates training only when the conditions are met.

4.2.1 Legal text classification

The samples used in the experimental dataset were collected from two main portals. The first dataset was collected from the Scientific Judicial Portal(SJP)[1], operated by the Ministry of Justice in Saudi Arabia. The SJP is the largest specialized information database in the field of justice in the Kingdom of Saudi Arabia. It is the ideal solution for specialists, including judges, lawyers, trained lawyers, academics, prosecutors, and graduate students, in the justice and legal domain. The second dataset collected was from the Board of Grievances(BoG) portal[2], where the following is stated in their website: *"The Board tested a judiciary academic series in the name of (judge library) and its distribution among the Board judges (hard copy and soft copy) to increase cognitive formation with them, a state which its effect shall be reflected on the judiciary verdicts they issue, including academic references in administrative, commercial and penal judiciary formed of 32 volumes in addition to judiciary verdicts"*.

Because existing documents in both datasets can belong to multiple categories depending on the submission details, they are suitable for the task of classifying lengthy legal documents. Three different classes of documents were selected from the SJP dataset and ten classes from the BoG dataset. Because all documents from certain classes are essentially headlined in the same manner, the classification task required that the parts of the document containing easily identifiable indicators of the class were trimmed. Owing to this omission, the model needs to analyze the entire content instead of deriving the conclusion based on just the first few lines. This modification was implemented for all classes.

4.2.2 Keyword Extraction

Unfortunately, compared with the data available for research in English and a few Latin languages, there are no ready-made and well-prepared data for research purposes in Arabic, especially for understanding the natural languages of legal texts. Therefore, we built our dataset for this task with the help of professionals in the Arab legal domain. This dataset consists of approximately 8,000 legal documents containing the most important keywords manually extracted by these professionals. We preprocessed and cleaned the data and extracted approximately 37640 sentences containing keywords and other words that formed the sentences. The average length of the sentences was no more than 65 words because we performed a sentence segmentation process to ensure that each sentence did not lose its meaning or was not trimmed. We tagged the keywords in the sentence with the number 1 and the others with the number 0.

4.2.3 Named Entity Recognition

This dataset was also generated in the research department of Elm, Saudi Arabia. It contains more than 311,000 sentences, including thousands of distinct entities of 17 different sequence tags manually labeled by multiple human annotators as a part of our CourtNLP project at Elm research[3]. All the classes used are shown in Figure 1. The main objective of the NER procedure is to assign a label belonging to a particular class to each of the included words. Furthermore, some complex named entities can span multiple words; however, they are always contained within a single sentence. The IOB format (short for inside, outside, beginning) is predominantly used to represent the sentences in this field, with words starting with the name of an entity marked as B, internally located words as I, and other tokens as O.

[1] https://sjp.moj.gov.sa/

[2] https://www.bog.gov.sa/en/ScientificContent/Pages/default.aspx

[3] https://www.elm.sa/en/research-and-innovation/Pages/Research.aspx

Table 2: Overall results of all fine-tuned models in the legal text classification task on BoG Dataset

Model / Macro-Average	Precision	Recall	F1-score
Arabertv2-Large (Antoun et al., 2020)	0.850387	0.810795	0.827078
ARBERT (Abdul-Mageed et al., 2020)	0.802514	0.821973	0.812820
mBERT (Devlin et al., 2018)	0.702017	0.635928	0.598267
AraLegal-BERT (base)	**0.89276**	**0.89173**	**0.89098**

Table 3: Overall results of all fine-tuned models in the legal text classification task on SJP Dataset

Model / Macro-Average	Precision	Recall	F1-score
Arabertv2-Large (Antoun et al., 2020)	0.885678	0.886816	0.884516
ARBERT (Abdul-Mageed et al., 2020)	0.837714	0.834804	0.843827
mBERT (Devlin et al., 2018)	0.814763	0.780226	0.782501
AraLegal-BERT (base)	**0.92395**	**0.92133**	**0.92210**

English Tag	Arabic Tag	Tag count
accusation	التهمة	19974
document	مستند	91058
evidence	دليل	67456
Hadith	حديث نبوي	10094
Qura'n	قرآن كريم	8019
job	وظيفة	46415
jurisprudence	فقة	15648
law	قانون	41694
location	موقع	9127
organization	منظمة/مؤسسة	73171
person	شخص	15685
Nationality	جنسية	26651
Currency	عملة	13456
Amount	مبلغ	17982
Date time	وقت وتاريخ	36548
citation	اقتباس	36133
verdict	حكم	38189

Figure 1: Main Arabic Legal Named Entity Tags

5 Results

5.1 Impact of pretraining

We trained two models from scratch: the first was a base model that contains 12 layers, and the second was a large model that consists of 24 layers, similar to the original BERT. As anticipated, the full-sized 24-layer model trained from scratch had a significantly better ability than that of the base model with 12 layers, to meet the pretraining objectives. However, after the completion of the pretraining stage, the base model displayed a level of loss similar to that of the original BERT model trained with general datasets. In particular, a model's ability to adapt to narrowly defined niches is faster, which can be a significant advantage for domain-focused applications such as those used for the legal domain. Therefore, the content of the training set plays a role in choosing the appropriate training method. We are yet to perform experiments on the large model, and all fine-tuning results were based on the base model because we found that it provides significantly higher accuracy than the general Arabic BERT models in the three defined NLU tasks.

5.2 Results and discussion

We divided the datasets for all three tasks into training, validation, and testing sets. In this section, we discuss the test results. The evaluation was conducted using standardized hyperparameters, such as batch size and sequence length, with different datasets suitable for legal text classification, keyword extraction, and named entity recognition.

The best option for the first task of legal text classification is determined based on experimental results. For example, using this method, we found that multiple strategies could be used to bypass BERT's sequence length limitation of 512 tokens; however, the "head & tails" strategy, where only the first 128 and the last 382 tokens are retained, exhibits the best performance, such as the work in (Sun et al., 2019). Tables 2 and 3 summarize the overall results of our model compared with those of the three BERT variants for the Arabic language on the classification task with two datasets, namely SJP and BoG. On the BoG dataset, AraLegal-BERT outperformed all models by 0.7% in terms of F1-Macro average, which is higher than ARABERT-v2large. Similarly, our model also outperformed the other models on the SJP dataset; it achieved approximately 0.4% higher F1-Macro average than that of ArabBERTv2-large.

Furthermore, for the tasks related to named entity recognition and keyword extraction, we followed the same procedure that was performed in our previous work (Al-Qurishi and Souissi, 2021); considering that no new layers were added to the model, a linear layer was used to make the words and sequence-level tagging. The results were extremely different for these two tasks; furthermore, there was a significant difference between the performance of AraLegal-BERT and the other models; AraLegal-BERT achieved 21% higher F1-Macro average than ARABERT-v2large (Antoun et al., 2020) in extracting named entities, as shown in Table 5. In addition, the difference was significantly higher in the keyword extraction task, where AraLegal-BERT outperformed the highest model, ARBERT (Abdul-Mageed et al., 2020), with a significant difference of almost 26% in F1-Macro average, as shown in Table 4.

We denote that the general BERT models exhibited not only a low F1-Macro score but also a low recall-macro score, where they were not able to retrieve most of the required words compared with those retrieved by AraLegal-BERT. Finally, we would like to highlight that AraLegal-BERT is the base version; yet, it outperformed the rest of the models in all three defined tasks, with low memory requirement, faster performance, and good accuracy.

6 Conclusions and future work

Our experimental results show that a BERT model pretrained for a specific domain is better than the typical language models, for specific NLU tasks. Therefore, we present AraLegal-BERT, which was trained exclusively for Arabic legal texts and is capable of making highly accurate predictions on three main NLU tasks: legal text classification, named entity recognition, and keyword extraction. Essentially, the level of difficulty of a task is correlated with the gains from choosing the right training strategy as the importance of domain-specific vocabulary and semantics becomes more pronounced. The tested version of AraLegal-BERT is the base, cost-efficient version suitable for a broad range of Arabic legal text applications. Our future work will focus on additional possibilities for pretraining other models, such as the Electra, Roberta and XLM-R models for several NLU tasks in the Arabic legal domain with small, base, and large versions.

Acknowledgements

This study was supported and funded by the research department of Elm.

References

Ahmed Abdelali, Kareem Darwish, Nadir Durrani, and Hamdy Mubarak. 2016. Farasa: A fast and furious segmenter for arabic. In *Proceedings of the 2016 conference of the North American chapter of the association for computational linguistics: Demonstrations*, pages 11–16.

Ahmed Abdelali, Sabit Hassan, Hamdy Mubarak, Kareem Darwish, and Younes Samih. 2021. Pre-training bert on arabic tweets: Practical considerations. *arXiv preprint arXiv:2102.10684*.

Muhammad Abdul-Mageed, AbdelRahim Elmadany, and El Moatez Billah Nagoudi. 2020. Arbert & marbert: deep bidirectional transformers for arabic. *arXiv preprint arXiv:2101.01785*.

Muhammad Saleh Al-Qurishi and Riad Souissi. 2021. Arabic named entity recognition using transformer-based-crf model. In *Proceedings of The Fourth International Conference on Natural Language and Speech Processing (ICNLSP 2021)*, pages 262–271.

Emily Alsentzer, John R Murphy, Willie Boag, Wei-Hung Weng, Di Jin, Tristan Naumann, and Matthew McDermott. 2019. Publicly available clinical bert embeddings. *arXiv preprint arXiv:1904.03323*.

Wissam Antoun, Fady Baly, and Hazem Hajj. 2020. Arabert: Transformer-based model for arabic language understanding. *arXiv preprint arXiv:2003.00104*.

Iz Beltagy, Kyle Lo, and Arman Cohan. 2019. Scibert: A pretrained language model for scientific text. *arXiv preprint arXiv:1903.10676*.

Tom Brown, Benjamin Mann, Nick Ryder, Melanie Subbiah, Jared D Kaplan, Prafulla Dhariwal, Arvind Neelakantan, Pranav Shyam, Girish Sastry, Amanda Askell, et al. 2020. Language models are few-shot learners. *Advances in neural information processing systems*, 33:1877–1901.

Ilias Chalkidis, Manos Fergadiotis, Prodromos Malakasiotis, Nikolaos Aletras, and Ion Androutsopoulos. 2020. Legal-bert: The muppets straight out of law school. *arXiv preprint arXiv:2010.02559*.

Jacob Devlin, Ming-Wei Chang, Kenton Lee, and Kristina Toutanova. 2018. Bert: Pre-training of deep bidirectional transformers for language understanding. *arXiv preprint arXiv:1810.04805*.

Table 4: Overall results of all fine-tuned models in the Keywords Extraction Task

Model / Macro-Average	Precision	Recall	F1-score
Arabertv2-Large (Antoun et al., 2020)	0.765979	0.470098	0.582625
ARBERT (Abdul-Mageed et al., 2020)	0.789460	0.524715	0.630420
mBERT (Devlin et al., 2018)	0.721356	0.375075	0.493533
AraLegal-BERT (base)	**0.93481**	**0.84449**	**0.88736**

Table 5: Overall results of all fine-tuned models in the Named Entity Recognition Task

Model / Macro-Average	Precision	Recall	F1-score
Arabertv2-Large (Antoun et al., 2020)	0.891934	0.450073	0.598261
ARBERT (Abdul-Mageed et al., 2020)	0.889916	0.413266	0.564423
mBERT (Devlin et al., 2018)	0.886825	0.326475	0.477254
AraLegal-BERT (base)	**0.89848**	**0.73644**	**0.80943**

Jinhyuk Lee, Wonjin Yoon, Sungdong Kim, Donghyeon Kim, Sunkyu Kim, Chan Ho So, and Jaewoo Kang. 2020. Biobert: a pre-trained biomedical language representation model for biomedical text mining. *Bioinformatics*, 36(4):1234–1240.

Anna Rogers, Olga Kovaleva, and Anna Rumshisky. 2020. A primer in bertology: What we know about how bert works. *Transactions of the Association for Computational Linguistics*, 8:842–866.

Raquel Silveira, CG Fernandes, João A Monteiro Neto, Vasco Furtado, and José Ernesto Pimentel Filho. 2021. Topic modelling of legal documents via legal-bert. *Proceedings http://ceur-ws org ISSN*, 1613:0073.

Xing Su, Shan Xue, Fanzhen Liu, Jia Wu, Jian Yang, Chuan Zhou, Wenbin Hu, Cecile Paris, Surya Nepal, Di Jin, et al. 2022. A comprehensive survey on community detection with deep learning. *IEEE Transactions on Neural Networks and Learning Systems*.

Chi Sun, Xipeng Qiu, Yige Xu, and Xuanjing Huang. 2019. How to fine-tune bert for text classification? In *China national conference on Chinese computational linguistics*, pages 194–206. Springer.

Ashish Vaswani, Noam Shazeer, Niki Parmar, Jakob Uszkoreit, Llion Jones, Aidan N Gomez, Łukasz Kaiser, and Illia Polosukhin. 2017. Attention is all you need. *Advances in neural information processing systems*, 30.

Sabine Wehnert, Shipra Dureja, Libin Kutty, Viju Sudhi, and Ernesto William De Luca. 2022. Applying bert embeddings to predict legal textual entailment. *The Review of Socionetwork Strategies*, 16(1):197–219.

Thomas Wolf, Lysandre Debut, Victor Sanh, Julien Chaumond, Clement Delangue, Anthony Moi, Pierric Cistac, Tim Rault, Rémi Louf, Morgan Funtowicz, et al. 2020. Transformers: State-of-the-art natural language processing. In *Proceedings of the 2020 conference on empirical methods in natural language processing: system demonstrations*, pages 38–45.

Chin Man Yeung. 2019. Effects of inserting domain vocabulary and fine-tuning bert for german legal language. Master's thesis, University of Twente.

Tom Young, Devamanyu Hazarika, Soujanya Poria, and Erik Cambria. 2018. Recent trends in deep learning based natural language processing. *ieee Computational intelligenCe magazine*, 13(3):55–75.

Gechuan Zhang, Paul Nulty, and David Lillis. 2022. Enhancing legal argument mining with domain pre-training and neural networks. *arXiv preprint arXiv:2202.13457*.

An Efficient Active Learning Pipeline for Legal Text Classification

Sepideh Mamooler and **Rémi Lebret** and **Stephane Massonnet** and **Karl Aberer**
School of Computer and Communication Sciences, EPFL, Switzerland

Abstract

Active Learning (AL) is a powerful tool for learning with less labeled data, in particular, for specialized domains, like legal documents, where unlabeled data is abundant, but the annotation requires domain expertise and is thus expensive. Recent works have shown the effectiveness of AL strategies for pre-trained language models. However, most AL strategies require a set of labeled samples to start with, which is expensive to acquire. In addition, pre-trained language models have been shown unstable during fine-tuning with small datasets, and their embeddings are not semantically meaningful. In this work, we propose a pipeline for effectively using active learning with pre-trained language models in the legal domain. To this end, we leverage the available *unlabeled* data in three phases. First, we continue pre-training the model to adapt it to the downstream task. Second, we use knowledge distillation to guide the model's embeddings to a semantically meaningful space. Finally, we propose a simple, yet effective, strategy to find the initial set of labeled samples with fewer actions compared to existing methods. Our experiments on Contract-NLI, adapted to the classification task, and LEDGAR benchmarks show that our approach outperforms standard AL strategies, and is more efficient. Furthermore, our pipeline reaches comparable results to the fully-supervised approach with a small performance gap, and dramatically reduced annotation cost. Code and the adapted data will be made available.

1 Introduction

With the advent of pre-trained transformer-based language models (Devlin et al., 2019; Liu et al., 2019; He et al., 2021), training models from scratch has been outperformed by fine-tuning pre-trained language models for several tasks in natural language processing, including text classification (Howard and Ruder, 2018). However, fine-tuning these models still needs large labeled datasets to perform well on the downstream task (Dodge et al., 2020; Zhang et al., 2021; Mosbach et al., 2021). Collecting a large annotated dataset is a highly expensive and time-consuming process in specialized domains, where annotation can only be performed by the domain experts, such as the legal domain (Hendrycks et al., 2021).

Active Learning (AL) has been proved effective for data-efficient fine-tuning of pre-trained language models in non-specialized domains like news, emotions, and movies (Ein-Dor et al., 2020; Margatina et al., 2022). In addition, Margatina et al. (2022) have shown that the unlabeled data can be used to adapt the pre-trained language model to the downstream task, thereby improving the active learning performance with no extra annotation cost. On the specialized domains, Chhatwal et al. (2017) have evaluated multiple AL strategies in the legal domain before the emergence of pre-trained language models. Nevertheless, to the best of our knowledge, the effectiveness of active learning in fine-tuning pre-trained language models in the legal domain has been poorly studied.

In this work, we focus on efficient legal text classification with RoBERTa (Liu et al., 2019) by leveraging existing AL strategies. We identify two challenges in deploying AL strategies in the legal domain; First, legal texts contain a specialized vocabulary that is not common in other domains, including the ones on which pre-trained language models are trained. Second, the annotation of legal texts is highly expensive and time-consuming due to the necessity of specialized training for understanding these texts. For example, Hendrycks et al. (2021) reported a cost of over $2 million for the annotation of the Contract Understanding Atticus Dataset (CUAD) consisting of around 500 contracts.

To account for the specialized vocabulary, inspired by Margatina et al.'s (2022) work, we leverage the available *unlabeled* data to adapt the pre-trained language model to the downstream

Proceedings of the Natural Legal Language Processing Workshop 2022, pages 345 - 358
December 8, 2022 ©2022 Association for Computational Linguistics

task. In addition, considering the limitations of pre-trained language models like BERT and RoBERTa in capturing semantics (Reimers and Gurevych, 2019), we use knowledge distillation to further improve the task-adapted model by mapping its embedding space to a semantically meaningful space. Our experiments demonstrate that AL strategies can benefit from semantically meaningful embeddings.

Concerning the cost and time constraints, we focus on the fact that many AL strategies (Lewis and Gale, 1994; Gal and Ghahramani, 2016; Gissin and Shalev-Shwartz, 2019) require an annotated set of N positive and negative samples to start with. In practice, acquiring this set is expensive for large and skewed datasets. We propose a strategy to make the first iteration more efficient by clustering the unlabeled samples and limiting the pull of candidates to the cluster medoids. Our experiments demonstrate we can achieve comparable results with the standard initial sampling approach with up to 63%, and 25% fewer actions on the skewed Contract-NLI (Koreeda and Manning, 2021), and balanced LEDGAR benchmarks (Tuggener et al., 2020) respectively.

Our contributions can be summarized as follows:

1. We design an efficient and effective active learning pipeline for legal text classification by leveraging the available unlabeled data using task-adaptation and knowledge distillation, which obtains comparable performance to fully-supervised fine-tuning with considerably reduced annotation effort.

2. We propose a strategy to reduce the number of actions in the first iteration of active learning by clustering the unlabeled data, and collecting the samples from cluster medoids, further increasing the efficiency of our approach.

3. We evaluate our approach over Contract-NLI and LEDGAR benchmarks. Our results illustrate an increase of 0.3346, and 0.1658 in the best obtained F1-score, compared to standard active learning strategies, for Contract-NLI and LEDGAR respectively.

2 Related Work

Active learning with pre-trained language models Multiple works have studied active learning for pre-trained language models like BERT. Ein-Dor et al. (2020) have evaluated various AL strategies for fine-tuning BERT for text classification, and showed that AL can boost BERT's performance especially for skewed datasets. However, they do not leverage the available unlabeled data to adapt the pre-trained language model to the task at hand, and only focus on non-specialized domains like news and sentiment analysis that do not require experts' knowledge.

Gururangan et al. (2020) have shown that task-adaptive pre-training using the available unlabeled data leads to performance gain when using pre-trained language models like BERT. Following this observation, Margatina et al. (2022) demonstrated the importance of task-adaptation for active learning for non-specialized texts like news, movies and sentiment analysis.

Inspired by these works, we leverage the available unlabeled data to effectively adapt RoBERTa to legal text classification, where the annotation demands experts' knowledge. In addition, we propose an additional step to map the embedding space of the task-adapted RoBERTa to a semantically meaningful space using sentence transformers.

Sentence transformers Reimers and Gurevych (2019) have shown that the embedding space of off-the-shelf pre-trained language models like BERT (Devlin et al., 2019) and RoBERTa (Liu et al., 2019) is not semantically meaningful, and thus, is not suitable for common sentence comparison measures like cosine similarity. To overcome this limitation, they propose sentence transformers, obtained by adding a pooling layer on top of pre-trained language models, and fine-tuning them in a Siamese network architecture with pairs of similar sentences. In this work, we use a RoBERTa-based sentence transformer as a teacher model and distill its knowledge to the task-adapted RoBERTa to produce sentence embeddings that capture the semantics and can be compared using cosine similarity.

Active learning strategies Numerous methods have been proposed to find proper labeling candidates for active learning. Majority of them belong to one or both of two categories: diversity-sampling, and uncertainty-sampling. Diversity-based methods (Sener and Savarese, 2018; Gissin and Shalev-Shwartz, 2019; Wang et al., 2017) aim to find labeling candidates that best represent the dataset, whereas uncertainty-based methods (Gal and Ghahramani, 2016; Kirsch et al., 2019; Zhang and Plank, 2021) target candidates about which the model is uncertain. BADGE (Ash et al., 2020) is a cluster-based AL strategy that belongs to both of these categories. It transforms data into gradient embeddings that encode model confidence and sentence feature at the same time. By applying kmeans++ on the gradient embeddings it can find samples that differ both in terms of semantics and predictive uncertainty. ALPS (Yuan et al., 2020) is another cluster-based AL strategy that leverages both uncertainty and diversity using the surprisal embeddings obtained by passing the sentences to the MLM head of the pre-trained language model, and computing the cross entropy loss for a random set of tokens against the target labels.

Existing AL strategies often require a set of labeled samples to start with, which is expensive to acquire. To overcome this high cost, we propose a clustering-based strategy to reduce the effort required to create the initial set of annotated samples.

3 Notation and Setting

In this section, we explain the structure shared between all AL strategies used in this work and fix the notation.

Active learning is an iterative process aiming to obtain a desired performance given an annotation budget. Here, we consider the annotation budget to be the number of actions performed by the annotator. In addition, we assume all annotators are legal experts, and that each annotator assigns perfect labels to text segments. Let U_0 and L_0 be the starting pool of unlabeled and labeled samples respectively. Initially, $L_0 = \emptyset$. At the first iteration, the annotator labels N sample, P positive and $N - P$ negative, to obtained L_1. Then, at each iteration i, the model is fine-tuned using L_i, and the AL strategy recommends a set of samples C_i for annotation. These samples are labeled and U_i and L_i are updated as $U_{i+1} = U_i \setminus C_i$, and $L_{i+1} = L_i \cup C_i$. The procedure is repeated until the annotation budget is exhausted, or the desired performance is achieved.

We base our work on the Low-Resource Text Classification Framework introduced by Ein-Dor et al. (2020). Following this work, we focus on binary text classification, given a small annotation budget and a potentially imbalanced dataset. This scenario matches common use cases in the legal domain, where the goal is to find phrases that correspond to a specific category, with the lowest possible number of actions, given a pool of unlabeled, imbalanced data. We perform 5 AL iterations, and assume a more restricted annotation budget compared to Ein-Dor et al. (2020), allowing only 10 annotations per iteration. For the first AL iteration, we assume that 5 positive and 5 negative samples need to be annotated.

4 Methodology

We propose an efficient active learning pipeline for fine-tuning pre-trained language models for legal text classification. Our approach leverages available unlabeled data in three phases to adapt the pre-trained model to the downstream task (Sec. 4.1), guide its embedding space to a semantically meaningful and comparable space (Sec. 4.2), and reduce the number of actions required to collect the initial labeled set (Sec. 4.3). Finally, it leverages existing AL strategies to efficiently fine-tune a classifier (Sec. 4.4). We now explain each step in detail. An overview of this pipeline can be found in Algorithm 1.

4.1 Task-Adaptation

It has been shown that fine-tuning off-the-shelf pre-trained language models with standard approaches is unstable for small training sets (Zhang et al., 2021; Dodge et al., 2020; Mosbach et al., 2021). As shown by Margatina et al. (2022), this can lead to poor performance when fine-tuning pre-trained language models with AL. In addition, existing pre-trained language models are often trained on texts that do not need specialized training to be understood. However, legal texts contain specialized words that are not common in other domains. Thus, task-adaptation is crucial for the effectiveness of active learning in legal text classification. In the first step of our proposed pipeline, we obtain the task-adapted pre-trained (TAPT) RoBERTa by continuing pre-training the model with unlabeled samples for the Masked Language Modeling (MLM) task, as suggested by Gururangan et al. (2020) and Margatina et al. (2022).

4.2 Knowledge Distillation

Previous works (Reimers and Gurevych, 2019; Li et al., 2020; Su et al., 2021) have shown that, without fine-tuning, the sentence embeddings produced by pre-trained language models poorly capture semantic meaning of sentences, and are not comparable using cosine similarity. To overcome this shortcoming, Reimers and Gurevych (2019) introduced sentence transformers by adding a pooling layer on top of pre-trained transformer-based language models, and training them in a

Algorithm 1 AL pipeline for text classification

Input: unlabeled samples U_0, PT RoBERTa, PT Sentence-RoBERTa, AL strategy α, # iterations T **Output:** text classifier CLS RoBERTa, acquired labeled dataset L_T

$L_0 \leftarrow \emptyset$
Phase 1: Task-adaptation with Masked Language Modeling (MLM)
TAPT RoBERTa $\leftarrow$ MLM(PT RoBERTa, U_0)
Phase 2: Knowledge distillation
DisTAPT RoBERTa $\leftarrow$ Distill(TAPT RoBERTa, PT Sentence-RoBERTa, U_0)
Phase 3: Initial sampling
cluster medoids $\leftarrow$ KMeans(DisTAPT RoBERTa, U_0)
$L_1 \leftarrow$ Sample(cluster medoids)
$U_1 \leftarrow U_0 \setminus L_1$
Phase 4: Active learning
for $i \leftarrow 1$ to T **do**
    CLS RoBERTa $\leftarrow$ Train(DisTAPT RoBERTa, L_i)
    $C_i \leftarrow \alpha$(CLS RoBERTa, U_i)
    $L_{i+1} \leftarrow L_i \cup C_i$
    $U_{i+1} \leftarrow U_i \setminus C_i$
end for

Siamese network architecture with pairs of similar sentences. Compared to out-of-the-box RoBERTa, a RoBERTa-based sentence transformer drives semantically comparable sentence embeddings.

As we will explain in Sec. 4.3, we cluster the normalized sentence embeddings based on their Euclidean distance to efficiently acquire the labeled samples for the initial iteration of AL. The Euclidean distance between normalized embeddings can be driven from their cosine similarity. Hence, sentence embeddings that are comparable with cosine similarity can result in clusters with higher quality. In addition, semantically meaningful sentence embeddings give a better initialization of the `[CLS]` token, thereby obtaining better classification performance with a smaller training set.

We use a pre-trained RoBERTa-based sentence transformer (PT Sentence-RoBERTa) as a teacher model, and distill its knowledge to the TAPT RoBERTa. The resulting distilled task-adapted pre-trained (DisTAPT) RoBERTa produces semantically meaningful embeddings that are comparable via cosine similarity, and, as shown by our experiments (Sec. 6.2), benefit the classification task.

4.3 Initial Sampling

Many AL strategies (Gissin and Shalev-Shwartz, 2019; Gal and Ghahramani, 2016) require an initial set of N labeled samples containing P positive and $N - P$ negative sentences, which is either assumed to be available, or obtained by randomly sampling the entire dataset until the desired number of positive and negative samples are found. This approach is highly expensive for large and skewed datasets. We propose a simple, yet effective, strategy to efficiently acquire the initial labeled set. To this end, we leverage the distilled task-adapted pre-trained RoBERTa to cluster the unlabeled samples using KMeans algorithm (MacQueen, 1967). The labeled set for the initial iteration is then driven from the cluster medoids. As a result, we shrink the pool of candidates from the entire dataset to the cluster medoids, therefore, reduce the number of actions for obtaining the initial annotated set, while achieving comparable performance with the standard approach for initial sampling.

4.4 Active Learning

In the last phase, we iteratively fine-tune the DisTAPT RoBERTa for the downstream task. The initial labeled set is used at the first iteration. Then, more samples are labeled in the following rounds using an AL acquisition strategy until the annotation budget is exhausted, or the classifier satisfies the expected performance.

Our proposed pipeline can be used with existing AL strategies and, as demonstrated by our experiments (Sec. 6.2), consistently outperforms standard AL approaches, regardless of the AL strategy used.

5 Experimental Setup

We evaluate our approach against four standard active learning strategies provided in the Low-Resource Text Classification Framework (Ein-Dor et al., 2020):

- **Random** At each iteration, this approach randomly chooses samples for annotation.
- **Hard-Mining** Selects instances that the model is uncertain about, based on the absolute difference of prediction score and 0.5.
- **Perceptron Dropout** (Gal and Ghahramani, 2016) Also selects instances for which the model is least certain. The uncertainty is calculated using Monte Carlo Dropout on 10 inference cycles.
- **Discriminative Active Learning (DAL)** (Gissin and Shalev-Shwartz, 2019) Deploys a binary classifier to select instances that best represent the entire unlabeled samples.

We consider pre-trained RoBERTa and LEGAL-BERT (Chalkidis et al., 2020) as the baselines. However, we only evaluate our strategy using the pre-trained RoBERTa as our goal is not to rely on domain-adapted models like LEGAL-BERT since they might not always be available. For example, if the data is in German, we can find a pre-trained RoBERTa in German, but the LEGAL-BERT is pre-trained on English text only.

5.1 Datasets

We evaluate our framework on Contract-NLI (Koreeda and Manning, 2021) and LEDGAR (Tuggener et al., 2020) benchmarks.

Contract-NLI (Koreeda and Manning, 2021) is a dataset for document-level natural language inference. It consists of 607 documents with 77.8 spans per document on average. Each span is checked against 17 hypotheses and classified as contradiction, entailment, or not mentioned. In this work, we adapt this dataset to the classification task by considering each hypothesis as a category. If a span is classified as contradiction or entailment for a hypothesis, we label it with the corresponding category. Following this approach, we end up with a classification dataset with 4,371 train, 614 development, and 1,188 test samples within 17 classes.

LEDGAR (Tuggener et al., 2020) is a text classification benchmark consisting of a corpus of legal provisions in contracts. The entire dataset consists of 846,274 provisions and 12,608 labels. We only consider a subset of this dataset that corresponds to provisions with labels that appeared at least 10,000 times in the corpus, resulting in 44,249 train, 7,375 development, and 12, 907 test samples across 5 categories. Similar to Tuggener et al. (2020), we perform a $70\% - 10\% - 20\%$ random split to obtain the train, development and test sets.

The class distributions of both datasets can be found in the appendix (Sec. A.1). Compared to Contract-NLI, LEDGAR has fewer categories, is an order of magnitude bigger, and is more balanced.

5.2 Implementation Details

We base our implementation on the Low-Resource Text Classification Framework provided by Ein-Dor et al. (2020)[1], and augment it with the task-adaptation, knowledge distillation, and initial sampling steps.

As the pre-trained model, we use `roberta-base`[2] (with 125M parameters), the RoBERTa (Liu et al., 2019) language model trained on the union of 5 datatsets: Book corpus (Zhu et al., 2015), English Wikipedia[3], CC-News (Mackenzie et al., 2020), OpenWebText Corpus (Gokaslan and Cohen), and Stories (Trinh and Le, 2018), none of which belong to the legal domain.

For LEGAL-BERT, we use the `nlpaueb/legal-bert-base-uncased`[4] (with 110M parameters), trained on six datasets containing legal docments across Europe and the US.

For task-adaptation, we continue pre-training RoBERTa for the MLM task using the available unlabeled data. We train for 10 epochs with batch-size 64, and the learning rate set to 3e−4. The task-adapted model has perplexity 4.9706 for Contract-NLI and 2.1628 for LEDGAR.

For model distillation, we use `stsb-roberta-base-v2` (with 125M parameters), a RoBERTa-based sentence transformer trained on the STS benchmark (Cer et al., 2017), as the teacher model, and the task-adapted RoBERTa as the student model. Mean Squared Error (MSE) is used as the loss function. The student model is trained for 10 epochs, with 10K warmup steps, 1e−4 learning

[1] https://github.com/IBM/low-resource-text-classification-framework

[2] https://huggingface.co/roberta-base

[3] https://dumps.wikimedia.org

[4] https://huggingface.co/nlpaueb/legal-bert-base-uncased

rate and no bias correction. The final MSE ($\times 100$) is 6.8607 for Contract-NLI, and 7.2003 for LEDGAR.

For clustering the normalized sentence embeddings we use the KMeans implementation by `scikit-learn`. We cluster the Contract-NLI and LEDGAR sentence embeddings into 437, and 442 groups respectively. The number of clusters are chosen based on the dataset size, and the number of categories, and to make initial sampling with cluster medoids manageable for experts.

In all the active learning experiments, we perform 5 AL iterations, starting with 10 initial samples, and increasing the size of the annotated data by 10 at each iteration. Adam optimizer (Kingma and Ba, 2015) is used with learning rate set to 5e−5. The model is trained for 100 epochs and early stopping is used with patience set to 10. To account for randomization, we repeat each experiment three times.

To compare our approach with standard AL methods, we use F1-score as the evaluation metric as it captures both precision and recall and is sensitive to data distribution.

6 Results and Discussion

In this section, we provide the results of our experiments, and explain them in detail. We start by comparing our approach with and without the initial medoid sampling against standard AL strategies (Sec. 6.1). Then, we show the effectiveness of knowledge distillation on top of task-adaptation (Sec. 6.2). In addition, we demonstrate the efficiency of the initial sampling with cluster medoids (Sec. 6.3). Finally, we evaluate how well our approach performs for different AL strategies (Sec. 6.4).

6.1 Efficient AL Pipeline

Figure 1 compares our approach with and without the initial sampling phase (DisTAPT with IS, and DisTAPT) to standard DAL with pre-trained (PT) and TAPT RoBERTa for Contract-NLI and LEDGAR benchmarks. We report the average F1-score over all categories. DAL is chosen due to its better performance, as shown in Figure 2. The results for other AL strategies can be found in the appendix (Sec. A.2).

Our experiments show the importance of task-adaptation and knowledge distillation for pre-trained language models prior to fine-tuning with active learning. Figure 1 illustrates that, for the same size of annotated data, our pipeline consistently achieves better performance than standard AL approaches.

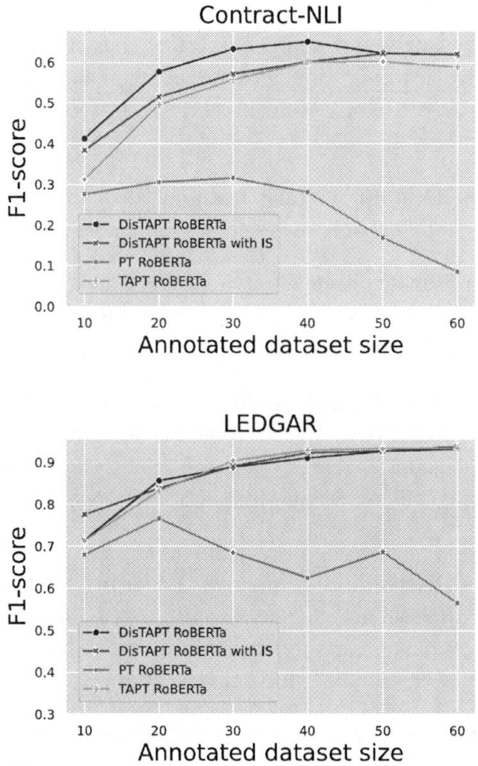

Figure 1: Test F1-score for **DAL** during AL iterations. The F1-score for the fully supervised fine-tuning is 0.6990 for Contract-NLI and 0.9538 for LEDGAR. The figure is best viewed in color.

For the Contract-NLI dataset, the F1-score obtained by fully-supervised fine-tuning (with 4,371 labeled samples) is 0.6990 for `roberta-base` and 0.7152 for `legal-bert-base-uncased`. DisTAPT RoBERTa reaches a F1-score as high as 0.6508 with only 40 labeled samples. The best F1-score obtained using pre-trained RoBERTa is 0.3162 with 30 labeled samples, which is 0.3165 lower than DisTAPT RoBERTa's F1-score for the same size of annotated data.

For the LEDGAR dataset, the F1-score obtained by the fully-supervised fine-tuning (with 44,249 labeled samples) is 0.9538 for `roberta-base` and 0.9588 for `legal-bert-base-uncased`. DisTAPT RoBERTa reaches a very close performance of 0.9321 F1-score with merely 60 labeled samples. The highest F1-score that pre-trained RoBERT reaches is 0.7663 with 20 annotated samples, which is 0.0904 lower than DisTAPT's performance with the same size of labeled data.

These results show that, for both datasets, there is only a small performance gap between our approach and the fully-supervised approach, indicating that our AL pipeline dramatically reduces the annotation cost, while achieving comparable performance with the fully-supervised fine-tuning.

In addition, It is observed that standard AL with off-the-shelf pre-trained RoBERTa is unstable. This is aligned with the previous works' observations (Mosbach et al., 2021; Zhang et al., 2021; Dodge et al., 2020). During fine-tuning, the pre-trained model should perform two tasks: adaptation to the legal domain with the new vocabulary, and classification. By performing task-adaptation and knowledge distillation before fine-tuning, we train the model in a curriculum learning approach, making the model stable even for small training sets.

6.2 Effect of Knowledge Distillation

To evaluate the effectiveness of knowledge distillation on the quality of obtained clusters, we compare the distribution of the Dunn Index of the clusters before and after knowledge distillation. For both datasets, after knowledge distillation, most of the clusters have higher Dunn Index which indicates that they are more compact and better separated than the clusters before knowledge distillation step. The results are provided in the appendix A.3 due to space constraints.

In addition, we evaluate the effect of knowledge distillation on the task-adapted pre-trained RoBERTa, and report the average F1-score over all classes for each dataset. Figure 1 shows that, for both datasets, DisTAPT RoBERTa outperforms TAPT RoBERTa at early iterations of active learning, and as the size of the labeled set increases, the two models' performance converge. This can be explained by the fact that, initially, DisTAPT RoBERTa's embeddings better capture the semantics of sentences, and thus result in better classification performance. As the labeled data grows, TAPT RoBERTa is fine-tuned and can produce semantically meaningful embeddings as well. Hence, for a highly restricted annotation budget, distilling the knowledge of a sentence transformer to the TAPT language model can lead to performance gain.

6.3 Efficiency of Initial Medoid Sampling

It was shown in Figure 1 that DisTAPT with IS obtains comparable performance with DisTAPT without IS. In this section, we evaluate the *efficiency* of the proposed sampling strategy for the initial iteration of AL.

To this end, we simulate the standard sampling strategy by randomly sampling text segments from the full dataset until 5 positive and 5 negative samples are found. The number of iterations is then considered as the number of annotations required to collect the labeled set for the initial AL iteration. Similarly, to simulate our proposed initial sampling, we randomly sample from cluster medoids until 5 positive and 5 negative samples are obtained. To account for randomness, we repeat the simulations 1000 times and report the median and the 90th percentile over all runs.

Table 1 illustrates the results of our simulations for Contract-NLI and LEDGAR. Due to the high number of classes in Contract-NLI, only eight categories of this dataset are presented in this table, and the results for other categories can be found in the appendix (Sec. A.4). For each class, in addition to the median and 90th percentile over 1000 runs, the difference in the 90th percentile between standard approach and our strategy (in %) is reported as the gain in annotation effort. For example, for the `Sharing with third-parties` class in Contract-NLI, the 90th percentile is 62% less when using medoids for initial sampling, meaning that, with 90% confidence, the annotators perform 62% fewer actions to acquire the initial labeled set using our approach.

It is observed that, for the skewed Contract-NLI dataset, our proposed initial sampling strategy reduces the number of actions performed by the annotator up to 63%. For LEDGAR however, which consists of balanced categories, the highest effort gain in sampling from cluster medoids is 25%. There are also few cases where using the entire dataset is more efficient than sampling from medoids. This happens when the class' frequency is higher in the full dataset than its frequency in the cluster medoids.

Overall, our results demonstrate the advantage of using the cluster medoids for collecting the initial annotated samples for a skewed dataset like Contract-NLI, which is a realistic use-case in the legal domain. It is noteworthy that the original version of LEDGAR dataset is also imbalanced, but as explained in Sec. 5.1, due to the drastically high number of classes, and for the sake of comparison with skewed datasets, only the most dominant categories are kept in this work.

Thanks to the semantically meaningful and

comparable sentence embeddings obtained after the knowledge distillation step, the cluster medoids well represent the entire dataset, and thus sampling among them drastically reduces the annotation effort without harming the performance. As a real life scenario, consider a company with hundreds of legal contracts aiming to classify their sentences into multiple categories, under a restricted budget. Reducing the annotation effort means lowering down the financial costs of annotation, which can be highly expensive in the legal domain (over \$2 million for annotating around 500 contracts according to Hendrycks et al. (2021)).

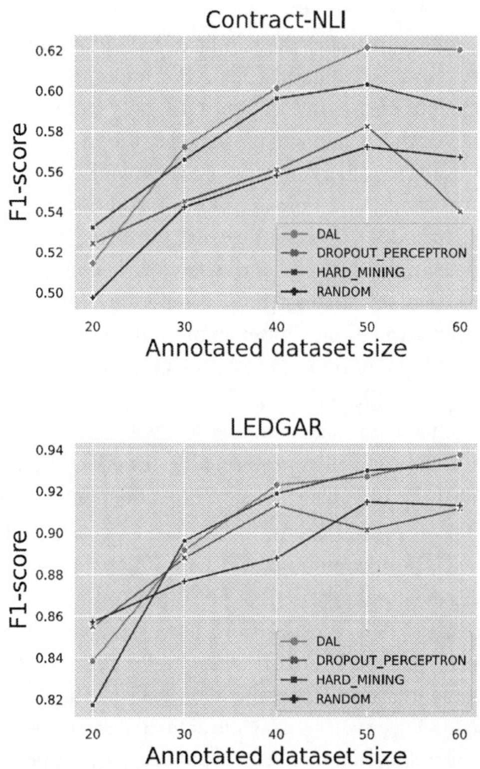

Figure 2: Comparison of four AL strategies when used with DisTAPT RoBERTa with IS.

6.4 Effect of AL strategy

Finally, we evaluate the generalizability of our approach over the four AL strategies mentioned in Sec. 5: DAL, Random, Hard-Mining, and Perceptron Dropout. As shown in Figure 2, DAL results in the best performance with at most 0.08 higher F1-score than other strategies with 60 labeled samples for Contract-NLI, and less than 0.04 higher F1-score with 40 annotated samples for LEDGAR. The small performance gap of these four AL methods in our pipeline indicates the generalizability of this approach to various AL strategies.

7 Conclusion

We propose an efficient active learning pipeline for legal text classification. Our approach leverages the available unlabeled data to adapt the pre-trained language model to the downstream task, and guide its embeddings to a semantically meaningful space before fine-tuning. We use model distillation to produce semantically comparable embeddings. A future work can study the effect of other approaches like BERT-Flow (Li et al., 2020) and whitening (Su et al., 2021) on AL with this pipeline. Moreover, we design a simple strategy to efficiently acquire a labeled set of positive and negative samples for the initial iteration of active learning.

Our experiments over Contract-NLI and LEDGAR benchmarks demonstrate the effectiveness of our approach compared to standard active learning strategies. Our results also show that our pipeline obtains very close performance to the fully-supervised approach with considerably less annotation cost. We test our methodology in the legal domain, and for four AL strategies, but we expect it to generalize to other strategies like ALPS and BADGE, and other specialized domains, like medicine. We leave this evaluation as a future work.

Limitations

In this work, we have shown the importance of task-adaptation and knowledge distillation, and that we can leverage the available unlabeled data to perform efficient fine-tuning via active learning and obtain better performance. The price to pay for this performance gain is time and computational power. The time taken by task-adaptation and distillation scales with the size of unlabeled data. On the other hand, more unlabeled samples result in more effective adaptation to the downstream task. Therefore, the user of this approach needs to find the best trade-off given their data, annotation budget, time and computational power. For, LEDGAR, the larger dataset used in this work, we performed the adaptation and distillation steps in 4 and 1 hour(s) respectively, using a single Nvidia GeForce GTX TITAN X GPU.

Moreover, we showed that by clustering the sentence embeddings produced by DisTAPT RoBERTa, the initial labeled set can be acquired

Dataset	Category	full dataset median	full dataset 90th%tile	medoids median	medoids 90th%tile	gain(%)
Contract-NLI	Inclusion of verbally conveyed information	75.0	125.0	35.5	59.0	52.8
	No licensing	64.0	108.0	68.5	109.1	-1.0
	No reverse engineering	342.0	568.0	144.0	209.1	63.2
	Notice on compelled disclosure	74.5	122.0	99.0	155.0	-27.0
	Sharing with employees	57.0	90.0	21.0	34.1	62.1
	Sharing with third-parties	54.0	92.1	21.0	35.0	62.0
	Survival of obligations	64.0	106.0	36.0	57.0	46.2
	Return of confidential information	116.0	189.0	61.0	99.0	47.6
LEDGAR	Amendments	23.0	37.1	21.0	33.0	10.8
	Counterparts	26.0	42.0	34.0	54.1	-28.8
	Entire agreements	26.0	42.0	33.0	55.0	-30.9
	Governing laws	17.5	28.0	14.0	21.0	25.0
	Notices	29.0	49.0	26.0	44.0	10.2

Table 1: Number of actions to acquire the initial labeled set for 8 categories of Contract-NLI, and LEDGAR when sampling from the full dataset (standard approach), and sampling from the cluster medoids (our approach).

more efficiently. Nevertheless, this approach inherits the limitations of clustering. Namely, the time complexity of clustering the embeddings scales with the data, and the number of clusters should be empirically chosen. In our experiments we spent 10 minutes to cluster the 44,249 samples belonging to LEDGAR dataset into 442 groups.

Ethics Statement

Industries have hundreds of contracts with tens of thousands of sentences that belong to various topics. Labeling all of these samples is a highly expensive and time-consuming process. In this work, we aim to reduce the resources spent on this task by leveraging recent advances in natural language processing, while keeping the human expert in the loop. The goal is to reduce the human effort in annotation so that the legal experts' time and knowledge can be used in another task at which humans are better than machines.

References

Jordan T. Ash, Chicheng Zhang, Akshay Krishnamurthy, John Langford, and Alekh Agarwal. 2020. Deep batch active learning by diverse, uncertain gradient lower bounds. *ArXiv*, abs/1906.03671.

Daniel Matthew Cer, Mona T. Diab, Eneko Agirre, Iñigo Lopez-Gazpio, and Lucia Specia. 2017. Semeval-2017 task 1: Semantic textual similarity multilingual and crosslingual focused evaluation. In *SemEval@ACL*.

Ilias Chalkidis, Manos Fergadiotis, Prodromos Malakasiotis, Nikolaos Aletras, and Ion Androutsopoulos. 2020. Legal-bert: The muppets straight out of law school. *ArXiv*, abs/2010.02559.

Rishi Chhatwal, Nathaniel Huber-Fliflet, Robert Keeling, Jianping Zhang, and Haozhen Zhao. 2017. Empirical evaluations of active learning strategies in legal document review. *2017 IEEE International Conference on Big Data (Big Data)*, pages 1428–1437.

Jacob Devlin, Ming-Wei Chang, Kenton Lee, and Kristina Toutanova. 2019. Bert: Pre-training of deep bidirectional transformers for language understanding. *ArXiv*, abs/1810.04805.

Jesse Dodge, Gabriel Ilharco, Roy Schwartz, Ali Farhadi, Hannaneh Hajishirzi, and Noah A. Smith. 2020. Fine-tuning pretrained language models: Weight initializations, data orders, and early stopping. *ArXiv*, abs/2002.06305.

Liat Ein-Dor, Alon Halfon, Ariel Gera, Eyal Shnarch, Lena Dankin, Leshem Choshen, Marina Danilevsky, Ranit Aharonov, Yoav Katz, and Noam Slonim. 2020. Active learning for bert: An empirical study. In *EMNLP*.

Yarin Gal and Zoubin Ghahramani. 2016. Dropout as a bayesian approximation: Representing model uncertainty in deep learning. *ArXiv*, abs/1506.02142.

Daniel Gissin and Shai Shalev-Shwartz. 2019. Discriminative active learning. *ArXiv*, abs/1907.06347.

Aaron Gokaslan and Vanya Cohen. Openwebtext corpus.

Suchin Gururangan, Ana Marasović, Swabha Swayamdipta, Kyle Lo, Iz Beltagy, Doug Downey, and Noah A. Smith. 2020. Don't stop pretraining: Adapt language models to domains and tasks. *ArXiv*, abs/2004.10964.

Pengcheng He, Xiaodong Liu, Jianfeng Gao, and Weizhu Chen. 2021. Deberta: Decoding-enhanced bert with disentangled attention. *ArXiv*, abs/2006.03654.

Dan Hendrycks, Collin Burns, Anya Chen, and Spencer Ball. 2021. Cuad: An expert-annotated nlp dataset for legal contract review. *ArXiv*, abs/2103.06268.

Jeremy Howard and Sebastian Ruder. 2018. Universal language model fine-tuning for text classification. In *ACL*.

Diederik P. Kingma and Jimmy Ba. 2015. Adam: A method for stochastic optimization. *CoRR*, abs/1412.6980.

Andreas Kirsch, Joost R. van Amersfoort, and Yarin Gal. 2019. Batchbald: Efficient and diverse batch acquisition for deep bayesian active learning. In *NeurIPS*.

Yuta Koreeda and Christopher D. Manning. 2021. Contractnli: A dataset for document-level natural language inference for contracts. *ArXiv*, abs/2110.01799.

David D. Lewis and William A. Gale. 1994. A sequential algorithm for training text classifiers. In *SIGIR '94*.

Bohan Li, Hao Zhou, Junxian He, Mingxuan Wang, Yiming Yang, and Lei Li. 2020. On the sentence embeddings from pre-trained language models. In *EMNLP*.

Yinhan Liu, Myle Ott, Naman Goyal, Jingfei Du, Mandar Joshi, Danqi Chen, Omer Levy, Mike Lewis, Luke Zettlemoyer, and Veselin Stoyanov. 2019. Roberta: A robustly optimized bert pretraining approach. *ArXiv*, abs/1907.11692.

Joel Mackenzie, Rodger Benham, Matthias Petri, Johanne R. Trippas, J. Shane Culpepper, and Alistair Moffat. 2020. Cc-news-en: A large english news corpus. *Proceedings of the 29th ACM International Conference on Information & Knowledge Management*.

J. MacQueen. 1967. Some methods for classification and analysis of multivariate observations.

Katerina Margatina, Loïc Barrault, and Nikolaos Aletras. 2022. On the importance of effectively adapting pretrained language models for active learning. In *ACL*.

Marius Mosbach, Maksym Andriushchenko, and Dietrich Klakow. 2021. On the stability of fine-tuning bert: Misconceptions, explanations, and strong baselines. *ArXiv*, abs/2006.04884.

Nils Reimers and Iryna Gurevych. 2019. Sentence-bert: Sentence embeddings using siamese bert-networks. *ArXiv*, abs/1908.10084.

Ozan Sener and Silvio Savarese. 2018. Active learning for convolutional neural networks: A core-set approach. *arXiv: Machine Learning*.

Jianlin Su, Jiarun Cao, Weijie Liu, and Yangyiwen Ou. 2021. Whitening sentence representations for better semantics and faster retrieval. *ArXiv*, abs/2103.15316.

Trieu H. Trinh and Quoc V. Le. 2018. A simple method for commonsense reasoning. *ArXiv*, abs/1806.02847.

Don Tuggener, Pius von Däniken, Thomas Peetz, and Mark Cieliebak. 2020. Ledgar: A large-scale multi-label corpus for text classification of legal provisions in contracts. In *LREC*.

Ran Wang, Xizhao Wang, Sam Tak Wu Kwong, and Chen Xu. 2017. Incorporating diversity and informativeness in multiple-instance active learning. *IEEE Transactions on Fuzzy Systems*, 25:1460–1475.

Michelle Yuan, Hsuan-Tien Lin, and Jordan L. Boyd-Graber. 2020. Cold-start active learning through self-supervised language modeling. *ArXiv*, abs/2010.09535.

Mike Zhang and Barbara Plank. 2021. Cartography active learning. In *EMNLP*.

Tianyi Zhang, Felix Wu, Arzoo Katiyar, Kilian Q. Weinberger, and Yoav Artzi. 2021. Revisiting few-sample bert fine-tuning. *ArXiv*, abs/2006.05987.

Yukun Zhu, Ryan Kiros, Richard S. Zemel, Ruslan Salakhutdinov, Raquel Urtasun, Antonio Torralba, and Sanja Fidler. 2015. Aligning books and movies: Towards story-like visual explanations by watching movies and reading books. *2015 IEEE International Conference on Computer Vision (ICCV)*, pages 19–27.

A Appendix

A.1 Dataset Distributions

We provide the details of class distributions for Contract-NLI and LEDGAR benchmarks in Table 2. As shown in this table, LEDGAR contains considerably larger categories compared to Contract-NLI and is more balanced.

A.2 Effective Fine-Tuning

Here we present the results of standard active learning and our approach for four AL strategies discussed in Sec. 5 including Random, Hard-Mining, and Perceptron Dropout. As before, we report the average F1-score over three runs. Figure 3 corresponds to Contract-NLI and Figure 4 illustrates the results for the LEDGAR dataset.

A.3 Effect of Knowledge Distillation

Figures 5 and 6 illustrate the comparison of the Dunn Index distribution that were not presented in the main paper.

A.4 Efficiency of Initial Sampling with Medoids

In Table 3 we provide the median and 90th percentile of number of actions performed to collect the initial labeled set, for the standard sampling approach, and our proposed strategy using cluster medoids,

Dataset	Category	Train Size	Dev Size	Test Size
Contract-NLI	Confidentiality of Agreement	161	29	46
	Explicit identification	203	29	60
	Inclusion of verbally conveyed information	274	45	76
	Limited use	371	53	110
	No licensing	327	39	86
	No reverse engineering	60	8	13
	No solicitation	93	11	28
	None-inclusion of non-technical information	332	50	94
	Notice on compelled disclosure	276	45	77
	Permissible acquirement of similar information	311	47	96
	Permissible copy	167	17	49
	Permissible development of similar information	263	40	73
	Permissible post-agreement possession	312	25	63
	Return of confidential information	182	24	38
	Sharing with employees	358	56	94
	Sharing with third-parties	370	53	102
	Survival of obligations	311	43	83
LEDGAR	Amendments	9,132	1,515	2,615
	Counterparts	8,033	1,312	2,363
	Entire agreements	8,094	1,361	2,370
	Governing laws	11,926	1,997	3,454
	Notices	7,064	1,190	2,105

Table 2: Category frequency for Contract-NLI adapted to classification task, and LEDGAR benchmarks.

for nine categories of Contract-NLI that were not included in Table 1 in Sec. 6.3. It is observed that, for most categories, there is a considerable reduction in the number of actions performed to acquire the annotated data for the initial AL iteration.

Category	full dataset		medoids		gain(%)
	median	90th%tile	median	90th%tile	
Confidentiality of Agreement	125.0	215.1	120.0	178.2	17.1
Explicit identification	100.0	161.1	48.0	77.0	52.2
Limited use	56.0	90.1	37.0	58.0	35.6
No solicitation	227.0	383.0	178.0	261.0	31.8
None-inclusion of non-technical information	61.0	101.1	39.0	64.0	36.7
Permissible acquirement of similar information	65.0	107.0	91.0	145.0	-35.5
Permissible copy	121.0	197.0	68.0	108.0	45.2
Permissible development of similar information	77.0	129.1	82.0	129.0	0.1
Permissible post-agreement possession	66.0	108.1	41.0	66.0	38.9

Table 3: Number of actions to acquire the initial labeled set for 9 categories of Contract-NLI when sampling from the full dataset (standard approach), and sampling from the cluster medoids.

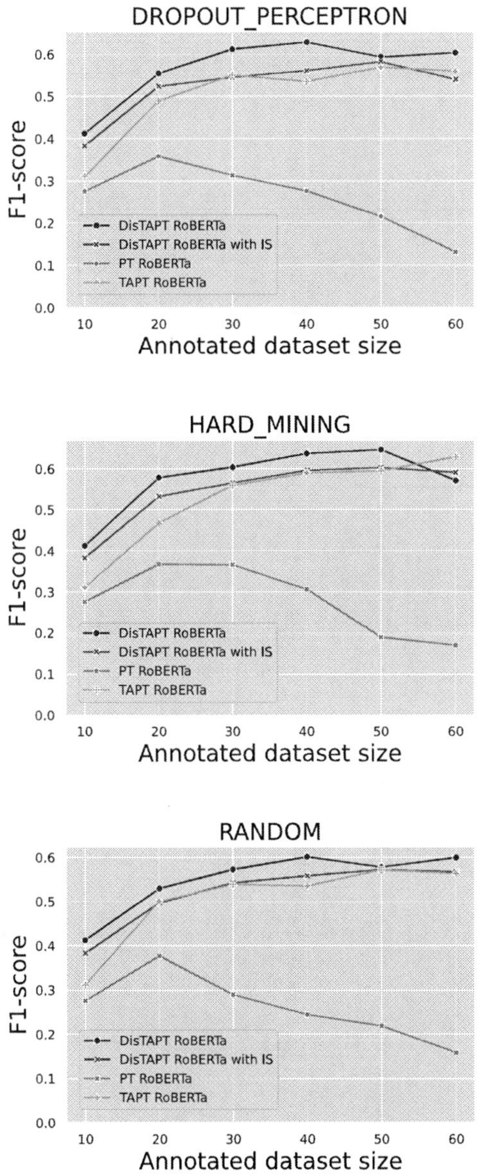

Figure 3: Test F1-score for **Contract-NLI** during AL iterations. The F1-score for the fully supervised fine-tuning is 0.6990.

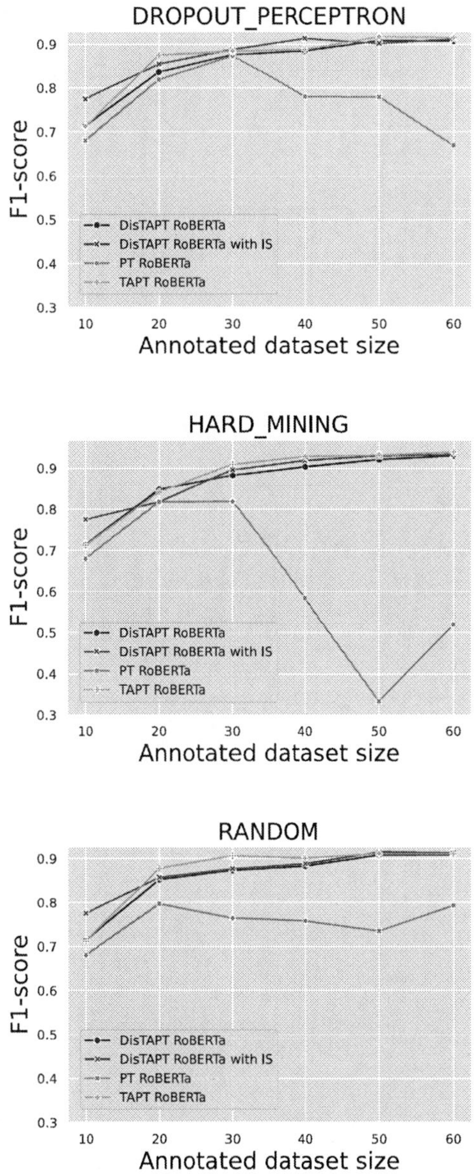

Figure 4: Test F1-score for **LEDGAR** during AL iterations. The F1-score for the fully supervised fine-tuning is 0.9538.

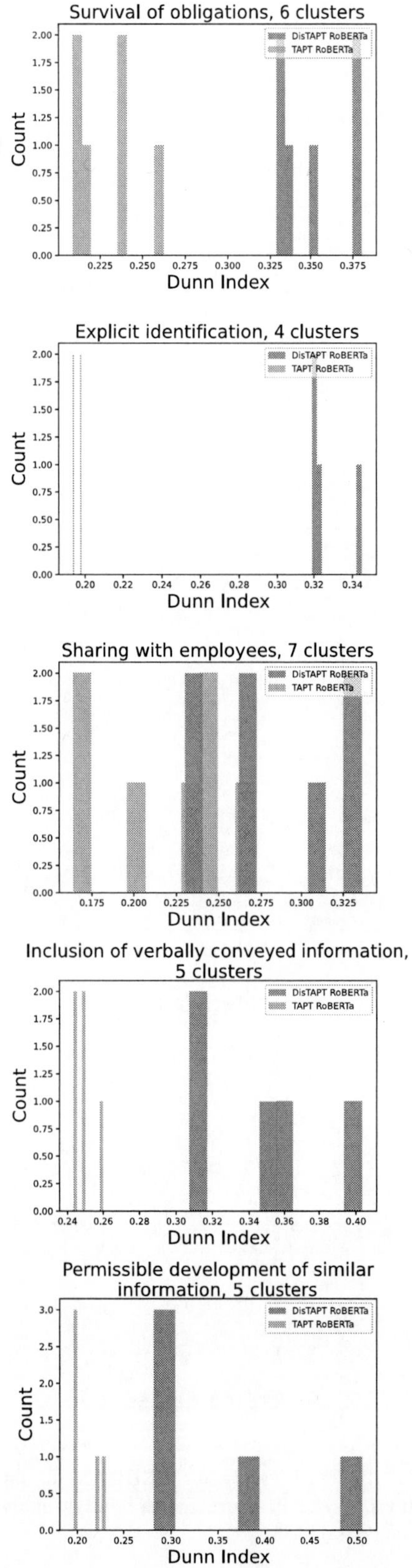

Figure 5: Comparison of the Dunn Index distribution before (TAPT RoBERTa) and after knowledge distillation (DisTAPT RoBERTa) for **Contract-NLI** dataset.

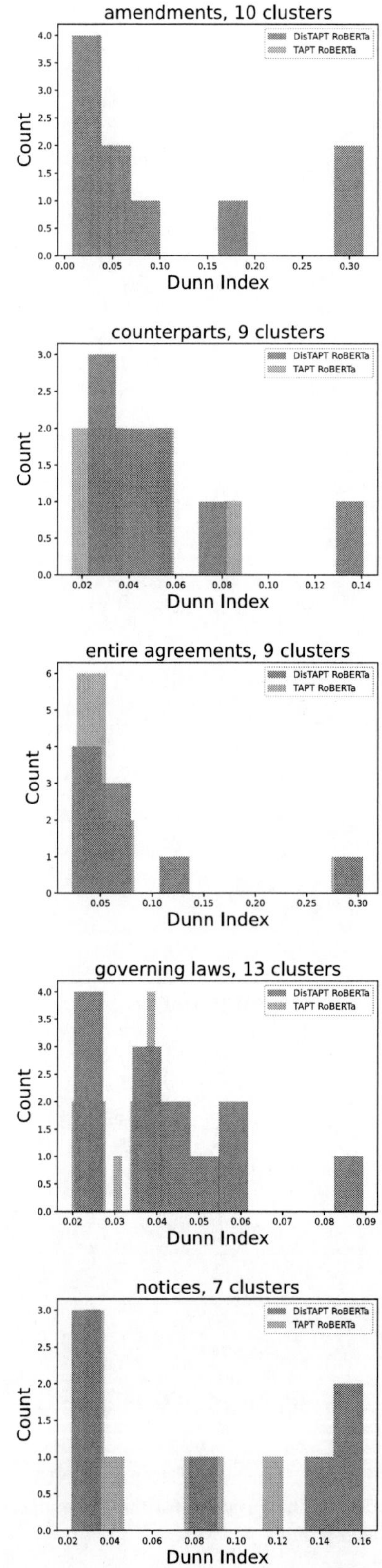

Figure 6: Comparison of the Dunn Index distribution before (TAPT RoBERTa) and after knowledge distillation (DisTAPT RoBERTa) for **LEDGAR** dataset.

Author Index

Aberer, Karl, 345
Agarwal, Astha, 184
Aggarwal, Vinay, 296
Akdag Salah, Almila, 287
Al-qurishi, Muhammad, 338
Allaway, Emily, 265
Alqaseemi, Sarah, 338
Alschner, Wolfgang, 256
Androutsopoulos, Ion, 130
Au, Ting Wai Terence, 246
Avila, Sandra, 228
Avram, Andrei-marius, 305

Balaji, Sumanth, 276
Bannihatti Kumar, Vinayshekhar, 111
Bergam, Noah, 265
Bernsohn, Dor, 31
Bex, Floris, 76
Bhambhoria, Rohan, 119
Bhattacharjee, Kasturi, 111
Bhattacharya, Arnab, 153
Bongard, Leonard, 194
Braun, Daniel, 218
Broda, Irina, 238

Cercel, Dumitru-clementin, 305
Cercel, Mihaela-claudia, 305
Chalkidis, Ilias, 88, 130
Chhaya, Niyati, 296
Cox, Ingemar, 246

De, Suparna, 65
Dinică, Ion-robert, 305

Eom, Saehee, 143

Galassi, Andrea, 47
Ganesh, Ananya, 296
Gangadharaiah, Rashmi, 111
Gao, Jiaxun, 256
Garimella, Aparna, 276, 296
Gatt, Albert, 287
Grabmair, Matthias, 238
Gubelmann, Reto, 12
Guha, Shouvik Kumar, 153
Gupta, Smita, 184

Habernal, Ivan, 172, 194
Haddad, Rashid, 238
Hagag, Ben, 31
Hamacher, Marius, 53
Handschuh, Siegfried, 12
Hayat, Gila, 31
Hazarika, Angshuman, 153
Held, Lena, 194
Hongler, Peter, 12
Hwang, Wonseok, 143

Inkpen, Diana, 256

Johnson, Jon, 65
Joshi, Sagar, 276

Kalamkar, Prathamesh, 184
Kambhatla, Nandakishore, 296
Karn, Saurabh, 184
Kloppenborg, Katharina, 53

L. Colombini, Esther, 228
Lagioia, Francesca, 47
Lampos, Vasileios, 246
Lebret, Rémi, 345
Lee, Hanuhl, 143
Legkas, Sotiris, 88
Li, Jonathan, 119
Li, Xiang, 256
Litman, Diane, 322
Lukose, Emilia, 65

M. Benatti, Raysa, 228
M. L. Villarroel, Camila, 228
Malakasiotis, Prodromos, 88
Malik, Vijit, 153
Mamakas, Dimitris, 130
Mamooler, Sepideh, 345
Margadant, Elina, 12
Maroudas, Stelios, 88
Massonnet, Stephane, 345
Mckeown, Kathleen, 265
Meyers, Adam, 1
Modi, Ashutosh, 153

Negrini, Marco, 238
Nigam, Shubham, 153
Niklaus, Joel, 31
Nirmala, S, 208

Nordquist, Sean, 1

Park, Hai Jin, 143
Perçin, Sezen, 47
Pop, Florin, 305
Prijs, Daniël, 76

Raghavan, Vivek, 184
Ruggeri, Federico, 47

Sancheti, Abhilasha, 296
Sanjay, Rishabh, 153
Santin, Piera, 47
Santos, Cristiana, 287
Sartor, Giovanni, 47
Schraagen, Marijn, 76
Semo, Gil, 31
Seo, Minjoon, 143
Severi, Fabiana, 228
Sheik, Reshma, 208
Smădu, Răzvan-alexandru, 305
Souissi, Riad, 338

T, Gokul, 208
Tiwari, Aman, 184
Torroni, Paolo, 47
Tsotsi, Petros, 130

Van De Luijtgaarden, Nick, 76
Van Hofslot, Marieke, 287
Varma, Vasudeva, 276

Xu, Shanshan, 238

Yin, Ying, 172

Zesch, Torsten, 53
Zhong, Yang, 322
Zhu, Xiaodan, 119
Zufall, Frederike, 53

Association for Computational Linguistics
209 N. Eighth Street
Stroudsburg, Pennsylvania 18360

ISBN 978-1-7138-9142-0

CURRAN ASSOCIATES INC.
proceedings.com